International Directory of
COMPANY
HISTORIES

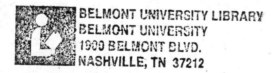

International Directory of
COMPANY
HISTORIES

VOLUME 69

Editor

Jay P. Pederson

ST. JAMES PRESS
An imprint of Thomson Gale, a part of The Thomson Corporation

Detroit • New York • San Francisco • San Diego • New Haven, Conn. • Waterville, Maine • London • Munich

THOMSON

GALE

International Directory of Company Histories, Volume 69

Jay P. Pederson, Editor

Project Editor
Miranda H. Ferrara

Editorial
Virgil Burton, Donna Craft, Louise Gagné, Peggy Geeseman, Julie Gough, Linda Hall, Sonya Hill, Keith Jones, Lynn Pearce, Maureen Puhl, Holly Selden, Justine Ventimiglia

Imaging and Multimedia
Randy Bassett, Lezlie Light

Manufacturing
Rhonda Dover

Product Manager
Gerald L. Sawchuk

LIBRARY OF CONGRESS CATALOG NUMBER 89-190943

ISBN: 1-55862-544-5

BRITISH LIBRARY CATALOGUING IN PUBLICATION DATA

International directory of company histories. Vol. 69
I. Jay P. Pederson
33.87409

Printed in the United States of America
10 9 8 7 6 5 4 3 2 1

CONTENTS

Company Histories

PREFACE

The St. James Press series *The International Directory of Company Histories (IDCH)* is intended for reference use by students, business people, librarians, historians, economists, investors, job candidates, and others who seek to learn more about the historical development of the world's most important companies. To date, *IDCH* has covered over 7,000 companies in 69 volumes.

Inclusion Criteria

Most companies chosen for inclusion in *IDCH* have achieved a minimum of US$25 million in annual sales and are leading influences in their industries or geographical locations. Companies may be publicly held, private, or nonprofit. State-owned companies that are important in their industries and that may operate much like public or private companies also are included. Wholly owned subsidiaries and divisions are profiled if they meet the requirements for inclusion. Entries on companies that have had major changes since they were last profiled may be selected for updating.

The *IDCH* series highlights 10% private and nonprofit companies, and features updated entries on approximately 50 companies per volume.

Entry Format

Each entry begins with the company's legal name, the address of its headquarters, its telephone, toll-free, and fax numbers, and its web site. A statement of public, private, state, or parent ownership follows. A company with a legal name in both English and the language of its headquarters country is listed by the English name, with the native-language name in parentheses.

The company's founding or earliest incorporation date, the number of employees, and the most recent available sales figures follow. Sales figures are given in local currencies with equivalents in U.S. dollars. For some private companies, sales figures are estimates and indicated by the abbreviation *est.* The entry lists the exchanges on which a company's stock is traded and its ticker symbol, as well as the company's NAIC codes.

Entries generally contain a *Company Perspectives* box which provides a short summary of the company's mission, goals, and ideals, a *Key Dates* box highlighting milestones in the company's history, lists of *Principal Subsidiaries, Principal Divisions, Principal Operating Units, Principal Competitors,* and articles for *Further Reading.*

American spelling is used throughout *IDCH*, and the word ''billion'' is used in its U.S. sense of one thousand million.

Sources

Entries have been compiled from publicly accessible sources both in print and on the Internet such as general and academic periodicals, books, annual reports, and material supplied by the companies themselves.

Cumulative Indexes

IDCH contains three indexes: the **Index to Companies**, which provides an alphabetical index to companies discussed in the text as well as to companies profiled, the **Index to Industries**, which allows researchers to locate companies by their principal industry, and the **Geographic Index**, which lists companies alphabetically by the country of their headquarters. The indexes are cumulative and specific instructions for using them are found immediately preceding each index.

Suggestions Welcome

Comments and suggestions from users of *IDCH* on any aspect of the product as well as suggestions for companies to be included or updated are cordially invited. Please write:

The Editor
International Directory of Company Histories
St. James Press
27500 Drake Rd.
Farmington Hills, Michigan 48331-3535

AB	Aktiebolag (Finland, Sweden)
AB Oy	Aktiebolag Osakeyhtiot (Finland)
A.E.	Anonimos Eteria (Greece)
AG	Aktiengesellschaft (Austria, Germany, Switzerland, Liechtenstein)
A.O.	Anonim Ortaklari/Ortakligi (Turkey)
ApS	Amparteselskab (Denmark)
A.Š.	Anonim Širketi (Turkey)
A/S	Aksjeselskap (Norway); Aktieselskab (Denmark, Sweden)
Ay	Avoinyhtio (Finland)
B.A.	Buttengewone Aansprakeiijkheid (The Netherlands)
Bhd.	Berhad (Malaysia, Brunei)
B.V.	Besloten Vennootschap (Belgium, The Netherlands)
C.A.	Compania Anonima (Ecuador, Venezuela)
C. de R.L.	Compania de Responsabilidad Limitada (Spain)
Co.	Company
Corp.	Corporation
CRL	Companhia a Responsabilidao Limitida (Portugal, Spain)
C.V.	Commanditairc Vcnnootschap (The Netherlands, Belgium)
G.I.E.	Groupement d'Interet Economique (France)
GmbH	Gesellschaft mit beschraenkter Haftung (Austria, Germany, Switzerland)
Inc.	Incorporated (United States, Canada)
I/S	Interessentselskab (Denmark); Intercsentselskap (Norway)
KG/KGaA	Kommanditgesellschaft/Kommanditgesellschaft auf Aktien (Austria, Germany, Switzerland)
KK	Kabushiki Kaisha (Japan)
K/S	Kommanditselskab (Denmark); Kommandittselskap (Norway)
Lda.	Limitada (Spain)
L.L.C.	Limited Liability Company (United States)
Ltd.	Limited (Various)
Ltda.	Limitada (Brazil, Portugal)
Ltee.	Limitee (Canada, France)
mbH	mit beschraenkter Haftung (Austria, Germany)
N.V.	Naamloze Vennootschap (Belgium, The Netherlands)
OAO	Otkrytoe Aktsionernoe Obshchestve (Russia)
OOO	Obschestvo s Ogranichennoi Otvetstvennostiu (Russia)
Oy	Osakeyhtiö (Finland)
PLC	Public Limited Co. (United Kingdom, Ireland)
Pty.	Proprietary (Australia, South Africa, United Kingdom)
S.A.	Société Anonyme (Belgium, France, Greece, Luxembourg, Switzerland, Arab speaking countries); Sociedad Anónima (Latin America [except Brazil], Spain, Mexico); Sociedades Anônimas (Brazil, Portugal)
SAA	Societe Anonyme Arabienne
S.A.R.L.	Sociedade Anonima de Responsabilidade Limitada (Brazil, Portugal); Société à Responsabilité Limitée (France, Belgium, Luxembourg)
S.A.S.	Societá in Accomandita Semplice (Italy); Societe Anonyme Syrienne (Arab speaking countries)
Sdn. Bhd.	Sendirian Berhad (Malaysia)
S.p.A.	Società per Azioni (Italy)
Sp. z.o.o.	Spólka z ograniczona odpowiedzialnoscia (Poland)
S.R.L.	Società a Responsabilità Limitata (Italy); Sociedad de Responsabilidad Limitada (Spain, Mexico, Latin America [except Brazil])
S.R.O.	Spolecnost s Rucenim Omezenym (Czechoslovakia
Ste.	Societe (France, Belgium, Luxembourg, Switzerland)
VAG	Verein der Arbeitgeber (Austria, Germany)
YK	Yugen Kaisha (Japan)
ZAO	Zakrytoe Aktsionernoe Obshchestve (Russia)

$	United States dollar	ISK	Icelandic krona
£	United Kingdom pound	ITL	Italian lira
¥	Japanese yen	JMD	Jamaican dollar
AED	Emirati dirham	KPW	North Korean won
ARS	Argentine peso	KRW	South Korean won
ATS	Austrian shilling	KWD	Kuwaiti dinar
AUD	Australian dollar	LUF	Luxembourg franc
BEF	Belgian franc	MUR	Mauritian rupee
BHD	Bahraini dinar	MXN	Mexican peso
BRL	Brazilian real	MYR	Malaysian ringgit
CAD	Canadian dollar	NGN	Nigerian naira
CHF	Swiss franc	NLG	Netherlands guilder
CNY	Chinese yuan	NOK	Norwegian krone
COP	Colombian peso	NZD	New Zealand dollar
CLP	Chilean peso	OMR	Omani rial
CZK	Czech koruna	PHP	Philippine peso
DEM	German deutsche mark	PKR	Pakistani rupee
DKK	Danish krone	PLN	Polish zloty
DZD	Algerian dinar	PTE	Portuguese escudo
EEK	Estonian Kroon	RMB	Chinese renminbi
EGP	Egyptian pound	RUB	Russian ruble
ESP	Spanish peseta	SAR	Saudi riyal
EUR	euro	SEK	Swedish krona
FIM	Finnish markka	SGD	Singapore dollar
FRF	French franc	THB	Thai baht
GRD	Greek drachma	TND	Tunisian dinar
HKD	Hong Kong dollar	TRL	Turkish lira
HUF	Hungarian forint	TWD	new Taiwan dollar
IDR	Indonesian rupiah	VEB	Venezuelan bolivar
IEP	Irish pound	VND	Vietnamese dong
ILS	new Israeli shekel	ZAR	South African rand
INR	Indian rupee	ZMK	Zambian kwacha

International Directory of

COMPANY

HISTORIES

Accor S.A.

2, rue de la Mare-Neuve
91000 Évry
France
Telephone: (33) 1 69 36 80 80
Toll Free: (800) 207-2542 (Accor North America
    Group)
Fax: (33) 1 69 36 79 00
Web site: http://www.accor.com

Public Company
Incorporated: 1983
Employees: 158,000
Sales: EUR 6.83 billion ($8.6 billion) (2003)
Stock Exchanges: Paris
Ticker Symbol: AC
NAIC: 721110 Hotels and Motels (Except Casino
    Hotels); 722110 Full-Service Restaurants; 722211
    Limited-Service Restaurants; 561510 Travel Agencies;
    713210 Casinos (Except Casino Hotels)

Paris-based Accor S.A. is Europe's leading hospitality group with almost 4,000 hotels in 85 countries around the world. Accor provides hotels in every range, from the five-star Sofitel chain to budget-priced Formule 1, Etap, and Ibis in Europe, Motel 6 and Red Roof Inns in the United States, and midrange Novotel and Mercure in Europe and the Asia/Pacific Rim region. In addition to its hotel properties, Accor is active in travel and leisure through its half-interest in Carlson Wagonlit Travel, offering package tours and resorts in 33 countries. Accor also provides its worldwide customer base with foodservices (restaurants and employee vouchers), casinos, and onboard railway services (sleeping berths and dining).

Early History: The 1960s and 1970s

In 1967 Gérard Pelisson and Paul Dubrule opened their first Novotel hotel on a roadside near Lille in northern France. Travel was booming in France in the 1960s and the hotel industry had not yet expanded to meet the demand. French hotels, in general, were either rural inns or luxury hotels in city centers. Dubrule decided to build American-style highway hotels in the medium price range and collaborated with Pelisson, a former head of market research at IBM-Europe. Through Pelisson's connections the partners were able to secure a bank loan, and the Novotel firm was launched. The company's ensuing success was in large part due to its being first to break into the unexploited European market for highway lodging. Each Novotel provided standardized rooms, ample parking facilities, and restaurants featuring local cuisine. Soon Novotels also were established at airports and popular vacation sites, such as the seaside and mountain areas.

Pelisson and Dubrule developed their expanding company with a philosophy of decentralized management and a unique dual chairmanship. Although to comply with French law the partners took turns holding the official position of chairman, they made all decisions jointly and shared responsibilities, immersing themselves in all aspects of the business. The company's specialty became variety, providing hotel chains to fit every need. In 1973 Sphere S.A. was created as a holding company for a new chain of two-star, no-frills hotels, called Ibis; the first Ibis was opened the following year. During this time, the company also acquired Courte Paille, a chain of roadside steakhouses founded in 1961, which reflected many of the same priorities as Novotel: practicality, easy parking, consistent quality, and quick service.

The acquisition of the Mercure hotel chain in 1975 pushed the company into metropolitan areas and the business traveler market, and these hotels varied according to regional demands in style, character, and restaurant offerings. By the end of the 1970s Novotel had become the premier hotel chain in Europe with 240 establishments in Europe, Africa, South America, and the Far East.

New Ventures in the Early 1980s

In 1980 Novotel invested in Jacques Borel International, which owned restaurants and the luxury Sofitel hotel chain. Jacques Borel had begun his career with the establishment of one restaurant in 1957 and by 1975, when he took over Bel-

Company Perspectives:

With 158,000 people in 140 countries, Accor is the European leader and a global operator in its two core businesses, Hotels and Services. It also operates in travel agencies, casinos, restaurants, and onboard train services.

gium's Sofitel chain, he was Europe's top restaurateur. After losses in the hotel business forced Borel to sell the Sofitel chain to Pelisson and Dubrule in 1982, Novotel and its holdings were incorporated under the name Accor and became one of the top ten hotel operators in the world, an elite group typically dominated by American firms. The merger doubled the partners' holdings and infused new talent into the senior management, as Bernard Westercamp became Accor's vice-president and general manager. Sofitel's luxury services, aimed at business and holiday travelers and located in the center of international cities, near airports, and in prestigious tourist areas, introduced Accor to the higher-priced end of the hospitality industry.

Accor's initial expansion into the American market, which began in 1979 with the opening of a hotel in Minneapolis, was not as successful as its ventures in Europe due to a saturated U.S. market and Accor's slow development. The company brought Novotel, Ibis, and Sofitel hotels to the United States, as well as a chain of eateries in California called Seafood Broiler, but all operated at a loss. Nonetheless, Pelisson and Dubrule made American-style service culture fundamental to their business in Europe. After visiting training schools at McDonald's Corporation and Disneyland, they opened Accor Academy at the company headquarters in Évry in 1985. The academy offered seminars ranging from phone etiquette to team-building skills and the exploration of new technologies. Accor spent a reported 2 percent of its annual payroll on training.

During the mid-1980s Accor developed investments in restaurant and travel businesses. The company opened Pizza del Arte, a chain of Italian restaurants, in 1983 in commercial and city centers and entered a partnership with the bakery and catering company Lenôtre two years later. Accor also entered the travel industry during this time, buying into Africatours, the largest tour operator to Africa, which became the third of its major investments, along with hotels and restaurants. The company expanded its tour operations to North and South America, Asia, and the South Pacific through the purchases of Americatours, Asiatours, and Ted Cook's Islands in the Sun. In an effort to attract weekend clientele in Europe, Accor developed Épisodes, an agency specializing in weekend rates for rooms usually occupied by business travelers during the week.

In 1985 Hotec, a subsidiary of Accor, brought forth a completely new idea in the hotel industry with the creation of Formule 1, a one-star budget hotel chain with no reception staff, no restaurant, and no private bathrooms. Travelers simply inserted a credit card at the entrance to gain access to the rooms, which were plain yet practical and cost $15 a night. Formule 1 hotels appealed to vacationing young people and families with limited financial resources. Costs were kept to a minimum by the use of prefabricated construction and staffs of only two to

run each 60-room hotel. Occupancy rates were high and ten Formule 1s were in operation by early 1987 with another 30 under construction across Europe.

Continued Expansion in the Late 1980s

By 1986 Accor's revenues had reached around $2 billion, with net profits of $32 million. Novotel, with hotels in 31 countries, remained the most profitable while Sofitel faced stiff competition in the luxury hotel market, particularly from American properties. Nevertheless, Accor expanded at a far swifter rate than its international rivals, becoming the largest operator in Europe. It led the market in France and West Germany, and expanded in the medium and economy range in Spain, Italy, and Britain with its $75 million investment budget. The company's European base provided three-quarters of its revenue, with more than half coming from hotels and the rest from its foodservices.

In 1985 Accor took control of Britain's Luncheon Voucher, the company that invented meal tickets, which companies distributed to their employees as a benefit. Accor overhauled the company's communications and management systems and restored its market presence through a new sales drive. By 1987 Accor was the world leader in restaurant vouchers for employees and was exploring similar voucher programs for child care and groceries.

In 1987 Accor exploited another growing market: homes for the elderly. The company's Hotelia homes provided 24-hour medical and nursing care, as well as more traditional hotel services. In addition, Accor created the successful Parthénon chain of residential hotels in Brazil, and initiated a large-scale reorganization to better cope with its diversification of products and growth. Accor was restructured according to product, so each chain had its own general management, though the company was still committed to decentralization and expected management to act autonomously. Pelisson and Dubrule maintained a flexible, dynamic structure and remained accessible to their expanding management teams.

The following year, in 1988, Accor invested in France Quick, ranked second in the French fast-food market, and launched the Free Time fast-food chain. With several partners Accor then invested in Cipal-Parc Astérix, a theme park north of Paris, based on a Gallic cartoon character, and expressed interest in providing catering and lodging for the then-projected EuroDisney amusement park. Accor's rapid growth was not without its setbacks, however, as it made a failed bid for the Hilton Hotels empire and an unsuccessful merger with Club Méditerranée.

As the restructuring took hold, Accor revenues improved with 1989 profits up 30 percent from 1988, on sales of $3.6 billion. Accor enjoyed 12 percent earnings-per-share increases annually from 1983 to 1989. Steady growth allowed the company to sell equity, including a $340 million issue in January 1990.

Acquisitions in the Early 1990s

Accor made a major move into the U.S. market when it purchased the Dallas, Texas-based budget hotel chain Motel 6 in 1990 for more than $1.3 billion. The deal made Accor the second largest hotel company in the world in terms of rooms

Key Dates:

1967: Gérard Pelisson and Paul Dubrule open the first Novotel hotel.
1973: Sphere S.A. is created as a holding company.
1974: The first Ibis hotel is opened.
1975: The Mercure hotel chain is acquired.
1979: Novotel opens its first U.S. hotel in Minneapolis.
1980: Novotel-SIEH acquires a stake in Jacques Borel International, owner of Sofitel hotels.
1982: Novotel-SIEH becomes the sole owner of the Sofitel chain.
1983: The Novotel, SIEH, and JBI holdings are incorporated as Accor S.A.
1985: Accor partners with Lenôtre, a baking and catering company.
1990: Motel 6 becomes part of the Accor family.
1992: Accor buys a majority stake in Belgium's Wagons-Lits.
1994: Accor's Wagonlit travel agency and Carlson Travel form a partnership.
1997: Carlson and Wagonlit merge with Accor's travel business; company retains a half-interest in the new firm, named Carlson Wagonlit Travel.
1999: Accor acquires the Red Roof Inn chain in the United States.
2000: Accor launches the Accorhotels.com web site.
2001: Accor partners with the Beijing Tourism Group and Zenith Hotel International for expansion in China.
2003: Carlson Wagonlit Travel and France's Protravel S.A. merge.
2005: Several Accor properties are damaged by a devastating tsunami in Southeast Asia.

(157,000) and represented an attempt by Pelisson and Dubrule to build an American hotel empire to match their successful European operations. Accor paid a hefty price to enter the crowded U.S. market and took on an additional $1 billion debt from the sale. The partners, however, were committed to expanding in the United States with the same cost-cutting measures that had worked so well for Formule 1, including credit card payment and limited maintenance staff.

Accor used a radio ad campaign and transatlantic marketing to lure Europeans to Motel 6. Although Accor agreed not to overhaul the management of Motel 6's parent company, Motel 6 G.P. Inc., it did sell a 60 percent stake in the budget chain to French investors. In 1991 Accor bought 53 Regal Inns and Affordable Inns from RHC Holding Corporation to make Motel 6 the preeminent budget hotel company in the world. Motel 6's success in the early 1990s was due in part to Accor's financial backing and ability to pay cash, as well as its decision to purchase company-owned properties outright rather than franchising them.

In 1990 Accor and Société Générale de Belgique bought a 26.7 percent stake in Wagons-Lits, a Belgian company that dominated the European railroad sleeping car business and was the second largest hotel chain in continental Europe, owning about 300 hotels in Europe, Thailand, and Indonesia. In 1992

the European Community approved Accor's nearly $1 billion bid for a 69.5 percent controlling interest in Wagons-Lits. At the end of the year, Accor became the world leader in its industry with 2,100 hotels, 6,000 restaurants, and 1,000 travel agencies.

With the privatization of industry in Hungary, Accor entered a partnership in 1993 to buy 51 percent of the hotel company Pannonia from the Hungarian government. Pannonia owned medium-priced hotels in Hungary, Germany, and Austria and gained exclusive rights to develop under Accor in Bulgaria, Albania, Romania, Slovakia, Hungary, and the former Soviet Union and Yugoslavia, as well as to develop the Mercure chain in Austria. Accor also launched the Coralia label in 1993 to distinguish holiday hotels from business hotels. Around 30 Accor hotels in the Mediterranean and Indian Ocean regions added the Coralia label by 1994 and more were planned in the Caribbean, Central America, and Venezuela.

In the early 1990s Accor's Atria subsidiary was developing economic centers in cities and towns composed of conference centers, offices, and hotels, particularly Novotels and Mercures, in conjunction with local chambers of commerce. The company also had investments in Thalassa International spas and luxury hotels and casinos in France. Accor began a hotel-rebranding strategy in June 1993 to eliminate the Pullman Hotels International chain, acquired in 1991, while expanding its Sofitel and Mercure brands. Through renovations, the company transformed 27 Pullman hotels into Sofitels, while another 25 Pullman hotels became Mercure hotels.

Accor similarly expanded its restaurant business in the early 1990s with L'Arche cafeterias, L'Écluse winebars, Boeuf Jardinier steakhouses, Café Route highway cafés, Actair airport restaurants, Terminal train station buffets, and Mcda's Grills in Spain. The company increased its partnership in France Quick and began building independent "villas" for Pizza del Arte. In 1994 Lenôtre, the bakery and catering chain Accor had developed in six countries, merged with Rosell, a chain specializing in organization, expansion, and management of catering services, for mutual advantages.

With the Dutch Wagons-Lits, Accor continued its expansion in restaurants and sleeping compartments on trains. In the car rental business, the company shared control of Europcar Interrent International with Volkswagen AG in 89 countries in Europe, Africa, and the Middle East. In March 1994 Accor agreed to merge its travel agency business with Carlson Travel Network, a subsidiary of Carlson Companies, to form a network of 4,000 agencies in 125 countries worth $10.8 billion. The new enterprise, named Carlson Wagonlit Travel, would be jointly owned (half-interest each) by Carlson and Accor. The integration of the two businesses occurred gradually over the next several years.

Divesting Assets in the Middle and Late 1990s

Accor's rapid expansion lost some momentum in the mid-1990s as its debt accumulated and a recession hit the travel industry. One of the first signs its steamrolling expansion would not continue was the loss of Accor's 1994 bid for a majority stake in the four-star Meridien hotel chain. Although Accor found funding through the Saudi hotel financier Prince Al Waleed, the company's bid still fell short.

In 1994 Accor sought to reduce its debt and free up funds for further expansion by selling some of its real estate and noncore businesses. Its principal strategy was to sell its expensive hotel real estate, but to continue managing the properties through leases. The same year Accor sold several Dutch Wagons-Lits enterprises and in 1995 sold its catering operations. Despite its divestments, Accor's nonhotel businesses were taking an increasingly prominent position in the conglomerate. The Carlson and Wagonlit Travel partnership was thriving, with sales rising from FRF 19.4 billion in 1993 to FRF 21 billion in 1995. Europcar, Accor's joint venture with Volkswagen, had become Europe's largest car rental company; in addition to its car rental fleet, by 1995 the company had 3.2 million leased vehicles. Net overall income for Accor had been rising since its 1993 low of FRF 423 million, to reach FRF 923 million in 1995.

Accor's hotel operations, however, remained the company's mainstay. By 1997 Accor operated 2,605 hotels with 289,200 rooms around the world. Sales from its hotel operations rose 16.6 percent in 1997 to FRF 18.6 billion. The company had placed its hotels in two groups: the business and leisure group, which consisted of Mercure (with 43,000 rooms), Novotel (with more than 50,000 rooms), Coralia (with 23,500 rooms), and Sofitel (with 20,500 rooms); and the economy group, which consisted of Motel 6 (84,500 rooms), Ibis (45,000 rooms), Formule 1 (22,000 rooms), and Etap Hotel (13,000 rooms). Accor continued to open new hotels, especially internationally. Its Asia-Pacific subsidiary, which the company had launched in 1993, controlled 144 hotels in 18 countries by 1996. With 56 more projects in the works, Accor Asia-Pacific had become that region's leading hotel group; its Africa/Middle East group operated 99 hotels by 1997, and its Latin America group, 89 units.

In 1997 the company's founders, Dubrule and Pelisson, reorganized the management of the company to reduce their involvement in the day-to-day decision making. The two chaired the new supervisory board but ceded the management board to Jean-Marc Espalioux. The same year, the merger of the travel agency businesses of Accor and Carlson was completed, making Carlson Wagonlit Travel one of the largest travel agencies in the world. Accor unveiled a restructuring plan in 1998 to substantially reduce its debt load through workforce reductions, selling numerous hotel properties in the United States and Europe (in favor of leasing them), and selling its Spanish concession restaurant subsidiary, General de Restaurantes S.A. Proceeds from these measures fueled expansion in the Asia/Pacific region and the 1998 acquisition of Postiljon, a Dutch hotel group the company planned to incorporate into its Mercure chain.

As the century drew to a close Accor made another pivotal move into the U.S. hospitality industry, buying Red Roof Inns for $1.1 billion. Red Roof, considered a step or so above Motel 6, brought in revenues of more than $375 million in 1998 and net income of more than $34 million. Accor had raised the majority of the funds by selling hundreds of its Motel 6 properties in lease-back deals to generate cash for the Red Roof Inn purchase and other hotel properties in Western Europe and Australia. Accor also entered a joint venture with the Moroccan and Tunisian governments to build and manage resorts and spas in those countries, with an investment of at least $250 million in 1999.

The New Millennium: The Early 2000s

In the first year of the new millennium, Accor was determined to lure Americans to its popular Sofitel luxury hotel brand. Five-star Sofitels were built in major metropolitan areas such as Chicago, Dallas, Houston, Los Angeles, Miami, New York City, San Francisco, and Washington, D.C., along with several European cities. Accor opened a total of 254 new hotels during 2000, of which 12 were Sofitels. The company also launched its first web site, Accorhotels.com, offering information and online booking services that received some 12 million hits during the year. In addition, Accor sold its half-ownership of Europcar, its car rental agency, to partner Volkswagen; opened a Novotel and an Ibis in the Sydney, Australia Olympic Village; and expanded into Israel through a stake in Clal Tourism. Accor finished 2000 with revenues of EUR 7.01 billion, with hotels bringing in EUR 4.74 billion, services EUR 437 million, and its travel agencies, casinos, restaurants, and onboard rail services the remaining EUR 1.83 billion.

By 2001 Accor took its Sofitel brand to Asia, opening luxe establishments in China and Vietnam, and bought a minority stake in Century International Hotels, based in Hong Kong. While its Asia/Pacific region experienced solid growth, Accor also expanded its reach in Latin America (opening its 100th hotel in Brazil), the Middle East (building new hotels in Dubai, Bahrain, and Yemen), and Australia (taking over a landmark hotel in Sydney). Revenues for 2001 reached EUR 7.29 billion with hotels, with the company's upscale and business establishments almost equal to the combined bookings of its economy accommodations in the United States and Europe: EUR 2.7 billion for the luxe rooms versus EUR 2.4 billion for the economies (EUR 1.02 billion in Europe, EUR 1.33 billion in the United States). Although all figures represented a relatively strong year, the last quarter of 2001 and first half of 2002 were greatly affected by the travel industry slump after the terrorist attacks in the United States on September 11.

For 2002 Accor continued its Asian expansion, buying the remaining interests in its Hong Kong partner, Century International, and China's Zenith International Hotels. The company also bought stakes in hotel chains in Poland (Orbis), Germany (Dorint AG), and Egypt (El-Gezira Hotels); opened 14 new Sofitel hotels in major metro areas; and its newest brand, Suitehotel (launched the previous year), designed for both the comfort and functionality of extended-stay customers, gained popularity in Europe. Revenues for 2002 rebounded nicely in the second half of the year to reach EUR 7.14 billion, with its U.S. holdings—Motel 6 and Red Roof Inn—down significantly from the previous year due to the terrorist attacks.

Accor continued its rapid expansion plans in the United States for its Motel 6, Red Roof Inn, and Sofitel brands, while concentrating on Novotel, Ibis, Sofitel, and Suitehotels in Europe and Asia. The company, which had seen its online reservations grow at breakneck speed, teamed with rivals Hilton International and Six Continents to launch a new reservations service called WorldRes.Europe. The new site, cleared by the European Commission in 2003, allowed travel agencies, hotel personnel, and travel sites to reserve and hold bookings for each hospitality giant in real-time. While hopes were high for the new web site, Accor and competitors were hurt by a sharp downturn in travel and tourism in Europe and Asia. In Asia the

SARS outbreak shut down travel in and out of the region, while the war in Iraq and political woes affected travel in France and the United Kingdom. Despite the circumstances, Accor maintained its expansion, hoping to bring its total number of hotels worldwide to 4,000 by the end of 2003.

At the close of 2003 Accor had almost met its goal with 3,894 hotels and 453,403 individual rooms worldwide. Revenues for 2003 were EUR 6.83 billion, with the company's European properties still outpacing its American holdings. The U.S. hotel chains (Motel 6 and Red Roof Inns) were down more than 18 percent from 2002 to 2003, while Accor's upscale and economy chains in Europe posted slight gains of 1.3 and 2.3 percent, respectively. All other segments—restaurants, casinos, rail, and travel agencies—experienced declines as well, with foodservice and gambling in the double digits (15.6 and 16.2 percent, respectively). Accor's travel agency unit was poised for major growth after the merger of Carlson Wagonlit Travel and the Lyon, France-based Protravel S.A. Accor hoped the merger would unseat American Express as one of France's top travel agencies. Combined revenues for Carlson and Protravel for 2003 were EUR 2.3 billion ($2.75 billion).

Accor opened its fifth Sofitel in Bangkok, Thailand, in 2004, bringing its total properties in Asia to more than 200 hotels in 15 countries. Worldwide, Accor was ranked fourth largest behind Cendant, InterContinental, and Marriott International, though the company was the leading hospitality firm in Europe, ahead of InterContinental, Best Western, and Hilton International. What distinguished Accor from its rivals, however, was its broad coverage of the hospitality and leisure market with establishments for all budgets, from one- to five-star properties. Formule 1, Etap, Motel 6, and Red Roof were bargain priced with few amenities; Ibis and Suitehotel offered more services at a reasonable price; Mercure and Novotel offered travelers midscale accommodations with comfort and a measure of sophistication; and Sofitel served the luxury market with gourmet restaurants and upscale architecture in major international locations.

As Accor entered the mid-2000s the company had not only gained worldwide respect for its burgeoning empire, but was able to settle an old score when it bought a 30 percent stake in Club Méditerranée S.A. for EUR 252 million ($305 million). Back in the 1980s Accor had tried, without success, to merge with Club Med at the height of its popularity; by 2004 Club Med had been upstaged by such rivals as Sandals Inc. and had fallen on hard times. Accor intended to bolster its presence in the leisure market, while continuing its plans of opening a total of about 200 hotels annually for the next several years, especially in Asia. These plans were disrupted, however, when a tsunami in December 2004 devastated many countries in the Asia/Pacific Rim region and hit Accor's Sofitel hotel in northern Phuket, Thailand, killing hundreds of employees and guests. Two other establishments in the area sustained damage but had no casualties. Accor immediately sent representatives with food, clothing, and water to the region.

Principal Subsidiaries

Académie Accor; Accor Asia Pacific Corp.; Accor Hotels Belgium; Accor Casinos S.A. (50%); Accor GmbH (Austria); Accor Hotels Denmark; Accor Hoteles Espange (Spain); Accor Hotellerie DTC (Germany); Accor Lodging North America; Accor Redevances; Accor Services Austria; Accor Services Chili (Chile); Accor Services Deutschland (Germany); Accor Services Empresariales (Mexico); Accor Services France; Accor Suisse (Switzerland); Accor TRB (Belgium); Accor UK; AS Australia; Carlson USA (50%); Carlson Canada (50%); ESA (Portugal); Frantour S.A.; Hotexco; Lenôtre; Luncheon Vouchers (U.K.); MMH Mercure (Netherlands); Nhere B.V. (Netherlands); Novotel Canada; Novotel Netherlands; Novotel USA; Pannonia (Hungary); Postiljon; Red Roof Inns; Rikskuponger (Sweden); SFPTH S.A.; SPHU (Hôtel Union, Senegal); Saudi Hotels Management; Scapa Italia (Italy); Servicios Ticket (Argentina); Sifalberghi (Italy); WLT Mexicana (Mexico); WLT Travel UK (50%).

Principal Competitors

Best Western Corporation; Cendant Corporation; Choice International; Hilton Hotels Corporation; InterContinental Hotels Group PLC; Marriott International Inc.; Starwood Hotels & Resorts Worldwide, Inc.

Further Reading

"Accor Becomes Partner in Beijing Tourist Board," *Travel Trade Gazette UK & Ireland,* August 23, 1999, p. 7.

"Accor Web Site Tops 12 Million Hits," *Lodging Hospitality,* March 15, 2001, p. 42.

Bergsman, Steve, "Accor Gains Ground with U.S. Acquisitions," *Hotel & Motel Management,* May 27, 1991, pp. 3, 60–61.

Bond, Helen, "Motel 6 Eyes More Moves," *Hotel & Motel Management,* May 27, 1991, pp. 1, 76.

Bruce, Leigh, "The Two-Headed Chairmanship That Keeps Accor Soaring," *International Management,* January 1987, pp. 26–28.

"Carlson Finalizes Deal," *Travel Weekly,* February 17, 1997, p. 38.

Casussus, Barbara, "Accor Plans Expansion After Huge Rise in Profit," *Travel Trade Gazette Europa,* April 8, 1999, p. 4.

"Circling the Wagons," *Economist,* January 27, 1990.

"Commission Clears Accor, Hilton, Six Continents Internet Bookings Joint Venture," *Europe Media,* May 20, 2003.

Daneshkhu, Scheherazade, "Hard to Find: Hotel Rooms and Profits," *Financial Times,* December 16, 1999, p. 37.

Evans, Richard, "Le Motel 6, C'est Moi: France's Accor Has Mastered the American Art of Mass Marketing," *Barron's,* April 30, 2001, p. 20.

Flowers, Grant, "Accor to Expand Sofitel Brand Worldwide," *Travel Weekly,* March 25, 1999, p. 1.

——, "Accor Unveils First New York City Property," *Travel Weekly,* August 7, 2000, p. 24.

"French Hotel Group Acquires 40-Percent Stake in Clal Tourism," *Israel Business Today,* May 2000, p. 17.

"French Travel Groups Merge," *Daily Deal,* November 28, 2003.

Huband, Marc, "Big Investment in Tourism: Accor Group," *Financial Times,* December 20, 1999, p. 6.

Jones, Sandra, "Accor Launches Rebranding, Proposes Venture with Air France," *Hotel & Motel Management,* July 3, 1993, p. 11.

Lever, Robert, "Viva la Capitalisme," *Barron's,* June 2001, p. 14.

Matlack, Carol, "It's Time for Accor to Get Some Respect," *Business Week,* September 22, 2003, p. 32.

McDowell, Edwin, "Not Just Leaving the Light On," *New York Times,* October 28, 1998, p. C1.

"Meat and Drink," *Economist,* July 8, 1995, p. 7.

"Playing Monopoly: Luxury Hotels," *Economist,* May 7, 1994, pp. 77–78.

Reier, Sharon, "Bedroom Eyes," *Financial World,* June 9, 1992, pp. 56–58.

"Rest Assured," *Economist,* January 10, 1998.

Riemer, Blanca, "This Buy-America Bandwagon Could Hit a Few Potholes," *Business Week,* July 30, 1990, p. 21.

Shundich, Steven, "Corporate 200: Through Mergers and Acquisitions, Consolidation Continues to Reshape Hospitality Industry Worldwide," *Hotels,* July 1997, p. 45.

Sidron, Jorge, "Accor, Century International Cobrand Five Properties," *Travel Weekly,* November 15, 2001, p. 20.

Strauss, Karen, "Accor's Pélisson: 'It's Only the Beginning,' " *Hotel,* September 2004, p. 32.

"Suitehotel Brings All-Suites to Europe Hotels," *Lodging Hospitality,* March 1, 2002, p. 12.

Toy, Stewart, "Accor Goes with the Modified American Plan," *Business Week,* October 1, 1990, pp. 78–79.

Walsh, John P., "Accor Plans Balanced Growth in U.S.," *Hotel & Management,* April 15, 2002, p. 3.

Whitford, Marty, "The Price Is Right," *Hotel & Motel Management,* August 9, 1999, p. 1.

—Jennifer Kerns
—updates: Susan Windisch Brown; Nelson Rhodes

Aerolíneas Argentinas S.A.

Calle Hipolito Bouchard 547
9th Floor
Buenos Aires
1106
Argentina
Telephone: + 54 (11) 4130-3000
Toll Free: (800) 333-0276; 0810-222-VOLAR (86527)
Web site: http://www.aerolineas.com.ar

Private Company
Incorporated: 1949
Employees: 5,100
Sales: $1 billion (2005 est.)
NAIC: 481111 Scheduled Passenger Air Transportation;
    481211 Nonscheduled Chartered Passenger Air
    Transportation; 488119 Other Airport Operations

Aerolíneas Argentinas S.A. is Argentina's leading airline, flown by more than five million passengers a year. The carrier struggled under foreign ownership through the 1990s, accumulating massive debts. This burden was reduced after Air Comet, a unit of Spanish tour operator Grupo Marsans, acquired control of Aerolíneas Argentinas in 2001. Since then, the company has returned to profitability and begun rebuilding and expanding its international route network.

Origins

Argentine civil aviation has its roots in the French airmail line Aéropostale and its South American subsidiaries, one of which was Aeroposta Argentina. Aeroposta was established in 1927 primarily as a mail carrier. Early flights in this country were often perilous; rudimentary equipment, strong winds, and poor landing strips inspired flying adventures of the kind recounted by the famous French aviator and writer Antoine de Saint-Exupéry. Moreover, the company was battered by worldwide economic depression in the early 1930s, during which time the French government withdrew much of its financial support for parent company Aéropostale. In 1932, control of Aeroposta underwent several changes, including temporary ownership by the Argen-

tinian post office, but the company ultimately survived as Aeroposta Argentina, S.A., the national airline of Argentina. In 1937, Aeroposta's economic woes were somewhat allayed when Argentina's Pueyrredon financial group, a conglomerate of banks and insurance companies, bought out the remaining French interests in the line. Although Aeroposta came under the control of Ernesto Pueyrredon, it also continued to receive a subsidy from the Argentinian government.

Beginning in the late 1930s, other airlines were starting to crop up in Argentina. In 1946, the government of Argentina imposed some organization on the country's airlines (and fended off competition from foreign airlines, such as the U.S.-based PANAGRA), forming a system of mixed-stock companies. Aside from Aeroposta, three new joint stock companies were created out of the airlines that had sprung up in the 1930s. The first was FAMA (Flota Aérea Mercante Argentina), which set the precedent for the nation's international air service. ALFA (Aviaciín del Litoral Fluvial Argentina) was formed by merging one private, one military, and one civil airline. ZONDA (Zonas Oeste y Norte de Aerolíneas Argentinas) took over PANAGRA's domestic trade network in the northwest.

1950s–70s: Striving to Stay Aloft Amidst Government Upheaval

On May 3, 1949, a new nationalistic government in Argentina, led by Juan Perón, merged the four joint-stock companies—Aeroposta Argentina, FAMA, ALFA, and ZONDA—into the new state airline, Aerolíneas Argentinas. This monopoly would last until 1956. After working to integrate the aircraft and routes of all four operations, Aerolíneas Argentinas achieved operating efficiencies and became a member of the International Air Transport Association (IATA).

When a military coup ousted Perón, however, a new provisional government liberalized the aviation market again. Competition ensued as Argentinian investors formed new airlines. Privately backed Transcontinental, S.A., for example, provided six years of competition before financial woes resulted in its being taken over by Austral, another new private carrier. Aerolíneas Ini and Transatlantica were two other competitors for Aerolíneas Argentina's business during this period.

Company Perspectives:

Could we ever have imagined, fifty years ago, such evolution, such route development? Was it a drive from within to fly across our vast country that gave us the impulse to reach out to the world? Was it the knowledge of our pilots or the spirit of the Argentines that gave this impulse to Aerolíneas? One thing we do know for sure is that the word 'impossible' does not exist. What we do know is that Aerolíneas, either with its present equipment or with the super-'Jumbos' yet to come, will expand into the future, on internal or overseas routes, and will be the main link for the business traveller and tourist alike with the rest of the world.

None of the new entrants had the experience or resources of Aerolíneas Argentinas (AR). AR was able to launch South America's first commercial jets in March 1959: six Comet IVs received to settle a bill for harboring British troops during World War II. Within a couple of years, however, half of these had crashed, and though no fatalities were reported the company's president was forced to resign. Under new leadership, AR continued to expand and modernize its fleet, retiring older aircraft and establishing service to popular resort destinations.

By the 1960s, AR was the leading South American airline, flying more than 600 million passenger-kilometers a year. Financial and managerial woes were emerging, however. In 1963, the airline dropped out of the International Air Transport Association (IATA), a cartel of world airlines, when that organization denied AR the right to impose a surcharge for flights on jets. Both AR and its competitor Austral had been losing money on the regulated domestic fares and had been granted government subsidies to help offset the losses. A new board of directors took over AR in June 1964 amid charges of mismanagement and corruption at the airline. The next year, the new leaders set about improving the airline's fleet, establishing a relationship with Boeing, by ordering several of that company's 707s, which would last for many years. AR rejoined the IATA during this time. The year 1966 saw yet another change of administration.

In 1967, in order that AR and Austral might co-exist under government control, a new Argentinian president divvied up domestic air routes between Austral-A.L.A.(Aerotransportes Litoral Argentina, its new partner) and AR. By now, AR's Boeing 707s were flying the world's longest nonstop scheduled flight at the time: 5,700 miles from Rio de Janeiro to Rome. Service to New York also had begun, and by the end of the decade, AR had obtained clearance to open service to the West Coast of the United States.

In 1972, Argentinian and U.S. authorities briefly locked horns over the rights of Pan American and Braniff airlines to serve Argentina. When Argentina officials denied these American airlines the right to expand their routes in Argentina, the U.S. government responded by attempting to curb AR's presence in the United States. Settlements over the routes were eventually made, and AR was able to add nonstop service to Miami and Cape Town in 1973, the latter in conjunction with South African Airways. In December, new management in-stalled by the returning Juan Perón (the second executive shuffle in a year) gave the airline a new emphasis on commercial viability in route selection and fare determination.

Although Perón died in 1974 and his wife, Isobel Perón, was overthrown in 1976, the structure of the airline remained relatively unchanged. The company continued to weather upheavals in management, intense competition from Austral, and ever-changing government policies. AR began operating massive Boeing 747 widebody jets to Madrid in January 1977, launching a period of expansion. After testing the route with charters, AR pioneered the first scheduled (monthly) service across Antarctica, to Auckland, New Zealand. AR began the 1980s as the third busiest airline in South America after VARIG and Mexicana, flying six billion passenger-kilometers a year.

The Path to Privatization in the 1980s

The disastrous Falklands War in April 1982 did not help Argentina's economy, which fell apart in the mid-1970s during Isobel Perón's rule. Inflation reached triple or quadruple digits, depending upon the estimate, and in 1986 the government of Argentina planned for the privatization of several large companies in order to satisfy its creditors. AR was to be one of the first.

In February 1988, the Directory of Public Enterprises (DEP) announced the sale of 40 percent of AR to SAS for $204 million. Cielos del Sur, which owned Austral, itself privatized in 1987, put forth an informal but well publicized counteroffer with the support of Swissair and Alitalia. SAS withdrew its bid in December 1988 after a highly politicized debate pitting President Raul Alfonsín against incumbent Carlos Menem. The Cielos del Sur group was not able to finalize its bid, however, due to a lack of financial disclosures from the government. Then, Swissair withdrew from the group, scuttling the offer. Menem renewed efforts to find a buyer after winning office in May 1989.

Menem's efforts were frustrated by the company's poor financial health; it was losing $10 million a month in 1990, which was a terrible year for the airline industry as a whole, with most of the world's major carriers posting losses. Nevertheless, a consortium led by Spain's carrier Iberia made a bid in June 1990, kicking off AR's tortuous, extended privatization process. In its initial offer, Iberia would control 30 percent, three Spanish banks another 19 percent, Argentinian investors 36 percent, employees 10 percent, and the government 5 percent, resulting in 51 percent Argentine ownership. Iberia and its partners agreed to pay more than $2 billion for their 85 percent share, including a $130 million initial cash payment. Not included in the new deal were AR's lucrative ramp service and duty-free businesses.

Several factors soured the deal for Iberia once it was committed to the buyout. When Enrique Pescarmon sold Cielos del Sur (and thus Austral) to Iberia in March 1991, leaving the partnership, his share was split between other Argentinian interests. Mounting losses through 1992 (when AR lost $189 million on revenues of $911 million) necessitated a capital infusion from the Spaniards and the Argentine government, diluting other shareholdings of the private local investors. The Spanish holdings, however, remained the same. The government owned 43 percent, which it intended to reduce to 10 percent once the

Key Dates:

1949: Aerolíneas Argentinas (AR) is created by the Juan Perón administration out of four existing airlines.
1959: AR introduces South America's first commercial jets.
1967: AR's Boeing 707s operate the world's longest non-stop scheduled flight.
1977: Widebody Boeing 747 service to Madrid begins; AR pioneers scheduled flights across Antarctica.
1982: The Falklands War badly affects Argentina's economy.
1988: SAS offers an unsuccessful bid for 40 percent of AR.
1990: A group led by Spanish carrier Iberia agrees to pay $2 billion for 85 percent of AR.
1998: AMR Corp. buys 10 percent of Interinvest, AR's holding company.
1999: The Iberia-led group unsuccessfully tries to sell off its stake.
2001: Spanish tour operator Grupo Marsans acquires control of the airline.
2002: AR posts its first operating profit in 25 years.
2003: A new Executive Jet service is unveiled using modified Boeing 737s.
2004: New headquarters are constructed as the airline expands.

market allowed. In addition, $2.1 billion of foreign debt, part of Iberia's purchase requirement, ended up costing more than originally estimated. Finally, postponed layoffs of 775 workers incited labor protests. Moreover, Iberia suffered serious losses at home, $264 million on 1992 revenues of $3.6 billion.

New Investors in the 1990s

As costly as it proved to Iberia, AR still controlled one-third of South America's air traffic, making it a somewhat attractive investment to global competitors. Since Iberia needed government subsidies for its own survival, the European Commission mandated that it reduce its holdings in AR. Merrill Lynch and Bankers Trust bought into the company in 1996, and American Airlines parent AMR Corporation beat out Continental to take a 10 percent share of Interinvest, AR's holding company, in 1998.

The number-crunching methodology of American Airlines (AA) brought quite a culture change to the airline, accustomed to decidedly less formal decision-making. AA managers immediately set out to reduce short-term debt of about $700 million and slashed the payroll. They also used AA standards to improve customer service, starting out a process that could make AR eligible for membership in the OneWorld global alliance. Reducing the number of aircraft types was also a priority; still, the company ordered a dozen Airbus A340s, a type new to Latin America, for its long-haul needs.

AR faced stiff international competition from LAN Chile and VARIG. New open skies agreements cleared the way for Continental and Delta into the Argentine market as well. A

recession at home compounded the carrier's difficulties in 1999, even as local cut-rate upstarts such as Southern Winds Líneas Aéreas plagued the airline. AR's owners had failed to find a buyer, or a way out, by the end of December. Interinvest, which then owned 85 percent of AR, was in turn 80 percent owned by the Spanish government via SEPI (Sociedad Estatal de Participaciones Industriales), 10 percent owned by Iberia, and 10 percent by AA. Employees owned 10 percent of AR and the Argentine government the remaining 5 percent. Nevertheless, company literature remained optimistic. Losses for 1999 reached $240 million as the Latin American aviation industry struggled through a recession.

Acquisition by Marsans in 2001

American Airlines stopped managing the airline in 2000. By the end of the year, Aerolíneas Argentinas had accumulated debts of nearly $1 billion. In October 2000, the Spanish government agreed to invest an additional $650 million in the airline.

SEPI proffered a restructuring plan that focused on cutting costs through scaling back services and cutting jobs and wages. Most of the airline's unions, reported *Airline Business,* preferred to have AR recapitalized and an international strategic partner enlisted, while expanding routes.

The fate of 6,700 employees at stake made the airline's fate a contentious political issue. As negotiations between the governments of Argentina and Spain dragged on, AR focused on preserving enough cash to keep flying. By the middle of 2001, AR was operating only half its scheduled international routes.

SEPI decided to sell off the airline, first placing it in bankruptcy protection, and in October 2001 chose Air Comet, a partial subsidiary of privately owned Spanish tour operator Grupo Marsans, from a field of several bidders. As part of the deal, Air Comet/Marsans agreed to keep all of the airline's employees on the payroll for two years. Marsans was acquiring 92 percent of shares in exchange for assuming half of AR's $1.8 billion debt. Marsans was planning to raise additional capital from private investors in Argentina, as well as through eventual international stock offerings.

LatinFinance remarked that this was AR's second privatization, by a second government. The publication also noted that the timing of the deal, after the September 11 terrorist attacks on the United States, was challenging. According to *Latin Trade,* however, Antonio Mata, AR's new head, was able to negotiate an average 60 percent discount with suppliers in the degraded aviation market. Mata was a veteran of Spain's tourism industry and founder of Air Comet.

The devaluation of the Argentine peso in 2001 boosted tourism, observed *Latin Trade.* The next year, Aerolíneas Argentinas was able to post its first operating profit in a quarter-century, about $22 million. AR had an 85 percent market share on domestic routes.

Passenger count rose 40 percent to 5.1 million in 2003. To help ward off competition from upstart airlines catering to the business crowd, a new "Executive Jet" service was unveiled during the year. This program used a fleet of three Boeing 737s modified to carry just 30 passengers in an extra level of comfort.

In 2004, the company began an ambitious $557 million fleet renewal plan that would see 49 aircraft acquired in three years. New aircraft included the most advanced Boeing 747 variant.

At the same time, the airline was adding a $3 million flight simulator to train Boeing 737 pilots for Aerolíneas Argentinas and other local airlines. AR had become more self-reliant in maintenance work.

A new $100 million headquarters called "Ciudad Aerolíneas" was being built. The company was expanding throughout the South American region, adding service to Chile, Bolivia, Paraguay, and Uruguay. Parent company Marsans was creating a new Chilean airline, Aerolineas del Sur, to operate in Aerolíneas Argentinas colors. A plan to acquire Pluna, a Uruguayan airline controlled by VARIG, was canceled.

Principal Subsidiaries

Aerohandling S.A.; Jet Paq S.A.

Principal Operating Units

Aerolíneas Cargo; Austral Líneas Aéreas.

Principal Competitors

LAN Chile S.A.; Southern Winds Airlines; TAM Linhas Aéreas S.A.; VARIG S.A.

Further Reading

"Aerolineas Plans Fresh Start As Marsans Steps In," *Airline Business,* November 1, 2001, p. 18.

Cameron, Doug, "Aerolineas Needs a Lift," *Airfinance Journal,* April 1996, p. 20.

Carey, Susan, "Europe's Airlines Giving Up on Mergers in Favor of Other Forms of Cooperation," *Wall Street Journal,* April 6, 1988, p. 1.

Christian, Shirley, "Argentina Closes Sale of Airline," *New York Times,* November 23, 1990, p. D1.

Davies, R.E.G., *Airlines of Latin America Since 1919,* Washington, D.C.: Smithsonian Institution, 1984.

"Don't Fly with Me, Argentina," *Economist* (U.S.), June 9, 2001, p. 3.

Footer, Kevin, "In Search of a Leader: What Keeps Aerolineas Argentinas Airborne? It Could Be the Most Recent Round of Funding—US$650 Million—But the Real Answer Is Politics," *Latin CEO: Executive Strategies for the Americas,* February 2001, pp. 48 + .

Forward, David C., "Aerolíneas Argentinas Does the Tango with Toulouse," *Airways,* October 1999, pp. 20–27.

Frascara, Ricardo, "52 Years," Buenos Aires: Aerolíneas Argentinas S.A.

Goodman, Joshua, "Over the Top: Amid Economic Recovery, Aerolineas Argentinas Sets Sights on Rival LAN," *Latin Trade,* August 2004, p. 54.

Grosse, Robert, "A Privatization Nightmare: Aerolíneas Argentinas," in *Privatizing Monopolies: Lessons from the Telecommunications and Transport Sectors in Latin America,* edited by Ravi Ramamurti, Baltimore: Johns Hopkins, 1996.

Kamm, Thomas, "Privatization Campaign in Argentina Bogs Down," *Wall Street Journal,* October 25, 1990, p. A16.

Knibb, Dave, "Aerolineas Argentinas Approaches Moment of Truth," *Airline Business,* August 1, 2001, p. 18.

——, "Aerolineas Tries to Find Middle Ground," *Airline Business,* October 1, 2000, p. 16.

Limo, Edvaldo Pereira, "Tango American," *Air Transport World,* October 1999, pp. 96–99.

——, "Tango Twosome," *Air Transport World,* December 1997, pp. 61–64.

O'Brien, Maria, "So Long, Farewell Aerolineas: The Argentine National Airline Is in Private Hands, 11 Years After It Was First Privatized," *LatinFinance,* November 2001, p. 54.

Page, Paul, "Troubled Tango," *Air Cargo World,* July 2001, p. 26.

Riding, Alan, "Argentina's Privatization Battle," *New York Times,* November 28, 1988, p. D8.

Schumacher, Edward, "Argentina's Chief Banker Is Held; Pressure Grows to Renounce Debt," *New York Times,* October 4, 1983, p. A1.

Vitzhum, Carlta, and Craig Torres, "Aerolineas Argentinas's Sale Deadline Is Set to Expire with No Buyer in Sight," *Wall Street Journal,* December 30, 1999, p. A3.

Warn, Ken, "SEPI in Aerolineas Rescue Plan," *Financial Times* (London), Companies & Finance: The Americas, June 14, 2000, p. 34.

—Frederick C. Ingram

Aerosonic Corporation

1212 North Hercules Avenue
Clearwater, Florida 33765
U.S.A.
Telephone: (727) 461-3000
Fax: (727) 447-5926
Web site: http://www.aerosonic.com

Public Company
Incorporated: 1968 as Instrument Technology
   Corporation
Employees: 269
Sales: $31.11 million (2004)
Stock Exchanges: American
Ticker Symbol: AIM
NAIC: 334511 Search, Detection, Navigation, Guidance,
   Aeronautical, and Nautical System and Instrument
   Manufacturing

Aerosonic Corporation is a producer of aircraft instruments and precision machined components. The company makes a variety of instruments including altimeters, airspeed indicators, rate of climb indicators, angle of attack/stall warning systems, engine vibration monitoring systems, and Integrated Multifunction Probes. The latter, a space- and weight-saving combination of several air pressure-related instruments, has found favor among makers of advanced business aircraft and jet fighters.

The company has four divisions in three locations. Flight instruments and precision machined components are made in Clearwater, Florida. Another aircraft instrument maker, Avionics Specialties of Charlottesville, Virginia, was acquired in 1993. Aerosonic maintains a test facility in Wichita, Kansas. About 32 percent of the company's equity is held by former Chairman and CEO J. Mervyn Nabors.

Origins

Herb Frank founded the company in Cincinnati in 1953; the business moved to Clearwater, Florida, in 1956. Aero-Sonic Instrument Corporation, an Ohio corporation, was formed in 1956

and the next year merged into Aerosonic Corp., a recently registered Florida corporation. In 1970, Aerosonic Corp. of Florida merged with Instrument Technology Corporation (ITC), which had incorporated as a Delaware corporation on October 3, 1969. ITC was renamed Aerosonic Corporation in November 1970.

Frank was a graduate of the University of Cincinnati and Cal Tech. He suffered partial paralysis on his left side, and his efforts in employing disabled workers were recognized by President Lyndon Johnson.

Aerosonic produced mechanical flight instruments such as altimeters (altitude indicators). By the 1980s, sales were in the $10 million range. The company posted net income of $395,000 on sales of $10.5 million in the fiscal year ended January 1982, but lost $223,000 in fiscal 1983 as sales slipped to $6.8 million.

Late 1980s Ordnance Venture

The company would be profitable again by the late 1980s. Net income was $107,000 in fiscal 1987 on sales of $9.2 million. Net income rose to $166,000 in fiscal 1988 on sales of $11.1 million.

In August 1989, Aerosonic won an Army contract to produce 4,000 aircraft clocks. It was later revealed that Aerosonic had used some Swiss-made mechanisms in fulfilling the contract, which specified 100 percent U.S. content. Aerosonic agreed to a fine of $200,000 in 1992 to settle the case.

The market for military and civil aircraft slowed in the late 1980s. A new business producing components (base closure assemblies) for 155-mm artillery shells was launched in 1988. Some shareholders criticized the timing, as the Soviet threat was then being defused through perestroika. This unit, however, would be responsible for raising Aerosonic's revenue to $29 million in 1992, thanks to Operation Desert Storm. In February 1991, the company received an $8 million Army contract for artillery shell parts.

Net sales were $11.1 million in the fiscal year ended January 1990; net income, $75,000. Sales reached $29.5 million for the fiscal year ended January 1992. Earnings were $1.6 million. Aerosonic had 320 employees in the early 1990s.

Acquiring Avionics Specialties in 1993

Aerosonic acquired the avionics business of Teledyne Industries Inc. in January 1993. Teledyne Avionics, based in Virginia, had been in business since the 1940s and produced angle of attack and stall warning systems, among other equipment. It employed 120 people. One product, the integrated multifunction probe (IMFP), combined several instruments in one unit. The new unit continued to operate independently, under the name Avionics Specialties Inc. The acquisition brought Aerosonic further into the jet aircraft market.

Aerosonic shares moved from the NASDAQ to the American Stock Exchange in March 1993. A Newport, Arkansas plant was sold to a group led by its managers in 1993. After earning $869,000 in 1993, Aerosonic posted a $211,000 loss in 1994, even as sales edged up 2 percent to $24.4 million. Avionics Specialties was the strongest unit, thanks to sales of its turbine-engine power analyzer and recorder system.

From mid-1992 to mid-1995, the CEO position was held by David S. Goldman, Herb Frank's son-in-law, who had been with Aerosonic since 1969. Goldman stepped down as chief executive in April 1995, returning to his position as chief financial officer.

Frank regained a seat on the board in March 1995, but died the next year. He was buried in the white smock he liked to wear around the factory, with one of the company's instruments in his hand. According to the *St. Petersburg Times,* he was remembered as a father figure to many in the company, including Merv Nabors, who came from a broken home and described Aerosonic as a second family.

Nabors became the company's CEO after Frank's death in April 1996. He also acquired the Frank family's shareholding for about $2 million. Nabors had been with the company since the 1960s when, according to the *Tampa Tribune,* he was recruited by Frank at age 16 to play third base on the company softball team. Nabors eventually became Aerosonic's largest shareholder, with 32 percent of shares, but he started, literally, in the mailroom, and worked a number of jobs in every department, from machining to accounting.

Going Digital in the Mid-1990s

In 1984, Nabors had launched American Instrument Co., a maker of electronic subassemblies, when Frank proved unwilling to enter the new digital realm. After the management shift, he was able to update the product line at Aerosonic.

Until then, the company's electromechanical instruments had used analog dials. Aerosonic began to produce digital instruments with digital displays—a much higher margin business, with units costing in the thousands, rather than hundreds, of dollars. They were also smaller, freeing up precious cockpit space. Aerosonic developed compact two-inch digital altimeters and airspeed indicators. Learjet Inc. and Beech Aircraft Corporation (later part of Raytheon Aircraft Company) were important early customers. There still remained something of a market for analog instruments, which were mandated as backups by the FAA.

Another important new technology was a probe capable of measuring speed, altitude, and angle of attack all in one unit. This was produced by Aerosonic subsidiary Avionics Specialties Inc. at its Charlottesville, Virginia plant. The integrated multifunction probe (IMFP) allowed for savings in cost as well as weight. It was chosen for inclusion in Honeywell Inc.'s new avionics system.

Nabors also streamlined the company after becoming CEO. The ordnance and automotive parts business was sold off in 1996. National Metalworking Corp., an affiliate of Lancaster, Pennsylvania-based Bulova Technologies LLC, bought the ordnance unit, which had lost $2 million on sales of $19 million in the prior year.

The administrative staff also was trimmed, while new talents in finance and marketing were brought in. Aerosonic had 300 employees before the divestment of the ordnance unit and other cuts, which brought the headcount down to 200.

Nabors succeeded in quickly steering the company to profitability. Aerosonic lost $1.8 million in 1995, but reported profits for the rest of the decade. By 1997, a recovery was well underway: The company posted income of $1.2 million on sales of $19.3 million. Revenues were $14.9 million in 1998, with net income of $389,000.

A rebound in the general aviation industry aided the recovery. Nevertheless, the company diversified somewhat, organizing its Precision Components division in August 1998. Most of its output of machined mechanical components would go to the optics industry.

More Military Work After 9/11

In the fiscal year ended January 2001, 71 percent of Aerosonic's $25 million in sales went to the private sector. The share of military work increased to about 50 percent within two years after the September 11, 2001 terrorist attacks on the United States.

According to the *St. Petersburg Times,* 80 percent of the parts for Aerosonic's products were being produced at the Clearwater site. The company had about 270 employees in all.

<table>
<tr><td colspan="2" align="center">**Key Dates:**</td></tr>
<tr><td>**1953:**</td><td>Aerosonic is formed in Cincinnati by Herb Frank.</td></tr>
<tr><td>**1956:**</td><td>The company moves to Clearwater, Florida.</td></tr>
<tr><td>**1970:**</td><td>Aerosonic is merged with Instrument Technology Corporation.</td></tr>
<tr><td>**1988:**</td><td>Artillery shell component production is started.</td></tr>
<tr><td>**1993:**</td><td>Avionics Specialties is acquired from Teledyne.</td></tr>
<tr><td>**1996:**</td><td>Merv Nabors becomes CEO and steers the company into digital instruments.</td></tr>
<tr><td>**1998:**</td><td>The Precision Components division is formed.</td></tr>
<tr><td>**2002:**</td><td>David Baldini succeeds Nabors as CEO and chairman.</td></tr>
</table>

John Mervyn Nabors resigned as company president in November 2002 and as chairman six months later. His CFO, Eric McCracken, resigned in October 2002. David A. Baldini replaced Nabors as president, CEO, and chairman.

The Securities and Exchange Commission (SEC) subsequently investigated Nabors and McCracken for overstating earnings through use of accounting gimmicks. Nabors paid a fine of $260,000 to settle the case against him without admitting guilt. No charges were brought against the company. Aerosonic filed restated reports from 2000 to 2004.

The company continued to land contracts, building its backlog to $54 million by the end of 2002. It agreed to supply flight instrument probes for Lockheed-Martin Aeronautics Co.'s Joint Strike Fighter. Lockheed-Martin had used similar probes in its most advanced F-16s. In May 2002, Aerosonic got its largest contract to date, a $19.6 million deal to produce 4,500 altimeters for the Army. Another large contract was won from the U.S. Army in November 2003. It involved overhauling encoding altimeters and had a potential value of $4.3 million over three years.

Sales rose 21 percent to $31.1 million in 2004, though net income dropped 50 percent to $500,000. Domestic sales accounted for 87 percent of the total, with the defense sector taking a little more than half.

Principal Divisions

Clearwater Instruments; Kansas Instruments; Avionics Specialties, Inc.; Precision Components.

Principal Competitors

Honeywell International Inc.; Rockwell Automation; Safe Flight Instrument Corporation.

Further Reading

"Aerosonic Buys Teledyne Avionics," *Flight International*, February 10, 1993, p. 16.

Coryell, George, "Aerosonic Files Suit vs. Ex-CEO," *Tampa Tribune*, October 4, 1996, p. 8.

Cosdon, Christina K., "Herbert Frank, Aerosonic Leader," *St. Petersburg Times*, April 20, 1996.

Goldstein, Alan, "Aerosonic Settles '83 Stock-Fraud Lawsuits," *St. Petersburg Times*, July 24, 1991, p. 1E.

——, "Aerosonic to Buy Teledyne Division," *St. Petersburg Times*, December 17, 1992, p. 1E.

——, "Pinellas Firm Gets Army Contract," *St. Petersburg Times*, February 8, 1991, p. 1E.

Hundley, Kris, "Aerosonic Adjusts on the Fly," *St. Petersburg Times*, September 13, 2001, p. 13A.

——, "Aerosonic Corp. Opens Revised Books," *St. Petersburg Times*, November 21, 2003, p. 2D.

——, "Aerosonic Looks at Its Books Again," *St. Petersburg Times*, March 18, 2003, p. 1E.

——, "As Many in Bay Area Close, Some Bustle," *St. Petersburg Times*, September 12, 2001, p. 21A.

Huntley, Helen, "St. Petersburg, Fla.-Area Mail Rooms Adjust to Anthrax Threat," *St. Petersburg Times*, October 16, 2001.

Jackovics, Ted, "Aerosonic Might Consider Buyout from Partnership," *Tampa Tribune*, July 20, 2002, p. 2.

——, "Aerosonic President Dead at 74," *Tampa Tribune*, April 20, 1996, p. 7.

——, "Aerosonic Scores High in Profits," *Tampa Tribune*, July 21, 2001, p. 2.

——, "Aerosonic to Market New Flight Information System," *Tampa Tribune*, May 14, 1998, p. 1.

——, "Clearwater Company Scores Army Contract," *Tampa Tribune*, May 17, 2002, p. 2.

——, "Ex-Aerosonic Officials Face Fraud Charges," *Tampa Tribune*, October 21, 2004, p. 1.

——, "Gauging His Future," *Tampa Tribune*, September 11, 2000, p. 8.

Norris, Kim, "Aerosonic CEO Gives Up Post in Revamping," *St. Petersburg Times*, April 7, 1995, p. 1E.

Phillips, Edward H., "Beech Selects Teledyne Avionics Stall Warning System for Starship," *Aviation Week & Space Technology*, May 2, 1988, p. 32.

Sachdev, Ameet, "Ex-CEO Pleads Guilty to Tax Evasion," *St. Petersburg Times*, June 24, 1999, p. 1E.

——, "Gauging Aerosonic's Future," *St. Petersburg Times*, February 8, 1999, p. 8.

——, "No Frills, No Perks—Yet," *St. Petersburg Times*, June 22, 1998, p. 3.

Sasso, Michael, "Aerosonic Head Resigns amid Errors," *Tampa Tribune*, May 23, 2003, p. 1.

——, "Aerosonic Shows Some Gains, But Faces Class-Action Suit," *Tampa Tribune*, November 22, 2003, p. 2.

Sokol, Marene, "Aerosonic Turning to Munitions for Profits," *St. Petersburg Times*, July 8, 1989, p. 6B.

Trigaux, Robert, "Aerosonic Accuses Ex-CEO of Fraud," *St. Petersburg Times*, October 4, 1996, p. 1E.

——, "Despite Posting Loss, Aerosonic Optimistic," *St. Petersburg Times*, April 27, 1996, p. 1E.

——, "Struggling Aerosonic Sheds Ordnance Division," *St. Petersburg Times*, June 14, 1996, p. 1E.

Wright, Fred W., Jr., "Gary Colbert," *St. Petersburg Times*, February 24, 2003, p. 4E.

—Frederick C. Ingram

American Girl

American Girl, Inc.

8400 Fairway Place
Middleton, Wisconsin 53562
U.S.A.
Telephone: (608) 836-4848
Fax: (608) 836-1999
Web site: http://www.americangirl.com

Wholly Owned Subsidiary of Mattel, Inc.
Incorporated: 1986 as Pleasant Company
Employees: 1,400
Sales: $350 million (2003 est.)
NAIC: 511120 Periodical Publishers; 454113 Mail-Order Houses

American Girl, Inc. is one of the most well respected brands in the U.S. toy and children's book industries. Headquartered in Middleton, Wisconsin, the company has as its primary focus the positive growth and well-being of girls ages three to 12. The corporate mission is simple: "to celebrate girls." When author and educator Pleasant Rowland founded the company in 1986, its only product line was historical fiction series books and high quality, 18-inch dolls representing each of the three heroines in the series books. The company has since expanded to include additional doll and character toy lines, contemporary clothing for girls, two large retail stores, and a publishing business that ranks among the top 15 children's book publishers in the country. American Girl publishes a bimonthly magazine, as well as an expansive collection of historical fiction, and contemporary fiction and nonfiction titles. Since 1998, the company has been a wholly owned subsidiary of Mattel, Inc.

American Girl is made up of four divisions: the Consumer Catalogue and E-commerce division; the Publications division; the Retail division; and the American Girl's Brand division. Most American Girl products are marketed exclusively through the American Girls catalogue, web site, and two proprietary retail stores. American Girl-published books are also distributed through several bookstores around the country. In addition to the Wisconsin headquarters, the company has warehouse and distribution sites in Wilmot and DeForest, Wisconsin, and Edison, New Jersey, as well as retail stores in Chicago and New York City.

Bringing History to Life: 1985

A trip to Colonial Williamsburg inspired Pleasant Rowland to create the American Girls Collection of books and dolls. At the time, Rowland, a former teacher and publisher of educational books, had been looking for just the right gifts for her young nieces, but she was disenchanted with what Barbie and the Cabbage Patch dolls had to offer young girls. With her American Girl concept, she sought to combine important history lessons with play to foster a child's developing creativity.

Her vision of something that would integrate play and learning, while emphasizing traditional American values materialized as the stories of three nine-year-old heroines living out their own adventures at pivotal times in American history. Though the books were fiction, with six stories in each series, each was thoughtfully written to be historically accurate and cover key events that were crucial in shaping the United States. Rowland created the American Girl Collection in 1985 with three unique and adventurous heroines. Those first heroines were Kirsten, a Swedish immigrant girl who lived in Minnesota in the 1850s; Molly, a girl living in Chicago during the 1940s with a father serving in World War II; and Samantha, an orphan girl who lived with her wealthy grandmother in New York City in 1904.

Rowland said her goal was to "bring history to life." When she first floated the idea for historical dolls with accompanying stories past a focus group of mothers, Rowland did not get an encouraging response. However, as soon as she displayed the prototype dolls, books, and accessories, the mothers were on board. Each doll came with one introductory novel about her life and the time in history, and five additional books each telling a tale of her adventures, challenges, and resulting growth.

Parents appeared willing to buy into Pleasant Company's products despite the nearly $100 price tag for a doll and her six books. Rowland believed her products were not only high quality, but were at the time one of the few things in a "tween" girl's world telling her not to grow up too fast, but rather encouraging her to remain a little girl. The company founder's

Company Perspectives:

"We give girls chocolate cake with vitamins. Our books are exciting, our magazine is fun, and the dolls and accessories are pretty. But more important, they give young girls a sense of self and an understanding of where they came from and who they are today."   —Pleasant T. Rowland, founder

hope was to prolong that fleeting period of childhood when girls play with dolls.

Sales Soar for "Wholesome Americana"

Early indicators made Rowland's American Girl Collection look like a winner. That first Christmas season, Pleasant Company sold $1.7 million worth of products through its mail-order catalogue. During the company's second year, sales reached $7.6 million. Pleasant Company soon outgrew its warehouse and had to find a bigger space. A *Time* magazine article later theorized about the company's success: "The genius behind American Girl's high-end products is that moms feel good about dropping a lot of cash on low-tech, wholesome Americana."

By 1991 sales had grown to $77 million based only on a direct mail catalog and word of mouth; the "buzz" factor among mothers was not insignificant. For the next five years sales grew approximately $50 million each year. The American Girl Collection eventually expanded to include Felicity, living in Colonial Williamsburg, Virginia, in 1774; Addy, a slave girl seeking freedom in the midst of the Civil War in the 1860s; Josefina, a Hispanic girl in colonial New Mexico in 1824; Kaya, a Nez Perce girl growing up in the Northwest in 1764; and Kit, a poor girl growing up in Depression Era 1934.

In 1992 Pleasant Company's publishing arm launched a bimonthly magazine called *American Girl*. According to company literature it was created to be an "age-appropriate, advertising-free publication designed to affirm self esteem, celebrate achievements, and foster creativity in today's girls." The magazine content included fiction and nonfiction articles, letters from readers, party and craft ideas, advice, and even a historical or modern-day paper doll in each issue. The magazines were sold through both subscription and bookstores.

As a relatively young company, Pleasant Company's soaring sales were noticed in the marketing world. In 1993 Pleasant Company was listed among *Advertising Age*'s Marketing 100, the "'best and brightest' marketers in America." The company's early success was impressive, especially given its limited distribution channels. Rowland and her vision were credited with much of the company's success. *Working Woman* put Rowland on its list of the top 50 women business owners for six years in a row, from 1993 through 1998.

Expanding the Brand to Contemporary Dolls and Books

In 1995 Pleasant Company branched out from its original historical product focus and debuted the "American Girls of Today" line, featuring 18-inch dolls which resembled the his-

torical heroines in size and quality, but looked more like modern girls. Girls could order the Girls of Today dolls with specific eye, hair, skin tone, and facial features so they could own a doll that looked most like them. With all the feature combinations, there were 21 dolls to choose from. Along with the Girls of Today dolls came a host of contemporary clothes and accessories. Books about contemporary girls were also added to the line, along with "history mysteries." These new dolls, their accouterments, and modern-day books reflected the diverse interests and lifestyles of girls at the dawn of the 21st century.

That year Pleasant Company also introduced the American Girl library, a collection of nonfiction advice and activity books with such titles as *A Smart Girl's Guide to Starting Middle School* and the *Slumber Party Book*. The American Girl library line grew out of favorite sections of the magazine, which had by that time become extremely popular with girls in the eight- to 12-year-old bracket and had increased subscription sales each year.

The company also introduced the Bitty Baby line of dolls targeted toward younger girls, ages three to six, and designed to encourage nurturing behavior. Bitty Babies were high quality, huggable, 15-inch baby dolls, that had their own coordinating clothes and accessories. Bitty Babies could be ordered with a variety of combinations of skin tones and hair and eye colors, and were priced lower than the 18-inch dolls, at about $40 apiece.

Throughout the 1990s, Pleasant Company's business boomed, capturing the attention of the corporate world, even those outside the toy industry. A 1995 article in the *Economist* described the American Girl heroines as "gutsy, spirited and articulate, taking life's challenges in their stride. None faces tougher challenges than Addy, a slave (possibly the best-dressed slave in history), who makes a perilous escape to freedom during the civil war." The *Economist* continued, "The company has sold more than 25 million books and 2 million dolls since 1986. In 1994, sales increased by 40% to $152 million. To meet demand during the holiday season, the workforce has swelled from 475 to some 2,000." The *Economist* article also noted that, ironically, American Girl dolls were produced in Germany and many of their accessories were made in other countries.

Going Retail with a Proprietary Store

In 1998, the company opened American Girl Place, a 35,000-square-foot retail store and entertainment venue which featured a "whimsical" café and a 150-seat theater. The store, which showcased the product lines from the company's extensive catalogue, was located in Chicago's hottest shopping area on Michigan Avenue, right across from the historic Water Tower. The store was part doll boutique, part museum with life-sized dioramas of the historical dolls in their settings. The theater performance was a one-hour musical revue which highlighted the historical heroines featured in the book and doll collection. Early on, it appeared that Pleasant Company's first foray into the retail store business was successful. Within a few months the store was selling out the theater performances, and dinner reservations were booked full. In 1999 American Girl Place was awarded a "THEA," the Outstanding Achievement Award from the Themed Entertainment Association.

The opening of American Girl Place had fulfilled much of Pleasant Rowland's original vision for her company, and she was ready to move on to new challenges. That same year, 1998, she sold the company named for her to Mattel, Inc, the world's leading toymaker and owner of the Barbie dynasty. Mattel paid an estimated $700 million for Pleasant Company, and has since operated it as an independent subsidiary. Rowland became vice-chairman of Mattel, but retired in 2000 to pursue new challenges. Mattel maintained Rowland's commitment to quality and limited avenues of distribution of American Girl products.

In 1999 the company gained publishing and merchandising rights to popular picture book character Angelina Ballerina from HIT Entertainment PLC. Angelina was a beloved mouse character. Pleasant Company created Angelina dolls with books and accessories. According to the company, picture books about Angelina were designed to "teach girls ages 3–7 gentle life lessons about growing up."

Testing the European Market

Pleasant Company established an office in London in 2000, and the publications arm of the business prepared to enter the European market. In 2001 the company marketed books from the American Girl historical collection, Amelia's journal-style books, and Angelina Ballerina books in the United Kingdom, with plans to pursue the French and German markets in subsequent years. Early on, it appeared "the more universal characters of Amelia and Angelina Ballerina were generating more interest than Pleasant Co.'s signature line," according to the *Book Publishing Report*.

The company continued to extend its American Girl brand with new lines. In 2001 they introduced heroine character dolls with a modern-day twist. Lindsey was the first in a line of limited-edition, modern-day character dolls. Lindsey came with her own story and of course clothes and accessories to match. Lindsey was a success, followed by Kailey and Marisol. The company also presented a new line of school-themed easy reader books with accompanying 16-inch posable dolls called the Hopscotch Hill School Collection. For real girls, not the doll variety, the company created American Girls Gear, or A.G. Gear, a clothing and accessory line for girls eight to 12, with apparel styles that matched both the modern and historical dolls.

Pleasant Company made business page headlines when *Fortune Small Business* reported that American Girl dolls were second only to Barbie as the most popular dolls in the country. In 2002 annual revenues for Pleasant Company reached $350 million, with sales coming exclusively through limited channels: the corporate web site, catalogue, and retail store. By 2003, American Girl Place was the top grossing retail site on Chicago's renowned Magnificent Mile, bringing in $40 million annually. Following the tremendous success of the Chicago retail store, Pleasant Company opened a second proprietary store in midtown Manhattan in 2003. The second American Girl Place was located across from Rockefeller Center.

Name Change, Ensuring Brand Consistency

In early 2004 Pleasant Company made a move to better highlight its well recognized brand by officially changing the company name to American Girl, Inc. It had been a gradual progression over the years. The catalogue name had changed to American Girl in 1998, the web site address was americangirl.com, and even the company phones were answered "American Girl." The company indicated that the name change would ensure better consistency of its identity with the public.

Statistics supported the company success story. More than 100 million American Girl books and ten million American Girl Dolls had been sold since Rowland first told the adventures of Kirsten in 1986. The americangirl.com web site logged 1.3 million visitors each month. American Girl Place in Chicago, in addition to grossing $40 million annually, welcomed more than a million visitors each year, making it Chicago's second most popular tourist attraction. By 2005, circulation of the *American Girl* magazine had reached 700,000. The magazine was ranked eighth among the top children's magazines and was the largest dedicated exclusively to girls in the seven to 12 age bracket. The editors received about 10,000 pieces of reader mail from subscribers after each issue. Perhaps most notable, according to company statistics, "over 95 percent of girls ages 7–12 are familiar with the American Girl dolls, which rank second only to Barbie in the dolls category." *Newsweek* said it best in 2003: "Barbie may be bigger. But the honor of best-loved doll goes to the American Girl, a flat-chested, makeup-free toy that comes packaged with an educational book."

Success Supporting Parent Company

Parent company Mattel was thrilled with the success of its 1998 acquisition. In fact, while sales of Barbie began to decline, Mattel leaders were pleased that American Girl sales remained strong, helping to boost the parent company's profit numbers. The New York and Chicago stores combined saw three million visitors in 2004. Mattel indicated that the New York store opening helped boost American Girl sales 18 percent. In addition, it was reported that Mattel was adding a story-based Barbie line, perhaps using the American Girl model.

Though American Girl had extended its brand well beyond the original historical concept, its flagship eight-character historical collection remained an integral part of the business, commanding a third of the total space in the catalogue. In late 2004, American Girl entered the media market with its first ever television movie aired on the WB network, featuring one of its most well-loved historical dolls, Samantha. The company was exploring additional movie opportunities for its other popular heroines.

Principal Divisions

Consumer Catalogue and E-commerce; Publications; Retail; American Girl's Brand.

Principal Competitors

Alexander Doll Company, Inc.; The Middleton Doll Company; Scholastic Corporation.

Further Reading

"American Girl and Other Pleasant Company Properties Head to Europe," *Book Publishing Report*, April 3, 2000, p. 5.

"'American Girl' Pleasant Rowland Purchases McKenzie-Childs, Ltd.," *Gifts and Decorative Accessories*, July 2001, p. 14.

"America Past and Pleasant," *Economist,* December 16, 1995, p. 62.

Balousek, Mary, "Pleasant Company Changes Name; Middleton Company Now Called American Girl to Reflect What Public Thinks," *Wisconsin State Journal*, January 11, 2004.

Hajewski, Doris, "American Girl Powers Mattel," *Milwaukee Journal Sentinel*, July 20, 2004, p. 3D.

O'Hara, Della, "It's a Girl Thing; American Girl's Avid Popularity Reaches Airwaves," *Chicago Sun-Times*, November 23, 2004, p. 52.

"Pleasant Company Launches Magazine," *Publishers Weekly*, June 1, 1992, p. 22.

Rawe, Julie, "American Girl: Rise of a Toy Classic," *Time*, December 8, 2003, p. 56.

"Santa Discloses What's Hot, What's Not with Toys This Year," *Pittsburgh Post – Gazette*, December 21, 2003, p. C1

Schumann, Michael, "Girls Day Out," *State Journal Register* (Springfield, Ill.), April 11, 2004, p. 45.

Sloane, Julie, "A New Twist on Timeless Toys," *Fortune Small Business*, October 2002, p. 70.

Springen, Karen, "They're History," *Newsweek*, December 8, 2003, p. 12.

Wilson, Marianne, "American Girl Has Charm," *Chain Store Age*, January 1999, p. 136.

—Mary Heer-Forsberg

American Pharmaceutical Partners, Inc.

1101 Perimeter Drive, Suite 300
Schaumburg, Illinois 60173-5837
U.S.A.
Telephone: (847) 969-2700
Toll Free: (888) 391-6300
Fax: (800) 743-7082
Web site: http://www.appdrugs.com

Public Company
Incorporated: 1996
Employees: 1,212
Sales: $351.3 million (2003)
Stock Exchanges: NASDAQ
Ticker Symbol: APPX
NAIC: 325412 Pharmaceutical Preparation Manufacturing

American Pharmaceutical Partners, Inc. (APP) is a publicly traded specialty pharmaceutical company based in Schaumburg, Illinois. Often during its brief history, the company has been at the center of controversy and at times skirted scandal. Its chairman, Dr. Patrick Soon-Shiong, owns about 70 percent of APP through his control of another company, American Bio-Science. Over the years, the results of much of his research have been questioned, and he also has been involved in a number of disputes with business partners, including an estranged brother who fired Soon-Shiong and sued him in the 1990s. Wall Street short-sellers have been gunning for APP since its 2001 initial public offering (IPO), convinced that Soon-Shiong's high-wire act was due for a fall. In particular, his doubters question claims about the effectiveness of a new cancer drug for which APP has been seeking Food and Drug Administration (FDA) approval, a case that has prompted the Securities and Exchange Commission to review and consider launching a formal investigation. Despite the notoriety surrounding its attempt to launch its first proprietary blockbuster drug, APP has developed a very profitable business in injectable pharmaceutical products, offering more than 150 generic injectables in more than 300 dosages, focusing primarily on the oncology, anti-infective, and critical care markets.

Founder's Launch of Entrepreneurial Career in the 1990s

Soon-Shiong was born in 1952 in South Africa, a child of parents who emigrated from China during World War II. He was a top student at the University of Witwatersrand's medical school, then became a resident at Johannesburg's General Hospital. He came to the United States in 1983 to take a faculty position at UCLA's medical school. After performing the school's first pancreas transplant, he was asked to start a transplant program, but he declined. Instead, he pursued less invasive ways to treat diabetes. He revisited a technique used a decade earlier, which transplanted islet cells capable of producing insulin inside the pancreas. Researchers had failed previously because the patient's immune system destroyed the cells before they could provide insulin. In 1987 Soon-Shiong devised a way to work around the problem by encapsulating the islets in a gel made from seaweed. He reported great success in his early research, but his peers were far from convinced. In 1991 Soon-Shiong left UCLA to form VivoRX Inc. and VivoRx Diabetes Inc. with his brother Terrence in order to continue his diabetes work, as well as to conduct research on encapsulating other drugs to prevent side effects.

In 1993 Soon-Shiong received permission from the FDA to conduct human trials, and he transplanted his alginate capsules in the pancreas of a 38-year-old patient named Steven Craig, who had been a severe diabetic since childhood. Craig was weaned off insulin over the next several months, then went an entire month without an injection. Soon-Shiong trumpeted his success to the press and became something of a minor celebrity on the TV talk show circuit and at diabetes conferences. By hyping his results before he had published his research in a peer-reviewed medical journal, Soon-Shiong angered many in the research community, but he did succeed in garnering the attention of Mylan Laboratories Inc., which in June 1994 paid $5 million for a 10 percent stake in the Los Angeles-based VivoRX companies and provided $200,000 a month in research funds. Mylan also paid for a license to market Soon-Shiong's diabetic treatment after it gained FDA approval. In addition, Soon-Shiong formed another company to pursue cancer research, VivoRx Pharmaceutical, in which Mylan acquired a 10 percent stake for just $1,000. The company would eventually change its name to American BioScience. Another company that decided to fund Soon-Shiong was Premiere Inc., a major hospital buying group, which in 1996 invested $4 million in his research companies.

Launching APP in 1996

Soon-Shiong was having difficulty reproducing the results he had achieved in Steven Craig, and he began turning his attention to cancer research and the launch of another venture, American Pharmaceutical Partners. (Craig in the meantime continued to praise Soon-Shiong's treatment, but in 1998 committed suicide, which according to his widow was the result of Craig's despondency over his poor health.) Premiere in 1996 helped to fund the start-up of APP, which soon began to broker generic drugs to hospitals, taking advantage of its relationship with Premiere to gain business. In July 1997, at a time when APP owned no factories, produced no drugs, and generated sales of just $85,000, Premiere named APP as one of its "corporate partners," putting the tiny company on a par with a select fraternity of multinational companies, including Merck and Johnson & Johnson. Because of its cozy relationship with Premiere, which benefited from APP's success by acquiring additional shares of stock based on sales, APP attracted customers such as Fujisawa USA, which correctly surmised that it would be able to do more business with Premiere, supplier to 1,500 hospitals, if it went through APP. In effect, APP became a "toll taker" for Premiere. APP then began working with other buying groups, including the largest, Novation, to which APP paid a fee based on its hospital sales.

In 1998 APP added a manufacturing base by acquiring Fujisawa USA, a money-losing injectable generic drug operation. APP picked up two manufacturing plants located in Melrose Park, Illinois, and Grand Island, New York, as well as 94 different product lines and 193 approved product codes. Fujisawa had lost money for nine straight years, yet APP, because of its ties to buying groups, was able to turn the business around in just six months. But the company was troubled with quality control problems that predated APP. In November 1998 APP had to withdraw its antibiotic gentamicin, which was making patients sick. Several months later the company resumed selling the drug only to have additional patients become sick. It fell upon the FDA to discover that one of APP's Chinese suppliers was in substandard condition. Once a change of suppliers was made, the problem was solved. But the company continued to have problems with other drugs as well. FDA inspectors in 1999 found Adenoscan was being produced in chipped and leaking glass vials, and APP was able to avoid legal action only by recalling the product. Another drug, oxytocin, also was recalled in 1999.

Even as Soon-Shiong was growing APP in 1998 through the Fujisawa acquisition, he was falling out with his original part-

ners, brother Terrence and Mylan, who were displeased that he had allowed his diabetes work to be ignored. Mylan sued both brothers, and Terrence in turn fired Dr. Patrick Soon-Shiong and sued him for fraud, accusing his brother of using VivoRX-paid consultants to conduct cancer research at American Bioscience. In early 1999 the matter was submitted to arbitration, clearing Patrick Soon-Shiong, who was then rehired by his brother. But a year later another suit was filed. The matter would not be settled until another year had passed, at which point Dr. Soon-Shiong agreed to pay $32 million to his brother and Mylan. But Soon-Shiong could well afford to pay after becoming a billionaire following an IPO of stock in APP.

The appeal of APP to investors was not the company's profitable and growing injectable generic drug business. Rather, it was an experimental cancer treatment called Abraxane, which Soon-Shiong had been developing through American Bioscience. Abraxane was similar to Soon-Shiong's diabetes treatment in that it encapsulated paclitaxel—the active ingredient found in Taxol, the best-selling chemotherapy drug—within a nanoparticle-size ball of human protein. The protein provided protection for the drug so that it could arrive in a concentrated form when it reached a cancerous cell. Moreover, one of Taxol's most toxic components was removed, which allowed Abraxane to deliver ever higher doses while eliminating side effects. In 1999 American Bioscience granted North American rights to APP for $60 million and another $25 million in milestone payments. It was an arrangement questioned by Soon-Shiong's detractors, who pointed out that the arrangement provided financial protection for Soon-Shiong and the other private investors of American Bioscience at the expense of APP shareholders. The prospectus for APP's 2001 offering disclosed the licensing terms, but investors were more attracted by the promise of Abraxane to be overly concerned about Soon-Shiong's less-than-savory downside protection scheme. He also was involved in another controversy relating to Abraxane. As Bristol-Myers's exclusive right to market Taxol neared expiration in 2000, Soon-Shiong applied for and received a patent for an experimental form of Taxol, then sued Florida-based Ivax Corp. to keep it and other firms from marketing a generic version of the drug. Ultimately a federal court removed the names of Soon-Shiong and two colleagues from the patent, ruling that the drug had been developed by Florida State University scientists. In 2000 the Federal Trade Commission (FTC) looked into the matter as well, to make sure APP had not colluded with Bristol-Myers in an effort to keep cheap generic versions of Taxol off the market. APP maintained that it had simply been attempting to protect its position regarding Abraxane. Then, in June 2002, 29 states sued Bristol-Myers, alleging that it conspired with APP to keep generic versions of Taxol off the market, thereby costing the states and cancer patients billions of dollars. Although APP was not a defendant in the case, it was named as a co-conspirator.

IPO in 2001

Despite the mounting questions surrounding APP and its chief executive, investors were not scared away. APP's initial offering was completed in December 2001, raising $144 million for the company. Yet controversy continued to dog the company, the result of a March 2002 *New York Times* exposé concerning the cozy relationship between Premiere and APP.

Key Dates:

1996: The company is formed.
1998: Fujisawa USA is acquired.
2001: The company is taken public.
2003: Phase three clinical trials for Abraxane are completed.

The FTC began looking into the matter, as did Congress. To relieve the pressure Premiere sold back its stake in APP to the company for $31.8 million. It also changed some of its practices, promising to discontinue investment in supply companies and to broaden the number of companies with which it contracted. Questions also arose for APP in 2002 regarding the clinical trials underway for Abraxane, which was being touted as having the potential to produce $500 million in annual sales for APP. During an October conference call with analysts it came to light that some of the cancer patients enrolled in the trials had never been treated with any chemotherapy. Although APP maintained that its patient mix had been approved by the FDA, there were still concerns that by using Abraxane as a first-line drug, the results would be skewed, making the treatment appear more effective than it might actually be. The company's stock dropped sharply following the revelation. It was mostly on Wall Street that APP was held with some suspicion, as short-sellers borrowed every available share in anticipation of the company's collapse. Small-time investors, on the other hand, the ones who populated the Yahoo! Financial message boards, were enamored with the company and believed that some people on Wall Street were conspiring to sabotage the stock. One analyst, Kevin McNamara of Sterling Financial Investment Group, wrote a critical assessment of APP in 2003 and became the recipient of abusive e-mails and phone calls that terrorized his family.

Despite the questions about the patient mix in Abraxane's clinical trial, the FDA granted the treatment fast-track status in January 2003. In the meantime, the company's injectable generic drug business was thriving, as it received FDA approval on numerous products. Sales totaled $192 million in 2001, then grew to $277.5 million in 2002, and $351.3 million in 2003. Net income during this period improved to $71.7 million in 2003. But many investors were still uncertain, focusing on APP's efforts with Abraxane. In September 2003, the company claimed in a press release that phase three clinical trials showed Abraxane outperforming Taxol, but because no supporting details were provided, Wall Street cut the price of APP's stock by a third, reducing the company's market value from $3 billion to $2 billion. Soon-Shiong said that he would provide details at a scientific meeting, but researchers also were dismayed by the omission. Shareholders were displeased as well, and APP was soon hit with shareholder lawsuits alleging the company had released misleading information about Abraxane and that Soon-Shiong had unloaded 300,000 shares before the stock tumbled.

Finally in December 2003, APP released the supporting data from the clinical trial, which on the surface showed Abraxane to be far more effective than Taxol in fighting breast cancer. The price of APP shares quickly rose, only to sink again as critics began to pick apart the study, in particular that fact that about 75 percent of the patients were from Russia, hardly the usual site for such a study. In addition, the Russian trial produced much lower results for Taxol than had been produced in other studies. The company still hoped to receive FDA approval based on this study, but the results were far from stunning, and due to emerging competition in the cancer field it was becoming far less likely that Abraxane would ever become the blockbuster product Soon-Shiong had envisioned. Moreover, APP was again the object of government scrutiny, as the SEC began to take a look at whether APP had misled investors by exaggerating Abraxane's potential. A formal investigation, however, would require approval from the SEC commissioners. As of September 2004, no such investigation had yet been launched. A few weeks later, Soon-Shiong stepped down as APP's CEO, turning over the job to Alan Heller, a former president of Global Renal operations at Baxter Healthcare Corporation and executive vice-president and president of G.D. Searle. Soon-Shiong stayed on as executive chairman, electing to concentrate on "strategic initiatives" and the researching of new proprietary injectable pharmaceutical products.

Principal Subsidiaries

Drug Source Co., LLC; Pharmaceutical Partners of Canada; WebDrugSource.com, Inc.

Principal Competitors

Bristol-Myers Squibb Company; Mayne Pharma (USA) Inc.

Further Reading

Arsmtrong, David, "Vindication," *Forbes,* October 6, 2003, p. 126.

Bogdanich, Walt, Barry Meier, and Mary Williams Walsh, "When a Buyer for Hospitals Has a Stake in Drugs It Buys," *New York Times,* March 26, 2002, p. A1.

Darmiento, Laurence, "Firm Mired in Lawsuits Mounts IPO," *Los Angeles Business Journal,* December 17, 2001, p. 1.

——, "New Doubts Raised by Trial Methods in Cancer Drug Study," *Los Angeles Business Journal,* January 5, 2004, p. 3.

——, "Uncertain Investors Keep Drug Firm's Stock on See-Saw Path," *Los Angeles Business Journal,* December 9, 2002, p. 30.

—Ed Dinger

AMERIGROUP Corporation

4425 Corporation Lane
Virginia Beach, Virginia 23461
U.S.A.
Telephone: (757) 490-6900
Toll Free: (800) 600-4441
Fax: (757) 490-7152
Web site: http://www.amerigrp.com

Public Company
Incorporated: 1994 as AMERICAID Community Care
Employees: 2,100
Sales: $1.62 billion (2003)
Stock Exchanges: New York
Ticker Symbol: AGP
NAIC: 515120 Health and Welfare Funds

With its headquarters in Virginia Beach, Virginia, AMERIGROUP Corporation (Amerigroup) is a managed healthcare company serving people enrolled in government-sponsored programs such as Medicaid (providing medical treatment to the poor), State Children's Health Insurance, and FamilyCare. The publicly traded company operates in Texas, Florida, Maryland, New Jersey, Illinois, and the District of Columbia. An October 2004 acquisition of a New York City health plan also positioned Amerigroup to enter New York state, home to the second largest Medicaid population in the United States. Amerigroup has realized strong profits by focusing on young people, who tend to be healthier than the general population and require fewer drugs. Unlike other health maintenance organizations (HMOs), however, Amerigroup extends its mission beyond mere healthcare, in some cases stepping in to provide other social services to benefit younger patients. For example, if indigent parents cannot afford to pay electric bills and, therefore, are unable to keep medicine refrigerated, Amerigroup has on occasion stepped in to restore service. Aside from being compassionate, such decisions save money in the long run, helping to make sure that patients receive the care they need and avoid more serious, and expensive to treat, illnesses. The company's principal product is Americaid,

geared toward low-income mothers and children. The Amerikids product serves uninsured children not eligible for Medicaid, Ameriplus is an HMO for Supplemental Security Income recipients, and Amerifam is a family care HMO for families of Medicaid children and participants in the State Children's Health Insurance Program. All told, Amerigroup serves more than 850,000 members.

Founder Entering the Healthcare Field in the Late 1970s

Born in Paducah, Kentucky, Amerigroup's founder, Jeffrey L. McWaters, became familiar with the challenges of the healthcare industry at an early age because his mother was employed by a group of physicians. He attended Paducah Community College before transferring to the University of Kentucky. After giving some thought to becoming a doctor, he earned a degree in accounting in 1978, then found work at Ernst & Young's Nashville branch before launching his career in the medical field. He joined Hospital Affiliates, owned by Insurance Co. of North America (now Cigna), just as it began acquiring and managing health maintenance organizations (HMOs). In the right place at the right time, McWaters was able to gain valuable experience at a young age about the inner workings of an emerging industry. He learned how an entrepreneur set about securing venture capital, and when he was sent to Dallas to help open an office for Hospital Affiliates, he learned how to build a business. He told *Managed Healthcare Executive* in 2002, "We didn't even have a checkbook to balance when we started. We had no policies or procedures, no infrastructure, no computer system, nothing. We did it all from scratch."

Everything McWaters learned at Hospital Affiliates would prove useful in his next venture in 1986 when he helped psychiatrist Ronald I. Dozoretz to found Options Mental Health, one of the first managed behavioral care companies in the country. McWaters became the chief executive officer of the Norfolk, Virginia-based company that developed customized mental health and substance abuse programs for federal, state, and local Medicaid populations. As he explained to *Managed Healthcare Executive,* "It became clear to me that the Medicaid and uninsured populations were both very large and growing. It was still being managed by a 1960s-era healthcare system. Patients couldn't be seen, and doctors weren't getting paid enough.'' When in the early 1990s a number of states began turning over their Medicaid populations to HMOs, McWaters sensed an opportunity. He struck out on his own in 1994 to start a new HMO dedicated to serving Medicaid recipients, primarily children and expectant mothers, literally working out the business plan on his kitchen table.

The approach McWaters took was similar to disease management, although the needs of the Medicaid population were not as constant. The HMO would concentrate on a few core disease states (perinatal, asthma, diabetes, and sickle cell anemia), but the essential thrust was to provide education and guidance, for instance, steering patients to a primary care physician with whom they could develop a beneficial relationship rather than relying on a hospital emergency room for routine healthcare. Moreover, Americaid would tackle other obstacles that stood in the way of patients receiving effective healthcare, relieving doctors of burdens normally shouldered by social workers, such as taking care of transportation and helping patients to find better housing. While McWaters was targeting a high-maintenance population, it was one that offered a higher margin than the general population, as well as being more cooperative, because it was younger, responded well to treatment, and recovered more quickly. It was also a market neglected by major HMOs, presenting McWaters with a significant niche opportunity.

For funding, McWaters turned to the San Francisco-based venture capital firm of New Enterprise Associates (NEA), which made the first financial commitment. NEA also helped to bring in other venture capital firms, Acadia Venture Partners and Sutter Hill Ventures, and lent its expertise to help McWaters flesh out his business model. In December 1994, McWaters incorporated the company, naming it Americaid Community Care. He decided to house his new company in Virginia Beach, Virginia, despite having no desire to serve the Virginia market. Rather, he chose the city because of its central location, quality of life, and educated workforce. McWaters then spent the next year applying for licenses in the states in which he wanted to operate, developing the products and necessary healthcare systems, and recruiting and training personnel.

Launch of the First Operations in 1996

The first Americaid operation was launched in New Jersey in February 1996. By the end of the year the subsidiary enrolled 10,000 members. Americaid Illinois followed in April 1996 and signed up 2,000 members in Chicago. Then in September 1996 Americaid Texas got started in Fort Worth and by the end of the year had 21,000 members. The company developed a consistent approach to entering a new market, starting out by inviting community leaders to focus groups and hiring some to serve as consultants to provide insights to the community and to act as outreach workers. The company also sought out the people to whom Medicaid recipients were likely to turn for advice, educating clergy and area social service workers about how the Americaid plan worked. Because most states did not permit Americaid to market itself directly to Medicaid markets, the company placed information where potential members were likely to frequent, such as churches, Head Start programs, daycare centers, and supermarkets. After the company achieved a toehold in the community it relied on word of mouth to build membership. During a partial year of doing business in 1996, Americaid generated nearly $23 million in revenues from premiums, losing $10.9 million, but the company was firmly established and poised for strong growth.

In 1997 Americaid completed another round of equity financing, raising $16.2 million and adding a new investor to the mix, Greenwich, Connecticut-based Health Care Capital Partners. Americaid won a bid to enroll Medicaid members in Fort Worth, Texas, signing up 2,000 by the end of the year. The company also began to branch out beyond the Medicaid population. According to federal law at least 25 percent of its membership had to be commercial enrollees. In addition, the company launched a Medicare HMO and another for ''dual-eligibles,'' people covered by both Medicaid and Medicare. Because of this product expansion, the company decided to change its name to something more inclusive, becoming Amerigroup Corporation. By the end of the year, it had 41,000 members and revenues increased to $64.9 million. The company lost $8.9 million but was on the verge of profitability.

Amerigroup enjoyed strong growth in 1998, as membership topped the 100,000 mark, reaching 113,000 by the end of the year. Membership in Illinois doubled to 10,000 while the New Jersey plan grew from 10,000 to 38,000, mostly the result of the company acquiring Oxford Health Plan's Medicaid business in the state. The greatest increases, however, were achieved in Houston, when in the first full year of the plan's operation 40,000 members were enrolled. As a result of these significant gains, Amerigroup all but tripled its premiums over the previous year to $186.8 million. The company also turned its first profit, nearly $3.5 million, albeit almost all of that amount resulted from investment income earned from cash on hand. Nevertheless, it was an impressive showing for a young company and, more important, just a taste of what was in store for 1999.

Amerigroup more than doubled in size in 1999, the result of acquisitions as well as entering markets from scratch. Early in the year, the company acquired the Prudential HealthCare's Medicaid business in Maryland followed by the Washington, D.C. operation. Amerigroup picked up 75,000 Medicaid recipients in Maryland and added another 8,000 by the end of the year. In the District of Columbia, Amerigroup acquired another 11,000 members and enrolled 1,000 over the next several months. Amerigroup also opened its Dallas Health Plan in July 1999 and by the end of the year signed up 34,000 members. Existing operations also saw gains: 10,000 in Fort Worth, 8,000 in New Jersey, and 10,000 in Illinois. Tallied together, Amerigroup's membership reached 268,000 by the end of 1999, while premiums for the year grew to $392.3 million and net income increased to $11.3 million. To keep up with its rapid growth, Amerigroup also opened a new service center in Virginia Beach in 1999, followed a year later by a technology center.

IPO Delay in 2000–01

Amerigroup launched its Amerikids healthcare product in Dallas and Houston in 2000 as well as Ameriplus in New Jersey. During the year the company achieved significant increases in enrollment in all of its markets, adding 1,000 new members in the District of Columbia, 7,000 in Fort Worth, 8,000 in Dallas, 9,000 in Chicago, 11,000 in New Jersey, 12,000 in Maryland, and 17,000 in Houston. Revenues for the year again showed strong growth, totaling $646.4 million, and net income improved to $26 million. The time seemed ripe for the company's initial investors to earn back their investments through a stock offering. In the spring of 2000 the company filed for an initial public offering (IPO) of stock with Deutsche Banc Alex. Brown serving as underwriter, but the timing proved unfortunate. After a significant bull-market run, the stock market was beginning to falter and IPOs became difficult to pull off. Amerigroup postponed its offering and for the next several months waited in vain for a window of opportunity to open. In the summer of 2001 new underwriters, Banc of America and UBS Warburg, stepped in, and in the first week of September an October date for the offering was set. But in the aftermath of the terrorist attacks of September 11, 2001, the offering again had to be postponed. It was not until November 2001, after submitting ten amendments to its original filing, that Amerigroup was able to complete its offering. In the end, the delays were beneficial to the company, which was able to grow profits and also take advantage of other healthcare companies that went to market before it, most of which performed well and helped Amerigroup to command a hefty premium. All told, the company netted $68.7 million, most of which was earmarked for general corporate needs and acquisitions, such as the $1.5 million purchase of MethodistCare Inc., a Houston Medicaid company, which added another 18,000 members after the deal was completed in 2002. When the year came to a close in 2001, Amerigroup had built its overall membership to 472,000, of which 150,000 were the result of acquisitions. Premiums improved to $889.5 million and net income exceeded $36 million.

In addition to the MethodistCare acquisition, in 2002 Amerigroup bought the District of Columbia Medicaid business of Capital Community Health Plan, the company's sixth acquisition, adding another 24,000 members. Amerigroup enjoyed significant growth in other markets as well, increasing enrollments in Maryland by 7,000, New Jersey by 11,000, Dallas by 20,000, Fort Worth by 23,000, and Houston by 39,000. Total memberships now approached 600,000, and as a result premiums topped the $1 billion mark to $1.15 billion, while net income improved to $47 million.

Amerigroup moved from the NASDAQ to the New York Stock Exchange in early 2003, in keeping with the company's financial status as well as its peers, which were listed already on the New York Stock Exchange. Moreover, the change gave the company greater exposure to a wider range of investors and would likely provide more long-term stability to its pricing. Later in the year, the company took advantage of its new listing to make a secondary offering of stock. What investors could not help but notice was Amerigroup's continued expansion in 2003. At the same time that it announced it was moving to the New York Stock Exchange, the company completed the $121 million purchase of Physicians Healthcare Plans Inc., adding 190,000 members in Florida, and moving into the Tampa, Orlando, and Miami/Fort Lauderdale markets. Later in the year, Amerigroup added another 28,000 Florida members by acquiring St. Augustine Medicaid, an AvMed Inc. division. During 2003 Amerigroup also enjoyed strong enrollment in some of its other markets, adding 5,000 new members in Houston, 9,000 in Dallas, and 33,000 in Fort Worth. Annual revenue from premiums topped $1.6 billion while net income in 2003 reached $67.3 million.

To support its expansion, Amerigroup added a chief operating officer and fresh executive talent, which it showed off to Wall Street analysts in a 2004 meeting. During the year, the company also reached an agreement to acquire a New York City health plan, CarePlus Health Plan, for $125 million, a deal that if approved by the government would give Amerigroup a presence in a potentially lucrative market, home to 1.3 million people eligible for Medicaid. The 114,000 members Amerigroup would pick up in the deal, the company's tenth in ten years, would push the company's membership rolls beyond the million mark and revenues to more than $2 billion. Flush with cash, Amerigroup was eyeing another 20 possible acquisitions. Other than Indiana, where the company had applied for a license, it was unclear what new markets the company planned to enter. There was little doubt, however, that Amerigroup was just beginning to realize its potential and strong growth would likely continue for some time to come.

Principal Subsidiaries

AMERIGROUP Florida, Inc.; AMERIGROUP Illinois, Inc.; AMERIGROUP New Jersey, Inc.; AMERIGROUP Texas, Inc.; AMERIGROUP Maryland, Inc.; AMERIGROUP District of Columbia, Inc.

Principal Competitors

Aetna Inc.; Blue Cross and Blue Shield Association; United-Health Group Incorporated.

Further Reading

Elliott, Alan R., "AMERIGROUP CORP. Virginia Beach, Virginia Low-Cost Health Care Drives Business Here," *Investor's Business Daily,* April 23, 2002, p. A10.

Franklin, Katrice, "Fired-Up Company Hires Away," *Virginian Pilot,* December 10, 1998, p. D1.

Gordon, Debra, "Health-Care Choices for Poor Americaid Community Care Continues to Grow As States Turn Their Medicaid Programs

Over to Managed-Care Companies,'' *Virginian Pilot,* July 25, 1997, p. D1.

Grugal, Robin M., ''Patience Pays Off for Medicaid HMO,'' *Investor's Business Daily,* November 7, 2001, p. A12.

Hennessey, Raymond, ''Offerings in the Offing: Survivor Gelt,'' *Barron's,* November 5, 2001, p. 35.

McCue, Michael T., ''Managing America's Toughest Challenges,'' *Managed Healthcare Executive,* January 2002, p. 16.

Walker, Joe, ''Virginia-Based Amerigroup Caters to 472,000 Disadvantaged Patients,'' *Paducah Sun,* March 4, 2002.

—Ed Dinger

Ameristar Casinos, Inc.

3773 Howard Hughes Parkway
Suite 490 South
Las Vegas, Nevada, 89109
U.S.A.
Telephone: (702) 567-7000
Fax: (702) 866-6397
Web site: http://www.ameristarcasinos.com

Public Company
Incorporated: 1993
Employees: 7,050
Sales: $854.7 million (2004)
Stock Exchanges: NASDAQ
Ticker Symbol: ASCA
NAIC: 713210 Casinos; 721120 Casino Hotels; 722110
Full Service Restaurants

Ameristar Casinos, Inc. owns and operates six casinos with adjacent hotels, as well as related food, beverage, and entertainment services, in Nevada, Iowa, Missouri, and Mississippi. On the high desert plateau of Jackpot Nevada, the Horseshoe Hotel and Casino provides gambling entertainment in a rustic, western setting, while Cactus Pete's Resort and Casino offers a desert theme. The Ameristar Vicksburg is a dockside casino in the style of an 1870s riverboat located on the Mississippi River in Vicksburg, Mississippi. Ameristar also operates a riverboat casino from Council Bluffs, Iowa, across the Missouri River from Omaha. Kansas City, Missouri, is home to the Ameristar Casino Kansas City and St. Charles, Missouri, houses the Ameristar Casino St. Charles.

Small-Time Operation to Public Corporation

Before the town of Jackpot, Nevada, had a name, Don French and "Cactus Pete" Piersanti moved their slot machine gaming operations to the high desert plateau from Idaho. In 1954, French opened the Horseshoe Casino, and Piersanti opened Cactus Pete's Desert Lodge; Cactus Pete's incorporated with three shareholders in 1956. The two tiny casinos prospered on the "grind," casino lingo for obtaining small profits from a large volume of customers who play slot machines, rather than on high stakes gamblers. Located on Highway 93 at the border of Idaho, the Horseshu and Cactus Pete's thrived on visitors from Idaho, Oregon, Washington, Montana, northern California, and southwestern Canada, as well as on middle-income travelers driving to and from Las Vegas and other points in the southwestern United States. The two gambling sites slowly expanded over the years, beginning with the 15-room Desert Inn Motel at Cactus Pete's in 1958. Table games, such as poker, blackjack, craps, and roulette were added at both properties over the years. Then, in 1964, the Horseshu came under the direction of Cactus Pete's.

The death of one of Cactus Pete's shareholders led to a change in ownership in 1967, with the addition of three new shareholders. When one of the new shareholders, Ray Neilsen, of Neilsen and Miller Construction, which had contracted work on the properties, died in 1971, his wife Gwen inherited Neilsen's shares, while his son Craig became involved in the daily operation of Cactus Pete's. Craig Neilsen became president in 1984, and ultimately sole owner of the corporation in 1987, which included both properties by that time.

As the casino industry became more competitive and market-oriented in the 1980s, Craig Neilsen adapted. In an increasingly market-driven industry, free food and drink were no longer sufficient to attract customers. A new marketing strategy included "slot club cards" which strengthened Cactus Pete's repeat-customer base. The personalized cards, inserted into the slot machines, provided the casino with information as to which machines regular customers preferred, and the amount of time and money spent at each machine. The amount of a customer's game play determined what free gift a customer might acquire, such as a free meal, free T-shirt, or free hotel stay. Personal information obtained when players signed up for a club card allowed casino managers to add a personal touch to customer retention. When a computer tracked a frequent player on a slot machine, the manager might send a casino employee over to offer a free meal or to send happy birthday wishes.

Neilsen initiated a $22 million expansion of Cactus Pete's in 1991, transforming it into a 25,000-square-foot casino and des-

Company Perspectives:

Ameristar Casinos, Inc. is an innovative, Las Vegas-based gaming, entertainment company known for its distinctive, quality-conscious hotel casinos and value orientation. The company roots go back nearly five decades to a tiny roadside casino in the high-plateau country that borders Idaho and Nevada. Publicly held since November 1993, the corporation owns and operates six properties in Nevada, Missouri, Iowa, and Mississippi.

tination resort for the northwestern United States. New amenities included a sports and keno lounge, the Bristlecone Emporium gift shop, the Ruby Mountain Ballroom, and an Olympic-sized swimming pool. In 1993 Cactus Pete's Resort Casino earned a Four Diamond rating from the American Automobile Association, and would receive that designation annually.

With the proliferation of legalized gambling in the early 1990s, Neilsen sought to expand his casino operations outside of Nevada. A public offering of stock in the fall of 1993 coincided with Ameristar Casinos' incorporation. Neilsen maintained 86.9 percent ownership of the casinos and became president and CEO of Ameristar. The stock offering funded final construction on the Ameristar Vicksburg casino, which opened in February 1994 in Vicksburg, Mississippi. The 35,000-square-foot dockside casino, permanently anchored on the Mississippi River, 45 miles west of Jackson, included four bars, two restaurants, a cabaret, and a showroom, as well as a restaurant on the bluff overlooking the casino, the Delta Point River Restaurant. Gaming included poker, blackjack, roulette, craps, and over 1,000 slot machines. The tourist traffic in this area involved passers-by on Interstate 20 and visitors to Vicksburg National Military Park. Local residents and residents from eastern Louisiana provided a more regular customer base. The project included acquisition of 18 acres across from the dock for future development and a 20-acre mobile home park to provide housing rentals for employees and other local residents.

In 1995 Ameristar obtained one of three gaming licenses to operate a riverboat casino in Council Bluffs, Iowa, on the Missouri River. Ameristar planned a complete destination resort and entertainment center for the region, designed in the architecture of a late 1800s rivertown much like Council Bluffs itself. The 272-foot-long and 98-foot wide riverboat casino encompassed 40,000 square feet on two levels, with high ceilings to create the grand, spacious atmosphere of a land-based casino. In addition to 1,098 slot machines, gaming activities included craps, blackjack, roulette, Caribbean stud, Spanish 21, Pai Gow, 21 Madness, and Let it Ride. A legal requirement for the riverboat casino involved two-hour cruises a minimum of 100 days during the excursion season, from April 1 to October 31. The Ameristar Council Bluffs casino opened for business in January 1996, after a voyage along the Mississippi and Missouri Rivers from Jennings, Louisiana.

Ameristar opened the Main Street Pavilion on the land adjacent to the riverboat dock in June 1996. The 68,000-square-foot Pavilion featured a main street designed in the style of the Victorian era, with restaurants and a variety of entertainment choices for children and adults. In a joint venture with New Horizon Kids Quest, the Pavilion included a 10,000-square-foot activity center for children, which provided childcare on an hourly basis while parents gambled. The center accommodated 200 children for up to five days with hours of operation from 10 a.m. to 10 p.m. daily, and until midnight on Friday and Saturday nights. The Main Street Pavilion also included a 160-room hotel, with panoramic views of the Missouri River, which opened in November after a five-month delay. Visitors had access to the riverboat via an enclosed ramp from the Pavilion.

The proliferation of gambling casinos increased competition as well as opportunities for Ameristar. Specifically, the casinos in Jackpot experienced competition from Native American casinos which opened in Pocatello, Idaho, western Washington, and northeastern Oregon, as well as from casinos in Alberta, Canada, which sought to attract customers from the same geographical areas, the northwestern states and southwestern Canada. Ameristar responded by upgrading the slot machines to state-of-the-art equipment, with touch screens and color and sound effects, by remodeling the 3,500-square-foot Horseshu casino, and by increasing its marketing efforts. The Ameristar Vicksburg faced competition from new casinos in Bossier City and Shreveport, Louisiana, as well as in Philadelphia, Mississippi.

Relocation to Las Vegas in 1996

Ameristar entered the casino market in the Las Vegas area through a merger with Gem Gaming, Inc. That company had begun construction on The Reserve casino in Henderson, Nevada, then a fast-growing suburb of Las Vegas and one of the fastest growing suburbs of the United States. Ameristar redesigned the project to elaborate on the African safari theme, to allow for more gambling space, and to enable possible expansion in the future. To oversee design of the new casino, Ameristar hired Henry Conversano, designer of the Mirage in Las Vegas and The Lost City at the Sun City Resort Hotel and Casino in Sun City, South Africa. The Reserve casino and hotel featured colorful murals, artificial aica trees, jungle sounds, and hand-carved statues of large animals, such as elephants and giraffes, with some statues designed as encasements for slot machines. Exotic murals covered the exterior of the building, while monkey gargoyles perched on the hotel towers and replicas of elephant tusks bracketed the 120-foot-tall sign.

The Reserve began as a $90 million project, but Ameristar's changes added $45 million in expenditures. The 42,000-square-foot casino included 1,380 slot machines, sports book keno, a bingo hall with 300 seats, and 25 table games, for roulette, blackjack, poker, and craps. Amenities included four restaurants, including Congo Jack's, where the front of a small airplane has appeared to have crashed among the tables, three bars, and a 224-room, nine-story hotel, which offered an introductory rate of $19.95 per night. Future expansion on the 53-acre property would involve additional hotel towers, multilevel parking, and additional restaurants and bars. Credit problems related to the acquisition of Gem Gaming delayed the opening of The Reserve until February 1998, but thereafter, Ameristar relocated its corporate offices from Twin Falls, Idaho, to Las Vegas in conjunction with entry into the Las Vegas market.

Key Dates:

1954: Don French and "Cactus Pete" Piersanti establish casinos in the Nevada desert, in an area that would become known as Jackpot.

1987: Craig Neilsen becomes sole owner of gaming properties in Jackpot, Nevada.

1991: Neilsen transforms Cactus Pete's into a destination resort.

1993: Neilsen incorporates properties as Ameristar Casinos Inc. and takes the company public.

1994: Company's first casino outside Nevada opens in Mississippi.

1998: Grand opening is held for The Reserve casino and hotel in Las Vegas.

1999: Ameristar Council Bluffs receives a AAA Four Diamond rating.

2000: Ameristar buys properties from Station Casinos in Kansas City and St. Charles, Missouri; sells The Reserve Casino to Station Casinos.

2001: Renovation is completed on Ameristar Casino Vicksburg; additional entertainment complex is added to St. Charles facility; Kansas City riverboats are joined into one major casino complex.

2002: Renovated Ameristar Casino St. Charles reopens.

2003: Improvements are made to the Kansas City complex.

For The Reserve's promotional campaign, Ameristar hired Seiniger Advertising, a specialist in the entertainment industry. Advertising for The Reserve amplified the African safari theme. The main tagline for print, local television, bus wraps, and outdoor advertisements described The Reserve as "A whole new breed of casino." A print advertisement showed an orangutan with a stoic look and underlying text which stated, "We know a good poker face when we see one." The text under a picture of a cheetah advertised The Reserve's restaurants saying, "If the food were any fresher, you'd have to chase it." A 30-second television promotion showed elephants, giraffes, and other animals running across the African plains towards the casino.

Marketing targeted local residents of the Henderson-Green Valley suburbs. With 70 percent of The Reserve's customer base expected to come from within a ten-mile radius, Ameristar introduced the first "self-comping" players club in the Las Vegas area. Like Cactus Pete's slot club cards, The Reserve players club allowed regular customers to earn free meals and discounts. The casino and hotel also attracted travelers along Lake Mead Parkway, with new road construction expected to increase traffic near the casino.

For its first ten months of operation, February 1, 1998 to December 31, 1998, operations at The Reserve resulted in a loss of $16 million, including pre-opening costs of $10.6 million, and a loss of $12.7 million for the company overall in 1998. Ameristar intensified its marketing efforts, adding cash-back opportunities for frequent players, and improved its operating margins, particularly in the area of foodservice.

Activities Outside Nevada in the Late 1990s

The controversy over legalized gambling had mixed effects on Ameristar. A 1998 Mississippi referendum to amend the state constitution to halt legalized gambling would have closed the Ameristar Vicksburg, but a state judge found the referendum invalid due to a mistake in its filing. Ameristar expected citizens to place a revised version of the referendum on the ballot in 2000. However, local concerns about gambling may have assisted the Ameristar Council Bluffs as the Iowa Racing and Gaming Commission regulated the number of gaming licenses to those already existing in 1998, thus eliminating any possibility of new competition without first overturning the regulation.

Ameristar maintained strong market positions at its casinos outside Nevada. Revenues at Council Bluffs increased steadily with growth in the gaming market there. Revenues increased 24.8 percent, from $70.3 million in 1996 to $87.8 million in 1997, followed by an additional 11 percent increase in 1998 with revenues of $97.7 million. At Vicksburg revenues declined from $66.2 million in 1996 to $64 million in 1997, largely attributed to a decline in the size of the gaming market there. Ameristar maintained a leading position, however. Revenues increased to $68.5 million in 1998 with a new hotel and increased gambling revenues.

Ameristar expanded hotel facilities adjacent to its casinos in Mississippi and Iowa. In June 1998 the company completed a hotel in Vicksburg. The eight-story, 144-room hotel included a presidential suite, four luxury suites, and 16 king spa suites. Ameristar leased property at Council Bluffs to Kinseth Hotel Corporation to build a Holiday Inn Suites. The 140-room, limited service hotel opened in March 1999, with an enclosed, climate controlled walkway to the Main Street Pavilion.

In July 1999 the company began construction to add a third floor gaming deck to the Ameristar II riverboat at Council Bluffs, as well as land-based entertainment and parking facilities. The $41 million project involved the creation of the first shipyard in Iowa where Lee Vac Shipyards fabricated the ship's deck, which the company maneuvered as a whole onto the riverboat, allowing the casino to remain open throughout the new construction. The expansion increased the size of the riverboat casino to 37,000 square feet, with a capacity for 2,830 people, making it the largest riverboat casino in Iowa. Ameristar increased the number of slot machines to 1,446 and the number of game tables to 51, and added 18 state-of-the-art video poker and video reel slot machines. The Center Sports Bar featured 19 televisions with flat plasma screens. The grand opening celebration in November 1999 included a traditional boat launching ceremony, with a christening and champagne toast. In December 1999 Ameristar signed an agreement with Players Network to provide a closed circuit television network for its hotel patrons in Council Bluffs. The Players Network programs included instruction on casino gaming, sports and racing events, entertainment, and promotions and events at the casino-hotel property.

In the fall of 1999 Ameristar sought to revive a casino project in south St. Louis County, along the Mississippi River in Missouri. The company signed a letter of intent with Futuresouth Inc. to take over the lease for a potential casino site in Lemay,

Missouri, on the Mississippi River. Ameristar expected the project to include restaurants, meeting facilities, and ample parking; it would be structured to enable future expansion of the casino and additional amenities. As construction would take place on the site of an old lead plant, clean-up was estimated at $1 million. As part of the deal, Futuresouth, a local group of business people, maintained an interest in the casino project, giving Ameristar some initial political strength over its competitors.

Several factors added complexity to the case, however, as Isle of Capri's Lady Luck Gaming acquisition gave that company a financial edge in its endeavor to attain a potential casino site farther south. Moreover, a citizens organization opposed the casino in Lemay, speaking to the Missouri Gaming Commission of their concerns that gambling would be detrimental to local businesses and destroy the town's quaint atmosphere. Another citizens group formed in favor of a casino development in Lemay, citing the funds gambling taxes would generate for schools and senior citizens and noting Ameristar's donations to computer programs for schools in Iowa City.

Growth and Record Winnings

In 1999, Ameristar Casino received a four diamond designation for its Council Bluffs, Iowa riverboat casino from the American Automobile Association. The prestigious AAA rating marked the first time a riverboat casino in Iowa had received such status.

That same year the company lost a longtime key player when Gwen Neilsen passed away. Neilsen had contributed greatly to the transformation of Ameristar Casino from its standing as a privately held company to its public offering on the NASDAQ stock exchange. The company also credited Neilsen with envisioning and implementing Ameristar's strategic expansion into the Midwest.

In 2000 Ameristar bought two properties from Station Casinos in an agreement in which Ameristar purchased a Kansas City gaming facility and a St. Charles, Missouri outfit from Station and Ameristar in turn selling Station Casinos one of its Las Vegas holdings known as The Reserve.

The Reserve deal was completed in 2001, and the company went on to complete several noteworthy projects that same year. Ameristar focused on making significant capital improvements to several of its properties including a $40 million renovation at its Ameristar Casino Vicksburg in Mississippi.

The company added an entertainment wing at its newly acquired St. Charles facility and in Kansas City the company joined together its two floating casinos forming a 130,000-square-foot complex. Previously the twin casinos, known as the King and Queen, floated separately along the river.

Ameristar's expansion brought the company increased revenue and in 2001 it posted income of $550 million. The *Nevada Business Journal*'s 2001 ranking placed Ameristar at number 14 among Nevada's top publicly traded companies.

In August 2003 Ameristar revenues had grown significantly. St. Louis, the major metropolitan area near the St. Charles operation, had become the eighth largest market for casinos and Ameristar led the way with its posh facility.

Company profits resonated with Wall Street and shares of Ameristar Casino stock tripled from 2003 to 2004. Analysts spoke highly of the company saying that Ameristar led its competitors in similar markets, and was clearly outperforming the industry as a whole.

Further expansion was in the works when in the summer of 2004 Ameristar agreed to acquire Mountain High Casino in Black Hawk, Colorado, for $115 million. In addition, Ameristar paid a cash dividend to investors in September 2004. The company announced the plans to pay out $.125 per share on its common stock.

Principal Subsidiaries

AC Food Services, Inc.; AC Hotel Corporation; Ameristar Casino Council Bluffs, Inc.; Ameristar Casino Las Vegas, Inc.; Ameristar Casino St. Charles, Inc.; Ameristar Casino Kansas City, Inc.; Ameristar Casino Vicksburg, Inc.; Cactus Pete's Inc.

Principal Competitors

Harrah's Entertainment, Inc.; Harveys Casino Resorts; Station Casinos, Inc.; Isle of Capri Casinos, Inc.

Further Reading

"Ameristar Breaks Ground for Hotel," *Biloxi Sun Herald,* April 13, 1997, p. G2.

"Ameristar Casinos Announces Settlement of Arbitration Proceedings with Former Gem Stockholders," *PR Newswire,* May 7, 1997.

"Ameristar Casinos, Inc. Responds to Jury Verdict in Pike County, Mississippi Litigation," *PR Newswire,* November 1, 1999.

"Ameristar Casinos Declares Cash Dividend," *PR Newswire*, August 17, 2004.

Berns, Dave, "At Last, The Reserve Opens," *Las Vegas Review-Journal,* February 12, 1998, p. 1D.

Buyikian, Teresa, "Seiniger's Wild West," *Adweek* (Western edition), February 23, 1998, p. 4.

Carey, Christopher, "Ameristar Casino Scores with Expansion,*" St. Louis Dispatch,* August 6, 2003.

——, "Ameristar Deals 3 of a Kind," *St. Louis Post Dispatch,* April 13, 2004.

Carroll, Chris, "Lady Luck Gaming's Sale Makes Casino More Likely, Leading Local Investor Says," *St. Louis Post-Dispatch,* October 25, 1999, p. 5.

"Casino to Provide Child Care," *Omaha World Herald,* June 11, 1996.

DeFrank, Sean, "King of the Jungle," *Las Vegas Review-Journal,* February 4, 1998, p. 1A.

Dorr, Robert, "Ameristar Faces Credit Pinch," *Omaha World Herald,* March 28, 1997, p. 16.

——, "Ameristar Plans $41 Million Expansion of Facilities," *Omaha World Herald,* April 15, 1998, p. 17.

——, "Ameristar Says Hotel Delay Hurt Profits," *Omaha World Herald,* February 21, 1997, p. 16.

Edwards, John G., "Earnings Rise for Casino Firms," *Las Vegas Review-Journal,* April 21, 1999, p. 1D.

Faust, Fred, "Company Proposes a New Casino South of Jefferson Barracks Bridge," *St. Louis Post-Dispatch,* August 25, 1999, p. C7.

——, "The Contest for the Next Casino License Gets an Interesting Twist," *St. Louis Post-Dispatch,* October 11, 1999, p. 2.

——, ''Las Vegas Company May Seek to Revive Lemay Casino Plan,'' *St. Louis Post-Dispatch,* August 24, 1999, p. C7.

Hansen, Mathew, ''The Great Casino Debate,'' *Lincoln Journal Star,* October 10, 2004, p 1.

Little, Joan, ''Lemay Residents' Group Opposes Proposed Casino,'' *St. Louis Post-Dispatch,* October 18, 1999, p. 2.

——, ''New Group Forms to Defend Virtues of a Casino in Lemay,'' *St. Louis Post-Dispatch,* November 1, 1999, p. 1.

Langfitt, Frank, ''Casinos Go from Sleazy to Slick—and They Want to Bring Their Act to Maryland,'' *Baltimore Morning Sun,* May 28, 1995, p. 1F.

''(No) Chance Encounters,'' *Advertising Age,* September 6, 1999, p. 42.

Palermo, Dave, ''Rough Going Along the Rivers Casinos Stifle Heritage Tourism, History Buffs Say,'' *Biloxi Sun Herald,* November 16, 1997, p. A1.

''Players Network Announces First Affiliate Contract Outside of Nevada,'' *PR Newswire,* December 7, 1999.

Trask, Mike, ''Ameristar Casinos Experience 76% Increase in Revenue,'' *St. Charles County Business Record,* February 11, 2003.

——, ''Ameristar Casinos St. Charles Outshines Competitors in July,'' *St. Charles County Business Record,* August 12, 2003.

—Mary Tradii
—update: Susan B. Culligan

AMICAS, Inc.

20 Guest St., Ste. 200
Boston, Massachusetts 02135
U.S.A.
Telephone: (617) 779-7878
Toll Free: (800) 490-8465
Fax: (617) 779-7879
Web site: http://www.amicas.com

Public Company
Incorporated: 1996 as InfoCure Corporation
Employees: 687
Sales: $111.5 million (2003)
Stock Exchanges: NASDAQ
Ticker Symbol: AMCS
NAIC: 511210 Software Publishers

AMICAS, Inc. provides practice management software systems to the healthcare industry, focusing on the radiology market. It offers both Windows-based and Java/browser-based systems, featuring a comprehensive medical records system, document imaging and management capabilities, custom reporting and decision support systems, web-based and wireless report distribution, picture archiving, and a billing system. The public company trades on the NASDAQ and, until early 2005, was known as VitalWorks, Inc. Since the sale of its medical division to Cerner Corporation, the company has relocated its headquarters to Boston.

Founders Entering the Medical Software Field in the 1980s

The company was founded by Frederick L. Fine and James K. Price, who had been fraternity brothers at the University of Georgia. The former earned a degree in Economics and the latter a degree in Marketing. After graduation, both went to work for two years as sales reps at Moore Business Systems, provider of practice management systems. They split up, with Fine becoming a regional manager with Informatics General Corporation, which produced accounting software, and Price serving as healthcare sales manager of a practice management

systems supplier, Executive Business Systems. In 1985 the two young men decided to team up and launch a business to develop and market computer systems aimed at small doctors offices, rather than hospitals and medical groups. They were turned away from a number of Atlanta banks, but ultimately secured funding from the Small Business Administration, which agreed to lend them $250,000. They founded International Computer Solutions, Inc. (ICS) in 1985 and set up shop in a small office in Atlanta, initially sharing the same desk.

Over the next 13 years, Fine and Price built up ICS's business, so that by 1996 it was providing DOS, Windows, and Unix-based practice management systems to about 2,500 healthcare providers. Ready to take the business to the next level, in November 1996 they formed InfoCure Corporation, VitalWorks' predecessor, to acquire ICS and several other medical software companies and to become a vehicle for acquiring additional companies serving small medical practices. It was an area ripe for consolidation and neglected by the major players in the field. In addition to ICS, InfoCure's five other founding companies included DR Software, Inc., an Atlanta-based company founded in 1983 to provide practice management systems to medical practices with just one to two providers; KComp Management Systems, Inc., a Los Angeles company founded in 1995 that catered to mid-sized dental and oral surgery practices; Healthcare Information Systems, Inc., a Kansas City, Kansas-based provider of UNIX-based practice management systems to mid-sized medical practices and clinics, founded in 1984; Rovak, Inc., a St. Elmo, Minnesota, company founded in 1984, providing practice management software primarily to orthodontists and oral surgeons; and Health Care Division, Inc., a company founded by Fine and Price in 1996 to acquire Charlotte, North Carolina-based Info Systems, which provided IBM AS/400-based practice management systems to mid-sized and large medical practices and clinics. The six companies had a combined established customer base of 17,000 doctors.

The acquisition of the founding companies coincided with InfoCure's initial public offering (IPO), which was completed in July 1997 and netted the company nearly $7 million. InfoCure used about $2.9 million to pay the cash portion of the purchase price for the six founding companies. All told, the

Company Perspectives:

AMICAS is all about people. Nowhere else will you find a more dedicated, more driven group of men and women. It's our people that make us special, and in turn make our products and services special.

founding companies were acquired for $10.9 million in cash and 3.7 million shares of InfoCure stock, plus the assumption of $2.3 million in debt. Just prior to the IPO, InfoCure also added the business of Millard-Wayne, Inc., when the holding company for ICS acquired the Atlanta-based company. Founded in 1977, Millard-Wayne sold IBM AS/400-based practice management systems to mid-sized and large medical practices and clinics, adding another 2,000 healthcare providers to InfoCure's customer base.

Late 1990s Acquisition Binge

After completing its offering, InfoCure was soon on the acquisition trail again. In October 1997 it added three companies: Professional On-Line Computer, Inc., a Michigan company providing medical management software to radiologists and others; Commercial Computers, Inc., provider of practice management systems in south Florida; and SoftEasy Software, Inc., a Philadelphia, Pennsylvania-area software company serving podiatrists. Not only did InfoCure grow its customer base, it also increased its talent pool by successfully retaining key technical and administrative personnel, a practice the company would attempt to follow in all of its acquisitions. Before 1997 came to a close, InfoCure made two more acquisitions: Pace Financial Corporation, a Cincinnati company with offices in Minneapolis and Rochester, Minnesota, marketing a proprietary medical office information system running on the IBM AS/400 platform; and the orthodontic practice management system business of Halis Services, Inc. Also of importance in 1997, InfoCure launched InfoFunds, a program to provide customer financing and drive additional sales.

In January 1998 InfoCure continued to act as a consolidator, adding Micro-Software Designs, Inc., which primarily served oral and maxillofacial surgery practices, and Medical Software Integrators, Inc., provider of practice management systems to anesthesiology practices. Later in the year, InfoCure acquired the Healthcare Systems division of the Reynolds and Reynolds Company, adding practice management systems geared toward radiology and anesthesiology practices. Then, to close the year, InfoCure acquired Radiology Management Systems, Inc., a Santa Monica, California-based company serving radiologists.

InfoCure picked up the pace in 1999, adding more than a dozen companies to the fold. In February it acquired Macon Systems Management, LLC, targeting dermatologists, and OMSystems, Inc., serving orthodontists. In June InfoCure acquired Strategicare, Inc. and its Disc Computers Systems, Inc. subsidiary, which provided practice management software for general medical practices. Three more acquisitions followed in August: Ardsley, M.I.S., serving orthodontists; Medfax Corporation, primarily serving radiologists; and Scientific Data Management, Inc., which provided practice management software

for general medical practices. In November 1999 InfoCure bought Datamedic Holding Corp., which focused its business on ophthalmologists and oncologists. InfoCure then ended the year with a flurry of deals. It added the dental businesses of National Data Corporation; Zila, Inc., which marketed its services under the Practice Works name; Kevin Kozlowski, Inc.; Unident Corporation; and InfoLogic, Inc. InfoCure also acquired Prism Data Systems, Inc., a provider of software to ophthalmologists, and CDL Healthcare Systems, Inc., which catered to general medical practices. In addition, InfoCure acquired VitalWorks Inc., a company that delivered practice management software to general medical practices through a browser-based interface over the Internet on a subscription basis. To help pay off some of the debt incurred in making these acquisitions, InfoCure conducted a secondary offering of stock in 1999, raising $112 million. The price of the company's stock continued to rise, prompting a 2-for-1 split in August. In this way it kept the price low to attract more investors while increasing the number of shares in circulation.

Much of the stock's growth was due to the potential of adding the power of the Internet to the company's mix. In July 1999 InfoCure signed an agreement with a subsidiary of Sybron International Corp., the largest supplier of dental products in the world, to allow InfoCure customers to buy orthodontic supplies online worldwide. It also reached an agreement with Hewlett-Packard to offer its software on HP personal computers and handhelds through Qwest's fiber-optics network. By now, InfoCure was serving orthodontic customers in Australia and 11 European customers, and hoped to apply its experience with Sybron to radiology and anesthesiology. It also wanted to expand into other practices, such as ophthalmology, dermatology, and oncology, while spreading its international reach, especially into Latin America. The addition of VitalWorks also marked a significant turning point for InfoCure. It formed VitalWorks.com and began moving the entire company toward an application service provider business model, so that now instead of buying software from InfoCure, customers rented access to the applications on a monthly or yearly subscription. To aid in making this transition, InfoCure forged an alliance with Qwest Communications International Inc. to offer the VitalWorks applications online to physicians, allowing them to handle billing and claims processing and connect to pharmacies and insurance companies. Rather than incurring major upfront costs in buying practice management software, paying as high as $100,000, physicians could now receive the services by paying a more manageable subscription price. The new strategy also included spinning off VitalWorks with an offering of stock in 2000. Moreover, the company wanted to package its dental practice business into another eCommerce subsidiary, PracticeWorks.com, which also was to be spun off with a public stock offering.

In early 2000 InfoCure lined up additional help in making its transition to a Web-based business when WebMD agreed to invest as much as $100 million in VitalWorks.com. WebMD paid $10 million upfront to acquire a 10 percent stake in VitalWorks.com, and was slated to invest another $90 million after the IPO, including $40 million in cash. Also of significance, InfoCure gained access to WebMD's transactions technology. The two parties agreed to jointly research and develop a way to integrate their technologies. For WebMD the alliance was advantageous because it desired access to InfoCure's base of customers, now totaling about 100,000 physicians.

VitalWorks was scheduled to sell 20 percent of its shares in a May 2000 offering, but the IPO was postponed because of poor market conditions for Internet stocks. In the meantime, InfoCure beefed up PracticeWorks by acquiring six new dental practice management companies. Making the transition to a Web-based business proved difficult, however, as InfoCure was hit with major restructuring charges. Sales were also adversely impacted by changes in government regulations covering patient privacy that had been delayed by more than a year and caused customers to put off adding practice management software until there was more clarity on the new requirements. The company reported a 15 percent drop in sales for the second quarter in 2000 and investors punished the stock, which lost 87 percent of its value from January to August 2000, dropping from a high of $37.38 to less than $5. In August 2000 InfoCure elected to cut 40 percent of its workforce, some 400 employees, in order to weather the storm.

New Century, New Name

InfoCure changed direction in the fall of 2000, announcing that VitalWorks would not be spun off. Instead, PracticeWorks would be spun off to shareholders and InfoCure would then assume the VitalWorks name and concentrate solely on providing management information technology and e-health services for medical practices. In March 2001, PracticeWorks was spun off to InfoCure shareholders, with James Price leaving to become PracticeWorks' chief executive. Also at that time, Frederick Fine turned over the CEO post to Joseph M. Walsh, who had been the head of one of InfoCure's acquisitions and had served as InfoCure's president since May 2000. Another CEO of an acquired company, Steve Kahane of Datamedic, became the company's chief strategic officer. Fine stayed on as InfoCure's chairman, but in June 2001 he gave up that post as well to Walsh. In August 2001 InfoCure assumed the VitalWorks name.

VitalWorks fell out with WebMD in 2001, leading VitalWorks to sue for breach of contract, alleging that WebMD refused to pay agreed-upon rebates. The matter would be resolved later in the year, with WebMD paying $2.5 million to VitalWorks to settle all claims. Over the next year or two the company also had to deal with several shareholder lawsuits related to some of the companies InfoCure bought during its acquisitions binge.

After suffering through two years of significant losses, VitalWorks returned to profitability in 2002, posting net income of $24.1 million on revenues of $114.8 million. Sales fell off in 2003 to $111.5 million and net income dropped to less than $8 million, but also during the course of the year the company made an acquisition that changed the direction of the company once again. In November 2003 it acquired Boston-based AMICAS, Inc., which developed Web-based diagnostic image management software, the addition of which allowed VitalWorks to offer radiologists a complete radiology data management system. The radiology sector of the company's business was so strong that in 2004 management decided to devote all of its attention to it.

VitalWorks first rearranged its management team, with Kahane replacing Walsh as CEO, while the latter stayed on as chairman. The company then announced that it planned to move its headquarters to Boston, where the company now had a significant presence because of the AMICAS operation. This decision would make more sense in light of the agreement the company announced a few weeks later that it was selling its medical division to Cerner Corporation for $100 million. In this way, the newly named AMICAS could focus all of its efforts on the radiology business. How the company would fare in a new home with a new business plan remained very much an open question.

Principal Competitors

Cerner Corporation; Eclipsys Corporation; IDX Systems Corporation.

Further Reading

Anderson, Charlie, "Cerner Will Buy Medical Division for $100M Cash," *Business Journal, Kansas City,* November 19, 2004, p. 6.

Grantham, Russell, "Declining Sales Lead to Job Cuts at InfoCure," *Atlanta-Constitution,* August 3, 2000, p. C1.

Hiland, Harriett, "InfoCure Is Taking Paper Out of Doctor's Offices," *Atlanta Business Chronicle,* November 14, 1997, p. 27A.

Robbins, Roni B., "Former Fraternity Brothers Score with Medical Software," *Atlanta Business Chronicle,* November 20, 1998, p. A20.

——, "InfoCure Looking at Stock Split, More Acquisitions," *Atlanta Business Chronicle,* July 30, 1999, p. 13A.

—Ed Dinger

Amkor Technology, Inc.

1345 Enterprise Drive
West Chester, Pennsylvania 19380
U.S.A.
Telephone: (610) 431-9600
Fax: (610) 431-5881
Web site: http://www.amkor.com

Public Company
Incorporated: 1997
Employees: 2,261
Sales: $1.6 billion (2003)
Stock Exchanges: NASDAQ
Ticker Symbol: AMKR
NAIC: 334413 Semiconductor and Related Devices

Amkor Technology, Inc. is a publicly traded company providing contract semiconductor assembly and test services. Assembly and testing are two of the three steps required to produce a finished integrated circuit ready for use in a host of electronic applications. After transistors and electronic circuitry are deposited onto a silicon wafer, the wafer is assembled, or ''packaged,'' by being cut into separate integrated circuits, which are connected electrically to a system board through a protective housing. The packaged integrated circuit is then subjected to testing to verify function, current, timing, and voltage. In addition, Amkor offers value-added services such as electrical package characterization and thermal package characterization, which help designers to learn how a device will perform in a finished package. The company also can help in the design of a package and provide other services, including die processing, package signal integrity analysis, failure analysis, and qualification testing. Amkor serves major global customers such as Agilent, Intel, Philips, Sony, and Toshiba. Amkor maintains its corporate headquarters in West Chester, Pennsylvania, where its founder and chairman, James J. Kim, lives, but most of the company's U.S. operations are located in Arizona, and manufacturing is conducted overseas in seven Asia-Pacific countries.

Founding the Company in the 1960s

James J. Kim was born Joo Jin Kim in 1936 in Seoul, Korea, the son of a Korean entrepreneur, Hwang Soo Kim. He started law school in Seoul in 1954 but soon realized he was not suited to the profession. A family friend suggested that he attend the Wharton School of business at the University of Pennsylvania, and in 1955, at the age of 19, Kim traveled to the United States. He spent a year in Colorado with a friend learning English before entering Wharton to study economics. He earned a B.S. in economics in 1959, followed by a master's degree in economics in 1961. In that same year, he married a Korean immigrant, Agnes Kim, who lived in the area, and they decided to stay in the United States. Kim then became an assistant professor at another Philadelphia school, Villanova University. The couple became U.S. citizens in 1971. In the meantime, Kim's father had started a company that provided workers to the mechanical manufacturing industries, and with the emergence of the Japanese electronics industry, he turned his attention to supplying labor for this sector. In 1968 Kim urged his father to become a manufacturer himself. The elder Kim agreed, starting a company called Anam Industrial Co. Ltd. and opening a factory in Seoul to assemble electronic packages.

Anam ran into problems in the late 1960s when a partner of Hwang Kim quit. In 1968 his son began to help by acting as Anam's marketing agent in the United States. James Kim would then give up his academic career, quitting his Villanova post in 1970. He set up an office in his garage and incorporated Amkor Electronics Inc. (Amkor standing for American-Korean). The company was formed to design semiconductor packages and provide packaging services, with Anam acting as supplier. During the day Kim worked with U.S. engineers in determining the best way to take advantage of Anam's facilities, and at night he sent instructions to Korea by way of a telex machine. Well versed in the intricacies of U.S. tax law, Kim also set up Amkor to receive fees for its services, which were taxed at a lower rate. He also established several other companies to provide fee-based services to Anam. In addition to running this small stable of Amkor-related companies, he became involved in a business launched in 1977 by his wife, who opened a kiosk in a Philadelphia-area shopping mall that sold calculators and digital watches. A retail chain called The Electronics Boutique grew out of this initial venture. It began to show strong growth after adding video games and then moved into the home computer market by offering both hardware and software. The chain was located in 25 malls by the early 1980s, generating revenues of $13 million.

Once both of his companies became too large to manage by himself, Kim turned over the presidency to outsiders—Amkor in 1980 and The Electronics Boutique in 1984. By the mid-1980s, Amkor had sales offices located around the world, selling to 100 European and Japanese semiconductor companies and producing sales in excess of $100 million. The business for both Amkor and Anam continued to grow at a fast clip well into the 1990s, due in large measure to the economic development policies pursued by the South Korean government. Another important factor was the hiring of John Boruch, the company's longtime president. He learned the semiconductor business at Motorola after earning a degree in economics from Cornell University, and joined Amkor in 1984 to take charge of worldwide sales. Five years later he was named president and began moving Amkor away from the commodity side of the semiconductor industry, instead focusing on the value-added semiconductor packaging business.

Launching an Expansion Program in the Early 1990s

Amkor worked with Anam to launch an expansion program. In 1991 they acquired a packaging plant in the Philippines from Advanced Micro Devices and bought a second plant in the country from American Microelectronics Inc. Amkor then built a third plant in the Philippines from scratch. Later the Amkor/Anam group built a fourth plant in Korea. As a result of increased production capacity, Amkor experienced rapid growth in the early 1990s and emerged as a world leader in the semiconductor packaging industry. Sales topped $300,000 in 1992, then improved to $442 million in 1993 and $573 million in 1994, before jumping to $932.4 million in 1995. Net income also reached $59.1 million in 1995. A year later sales topped the $1 billion mark, totaling $1.2 billion, or about one-third of a $4.4 billion semiconductor packaging market. Because of the rising need for integrated circuits for home computers, cell phones, and other consumer electronics, the demand for semiconductor packaging services was growing steadily, boding well for Amkor and Anam despite the influx of new competition.

Although there was strong demand for their products, the health of Amkor and Anam was jeopardized by an economic meltdown in Korea that led to a currency devaluation. The fate of the companies was in jeopardy because they had taken on a considerable amount of debt, mostly from Korean banks, in expanding production capacity. Amkor owed more than $500

million, and Anam was especially overextended, owing more than $1.2 billion. James Kim, who had become Anam's chairman in 1992, now took steps to relieve the situation by taking Amkor public to raise funds to pay off a major portion of that debt.

Going Public in 1998

In September 1997 Kim formed a holding company, Amkor Technology, Inc., incorporated in Delaware, then filed for an initial public offering (IPO) of stock to be conducted in November 1997. After a delay of several months, the IPO was back on track, and in preparation the various Amkor companies were merged with the new Amkor Technology entity. Then, in May 1998, the IPO was conducted, with Salomon Smith Barney acting as lead manager. Amkor netted about $300 million from the sale of stock and also raised another $180 million in convertible subordinated notes. The company earmarked $313 million to pay down debt, with the balance providing working capital. Later in 1998 bankrupt Anam underwent a restructuring of its debt with Korean financial institutions.

As part of the plan to rescue Anam, Amkor arranged to buy the largest and newest Anam manufacturing plant, located in Kwangju, Korea, for $600 million and the assumption of another $7 million in debt. Amkor also purchased Anam's interest in a Philippine facility, and two months after its IPO Amkor paid $9.5 million to acquire Anam affiliate Anam/Amkor Precision Machine Company Inc. In the second quarter of 1999 Amkor agreed to purchase a stake in Anam worth $150 million. Amkor acquired more Anam assets in early 2000, paying $1.4 billion to add Anam's three remaining packaging and test factories. Thus the once dominant partner in the Anam-Amkor relationship was now just a foundry services provider for Amkor, manufacturing 17,000 silicon wafers each month contracted to Texas Instruments Inc. Some of the money that Amkor poured into Anam, however, was intended to increase the foundry's production capacity to around 30,000 wafers each month, hopefully to allow the former giant to make inroads in the foundry business.

While Anam was fortunate to be saved, Amkor emerged as the leading semiconductor packaging-and-test services provider in the world. Revenues topped $1.5 billion in 1998, reached $1.9 billion in 1999, and approached $2.4 billion in 2000. Net income during this period grew from $75.6 million in 1998 to $154.2 million in 2000. Amkor took steps in 2000 to increase production capacity of its plants in Korea and the Philippines by more than 800,000 square feet. In 2001 the company also began to grow externally through acquisitions in an effort to expand its geographic presence to better serve its customers as well as to capitalize on the opportunities in new markets. In January 2001 an Amkor subsidiary launched operations in Japan after acquiring a Toshiba Corporation packaging and test facility as part of a joint venture with Toshiba formed in December 2000. Later in 2001 Amkor established a manufacturing presence in Taiwan through a pair of acquisitions at a total cost of $145 million in stock. It acquired a 69 percent interest in Taiwan Semiconductor Technology Corporation and a 98 percent stake in Sampo Semiconductor Corporation. Entering the Taiwan semiconductor market was important because it was home to the largest silicon foundries in the world, and it also allowed Amkor to serve the major chip manufacturers located there as well. Amkor further bolstered its Asian presence in 2001 with the opening of a new packaging and testing plant in Shanghai, China, to provide integrated circuits for the country's burgeoning cell phone and computer industries. In the meantime, Amkor did not lose sight of the European market. In 2001 it formed an alliance with Netherlands-based Philips Semiconductors, which included a technology exchange and joint product development efforts.

But even as Amkor was expanding its production capacity, it had to contend with another rough patch in the volatile semiconductor industry, which had suffered down cycles in 1975, 1985, 1996, and 1998. Late in 2000 demand began to soften and the situation grew worse in 2001, as the industry lost about one-third of its worldwide market. To compensate for falling sales, Amkor cut its payroll by 10 percent. As a result of the recession, revenues dropped to $1.3 billion and the company took a net loss of more than $450 million in 2001. The following year brought only a slight improvement, with sales reaching $1.4 billion. Amkor completed a pair of acquisitions in 2002, part of a trend in which integrated device manufacturers outsourced their packaging and test operations to outside providers. Amkor added Agilent Technologies' assembly business for semiconductor packages used in printers, and also acquired the Japanese semiconductor packaging business of Citizen Watch Co., Ltd. A deal to add the Fujitsu Ltd. operations in Japan fell through, however.

In 2003 Amkor sold back the wafer fabrication services business to Anam for $62 million and obtained a release from Texas Instruments on the foundry's contractual obligations. The money helped to shore up Amkor's finances, as did the sale of a 21 percent stake in Anam to Korea's Dongbu Group for $93 million in cash and notes. Amkor still owned 21 percent of Anam, but Amkor was expected to eventually divest itself of that interest as well. The sale of the wafer foundry also marked the end of the idea that Amkor could grow into a full fabrication and packaging services provider. The company was too much in debt, and demand for semiconductors was too soft to support that concept. Moreover, no synergy had ever been created between chip fabrication and the assembly and testing sides of the business.

Sales showed some improvement in 2003, increasing by 14.1 percent, or $197.6 million, to $1.6 billion. Business continued to rebound in 2004, and the company's long-term prospects were buoyed by an agreement Amkor signed to acquire an IBM assembly plant in Shanghai and a testing facility in Singapore; in return IBM contracted for about $1.5 billion in assembly and testing revenues over the next several years. After a difficult period, Amkor appeared to be ready to resume its extended trend of growth.

Principal Subsidiaries

Amkor Technology Hong Kong, Ltd.; Amkor Technology Singapore Pte. Ltd.; Amkor Technology Japan, KK; Amkor Technology Philippines (60%); Amkor Technology Taiwan Ltd. (84%); Amkor Technology Greater China, Ltd.

Principal Competitors

ASE Test Limited; Siliconware Precision Industries Co. Ltd.; STATS ChipPAC Ltd.

Further Reading

Abelson, Reed, "Native Korean Plugged in to S.S. Electronics Market," *Philadelphia Business Journal,* November 17, 1986, p. 10.

Fernandez, Bob, "Philadelphia-Based Retail Mogul Takes $3 Billion Loss in Stride," *Philadelphia Inquirer,* April 4, 2001.

Ojo, Bolaji, "Amkor Secures Its Fate by Rescuing Anam," *Electronic Buyers' News,* December 6, 1999, p. 5.

Steffora, Ann, "Amkor's Dilemma—IPO or Sell," *Electronic News,* April 20, 1998, p. 48.

Young, Lewis H., "An American-Korean One-Two Punch," *Electronic Business Today,* October 1997, p. 55.

—Ed Dinger

AptarGroup, Inc.

475 West Terra Cotta Avenue, Suite E.
Crystal Lake, Illinois 60014
U.S.A.
Telephone: (815) 477-0424
Fax: (815) 477-0481
Web site: http://www.aptar.com

Public Company
Incorporated: 1993
Employees: 6,600
Sales: $1.11 billion (2003)
Stock Exchanges: New York
Ticker Symbol: ATR
NAIC: 326122 Plastics Pipe and Pipe Fitting
    Manufacturing; 332115 Crown and Closure
    Manufacturing; 332919 Other Metal Valve and Pipe
    Fitting Manufacturing; 332999 All Other
    Miscellaneous Metal Product Manufacturing; 333913
    Measuring and Dispensing Pump Manufacturing;
    339999 All Other Miscellaneous Manufacturing

AptarGroup, Inc. makes a number of dispensing systems for consumer products in the personal care, fragrance/cosmetic, food/beverage, pharmaceutical, and household markets. AptarGroup's business is divided in three segments, aerosol valves, pumps, and dispensing closures. The company counts itself as the largest supplier of fine mist pumps in the world, the largest supplier of aerosol valves in North America, and the largest supplier of dispensing closures in the United States. AptarGroup maintains manufacturing facilities in North America, Europe, Asia, and South America, serving more than 5,000 customers. International sales account for 60 percent of the company's annual sales. Pumps represent AptarGroup's biggest business segment, accounting for 58 percent of its total sales. Dispensing closures and aerosol valves account for 23 percent and 14 percent of total sales, respectively.

Origins

AptarGroup comprises a collection of companies founded at different times in distinct business niches that, over the course of decades, came together under the AptarGroup corporate banner, which first was unfurled in 1993. AptarGroup's lineage included the names Werner Die & Stamping, Seaquist Manufacturing Company, Pfeiffer GmbH, and Valois S.A.—U.S., German, and French companies that together gave AptarGroup its 21st century profile of a company reliant on aerosol valves, spray pumps, and dispensing closures. Aerosol valves represented the oldest facet of AptarGroup's business, a chapter of the company's history that was begun by Werner Die & Stamping.

Several months after the end of World War II, Nels Werner Seaquist and Alex Werner Carlson set in motion the events that led to AptarGroup's formation a half century later. Both men worked for a company named Oak Manufacturing Co. in Crystal Lake, Illinois, where they developed their skills in tool and die manufacturing. Seaquist and Carlson possessed enough confidence in their abilities to leave Oak Manufacturing and start their own company, using their shared middle names to christen the enterprise Werner Die & Stamping. In January 1946, the company began operating in Cary, Illinois, occupying a 20-foot by 30-foot garage where Seaquist and Carlson began working on a line of aerosol valves. The entrepreneurs made their first shipment in 1948, when they supplied a company in Chicago named Continental Can Company with low-pressure aerosol valves. By the end of the year, Werner Die produced six million aerosol valves, enabling the company to finance the construction of a 5,000-square-foot manufacturing plant in 1949.

Seaquist decided to go it alone several years after working with Carlson. In 1952, after acquiring tooling from Continental Can Co., he formed his own company, Seaquist Manufacturing Company. Under Seaquist's guidance, the company developed a new valve comprising parts made of molded plastics with molded orifices, a product known as the NS-31. Seaquist's innovative work caught the attention of a privately held, family-controlled company in Chicago named Pittway Corporation. Founded by the Harris family, Pittway eventually became the world's largest manufacturer of fire and burglar alarm systems, but the company delved into other businesses as well, developing interests in publishing, trade show presentations, and consumer electronics. Pittway's acquisition of Seaquist Manufacturing, which subsequently was renamed Seaquist Valve,

---

Company Perspectives:

AptarGroup delivers solutions that bring convenience to life. Your life. We supply leading multinational companies with innovative spray pumps, dispensing closures, nasal pumps, aerosol valves and lotion pumps. We partner with customers at the early phase of a product's packaging design and aid them in selecting the best solution for their needs. Our dispensing systems are assembled using sophisticated high-speed machines and robots and our plastic injection molding expertise achieves extraordinary results.

---

became the foundation of its packaging operations, an arm of the company that would increase in size and scope during the ensuing decades.

Expansion Through Acquisitions in the 1970s

With the financial help of a larger parent company, Seaquist Valve expanded, developing business arms of its own. The first division of the company was established in 1968, when Seaquist Canada was formed. The international dimension to the company's business—an important facet of AptarGroup decades later—widened in scope when Pittway began augmenting Seaquist Valve's growth with acquisitions. These acquisitions represented the constituents of the modern-day AptarGroup. The first to arrive was a French company named Valois S.A. The company was founded in 1947 by Jean Ramis, who held a patent on a plastic aerosol valve. Pittway acquired the company in 1970, giving its packaging operations a presence in the United States through Seaquist and in Europe through Valois. Pittway, at this point, had limited its packaging operations to the production of aerosol valves, but in the mid-1970s the company began to diversify, giving its packaging operations the same three business pillars that supported AptarGroup. In 1976, Seaquist Closures was established as a separate division, assigned to manufacture dispensing closures, which were plastic caps typically used for squeezable containers that allowed a product to be dispensed without removing the cap. That same year, Pittway purchased a 35 percent stake in Pfeiffer GmbH, a German company engaged in the manufacture of pumps—finger-actuated dispensing systems that dispersed spray or lotion from non-pressurized containers. Pfeiffer, like Valois, was founded in 1947, starting in Munich where its founder, Erich Pfeiffer, began building one of the packaging industry's pioneers. Pfeiffer GmbH developed the first metal pump in 1952 and the first leak-proof dispenser pump in 1960. Several years before Pittway acquired the company, Pfeiffer GmbH developed the first nasal spray pump, presumably the reason the Harris family took an interest in the company.

During the 1970s, Pittway diversified its packaging operations. In the 1980s, the company entrenched its position in three main product lines: aerosol valves, spray pumps, and dispensing closures. The company did so through internal expansion by fostering the growth of Seaquist divisions, Valois, and, to a lesser extent, through its partially owned pump maker, Pfeiffer. Pittway also solidified the three business segments by completing acquisitions of other companies, acquisitions that added

technology, new markets, and manufacturing capacity to its packaging operations. In 1981, Pittway acquired two U.S. companies, AR Valve, a manufacturer of aerosol valves, and RDW Industries, a maker of dispensing closures. Through Valois, Pittway purchased a French manufacturer of spray pumps named STEP S.A., completing the acquisition in 1983. In 1989, Pittway completed the purchase of another spray pump manufacturer, acquiring an Italian company, SAR S.p.A.

The 1990s saw Pittway's packaging operations gain their independence, the moment that marked the birth of AptarGroup. Pittway, for its own strategic reasons, was peeling off layers of itself, embarking on a divestiture program that would see it shed its diversity. The company sold its consumer electronics business and packaging operations during the early 1990s, a subsidiary named First Alert, Inc. in 1994, and its publishing and trade show assets in 1998. At the close of the century, after winnowing its business scope, Pittway was acquired by Honeywell, Inc.

AptarGroup's Debut in 1993

The multi-step process that resulted in the formation of AptarGroup began at the beginning of Pittway's divestiture program. In 1992, Seaquist Valve and Seaquist Pump, a division formed in 1987, were merged, creating Seaquist Dispensing, a subsidiary of Seaquist Group. In April 1993, Pittway spun off Seaquist Group and concurrently acquired the 65 percent of Pfeiffer it did not already own. The new, independent company, which began trading on the New York Stock Exchange, was renamed AptarGroup, a reference to the Latin word "aptare," to "adapt and respond." The company debuted with more than $400 million in annual sales.

On its own for the first time in 30 years, the packaging operations expanded, achieving significant growth during its first decade of independence. The company's established presence in Europe was augmented by expansion into other areas of the world, as AptarGroup acquired manufacturing space in Mexico, the Czech Republic, China, Argentina, and Brazil. In 1995, the company acquired 35 percent of Loffler Kunststoffwerk GmbH & Co., a leading manufacturer of dispensing closures in Europe.

As AptarGroup entered the late 1990s, the company represented a formidable, global force in the consumer products packaging industry. By the end of 1996, AptarGroup served more than 1,000 customers, supplying three categories of products to a variety of markets. Pumps represented the single most important facet of the company's business, accounting for 63 percent of the $615 million collected in sales in 1996. More than 90 percent of the company's pumps were manufactured in Europe. AptarGroup's pumps were sold to the fragrance/cosmetics market, the pharmaceutical market, and the personal care market. In each of these markets, the company held a leading position. AptarGroup counted itself as the largest supplier of pumps to the fragrance/cosmetics market in Europe. The company ranked as the world's largest supplier of pumps to the pharmaceutical market, relying on clean-room manufacturing facilities in France, Germany, and Switzerland. In the personal care market, AptarGroup ranked as the largest supplier of fine mist pumps in North America and a leading supplier of lotion pumps in Europe.

For the remaining 37 percent of its revenue, AptarGroup relied on the sale of dispensing closures and aerosol valves, its original product line. The company sold its closures to the same markets it sold its pumps, but the majority of its customers operated in the personal care market. AptarGroup manufactured nearly 80 percent of its closures in North America, ranking as the largest supplier of closures on the continent. The product line accounted for approximately 18 percent of AptarGroup's total sales. The company's aerosol valve business, which contributed 17 percent of total sales, ranked as the largest in North America. AptarGroup manufactured nearly 60 percent of its aerosol valves in North America, selling the product line to the personal care, household, and pharmaceutical markets.

Expansion in Late 1990s and 2000s

AptarGroup expanded its business base during the late 1990s, completing a series of acquisitions and starting several ventures of its own that yielded consecutive years of record financial totals. In 1997, the company established two start-up operations, CosterSeaquist L.L.C., a U.S.-based aerosol spray cap manufacturer started as a joint venture company, and Aptar Suzhou Dispensing Systems, Co., Ltd., a company based in China that manufactured all three categories of AptarGroup's products.

AptarGroup ended the 1990s by using a combination of acquisitions and start-up ventures to help push annual sales past the $800 million mark. The company's emerging presence in South America was bolstered by the founding of a subsidiary in Brazil in 1999, Seaquist-Valois do Brasil Ltda., which manufactured dispensing closures and pumps. The year also included the acquisition of Somova, S.r.l., a Milan-based manufacturer of pumps and aerosol spray caps, and the purchase of an 80 percent stake in a Swiss research and development company, Microflow Engineering S.A. The year's biggest deal was completed in February, when AptarGroup purchased a U.S.-based perfume pump maker named Emson Research Inc. The acquisition, a $150 million deal, gave AptarGroup a handful of manufacturing plants in Connecticut, but the greatest contribution to the company's operations was Emson's strong presence in the mainstream U.S. fragrance pump market. At the time of the acquisi-

tion, AptarGroup derived 55 percent of its fragrance pump sales from Europe, maintaining a solid position in the U.S. market only in the smaller upscale end. Emson, which generated $85 million in sales before its acquisition by AptarGroup, derived 75 percent of its sales from the United States, ranking as the largest manufacturer of fragrance/cosmetics pumps in the country. "This acquisition gave us balance," AptarGroup's chief financial officer said in a February 22, 1999 interview with *Plastics News*.

As AptarGroup moved toward its tenth anniversary, the company was recording impressive financial growth. Innovations such as AptarGroup's design of a squeeze bottle with a silicon valve dispenser on the bottom for ketchup maker H.J. Heinz Co. and for mayonnaise maker Kraft Foods Inc. sparked growth in the company's business. In 2003, thanks to a 20 percent increase in revenues, the company eclipsed the $1 billion-in-sales mark, recording $1.11 billion in sales. To maintain its stalwart market position, AptarGroup planned to keep entering new markets and develop innovative solutions for consumer products packaging, as it attempted to remain on the vanguard of an industry it had helped advance for nearly 60 years. Toward this end, the company was moving into new markets as it entered the mid-2000s. In the first half of 2004, AptarGroup opened its first plant in Russia, a 50-employee factory in Vladimir that made dispensing closures for food and beverage and personal care companies. As the company plotted its future development, growth in markets outside of the United States and Western Europe represented one of the objectives to be fulfilled. AptarGroup generated only 9 percent of its sales outside of the United States and Western Europe in 2004, a percentage that the company's president and chief executive officer, Carl A. Siebel, wanted to increase. "The goal is for the rest of the world, Eastern Europe included, to represent at least 20 percent of our sales within five years," Siebel said in a May 17, 2004 interview with *Crain's Chicago Business*.

Principal Subsidiaries

AptarGroup International L.L.C.; AptarGroup International Holding B.V. (Netherlands); AptarGroup Holding S.A.S. (France); Valois S.A.S. (France); Asia Pacific Inspection Center (Suzhou) Co. Ltd. (China; 55%); Aptar Suzhou Dispensing Systems Co. Ltd. (China); SeaquistPerfect Molding L.L.C.; Emson Research, Inc.; Global Precision, Inc.; Liquid Molding Systems, Inc.; Philson, Inc.; Pfeiffer of America, Inc.; P Merger Corporation; Seaquist Closures L.L.C.; Seaquist Closures Foreign, Inc.; Seaquist de Mexico S.A. de C.V. (80%); SeaquistPerfect Dispensing L.L.C.; SeaquistPerfect Dispensing Foreign, Inc.; Valois of America, Inc.

Principal Competitors

Amcor Limited; Crown Holdings, Inc.; Rexam Plc.

Further Reading

"AptarGroup Adds Emson Research's Pumps," *Soap & Cosmetics,* May 1999, p. 56.
"AptarGroup, Inc. Acquires Somova," *Global Cosmetic Industry,* August 1999, p. 8.

Bowe, Christopher, ''The Americas: Honeywell to Buy Pittway for Dollars 2Bn,'' *Financial Times,* December 21, 1999, p. 26.

Hardin, Angela Y., ''Penton Puts Stock in Spinoff,'' *Crain's Cleveland Business,* August 10, 1998, p. 3.

Murphy, H. Lee, ''AptarGroup Counts on Bottle Design to Dress Up Results,'' *Crain's Chicago Business,* May 19, 2003, p. 16.

''Russian, E. European Markets Lure AptarGroup,'' *Crain's Chicago Business,* May 17, 2004, p. 40.

Scott, Chris, ''Magazine Sale May Spell Change for Pittway's Publishing Division,'' *Crain's Chicago Business,* January 29, 1996, p. 6.

Smith, Sarah S., ''Aptar Acquires Emson Research,'' *Plastics News,* February 22, 1999, p. 4.

Tita, Bob, ''New Dispensers Pumping Up Aptar,'' *Crain's Chicago Business,* November 15, 2004, p. 4.

—Jeffrey L. Covell

Arriva PLC

Admiral Way, Doxford Internation
Sunderland
SR3 3XP
United Kingdom
Telephone: +44 191 520 4000
Fax: 44 191 520 4001
Web site: http://www.arriva.co.uk

Public Company
Incorporated: 1938
Employees: 28,552
Sales: £1.53 billion ($3.25 billion) (2003)
Stock Exchanges: London
Ticker Symbol: ARI
NAIC: 485210 Interurban and Rural Bus Lines; 423110
Automobile and Other Motor Vehicle Merchant
Wholesalers; 423120 Motor Vehicle Supplies and
New Parts Merchant Wholesalers; 447110 Gasoline
Stations with Convenience Stores; 485510 Charter
Bus Industry; 522298 All Other Non-Depository
Credit Intermediation; 531190 Lessors of Other Real
Estate Property; 532111 Passenger Cars Rental;
532112 Passenger Cars Leasing; 551112 Offices of
Other Holding Companies; 811111 General
Automotive Repair

Arriva PLC is one of Europe's leading and fastest-growing publicly traded transportation companies. The Sunderland, England-based company is one of the United Kingdom's top three transportation groups, behind Stagecoach and Go-Ahead. Arriva's U.K. operations include the operation of more than 6,000 buses—the company is the leading bus operator in London, and also operates bus lines in the Northeast, Northwest, Midlands, Yorkshire, and Southeast of England, as well as in Wales and Scotland. Arriva is also a major operator of trains in England, conducting interurban, rural, and commuter passenger rail services in Wales, and in Liverpool and Manchester and throughout the north of England. The company also operates more than 235 railroad stations in the United Kingdom. Limited

future growth in the United Kingdom has led Arriva to the European continent, where the privatization of the public transportation infrastructure was underway in the 2000s. Arriva is already a leading bus operator in The Netherlands, with some 20 percent of that country's regional market, and provides rail, taxi, and water bus services as well. In Denmark, Arriva became the first private (non-government-owned) company to receive a passenger rail contract in that country, providing service in the Mid- and North Jutland regions. Arriva's Scandinavian presence also includes bus services in Sweden. Elsewhere in Europe, the company provides bus services in Spain and Portugal, and is the leading private bus group in Italy. Arriva also operates a bus and coach leasing business. The company's corporate leasing arm oversees a fleet of some 11,000 cars and vans. Quoted on the London Stock Exchange, Arriva is led by Managing Director R.J Davies. In 2003, the company posted revenues of £1.53 billion ($3 billion).

Motorbikes in the 1930s

Tom Cowie started out his working life repairing and selling motorcycles for his father, also named Tom, in the backyard of the family's home through the 1920s and 1930s. In 1938, the senior Cowie opened his own shop selling used motorcycles. Tom Cowie was called up for military service soon after; returning from the army in 1946, Cowie used his £1,000 in savings to take over the family business and expand it. Over the next decade, Cowie's company emerged as a major U.K. motorcycle retailer.

Cowie prepared to expand the company still further at the end of the 1950s. In 1950, Cowie added a new automobile retailing operation, which quickly overtook the company's original motorcycle business in sales. Cowie quickly began expanding, adding new showrooms throughout its home region. From the beginning, however, Cowie's automobile sales leaned heavily toward the lease-to-own and corporate markets. That effort was supported by the company's public offering in 1965. In 1969, the company, known as T. Cowie, sold more than 42 percent of its stock to Mercantile Bank.

Cowie continued adding dealerships and showrooms through the 1970s, moving into the Midlands region. Cowie

Company Perspectives:

With activities in eight different European countries, our vision is to be recognised as the leading transport services organisation in Europe. We are working to achieve our vision by growing the business through organic growth, acquisition, better service delivery, innovation and marketing.

also built up a strong automobile financing business, called Red Dragon Securities. By the middle of that decade the company had raised its annual sales to more than £18 million. In 1977, the company became determined to expand beyond its core northern markets, and it launched a takeover attempt on Colemore Investments. That acquisition would have permitted the company to expand its dealer network into the southern regions of the United Kingdom, and also introduced Cowie to the European market with a number of Fiat dealerships. Yet the attempt was rejected by Colemore's shareholders.

Instead, Cowie began focusing on a different acquisition target. By 1980, the company had built up a 30 percent stake in the George Ewer group, which operated a number of automobile dealerships, and included franchises for makes such as Vauxhall, Ford, and British Leyland. The Ewer group had another significant holding—the Grey-Green fleet of motor coaches.

The bid for Ewer quickly turned hostile, however, after Cowie opposed Ewer's purchase of struggling farm machinery group Eastern Tractors. Cowie ultimately triumphed, succeeding in gaining more than 51 percent of Ewer's shares by the end of 1980. The acquisition added some £14 million to Cowie's annual sales, which topped £91 million by the end of the group's 1981 fiscal year. Cowie quickly restructured its new acquisition, shutting down Ewer's money-losing dealerships.

Cowie ultimately sold off the money-losing Eastern Tractors operation. More successful for the company was its financing business, which grew strongly into the mid-1980s, emerging as a major U.K. corporate fleet operator. The company considered spinning off that business as a separate, publicly listed entity, in part to improve the value of its own stock, but ultimately retained full control.

Public Transporter in the 1990s

In the early 1990s, Cowie's finance operation proved its primary profit driver, with margins as high as 10 percent, compared with just 2 percent from its motor dealerships. Cowie also expanded into a related area, that of vehicle rentals, including rentals of buses and motor coaches, in 1991.

Yet the company's bus operations pointed the way to its future as Arriva. The United Kingdom had been undergoing a vast privatization and deregulation program under the Thatcher government in the 1980s and early 1990s. As part of that process, the country became a pioneer in the privatization of its public transportation infrastructure, including its bus and rail networks.

Cowie began looking for new acquisition opportunities to boost its bus business in the early 1990s. In 1994, the company

paid nearly £30 million to acquire Leaside Bus Company—previously operated by the London Regional Transport authority—adding routes in north and central London. Leaside's £43 million in revenues per year tripled Cowie's bus revenues.

Soon after the Leaside acquisition, Cowie spotted a fresh opportunity. In December 1994, the company agreed to pay £16.3 million to acquire South London Transport, also from the London Regional Transport authority. South London added a fleet of 400 buses and routes in Brixton, Norwood, Croydon, and Thornton Heath. The addition of South London established Cowie as the leading bus operator in the London area, with a market share of 18 percent.

Cowie leapt into the big leagues with the acquisition of the British Bus Group in 1996. Paying £282 million, Cowie took over the United Kingdom's third largest bus company, with some 12 percent of the U.K. market. The addition of British Bus boosted Cowie's total market share to more than 16.5 percent nationwide, with a fleet of more than 6,400 buses, and new markets including Yorkshire, Essex, Derbyshire, Northumbria, Scotland, and Wales.

The company's shifting direction led to conflict in the boardroom and the ouster of founder Tom Cowie (by then Sir Tom Cowie) in 1997. Soon after Cowie's departure, the company announced its decision to change its name, uniting its different operations under the single Arriva banner. By the end of that year, Arriva had made its first purchase, paying £5 million for the Original London Sightseeing Tour and its fleet of 81 double-decker buses.

International Transport Leader in the New Century

The new name also pointed toward a new shift in the company's strategy. With future growth prospects in the United Kingdom limited by monopoly concerns, Arriva began eyeing the continental European markets. Under pressure from the European Union, these markets were expected to begin opening up their own transport networks to private competitors in the early 2000s.

Arriva made its first move into the larger European market with the purchase of Unibus, based in Denmark, in 1997. In 1998, Arriva entered The Netherlands, acquiring 75 percent of Vancom Nederland, part of U.S.-based ATC Vancom and then the largest private public transportation group in that country. The Vancom purchase gave Arriva control of routes in the Flevoland, Groningen, and Maastricht regions.

Arriva continued building its presence in The Netherlands, adding the Veonn & Hanze bus group in 1998. The company also entered rail services operations for the first time, starting in Groningen, and, in a joint venture, launching combined bus and train services in Friesland.

Arriva announced its decision to sell off its car leasing business in 1999 as it moved toward becoming a specialty transport operator for the new century. The company continued targeting Europe, buying Bus Danmark for £13.7 million in 1999. The purchase boosted the company's share of the Danish market to 18 percent, and also gave it a foothold in the bus market in Sweden. In that year, also, the company bought two

Key Dates:

1938: The Cowie family begins selling used motorcycles.
1946: Tom Cowie takes over the family business.
1960: Cowie launches sales of automobiles.
1965: Cowie goes public on the London Stock Exchange.
1980: The acquisition of George Ewer leads Cowie into the bus market, through Grey-Green bus lines.
1991: Cowie launches an automotive rental business.
1994: Cowie acquires the Leaside and South London bus companies, becoming a leader in the London market.
1996: Cowie acquires British Bus, the third largest bus company in the United Kingdom.
1997: The company changes its name to Arriva; the company acquires its first overseas bus operation, Unibus, in Denmark.
1998: Arriva enters the Netherlands market through the acquisition of Vancom Nederland and Veonn & Hanze.
1999: The company sells off its car leasing business to focus on the public transportation market; Bus Danmark is acquired; the company enters Spain.
2000: The company launches U.K. rail operations and enters the Portuguese bus market.
2002: The company begins operating a rail franchise in Denmark.
2003: The company begins a 15-year contract to operate rail service in Wales.
2004: The company acquires Prignitzer Eisenbahn Gruppe and Regentalbahn in Germany.

bus operators in the Galicia region in Spain. By 2000, the company had extended its Iberian presence with the purchase of four bus companies in Portugal, giving it routes in Famalicao, Guimaraes, and Braga.

The liberalization of the U.K. rail market brought Arriva's attention back home in 2000, when it launched its Arriva Trains Northern division in the north of England. The company further boosted its U.K. rail business with the 15-year contract to operate the passenger rail network in Wales in 2003. In a further extension of its rail operations, the company won the franchise to operate the Jutland-region passenger train service in Denmark.

By then, Arriva had gained a leading share in the Danish bus market, through its acquisition of Combus in 2001. The following year, Arriva boosted its Iberian operations with the purchase of Autocares Mallorca and the acquisition of majority control of Portugal's Transportes Sul do Tejo, a leading bus operator in the Lisbon area. In 2002, also, Arriva entered Italy, buying up SAB Autoservizi, the leading Italian bus operation in the Lombardy region.

As it shed its remaining noncore holdings, Arriva emerged as one of Europe's leading pure-play public transport operators. In 2004, the company established a beachhead in Germany, the largest single European market, with the purchase of Prignitzer Eisenbahn Gruppe. By the end of that year, the company had extended its German presence to the Bavarian region, with the acquisition of 76.9 percent of Regentalbahn AG. That purchase also gave Arriva operations extending into the Czech Republic. Arriva clearly had arrived as a leading European transport group for the new century.

Principal Subsidiaries

Arriva Bus & Coach Limited; Arriva Bus & Coach Rental (1) Limited; Arriva Bus & Coach Rental (2) Limited; Arriva Bus & Coach Rental (3) Limited; Arriva Bus & Coach Rental (4) Limited; Arriva Croydon & North Surrey Limited; Arriva Cymru Limited; Arriva Danmark A/S1 (Denmark); Arriva Derby Limited; Arriva Durham County Limited; Arriva East Herts & Essex Limited; Arriva Findiv Limited; Arriva Fox County Limited; Arriva International Limited; Arriva Kent & Sussex Limited; Arriva Kent Thameside Limited; Arriva London North East Limited; Arriva London North Limited; Arriva London South Limited; Arriva Manchester Limited; Arriva Merseyside Limited; Arriva Midlands North Limited; Arriva Motor Holdings Limited; Arriva Motor Retailing Limited; Arriva Noroeste SL2; Arriva North East Limited; Arriva North West Limited; Arriva Northumbria Limited; Arriva Passenger Services Limited; Arriva Personvervoer Nederland B.V.3 (Netherlands); Arriva Portugal – Transportes, LDA6; Arriva Scotland West Limited4; Arriva Sverige AB5 (Sweden); Arriva Tees & District Limited; Arriva Teesside Limited; Arriva The Shires Limited; Arriva Trains Limited; Arriva Trains Northern Limited; Arriva Trains Wales/Trenau Arriva Cymru Limited; Arriva Vehicle Rental Limited; Arriva Yorkshire Limited; Arriva Yorkshire West Limited; British Bus (Properties) Limited; British Bus Group Limited; London Pride Sightseeing Limited; Londonlinks Buses Limited; MTL Services Limited; SAB Autoservizi S.r.L.7; Stevensons of Uttoxeter Limited; The Original London Sightseeing Tour Limited; Transportes Sul do Tejo S.A.6.

Principal Competitors

FirstGroup PLC; Stagecoach Group PLC; Go-Ahead Group PLC; Azienda Trasporti Municipali; Keolis; Swebus AB; Nettbuss A.S.; Bus Eireann; Transports Verney.

Further Reading

Canovan, Cherry, "Driving into Europe," *Acquisitions Monthly,* August 2002, p. 48.
"Cowie Group," *Times,* March 2, 1994, p. 27.
Davidson, Andrew, "Arriva Chief Says Drive into Europe Is Just the Ticket," *Sunday Times,* October 10, 2004, p. 13.
Emling, Shelley, "Arriva's Horizons," *International Herald Tribune,* April 3, 2004, p. 19.
Geary, Joanna, "Arriva Set to Expand After Strong Showing," *Birmingham Post,* December 18, 2004, p. 15.
Martin, P., *The Tom Cowie Story,* London: James and James, 1988.
Mason, John, "Expanding Arriva Ahead of Expectations," *Financial Times,* December 18, 2004, p. 3.
Richardson, Denise, *Sir Tom Cowie: A True Entrepreneur,* Sunderland: University of Sunderland Press, 2004.
Wright, Johanna, "Drivers Test Arriva's Danish Rail Adventure," *Financial Times,* January 2, 2004, p. 18.

—M.L. Cohen

Atos Origin S.A.

Immeuble Les Miroirs
18, avenue d'Alsace
92926 Paris La Défense Cedex
France
Telephone: +33 1 55 91 20 00
Fax: +33 1 55 91 20 05
Web site: http://www.atosorigin.com

Public Company
Incorporated: 2000
Employees: 26,473
Sales: EUR 5.3 billion ($6 billion) (2004)
Stock Exchanges: Euronext Paris
Ticker Symbol: ATO
NAIC: 541611 Administrative Management and General
   Management Consulting Services

Atos Origin S.A. has emerged as Europe's third largest IT services company, and ranks among the world's top 20 IT consultancy companies. Atos Origin is a full-service systems integration provider in three primary areas: consulting, systems integration, and managed operations. The company focuses particularly on the following markets: financial services; consumer packaged goods/retail; discrete manufacturing; process industries; telecoms, media, and utilities; and the public sector. Major customers include ABN AMRO; BNP Paribas; Euronext; PPR; Procter & Gamble; Unilever; Alstom, BMW, and Renault; Akzo Nobel, Schlumberger, and Shell; France Telecom; KPN and Telecom Italia; and the French Ministry of Education and the UK Metropolitan police. Atos Origin is highly focused on Europe, which accounted for 90 percent of its EUR 5.3 billion ($6 billion) in revenues in 2004. France remains the company's single largest market, at 27 percent of sales, while the U.K. and Benelux markets each add about 20 percent. Managed operations, such as IT systems for the 2004 and 2008 Olympic Games, represent 50 percent of the group's sales, and systems integration adds 41 percent. Consulting, the company's newest area of operation, adds 9 percent to sales. Atos Origin is the result of a string of acquisitions, including the purchase of

KPMG Consulting in 2002 and SchlumbergerSema in 2004. Atos Origin is listed on the Euronext Paris Stock Exchange.

Early French IT Entrants in the 1970s

Although Atos Origin itself was formed in 2000 through the merger of France's Atos and The Netherlands' Origin, its own origins reached back to the earliest days of the information technology market. A result of a long series of mergers and acquisitions, Atos Origin emerged as a major European IT company, before joining the ranks of the global leaders in the mid-2000s.

The first major merger leading toward the later Atos Origin occurred in 1972, when French management systems pioneer Cegos Informatique, founded in 1962 as part of the Cegos consultancy, merged with Sliga, the subsidiary responsible for the growing data processing operations of Crédit Lyonnais, formed in 1970. The merged company was then named Sligos, with Crédit Lyonnais retaining majority control.

Sligos grew into one of France's leading IT companies during the 1970s. A major factor in the company's success was its participation in the development of the country's banking card system. In 1973, Sligos was chosen by the country's bank to develop the data processing backbone for the proposed Carte Bleue, which allowed credit card-like purchases throughout the country. By 1975, Sligos's system processed some 2.5 million transactions per year—a number that was to increase to more than 30 million per year by 1980. The development of the microchip permitted Sligos, which also began fabricating cards, to roll out electronic "smart" card processing systems during the 1980s. By the end of that decade, the Carte Bleue system had been extended nationwide, and the company's card production neared 50 million cards.

Sligos went public in 1986, and then, at the end of the decade, began expanding beyond France. By the early 1990s, Sligos had entered the United Kingdom through its purchase of Signet in 1991, and Germany through the Marben Group, as well as Italy and Spain. Into the mid-1990s, Sligos began a restructuring, exiting a number of operations, including the production of smart cards, in order to refocus its business around a core of systems integration services.

By then, the French IT industry was in the midst of a long consolidation effort, which saw the emergence of a small number of larger groups capable of competing on a European, and even global, scale. Among these groups was Axime, which proposed to merge with Sligos in 1996.

Axime stemmed from the creation of Sodinforg in 1981 by four associates at the Centre Technique Régionale Carte Bleue in Nancy. That company grew quickly through the 1980s, making a number of acquisitions, including Perbanq in 1984, Sedap in 1986, Segime Industrie in 1987, and Stratégie Informatique in 1989. By the end of the 1980s Sodinforg had become France's third largest smart card systems developer.

In 1991, Sodinforg agreed to merge with the number four in the French market, Segin, and another important IT services group, SITB. The merged company, led by Bernard Bourigeaud, then underwent a restructuring to focus on three core operations: electronic transaction processing; software engineering; and systems integration. As part of its restructuring, Axime sold off a number of businesses, including its check personalization and POS terminal businesses, representing some 50 percent of its total revenues.

Creating Atos in the 1990s

Instead, Axime began reinforcing its core businesses, while extending its operations to include online multimedia and outsourcing services. As part of that effort, the company acquired stakes in a number of businesses, and also began expanding beyond France, notably with the establishment of Segin Italie in 1991.

In 1993, the merged company formally adopted the name Axime, replacing Segin's listing on the Paris Bourse's secondary market. In that year, the company acquired CTL and its subsidiary Finaxine. Axime also acquired the network of offices operated by Comelog in the south of France that year. In 1995, Axime moved its listing to the Paris Bourse's monthly settlement market. Soon after, Paribas, which had held 88 percent of its stock in Axime, began selling off its holding, reducing its shares to 26 percent by the following year.

Axime continued making acquisitions, such as Iris in 1995. The company also acquired stakes in a number of other businesses, such as 30 percent of Carte Jeunes, while boosting its stakes in others, such as ODS (raised to nearly 73 percent) and Altek (to 100 percent). Axime also gained a boost to its outsourcing operation with the acquisition of the outsourcing division of ADP-GSI, which enabled Axime to gain the contract for operating the Paris Bourse's quotation and clearing systems. The company then set up a joint venture, later renamed as Euronext, with the Société des Bourses Françaises to develop these systems.

Bourigeaud now sought to raise Axime's profile still further. In 1996, Bourigeaud led Axime into merger talks with Sligos. That merger was completed by mid-1997, and by September 1997, the new, larger company had settled on a new name, Atos.

Following the merger, Atos launched a reorganization effort, including the creation of four strategic divisions: Services, Multimedia, Outsourcing, and Systems Integration. The company also sold off a number of noncore holdings at that time, including a computer hardware retailing operation, a direct marketing company, and its network interconnection software development business. At the same time, Atos made a number of strategic investments, buying up Sesam in Italy and buying out its minority partners in a number of subsidiaries.

Global Player at the Beginning of the 21st Century

Atos continued seeking acquisition opportunities into the new century. In 2000, for example, Atos acquired Odyssée, which focused on providing consulting services for the financial and banking sectors. Atos also made strong gains in its outsourcing and e-business operations, picking up a number of important clients, such as Vivendi and Peugeot. By the beginning of the 2000s, Atos was one of Europe's e-business systems providers.

Nonetheless, Atos remained focused, in large part, on the French market and enjoyed little name recognition elsewhere. That situation changed dramatically in 2000, when the company agreed to acquire Origin, owned by Royal Philips Electronics. Origin had been formed only in 1996, when BSO, founded in 1976, merged with Philips's Communications and Processing Services division, which itself had been formed in 1991. The merged company now became a player in the European market, claiming the number three spot among the continent's IT groups, with annual revenues of EUR 2.8 billion.

Atos Origin, still guided by Bernard Bourigeaud, now joined a trend in the IT services industry toward the convergence of traditional systems integration and management with consulting services. In 2002, the company acquired the U.K. and Netherlands operations of KPMG Consulting, which began operating as ATOS KPMG. The acquisition, which cost the company EUR 657 million ($620 million) helped raise Atos Origin's profile, boosting it to the number ten position among IT services providers in Europe. Atos Origin also scored an important outsourcing contract that year, agreeing with the Netherlands' KPN to take over nearly all of its IT operations. This contract, worth more than EUR 1 billion, helped Atos Origin consolidate its position as the number two native European IT services company.

By the end of 2003, Atos Origin was ready to move into global big leagues. In September 2003, the company announced that it had reached an agreement to acquire SchlumbergerSema, a leading provider of IT services to the oil industry, as well as the holder of contracts to supply the IT systems for the 2004

Key Dates:

1962: Cegos Informatique (subsidiary of Cegos) is created.
1970: Sliga (subsidiary of Crédit Lyonnais) is created.
1972: Cegos Informatique and Sliga merge, creating Sligos.
1973: Sligos is awarded a contract to develop the data processing backbone of the Carte Bleue.
1976: BSO (Netherlands) is founded.
1981: Sodinforg is created.
1991: Sodinforg, Segin, and SITB merge to create Axime; Philips C&P is created.
1993: Axime formally adopts its name and lists on the Paris Bourse's secondary market.
1996: Axime and Sligos agree to merge; BSO and Philips C&P merge to form Origin.
1997: The merger of Axime and Sligos creates Atos.
2000: Atos acquires Odyssée; Atos and Origin merge to form Atos Origin.
2002: Atos Origin acquires the U.K. and Netherlands businesses of KPMG Consulting for EUR 657 million.
2004: Atos Origin acquires SchlumbergerSema, becoming the largest European IT services company.

and 2008 Olympic games. The addition of SchlumbergerSema's operations catapulted Atos Origin's revenues past EUR 5 billion.

The 2004 Olympic Games represented an opportunity for Atos Origin to raise its international profile. At the same time, the SchlumbergerSema acquisition allowed Atos Origin to penetrate a new and potentially vast market: China. Atos Origin inherited SchlumbergerSema's contract to provide IT support services for six of the ten Chinese credit card-issuing banks. Atos Origin now made plans for further expansion in China,

expecting to quadruple its operations there by as early as 2006. With a history of successful mergers behind it, Atos Origin had taken a place as global IT services leader for the new century.

Principal Subsidiaries

Atos Investissement; Atos Multimédia (Italy); Atos Odyssée; Atos Origin (The Netherlands); Atos Origin Formation; Atos Origin GMBH (Germany); Atos Origin Infogérance; Atos Origin Intégration; Atos Origin International; Atos Service N.V. (Benelux); Atos S.p.A. (Italy); Atos TPI; Atos Worldline; AtosEuronext; Atos-ODS Origin (Spain); GTI (Spain); Immobilière Industrielle Faidherbe; Origin France; St. Louis RE (Benelux).

Principal Competitors

Pinkerton Computer Consultants Inc.; KPMG Deutsche Treuhand-Gesellschaft Aktiengesellschaft; PwC Deutsche Revision AG; Ernst and Young L.L.P.; Deloitte & Touche LLP; Cap Gemini S.A.

Further Reading

"A Desperate Embrace," *Economist*, November 13, 2004, p. 8.

Harvey, Fiona, "Slivers of Silver Linings on a Cloudy Horizon," *Financial Times*, May 7, 2003, p. 6.

——, "Swimming in Murky Waters," *Financial Times*, March 19, 2003, p. 5.

Minder, Raphael, "IT Group Learns from Others' Mistakes," *Financial Times*, June 6, 2002, p. 32.

Saltonstall, David, "Atos Origin Bets on Local Factory for Offshoring," *Business News Americas*, December 19, 2003.

Schenker, Jennifer L., "Looking to Vault into the Top Tier," *International Herald Tribune*, July 28, 2004, p. 16.

Walton, Christopher, "Atos Acquisition to Send European Status Soaring," *MicroScope*, September 29, 2003, p. 3.

——, "Atos Origin Buys in New Strength," *MicroScope*, February 9, 2004, p. 1.

—M.L. Cohen

Avista Corporation

1411 East Mission Avenue
Spokane, Washington 99220
U.S.A.
Telephone: (509) 495-4817
Fax: (509) 495-8725
Web site: http://www.avistacorp.com

Public Company
Incorporated: 1889 as The Washington Water Power
   Company
Employees: 1,450
Sales: $1.12 billion (2003)
Stock Exchanges: New York
Ticker Symbol: AVA
NAIC: 221122 Electric Power Distribution; 517212
   Cellular and Other Wireless Communications; 541512
   Computer Systems Design Services; 551112 Offices
   of Other Holding Companies

Avista Corporation operates as a generator, transmitter, and distributor of energy, providing electricity and natural gas to customers in eastern Washington and northern Idaho, a region known as the Inland Northwest. Avista provides electricity to 325,000 customers and natural gas to 300,000 customers. The company owns and operates eight hydroelectric facilities, a wood-waste fueled generating station, and a two-unit natural gas-fired combustion turbine generation facility. The investor-owned utility operations are conducted through a subsidiary named Avista Utilities, one of four business segments composing the company's operations. The other facets of the company's business are operated through Energy Marketing and Resource Management, Avista Advantage, and Avista Capital, which governs the company's interests in nonutility businesses. Energy Marketing and Resource Management markets and trades electricity and natural gas in a territory encompassing 11 western states and the Canadian provinces of British Columbia and Alberta. Avista Advantage provides utility bill processing and payment and information services throughout North America.

Origins

For more than a century, Avista operated under the name The Washington Water Power Company (WWP), a utility whose growth mirrored the growth of the region it served. During the years immediately preceding WWP's formation, the young city of Spokane (then known as Spokane Falls) was beginning its development into what it later became: the commercial center of eastern Washington and northern Idaho, a hub for the agricultural, horticultural, cattle-raising, and lumber activities that gave the region its economic might. Spokane, situated at the foot of an eponymous valley located midway between the beginning and the end of the Spokane River, was incorporated in 1881, the same year the Northern Pacific Railway reached the region, a confluence of events that were directly related.

The arrival of the railroad brought people and goods, invigorated trade, and ignited the growth of a city. As more people moved to Spokane and the city's business activity bustled, the need for electricity increased commensurately, stretching the limits of capacity. The trustees of the local power company, the Edison Electric Illuminating Company, foresaw the need for electricity and its supply moving in opposite directions, quickly heading toward a point when the capacity of Edison Electric could not meet the demands of Spokane's residents and businesses. In 1889, they voiced their concerns to Edison Electric's financial backers, a consortium of businessmen based in New York. The trustees proposed building a power station on the Spokane River, offering hydro-generated electricity as a solution to the impending energy crisis and as a new means to fuel Edison Electric's financial growth. The response from the East Coast dashed plans for a hydroelectric power station. Water power, the trustees were informed by the New York financiers, held little or no value.

The idea of a power station on the Spokane River did not die when the Spokane businessmen received their dismissive reply. Perhaps more out of necessity than rebellion, ten Edison Electric shareholders pooled their money and formed WWP, incorporating the company in 1889. More electricity was needed, and needed quickly, a need impressed upon Henry Herrick, one of WWP's first engineers. Herrick oversaw the construction of

Company Perspectives:

Avista's purpose is to improve life's quality by providing energy and energy-related services. We do this by safely and reliably delivering these services at a competitive price and by helping our customers get the most value from their energy dollar, while providing our investors a fair return.

WWP's first power station, dubbed the Monroe Street power station, overcoming calamity to get the project completed. A fire destroyed more than 30 city blocks in August 1889, razing much of Spokane, but Herrick pressed ahead, completing Monroe Street and bringing the hydroelectric project on line on November 12, 1890, the day WWP became operational.

The most telling evidence of the prudence of hydroelectricity in Spokane Valley was provided shortly after WWP's Monroe Street station began producing power. In 1891, the not-to-be-dissuaded Edison Electric stockholders, who decided to take their own destiny in their hands, purchased a controlling interest in Edison Electric, trumping the financial backers in New York who disregarded the value of the project that forced their retreat. The directors of WWP wasted little time on vindication, however, concentrating their energies instead on aggrandizing their new concern. To make WWP bigger, company officials needed to increase the demand for their product, a need that was fulfilled by promoting the growth of Spokane. Not long after acquiring control of Edison Electric, WWP acquired the Spokane Street Railway Company, seeing the asset as a way both to increase energy consumption and to promote the growth of Spokane. In 1895, shortly after purchasing the streetcar company, WWP created Natatorium Park, a streetcar-accessible destination that offered entertainment and recreational attractions. Both investments fulfilled the expectations of their worth: At its peak the streetcar system served nearly 25 million passengers annually; Natatorium Park remained a WWP property until 1968.

Extensive Expansion Beginning in 1900

WWP entered its most impressive period of expansion after the dawn of the 20th century, when Spokane recorded its own explosive growth. The population of Spokane rose dramatically during the century's first decade, swelling from 36,800 to nearly 105,000. In response, WWP officials directed the utility's efforts toward expansion to serve the rapidly growing city and the businesses and industries in outlying areas. In 1903, WWP constructed a 117-mile transmission line—the longest high-voltage line in the world at the time—to provide power to mining operations in northern Idaho. Other rural areas were connected to WWP service during this period, a period of perpetual expansion that continued into the 1930s. During these defining decades, the utility constructed more than 1,500 miles of transmission lines and also constructed the hydroelectric facilities that supported it in the 21st century. Hydroelectric projects completed during this period included Post Falls, Nine Mile, Post Street, Little Falls, Long Lake, and Upper Falls—all operated by Avista a century later. The scope of each of the projects was immense, requiring legions of workers and vast resources. The Long Lake facility, for instance, boasted 170-foot spillways, the tallest in the world when they were built, and the largest turbines in use at the time. The construction camp for the workers represented a town of its own, complete with a general store, post office, cement laboratory, steam laundry, hotel, barbershop, and 250-seat dining room near a clubhouse that showed movies and presented vaudeville acts.

WWP complemented its tremendous physical expansion during the first three decades of the century with a number of acquisitions that enabled it to convey the power it produced to customers. Between 1900 and 1936, the utility acquired 40 operating units or electrical systems operated by other power companies. WWP's acquisitive appetite put it into the position to link with the systems of the Puget Sound Power and Light Company in western Washington and the Montana Power Company in 1923, which enabled each of the three utilities to lend assistance to the others in case of an emergency. This relationship formed the basis for the Northwest Power Pool, established in 1941, that served as an electric interchange between five western states and the province of British Columbia.

The exhaustive work completed between 1900 and 1930 established WWP as the provider of power to one of the most important financial and transportation centers in the western United States. Its next significant period of development occurred after World War II, when the utility bolstered its energy interests and diversified into non-energy business areas.

The demand for power increased substantially following World War II, as the region served by WWP experienced an increase in population and in commercial and industrial activity. To meet the growing demand, WWP officials planned another major construction project, applying in 1950 for a license from the Federal Power Commission to build a dam at Cabinet Gorge on the Clark Fork River in Montana. Shifts of work crews worked 24 hours a day building the dam, a 208-foot-high, 600-foot-wide structure that was completed in 21 months. While construction of the Cabinet Gorge dam was underway, WWP work crews were laboring 22 miles upstream building the first of three hydroelectric projects on the Noxon Rapids. The first of these three projects, which ranked as the utility's largest power-producing facility in the 21st century, was brought on line in 1959.

WWP officials did not content themselves with the large-scale construction activity on the Clark Fork River during the 1950s. Management wanted to add natural gas assets to the utility's portfolio, a source of energy first delivered to the Pacific Northwest in 1955. WWP took the most expedient way to add natural gas to its energy mix by acquiring another company, purchasing the Spokane Natural Gas Company in 1958. The company also expanded into other areas through acquisition, developing a portfolio of non-energy assets that provided a meaningful stream of revenue. WWP's acquisition of the Spokane Street Railway Co. and the development of Natatorium Park in the late 19th century marked the beginning of the utility's involvement in non-energy interests, but the modern version of a diversified WWP began shortly after it delved into natural gas. In 1960, the utility acquired the Spokane Industrial Park, becoming a landlord for a facility that housed dozens of businesses. In 1977, the company formed Itron, a company involved in developing technology used in meter-reading equipment.

Key Dates:

1889: The Washington Water Power Company is incorporated.

1900: During the ensuing three decades most of the hydroelectric facilities operated by the utility are built.

1950: Construction of the Cabinet Gorge dam begins.

1958: The acquisition of the Spokane Natural Gas Company marks the utility's entry into the natural gas business.

1996: The utility wins federal approval to market electricity nationally.

1999: The utility changes its name to Avista Corporation.

2000: Gary Ely is named president, chief executive officer, and chairman of Avista Corp.

Profound Change in the 1990s

Avista celebrated its 100th anniversary as a more than $500-million-in-sales company. The company's utility business provided electricity to 250,000 customers and natural gas to 85,000 customers. Its nonutility business was governed in large part through a subsidiary named Pentzer Corporation, which held interests in a variety of businesses, including energy services, telecommunications, real estate development, and electronics. In the decade following the centennial celebrations in Spokane, both segments of WWP's business underwent significant change, as the company abandoned the corporate title that had identified it since the late 19th century and reorganized its business to compete in the future, a future in which the Inland Northwest's utility company would operate under the name Avista Corporation.

WWP's decade of profound change saw growth on all fronts. The growth of the company's natural gas business stood as the highlight of the first half of the 1990s, as the number of natural gas customers increased from 85,000 to 230,000 between 1989 and 1995. Midway through the decade, however, the company's electricity business moved to the forefront, marking the beginning of a new era in WWP's existence. In 1996, the utility won federal regulatory approval to market wholesale electric power nationally. A new subsidiary was formed, WWP Resource Services, to spearhead the company's entry into the ranks of power marketers certified by the Federal Energy Regulatory Commission (FERC), a move that industry observers perceived as crucial to WWP's survival in an industry transitioning away from monopoly and toward competition. By the end of 1996, WWP planned to begin brokering electricity in the southeastern United States, the first step toward developing into a utility involved in markets throughout North America.

In the wake of the approval from the FERC, a new alignment of companies emerged that gave WWP a national profile. In 1997, the company formed Avista Energy, a nationally oriented energy trading and marketing subsidiary. One year later, Avista Advantage was formed, giving WWP a national energy services subsidiary. At the start of 1999, WWP adopted the name used by its new subsidiaries and changed its official corporate title to Avista Corporation.

As Avista entered the 21st century, a new leader took command. In 2000, Gary G. Ely was named president, chief executive officer, and chairman of Avista, earning the top three posts after spending 33 years working for the utility. Under Ely's leadership, Avista's objective was to secure a lasting and prominent role as a national power broker. The company's century-old utility business in the Inland Northwest provided a reliable and sturdy business foundation, but continued success for the company meant realizing its potential in markets far removed from eastern Washington and northern Idaho.

Principal Subsidiaries

Avista Capital, Inc.; Avista Advantage, Inc.; Avista Communications, Inc.; Avista Development, Inc.; Avista Energy, Inc.; Avista Energy Canada Ltd.; Copac Management, Inc. (Canada); Avista Power L.L.C.; Avista Services, Inc.; Avista Turbine Power, Inc.; Avista Rathdrum, L.L.C.; Coyote Springs 2, L.L.C.; Rathdrum Power, L.L.C.; Avista Ventures, Inc.; Pentzer Corporation; Pentzer Venture Holdings II, Inc.; Bay Area Manufacturing, Inc.; Advanced Manufacturing and Development, Inc.; Avista Receivables Corporation; WP Funding LP; Spokane Energy, L.L.C.

Principal Competitors

IDACORP, Inc.; PG&E Corporation; Puget Energy, Inc.

Further Reading

Caldwell, Bert, "Washington State Utility Company Prospers Due to Energy Trading Business," *Spokesman-Review,* March 26, 2001, p. B3.

Davis, Tina, "Energy: Avista Plans Fuel Cell Spin-Off," *New Technology,* May 15, 2000, p. 32.

Ernst, Steve, "Crunch Time at Avista Corp.," *Puget Sound Business Journal,* September 8, 2000, p. 1.

Lobsenz, George, "Avista CEO Resigns in Wake of Tough Regulatory Ruling," *Energy Daily,* October 23, 2000, p. 1.

Nabbefeld, Joe, "Redmond Will Retire After 32 Years at Wash. Water Power," *Puget Sound Business Journal,* August 22, 1997, p. 47.

Neurath, Peter, "Competition Sparks Utility Merger," *Puget Sound Business Journal,* July 8, 1994, p. 1.

"Spokane, Wash., Utility Company Replaces Its Chief Executive," *Spokesman-Review,* October 20, 2000, p. B2.

—Bruce Vernyi
—update: Jeffrey L. Covell

Babcock International Group PLC

2 Cavendish Square
London W1G OPX
United Kingdom
Telephone: +44 20 7291 5000
Fax: +44 20 7291 5055
Web site: http://www.babcock.co.uk

Public Company
Incorporated: 1891 as Babcock & Wilcox Ltd.
Employees: 6,110
Sales: £452.0 million ($833.95 million) (2004)
Stock Exchanges: London
Ticker Symbol: EPIC:BAB
NAIC: 336611 Ship Building and Repairing; 541330 Engineering Services; 551112 Offices of Other Holding Companies

Babcock International Group PLC is one of the world's leading support services groups. Traditionally specializing in military work, the company has bolstered its commercial offerings through the acquisition of Peterhouse Group, a leader in civil infrastructure services. Based in the United Kingdom, which accounted for three-quarters of 2004 sales, Babcock also has operations in continental Europe, Africa, and North America.

Origins

Babcock International Group PLC can trace its origins to the British offshoot of the American steam boiler manufacturer, Babcock & Wilcox Co. (Babcock & Wilcox is now a completely separate company.) George Herman Babcock and Stephen Wilcox formed Babcock & Wilcox Co. after introducing a design for a steam boiler in 1867. A sales office opened in Glasgow in 1881 and within two years the firm was sourcing components from local contractors. Clydebank's Singer Works began building complete boilers in 1885.

A new company was established in Britain on July 4, 1891, to supply the boilers outside the United States and Cuba. Babcock & Wilcox Ltd. launched a factory of its own at Renfrew, Scotland, in 1895. In 1900, the start-up capital of £240,000 was raised to £1.57 million as the firm embarked on a century of leadership in the global boiler markets, establishing operations in a number of other countries.

According to a profile in *Manufacturing,* Babcock began its involvement with the Rosyth Dockyard in 1913 when it won a bid to build a steam raising plant there. The plant eventually became the base for extensive ship repairing operations.

Babcock was a leader in supplying boilers for conventional and nuclear power plants from the 1950s on. The company also diversified into a number of international businesses.

International in the 1970s and 1980s

In the mid-1970s, Babcock began to increase its investments in North America. By 1979, the company's North American subsidiary accounted for one-third of total sales (£844 million) and more than half of profits. During the year, the firm acquired Toronto construction equipment manufacturer Allatt Ltd. as well as Keeler Corporation, a Michigan-based metal casting company.

While Babcock was increasing overseas production, it was also raising overseas sales of U.K. plants, such as the Babcock Renfrew boiler making operation in Scotland. Renfrew was where huge boilers for conventional and nuclear power plants were constructed. The factory's exports rose from 10 percent of output in 1975 to 65 percent in 1983, noted the *Economist,* as the British economy slugged its way through a recession.

British power stations, Babcock's traditional main customer, would be slow to place orders for new boilers for the next ten years. In 1977, 1,100 workers at Renfrew had been laid off due to declining orders. Six years later, 300 white-collar employees were let go. The company was investing in new equipment to remain competitive.

Babcock's Materials Handling group supplied large conveyor belts to the auto industry through its Acco Industries, Inc. subsidiary in the United States. Acco, acquired in 1975, traced its origins back to 1904. (Acco would go to FKI after its demerger from Babcock in 1989.)

Company Perspectives:

Our vision is to become the partner of choice for supporting the outsourcing needs of government and private sector customers who have exacting technical and operational requirements.

Our mission is to deliver high quality support services solutions through applying specialist knowledge, expertise and original thinking to the challenges of public and private sector customers.

Babcock International's turnover was £1.1 billion in 1985. The company's subsidiaries were active in projects such as power stations in Brazil and coal reclaiming equipment in Australia. FATA European Group, based in Turin, Italy, provided materials handling equipment for the European market (it was divested in the late 1980s). There was also the Babcock Africa boiler-related business and a contracting business in South Africa.

Claudius Peters was the center of Babcock International's materials handling business. It had been unprofitable since the early 1970s and in 1986 got a new managing director, Rainer Herold, formerly of Siemens. A round of staff cuts and restructuring followed. Babcock's considerable contracting operations, which managed long-term construction and engineering projects, also included the British firm Woodall Duckham.

Late 1980s Merger/Demerger

The firm was acquired in August 1987 by FKI Electricals for £415 million. Lord King, Babcock chairman since 1972 (and also chairman of British Airways beginning in 1981), became chairman of the new combined company, called FKI Babcock. FKI Chairman Tony Gartland was the chief executive. About 6,000 jobs, more than half of them in the United Kingdom, were subsequently cut at Babcock International's operations, reducing the workforce to less than 30,000. Its head office in London and more than two-dozen plants were closed. Some of these operations were shifted to other FKI Babcock sites.

With annual sales of £84 million, FKI had been much, much smaller than £1.2 billion Babcock International before the merger. It was a diversified group, though, with interests ranging from the Fisher-Karpark parking meter business, to tea plantations, to lighting controls. FKI specialized in acquiring loss-making companies and turning them around. In the mid-1980s, it bought engineering businesses from Thorn EMI, four transport companies from TI Group, and a maker of boiler components called Laurence Scott. Systems engineer Stone International was acquired earlier in 1987.

After two years, FKI and Babcock were demerged in August 1989. Oliver Whitehead then became Babcock's chief executive.

Acquisitive in the 1990s

Babcock International had sales of £46.7 million in 1990. The company's plant at Renfrew had expanded beyond boilers, producing other large objects such as wind tunnels and ships' propellers.

Babcock International made a number of acquisitions in the early 1990s. Coventry-based Tickford Rail, which refurbished train carriages, was bought in 1991. King Wilkinson, an energy industry contractor in the Middle East, was added in April 1992. The Swedish-based ship-to-shore handling business Consilium was acquired by Claudius Peters in 1992. Consilium also produced wood processing equipment.

In October 1993, Babcock got a new chief executive, John Parker, formerly head of Belfast shipbuilder Harland and Wolff. He was joined by Managing Director Nick Salmon, formerly an executive with GEC Alsthom. Parker became chairman in 1994, succeeding Lord King, while Salmon was named CEO. Salmon left three years later to return to GEC Alsthom.

The materials handling business, based in Germany, was reorganized in fiscal 1994, when the division's sales reached £153 million. Renamed Babcock Materials Handling (BMH), it produced equipment for moving things such as paper, pulp, cement, and coal. Customers included ports, steel plants, and power stations.

Babcock held a joint contract to manage the Rosyth Royal Dockyard in Scotland with Thorn EMI. Rosyth, which refurbished warships, was the base for Babcock's facilities management division. In 1994, Babcock bought out Thorn EMI's 35 percent interest, creating Babcock Rosyth Defence, which subsequently won a ten-year contract to run New Zealand's Devonport Dockyard.

Losing Energy in the Mid-1990s

Babcock had a £42 million loss on sales of £805 million for the fiscal year ended March 1994. Much of this was from the troubled energy division, including a $15 million loss on a £420 million flue gas desulphurization contract at the Drax power station. This prompted a change of strategy. Afterward, Babcock shied away from contracts that large, unless the risk was shared with other partners.

The company also sold off risky businesses altogether. In 1995, Babcock sold a 75 percent stake in the entire energy division—including the historic boilermaking operation at Renfrew—to Mitsui Engineering & Shipbuilding (MES) of Japan. MES paid £56 million in cash. The unit was then renamed Mitsui Babcock Energy. The deal included a schedule to allow MES to eventually acquire the remainder of the division for another £14 million.

There were also big changes in the works at Rosyth. The company began seeking civil business in the oil industry through Babcock OGL, a joint venture with Laing Oil and Gas. In late 1996, Babcock bought Rosyth from the Ministry of Defence at a net cost of just £21 million ($33 million). The facility then employed 3,200 people, down from 7,000 when the management contract started in 1987. Its sales exceeded £200 million a year. The deal came complete with another ten years of business from the government, worth up to £1.5 billion. The company also joined A&P International, the largest ship repair company in the United Kingdom, in a bid to acquire New Zealand's Devonport Dockyard, where Babcock held a management contract.

By this time, Babcock had 10,000 employees around the world. It was working contracts in 60 countries and had offices in 25. A new Environmental division, made up of one plant in Texas, was developing ways to recycle electric arc furnace dust. Babcock soon divested this unprofitable unit. In-house manufacturing activities at the company's materials handling business in Germany were also scaled back.

After two dozen or so divestments in the previous five years, Babcock had sales of £500 million in 1998. It then specialized in just two areas of operation: materials handling and facilities management. The latter category, based at Rosyth, included a massive, three-year refurbishment project for the *HMS Ark Royal* aircraft carrier.

New Focus Beyond 2000

Babcock strengthened its shipbuilding capabilities in 2000. It acquired Armstrong Technology, a Newcastle warship designer, and FBM Marine, a producer of smaller vessels based in Cowes. FBM's shipyard was not included in the deal, and its staff was transferred to new offices at Southampton and Babcock's other facilities.

The company's rail division, also based at Rosyth, was developing innovative, flexible rail wagons. In January 2001, Babcock signed a deal to run naval maintenance at Faslane, a base for four British Vanguard class nuclear submarines.

Babcock acquired Hunting Contract Services (HCS), the military support services business of Hunting, an oil services provider, in 2001. The deal was worth £60.9 million, and included the transfer of 1,800 employees to Babcock. The acquisition was part of a new strategic focus on support services, rather than engineering.

The entire materials handling business was slated for sale in 2001, but a slowing global economy scuttled the offering, recorded *Sunday Business*. The Scandinavian wood pulp-handling business was divested, however.

SGI, a civil support services group, was acquired in 2002. Military work continued to keep the Rosyth shipyard busy, and Executive Chairman Gordon Campbell (appointed in 2001) was making government work the company's main strategic focus, according to the *Evening Standard*. Babcock also managed

several army bases and helped train pilots, the latter business picked up in the Hunting acquisition.

After losing £7.3 million in fiscal 2001 and £13.9 million in 2002, Babcock posted a pretax profit of £13.4 million in fiscal 2003. Sales rose 25 percent to £409 million.

Peterhouse Group PLC was acquired in June 2003 for £99 million. Peterhouse had formerly competed with Babcock in the support services business but was stronger in the civil sector.

Babcock posted sales of £452 million ($825.3 million) in the 2004 fiscal year, up 23.8 percent. Net income rose 130 percent to £16.4 million ($30.3 million).

Babcock won contracts to refit four British warships in the 2004 calendar year. The news was accompanied by layoffs of nearly 300 workers at Rosyth, part of the restructuring meant to make the company more competitive in such bids.

Principal Subsidiaries

Babcock Eagleton, Inc.; Certas PLC; Peterhouse Group PLC.

Principal Divisions

Babcock Defence Services; Babcock Engineering Services; Eve Group; First Engineering; Babcock Infrastructure Services; Babcock Naval Services.

Principal Competitors

BAE Systems PLC; Capita; DML Group; Serco Group; VT Group PLC; Weir Group.

Further Reading

Allen, Sam, "The Changing Face of Rosyth," *Manufacturer,* April 2003.
"The Babcock Family," *Economist,* May 5, 1984, p. 27.
"Babcock Swings into FY Profit with Completion of Business Transformation," *AFX International Focus,* June 12, 2003.
Baxter, Andrew, "City Sets Sights on a Less Exciting Future," *Financial Times* (London), U.K. Company News, April 28, 1994. p. 30.
——, "Clean, Tidy and Ready for New Brooms," *Financial Times* (London), U.K. Company News, October 4, 1993, p. 16.
——, "Looking for the Right Mix," *Financial Times* (London), Management Sec., April 21, 1995, p. 20.
——, "Sale Insulates Babcock from Energy Risk," *Financial Times* (London), U.K. Company News, September 1, 1995, p. 15.
Burt, Tim, "Babcock Chief Resigns to Rejoin GEC Alsthom," *Financial Times* (London), Companies & Finance Sec., March 15, 1997, p. 19.
"Engineers Say Goodbye Britain, Hello World," *Economist,* May 3, 1980, p. 81.
Fuller, Jane, "Go, Stop, Go, Stick in a Stuck Go-Go Stock," *Financial Times* (London), Sec. I, U.K. Company News, November 16, 1991, p. 10.
——, "Making the Most of a Power Base," *Financial Times* (London), Sec. I, U.K. Company News, December 18, 1991, p. 20.
Gray, Tony, "Babcock Returns to the Big League: The Acquisition of Rosyth Royal Dockyard by Babcock International Has Been Dubbed a 'Goldmine' by One Analyst," *Lloyd's List,* December 28, 1996, p. 2.

Harris, Clay, ''Bringing in New Thinking for a New Future,'' *Financial Times* (London), Sec. I, U.K. Company News, July 22, 1987, p. 22.

——, ''FKI Babcock to Shed 4,000 Jobs Worldwide,'' *Financial Times* (London), Sec. I, November 27, 1987, p. 1.

Leitch, John, ''Peterhouse Delivers Goods for Babcock,'' *Contract Journal,* December 1, 2004, p. 8.

Lorenz, Andrew, ''Parker Puts Babcock Back on an Even Keel,'' *Sunday Times* (London), May 23, 1999.

Nicoll, Alexander, ''Babcock to Buy Hunting Offshoot,'' *Financial Times* (London), Companies & Finance U.K., February 16, 2001, p. 22.

——, ''Babcock to Take Over Management of Maintenance at Faslane Submarine Base,'' *Financial Times* (London), National Sec., January 23, 2001, p. 8.

''North America Lifts Babcock to £35 Million,'' *Financial Times* (London), Sec. I, U.K. Company News, March 27, 1986, p. 24.

Tieman, Ross, ''Yachtsmen on a Long-Term Voyage to Recovery,'' *Times,* Bus. Sec., November 5, 1994.

''290 Jobs Are Axed at Naval Dockyard,'' *Times*, Home News Sec., July 24, 2004, p. 7.

Waller, David, ''Too Many Cooks in the Boiler,'' *Financial Times* (London), Sec. I, Management, September 21, 1988, p. 22.

Wells, Mike, ''From Yardarms to Ploughshares,'' *Euroil,* June 1995, p. 34.

Withers, Malcolm, ''British Defence Giant Babcock to Buy Division of Rival Company,'' *Evening Standard* (U.K.), February 15, 2001.

——, ''Defence Work Gives Babcock International Full Order Book in Britain,'' *Evening Standard* (U.K.), June 18, 2002.

Wootliff, Benjamin, ''Newly Appointed Executive Seeks to Revive British-Based Babcock's Glory,'' *Sunday Business* (U.K.), October 21, 2001.

—Frederick C. Ingram

Banco de Chile

Ahumada 251
Santiago
Chile
Telephone: (56) (2) 637-1111
Toll Free: (56) (600) 637-3000
Fax: (56) (2) 637-3034
Web site: http://www.bancochile.cl

Public Company
Founded: 1893 as S.A. Banco de Chile
Employees: 9,133
Total Assets: $15.55 billion (2003)
Stock Exchanges: Bolsa de Comercio de Santiago
    London Bolsa de Madrid New York
Ticker Symbol: CHILE (Santiago); BCH (New York)
NAIC: 522110 Commercial Banking; 522210 Credit Card
    Issuing; 522291 Consumer Lending; 522310
    Mortgage and Other Loan Brokers; 523120 Securities
    Brokerage; 523920 Portfolio Management; 523930
    Investment Advice; 524113 Direct Life Insurance
    Carriers; 561400 Collection Agencies

Banco de Chile is the second largest private bank in Chile and the largest that remains under Chilean ownership. As a full-service bank its activities include commercial loans, foreign exchange, capital-market services, cash management, and noncredit services such as payroll and payment. A wide variety of treasury and risk-management products are offered to corporate customers. Personal banking products include credit cards and residential mortgage, auto, and consumer loans as well as deposit services such as checking and savings accounts and time deposits. Through its subsidiaries, Banco de Chile offers services such as securities and insurance brokerage, mutual-fund management, financial advisory services, and factoring.

First Banco de Chile: 1893–2001

Banco de Chile was founded in 1893 by the merger of three of the oldest banks existing at the time: Banco Nacional de Chile, Banco Agricola, and Banco de Valparaiso. It opened its doors at the beginning of the following year in 25 cities. A London office was opened in 1906. Banco de Chile quickly established itself as the nation's foremost private bank. In 1964 it held 29.5 percent of the deposits in all 24 domestic commercial banks and 43.5 percent of the assets, an amount almost equal to the next nine ranking banks. No individual held as much as 3 percent of the bank stock, but 30 shareholders held 20 percent. In their book *Landlords & Capitalists,* Maurice Zeitlin and Richard Earl Ratcliff concluded that the bank "is under the joint control of several dominant owning families, whose diverse economic interests transcend industry, commerce, agriculture, and banking. These families, indeed, are 'finance capital' personified." The authors specifically mentioned in this regard "the Larraín, Matte, and Valdés families, among whom are the descendants of the founders of the three original banks that merged to form the Bank of Chile . . . in collaboration with the Cortés and Cousiño families, with whom they also have close kinship ties."

Unlike most other Chilean banks, Banco de Chile was not nationalized by the left-wing government of President Salvador Allende Gossens in the early 1970s, but the state took a stake of more than 45 percent of the shares. After the military coup that overthrew this government in 1973, an economic program of virtually unfettered free enterprise was adopted. Between 1975 and 1978, when, in terms of net worth, Banco de Chile was the third largest private enterprise in the nation, the government's shares were placed on auction and purchased by a group led by Javier Vial Castillo. The bank's resources enabled Vial—who became its president—to form the second largest conglomerate in Chile, taking in 25 of the nation's largest 250 private enterprises. Leasing Andino S.A., established in 1977 as an affiliate (and later absorbed by its parent), became the largest company in its field.

Chile's rapid economic expansion in this period proved unsustainable when the United States began raising interest rates in 1979 to end the inflation that had resulted from sharp increases in the price of oil. By 1982 almost all of the capital and reserves of Chile's banks and finance companies had been committed to loans that could not be repaid. In the case of

Banco de Chile, nonperforming loans in 1983 took up more than twice its capital and reserves. Vial's BHC group, which held 25 percent of the bank, owed it about CLP 19 billion ($487 million). Banco de Chile was turned over to the government that year. The central bank bought at least $1 billion of Banco de Chile's nonperforming loans at book value, issuing ten-year bonds on condition that the shareholders divert future dividends to pay off the debt.

Under a "popular capitalism" program, the government in 1985 lent money at zero real-interest rates to encourage taxpayers to buy stock in Banco de Chile (and four other banks). Some 39,000 did so, reducing the stake of the previous 16,000 shareholders to just 12 percent. Vial was sentenced to jail for fraud and served nine months. In 1996 the bank still owed the nation's central bank CLP 706.48 trillion ($1.74 billion). At this point the debt was rescheduled and assigned to a subsidiary of Banco de Chile, which agreed to pay it off from funds allotted to dividends over 40 years at 5 percent interest. Meanwhile, the central bank held 64 percent of Banco de Chile's shares as collateral and was essentially a preferred shareholder.

Although no private shareholder held a dominant position in Banco de Chile, leadership had passed to Empresas Penta S.A., a holding company based on the acquisition of an insurance company in 1982 by five former executives of the Cruzat-Larraín conglomerate, which also had collapsed in the wake of the national financial crisis. Following a 1987 law that expanded the services that banks were allowed to offer, Banco de Chile established four subsidiaries for purposes such as brokering securities, managing mutual funds, and offering financial advice. During 1996–97 the bank's subsidiaries had a larger share of mutual-fund management and leasing contracts than those of any other bank. A 1997 law extended further the activities in which banks could take part, following which Banco de Chile established subsidiaries for purposes such as factoring and insurance brokerage. It also had a significant presence abroad, with a branch in New York City, an agency in Miami, and offices in Buenos Aires, Mexico City, and Sao Paulo. Although the bank had dropped from first to third in size due to mergers in the industry, it was still Chile's most efficient and profitable financial institution, according to *LatinFinance,* which awarded it the title "Best Bank in Chile" in 1997. The previous year it achieved an impressive 27.62 percent return on equity.

Empresas Penta, the bank's leading shareholder with 5.7 percent of the stock in 1996, raised its stake to 14 percent in 1999. A working alliance with other shareholders and directors commanded approximately 30 percent of the shares (excluding the central bank's) and thereby appeared to offer security against the prospect that the bank might be taken over by an outsider. Nevertheless, the Luksic group—backed by the re-sources of Quiñenco S.A., one of the two or three biggest holding companies in Chile—began buying the bank's stock in 1999, setting off a bidding war with Penta. Quiñenco, which had only recently acquired another big Chilean bank, Banco de A. Edwards, held 13 percent of Banco de Chile in December 2000, when it purchased Penta's stake (now 35 percent) for $541 million. Banco de Chile and Banco de A. Edwards were merged at the beginning of 2002 to form, at the time, Chile's largest bank. It retained the Banco de Chile name.

Banco de A. Edwards: 1866–2001

George Edwards was the physician on a British craft raiding Spanish possessions along the Pacific coast of South America in 1803, when he fell in love with a young Chilean woman and deserted ship. Of their eight children, the most financially successful was Agustín Edwards Ossandón, who sold goods to the miners who worked for his father and became a millionaire by age 30. After making still more money with an ironworks supplying a railroad, he turned to finance, founding Chile's first insurance company in 1853 and Banco de A. Edwards y Cia in 1866. (Some sources give an earlier date and credit Edwards as the nation's first private bank.) He also played a leading role in developing Chile's nitrate deposits and cornered the world copper market in 1871–72. Banco Edwards was highly lucrative; although it held only 8 percent of the nation's banking market during 1870–85, it accounted for 30 percent of the profits.

Edwards family members not only owned the bank that bore their name and large landed estates but also investments in railroads, telegraph lines, newspapers, copper mines, and nitrate fields. Agustín Edwards Ross, son of the founder, established partnerships between the family's nitrate and railway holdings and the most powerful English firms. Agustín Edwards Mc-Clure, his son, cultivated the family's close relations with England during his long term as Chile's ambassador in London. In 1920 he added to the family fortune by selling its 60 percent share of the bank to the Anglo-South American Bank Ltd. The Edwardses eventually regained control of the bank during the 1930s or 1940s, when British economic involvement in Latin America was sharply reduced, first by the Great Depression, then by World War II. In the mid-1960s the Edwards interests held at least 42.75 percent of the shares. Agustín Edwards Eastman, grandson of Agustín Edwards McClure, was vice-president of the bank. The president was Arturo Lyon Edwards, his first cousin once-removed. Banco Edwards was the nation's fifth largest bank at the time.

After President Salvador Allende took office in 1970, his left-wing government nationalized the bank, expropriating its assets and turning the proceeds over to the newly established Banco Nacional de Curicó, which later became Banco Nacional. A military coup overthrew Allende's government in 1973. At the end of the decade, the Edwards family acquired Banco Constitución and reopened it under the Banco Edwards name. Because, unlike Banco de Chile, Banco Edwards did not, relatively speaking, make reckless loans or engage in ultimately disastrous dollar borrowing, it survived the national banking crisis of 1982. The controlling interest, however, fell into the hands of the Ergas family in 1986. Banco Edwards expanded its scope when a 1987 law allowed the nation's banks to enter fields such as stock brokerage and mutual-fund management.

During the first half of the 1990s it fared well, exceeding the banking system as a whole in capital growth and profit margin.

In 1995 Banco Edwards offered American depositary receipts (the equivalent of common stock) in New York and other international markets. The sum raised enabled the bank to pay off its debt of CLP 51.09 billion (about $128 million), stemming from the earlier banking crisis, to the central bank. Agustín Edwards del Rio, son of Agustín Edwards Eastman, opposed the share offering and, on not prevailing, resigned as bank president. After another law, in 1997, allowed banks to expand their operations still further, Banco Edwards was one of the first to establish subsidiaries for leasing and factoring.

Members of the Ergas family held 51 percent of the shares in 1998, while the Edwards clan held 16.5 percent. With the growing concentration of the Chilean banking system into fewer hands and dissension within the Ergas family, a takeover bid became inevitable. It came from the Luksic group, which, acting through its chief holding company, Quiñenco S.A., purchased a majority share of the bank in 1999 for $283.3 million.

Merged Bank of Chile: 2002–03

After purchasing the controlling interest in Banco de Chile in 2000, Quiñenco merged it with Banco Edwards into a combined Banco de Chile effected at the beginning of 2002. The former had been the nation's third largest, and the latter the nation's sixth largest, bank at the time. The merged entity was briefly Chile's largest bank, but in 2002 Banco Santiago and Banco Santander Chile were merged into a combined Banco Santander Chile that was majority-owned by the Spanish bank Banco Santander Centro Hispano.

Under the merger terms, shareholders of Banco de Chile received shares equivalent to 66 percent of the merged bank and shareholders of Banco Edwards shares equivalent to the remaining 34 percent. Banco Edwards's earnings of $5.3 million in 2000 compared poorly with Banco de Chile's $143 million, and its return on equity of 1.44 percent was even worse compared with the latter's 27.27 percent, which had made it the best-performing bank in Chile in 2000. On the other hand, the old Banco de Chile brought with it the considerable liability of its debt to the central bank, although with the merger the central bank's holding of the merged bank's shares fell to 42 percent. Each bank brought different strengths to the merger. While Banco de Chile offered a full range of services to both individuals and corporate customers, Banco Edwards had traditionally targeted wealthy individuals and midsized companies, and the merged bank planned to retain the Edwards name for high-end products. ("Banco Creditchile" was the brand name given to Banco de Chile's services to lower-income individual customers.) By the end of 2002, more than 50 branches had been merged. At the end of 2003, the new Banco de Chile had 224 branches. It earned CLP 130.55 billion ($217.8 million) that year.

Principal Subsidiaries

Banchile Administradora General de Fondos S.A.; Banchile Asesoria Financiera S.A.; Banchile Corredores de Bolsa S.A.; Banchile Corredores de Seguros Ltda.; Banchile Factoring S.A.; Banchile Securitiadora S.A.; Promarket S.A.; Socofia S.A.

Principal Divisions

Agreements and Special Business; Company Banking; Creditchile; Corporate and International; Credit Risk; Finance; Marketing; Operations and Technology; Personal and Branch Banking.

Principal Competitors

Banco Santander Chile.

Further Reading

"Best Bank in Chile," *LatinFinance,* October 1997, p. 34.
Fazio, Hugo, *Mapa actual de la extrema riqueza en Chile,* Santiago: LOM-Arcis, 1997, pp. 307–11.
——, *La transformación de la economía chileno,* Santiago: LOM Ediciones, 2000, pp. 175–77.
Galloway, Jennifer, "Day of Reckoning," *LatinFinance,* November 1999, pp. 27–29.
——, "Fair Market Value for All?," *LatinFinance,* December 2001, pp. 29–31.
Kinzer, Stephen, "Chilean's Bid for a Comeback," *New York Times,* September 19, 1983, pp. D1, D8.
Merino, Robert, "La saga de los Agustines," *Capital,* May 2000, pp. 28–31.
"Nice Economy," *Banker,* October 1988, pp. 122–24.
Pérez Villamil, Ximena, "Asuntos de familias," *Capital,* August 1998, pp. 32–37.
Soto, Héctor, "Cambio de mando," *Capital,* January 2001, pp. 18–23.
Zeitlin, Maurice, and Richard Earl Ratcliff, *Landlords & Capitalists,* Princeton, N.J.: Princeton University Press, 1988, p. 66 and pp. 119–25.

—Robert Halasz

Barnes Group Inc.

123 Main Street
P.O. Box 489
Bristol, Connecticut 06011-0489
U.S.A.
Telephone: (860) 583-7070
Fax: (860) 589-3507
Web site: http://www.barnesgroupinc.com

Public Company
Incorporated: 1922 as Associated Spring Co.
Employees: 6,100
Sales: $890.82 million (2003)
Stock Exchanges: New York
Ticker Symbol: B
NAIC: 332116 Metal Stamping; 332611 Spring (Heavy Gauge) Manufacturing; 332999 All Other Miscellaneous Fabricated Metal Product Manufacturing; 551112 Offices of Other Holding Companies

Barnes Group Inc. serves diversified industrial markets throughout the world. It is the largest manufacturer of springs in North America, for example, and is a leading distributor of maintenance, repair, and overhaul parts and services in the United States. Barnes also sells specialized aerospace parts and services. The company's rich history is illustrative of the Yankee ingenuity that built the American industrial machine. Barnes is organized into three business units: Associated Spring, Barnes Aerospace, and Barnes Distribution.

Bristol Origins

The founder of what would eventually become a *Fortune* 500 company was Wallace Barnes. Wallace, nicknamed "Bub," was born on Christmas Day in 1827 and grew up in Bristol, Connecticut, where his ancestors had settled in the mid-1600s after arriving from England in 1630. Wallace's ancestor Thomas Barns (the name was later changed to Barnes), the original settler who arrived from England, fought in the Pequot War. After bearing three children, his wife Mary was put to death by hanging in 1662 for "entertaining familiarity with Satan." One of Thomas Barns's children became the first settler of Bristol and that town's first tavern keeper. Succeeding Barnes family members became war heroes, political figures, and noted businessmen.

Wallace Barnes began working for both his father Alphonso and grandfather Thomas in the family hotel and general store. The general store specialized in clocks, but it also sold drugs and general merchandise. Wallace eventually became skilled as a druggist. Partly because he and his father did not get along, however, he left to start his own druggist shop in a nearby town. Lackluster returns from that venture prompted him to try his hand at a new business, clockmaking. Wallace started out contracting to supply cut glass, doors, and parts to different clockmakers who were part of the bustling clock trade that had developed in Bristol; in fact, Bristol was known as the clockmaking capital of the United States at the time. Unfortunately, the local clock industry fell on hard times when the Panic of 1857 caused a severe depression.

At the time of the Panic, Wallace was working for clockmaker A.S. Platt. Platt, for whom Wallace had been working at the rate of $1.25 per day, became unable to pay him for his services. Instead of cash, Barnes accepted some hoop-skirt wire as compensation. In a move that demonstrated his dealmaking savvy, Wallace hauled the wire in a wagon to nearby Albany. There, he traded the wire for a financially troubled haberdashery store. Rather than stay to run the store himself, Wallace turned around and traded it for a Missouri farm that he had never seen. Upon returning to Bristol, he managed to trade the farm for a blacksmith shop, which he sold for the handsome sum of $1,600. Incredibly, Wallace used the money to purchase the troubled A.S. Platt, the company that had given him the wire in the first place.

Barnes's new purchase included a bevy of equipment and raw materials. Importantly, Barnes also received the rights to a secret method of tempering steel springs that involved heating the springs and then quenching them in oil. Wallace wisely partnered with E.L Dunbar, a more experienced manufacturer who was also Wallace's longtime friend. They each contributed $2,000 to the venture and set up shop in a two-story building in Bristol. They started with a handful of employees making springs and hoops for

Company Perspectives:

Management has embraced a corporate culture within Barnes Group that has as its common goals the generation of sustainable, profitable growth and building lasting value for its stockholders. The Company's strategies for generating growth include organic growth from new products and services, markets and customers; and growth from strategic acquisitions, of which eight have been completed since 1999.

skirts, but their workforce quickly expanded when the demand for hoops exploded in the wake of a fashion craze. Wallace and his partner scrambled to relocate in a bigger shop, and by the end of the year had 150 workers manning three eight-hour shifts six days a week. Although the hoopskirt fad died out before the start of the Civil War in 1861, Barnes and Dunbar managed to reap profits of about $225,000 in 1859 alone.

When the Civil War started, Wallace and Dunbar switched to making musket springs and powder horns, among other items. Although the company was still making money, the two partners split in 1863; political differences may have forced the departure of Dunbar, a "Copperhead" who sympathized with the South and differed from the staunchly Republican Barnes. Barnes continued to operate the business during the next several years, expanding into new product lines and even patenting several new springs and production techniques. Despite a discouraging fire that destroyed his factory in 1866, Wallace persevered with his springmaking operations and was employing a workforce of 35 by the mid-1870s.

Interestingly, the intense and optimistic Wallace Barnes was known in his community during this time more as a trader of Jersey cattle than as a manufacturer. In fact, Wallace was much more of a tinkerer, trader, and venturer than he was a businessman. During the 1880s, when his spring business was faltering, Wallace was probably making more money from the new livestock drug that he had developed and patented and was selling throughout the world. Thus, the success of his spring business was not necessarily paramount. Other interests included a theater that he built in downtown Bristol and coon hunting, a favorite hobby to which he devoted significant energy. When Wallace died in 1893 at the age of 65, he left an estate appraised at about $70,000—not as much as one might expect from such an active businessman, but reflective of his varied interests.

Carlyle Fuller (C.F.) Barnes, the eldest of Wallace's five sons, had become active in the spring business in the 1880s. He and his brothers changed the name (and focus) of the business, in fact, to the Barnes Brothers Clock Company, although that venture lasted only four years and the brothers returned to making springs instead of clocks. Part of the problem had been that their father had a habit of taking money from that business to cover debts related to other ventures. In any event, C.F was credited with saving the company from bankruptcy following Wallace's death. Despite economic turbulence at the time, he was able to get his creditors to back his foray into manufacturing bicycle wheels and related parts. The Barnes Company, as it had become known, cashed in on the bicycle fad and generated

much needed profits in the late 1890s. That put the company in good financial shape going into the 1900s.

The fading bicycle boom was replaced in the early 1900s by the emerging automobile industry. Barnes benefited from strong demand for motorcar springs for valves, clutches, starters, suspensions, and hundreds of other items. At the same time, Americans were increasingly purchasing other items, introduced en masse during the Industrial Revolution, that required springs, such as typewriters, telephones, ice-cream makers, electric sewing machines, and more. As demand for Barnes's various springs grew, the company expanded, adding new production facilities and even building its own steel mill. By 1910, when C.F Barnes's son Fuller joined the company, Barnes was employing a workforce of about 200. Fuller's younger brother Harry also started working for the company in 1913. The two brothers helped steer the company through its biggest expansion wave during the next few years, as demand for springs spiraled during World War I, and the company's workforce temporarily soared to 1,400. Barnes churned out an estimated 90 million springs for the U.S. government during that war.

Formation of Associated Spring: 1922

Although sales slowed after the war, they were soon supplanted by demand unleashed during the Roaring Twenties. Barnes was reaping about $2 million in revenues annually by the early 1920s and was rapidly expanding its product lines and production facilities. Barnes's primary area of interest, however, was still the automobile industry. Still, the brothers thought their company lacked the size needed to take a leadership role as a supplier of springs to that industry. Consequently, the Barnes brothers engineered the November 1922 merger of three companies to form Associated Spring Co., with Fuller Barnes as president. The new company grew rapidly during the 1920s, increasing sales 85 percent and broadening its scope to include all types of appliance and aviation industries. Associated Spring also purchased other competitors, including the descendant of a springmaking firm created by E.L Dunbar after he had split from Wallace Barnes.

The stock market crash of 1929 and the resulting Great Depression battered Associated Spring. After nearly a decade of success, the company posted a crushing $43,585 loss in 1931 and then a $482,925 shortfall in 1932. Salary cuts, layoffs, and restructuring allowed the company to survive the Depression. During that period, Barnes was separated from the other two companies with which it had merged, although all three subsidiaries were still under the same corporate umbrella.

By the late 1930s the Barnes factories were humming once again as the United States geared up for World War II. Throughout the war, Barnes delivered millions of springs for airplanes, tanks, trucks, and jeeps. In addition, its steel mill cranked out products ranging from band saws to machine-gun ammunition clips. Associated's total payroll jumped to 6,000 in 1943, when shipments hit an all-time high of $31 million.

Public in 1946; NYSE-Listed in 1963

When the war ended, Associated Spring and its Barnes subsidiary enjoyed steady demand as peacetime markets surged. Sales in 1946 hit $22.6 million and the company was still employing more than 4,000 workers. To fund growth, Associated went public and sold its shares over-the-counter. It used the cash to expand its factories, open new sales and distribution offices, and to buy other companies. By 1953 the company was capturing about $50 million in annual sales. In that year, Carlyle F. ("Hap") Barnes, Fuller's son, was made president of Associated; he would become CEO in 1964. Under his direction, the company expanded internationally, first into Puerto Rico and then into Argentina, England, Japan, and Mexico by the early 1960s. Throughout the 1950s and 1960s, Barnes sustained its legacy of innovation in the spring industry. By 1963, in fact, the company was employing 5,200 workers and was selling its shares on the New York Stock Exchange.

Hap Barnes, who had been joined at the executive level by his cousin Wallace (Wally), was satisfied with Associated's performance by the early 1960s. But he also realized that it was time for a change, mostly because the company had become overly dependent on the automotive industry. To reduce the dependency, he decided that the organization should diversify into distribution, which was more closely tied to the counter-cyclical replacement and overhaul market. To that end, Associated purchased Bowman Products Company in 1964, giving it an instant and significant stature as a distributor of repair and replacement parts. Several acquisitions followed during the mid- and late 1960s, but Bowman proved to be among the most successful. By 1968 Associated was doing $100 million in sales annually, and by the early 1970s was employing 6,000 workers in 41 locations in the United States and abroad. It was even listed on the London Stock Exchange.

Global Expansion in the 1970s and 1980s

During the 1970s Associated stepped up its global expansion efforts. It purchased major spring producers in England and Sweden in the early 1970s, for example, that added about 1,500 workers and more than $11 million in new sales to its portfolio. In the mid-1970s, moreover, Barnes bought companies in South America, Germany, and India. Because of the widened scope of the organization, its name was changed in 1976 from Associated Spring to Barnes Group Inc. One year later, Hap Barnes

stepped aside as chief executive and handed the reigns to his cousin, Wally Barnes; Hap remained a senior officer at the company until 1989, his 41st year at Barnes. Wally oversaw the opening of a new $3 million international headquarters in downtown Bristol in 1979.

Under Wally Barnes's direction, Barnes Group continued to expand and acquire companies. In 1979, in fact, Barnes achieved record sales of $432 million, making that its eight consecutive annual rise in both sales and earnings. The sales figure placed Barnes on the *Fortune* 500 list for the first time. Although Barnes's growth was impressive to many, critics were concerned that the company had expanded too rapidly. Their concerns were confirmed in 1981, when net income plunged from $24 million to just $5 million. One year later that figure dipped to an embarrassing deficit of $5.5 million. Although a recession was partly to blame, Barnes executives realized that changes were needed. Barnes shuttered several poorly performing plants and divisions in 1983 and sold off several interests that no longer complemented its corporate goals. After showing a loss of $2.6 million in 1983, Barnes enjoyed a profit recovery in 1984 as net income increased to $15.7 million.

Barnes continued to make acquisitions and expand certain operations, particularly those related to aerospace, in the mid- and late 1980s. But it also sustained a concerted effort to cut costs, focus on customer service, and jettison badly performing businesses. It sold a major portion of its distribution business, for example, and got completely out of the steelmaking industry. The end result of restructuring was steady sales growth and healthy profits during most of the 1980s. Revenues increased from about $420 million in 1984 to about $545 million in 1990, while net income hovered between about $13 million and $18 million. Wally Barnes announced his retirement as chief executive in 1990, to become effective in 1991, leaving leadership of the company to someone outside of the Barnes family.

Turbulence in the 1990s

Barnes Group Inc. was hurt by the global economic downturn of the early 1990s. Sales slipped to about $500 million by 1993, and Barnes was forced to post a loss in 1992 as a result of restructuring charges and accounting changes. Barnes stepped up cost-cutting efforts during the period and closed some operations, among other reactions to the downturn. Total Barnes employment fell from about 4,500 to 4,200 during the period. In 1994, however, Barnes rebounded and managed to record its highest profit since 1980. After a few years of turbulence in the executive ranks, Barnes's board named Theodore E. Martin president and chief executive in 1995. Martin had served stints with several manufacturers before joining Barnes in 1990.

Going into the mid-1990s, Barnes was still a global leader in the spring business, which had been its mainstay for most of its history. Its Associated Spring division, which operated 11 plants in five countries and served a wide range of industries, was accounting for roughly half of corporate revenues in 1995 and the large majority of profit. Through its Bowman division, Barnes was also a top distributor of repair and maintenance parts. Bowman was contributing about 40 percent of sales and about one-third of corporate income. Meanwhile, Barnes's aerospace division was a leading producer of titanium and precision parts for jet engines, and also provided jet-engine refurbishing services. That struggling division lost money during the defense industry downturn in the early 1990s, but was rapidly improving going into the mid-1990s.

Acquisitions Path in the Late 1990s

Edmund M. Carpenter, formerly head of General Signal Corporation, became Barnes Group's president and CEO in 1998. He promptly set the company on an acquisition path. Cleveland area-based Nitrogen Gas Products, the nitrogen gas spring operation of Teledyne Fluid Systems, was acquired in August 1999.

Curtis Industries, Inc., a nearby Mayfield Heights, Ohio-based distributor of MRO (maintenance, repair and operating) supplies, was bought in May 2000 and combined with Bowman Distribution to form Barnes Distribution. Curtis had sales of more than $80 million a year. Curtis CEO A. Keith Drewett was picked to head the combined business.

The Bowman Distribution and Curtis Industries brand names remained in place, as did the Mechanic's Choice, a line Curtis had acquired from Avnet in 1996. According to *Industrial Distribution*, Curtis was stronger in automotive markets, while Bowman catered to the aerospace and railroad industries.

Two units were acquired from Aviation Sales Company and added to Barnes Aerospace in September 2000. Kratz-Wilde Machine Company and Apex Manufacturing Inc. produced precision machined components for the aerospace industry. The deal was worth $41 million and boosted Barnes Group's involvement with the booming regional jet industry.

Barnes's three businesses had net sales of $740 million in 2000, up 19 percent from the previous year. Net income rose 25 percent to $35.7 million. Associated Spring was the largest division, with sales of $327 million. Barnes Aerospace did $135 million worth of business, while Barnes Distribution contributed $291 million to revenues. Each was profitable.

Still Expanding After 2000

England's Euro Stock Springs & Components Ltd. was acquired in 2001, as was Forward Industries of Michigan. Euro Stock, a distributor of springs, had fewer than 20 employees. Nearly all of the manufacturing assets of Seeger-Orbis GmbH & Co. OHG, a retaining ring manufacturer in Germany, were acquired in February 2002.

Spectrum Plastics Molding Resources Inc. of Connecticut was also added a month later. The Spectrum buy brought metal-in-plastic and plastic-on-metal parts to the Associated Spring product line. Spectrum employed 120 people and had sales of about $17 million a year.

Des Plaines, Illinois-based MRO supplies distributor Kar Products was also acquired in 2002 for $78.5 million. It had sales of $122 million that year and employed a sales force of 600 people. As the *Waterbury Republican-American* noted, the deal brought Barnes 40,000 new customers throughout the United States.

By 2003 the acquisition drive had raised the number of employees to 6,100 at 60 sites around the world. Barnes had also trimmed some of its operations during this time, shutting down a spring plant in Dallas that had employed 100 people. The Aerospace Division had its workforce cut by 20 percent, or 260 employees.

Such cost-cutting helped boost Barnes Group's profits 42 percent to $27.2 million in 2002, even as sales fell at the aerospace and distribution units. Total sales were $784 million. Net income rose 22 percent in 2003 to $33 million. Sales, up 14 percent, reached a record $890.8 million during the year.

Things were rolling particularly smoothly at Barnes Group's joint venture with NKH Spring Co., Ltd. Formed in 1986, NASCO NHK-Associated Spring Suspension Components Inc. produced automotive springs at a plant in Bowling Green, Kentucky. It was investing $18 million to expand the facility to keep up with the SUV craze. The plant, which employed more than people, also supplied Honda and Toyota sedans.

The acquisitions continued in 2004. In September, Barnes bought Troy, Michigan-based DE-STA-CO Manufacturing from Dover Corp. for $17 million. DE-STA-CO designed and produced reed valves for air conditioning compressors and shock disks for automotive ride control systems at plants in Michigan, Thailand, and the United Kingdom. It had sales of about $28 million a year.

Principal Subsidiaries

Associated Spring-Asia PTE. LTD. (Singapore); Associated Spring do Brasil Ltda. (Brazil); Associated Spring Mexico, S.A.; Associated Spring (Tianjin) Company, Limited (China); Barnes Financing Delaware LLC; Barnes Group (Bermuda) Limited; Barnes Group Canada Corp.; Barnes Group (Delaware) LLC; Barnes Group France S.A.; Barnes Group Finance Company (Bermuda) Limited; Barnes Group Finance Company (Delaware); Barnes Group (Germany) GmbH; Barnes Group Holding B.V. (Netherlands); Barnes Group Spain SRL; Barnes Group Trading Ltd. (Bermuda); Barnes Group (U.K.) Limited; Barnes Sweden Holding Company AB; Euro Stock Springs & Components Limited (U.K.); Kar Products, LLC; Raymond Distribution (Ireland) Limited; Raymond Distribution-Mexico, S.A. de C.V.; Ressorts SPEC, SARL (France); Seeger-Orbis GmbH & Co. OHG (Germany); Spectrum Plastics Molding Resources, Inc.; Stromsholmen AB (Sweden); The Wallace Barnes Company; Windsor Airmotive Asia PTE. LTD. (Singapore); 3031786 Nova Scotia Company (Canada); 3032350 Nova Scotia Limited (Canada).

Principal Operating Units

Associated Spring; Barnes Aerospace; Barnes Distribution.

Principal Competitors

Harbour Group Industries, Inc.; Howmet Castings; W.W. Grainger, Inc.

Further Reading

Ambronsini, Dana, ''Bristol, Conn.-Based Metal-Parts Maker Buys Out Plastic-Molding Firm,'' *Connecticut Post* (Bridgeport), March 21, 2002.

——, "Markets Inspired Spectrum Purchase," *Connecticut Post* (Bridgeport), March 22, 2002.

"Barnes Group Acquires Troy, Mich., Manufacturer of Reed Valves, Shock Disks," *Hartford Courant,* September 18, 2004.

Bullard, Stan, "Bowman Leaving City for Valley View Site," *Crain's Cleveland Business,* February 8, 1993, p. 3.

Fraza, Victoria, "Joining Forces; Barnes Distribution, Formed by Last Year's Marriage of Bowman Distribution and Curtis Industries, Is Looking to Capture a Bigger Piece of the MRO Pie," *Industrial Distribution,* June 1, 2001, p. 50.

French, Howard, "Navy Raids Local Factory: Agents Search Through Windsor Manufacturing's Records," *Journal Inquirer,* April 13, 1994, p. A24.

Khermouch, Gerry, "Barnes' Jet Die Unit Cleans Up Its Act; Tough Transition Nears End," *Metalworking News,* November 20, 1989, p. 1.

Marks, Brenda, "International Metal Parts Maker Finalizes Purchase of British Company," *Waterbury Republican-American,* January 12, 2001.

Miller, Christopher, "Suspension Spring Maker to Add Production Line to Bowling Green, Ky., Plant," *Bowling Green Daily News,* May 18, 2004.

Sand, J.F., Jr., "Barnes Group Selects Theodore E. Martin Chief Executive," *Business Wire,* April 5, 1995.

Silvestrini, Marc, "Bristol, Conn.-Based Metal-Parts Manufacturer Selling Stock," *Waterbury Republican-American,* May 8, 2003.

Smith, David A., "Bristol, Conn.-Based Metal Parts Maker Sees 2002 Profits Climb 42 Percent," *Waterbury Republican-American,* February 15, 2003.

Tanner, Ogden, *Barnes: An American Enterprise,* East Haven, Conn.: Eastern Press, Inc.

—David Wentz
—update: Frederick C. Ingram

Bell Microproducts Inc.

1941 Ringwood Avenue
San Jose, California 95131
U.S.A.
Telephone: (408) 451-9400
Toll Free: (800) 800-1513
Fax: (408) 451-1600
Web site: http://www.bellmicro.com

Public Company
Incorporated: 1987
Employees: 1,294
Sales: $2.23 billion (2003)
Stock Exchanges: NASDAQ
Ticker Symbol: BELM
NAIC: 423690 Other Electronic Parts and Equipment
   Merchant Wholesalers

Bell Microproducts Inc. is a distributor of computer components and value-added services. Bell Micro carries more than 150 brand name product lines, distributing disk drives, semiconductors, panel displays, and a host of other computer products and peripherals, but the company focuses on storage products and semiconductors, storage products in particular. The company's ''storage-centric'' product mix is complemented by a services segment that provides system design, integration, installation, and maintenance services to its commercial and industrial customers. The company also distributes two proprietary brands, its Rorke Data storage products and its Markvision memory modules. Bell Micro operates domestically and internationally, distributing its products to original equipment manufacturers (OEMs), value-added resellers (VARs), and contract electronic manufacturing services (EMS) customers in North America, Latin America, and Europe.

Origins

W. Donald Bell spent more than 20 years working in the electronics industry before he founded his own company. Bell served as a senior executive at several companies during his career, including Texas Instruments, American Microsystems, and Electronic Arrays. He reached the summit of the executive management ranks after distinguishing himself at a company named Kierulff Electronics. Bell joined the company in 1980, hired as an executive vice-president. The following year, he was named president of Kierulff. Bell spent five years in charge of the electronics company before the directors of Kierulff's parent company, Ducommun Inc., promoted him to the posts of president and chief operating officer of Ducommun. Bell occupied his new office in early 1986, but held onto his executive titles for little more than a year. In April 1987, Bell was fired after butting heads with Ducommun's chairman, Wallace Booth. Bell and Booth, according to the business press, clashed over policy differences.

After decades of working for others, Bell decided to start his own company following his departure from Ducommun. Before the end of 1987, he incorporated Bell Micro, financing the venture with his own money, investments from private individuals, and an unspecified line of bank credit. To help him start the company, Bell enlisted the services of two former Kierulff executives, Gary Bickers and Gary Cebrian. Bickers, who was fired one month after Bell, had served as regional vice-president at Kierulff. Bell appointed him vice-president of field operations at his new company. Cebrian, who had served as corporate marketing manager at Kierulff, was appointed as Bell Micro's operations manager.

When Bell's business began operating at the start of 1988, Bell Micro represented the newest entrant in the electronics distribution business. A 20,000-square-foot headquarters facility was established in Milpitas, California, near San Jose. The complex served as the company's stocking hub. Within a month, an office was opened just south of Los Angeles, in Fountain Valley, California, the first step toward completing Bell's expansion plan. ''We're building a nationwide distribution company,'' Bell announced in a January 25, 1988 interview with *Electronic News*. ''We plan to expand into two or three other locations in the central United States and the East Coast in 1988,'' he added.

Bell's original business plan was based on fulfilling a need other distributors left unfulfilled. He believed that semiconductors manufactured in Asia were underrepresented in the United States. Bell intended to focus on selling such products to OEMs and VARs in the United States, signing agreements with three Asian manufacturers, NEC Microelectronics, the Sony Components Products division, and Oki Semiconductor, within his first month in business. Aside from semiconductors, Bell Micro distributed disk drives, printers, terminals, and personal computers, but Bell, from the start, was inclined to limit the breadth of the goods he sold. "In the beginning," he said in his January 25, 1988 interview with *Electronic News,* "we'll have 10 to 15 product lines. We'll never have more than 25 product lines." (Bell Micro eventually distributed more than five times the limit Bell set in 1988, but one of the hallmarks of the company's success nearly 20 years later was its emphasis on depth rather than breadth in its product lines.)

Bell Micro in the Early 1990s

In comparison to later years, Bell Micro's expansion during the late 1980s and early 1990s occurred at a moderate pace. The company did manage, however, to establish a presence from coast to coast during its first five years in business, an anniversary that was marked by its initial public offering (IPO) of stock. When the public was first offered the opportunity to invest in Bell's business strategy in 1993, Bell Micro was beginning to record the impressive financial growth that later galvanized Wall Street. The company generated $65 million in sales in 1992 before nearly doubling its revenue to $125 million in 1993. Bell Micro by this point ranked as the 14th largest distributor in the nation, a standing that Bell was intent on improving. As he had articulated at the inception of the company, Bell wanted to create a nationwide distribution company. His primary means of achieving his goal was by acquiring other distributors, a strategy employed not long after the company's IPO.

By the time of Bell Micro's IPO, the company had offices stretching from California to New Jersey, but it was far from being a true nationwide enterprise. There were many markets that Bell Micro had yet to penetrate, and the acquisition of other distributors presented Bell with the most expedient way of fleshing out his company's national presence. After acquiring a personal computer reseller named LMB Microcomputers, Bell signed an agreement in February 1994 to purchase a Clifton, New Jersey-based distributor named Vantage Components for $13 million. At this point, Bell Micro had three facilities in California supported by other satellite offices in Seattle; Dallas; Minneapolis; Wilmington, Massachusetts; Chantilly, Virginia; and Parsippany, New Jersey. The acquisition of Vantage helped Bell significantly expand his presence in New England and New Jersey and give him entry into markets in Long Island, Florida, and Maryland. Vantage, with $33 million in sales in 1993, operated in Clifton; Billerica, Massachusetts; Columbia, Maryland; Smithtown, New York; and Fort Lauderdale, Florida. Bell

commented on the importance of the Vantage purchase, explaining its contribution to the execution of Bell Micro's growth strategy in a February 7, 1994 interview with *Electronic News.* "The acquisition of Vantage is part of our strategy to expand our products and services offering to customers throughout the United States," he said. "The synergy to be realized by this combination will enable us to make significant progress toward achieving a Bell Microproducts goal of cracking into the top 10 list of electronic distributors by the end of 1995."

After purchasing Advantage, Bell waited four years before completing another acquisition. The hiatus from acquisitive activity did not mean Bell Micro's growth stagnated, however. The company grew enormously during the mid-1990s. By 1997, Bell Micro was generating $533 million in revenue, having more than quadrupled its sales volume in the three years since the Vantage acquisition. The company's chief financial officer, Bruce Jaffe, commented on the feverish growth of the company during Bell Micro's tenth anniversary when the financial results were released to the public. In a September 28, 1998 interview with *Computer Reseller News,* Jaffe remarked, "We went from nothing to half a billion dollars in sales in 10 years. With a good mix of organic and external growth, we expect to get to a billion dollars quicker than it took to get to half a billion."

Rapid Expansion in the Late 1990s

Jaffe's comments were made at a crucial stage in Bell Micro's development. The computer industry, and by extension the distribution industry that it served, was experiencing phenomenal growth by the late 1990s. The popularity of personal computers combined with the widespread embrace of the Internet, the emergence of e-commerce, and the proliferation of computer networking in the business place, ignited the growth of the electronics industry and exponentially increased the amount of data used in commercial and industrial sectors. In response, Bell sharpened his company's focus on carrying storage products, making Bell Micro what company officials referred to as a "storage-centric" distributor.

The billions of dollars to be made in the distribution of computers and peripherals during the late 1990s forced the industry to consolidate. As big companies acquired medium-sized companies and medium-sized companies acquired small companies, Bell found himself at a crossroads in 1998. He paused, deciding whether to acquire or be acquired, realizing that if he pressed forward there would be no turning back. This was the critical juncture of Bell Micro's development, which coincided with the company's tenth anniversary. Bell decided to make Bell Micro one of the industry's consolidators, a decision that touched off an ambitious acquisition spree and fueled Jaffe's belief that the company would reach $1 billion in sales faster than it had reached $500 million.

Bell Micro's expansion drive saw it flesh out its presence domestically and establish itself as a multinational company. The acquisition campaign began in the fall of 1998, when the company purchased the computer product division of Almo Corp., which distributed disk drives, monitors, and other computer components. The acquisition, the first since 1994, strengthened the company's presence in the midwestern and eastern United States. Before the end of the year, the company

pany for its sharp focus on distributing storage products, a focus

Key Dates:

1987: Bell Microproducts is incorporated.
1993: Bell Microproducts completes its initial public offering of stock.
1998: An acquisition campaign begins amid industry consolidation.
1999: After entering Canada the previous year, Bell Microproducts enters the Latin American market through the purchase of Future Tech International.
2000: The acquisition of Ideal Hardware Ltd. establishes a European presence.
2002: Bell Microproducts completes a companywide reorganization.

pany for its sharp focus on distributing storage products, a focus that the founder intended to keep as he endeavored to increase his company's stature both through internal and external means.

Principal Subsidiaries

Bell Microproducts Canada Inc.; Tenex Data ULC (Canada); Future Tech, Inc.; Don Bell Microproducts Chile, S.A.; Bell Microproducts do Brasil, Ltda. (Brazil); Bell Microproducts Mexico S.A. de C.V.; Rorke Data, Inc.; Bell Microproducts Europe Inc.; Bell Microproducts Europe Partners C.V. (Netherlands); Bell Microproducts Europe Limited (U.K.); Ideal Hardware Limited (U.K.); Bell Microproducts Europe Export Limited (U.K.); Unifund Limited (U.K.); Ideal UniSolve Limited (U.K.); Bell Microproducts Solutions B.V. (Netherlands); Bell Microproducts Solutions N.V. (Belgium); Bell Microproducts Solutions GmbH (Germany); Bell Microproducts Solutions GmbH (Austria); Bell Microproducts B.V. (Netherlands); Rorke Data Italy s.r.l.; Bell Microproducts SARL (France); Bell Microproducts GmbH (Germany); Bell Microproducts s.r.l. (Italy); Bell Microproducts AB (Sweden); Bell Microproducts BVBA (Belgium); Bell Microproducts ApS (Denmark); Bell Microproducts Limited (U.K.); Total Tec Systems, Inc.

Principal Competitors

Arrow Electronics, Inc.; Avnet, Inc.; Ingram Micro Inc.; Tech Data Corporation.

entered Canada by acquiring Tenex Data, a leading Canadian distributor. In 1999, Bell Micro entered the Latin American market by acquiring Future Tech International. Sales by the end of the year eclipsed $1 billion. The following year, after completing five acquisitions since 1998, the company's sixth acquisition, Ideal Hardware Ltd., paved its entry into the United Kingdom and the European continent. Also in 2000 the company acquired Minneapolis-based Rorke Data, which maintained offices in The Netherlands and Italy. Bell Micro ended 2000 with $1.8 billion in revenue.

Bell's expansion spree continued in 2001, pushing Bell Micro's sales beyond the $2 billion mark only two years after the company had eclipsed $1 billion in sales. During the year, the company acquired TTP Group, a company based in The Netherlands with offices in several European countries. The company's Canadian operations were bolstered by the purchase of Forefront Graphics and its domestic operations were strengthened by the acquisition of Total Tec Systems, which operated in the eastern and southern United States. Bell also expanded through internal means during 2001, complementing the gains made by purchasing other companies. A technology center was opened in Montgomery, Alabama, during the year, while sales offices were established overseas in Belgium, France, Germany, Italy, Sweden, and The Netherlands.

After four years of frenzy, Bell Micro's acquisition campaign halted in 2002. The company spent much of the year completing a sweeping reorganization plan aimed at improving its service to its core geographies in the Americas and Europe. The company announced in 2002 that it was considering entering Asia in 2003, but economic conditions kept the company from following through on its plans. In October 2003, Bell Micro acquired EBM Mayorista, a Merida, Mexico-based distributor of computer hardware and software. The completion of the acquisition hinted that the company might be resuming its acquisition campaign, but no further purchases immediately followed the EBM deal.

As Bell Micro completed its first 15 years of business and planned for the future, there was justifiable cause for celebration. Within a decade, the company grew from a $65 million-in-sales company to an international force generating more than $2 billion in annual revenues. The business press hailed the com-

Further Reading

"Bell Microproducts Announces the Completion of the Acquisition of UK-Based Ideal Hardware," *Canadian Corporate News,* August 11, 2000.

Campbell, Scott, "Aims to Strengthen Eastern, Midwestern Presence—Bell Micro to Buy Almo CPD," *Computer Reseller News,* September 28, 1998, p. 81.

Cruz, Mike, "Storage Has Them Singing," *Computer Reseller News,* May 7, 2001, p. 103.

Douglass, Michelle, "Bell Micro on the Move," *Computer Dealer News,* March 14, 2000, p. 1.

"Ex-Kierulff President Starts His Own Firm," *Electronic News,* January 25, 1988, p. 39.

Fernandes, Lorna, "Corridor Attracts Another Resident," *Business Journal,* December 2, 1996, p. 1.

Kovar, Joseph F., "Serving Up Storage," *Computer Reseller News,* October 4, 2004, p. 60.

Kunert, Paul, "Bell Microproducts Splits Europe into Two Brands," *MicroScope,* February 12, 2002, p. P2.

Levine, Bernard, "Bell Micro to Buy Vantage As Buyout Drive Intensifies," *Electronic News (1991),* February 7, 1994, p. 1.

McKernan, Ron, "Bell Micro Stays Its Course," *Electronic News (1991),* July 24, 2000, p. 48.

Nash, Jim, "Bell Micro Hopes to Ring Up Software Sales with New Acquisition," *Business Journal,* February 14, 1994, p. 9.

Spiegel, Rob, "Bell Acquires Storage Solutions Provider," *Electronic News (1991),* May 28, 2001, p. 6.

Sullivan, Laurie, "Bell Moves to Storage Front," *EBN,* June 4, 2001, p. 14.

——, "Makeover Nearly Completed," *EBN,* April 1, 2002, p. 38.

Watkins, Steve, "Bell Microproducts Inc.," *Investor's Business Daily,* October 3, 2000, p. A12.

—Jeffrey L. Covell

Birds Eye Foods, Inc.

90 Linden Oaks
Rochester, New York 14625
U.S.A.
Telephone: (585) 383-1850
Toll Free: (800) 999-5044
Fax: (585) 385-2857
Web site: http://www.birdseyefoods.com

Private Company
Incorporated: 1961 as Curtice-Burns Foods, Inc.
Employees: 2,750
Sales: $843.4 million (2004)
NAIC: 311411 Frozen Fruit, Juice, and Vegetable
    Manufacturing; 311421 Fruit and Vegetable Canning;
    311919 Other Snack Food Manufacturing

Birds Eye Foods, Inc., formerly Agrilink Foods, Inc., is the country's top producer of frozen vegetables. Approximately 60 percent of the company is owned by Vestar Holdings. Agrilink was formed from two existing businesses in 1961 to process and market produce for the Pro-Fac agricultural cooperative, which owns a 40 percent interest.

Aside from its namesake, Birds Eye Foods has acquired other regionally strong brands of canned and frozen vegetables, such as C&W (also known as California & Western) and McKenzie's (based in the South). Greenwood Beets (mostly distributed in the East) is the country's best-selling brand of pickled beets. Birds Eye Foods has extended the well-known Birds Eye brand into value-added categories such as Voilà packaged meat and vegetable dinners. The brand also appears on some packages of fresh vegetables. (The European Birds Eye business was taken over by Unilever in 1943.) Nonfrozen lines owned by the company include Bernstein's Salad Dressings; Brooks chili beans; Husman's potato chips; Mariners Cove clam chowder; Nalley Products, which makes canned chili and 1,300 other items; Riviera soup (San Francisco); Snyder of Berlin (potato chips and other snacks, Pennsylvania); Tim's Cascade Snacks (potato chips and other snacks, the Northwest); and Comstock/Wilderness, the world's largest pie filling producer.

Tracing Company Roots to Curtice Brothers and Burns-Alton Corp.

The fruit and vegetable processor got started through the work of the Curtice brothers and the Burns-Alton Corp. late in the 19th century. First, in 1868, brothers Simeon and Edgar Curtice founded a small grocery store in Rochester, New York. Soon thereafter, they formed a canning business called Curtice Brothers to save surplus vegetables and fruits they could not sell in the store. Working first from a Water Street plant, the business expanded to Curtice Street, and before long additional plants were built in Vernon, New York, and in Woodstown, New Jersey.

At this time, the commercial tinning and canning industry was still developing. Technology for mass-market preserving was rudimentary, and the use of chemical preservatives brought occasional digestive side effects. Nevertheless the Curtice Brothers business grew; the company, along with other food processors, discovered that products tastefully packaged could find strategic markets.

In 1920, both Curtice brothers having died, control of the company was handed over to the Security Trust Company, which shortly thereafter sold its stake to Douglas C. Townson.

The Burns half of Curtice-Burns began as the Burns-Alton Corp. in Alton, New York. In 1900 founder C.F. Burns began packing dried and fresh apples and dried beans. His son Ed joined the family business in 1925, and the company's name was changed to C.F Burns and Son, Inc. Much of the company's food products at this time were shipped to Europe, a market that slowly shrank during the 1920s. In 1927 the Burns's plant was re-equipped to process applesauce. One year later, 50,500 cases, mostly applesauce, had been processed at the plant.

Creation of Curtice-Burns Through Merger in 1961

The merger of the Curtice Brothers and C.F. Burns & Son operations occurred in the early 1960s. Both companies were active in the fruit and vegetable growing regions in central and western New York State. They and other food processors were adjusting to the end of lucrative government contracts for canned food during World War II. With sales down, companies found fixed and overhead costs rising.

A shakeout of the regional industry was inevitable, with resulting mergers among rivals. One consolidation involved talks beginning in 1958 between Curtice Brothers, Burns-Alton Corp., and Haxton Foods Inc. of Oakfield, New York. All of the owners of these companies were approaching retirement age, so their main goal was to find a buyer for their companies. Additional aims were locating capital to fund the purchase of new labor-saving equipment and obtaining an increased market share in the expanding frozen food business. The obstacle was continuing price-cutting in the marketplace, which further dented already slender profit lines achieved by each company.

The merger talks did not progress well. A large agricultural cooperative, Cooperative Grange League Federation Inc. (GLF) of Ithaca, New York, was recruited in early 1959 to seek ways to establish a joint venture of farmers and processors involving the three companies. That year, the death of George W. Haxton led to the withdrawal of Haxton Foods from the joint venture talks. GLF consultants were left to establish the processing venture with Curtice Brothers and Burns-Alton.

Further study concluded that the best solution would be to merge Curtice Brothers and Burns-Alton into a new operating company with a contractual arrangement with an agricultural cooperative, owned and operated by farmers. Thus, in October 1960, Pro-Fac Cooperative, Inc. opened for business (''Pro'' standing for producers and ''Fac'' for the facilities owned by them). By March 31, 1961, more than 500 central and western New York state fruit and vegetable farmers had bought common stock in Pro-Fac. They pledged to deliver a predetermined tonnage of raw produce to the cooperative over the next three years.

This agreement meant that Curtice-Burns would be incorporated to process and sell products grown and delivered by Pro-Fac Cooperative. Achieving this vertical integration called for Pro-Fac to acquire the plants and equipment of the former Curtice Brothers and Burns-Alton operations for approximately $3 million. The new, merged company achieved sales of $13 million in 1962, its first fiscal year.

In June 1962, Haxton Foods was ultimately bought by Pro-Fac and Curtice-Burns for $1.5 million. Haxton Foods brought to the deal such branded products as its Blue Boy food line as well as several operating plants.

Regional Focus in the 1960s

Beginning in 1962, Curtice-Burns, under the leadership of President Stanley Macklem, set about becoming a regionally focused company. The idea was to operate a series of small, locally based businesses on a cost-effective basis, enabling Curtice-Burns to become a national force serving regional markets in ways that large, national competitors could not.

The company came by this strategy the hard way. Beginning as a processor and marketer of Pro-Fac products, Curtice-Burns served the private-label business, marketing canned string beans, beets, corn, and applesauce to supermarket chains such as Shop Rite Foods Inc. and Grand Union stores. Selling private-label products was profitable when national brands were in short supply. But in periods of oversupply, Curtice-Burns suffered. In 1962, for example, the company's second year of business, prices for private-label food products plummeted, and the company lost money. Worse, Pro-Fac growers received 15 percent below the average market price for their raw product.

Curtice-Burns sought to establish a regional edge to stabilize its earnings. A mere 10 percent fluctuation in the national supply of a product group could greatly alter a company's profit and loss statement. The unpredictability of supplies is often driven by crop yields, themselves subject to weather and annual planting patterns. A plan to diversify regionally allowed Curtice-Burns to give Pro-Fac members more than full market value for their raw product in all but two years between 1962 and 1980. Curtice-Burns began offering frozen vegetable products with regional appeal, marketing, for example, southern-style frozen vegetables in the southern United States. The company also could provide quick delivery of products.

In 1963 Morton Adams, who had been executive vice-president of Burns-Alton when it merged with Curtice Brothers in 1961, became president of Curtice-Burns. Two years later, in September 1965, Curtice-Burns purchased the canned sauerkraut maker Empire State Pickling Company, based in Phelps, New York, adding the well-known Silver Floss label. The company also added can-maker Finger Lakes Packaging to its operations portfolio. Pro-Fac built two can-making plants in Alton and LeRoy, New York, that year and leased them to Continental Can Co.

In February 1967 Curtice-Burns expanded outside New York State when it purchased the P.J. Ritter Company, headquartered in Bridgeton, New Jersey. Along with Indiana-based subsidiary Brooks Foods, P.J Ritter made branded tomato ketchup and specialty bean products under the Brooks label. P.J Ritter/Brooks products were sold in one-third of the U.S. market. Acquiring them allowed Curtice-Burns to further diversify regionally in the United States and decrease its weather and national oversupply risks by adding branded commodity products and growing areas to its portfolio.

Acquisition Activities Dominating the 1970s and 1980s

Curtice-Burns's next big acquisition came in June 1972 with the purchase of Pennsylvania-based Snyder's Potato Chips. Snyder's packaged its chip products in foil bags aimed at the convenience food market. The company also sold other potato chip, corn chip, and snack products.

A year later, Curtice-Burns issued 220,000 shares of common stock with a value of $10.50 each. The shares were to be listed on the NASDAQ. The proceeds of the 1973 issue helped in that year's purchase of Michigan Fruit Canners, headquartered in Benton Harbor, Michigan. The acquired company's products, marketed mainly under the Thank You brand label, brought Curtice-Burns into markets ranging from Denver to Pittsburgh and Atlanta.

In July 1975, Curtice-Burns moved west by purchasing Nalley's Fine Foods, based in Tacoma, Washington. Bought from W.R Grace & Co., Nalley's had four main product groups: canned meats, pickles, salad dressings, and snack foods. Nalley's brand products were sold mostly in the western U.S. market. Later the same year Curtice-Burns made a second public offering of 413,294 shares, valued at $11.50 each. Early in the following year, the company's stock gained a listing on the American Stock Exchange.

More companies were brought under the Curtice-Burns umbrella in the ensuing years. In 1976 the company acquired Nalley's Canada Ltd., based in Vancouver, British Columbia. In May 1977 Curtice-Burns acquired Comstock Foods, headquartered in Newark, New Jersey, from Borden. A year later, the Canadian arm of Curtice-Burns purchased Bonus Foods for $428,000.

Curtice-Burns had by now installed Hugh Cummings as president of the company. He oversaw the June 1979 acquisition of National Brands Beverage Division, which was bought from Canada Dry Bottling Co. of Syracuse, New York, for approximately $1.7 million. For the first time, Curtice-Burns had entered into the branded soft drinks market, initially in New York State.

Earnings at Curtice-Burns were dented by the early 1980s slowdown in the U.S. economy, which squeezed profit margins. Company sales in 1980 totaled $357.6 million, compared with $303.7 million posted a year earlier. Net income fell in that period from $5.13 million in 1979 to $4.6 million in 1980. Curtice-Burns recognized, however, that a slumping market is a good time to buy struggling rivals. In January 1980, the Na-

tional Oats Co. Inc., headquartered in Cedar Rapids, Iowa, was picked up from the Liggett Group. National Oats produced milled oat food products and corn for popping.

Curtice-Burns's U.S. expansion was furthered a year later when Lucca Packing Company, a California-based canned and frozen Italian and Mexican food maker, was purchased. Soon thereafter, Curtice-Burns bought the southern division of Seabrook Foods Company. Renamed the Southern Frozen Foods division of Curtice-Burns, the newly acquired company sold primarily McKenzie's brand southern-style frozen vegetables in 11 southeastern states.

In February 1984 Curtice-Burns purchased the 7-Up Bottling Company of Binghamton Inc. from a private concern for $1.15 million. Two years later, the company added fruit fillings, frozen fruits, and maraschino cherries to its line when it bought for $41 million the assets of Wilderness Foods, Naturally Good Foods, and Cerise Foods Divisions of Cherry Central Cooperative Inc. The acquired company served markets in the western United States from its Sodus, Michigan headquarters.

The acquisitions were meant to serve the company's long-term growth. As company President David McDonald expressed in 1988, "Our principal focus in any year is not on short term earnings, but on the structuring of Curtice-Burns in a manner that will, over the long term, maintain a rate of growth that is at the top of the industry." Curtice-Burns's marketing strategy included achieving dominant positions in niche food categories; for example, two meat snack companies were purchased, the Smoke Craft Division of International Multifoods, in December 1986, and, in December 1988, Lowrey's Meat Specialties, Inc., based in Denver. Lowrey's was the leading maker of meat snack products, including beef jerky, for which Curtice-Burns became the largest supplier in the U.S. market. The two companies later merged to form the Curtice-Burns Meat Snacks division. Other important acquisitions in this period were Adams, a producer of natural branded peanut butter, and Farman Brothers Pickle Co.

Another niche market was Mexican frozen food products, part of the larger frozen dinner market then becoming popular in the United States. In January 1989 the company acquired from Pillsbury the Van de Kamp Mexican Frozen Dinner line. Sales of frozen Mexican food were then increasing 16 percent annually in the U.S. market. Eighty percent of sales was made in the growing San Francisco and Los Angeles markets.

The company also was making cuts wherever possible to remain a low-cost producer. Due to a variety of factors, mainly competitive, Curtice-Burns exited the branded soft drinks market in 1988 when it sold its National Brands Beverage business to 11 separate bottlers. Only private labels were retained in a series of deals that netted the company $6.6 million in profit.

Perhaps more important, the company was focusing on growing low per capita food categories in its regional brand marketing. For example, in 1988, sales of canned vegetables nationwide reached around $63 million, and canned desserts attained $105 million in sales. Although small in size, Curtice-Burns believed no food processing giant could make inroads in such markets by advertising on television at great cost. The battleground for products such as sauerkraut and fruit toppings shifted from the living room to the grocery store shelf, where Curtice-Burns's cost-effective operations could successfully outplay bigger companies in the market.

The company's two-year acquisitions spree that began in 1986 led to a sales increase that in 1989 reached $807.2 million. Reflecting this growth, stock in Curtice-Burns soared 34 percent, to $32. By now, the Pro-Fac Cooperative numbered 774 members; Curtice-Burns itself had more than 7,000 full and seasonal employees on its payroll.

Streamlining and Change of Ownership in the 1990s

Adverse weather conditions and high raw product costs contributed to earnings falling 22 percent to $11.6 million in 1990. The early effects of the recession in North American markets was being felt. That year, the company was decentralized into ten major operating divisions: Southern Frozen Foods, headquartered in Montezuma, Georgia; Comstock Michigan Fruit, based in Rochester, New York; Finger Lakes Packaging, operating out of Lyons, New York; Snack Foods Group, headquartered in Rochester; Curtice-Burns Meat Snacks of Denver; Nalley's Fine Foods, based in Tacoma, Washington; Nalley's Canada Ltd. in Vancouver; Brooks Foods, headquartered in Mount Summit, Indiana; Lucca Packing of San Francisco; and National Oats Company, based in Cedar Rapids, Iowa.

Curtice-Burns's acquisitions continued apace. David Mc-Donald, the company's president and chief executive officer, announced in July 1992, according to *Refrigerated & Frozen Foods:* "If we could find an acquisition that would get us into another part of the country on an economic basis, we would make that acquisition. We'd buy any size company. We've bought them as small as a couple of million or as big as $100 million. It depends on the company."

McDonald's boldness came at a time when the recession was further affecting the company's balance sheet. Sales in 1991 remained stagnant at $933 million, compared with $926.8 million a year earlier. Profits were down from $7.4 million in 1990 to $3.6 million in 1991. The earnings decline was most pronounced in oat cereal sales. Following an oat bran craze that required increased plant capacity, demand nationally for oat products decreased, and the company had to adjust its National Oats division to market erosion and reduced profit margins. Two other major factors in the earnings decline were oversupply in vegetables and high material costs for meat snacks.

The early 1990s recession also meant widespread price-cutting in the snack food industry and record low earnings by North American food retailers that the company served with private-label products. In 1992 Curtice-Burns achieved a 68 percent jump in earnings to $6.14 million, but this profit was well below the levels of the 1980s, when sales were much lower. Return on average shareholders' equity was only 5.8 percent in 1992, less than half of the 1986 figure of 12.1 percent, which itself was the low mark of the period from 1983 to 1989. Results for 1992 were helped somewhat by cost efficiencies made possible with the opening that year of the company's first national sales office.

The competitive pressures of the food industry forced Curtice-Burns to take a hard look at its operations portfolio in 1993. That year, the company embarked on a restructuring program in order to shed unprofitable businesses. Early in the year Lucca Frozen Foods was divested, and in November the oats portion of the National Oats division was sold to Ralston Purina for $39 million, with National Oats' popcorn business being transferred to Comstock Michigan Fruit. Also in November, the Hiland potato chip business was sold for $3 million. In February 1994 Curtice-Burns sold its meat snacks business for $5 million, and the following year the company sold Nalley Canada Ltd. and the snack food line of its Nalley's Fine Foods division. Following these divestments, Curtice-Burns had six divisions: Comstock Michigan Fruit, Nalley's Fine Foods, Southern Frozen Foods, Snack Foods Group, Brooks Foods, and Finger Lakes Packaging. In October 1996, to further focus on core operations, Curtice-Burns sold Finger Lakes, a maker of sanitary food cans, to Silgan Containers Corporation for $30 million.

Meanwhile, during the early stages of this restructuring, Curtice-Burns itself was for sale. This change-of-control process was initiated in April 1993 when Agway Inc. announced its own restructuring and its intention to sell its controlling stake in Curtice-Burns, about one-third of the company's stock. Agway was a farm supply cooperative based in Syracuse, New York, which had played a key role in the formation of Curtice-Burns and in the establishment of the relationship between Curtice-Burns and Pro-Fac. It initially appeared that Curtice-Burns would be bought by Dean Foods Company, which in June 1994 offered $20 per share, or about $456 million. But disputes between Curtice-Burns and Pro-Fac over how much of the proceeds from the sale should go to Pro-Fac members led Dean Foods to withdraw its offer. Then, in September 1994, Curtice-Burns accepted a $19 per share offer from Pro-Fac, about $433 million, and became a wholly owned Pro-Fac subsidiary, thus cementing the longstanding relationship between the two firms.

With the restructuring complete, in large part, and the question of ownership resolved, Curtice-Burns set out in the mid-1990s to bolster its core businesses and solidify its relationship with Pro-Fac by making acquisitions and entering into partnerships that would enable it to buy more crops from Pro-Fac members. In July 1995 Michigan-based food processor Packer Foods was acquired for $5.4 million and was merged into Comstock Michigan Fruit. In mid-1996 Curtice-Burns bought Matthews Candy Co., which was placed in the Snack Foods Group. In April 1997 the company entered into a partnership with Flanagan Brothers, Inc., of Bear Creek, Wisconsin, through which the two companies would merge their sauerkraut production operations.

In January 1997 Dennis M. Mullen took over as CEO of Curtice-Burns. Mullen aimed to reduce debt at the company, improve its profitability, and eventually increase sales from the $739 million of 1996 to $1 billion. As part of his recovery program, Mullen sold off the canned vegetable business to Seneca Foods Corp. and divested can manufacturing unit Finger Lakes Packaging Inc.

Renamed Agrilink Foods in 1997

Curtice-Burns Foods, Inc. was renamed Agrilink Foods, Inc. in September 1997, while three of its businesses—Comstock Michigan Fruit, Southern Frozen Foods, and Brooks Foods—

were consolidated into one business unit under the name Curtice-Burns Foods. The newly named fruit and vegetable processing unit accounted for more than half of Agrilink's business. (The other units were Nalley's Fine Foods and Tim's Cascade Chips, Snyder of Berlin, and Husman Snack Foods.)

Agrilink made a number of important acquisitions in 1998. It bought Delaware's DelAgra Corp., a family-owned processor of private-label frozen vegetables, in March of that year. Another privately owned business, C&O Distributing Company of Canton, Ohio, was acquired in the same month. C&O had been a snacks distributor for Agrilink's Snyder of Berlin unit since 1975. Another longtime Snyder distributor, J.A Hopay Distributing Co., Inc. of Pittsburgh, was added in July 1998. Seyfert Foods Inc. was acquired from Heath Capital Investment in April 1998. Seyfert employed 275 people and made snacks under its own brand and private labels. The company was founded in 1934 and, between 1982 and 1994, had been owned by Borden Inc.

Agrilink's largest acquisition was the purchase of Dean Foods Vegetable Company (DFVC) in September 1998. DFVC had sales of more than $500 million a year and owned the venerable Birds Eye brand. Agrilink gave Dean Foods Co. $400 million, plus its $100 million aseptic business. DFVC also owned the Freshlike and Veg-All brands. The Dean acquisition also brought Agrilink into the market for "home meal replacements," or one-step frozen meat and vegetable combinations, via the new Voila! brand. The buy made Agrilink a $1 billion business.

Origins of Birds Eye and the Frozen Foods Industry

The Birds Eye brand dated back to the 1920s. Clarence Birdseye ("Bob" to his friends) was considered the founder of the modern frozen foods industry as well as the company that bore his name. Birdseye's innovations extended to machines for automatically cleaning and trimming fish filets.

Like many innovators, Clarence Birdseye was a man of eclectic interests. "I have more hobbies than the law allows. Some are sissy. Some have hair on their chest." Birdseye's activities as a naturalist can be filed among the latter.

Birdseye was born in Brooklyn on December 9, 1886, into an Episcopalian family of English descent. He was an avid outdoorsman from his youth. During his three years at Amherst College (which in 1941 would award him an honorary Master of Arts degree), he picked up the nickname "Bugs." He left college in 1910 due to financial pressures. He then began working summers as a field naturalist for the U.S. Biological Survey of the U.S. Department of Agriculture; his postings included the Southwest and Montana. During winters he held a variety of jobs back east.

He began trading in furs during this time, and spent several years collecting fox pelts in Labrador. There he observed natives' methods of freezing fish, and experimented with freezing cabbage and fish to provide for his new family, who had joined him in Labrador in 1916.

The Birdseyes returned to the States after the United States entered World War I in 1917. Clarence held various jobs in Washington, D.C., before becoming involved with the wholesale fish industry in 1922.

Clarence Birdseye was not the first to try to commercially produce frozen foods, but he was the first to make quick freezing practical. Since the Civil War, fishermen from northern Norway had shipped their naturally flash-frozen catch to the East Coast of the United States packed in barrels of ice and salt. A trade in "cold pack" fruits in the Northwest dated back to 1912, according to *Quick Frozen Foods.*

An early venture, Birdseye Seafoods Inc., began operating in 1922 out of Manhattan's Fulton Fish Market. According to the detailed profile of his life in the March 1980 issue of *Quick Frozen Foods,* Birdseye pioneered shipping techniques there, packing insulated cartons with fish and dry ice and sending them as far west as Chicago. This particular venture failed after two years, however, due to the bankruptcy of one of its backers.

Birdseye continued to innovate. According to *Quick Frozen Foods,* he conducted some of his research at the Bayonne, New Jersey plant of the Clothel Refrigerating Company, a division of the Electric Boat Company, the famed submarine manufacturer. He eventually developed the technique of freezing foods packed in cartons under pressure. Calcium chloride brine was used as the refrigerant for the metal plates that chilled the food. General Seafood Corporation was formed in 1924 to market this new process. Birdseye soon invented the double belt freezer (he called it a "froster"), which is considered the beginning of the modern frozen foods industry. In 1925, a plant was established in Gloucester, Massachusetts, a leading fishing port. General Foods Company was later created as a parent company for General Seafood. His company produced 1.7 million pounds of frozen fish in 1928, more than it could distribute.

In June 1929, a venture between the Postum Company and Goldman-Sachs Trading Corporation bought General Seafood for $22 million, renaming it General Foods Corporation. The patents alone accounted for $20 million, believed to have been a record at the time. Clarence Birdseye's personal share was less than $1 million, according to *Quick Frozen Foods.* Postum Company was renamed General Foods Corporation later in 1929.

Clarence Birdseye remained active in the research and development department of the Birds Eye Frosted Foods division. He soon hired Donald K. Tressler, an accomplished pioneering food technologist. (From 1930 to 1934, Birdseye also operated a company to market a window display lamp of his own design.)

Building a Market in the 1930s

A range of Birds Eye frozen foods (primarily fish and meats, but also berries, peas, and spinach) was test marketed in a number of stores (reported as either ten or 18) in Springfield, Massachusetts, beginning on March 6, 1930. The participating stores were given display freezers worth $1,500 and allowed to sell the products on consignment. The test campaign lasted 40 weeks, according to *Quick Frozen Foods;* other trials followed four years later in Syracuse and Rochester, New York.

For many consumers of the day, freezing was synonymous with the spoilage that accompanied frosts. In New York, there were even laws against the sale of frozen food. The reason slowly frozen food tasted bad was because ice crystals formed, destroying the cell walls. Birdseye's process froze more quickly at much lower temperatures, avoiding this outcome.

Frozen foods were slow to catch on in the retail sector during the Depression since refrigeration was expensive. Birds Eye hired American Radiator Corporation to produce affordable display freezers in 1934. These were rented to stores for $10 to $12.50 per month.

In 1933, the company had 516 outlets, most in New England, noted Michael Gershman in *Getting It Right the Second Time.* According to Gershman, the turning point for the company was its focus on the institutional market. Cafeterias embraced frozen foods for the convenience they brought to foodservice. Institutions were also a good venue in which to introduce the product to large numbers of consumers. The famous Waldorf-Astoria Hotel began buying, giving Birds Eye a valuable endorsement. Another future industry leader, Seabrook Farms in southern New Jersey, began packing frozen lima beans in 1931 using equipment obtained from Birds Eye.

Birds Eye made its first profit in 1937, according to Gershman. In the late 1930s, noted *Quick Frozen Foods,* 60 percent of the frozen food industry's sales were to bulk users such as makers of preserves, ice cream, and baked goods. Institutions accounted for 30 percent; only 10 percent went to grocery stores.

1940s Acceptance

Acceptance was growing. Even department stores were beginning to sell frozen foods, some 60 years before the megastore phenomenon. Macy's installed a freezer at its New York store in 1940, according to *Quick Frozen Foods;* it sold a short-lived, second line from Birds Eye called ''Coldseal.''

Birds Eye stopped leasing display freezers to retailers in 1940 in favor of outright sales. The company also began allowing stores to set their own retail prices. By 1941, reported *Quick Frozen Foods,* the industry had up to 15,000 freezer cabinets installed at retail stores.

During World War II, noted Gershman, Birds Eye was able to keep going by pointing out to the U.S. government that frozen foods were a great alternative to canned, since they were packed in paper, not valuable steel. Birdseye worked to develop a new, anhydrous process for dehydrating foods to satisfy a government mandate. It was not ready until after the war, when demand evaporated. The company also pioneered refrigerated shipping when it leased insulated railway cars in 1944.

Birds Eye spawned a separate, industry-leading business in Europe. Frosted Foods Ltd. was formed in 1938 to develop the Birds Eye brand in the United Kingdom. General Foods was partial owner. Unilever took over the Birds Eye brand in Britain in 1943; food rationing from 1940 to 1954, however, presented unique challenges. Around 1945, the first Birds Eye factory in Europe was established at Yarmouth, in southern England. By the end of the decade, 900 shops were carrying Birds Eye products in Europe. The operation was packing about 12 million pounds of frozen foods a year. European sales were about $3 million in 1951, when the business turned a profit of about $300,000. The number of shops had grown to 4,600, according to *Quick Frozen Foods.* The Birds Eye brand in Europe, controlled by Unilever, did $120 million in business in 1963, according to *Quick Frozen Foods.* By the end of the decade, British Birds Eye would be larger than its American counterpart or any other frozen food company in the world.

Clarence Birdseye passed away on October 7, 1956. He had maintained a wide variety of interests, forming a light bulb business that became part of Sylvania Company, and introducing innovations in fishing gear and paper manufacturing.

Philip Morris acquired General Foods, owner of Birds Eye, in 1985. Philip Morris bought Kraft Inc. three years later. Kraft General Foods sold Birds Eye to Dean Foods Company in 1993 for about $140 million. This was the first national brand for Dean, which dated back to the 1920s. Private-label business accounted for a large part of its $200 million in annual sales. Birds Eye added sales of $290 million a year.

Agrilink's Reorganization: 1998–2002

Agrilink made a number of other acquisitions following the 1998 purchase of DFVC/Birds Eye, and also divested some units. Agrilink sold its Adams Peanut Butter to the J.M. Smucker Company in January 1999. It acquired Erin's Gourmet Popcorn of Seattle soon after, to be combined with the Tim's Cascade Chips unit.

In 1999, Agrilink owner Pro-Fac Cooperative acquired the frozen vegetable business of troubled Agripac, Inc. of Oregon, while parts of Agrilink's Midwest private-label canned vegetable business were sold off. Agrilink reorganized under a one-company structure in July 1999. In 2000, the company's Tacoma, Washington pickle business was sold to Dean Foods Co. and a Wisconsin cannery was closed.

Around this time, the Birds Eye brand was extended into fresh produce through a deal with Rexburg, Idaho's Wilcox Marketing Group. Several different vegetable suppliers were involved.

The Birds Eye brand was extended further into the prepared foods category with the October 2002 test market of a new line of single-serving, microwaveable frozen soups called Hearty Spoonfuls. Until then, frozen soups had been offered mostly by regional players in the United States. Agrilink also had begun offering grilled vegetables under the Simply Grillin' brand.

Renaming As Birds Eye Foods in 2003

Vestar Capital Partners acquired majority control of Agrilink from Pro-Fac Cooperative in 2002. Pro-Fac continued to be Birds Eye's largest supplier and a significant minority owner. Agrilink Foods, the largest processor of frozen vegetables in the United States, was renamed Birds Eye Foods, Inc. effective February 10, 2003.

Several plants were closed during the year. Birds Eye divested a few other lines of business in 2003: Veg-All, sold to Arkansas-based Allen Canning Company in July; popcorn, sold to Gilster-Mary Lee; and applesauce, sold to Knouse Foods. Flanagan Brothers, based in Wisconsin, bought out Birds Eye's share of the Great Lakes Kraut L.L.C. joint venture. Freshlike canned food was sold to Allen in August 2004.

Net income rose 53 percent to $31.9 million in fiscal 2004; sales were $843.4 million, down 2.3 percent. During the year, Birds Eye Foods bolstered its West Coast operations with the acquisition of California & Washington Company, which produced the region-leading C&W brand of frozen vegetables.

Principal Competitors

ConAgra Foods, Inc.; Green Giant (General Mills Inc.); Kraft Foods, Inc.; Nestlé S.A.

Further Reading

Adelson, Andrea, "Food Maker Turns Down Dean Foods," *New York Times,* September 24, 1994, p. C5(N).

"Agrilink Prepped for Growth Following Recap," *Loan Market Week,* October 7, 2002, p. 5.

Burns, Greg, "Dean Buys Birds Eye from Kraft," *Chicago Sun-Times,* Financial Sec., November 2, 1993, p. 37.

Chao, Mary, "Aggressive Restructuring Pays Off at Agrilink," *Rochester Business Journal,* April 24, 1998, p. 1.

Cochran, Thomas N., and Pauline Yuelys, "Curtice-Burns Foods Inc.: Its Secret Is in Finding the Sauerkraut Markets," *Barron's,* September 26, 1988, p. 63.

Cook, James, "Tea for Two," *Forbes,* March 2, 1981, p. 78.

Ennen, Steve, "Frozen Assets: Teamwork Builds First-Ever Frozen Soup," *Food Processing,* October 1, 2002, p. 34.

"Engaging the Troops," *Chief Executive,* August 1, 2004, p. 62.

Frazier, Lynne McKenna, "New York Cooperative to Buy Seyfert Foods of Fort Wayne, Ind.," *News-Sentinel* (Fort Wayne, Ind.), March 26, 1998.

"Frozen Soups by Birds Eye First for Big Name Brand," *Quick Frozen Foods International,* October 1, 2002, p. 85.

Gershman, Michael, "Birds Eye Foods: Frozen Assets," *Getting It Right the Second Time: How American Ingenuity Transformed Forty-Nine Marketing Failures into Some of Our Most Successful Products,* New York: Addison-Wesley, 1990.

Hill, Jim, "New York Firm to Acquire Salem, Ore.-Based Food Cooperative," *Oregonian* (Portland), December 18, 1998.

Holman, Kelly, "Vestar Completes $800M Agrilink Acquisition," *Daily Deal,* August 20, 2002.

——, "Vestar Connects with Agrilink," *Daily Deal,* June 22, 2002.

"Inventors Hall of Fame Honors Frozen Food Innovator Clarence Birdseye," http://www.birdseyefoods.com/scripts/press/view.asp?ID=334, February 10, 2005.

Ivan, Chris, "New Soup Adds 20 Jobs to Fulton Plant," *Post-Standard* (Syracuse, N.Y.), July 24, 2002, p. B1.

Jaffe, Thomas, "Sleeper," *Forbes,* December 26, 1988, p. 154.

Kosman, Josh, "Vestar Close to Bagging Birds Eye Foods," *Daily Deal,* March 9, 2002.

Lively, Janet, "Curtice Burns Prospects Blossom," *Democrat and Chronicle* (Rochester, N.Y.), July 15, 1997, pp. 8B, 10B.

Martin, Sam, and Kellogg G. Birdseye, "Clarence Birdseye: The Man and His Achievements," *Quick Frozen Foods,* March 1980, pp. 39–60, 78.

"More Fresh Produce to Carry Birds Eye Name," *Food Institute Report,* September 17, 2001, p. 3.

Pollack, Judann, "Birds Eye Spot Works to Stir Up One-Step Meals: Agrilink Brand Battles Nestle, Pillsbury Entries," *Advertising Age,* February 8, 1999, p. 12.

"Regional Edge," *Refrigerated & Frozen Foods,* July 1992.

Shephard, Sue, "The Father of Frozen Foods," *Pickled, Potted, and Canned: How the Art and Science of Food Preserving Changed the World,* New York: Simon & Schuster, 2000, pp. 303–10.

"This Co-op Really Cooperates," *Food Processing,* March 1996, pp. 78–79.

Tressler, Donald K., "How Clarence Birdseye Paved the Way for a Thriving Frozen Food Industry," *Quick Frozen Foods,* February 1977, pp. 53, 64, 78.

Williams, E.W., "The Biography of an Industry, and the Magazine That Grew Up with It: The History of Frozen Foods 1938–1963," *Quick Frozen Foods,* August 1963, pp. 143–308.

——, "A Biography of Frozen Foods Covering 30 Years," *Quick Frozen Foods,* August 1968, pp. 51–105.

—Etan Vlessing
—updates: David E. Salamie; Frederick C. Ingram

BOYS & GIRLS CLUBS
OF AMERICA

Boys & Girls Clubs of America

1230 Peachtree Street, NW
Atlanta, Georgia 30309
U.S.A.
Telephone: (404) 487-5700
Fax: (404) 487-5705
Web site: http://www.bgca.org

Nonprofit Company
Founded: 1906 as Federated Boys' Clubs
Employees: 42,000
Sales: $105.9 million (2003)
NAIC: 624110 Child and Youth Services

Boys & Girls Clubs of America (BGCA) is a nonprofit organization that runs after-school clubs, serving more than four million children at 3,400 facilities located in all 50 states as well as Puerto Rico and the Virgin Islands. In addition, BGCA has about 150 clubs located on Native American tribal lands and nearly 400 clubs on military bases spread around the world. The organization and its predecessors have been combating juvenile delinquency for more than a century. Famous alumni include entertainers Bill Cosby, Brad Pitt, Martin Sheen, Neil Diamond, and Denzel Washington; athletes Michael Jordan, Jackie Joyner-Kersee, Derek Jeter, and Alex Rodriguez; as well as former President Bill Clinton. The clubs are open every day after school and on weekends, operated by full-time youth development professionals and supplemented by community volunteers. Dues are kept to a minimum, averaging less than $10 per year. Although much of BGCA's activities center around sports and recreational activities, the organization also emphasizes school work and offers programs on character and leadership development, the arts, health and life skills, and computer skills. BGCA maintains its national headquarters in Atlanta, six regional service centers, and a government relations office in Washington, D.C.

Roots of BGCA Dating to the 19th Century

BGCA traces its lineage to 1860 and Hartford, Connecticut, a mill town where often both father and mother were employed, leaving young boys to fend for themselves and often to get into trouble. Some civic-minded women started a recreational program for the boys, calling it the Dashaway Club, the first recorded attempt in the United States to provide out-of-school activities for children. With the advent of the Civil War, the club operated only sporadically and soon disbanded. It was reorganized in 1880 as the Good Will Boys' Club. In the meantime, the Union for Christian Work in Providence, Rhode Island, founded its own volunteer organization in 1868, offering boys an activity room, reading room, classroom, and meeting room. Salem, Massachusetts followed suit a year later. It was not until 1876 that the first group used ''Boys Club'' in its name. The Boys' Club of New York was founded by railroad magnate E.H Harriman in Manhattan's rough lower East Side. According to lore, Harriman was paying a visit to the superintendent of the Wilson Mission School for Girls located on Avenue A when a rock sailed through a window and landed on his lap. He was told such events were a regular occurrence because of the large number of street boys who had nothing better to do than tease the schoolgirls. Harriman supposedly said, ''Well, I can't blame the boy any more than I can blame this rock. But for the want of a little excitement and something to do, the boy wouldn't have thrown it.'' Harriman enlisted the help of influential friends to start a boys' club, which proved so popular that in 1887 the group moved into a five-story building.

Most of the early Boys' Clubs were located in the more densely populated East Coast cities. In 1906 representatives from 53 of these clubs met in Boston to bring some organization to the movement. They formed the Federated Boys' Clubs, and launched a drive to spread the concept across the country. It was fitting that the first president of the organization was Jacob Riis, the world famous muckraking journalist and social activist. Born in Denmark, he came to the United States in 1870 at the age of 21. He had learned something about journalism from his father, a schoolteacher who wrote for a weekly newspaper, and he was able to find work in New York City as a police reporter. In his job he became all too familiar with the squalid conditions of the city's tenements and the spiritual and moral degradation that resulted. Determined to do what he could to improve the plight of the poor, he used his pen, and more important, he used the camera and the new flash technology to take candid pictures of ghetto life in every dark corner. In 1890 he published a book of his photographs and stark text describing the plight of the

Company Perspectives:

Our mission is the Boys and Girls Club Movements reason for being: to inspire and enable all young people, especially those from disadvantaged circumstances, to realize their full potential as productive, responsible and caring citizens.

city's poor. He called it *How the Other Half Lives*. It presented so powerful a message, the photographs were so heart-wrenching, that the better half of New York society was thoroughly ashamed of its previous indifference. The publication of the book was a seminal moment in the progressive movement of the era. Riis continued to write and to fight against child-labor laws, and to support health code regulations, the building of playgrounds, and making city classrooms available for boys' clubs. In 1904 he began to suffer from heart disease, which because of his heavy workload and travel schedule began to take its toll. He retired as president of the Federated Boys' Clubs in 1909 and died five years later.

In 1915 Federated Boys' Clubs changed its name to Boys' Clubs Federation. A year later William Edwin Hall was named national president. A practicing attorney with degrees from both Yale University and Harvard University, Hall still found time to be an energetic president, a title he would hold for the next 38 years. Without doubt, his would be the greatest contribution to the establishment and growth of the Boys' Clubs movement. He took over an organization that encompassed just 43 clubs and operated with a budget of only $3,500.

Shortly after Hall assumed the presidency of the Boys' Clubs Federation, the United States entered World War I, and he was stretched even further by taking on governmental work. He agreed to head a commission to provide food to starving Belgium, and his later work with the Commission for Relief in Belgium resulted in a medal of merit awarded to him by King Albert of Belgium. It was also during the course of this work that Hall became friends with Herbert Hoover, future president of the United States. Hall found a way to combine his war work with his commitment to helping boys by becoming national director of the United States Boys' Working Reserve, a program that sent 200,000 boys, 16 years and older, to work on farms, thus allowing older men to join the armed forces. Younger members of Boys' Clubs helped out by tending "war gardens."

Barely Surviving the Post-World War I Era

When World War I came to a close, Boys' Clubs Federation was far from an established organization. For several years it was only able to stay afloat because of Hall's willingness to pay operating expenses and salaries out of his own pocket. Moreover, when the organization was between administrative leaders he shouldered that burden as well. In 1919 he met with the Chicago Union League Club, but when one executive tried to offer a check as a contribution, Hall passed it back, explaining, "We are not out to raise money. We want to see the Union League Club of Chicago sponsor a Boys' Club of its own." The Union League complied and opened a club. A year later it added a swimming pool, and then opened a second club. Hall next convinced the Union League Club in Detroit to follow the example of its Chicago brethren. In the late 1920s Hall went on

a barnstorming tour in an effort to establish Boys' Clubs across the country, especially in the South. Along the way he visited reformatories and boys' schools, many of which were poorly maintained and run, and he took time out to find local leaders to upgrade these facilities. Early in the 1930s he turned his attention to the New England states to urge the Boys' Clubs in this area to support the national organization. It was a key moment in the history of the organization, as the scope of the Boys' Clubs movement came into focus and everyone involved came to understand the need for a strong central organization. In 1931 the Boys' Club Federation of America was reorganized and in 1932 took the name of the Boys' Clubs of America. The Boys' Clubs movement would soon spread to Canada and Great Britain, where similar national organizations were established. In the United States in 1932 there were some 275 Boys' Clubs serving a quarter-million boys. New York had the most with 57 clubs, followed by Massachusetts with 40, and Pennsylvania with 32. The new organization added field staff, which spread out in an effort to establish more clubs around the country.

But it was a difficult time to think about expansion. Because of the Great Depression of the 1930s the Boys' Clubs were called on to do more than just provide after-school activities. They now fed the children, offering sandwiches, milk, and fruit, and even provided clothing. Staff took wage cuts and community benefactors remained committed to supporting the work despite the financial hardship. As a result, not one of the clubs was forced to close during this difficult period. In 1936 Hall was able to convince his old friend, Herbert Hoover, to become chairman of the organization's national board of directors. The former president was more than a figurehead, however. He oversaw a reorganization of the business side of the Boys' Clubs in order to fund the current work and an expansion of the program. Hoover's fund-raising efforts culminated in the establishment of the "National Associates of the Boys' Clubs of America" program, which recruited influential businessmen and government officials around the country. They in turn wrote personal letters on company stationery to members of their communities requesting financial contributions. The National Associates also solicited funds from corporations and foundations. As a result of these efforts, the Boys' Clubs organization was eventually put on a solid financial footing.

More than 150,000 members of Boys' Clubs served in the Armed Forces during World War II. Those too young to serve took part in the "Victory Volunteers" program, collecting such materials as aluminum, paper, rubber, scrap iron, and tin; collecting phonograph albums, books, and crossword puzzles for servicemen; and drumming up sales of War Bonds. After the war, the Boys' Clubs continued to spread across the country, so that by the time Hall retired in 1954 the number of clubs had grown to 375 and the budget increased to $8 million. As a result of his four decades of leadership, the Boys' Clubs had become part of the fabric of the country, prompting the U.S. Congress in 1956, on the 50th anniversary of the formation of the Federated Boys' Clubs, to award it a Congressional Charter. Herbert Hoover stayed on as chairman, eventually serving more than a quarter-century in the post. In 1960 the organization celebrated the 100th anniversary since the founding of the first Dashaway Club, and opened a new national headquarters building in New York, located across from the United Nations Building. It was named the Herbert Hoover Building.

Key Dates:

1860: The Dashaway Club is formed in Hartford, Connecticut.
1876: New York City founds the first youth group to use the Boys Club name.
1906: A national organization is established as Federated Boys' Clubs.
1932: The organization is renamed Boys' Clubs of America.
1936: Former president Herbert Hoover is named national chairman.
1956: Boys' Clubs receives a Congressional charter.
1990: The name is changed to Boys and Girls Clubs of America.
1996: Roxanne Spillett becomes the first woman to head the organization.
2004: BGCA launches its One Campaign plan to raise funds for local clubs as well as to raise public awareness.

Girls Becoming Involved in the 1950s

During the second half of the 20th century, the Boys' Clubs movement continued to spread while adjusting to the changing times. Girls first started participating in programs in the 1950s and their numbers steadily increased. The organization established a target of 1,000 clubs serving one million children, a goal that was met in 1972. In 1975 the national organization underwent a reorganization in order to improve services to local clubs. Spearheading this effort was Thomas G. Garth, who had dropped out of the University of Illinois to go to work for a local club and ten years later joined the national office. He would spend his entire working life with Boys' Clubs and become one of the greatest influences in the organization's growth during the final decades of the century.

In 1980 Boys' Clubs of America dropped the apostrophe, becoming Boys Clubs of America, but that name would soon be superseded as well. The number of girls involved in the clubs had become substantial, so that by 1985 the organization served one million boys and 321,000 girls. Garth, who was named national director in 1988, not only supported the increased participation of girls but also made an effort to bring clubs to where children most needed them. During the eight years that he headed the organization, the number of clubs operating in housing projects grew from 40 to 280. He also opened clubs on Native American lands, and in locations not generally associated with Boys Clubs, such as military bases, a homeless shelter, a shopping mall, and even inside a correctional facility for youthful offenders. To help determine the best place to open new clubs, the organization also began to take advantage of technology, using computer mapping and demographic analysis to reveal the number of potential members in a neighborhood.

In 1988 Boys Clubs of America decided to change its name to Boys & Girls Clubs of America to more accurately reflect the contemporary nature of the organization, which now served some 400,000 girls. Girls Clubs of America Inc., a 43-year-old organization, objected to the change, however, and received a temporary restraining order from a federal judge. Girls Clubs contended that the name change would confuse the public and hurt its fund-raising efforts. Girls Clubs operated 110 local units with a total membership of 250,000 girls, while affiliates had 40,000 boys as members, some of whom also belonged to Boys Clubs. The matter was settled out of court in October 1989, with Boys Clubs agreeing to pay Girls Clubs $740,000 for the uncontested right to use the Boys & Girls Clubs of America name, effective September 1990.

In the late 1980s BGCA launched its Outreach '91 effort to increase its membership to two million. The goal was reached in 1993, as the number of clubs topped the 1,500 mark. A year later the national organization moved its headquarters to Atlanta, Georgia. Garth relocated as well, but soon his health failed. He retired and in January 1996 he succumbed to cancer at the age of 60.

In 1996 Roxanne Spillett was named BGCA's new president, becoming the first woman to lead the organization. She took over during a major growth spurt: During 1995 and 1996 the organization added 300 new clubs and membership reached 2.5 million. Although BGCA was established in response to 19th-century conditions, it was clear that the organization's mission remained relevant as the country moved into the 21st century. But BGCA also kept pace with the times. It established an alliance with Computer City in the mid-1990s to provide computer training. In 2000 Microsoft donated $100 million to BGCA to make every club "technology able." The organization enjoyed strong success in raising funds, a far cry from the days when William Hall had to draw on his own funds to keep the organization afloat. Donors were also confident that their money would be put to good use. In 2001 and 2002, *Worth* magazine ranked BGCA as one of the "100 Best Charities in America" because of its financial efficiency, strength of reputation, and program effectiveness. For ten consecutive years the "Philanthropy 400" report, *The Chronicle of Philanthropy*, ranked BGCA as the number one youth organization and among the top 15 of all nonprofit organizations.

The traditional purpose of BGCA was to start clubs and serve the local affiliates, but the organization also began striving to create value as well, passing through government grants and charitable funds. In 2003, for instance, BGCA passed through a total of $104.2 million in money, technology, and holiday toys to the local affiliates, which in turn paid just $5 million in dues. In an effort to fulfill its mission to serve American youth, BGCA launched its One Campaign plan in 2004 to raise funds for local clubs as well as to raise public awareness, a drive that would culminate with celebrations during 2006 marking the 100th anniversary of BGCA as a national organization.

Further Reading

Browne, J. Zamgba, "Microsoft Donates $100M to Boys and Girls Clubs to Shrink Digital Divide," *New York Amsterdam News*, December 7, 2000, p. 6.

Hall, William Edwin, *100 Years and Millions of Boys*, New York: Farrar, Straus and Cudahy, 1961.

Rothman, Andrea, "Group's Suit Wants No 'Girls' Allowed in Boys Clubs Names," *Wall Street Journal*, March 2, 1988, p. 1.

Saxon, Wolfgang, "Thomas G. Garth Is Dead at 60; Headed the Boys and Girls Clubs," *New York Times*, January 5, 1996, p. D21.

—Ed Dinger

Cal-Maine Foods, Inc.

3320 Woodrow Wilson Avenue
Jackson, Mississippi 39209
U.S.A.
Telephone: (601) 948-6813
Fax: (601) 969-0905
Web site: http://www.calmainefoods.com

Public Company
Incorporated: 1969
Employees: 1,520
Sales: $572.3 million (2004)
Stock Exchanges: NASDAQ
Ticker Symbol: CALM
NAIC: 112310 Chicken Egg Production

Cal-Maine Foods, Inc. is the largest fresh egg producer in the United States. The Jackson, Mississippi-based company controls 13 percent of the market, selling more than 600 million dozen shell eggs each year in 28 states, mostly in mid-Atlantic, midwestern, southeastern, and southwestern states. Cal-Maine eggs are sold to supermarket chains, club stores, foodservice distributors, and egg product manufacturers, and marketed under several names: Cal-Maine, Rio Grande, and Sunups. The company also produces and markets specialty shell eggs under two brands: Egg-Land's Best for low-cholesterol eggs, and Farmhouse for eggs laid by uncaged hens. The Cal-Maine flock consists of 20 million laying hens and another five million young female chickens (pullets) and breeders. Cal-Maine is a public company trading on the NASDAQ, headed by its founder, Fred R. Adams, Jr., whose family owns a controlling interest.

Eggs Becoming Big Business in the 20th Century

Although Cal-Maine's laying hens produce on average almost one egg each day, laying a large number of eggs is far from a natural instinct for birds. Thousands of years ago people discovered that removing an egg from a nest prompted a hen to lay a compensatory egg, a process that could be repeated for an extended period of time. As a result, chickens were domesticated and bred for their eggs as well as their meat. Chickens were brought to the United States by European settlers and were raised on almost every farm, mostly for family consumption, while excess products were sold or traded. Many townspeople also kept chickens. It was not until the post–Civil War era that a large-scale poultry industry began to develop, but even then eggs were considered the province of women and children. Not until the 1920s when poultry science programs were started at American colleges were mass production techniques developed, so that the small-farm chicken enterprises run by women and children gave way to large organizations. Hatcheries gained wide use in the 1920s, as did research facilities funded by the major feed companies. In 1934 Kimber Farms in California began conducting genetic research on chickens to breed hens capable of laying a large number of eggs. Because chickens' immune systems were compromised by genetic hybridization, researchers also developed vaccines, which were made even more necessary because of the crowded conditions under which chickens were now kept. Battery cages arranged in rows and tiers became standard in the 1940s, a practice that helped to meet the increased demand for poultry and eggs in response to red meat rationing during World War II. People continued to eat eggs and chicken in large numbers after the war, resulting in many dairy barns being converted to the factory system to keep up with demand. But with the years, consumers began cutting back on eggs and eating more chicken, tipping the balance in the poultry industry.

The Launch of Fred Adams's Egg Business in the Late 1950s

Fred Adams was well versed with the egg business. After college he spent three years at Ralston Purina Company working in feed sales, and in 1957 he started his own egg operation in Mississippi. He then merged his company with a company in Maine and another in California in 1969 in an effort to launch a business with a national scope. A contest was held to name the new company and Cal-Maine was the winning entry. The egg business was still very much fragmented with a multitude of small operations dominating the marketplace. But consolidation would take on increasing importance in the industry, as demand for eggs dropped and along with it prices and profit margins. Per capita consumption peaked at about 400 eggs around World

War II, then slipped to 321 eggs by 1960. Annual consumption by 1990 totaled just 234 eggs per person. As a result, limiting costs through economies of scale was paramount, and Cal-Maine became one of the industry's leading consolidators. To a much smaller degree, for the sake of diversity, the company also owned a dairy farm in Edwards, Mississippi, and a pork farm in Meadow, Georgia. Still, egg production accounted for about 95 percent of the company's revenues and was Adams's clear focus.

In 1988 Cal-Maine had a flock size of 6.8 million birds, which produced 117.5 million dozen eggs that year. The company now embarked on an aggressive expansion program. In fiscal 1989 it paid $6.7 million to acquire an Arkansas company, Egg City, Inc., to add 1.3 million laying hens to its flock. A year later, in 1990, Cal-Maine completed a purchase that almost doubled its size, paying $21.6 million for Sunny Fresh Foods, Inc. Sunny Fresh controlled a flock of 7.5 million layers spread across operations located in Alabama, Arkansas, Kansas, New Mexico, North Carolina, Oklahoma, and Texas. Thus in one stroke Cal-Maine expanded its reach to the Southwest, Midwest, and mid-Atlantic areas. The company also grew internally in fiscal 1990, spending $10 million to build an egg production and processing facility in Mississippi, thus adding another one million layers to its flock.

Aside from industry consolidation, Cal-Maine faced other challenges during this period. Much of the decline in egg consumption during recent years was the result of time-pressed Americans electing to forgo large breakfasts, but there were also health concerns, in particular the amount of cholesterol found in eggs and the impact of cholesterol on heart disease. To make matters worse, in 1990 there were more than 2,000 cases of food poisoning and at least two deaths caused by salmonella poisoning (passed from the hen to the egg even before the shell was formed). Thus Cal-Maine and its competitors began to look for ways to allay consumer concerns. In the early 1990s a Pennsylvania company began to sell C.R. Eggs, produced by chickens fed on kelp and canola oil, with the promise that the eggs could help lower cholesterol levels. By 1991, however, the eggs were pulled off the shelves when it was learned that they contained extremely high levels of iodine. The Food and Drug Administration was also unhappy with the name, because "C.R." represented "cholesterol reduced," and the agency opposed health claims on packaging. As a result, C.R. Eggs became Egg-Land's Best and the iodine levels were reduced well below the recommended daily allowance. In 1992, Cal-Maine became an Egg-Land's franchisee.

Cal-Maine continued to add production capacity in the early 1990s. In 1991 it paid $6 million to acquire North Carolina-based Sunnyside Eggs, Inc., adding 1.8 million laying hens to the flock. The company then opened a pair of facilities in 1992: a $10 million Louisiana egg production facility with a layer capacity of one million, and a $3.5 million pullet growing site in

Mississippi capable of handling 500,000 young female chickens. As a result of these investments, Cal-Maine's net sales reached $235.9 million in fiscal 1993 (which ended May 29, 1993). Net income totaled $3.1 million. Although it did not increase capacity during calendar 1993, Cal-Maine continued an effort to increase productivity by introducing the most automated, labor-saving technology available. Hens were housed in environmentally controlled units to avoid the problem of layers being affected by extreme hot or cold weather. Now egg production remained steady throughout the year. Moreover, automation played an increasing role in the industry, as described by the *Mississippi Business Journal* in a 2000 profile of Cal-Maine: "Eggs purchased by consumers have never been touched by human hands. Eggs are produced, rolled out on a conveyor belt to an egg washer and grader and inspection station. Then the eggs are sized automatically and moved right into the final package."

Cal-Maine resumed its expansion in the mid-1990s, opening another Mississippi egg production facility in 1994 with a one million layer capacity at a cost of $9.2 million. Also in fiscal 1994 the company paid nearly $12.2 million to acquire Wayne Detling Farms, an Ohio operation with 1.5 million laying hens. Next, in June 1994, Cal-Maine paid nearly $2.9 million for Kentucky-based A&G Farms, adding another million layers to the flock. The company then spent $14 million in 1996 to build a Texas facility capable of housing one million layers and 250,000 pullets. Revenues during this period grew to $254.7 million in fiscal 1994, then dipped to $242.6 million a year later, before rebounding to $282.8 million in fiscal 1996, when the company also turned a net profit of $10.9 million.

Going Public in the Mid-1990s

To fuel further growth, Cal-Maine filed for an initial public offering of stock in December 1996. Underwritten by Paulson Investment Company Inc., the offering placed 1.4 million shares of common stock in December 1996, followed by another 330,000 shares in January 1997. Altogether, Cal-Maine netted $10.6 million, money that was put to use in April 1997 when the company spent $10.6 million to acquire Southern Egg Farm, Inc. The 40-year-old Georgia-based company had 1.3 million laying hens and established supermarket and institutional accounts in Georgia, South Carolina, and other southeastern states. In November 1997, Cal-Maine bought two more Georgia companies, paying $2 million for J&S Farms Inc. and $3.7 million for Savannah Valley Company Inc., adding a total of 900,000 layers to the flock.

By 1998, 61 egg companies were estimated to control about three-quarters of the country's flock of laying hens. Nevertheless, the industry remained fragmented, with many of the operations still family-owned and lacking succession plans. In addition, competition was increasing, making it more difficult for smaller producers to survive. With a solid management system in place, which management believed was capable of operating anywhere in the country, Cal-Maine was well positioned to take advantage of these conditions to achieve even greater growth. In June 1999 Cal-Maine added 1.2 million layers by acquiring Kentucky-based Hudson Brothers, Inc., followed in September 1999 by the purchase of Smith Farms, adding 3.9 million layers in Texas and Arkansas. Also during fiscal 1999 the company

Key Dates:

1969: The company is incorporated.
1990: Cal-Maine acquires Sunny Fresh Foods for $21.6 million.
1992: Cal-Maine becomes an Egg-Land's Best franchisee.
1996: The company is taken public.
1999: Smith Farms, Inc. is acquired.
2003: The company decides not to return to private status.

opened a new Kansas facility with a layer capacity of 1.25 million and pullet capacity of 250,000.

A growing concern for Cal-Maine in the late 1990s was lower egg prices, the result of increased supplies and a reduction in export sales. The company was further troubled by a sluggish stock price and began buying back shares, which management believed were undervalued. Revenues grew to more than $309 million in fiscal 1998, and then slipped to $288 million in fiscal 1999 and $287 million in fiscal 2000, when the company lost $17.4 million. Cal-Maine returned to the black in fiscal 2001, due in large measure to better egg prices, as sales soared to $358.4 million and the company posted net income of $6.8 million. Still dissatisfied with the price of its stock, however, Cal-Maine began in September 2001 to explore the possibility of returning the company to private status, but several weeks later dismissed the idea.

Business fell off again in fiscal 2002, as sales dropped to $326.2 million and Cal-Maine lost $10.6 million. Then demand for eggs began to surge due to the sudden popularity of the Atkins diet, which placed an emphasis on sources of protein, making eggs once again highly popular. As a result the price of eggs spiked, leading to an increase in Cal-Maine's revenues to $387.5 million in fiscal 2003 and a $12.2 million profit. The trend continued in fiscal 2004, even as Cal-Maine was taking steps once again to go private, due in part to the high cost of being a public company given the regulatory changes in the wake of the Enron and Worldcom accounting scandals. In August 2003 the board approved a 1-for-2,500 reverse split of the company's common shares in order to take the company private. Cal-Maine shareholders who owned less than 2,500 shares were to receive $7.35 for each share. Some shareholders cried foul and sued to stop the split, alleging that Cal-Maine was

on the verge of seeing its stock price skyrocket because of increasing egg prices and was taking advantage of its management-owned status to squeeze out minority investors. In November 2003 the board reconsidered the privatization plan and terminated it. According to Adams, the board changed direction because the price of Cal-Maine's stock finally began to reflect what he thought was an appropriate value.

As a result of continued interest in the Atkins diet, Cal-Maine's sales reach $572.3 million in fiscal 2004, and net income totaled $66.4 million. But the popularity of the diet began to wane and egg prices, which had more than doubled over the course of several months, began to fall off in December 2003. The drop in prices also brought out the short-sellers on Wall Street, who were convinced that the price of Cal-Maine's stock, which reached an all-time high of $45.60 in February 2004, was due for a fall. Further interest was fueled when Adams and other insiders took advantage of the high stock price to sell some of their shares. Despite the intense speculation over the price of its stock, Cal-Maine remained a leader in the shell egg market and was well positioned to enjoy a dominant position for years to come.

Principal Subsidiaries

Cal-Maine Farms, Inc.; Southern Equipment Distributors, Inc.; South Texas Applicators, Inc.; Cal-Maine Partnership, Ltd.; CMF of Kansas, LLC.

Principal Competitors

Michael Foods, Inc.; MoArk LLC; Rose Acre Farms, Inc.

Further Reading

Jeter, Lynne Wilbanks, "Mississippi's Cal-Maine Still Leading in Egg Business," *Mississippi Business Journal,* September 6, 1999, p. 12.

McCann, Nita Chilton, "Cal-Maine Grows Slowly But Surely Despite Changing Lifestyles," *Mississippi Business Journal,* August 1, 1994, p. 27.

McKay, Peter A., "Is Cal-Maine About to Lay an Egg?," *Wall Street Journal,* April 26, 2004, p. C3.

Much, Marilyn, "Egg Producer Sizzling After Long, Slow Burn," *Investor's Business Daily,* March 8, 2004, p. A10.

Smith, Rod, "Cal-Maine Reports Decade of 'Aggressive' Company Growth," *Feedstuffs,* October 4, 1999, p. 6.

—Ed Dinger

Capita Group PLC

71 Victoria Street, Westminster
London SW1H 0XA
United Kingdom
Telephone: +44 20 7799 1525
Fax: +44 20 7799 1526
Web site: http://www.capita.co.uk

Public Company
Incorporated: 1984 as CCS
Employees: 16,936
Sales: £1.08 billion ($1.99 billion) (2003)
Stock Exchanges: London
Ticker Symbol: CPI
NAIC: 541611 Administrative Management and General
  Management Consulting Services

Capita Group PLC is the leading business process outsourcing services provider in the United Kingdom, a market the company was instrumental in creating and developing. Capita offers a wide range of front office and back office services for both the public and private sectors. The company's clients include regional, local, and central governmental departments and services, and public and private clients within the health, education, transportation, insurance and pensions, and other industries. The company counts more than 20,000 clients, and a significant number of long-term and recurring contracts. Capita's business process outsourcing (BPO) operations range widely. For example, the company's Payrolls and Pensions unit processes payments for more than three million people, and provides payroll services for more than 1.65 million people. In the insurance field, the company operates call centers handling more than three million assistance calls and 250,000 emergency assistance calls per year; the company provides claims settlement and other support services for more than 30 insurance companies and oversees nearly one million life insurance and pension policies. Capita's shareholder services section supports more than 2,000 corporations, providing shareholder communication, share transfer, and other services. Capita develops and delivers software and other IT services for more than 23,000 public and private

schools, as well as tax and other administrative software and support services to housing councils overseeing more than 30 million people, backed by 21 call centers handling more than 26 million inquiries per year. The company also provides support for conferences and training programs—in 2003 alone the company organized 1,700 conferences and training courses, and provided training for more than 50,000 people. Capita also has achieved notoriety as the bill collector for a number of British organizations, such as the BBC licensing fee, and the London city congestion charge program instituted in 2003. With the United Kingdom's BPO market expected to be worth as much as £40 million in the early part of the 21st century, Capita has limited its geographic focus to the domestic market, where it expects to continue doubling its sales each year for some time to come. In 2003, Capita's sales neared £1.1 billion ($1.99 billion). The company is led by founder and Chairman Rod Aldridge and is listed on the London Stock Exchange.

Outsourcing Pioneer in the 1980s

Rod Aldridge was credited as pioneering the business process outsourcing (BPO) market in the United Kingdom in the 1980s. Aldridge, whose father was a sheet metal worker, had failed his 11-plus exams that would have allowed him to advance to higher-level schooling under England's former two-tiered educational system. As Aldridge himself described it to the *Sunday Times:* "My options were being closed down."

After leaving school at the age of 16, Aldridge went to work in the mail room at a local council office. Yet Aldridge sought more for himself, and began attending night school to study to become an accountant. Part of Aldridge's inspiration was watching his father, who was laid off after 38 years with the same company, launch a new career at the age of 52. As Aldridge said: "He started his own business in painting and decorating. His courage still fills me with awe."

With encouragement from his family, Aldridge earned his accountant's qualifications at the age of 23. Aldridge began working for the local council authority; his ambitions remained modest, and for the next decade, Aldridge continued to work for the public sector. In the early 1970s, however, Aldridge decided to broaden his horizons, and in 1972 took a job in London with the Chartered

---

Company Perspectives:

Vision and Strategy

   Capita is a constantly evolving company and we pride ourselves on being innovative and at the leading edge of service transformation.

   Delivering excellence in all we do, we aim to enhance and modernise customer services, support the raising of education standards and assist our commercial customers to remain competitive.

   Both locally and through a national network of customer service centres, we harness the best of technology and business process, to provide efficient, responsive, accessible services. We play a key role in regenerating local communities and focus on acting in a responsible manner, growing a sustainable business.

Institute of Public Finance and Accountancy, or Cipfa. By 1974, Aldridge held a technical director's position with Cipfa.

Cipfa's revenues came almost exclusively from membership fees. In the early 1980s, Aldridge was asked to investigate the possibilities of raising additional revenues from other sources. Aldridge quickly spotted an opportunity.

The Thatcher government was then in the process of dismantling much of the centralized, nationalized system developed by Labour governments over the previous decades. The new privatization effort also extended to the country's 450 local council governments, which found themselves confronting new legislation and the demand to contract out for services previously handled entirely by the government. At the same time, the use of computer-based information systems had become a vital component of government and bureaucratic life, and many council governments were struggling with requirements to install their own computer networks and systems.

Aldridge understood that local governments would need help to meet the new legislative imperatives and to integrate the new information technologies. In 1984, Aldridge convinced Cipfa to allow him to create CCS, Cipfa computer services division. Starting with a staff of just two people, including Aldridge himself, CCS quickly signed on customers—including 160 of the country's local councils.

By 1987, CCS's staff had grown to 33 people, and the division was generating profits of nearly £60,000 on annual revenues of £2 million. Yet Aldridge had begun to feel the constraints of operating from within Cipfa. For one thing, he had become impatient with his own prospects, having been passed up for senior executive positions. For another, the CCS had begun to receive inquiries from private companies seeking its services—a market that was outside of Cipfa's sphere of operations.

In 1987, Aldridge and three co-workers approached Cipfa's management with an offer to buy out 80 percent of CCS. Cipfa angrily refused the offer. Aldridge, however, then 40 years old, decided to call Cipfa's bluff. He came back with a new offer— sell him 100 percent of CCS, or he would simply launch a new company.

Cipfa backed down, and agreed to sell CCS for £330,000. Venture capital firm 3i provided most of the backing capital for the management buyout. Yet Aldridge contributed some £24,000 of his own, raised by taking out a second mortgage on his home—despite the imminent birth of his fourth child. As Aldridge stated to the *Sunday Times:* "There was no way I was going to fail."

Renamed as Capita, the company grew rapidly, posting profits of £1.5 million by 1989. In that year, Capita went public, with a listing on the Unlimited Securities Market, in an offering that valued the company at £8 million. Just two years later, as its revenues swelled to £25 million, Capita moved its listing to the London main board. By then, the company employed 320 people—many of whom came to Capita from the government services the company had taken on—at 11 sites in England.

Building Success in the 1990s

Capita quickly began expanding its range of services. In the early 1990s, for example, the company developed a strong property consultancy arm, which provided services especially to local governments and city councils, by acquiring a number of existing operations. In 1992, the company began managing revenues for the East Cambridgeshire District Council, marking the first time a council had outsourced this service. The following year, the company began administering benefits for Bromley council.

The national government also became a major Capita client. In 1996, for example, the company was awarded the contract to establish and administer the theory portion of the country's driver's license testing program for the Driving Standards Agency. The company also acquired the Recruitment & Assessment Service for HM Government, establishing Capita's involvement in the human resources sector. By the end of that year, Capita's revenues had jumped to £112 million, with profits of more than £12 million, and the company employed some 3,500 people at more than 60 locations.

By 1998, Capita's market value had soared past £1 billion. The company's revenues and profits had more than doubled, as the company added a number of new, large-scale contracts— such as a £230 million contract to provide IT training to U.K. teachers, and a contract with the Metropolitan Police Service to take over its payroll and pension service. By the end of 1999, Capita employed more than 7,000 people at 100 locations throughout the United Kingdom.

Acquiring Leadership in the New Century

As it entered the new century, Capita began a more ambitious program of expanding its range of services. Acquisitions played an important role in the company's quest to extend itself into new areas of operations. In 2000, for example, the company acquired Eastgate, which provided outsourcing services to insurance providers, and IRG PLC, which specialized in administrating employee share benefits programs for the private sector. Capita boosted the latter operation, renamed as Capita IRG, the following year when it paid Royal & Sun Alliance £24 million for its share trust operations. At the same time, Capita bought full control of aMyshares, which developed software for employee share plans. These additions enabled Capita to claim the

Key Dates:

1972: Rod Aldridge joins Cipfa.

1984: The CCS computer services division of Cipfa is launched to raise additional revenues.

1987: Aldridge leads a management buyout of CCS, renamed as Capita.

1989: An initial public offering is made on the Unlisted Securities Market.

1991: Capita transfers to a full listing on the London Stock Exchange.

1996: Capita receives a contract to develop and administer a new written driving test in England.

1998: Turnover tops £238 million.

2000: Eastgate and IRG PLC are acquired.

2001: McLarens Toplis is acquired.

2002: Mission Testing PLC is acquired; City Financial Group Ltd. is acquired and Capita Financial is established.

2003: Aurora Corporate Services Ltd. is acquired.

leading spot in the United Kingdom's corporate trustee sector. By the end of that year, Capita's revenues had jumped again, to £453 million, while the company's payroll counted more than 13,000. The boom in high-tech stocks during that period also was reflected in the company's market valuation, which reached a peak of £4.3 billion that year.

Other acquisitions followed, including those of loss adjusting company McLarens Toplis in 2001 and Mission Testing PLC in 2002. In that year, also, Capita acquired City Financial Group Ltd., the United Kingdom's leading independent collective fund administrator, which formed the foundation of the group's new Capita Financial subsidiary. In 2003, Capita added Aurora Corporate Services Ltd., which provided services to the insurance industry.

By 2004, Capita estimated that its range of services touched the lives of more than 30 million people in the United Kingdom. Yet the company's ubiquity came at a price—as the interface between the public and an increasingly varied range of government services, Capita often found itself embroiled in controversy. Such was the case in 2003, when the company, hired to conduct teacher screening services for the nation's school system, was unable to complete the screening in time for the new school year. In that year, also, Capita began implementing and managing the new anti-congestion payment system for the city

of London. These helped the company earn the nickname "Crapita" from *Private Eye* magazine.

In part in response to its difficulties in the public sector, Capita began stepping up its efforts to convert more of the United Kingdom's private sector to the outsourcing model. Capita, with revenues of nearly £1.1 billion, had clearly established itself as a leader in one of the most vibrant outsourcing markets in the world. With the U.K. market alone expected to rise to as much as £50 billion or more in the near future, Capita moved solidly into the new century.

Principal Subsidiaries

Capita Absence Management Services Limited; Capita Business Services Limited; Capita Gwent Consultancy Limited (51%); Capita Insurance Services Group Limited; Capita Insurance Services Limited; Capita IRG PLC; Capita IRG Trustees Limited; Capita Life & Pensions Services (Ireland) Limited; Capita Life & Pensions Services Limited; Capita Property Consultancy Limited; Capita Trust Company Limited; Cost Auditing Limited; Equita Limited; Management Services Limited (Ireland); Northern Administration Limited; Northern Registrars Limited; Sector Treasury Services Limited.

Principal Competitors

Pinkerton Computer Consultants Inc.; KPMG Deutsche Treuhand-Gesellschaft Aktiengesellschaft; PwC Deutsche Revision AG; KPMG L.L.P.; Ernst and Young L.L.P.; Deloitte & Touche LLP; PricewaterhouseCoopers Associates Proprietary Ltd.; Lagardere S.C.A.

Further Reading

Blackhurts, Chris, "The Ultimate Delivery Man," *Evening Standard,* February 13, 2003.

Davidson, Andrew, "Unstoppable Rise of a Serial Organiser," *Sunday Times,* April 13, 2003, p. 7.

Foley, Stephen, "Capita Plans Expansion into the National Health Service," *Independent,* July 26, 2002, p. 23.

Macleod, Hugh, "Capita to Take Congestion Charge Outside of London," *Independent,* February 21, 2003, p. 23.

Parkinson, Gary, "Capita Hits 2002 Target in First Six Weeks," *Daily Telegraph,* February 22, 2002.

Peston, Robert, "Private Man Who Is Big in Public Sector," *Sunday Times,* September 16, 2001, p. 9.

Wild, Damian, "Capita—Profits Despite Adversity," *Accountancy Age,* June 16, 2004.

—M.L. Cohen

Carlson Restaurants Worldwide

4201 Marsh Lane
Carrollton, Texas 75007
U.S.A.
Telephone: (972) 662-5400
Toll Free: (800) 374-3297
Fax: (972) 307-2822
Web site: http://www.fridays.com

Wholly Owned Subsidiary of Carlson Companies, Inc.
Founded: 1965
Employees: 20,000
Sales: $2.4 billion (2004 est.)
NAIC: 722110 Full-Service Restaurants; 533110 Owners
and Lessors of Other Non-Financial Assets

Carlson Restaurants Worldwide boasts a roster of 820 restaurants in 55 countries, with annual sales exceeding $2 billion. It is one of the largest international restaurant chains. With headquarters in Texas, the company is a private subsidiary of the Carlson Hospitality Worldwide division of Minnesota-based conglomerate Carlson Companies, Inc., a global leader in the fields of hospitality, travel, and marketing. The company's three restaurant divisions are T.G.I. Friday's U.S.A., T.G.I. Friday's International, and Pick Up Stix. The principal brand is T.G.I. Friday's casual dining restaurants, with both company-owned and franchised stores. Friday's restaurants have a 21- to 49-year-old guest base, and offer a wide selection of appetizers, entrées, salads, and pasta dishes in a vibrant bar-like atmosphere. The Friday's restaurant concept has also evolved to include Friday's Front Row Sports Grill and Friday's American Bar.

The company's inception was in 1965 when Alan Stillman opened the first T.G.I. Friday's restaurant in New York City. The Friday's brand has grown steadily as company leaders have worked to maintain the original energy and innovation upon which it was founded. It was one of the first American restaurant chains to penetrate the European market. The company acquired Pick Up Stix, a "fast-casual" chain of Chinese restaurants, in 2001, providing another avenue for corporate growth.

Opening a Festive Place to Meet, Eat, and Drink: 1965

Manhattan's upper east side was the location Alan Stillman chose to open the first T.G.I. Friday's restaurant in 1965. An experienced salesman, Stillman designed his restaurant to be the ideal place for men to meet local single women. He created a "jazzed up" restaurant and bar, designed to appeal to a professional crowd, with the latest food and beverage selections offered in a friendly, vibrant, and energetic atmosphere. Stillman's restaurant concept was an immediate hit with the locals. T.G.I. Friday's soon became a hot spot for the city's single professionals, and some credit it with bringing about the country's singles bar scene that would continue well into the 1970s and 1980s. First-year revenues for the bar and eatery reached $1 million.

The concept worked, and five years later a second T.G.I. Friday's opened in Memphis, Tennessee, followed two years later by a Friday's restaurant in Dallas. The Texas Friday's sales reached $2 million that first year. A year later another Friday's opened in Houston. Catering to the American fascination with astronauts and space exploration at the time, the grand opening of the Houston T.G.I. Friday's restaurant featured seven NASA astronauts, including Alan Shephard.

T.G.I. Friday's restaurants sprang up in other cities around the country, with the eatery's signature red and white awnings, blue exterior, interior wooden floors, Tiffany-style lamps, brass rails and fixtures, and stained glass décor. By 1975 T.G.I. Friday's had evolved to 12 restaurants in nine states. The chain caught the attention of Minnesota-based hospitality giant Carlson Companies, Inc., which purchased the Friday's line, with plans for expansion. Carlson Companies operated the chain as a private subsidiary, Friday's Restaurants Worldwide. T.G.I. Friday's continued to grow with the surge of the singles scene, expanding to Colorado, Florida, Illinois, and Missouri by 1978.

Beginning International Expansion: 1980s

By 1984, the nearly 20-year-old company had grown exponentially to 105 restaurants, and continued to refine its menu with innovative food and beverage selections. In 1985 the company began exploring the possibility of European expansion, forging business relationships in Great Britain. A year later British partner Whitbread & Co. PLC opened the chain's first international locale in Birmingham, England, followed a year later by a Friday's in London's Covent Garden district. That restaurant soon became the highest dollar volume store in the chain. By 1989, the Friday's concept had reached Asia.

Steady and consistent growth of the Friday's chain continued into the 1990s. In 1990 there were 169 restaurants in the T.G.I. Friday's system. By 1993 there were 243 Friday's in the United States, and 20 more restaurants abroad. T.G.I. Fridays had plans and a signed agreement for developing a presence in China in the mid-1990s. To improve brand identity and recognition within the United States the company began to invest in national network media for advertising exposure, first using radio, to promote increased traffic into restaurants as well as penetrating new markets. Their advertising later expanded to billboard, local and national print, and coast to coast exposure through network television ads. The advertising appeared to be effective at generating interest in Friday's restaurants.

In the mid-1990s, Friday's Restaurants Worldwide organized into three divisions: T.G.I. Friday's, T.G.I. Friday's Front Row Sports Grill, and Friday's American Bar. They were three slightly different models of the Friday's concept.

Creating New Friday's Concepts: 1990s

The company's first Friday's Front Row Sports Grill opened in Texas in 1994. The sports grills were generously decorated with sports memorabilia, often depicting favorite American pastimes. They also featured state-of-the-art technology and media equipment for patrons to view a variety of televised sporting events. The active, dynamic sports grills also offered video games, billiards, and boardwalk games for adults and children. Through the mid-1990s the Front Row Sports Grill concept expanded, with the largest opening in Orlando in 1995, and the first international venue in Jakarta, Indonesia, in 1997. Others cropped up within major league sports stadiums such as the Diamondbacks' home field in Phoenix, and the Brewers' Miller Park in Milwaukee,

Friday's Restaurants also extended its brand into a neighborhood "corner bar" type of gathering place through opening Friday's American Bar in several locations. The intent was to replicate the small corner bar feel and infuse it with the festive energy, decorative ambiance, and high quality menu and service of the Friday's brand. This Friday's concept was a smaller, more intimate, yet still dynamic venue. The menu was an abbreviated version of T.G.I. Friday's restaurants, with a wider variety of beverage choices than most neighborhood bars.

By 1995 Friday's systemwide revenues had exceeded $1 billion. The company had opened facilities in eight foreign

countries, including Australia, Brazil, China, Indonesia, and Switzerland. The following year Friday's continued with international expansion, with restaurants cropping up in Honduras, India, South Africa, Turkey, and elsewhere. The company's domestic growth curve climbed as well. In 1996 *Success* magazine ranked T.G.I. Friday's among the top 100 franchisers for the second year in a row.

Friday's was the first American casual eatery to open in Moscow, Russia, in 1997. At home in the United States, the company achieved other milestones, reaching $1 billion in domestic system sales. In 1997 Fridays had 101 international restaurants, posting $260 million in international sales, with hopes of adding 50 new restaurants abroad each year. That year the company had established 65 new restaurants, the majority opening overseas.

New Focus on Smaller Emerging Brands

The company shifted focus a bit in 1998 when it changed its name from Friday's Hospitality Worldwide to Carlson Restaurants Worldwide and implemented a multiple-brand strategy indicative of a broader vision for the company. To diversify its portfolio of restaurants, Carlson Restaurants created three operating divisions: domestic restaurants, dining brands outside of the United States, and emerging brands, named e.Brands.

The new corporate strategy involved purchasing or creating a number of smaller, slightly more upscale brands for expansion. Company leaders believed that rather than developing a second large brand like Fridays, they wanted to pursue growth through smaller, more diverse restaurants. Management also felt the multiple brand strategy would benefit from strong in-house support resources and infrastructure.

Looking for more sophisticated dining concepts, the company purchased Star Canyon and Aqua-Knox upscale restaurants in Dallas and Las Vegas as part of its emerging brands. Carlson Restaurants Worldwide also planned to develop its own smaller brands, such as Timpano Italian Chophouse, a restaurant reminiscent of the classic restaurants and clubs of the mid-1950s to early 1960s, located in Rockville, Maryland. The company also had in its portfolio at the time 18 Italiani's classic Italian restaurants in the United States and abroad, the Samba Room in Dallas, and the Taqueria Canoñita Mexican restaurant open in Las Vegas, Nevada.

Nation's Restaurant News credited then CEO Wallace Doolin with energizing, extending, and transforming the 33-year-old restaurant concept into a business which could boast annual sales of $1.5 billion. Doolin's revitalization included continuing a strong corporate commitment to excellence which was admired by peers in the restaurant business. Carlson's restaurants also continued innovating with food and beverage selections, adding menu items to stimulate sales, such as Jack Daniels grilled entrées and non-alcoholic fruity beverages. Friday's restaurants had implemented a Frequent Friday's program to cater to repeat or regular visitors. The restaurants also installed booths and dividers to meet guests' needs for more privacy.

In 1999 Carlson Restaurants Worldwide had reached more than $1.5 billion in systemwide revenues. Carlson Restaurants hoped to double the number of restaurants on its roster by the

Key Dates:

1965: Alan Stillman opens T.G.I. Friday's in New York City.

1975: Carlson Companies, Inc. purchases T.G.I. Friday's chain.

1985: Friday's Hospitality Worldwide lays groundwork for international expansion.

1986: T.G.I. Fridays opens in Birmingham, England.

1994: Friday's Restaurants Worldwide is organized into three divisions; first T.G.I. Friday's Front Row Sports Grill opens in Texas.

1998: Company changes its name to Carlson Restaurants Worldwide.

2001: Company acquires Pick Up Stix chain.

2002: Company begins revitalization plan for the Fridays chain.

2003: Carlson Worldwide divests e.Brands division; company partners with Atkins Nutritionals to create low carb menu.

2004: Carlson Restaurants earns Golden Chain Award and CEO is named Operator of the Year.

end of 2000. Company leaders had plans to open 50 new restaurants internationally.

Over the years, T.G.I. Friday's had grown to become a popular spot for families as well as singles, and the company was committed to catering to both market segments. In late 2000 the company established a formal partnership with SocialNet.com, a ''leading online social portal'' whose members were interested in making connections for dating, activities, and networking. The partnership was intended to encourage connections online, on the co-branded web site, and offline at a local T.G.I. Friday's restaurant.

Acquiring a Second Large Brand: 2001

In 2001 Carlson Restaurants Worldwide acquired Pick Up Stix, a ''fast casual'' Chinese takeout business based in California. The company anticipated growth potential in the to-go market catering to the on-the-go American lifestyle. Fast-casual restaurants are characterized by menu selections that are of higher quality than fast food, and dining room atmospheres that are more comfortable and visually appealing.

The Pick Up Stix chain was founded by Charlie Zhang, who opened a Stix (Americanized Asian) restaurant in Laguna Nigel, California, in 1989. Zhang's restaurant provided the best of traditional Chinese food, adapted to American tastes. The restaurants featured exhibition kitchens where guests could watch their food being prepared. Meals were cooked to order in Woks using lighter, healthier fare with less oil and sodium and no MSG. When the Stix founder realized that 65 percent of his business was takeout, he adapted his concept to become Pick Up Stix, opening the first one in Rancho Santa Margarita, California, in 1990. When Carlson purchased the chain there were 51 Pick Up Stix restaurants, primarily in Southern California, with a few in Las Vegas. Zhang continued to manage the chain, but it was under the Carlson Restaurants umbrella.

The acquisition was beneficial for Pick Up Stix, giving the chain more resources to help finance growth plans in hopes of expanding nationally beyond the California and Nevada locations. The small company also could benefit from strategies Carlson had used to grow a large restaurant chain. Pick Up Stix became its own division within Carlson Restaurants Worldwide.

Divesting e.Brands Group to Refocus on Big Chains

After just three years, Carlson Restaurants decided to reverse its focus on the emerging brands it had acquired and created to reach a more diverse dining market. The company chose to divest the entire emerging brands sector. The decision also involved focusing more on its core concept Friday's and Pick Up Stix brands. A year later Carlson found a buyer for its 12-restaurant e.Brands group, a group of investors, E-Brands Acquisitions LLC, based in Orlando, Florida.

Despite the middle-aged feel of T.G.I.Friday's restaurants and growing competition from similar casual dining chains such as Applebee's and Chili's, Friday's was often a local favorite, winning awards and recognition in cities all over the country for best late night restaurant, best location for kids parties, best happy hour, best burgers, best kids menu, best gourmet burger, best appetizers, and so on.

Facelifts for Friday's: 2002

In 2002 Carlson Restaurants Worldwide implemented a revitalization plan for its Friday's restaurants under the direction of President and CEO Richard Snead. For an estimated cost of $200 million, Friday's planned a systemwide makeover featuring a more modern look—less brass and more chrome, less decorative clutter, and more class. The makeover included redesigning the look of each Friday's restaurant inside and out, new music, menu layout, and menu selections. Company leaders wanted to keep the brand's tradition of an energetic and comfortable image, while making it more contemporary to attract younger clientele. In its advertising, Friday's highlighted the tagline ''Everyone could use more Fridays.'' The system-wide revitalization was expected to continue through 2006.

Friday's responded to the nation's fascination with low-carbohydrate eating in late 2003. Carlson Restaurants partnered with Atkins Nutritionals to develop low carb, high protein menu items. A survey of Friday's customers had revealed that more than 40 percent of them were dieters and 60 percent of those potential guests indicated an interest in an Atkins low carb menu. The partners created some totally new menu selections and altered other popular choices to make them more low carb. The goal was to make it easier for customers to maintain a low carb lifestyle, with low carb entrées, appetizers, and entrée salads. The selections eventually included low carb margaritas, wines, and even a low carb cheesecake. Atkins benefited through broad name brand recognition, including the placement of its trademark on the Friday's menu.

By 2004 Carlson Restaurants Worldwide had helped grow the Pick Up Stix restaurant chain to more than 90 sites in California, Arizona, Nevada, and Illinois. In November of that year Pick Up Stix opened a new prototype eatery in San Juan Capistrano. The new model had a warmer, more intimate, classy atmosphere, but supported quicker takeout service. Corporate leaders expected the new Stix model to be successful and had plans to establish 100 more restaurants like it over a three-year period.

The company also launched a new, more interactive web site that year, designed to strengthen connections to its customer base and make it easier for customers to find the information they needed. The site was user-friendly and highlighted special promotions. Carlson received an award for its redesigned website, the "Standard of Excellence for outstanding achievement in website development" award from the Web Marketing Association.

Company President and CEO Richard Snead also received industry recognition by being awarded the 2004 Golden Chain award by the *Nation's Restaurant News*. The company web site lauded Snead's selection: "Richard was recognized for leading the revitalization of the T.G.I. Friday's brand, including new restaurant and menu designs. He was also noted for championing development of the concept to 55 countries and launching a unique partnership between Fridays and Atkins Nutritionals." Snead also was chosen as Operator of the Year at the annual meeting of the Multi-Unit Foodservice Operators.

Carlson Restaurants Worldwide finished 2004 financially strong with $2.4 billion in sales, a nearly 8 percent increase over the previous year thanks in large part to strong international sales figures. At the start of 2005 the company had 820 total restaurants in its portfolio and was committed to continuing its revitalization of the Friday's sites and expanding both the Friday's and Pick Up Stix chains.

Principal Divisions

T.G.I. Friday's U.S.A.; T.G.I. Friday's International; Pick Up Stix.

Principal Competitors

Applebee's Neighborhood Grill and Bar; Chili's Grill and Bar; Brinker; Metromedia Restaurant Group.

Further Reading

"Carlson Sells e.Brands Group," *Restaurants & Institutions*, February 15, 2003, p. 22.

Hayes, Jack, "Overdiversification," *Nation's Restaurant News,* May 20, 2002, p. 92.

"New Game Plan in the Works for San Clemente, Calif.-Based Asian Eatery Chain," *Knight-Ridder/Tribune Business News*, December 16, 2004.

Papiernik, Richard, "U.S. Chains Capitalize on 'New' Europe After Fall of Berlin Wall," *Nation's Restaurant News*, November 22, 1999, p. 36.

Ruggless, Ron, "Carlson Celebrates 60th, Talks Strategy at Summit," *Nation's Restaurant News*, April 6, 1998, p. 6.

——, "Carlson Eyes Diversification with Pick-up of Pick Up Stix," *Nation's Restaurant News*, June 18, 2001, p.1.

——, "Expanding Carlson Restaurants into an International Powerhouse," *Nation's Restaurant News*, September 14 1998, p. 210.

——, "Newly Formed Carlson Restaurants Worldwide Plans Concept Addition," *Nation's Restaurant News*, March 9, 1998, p. 3.

——, "Richard Snead," *Nation's Restaurant News*, October 4, 2004, p. 128.

"T.G.I. Friday's Plans Massive Makeover," *Knight-Ridder/Tribune Business News*, February 10, 2005.

"T.G.I. Friday's /SocialNet.com Partnership Links the Hottest Online and Offline Meeting Spots," *Hospitalitynet.org*, November 7, 2000.

—Mary Heer-Forsberg

Carrier Corporation

One Carrier Place
Farmington, Connecticut 06032-2562
U.S.A.
Toll Free: (800) 227-7437
Fax: (860) 674-3139
Web site: http://www.carrier.com

Wholly Owned Subsidiary of United Technologies
Corporation
Incorporated: 1915 as Carrier Engineering Corporation
Employees: 38,977
Sales: $9.25 billion (2003)
NAIC: 333415 Air-Conditioning and Warm Air Heating
Equipment and Commercial and Industrial
Refrigeration Equipment Manufacturing; 333994
Industrial Process Furnace and Oven Manufacturing

Carrier Corporation leads the world in the manufacture of residential and commercial heating, ventilating, and air conditioning (HVAC) systems and equipment. Its businesses also include commercial, industrial, and transport refrigeration and cooling products. Carrier manufactures, sells, and services around 50 brands of products, among them heat pumps, furnaces, room air conditioners, packaged terminal air conditioners, chillers, ducted and ductless systems, compressors, condensers, and air cleaners. These products are manufactured at 80 facilities around the world, including 28 in the United States. Carrier maintains distribution channels and dealers in more than 172 countries; just in North America, the company has more than 200 distributors and 20,000 dealers. More than half of Carrier's workforce is employed outside the United States, while 40 percent of its revenues are generated abroad.

On July 6, 1979, Carrier Corporation became a wholly owned subsidiary of United Technologies Corporation (UTC), the Hartford-based diversified manufacturing giant perhaps best known for its Pratt & Whitney jet engine division, in a contentious takeover that drew the attention of the federal government. Carrier is one of UTC's five global enterprises, and in 2003 it accounted for 29 percent of UTC's revenues, making Carrier the largest of the five.

Willis Carrier, the Father of Air Conditioning

Though incorporated under its present name in 1930, the organization's roots extend back to the beginning of the 20th century when a newly graduated Cornell engineer, Willis Haviland Carrier, started work at the Buffalo Forge Company, Buffalo, New York, on July 1, 1901. The story of Carrier Corporation begins with its founder, who, by being the first researcher to combine air cooling with humidity control, became known as the inventor of modern air conditioning. Born November 26, 1876, on a farm in Angola, New York, a community in rural Erie County, Willis Haviland Carrier was the only child of Duane Carrier—who taught music to native Americans, tried running a general store, served a brief stint as postmaster, then took up farming—and his wife, Elizabeth Haviland, a descendent of a family of New England Quakers. Willis Carrier believed that he inherited his mechanical ability from his mother; she passed away when he was 11 years old.

Carrier graduated from Angola Academy, the local high school, in 1894 in the midst of a financial depression. Despite the problematic economics of his situation, he aspired to attend Cornell University, in Ithaca, New York. Carrier moved in with relatives in Buffalo and spent a year (1896–97) at Central High School in that city. In 1897 Carrier enrolled at Cornell on scholarships he had won through competitive examinations, graduating four years later with a degree in electrical engineering. He worked at odd jobs while in college to earn money for his living expenses.

Upon joining the Buffalo Forge Company shortly after graduation, Carrier was put to work on designs for a heating plant, boilers, and various types of systems for drying materials. He also began early on to pursue valuable research for his employer on the heat absorption of air when it circulated over steam-heating coils. Not surprisingly, the young engineer's first concentration, both practical and theoretical, was on heat, the core of Buffalo Forge's business.

The importance of Carrier's research activities was not lost on his managers and colleagues at Buffalo Forge. The company inaugurated a research program in 1902, with Willis Carrier as its unofficial director. That spring, Carrier's experiments drew the attention of a man who would become perhaps the most important figure in Carrier's career: J. Irvine Lyle, who was involved in sales and management for Buffalo Forge and in 1902 headed up the New York office. Like Carrier, Irvine Lyle was a farm boy; he grew up in Woodford County, Kentucky, and earned a degree in mechanical engineering in 1896. What prompted Lyle to seek out Carrier was a problem brought to Lyle by a consulting engineer working on behalf of the Sackett-Wilhelms Lithographing and Publishing Company of Brooklyn. High humidity levels in Sackett-Wilhelm's plant were causing production problems and the company was looking for a way to control airborne moisture.

Carrier threw himself into research on air dehumidification and by July 17, 1902, had completed drawings for what came to be recognized as the world's first scientific air conditioning system. Designed for Sackett-Wilhelms, the system was installed beginning in the summer of 1902 and continuing into 1903. By October 1903, Lyle was able to report back to Buffalo Forge's home office on the success of the first modern air conditioner. In the words of Carrier's biographer, "Out of Willis Carrier's research and ingenuity and Irvine Lyle's faith and salesmanship, a new industry was conceived and given birth."

Carrier continued to develop his ideas for conditioning air by controlling moisture. On September 16, 1904, he applied for a patent on an invention he called an "Apparatus for Treating Air"; U.S. patent number 808897 was issued for the device on January 2, 1906. The "Apparatus for Treating Air" was the first spray-type air conditioning equipment, designed to humidify or dehumidify air by heating or cooling water. It "was to open thousands of industrial doors." The LaCrosse National Bank of LaCrosse, Wisconsin, became the first purchaser of the system in 1904. By 1907, the spray-type air conditioning equipment had been installed for a number of significant customers, principally manufacturers in such businesses as textiles, shoes, and pharmaceuticals. The Wayland silk mill in Wayland, New York, acquired the first automatically operated modern air conditioning system, which took into account the added heat of the sun. Air conditioning had also found its way overseas to a silk mill in Yokohama, Japan.

At the end of 1907, Carrier came up with another "invention"—a new company. He proposed the idea of creating a spinoff of Buffalo Forge to engineer and market air conditioning systems. In early 1908, Carrier Air Conditioning Company of America, a wholly owned subsidiary of Buffalo Forge Company, was in actual operation. The suggestion that the fledgling venture bear Carrier's name came from Lyle, perhaps with the intention of shielding the parent company if the air conditioning business failed. In any event, Carrier be-

came vice-president of the subsidiary, although he remained in the employ of Buffalo Forge as its chief engineer and director of research, positions he had held since 1905. The sales manager of Carrier Air Conditioning Company of America, with headquarters in New York, was Irvine Lyle; the construction superintendent was Edmund P. Heckel; and the members of Lyle's staff included Boston-based Ernest T. Lyle, Irvine's younger brother and an experienced Buffalo Forge salesman, and Philadelphia-based Edward T. Murphy. In New York, Alfred E. Stacey, Jr., was chief engineer. When Stacey was transferred to Chicago in 1909, L. Logan Lewis joined the company as chief engineer. Murphy had worked with Carrier and Lyle in 1902 on the first air conditioner installation at Sackett-Wilhelms; Stacey and Heckel had worked with them on the Wayland silk mill system. Together, these men—the "original seven"—who had been together on the very first air conditioning projects would later found the organization that was the immediate precursor of Carrier Corporation.

By the end of Carrier Air Conditioning Company of America's first year in existence, the foundation of the air conditioning industry was firmly in place. Between 1908 and 1914, the firm took on one industry after another: tobacco, steel, and hospitality, among others. It sold air conditioning systems to paper mills, breweries, department stores, hotels, soap and rubber factories, candy and processed food plants, film studios, bakeries, and meatpackers—more than doubling its sales in the two-year period from 1912 to 1914. Despite this success, however, the Buffalo Forge Company decided in 1914, on the cusp of world war, to confine its activity to manufacturing. This alteration would require major changes at the air conditioning subsidiary. All the employees of Carrier Air Conditioning Company of America were to be discharged except Irvine Lyle, who was to be offered his old job as manager of Buffalo Forge's sales office in New York, and Willis Carrier, who was actually an employee of the parent company.

Independence from Buffalo Forge, 1915

Although secure in their positions at Buffalo Forge Company, Carrier and Lyle decided that they could not simply let go of the new industry they had built. Moving forward with their air conditioning venture necessitated moving away from Buffalo Forge. On June 26, 1915, Carrier Engineering Corporation was officially formed under the laws of New York State, and the "original seven" were in business for themselves. The founders were Willis Carrier, Irvine Lyle, Edward Murphy, L. Logan Lewis, Ernest Lyle, A.E Stacey, Jr., and Edmund Heckel; Carrier was president and Irvine Lyle assumed the positions of treasurer and general manager. Carrier Engineering Corporation opened its headquarters in Buffalo and its offices in New York, Chicago, Philadelphia, and Boston on July 1, 1915. The original capital was stock subscriptions totaling $2,500.

The new corporation's first decade saw not only a continuation of the previous success achieved in the air conditioning business (Carrier Engineering closed 40 contracts by the end of 1915), but also a breakthrough in refrigeration technology, another result of Willis Carrier's research creativity. In 1922 Carrier Engineering Corporation began manufacturing and selling the centrifugal refrigeration machines that its president and engineers had developed, equipment that represented the

Key Dates:

1902: Willis Haviland Carrier, then working for Buffalo Forge Company, designs the world's first scientific air conditioning system; it is installed at a printing plant in Brooklyn.

1906: Carrier receives a U.S. patent for an "Apparatus for Treating Air."

1908: Carrier Air Conditioning Company of America begins operating as a wholly owned subsidiary of Buffalo Forge.

1915: Carrier and colleagues leave Buffalo Forge to set up an independent air conditioning venture, Carrier Engineering Corporation, based in Buffalo.

1922: Company begins selling centrifugal refrigeration systems.

1924: Company sells its first "comfort air conditioning" job, to the J.L. Hudson Department Store in Detroit; Carrier makes its first installation at a movie theater.

1929: Carrier completes installation of the first air conditioning systems in the U.S. Senate and House of Representatives.

1930: Company is incorporated in Delaware as Carrier Corporation.

1937: Headquarters are shifted from New Jersey to Syracuse, New York.

1979: Carrier is acquired by United Technologies Corporation (UTC) in a hostile takeover.

Mid-1980s: Carrier's white-collar workforce is reduced by 30 percent as part of a massive restructuring effort.

1990: Carrier's headquarters are moved to Hartford, Connecticut, where UTC is based.

1994: Carrier announces a worldwide chlorofluorocarbons (CFC) phaseout.

1999: International Comfort Products Corporation is acquired; Toshiba Carrier Corporation joint venture is established with Japan's Toshiba Corporation.

2000: Carrier acquires Specialty Equipment Companies, Inc.

2003: Company closes its manufacturing plant located outside of Syracuse.

2004: Linde Refrigeration is acquired from the German firm Linde AG.

first major advance in mechanical refrigeration since David Boyle introduced the original ammonia compressor in 1872. The first sale of the centrifugal refrigeration system was to Stephen F. Whitman & Sons of Philadelphia, a candymaker.

While 1921 was a productive year for the highly promising refrigeration product line, it was a key year in other areas as well. Seeking space for expansion into manufacturing to produce the centrifugal refrigerators as well as for offices to house the company's headquarters, Carrier Engineering bought a building on Frelinghuysen Avenue in Newark, New Jersey. Willis Carrier went to Europe in search of low-cost suppliers of components for the refrigeration system and to help complete the organization of Carrier Engineering Company, Ltd., of England. Much was riding on the success of Carrier centrifugal

refrigerating machine, which at that time was barely off the drawing boards.

Once that success was assured, Carrier Engineering set a new goal for the mid-1920s and beyond: to pioneer into a new market—comfort air conditioning. This market began to open in 1924 when Irvine Lyle sold the company's first "comfort job," a centrifugal refrigeration system to cool the J.L. Hudson Department Store in Detroit. It was the introduction of the new centrifugal systems to movie houses, however, that truly launched comfort cooling. Carrier Engineering's first such installation was at the Palace Theater in Dallas in the summer of 1924. Perhaps the firm's crowning contract in the new comfort market was its installation, completed in 1929, of the first air conditioning systems in the U.S. Senate and House of Representatives.

Growth Through Consolidation and Acquisition: 1930s–60s

The history of the company that operates today under the UTC umbrella dates to the following year—October 31, 1930—when Carrier Corporation was incorporated in Delaware. The new entity was a consolidation of the Carrier Engineering Corporation and its subsidiaries, Carrier Construction Company, Inc., and W.J. Gamble Corporation, as well as several refrigeration and heating companies. Carrier Corporation's growth through the next three decades can be traced in the continuation of its merger and acquisition activities, which brought in, among other additions: Affiliated Gas Equipment, Inc., of Cleveland in 1955; the Elliott Company, a major subsidiary, in 1957; and a significant number of overseas organizations throughout the 1960s and 1970s. By the fourth quarter of 1977, shortly before UTC's unsolicited overtures, Carrier Corporation had more than 38 subsidiaries in locations as far flung as Japan, Singapore, and Australia; it operated, from its Syracuse, New York, headquarters (established in 1937), more than ten million square feet of manufacturing, warehouse, and office facilities in 23 states and 12 foreign countries; and it had diversified into a range of businesses that included energy process equipment (e.g., centrifugal air, gas compressors, and turbines), solid waste handling equipment, potentiometers (i.e., instruments for measuring electromotive forces), large electric motors, chemical specialty products for industry (e.g., inks and paints), and finance.

A "snapshot" view of Carrier Corporation in 1965 shows it riding the crest of the construction wave that swept households and businesses from the cities to the suburbs in the period of rapid economic expansion following World War II. During that year one in every four new houses in the United States was air conditioned, up from one in nine just five years earlier, boosting total domestic home air conditioner sales to a record $1.2 billion. Commercial air conditioning represented a $1.15 billion market in 1965, with one new industrial plant in three being HVAC equipped. Even schools had become potential customers for systems that were now capable of cooling, heating, controlling humidity, eliminating dust, and reducing noise. Carrier Corporation, number one in this burgeoning U.S. air conditioning market in the mid-1960s, reported a jump in sales in fiscal year 1964 to $325 million, up 9 percent, as well as a 22 percent increase in new orders and a 58 percent increase in profits during the first quarter of 1965. Exports, particularly to reverse-season continents such as Australia and South America, had helped make air conditioning a year-round enterprise by the 1960s, fueling the growth of all the firms offering HVAC products. Moreover, Carrier Corporation had landed several large, high-profile air conditioning projects, including the Houston Astrodome, the 19-building complex to house New York State's governmental offices in Albany, and the new London headquarters of Scotland Yard.

Takeover by United Technologies: 1979

In the following decade, however, the U.S. growth curve began heading downward, bringing slower activity in the industrial and construction sectors that were so vital to Carrier Corporation's health. In the aftermath of UTC's hostile takeover of the company—a protracted and bitter struggle that finally ended with Carrier's becoming a wholly owned subsidiary of UTC on July 6, 1979—the decade of the 1980s saw Carrier Corporation in a deteriorating competitive position: it lagged well behind the other companies in the industry in new product development, its costs were as much as 10 percent higher than the competition's, and it had developed a reputation among dealers for poor quality and service. These problems were compounded by a shrinking U.S. market for air conditioning and heating equipment as new home sales dropped 10.1 percent between 1989 and 1990 alone and the overbuilt office and commercial real estate markets depressed demand for Carrier's products by as much as 30 percent.

After assuming the chairmanship of UTC in 1986, Robert F. Daniell went to work on the Carrier subsidiary as part of his efforts to give the parent company an overhaul. This involved $600 million worth of cost cuts at UTC and the sale of more than $1.5 billion of its assets. By 1990, Daniell had disposed of unrelated Carrier Corporation businesses such as trout farming and dumpsters and eliminated $100 million in overhead. Carrier President William A. Wilson reduced the number of white-collar employees by 30 percent during his six-year tenure, which ended in 1990. He also initiated an updating of Carrier's product line, with the result that in 1990 new or redesigned products represented 75 percent of North American sales. Among the new offerings were a residential furnace designed to cut home energy costs by 45 percent and a home air conditioner featuring a 25 percent reduction in noise. Research and development initiatives included office air conditioning systems to cool the air without releasing the chlorofluorocarbons (CFCs) that deplete the atmosphere's ozone layer, as well as a $100 million investment in a new compressor to be manufactured in a state-of-the-art plant in the United States rather than in Japan, where such components had traditionally been purchased by air conditioner makers. Also in 1990, Carrier moved its corporate headquarters from Syracuse to Hartford, Connecticut, where UTC was based.

Early 1990s Restructuring

In 1992, after a four-year slide and despite downsizings and reorganizations, Carrier Corporation remained a troubled subsidiary and a drag on the parent's performance. Nevertheless, UTC cited the end of a lengthy recession and indications of a turnaround in UTC's overall operations as signs that its decision to hold onto its units, including Carrier, was going to pay off. In early 1992 it unveiled an ambitious restructuring plan in which more than 100 plants were to be closed or merged and 11,000 jobs cut. At the Carrier division, the push to add new products and to reduce both inventories and delivery time to customers meant consolidating and reengineering production processes and installing new technology at its manufacturing sites. In line with the plans of many U.S. corporations in the early 1990s, the goal at Carrier was to maintain current output with fewer workers and less space at lower costs. At a Carrier facility in Indianapolis, where assembly lines were reconfigured and component manufacturing was moved nearby, annual inventory was reduced by $12 million and productivity improved by as much as 20 percent.

As UTC anticipated the world market for HVAC equipment to grow by more than 65 percent, to approximately $40 billion, by the year 2000, with more than half that total market centered in the Asia-Pacific region, the blueprint for Carrier Corporation called for expansion outside slow-growth markets to secure a presence in developing areas globally. Quality and customer-satisfaction initiatives also continued to be emphasized, with the result that quality problems, and the accompanying warranty-claims costs, connected with new installations of the company's main line of home air conditioning compressors had declined by half from 1986 to 1992. To meet its goal of greater responsiveness to changing customer requirements, Carrier was building the add-on and replacement segments of the heating and air conditioning business (both residential and commercial). Research and development was another area in which Carrier was concentrating, spending $100 million on research in 1991 and committing itself to an additional $550 million research and development investment during the five subsequent years. The strategic focus was on such core technologies as compression, electronics and controls, refrigerants (particularly non-ozone-depleting alternatives), air management, heat transfer, and indoor air quality.

By the mid-1990s Carrier's various restructuring efforts were beginning to pay off. Backed by new product introductions, including a line of lighter, more efficient home air conditioners—that line's first major overhaul in a decade—Carrier boosted its revenues from $4.3 billion in 1992 to nearly $5 billion in 1994. The cuts in the workforce and the worldwide system of plants (14 factories having been closed from 1991 to 1995), painful as they had been, reduced overhead by more than 12 percent; operating profits tripled from 1992 to 1995. As a result of the company's aggressive pursuit of business in emerging markets—including making early entries into such countries as India, China, and Vietnam—more than 50 percent of sales occurred outside the United States in 1995, compared to just 10 percent 15 years earlier. Most of the products sold outside the United States were also made at overseas factories, in contrast to the earlier period, which was characterized by export sales of U.S.-made products. By mid-1996, Carrier had 33 companies, 17 joint ventures, 15 factories, more than 6,000 outlets, and thousands of employees in the Far East alone. The company also continued to tout its installations at high-profile buildings around the world. In 1993, for instance, Pope John Paul II dedicated a climate control system for the Sistine Chapel that had been designed by Carrier to protect Michelangelo's frescoes from dust and humidity. In 1994 the company announced that it would begin phasing out the use of CFCs worldwide, well in advance of when this would be required in many markets. Also in 1994 George David succeeded Robert F. Daniell as CEO of UTC, and one year later John R. Lord was named president of Carrier, succeeding William Frago. Lord had joined UTC in 1975, later held executive positions at Carrier and at UTC's Otis Elevator Company, Inc. subsidiary, and in 1992 was named president of Carrier's North American operations.

Acquisitions and Further Restructuring Efforts in the Late 1990s and Early 2000s

Revenues grew steadily through 2000, reaching $8.43 billion by that year. Part of this growth was fueled by acquisitions, several of which were particularly noteworthy. In August 1999 Carrier paid about $490 million in cash and assumed approximately $230 million in debt for International Comfort Products Corporation (ICP). Based in Nashville, Tennessee, ICP specialized in residential and light commercial HVAC equipment, and its 1998 worldwide revenues totaled $733.5 million. In early 2000 Carrier acquired Electrolux Commercial Refrigeration from AB Electrolux for approximately $145 million. The acquired unit, generator of $300 million in 1998 sales, produced refrigeration equipment for commercial customers within the supermarket, convenience store, food, and beverage markets. Carrier also purchased Specialty Equipment Companies, Inc. in late 2000 for approximately $700 million in cash and assumed debt. Aurora, Illinois-based Specialty Equipment manufactured refrigeration equipment, soft-serve ice cream and frozen dessert dispensers, and commercial cooking and holding equipment for the fast-food, convenience store, specialty chain, soft-drink, brewery, and institutional foodservice markets. Specialty's revenues for fiscal 2000 exceeded $500 million.

Carrier also formed a joint venture with Toshiba Corporation in 1999. The new Toshiba Carrier Corporation, based in Japan, represented a merger of Toshiba's air conditioning equipment division, which had annual sales of $1.1 billion, with Carrier's Japanese subsidiary, Toyo Carrier, which had about $200 million in yearly revenues. Carrier and Toshiba Carrier also formed manufacturing joint ventures in the United Kingdom and Thailand. Also at the beginning of 2000, Lord retired from the company and was replaced by Jonathan W. Ayers, who had been president of Carrier's Asian-Pacific operations since 1997.

The economic downturn of the early 2000s hit Carrier hard as sales of air conditioning and heating systems were dampened. Although the company's profitability was improving, other UTC units were doing much better, prompting David to replace Ayers with Geraud Darnis in October 2001. Darnis, a Frenchman, had served in a number of financial and management positions at Carrier before becoming president of Asian-Pacific operations in 1999 and then being named head of UTC's power group in early 2001. Continuing its cost-cutting efforts, Carrier announced the closure of its heating and air conditioning plant in Lewisburg, Tennessee, in March 2002. Then in October 2003 the firm revealed plans to close down its air conditioning and refrigeration manufacturing plant located just outside of Syracuse and shift the production to plants in China and Singapore—ending 66 years of Carrier manufacturing in the Syracuse area. The company planned to leave behind a reduced workforce of 1,600 people employed in marketing, sales, product support, warehousing, engineering, and research. Between 2001 and 2003, these and other bottom-line-oriented

initiatives yielded results: operating profits jumped 54 percent, from $590 million to $911 million. During the same period, revenues were relatively stagnant, increasing only 4 percent, from $8.9 billion to $9.25 billion.

Carrier continued along a similar path in 2004. A commercial air conditioning and ventilation products plant in McMinnville, Tennessee, was closed. In October Carrier acquired Linde Refrigeration, a division of the German firm Linde AG for approximately EUR 325 million ($390 million). Based in Cologne, Germany, Linde Refrigeration was a leader in commercial refrigeration in Europe, with annual sales of about EUR 866 million ($1 billion), and had manufacturing facilities and sales networks throughout Europe, Asia, and South America. In December 2004 Toshiba Carrier acquired a 20 percent interest in the air conditioning division of Guangdong Midea Electric Appliances Co., Ltd. Midea Air Conditioning, with sales of $1.2 billion, was the second largest producer of air conditioning systems in China and held positions in both the residential and light commercial markets. This marked Carrier's first penetration of the residential air conditioning sector in the fast-growing Chinese market.

Principal Subsidiaries

Carrier Air Conditioning Pty. Limited (Australia); Carrier Aircon Limited (India); Carrier China Limited (Hong Kong); Carrier Commercial Refrigeration, Inc.; Carrier Espana, SL (Spain); Carrier HVACR Investments B.V. (Netherlands); Carrier LG Limited (South Korea); Carrier Ltd. (South Korea); Carrier Mexico S.A. de C.V.; Carrier Nederland BV (Netherlands); Carrier Sales and Distribution, LLC; Carrier SAS (France); Carrier SpA (Italy); Carrier Singapore (PTE) Limited; Carrier Transicold Europe S.A.S. (France); International Comfort Products, LLC; Misr Refrigeration and Air Conditioning Manufacturing Company S.A.E. (Egypt).

Principal Competitors

American Standard Companies Inc.; York International Corporation; Lennox International Inc.; Daikin Industries, Ltd.; Paloma Industries, Limited.

Further Reading

Brady, Diane, "The Unsung CEO," *Business Week,* October 25, 2004, pp. 74+.

Davis, Dan, "Better to Be First," *Appliance,* October 1996, pp. PC6+.

Duffy, Gordon D., "A Leaner Carrier Eyes Global Expansion," *Air Conditioning, Heating, and Refrigeration News,* May 4, 1987, pp. 3+.

Gustaitis, Joseph, "The Man Who Cooled America," *American History,* August 1994, pp. 62+.

Hannagan, Charley, "Carrier Closing Manufacturing: DeWitt Factories Will Lose 1,200 Jobs," *Syracuse (N.Y.) Post-Standard/Herald-Journal,* October 7, 2003, p. A1.

——, "Hot and Cold: United Technologies, Carrier Corp.'s Parent, Tries to Overcome Downturn," *Syracuse (N.Y.) Post-Standard,* July 16, 2001, p. 11.

Hannagan, Charley, and Rick Moriarty, "End Is Near, Union Told," *Syracuse (N.Y.) Post-Standard,* May 12, 1998, p. A1.

Ingels, Margaret, *Willis Haviland Carrier: Father of Air Conditioning,* New York, Country Life Press, 1952.

Ivins, Molly, "King of Cool: Willis Carrier," *Time,* December 7, 1998, p. 109.

Jancsurak, Joe, "Quest for Global Comfort: When It Comes to HVAC, No One Company Does More Business Outside North America, or Spends More on R&D, Than Carrier," *Appliance Manufacturer,* August 1998, pp. C7+.

Johnson, Wayne, "Carrier Says Cutbacks Will Help It Compete," *Air Conditioning, Heating, and Refrigeration News,* January 27, 1992, pp. 3+.

Mader, Robert P., "Carrier Corp. Buys ICP," *Contractor,* August 1999, pp. 3+.

Naj, Amal Kumar, "United Technologies Navigates a Turnaround Course," *Wall Street Journal,* April 7, 1992.

"New Toshiba Carrier Corp. Looks for Global Expansion," *Air Conditioning, Heating, and Refrigeration News,* September 7, 1998, p. 1.

Smart, Tim, "UTC Gets a Lift from Its Smaller Engines," *Business Week,* December 20, 1993, pp. 109–10.

"UTC Streamlines with Retirement, Job Cuts," *Air Conditioning, Heating, and Refrigeration News,* July 26, 1999, p. 1.

Vogel, Todd, "Can Carrier Corp. Turn Up the Juice?" *Business Week,* September 3, 1990.

Wampler, Cloud, *Dr. Willis H. Carrier, Father of Air Conditioning,* New York: Newcomen Society of England, American Branch, 1949, 32 p.

"Warm News at Carrier," *Time,* March 5, 1965.

—Nancy Hitchner
—update: David E. Salamie

Cencosud S.A.

Avenida Kennedy 9001
Las Condes, Santiago
Chile
Telephone: (56) (2) 299-6999
Fax: (56) (2) 299-6978
Web site: http://www.cencosud.com.ar

Public Company
Incorporated: 1978
Employees: 27,700
Sales: CLP 921.29 billion ($1.55 billion) (2003)
Stock Exchanges: Bolsa de Comercio de Santiago New
    York
NAIC: 444110 Home Centers; 445110 Supermarkets and
    Other Grocery (Except Convenience) Stores; 522210
    Credit Card Issuing; 531120 Lessors of Nonresidential
    Buildings (Except Miniwarehouses); 713110
    Amusement and Theme Parks

Cencosud S.A. is one of the largest retailers in Chile and Argentina, with Jumbo hypermarkets (supersized supermarkets), Easy home centers, commercial centers (shopping malls), and theme parks in both countries. Founded by Horst Paulmann Kemna, an immigrant, Cencosud also owns the Santa Isabel and Las Brisas supermarket chains in Chile and issues its own credit card there. Subsidiaries arrange for the siting, development, and construction of its stores, and for the purchase, distribution, and sale of its perishable merchandise. The company's name is a contraction of Centros Comerciales Sudamericanos.

Hardscrabble Beginnings: 1957–75

Born in Germany, Paulmann came to Argentina in 1948 in the wake of World War II as a boy of 13, with his parents and six brothers and sisters. When the Perónist regime prohibited the imports on which his father's business depended, the family moved to Chile, where his parents had obtained the concession to operate a property that consisted of a hotel, restaurant, and bar. After three years of hard work, Paulmann's father and a brother-in-law were able to buy a small restaurant called Las Brisas, in

Temuco, and the whole family moved there. Following the death of Horst's father in 1957, he and his older brother Jurgen took over the business. Interviewed for the Chilean business magazine *Capital,* Paulmann, speaking in a marked German accent despite a half-century in South America, recalled to M. Angelica Zegers, "The first years in the restaurant I was in the kitchen and between 25 and 35 I got up every day at four in the morning to arrive at five sharp in the central market for the best deals. That's what's known as the university of life."

The brothers added a takeout rotisserie in 1959 and closed the restaurant two years later, converting it to their first Las Brisas supermarket. Horst Paulmann told Zegers how he plied the streets with a microphone, mooing like a cow to tell people they could buy condensed milk for 2 pesos, 20 centavos at the store. Asked what was most important in managing a supermarket—the relation with the suppliers, the employees, the customers, the products, or the prices—he replied: "First, the customers; second, the customers; and third, the customers." Jurgen and Horst Paulmann opened Las Brisas supermarkets in Concepción in 1965 and Valdivia in 1967. Two years later they installed a purchasing center in Santiago, which allowed them better control over their supplies and prices. In 1970 they opened another store in Concepción and one in Temuco, and in 1974 they opened two stores in Santiago: one a supermarket and the other, the first self-service store for wholesalers purchasing goods in large quantities.

Hypermarkets and More: 1975–95

Toward the end of 1975, the Paulmann brothers started construction of the first hypermarket in Chile, a Jumbo in the Las Condes neighborhood of Santiago. At the same time, however, the two decided to separate, because Jurgen did not like taking the risk of building a store of 7,000 square meters (about 75,000 square feet) in an area that was then almost depopulated. He retained the five Las Brisas supermarkets in southern Chile, while Horst kept the stores in Santiago. On the heels of years of political and economic crisis, Paulmann gambled, successfully, that the military government was ready to end import restrictions and thereby allow him to stock the store with high-quality imported items previously unavailable, as well as domestic delicacies such as fresh trout and lobster. In addition, he was aided by his suppliers in a time of high inflation; they warned him when a product was going to climb in price, and he bought in great quantities before it did so.

The success of the first Jumbo allowed Paulmann to build a second one on the site, which he bought very cheap, of a failing Santiago trolley-bus line. With prosperity returning, residents of Chile's capital and largest city flocked to it, buying large quantities of its meat, fish, vegetables, baked goods, pasta, and deli items. At about the same time he established Inmobilaria Las Verbenas, which began to act as a holding company and in which he grouped the properties of his enterprise. Incredibly, considering the severity of the economic crisis that struck Chile in 1982, Paulmann had sufficient resources to keep expanding. He now looked, however, toward Argentina. The country had its own problems—including triple-digit inflation—but the greater Buenos Aires area had in itself more inhabitants than all of Chile. He opened the first Jumbo in Argentina in 1982, a 9,282-square-meter (almost 100,000-square-foot) store in the Parque Brown area of Buenos Aires. Unicenter, the first regional shopping center in Argentina, was constructed in 1988 in suburban Martínez and eventually grew to 91,771 square meters (987,811 square feet) of rentable space. The success of this gigantic project led Paulmann to build an $80 million, 110,000-square-meter (1.18-million-square-foot) shopping center, Alto Las Condes, near the first Jumbo in Santiago.

Paulmann introduced the Easy chain, offering products for the home and garden, in 1993. The ''do-it-yourself'' concept of materials for construction, remodeling, and decoration was slow to catch on in Chile and Easy lost money during the first five years of its existence. Also, by 1993, Paulmann had established Aventura Play Centers. Run by his daughter, Heike, they eventually grew into theme parks located in both Chile and Argentina.

During these years Paulmann—a perfectionist obsessed with getting every detail right—acquired a reputation as difficult to deal with. Although extremely rational on one hand, he was given to micromanagement—even seen directing traffic in the parking lots of his malls—and to unexpected changes in direction on a moment's notice. Often he would call his subordinates late at night or in the early hours of the morning. On at least one occasion he dispatched his Chilean executives to an urgent meeting in Argentina, then, once they had arrived, postponed the meeting until the next day. One of Paulmann's closest associates quit after 18 years, seemingly because he tired of presenting projects that in the end never came to fruition. After longtime aide Oscar Wandanter resigned from Cencosud in 1996, the organization was left without a visible second in command. Self-financing was another key component of Paulmann's go-it-alone entrepreneurial style. ''The banks loan umbrellas when the sun shines and not when it rains,'' he told Zegers in 2001. ''That's why we have

been able to construct an enterprise where more than 12,000 people work in Chile and Argentina today and where we have always invested our own resources.''

But for all his efforts, Paulmann could not foresee every difficulty. While planning the Costanera Center mall in Santiago, he fired the local architectural firm after working with them for almost two years, then hired an office of better-known U.S. architects and ended with the same result. Even seemingly routine commissions could result in unforeseen problems. After Cencosud turned to an experienced Canadian firm for the redesign of a Jumbo, its staffers were stunned to find aisles at least 12 feet wide to handle the crush of shoppers, and 50 to 70 checkout lanes in service. Fixtures and materials had to be designed to withstand much heavier levels of traffic than American retailers experience. Nor did completed projects always meet expectations. In 1994 Cencosud announced that it would build the biggest mall in Chile, Alto La Florida in Santiago, with more than 200,000 square meters (nearly 2.2 million square feet) of space, at a cost of almost $100 million. The plan included a Jumbo, an Easy, a 16-screen cinema, and an office tower. This proved to be more space than even Paulmann could fill with his own retail chains, so he had to rent to rival ones.

Shuttling Between Argentina and Chile: 1993–2004

At the end of 1996 Cencosud opened another Santiago mall, Maipú, but most of the company's activity during the decade was in Argentina, where inflation had ended with the tying of the nation's peso to the dollar. In 1993 Cencosud opened Lomas Center, the first commercial center in the southern part of greater Buenos Aires, and in 1994 San Martín Factory. During 1996–97 Cencosud invested more than $200 million to raise four commercial centers in the province of Buenos Aires, which surrounds the city on three sides. Centro Comercial Palermo, located in the Buenos Aires neighborhood of that name, opened in 1996, and in 1997 the first mall in the western part of greater Buenos Aires, Plaza Oeste Shopping, opened its doors. Between 1997 and 2001 Cencosud completed Quilmes Factory, Las Palmas del Pilar, and El Portal de Escobar, all in the province of Buenos Aires; Portal de la Patagonia, in the province of Neuquén; and Portal de los Andes, in the city of Mendoza.

Cencosud bought Home Depot's four Argentine stores for $90 million in 2001, converting them into Easy units and taking out a $125 million syndicated loan from four banks to help pay for the acquisition. This was the first significant debt that Paulmann had taken on, but by the end of the year his company had issued bonds equivalent to another $144 million. Although Cencosud owned large tracts of property in the Chilean cities of Puerto Montt, Rancagua, Temoco, and Viña del Mar as well as Santiago, Paulmann was spending 80 percent of his time in Argentina, and his two chief lieutenants also were based there. Argentina accounted for some 70 percent of Cencosud's sales as late as 2001. Although the Chilean business press expressed pique at this development, *Capital* named him its entrepreneur of 2001.

As Argentina fell into recession, Cencosud turned back to Chile for a $250 million program of expansion through 2003 to include four commercial centers, two Easy stores, and a Jumbo. Portal Rancagua, a shopping mall in the city of that name, was completed in 2000. Three years later, the company owned

Key Dates:

1961: Jurgen and Horst Paulmann open their first super-market, in Temuco, Chile.
1975: The two brothers open the first Jumbo hypermarket, in Santiago, Chile's capital.
1982: Horst Paulmann opens the first Jumbo in Argentina.
1988: Unicenter, Argentina's first regional shopping mall, is inaugurated.
1993: The Easy home-center chain is introduced in Chile.
1996–97: Cencosud builds four commercial centers in the province of Buenos Aires, Argentina.
2001: The company buys Home Depot's four Argentine stores and converts them to Easy units.
2003: Cencosud buys Santa Isabel, a chain of 75 Chilean supermarkets.
2004: Cencosud becomes a public company, selling about 20 percent of its common stock.

Portal La Dehesa, a $130 million mall in the eastern part of Santiago with 45 checkout counters on two floors, five movie screens with 1,180 seats, a bowling alley, a food court, and a game room. Also in 2003, Cencosud bought Santa Isabel S.A., a 75-unit chain of Chilean supermarkets, from the Dutch retailer Koninklijke Ahold N.V. for $94.5 million. By 1996 this chain had become the largest of its kind in Chile but had subsequently lost market share and fallen into the red. The purchase made Cencosud the second largest operator of supermarkets in Chile, with 19 percent of the total sales volume. Then, in January 2004, Paulmann acquired the 17-unit Las Brisas chain from his brother Jurgen for about $30 million. In August Cencosud purchased Supermercados Montecarlo S.A., a chain of 14 Santiago units, for $78.5 million. These additions raised its share of Chilean supermarket sales to 24 percent.

Cencosud, in December 2003, took out a syndicated loan of $243 million from international and local banks. It became a public company in 2004 with an initial offering of shares on the Borsa de Comercio de Santiago. The offer to sell 20 percent of the company, eight times oversubscribed, raised $228.19 million and was accompanied by a sale of American depositary receipts in the United States that raised an additional $105.38 million. These funds were expected to be used in investments of about $133 million between 2004 and 2006 to build eight supermarkets and seven Easy stores in Chile. Some $25 million was spent to complete a Jumbo and Easy in La Serena in 2004. Due to open before the end of the year were Jumbo units in Temuco and Chillán, with others pending in Antofagasta and Valparaiso. A Cencosud shopping center in Rosario, Argentina, also opened in 2004.

Cencosud made even bigger news in 2004 with the announcement that it hoped to buy the Disco supermarket chain in Argentina—the nation's second largest retailer—from Koninklijke Ahold. Such a transaction, at a cost of $315 million, would add no less than 237 units to the company portfolio and raise Cencosud's annual sales to at least $2.2 billion and perhaps $3 billion. Because of antitrust issues the sale was not expected to close until 2005, if at all.

At the end of 2003 Cencosud had 21 Jumbo hypermarkets, 72 Santa Isabel supermarkets, 35 Easy home centers, 17 commercial centers (all of which had a Jumbo and an Easy), and seven Aventura Centers, totaling about one million square meters (nearly 11 million square feet) of selling space in 35 cities. In that year the company issued its own credit card, Jumbo Más, in Chile. The card allowed its holders to make credit purchases in Jumbo and Easy, paying monthly without interest over a period as long as 36 months.

Cencosud's sales came to CLP 921.29 billion ($1.55 billion) in 2003, and its net income to CLP 44.17 billion ($74.38 million). Chile now accounted for 65 percent of the total and Argentina only 35 percent. Jumbo sales came to 54 percent of the total, Easy to 27 percent, Santa Isabel to 14 percent, and the commercial centers to the remaining 5 percent. The long-term debt at the end of the year was CLP 303.33 billion ($510.8 million). By late 2004 company holdings were considerably larger, with the addition of the 17 Las Brisas and 14 Montecarlo units, plus another Jumbo and Santa Isabel and six more Easy units. The number of employees had now reached 27,700.

Principal Subsidiaries

Cencosud S.A.; Cencosud Internacional S.A.; Cencosud Shopping Centers S.A. (93%); Easy Argentina S.R.L. (Argentina); Inversiones Jumbo S.A. (Argentina); Jumbo S.A. (92%); Santa Isabel S.A.

Principal Divisions

Commercial Centers; Credit Card; Real Estate; Supermarkets.

Principal Competitors

Coto C.I.C.S.A.; Disco S.A.; Empresa D&S S.A.; S.A.C.I. Falabella.

Further Reading

Burgos, Sandra, "A la espera de un milagro," *Capital*, July 19–August 1, 2002, pp. 60–62.
"La caja inagotable," *Capital*, November 7-20, 2003, pp. 30–32.
Fenley, Gareth, "Jumbo's Shopping Spree," *Display & Design Ideas*, August 2002, pp. 30+.
Medel, Lorena, "Golpe a la catedra," *Capital*, December 28, 2001–January 31, 2002, pp. 50–51.
O'Brien, Marie, "Cencosud Bags Retail Investors," *LatinFinance*, June 2004, p. 45.
"El Revolutionario del Retail Chileno," *Gestión*, September 2004, pp. 14–16, 18.
Riquelme, Silvia, *Como ganar dinero en Chile*, Santiago: Editora Zig-Zag, 1994, pp. 165–70.
Soto, Héctor, "Un emporio Un imperio," *Capital*, October 1996, pp. 18–22, 25.
Zegers V., and M. Angelica, "La anti crisis de Paulmann," *Capital*, December 20–29, 2002, pp. 80–82.
——, "Hiper Paulmann," *Capital*, November 2–15, 2001, pp. 16–20, 22.
——, "Llanero Solitario," *Capital*, July 1999, pp. 36–40.

—Robert Halasz

Clearwire, Inc.

5808 Lake Washington Blvd. NE, Suite 300
Kirkland, Washington 98033
U.S.A.
Telephone: (425) 216-7600
Toll Free: (800) 305-5873
Fax: (425) 216-7900
Web site: http://www.clearwire.com

Private Company
Incorporated: 1998 as Clearwire Technologies Inc.
NAIC: 518111 Internet Service Providers

Clearwire, Inc. is a provider of wireless, broadband Internet service to consumers and small businesses, using central base stations to transmit radio signals to small, wireless modems connected to a customer's computer. Clearwire's wireless technology, developed by its subsidiary, Minneapolis-based NextNet Wireless, Inc., features plug-and-play installation and non-line-of-sight access. Clearwire, managed and owned by cellular pioneer Craig McCaw, operates as an Internet service provider in Jacksonville, Florida; St. Cloud, Minnesota; and Abilene, Texas—the first service areas of an expected national and international rollout of wireless Internet service.

Origins

When Craig McCaw directed his vast financial resources toward the development of Clearwire in the summer of 2004, the business press took notice. McCaw, the father of cellular telecommunications, founded McCaw Cellular Communications in the early 1980s and created the first national cellular network. McCaw sold his company to AT&T Corp. in 1994, a transaction that created AT&T Wireless and netted McCaw $11.5 billion. From that point forward, McCaw's actions were followed closely, as the "reclusive billionaire"—the description often used when mentioning McCaw—parlayed his fortune to fashion a business career in the wake of McCaw Cellular. McCaw, as described in the June 28, 2004 issue of *Fortune,* became a "serial entrepreneur and investor," enjoying success and failure.

McCaw founded Teledesic, which was meant to be a satellite-based, broadband-service phone company, but it declared bankruptcy in 2002 without ever launching a satellite. XO Communications, a broadband company McCaw founded the year he sold his cellular business, also declared bankruptcy in 2002 after incurring liabilities of more than $8 billion. In 1995, he registered a much-hailed success by investing $1.1 billion in troubled Nextel Communications, an intervention that was credited with transforming the cellular provider into an industry leader. McCaw's spectacular successes and failures, all supported by his enormous wealth, created a stir of interest whenever he emerged from hiding to spearhead a new venture. In Clearwire's case, the frenzied interest obscured the origins of the company. Most of the business press in the summer of 2004 referred to Clearwire as a company started by McCaw, but the company began operating six years before McCaw entered the picture. Clearwire's founder was not McCaw, but a Buffalo, New York company named Sierra Technologies Inc.

The name and essence of Clearwire were born within offices of Sierra Technologies, owned jointly by James Gero and Edward "Rusty" Rose III. Gero and Rose, who along with George W. Bush owned the Texas Rangers baseball club, formed Sierra Technologies in 1991 specifically to acquire Buffalo-based Sierra Research, a company founded in the late 1950s. When Gero and Rose acquired Sierra Research, the company operated as a division of LTV Corp., manufacturing electronic and avionic equipment for military and commercial customers. As the 1990s progressed, the company, operating as Sierra Technologies, distinguished itself as a developer and manufacturer of sophisticated radio-frequency products and systems for military and civilian applications—the technological foundation of Clearwire. Clearwire was formed in 1998 as a spinoff of Sierra Technologies, beginning as a company based in Arlington, Texas, whose secure transmission technology grew out of defense electronics used to link ships with aircraft trying to locate submarines.

The original version of Clearwire operated as Clearwire Technologies Inc. Financially backed by individual investors, the company set out on its own to provide high-speed, wireless Internet connections. Clearwire's system involved placing a cen-

95

Company Perspectives:

The Internet gives us all a profound freedom to communicate, explore and share ideas. But until now, Internet service has been, well, kind of a let down. That's why we created Clearwire. Clearwire is here to provide Internet service that's as amazing as the Internet itself. Now you can enjoy a high-speed broadband Internet connection on your terms—with a solution that's simple, flexible, reliable and affordable. Best of all, you won't be tethered to a cord or cable coming out of the wall because with Clearwire, you can connect to the Internet anywhere in the service area. In a nutshell, this is the Internet the way it oughta be.

tral base station on top of a building that sent a signal to low-power transmitters, usually placed on a windowsill, on the customer's premise. The company sold its systems to Internet service providers (ISPs), marketing its wireless service, which was capable of service up to 640 kilobytes per second (Kbps), as less expensive and easier to install than broadband Internet service provided through cable modems and digital subscriber lines (DSLs). Clearwire's service, ten times as fast as a dial-up modem and less expensive than competing broadband connections such as ISDN, T1, cable, and DSL, was geared for medium- and small-sized businesses. These customers typically paid a set-up fee of $500 and monthly charges ranging between $230 and $500. For business customers who paid as much as $1,200 per month to landline providers, Clearwire's wireless service offered price benefits. To those who had the option of paying for other types of connections, Clearwire's service made financial sense, and to those located in areas lacking the cable and phone line infrastructure to provide broadband service, it offered the only choice.

Clearwire's First Service Launch in 1999

Starting out, Clearwire offered its service to the two areas that represented the company's geographic background. In March 1999, it launched its first wireless service in Dallas using the unlicensed 2.4-gigahertz (GHz) bandwidth of the radio spectrum. In August 1999, the company offered its small-business oriented service to customers in Buffalo, using a base station in the city's downtown area that was capable of serving customers within 25 miles of the transmitter.

After releasing its first two systems, Clearwire adopted an expansion strategy more attuned to the advantages offered by wireless service. Large metropolitan areas such as Dallas were not the ideal locations for Clearwire service. Instead, the company targeted smaller cities, choosing to deploy its service in what were referred to as second- and third-tier cities. In many of these areas, the infrastructure to provide broadband service had not been built; trenches to lay cable needed to be dug, high-speed phone lines needed to be installed. Clearwire moved into these areas, establishing service in cities such as Albuquerque, New Mexico, and Columbus, Ohio.

As Clearwire began expanding into other markets, the company financed its growth through private investments. The first infusion of capital occurred at the end of 2000, when Dallas-based Cardinal Investments Inc. provided $22 million to help fund the establishment of Clearwire systems in new markets. A second round of financing occurred in April 2001, when an effort led by Goldman, Sachs & Co. and Liberty Associated Partners L.P. realized a capital injection of $97 million. The funds were earmarked for the development of new transmission equipment that was expected to double Clearwire's existing speed of service.

At roughly the same time Clearwire secured its $97 million in financing, the company brokered an important agreement, one that held particular importance for McCaw's version of Clearwire. During its first years in business, Clearwire operated in the unlicensed 2.4-GHz frequency, which was subject to interference and forced the company to compete with such powerhouses as Sprint and WorldCom for bandwidth. In early 2001, the company signed an agreement to share radio frequencies with the Instructional Television Fixed Service Spectrum Development Alliance (ITFS), a group of instructional television providers allotted bandwidth by the Federal Communications Commission in the 1960s. The agreement allowed Clearwire to lease wireless spectrum in the 2.5- to 2.7-GHz spectrum, giving it access to the frequency rights held by ITFS in roughly 100 cities.

With a fresh infusion of cash and the ability to obtain licenses in scores of markets, Clearwire plotted an ambitious program. The company planned to launch its service in 80 markets, expecting to begin its rollout in 2002, but before the expansion program was implemented, Clearwire stumbled. In October 2001, just six months after receiving $97 million, the company shut down service in three of its four markets, maintaining its service in Albuquerque. The company laid off 55 of its employees, a cutback that represented 55 percent of its workforce. Only a cursory explanation was given by Clearwire for its sudden retreat, an episode in the company's development that marked the beginning of the end for the Arlington-based Clearwire Technologies and its later emergence as the McCaw-led, Kirkland, Washington-based Clearwire, Inc. "We felt it was the smart thing to do due to the relative short-term uncertainty in the economy and the telecommunications markets," a Clearwire official said in an October 2001 interview with *Dallas Business Journal.*

Craig McCaw Starting a New Clearwire Era in 2004

The Clearwire name received a second chance in the wireless broadband sector when McCaw emerged as an interested suitor. In March 2004, McCaw merged his Flux Fixed Wireless company with Clearwire Holdings, the parent company of Clearwire Technologies, and installed himself as chief executive officer and chairman of his new company, Clearwire, Inc. It was the first time McCaw served as chief executive since he had last led McCaw Cellular a decade earlier. Aside from the slight variation in the name of the company, there were meaningful differences between the Texas-based Clearwire and McCaw's Clearwire. The Texas version of the company focused on serving business customers. McCaw intended to target residential customers. Further, the original Clearwire operated almost exclusively on the unlicensed range of the radio spectrum, barely having a chance to exploit its agreement with ITFS. McCaw intended to operate on the licensed bandwidth allotted to schools and nonprofit organizations, which gave him access to the approximately 100 markets realized from Clearwire's 2001 agreement with ITFS.

Key Dates:

1998: Clearwire is spun off from Sierra Technologies Inc.
1999: Clearwire offers wireless Internet service in Dallas.
2001: Clearwire signs an agreement to lease space on licensed frequencies of the broadcast spectrum.
2004: Craig McCaw purchases Clearwire, leading to the launch of service to Jacksonville, Florida; St. Cloud, Minnesota; and Abilene, Texas, by the end of the year.

Perhaps the most striking difference between the two versions of Clearwire was the technology McCaw intended to use. In December 2001, Clearwire spun off its equipment manufacturing arm, leaving McCaw to find a replacement. He chose a superior technology, acquiring Minneapolis-based NextNet Wireless, Inc. in June 2004, making the company a Clearwire subsidiary. Founded in 1998, NextNet introduced the first non-line-of-sight (NLOS) plug-and-play system for delivering high-speed, wireless Internet services. Clearwire's original technology only worked if the path between the base station and the windowsill transmitters was unobstructed, but NextNet's system worked regardless of obstructions. NextNet's technology proved to be effective and popular, used over licensed frequencies in Asia, Africa, Canada, and Latin America before McCaw purchased the company.

With the aid of the licensing rights controlled by Clearwire and the equipment made by NextNet, McCaw announced that he would deploy wireless broadband service in select markets throughout the country. By this point, the wireless technology employed enabled service up to 1.5 million bits per second (Mbps), providing a connection that neared the speed of DSL and cable modems. McCaw was in pursuit of the estimated 70 percent of residences in the United States that did not subscribe to the Internet through a broadband connection because of cost or availability barriers. For his first demonstration of the capabilities of the new Clearwire and NextNet technology, McCaw chose Jacksonville, Florida, aping the expansion strategy of targeting second- and third-tier cities formulated by Clearwire's management team during the late 1990s.

The launch of Clearwire's service in Jacksonville was marked by the symbolic cutting of ribbon fashioned out of coaxial cable and telephone cord. The event occurred on August 26, 2004, when the company's service became available to more than 120,000 homes in an area measuring more than 100 square miles. "Clearwire offers simplicity, affordability, and flexibility," a company press release announced on the day of the launch. "You can buy the service at select local retailers, take it home, set it up and be online in minutes," the statement continued. "It's plug-and-play as far as installation—no need for a technician to come to your home and no need to load software onto your computer to make it work."

As McCaw embarked on his expansion campaign, Clearwire benefited from the esteem accorded to its chief executive. In August 2004, as the launch in Jacksonville neared, 23 investors in nine states provided $160 million to finance Clearwater's expansion, with the bulk of the money coming from investors residing in McCaw's home state of Washington. In October 2004, when Clearwire expanded its coverage area in Jacksonville to include 75,000 additional homes, chip maker Intel Corporation invested an undisclosed amount in McCaw's Clearwire as part of an agreement to jointly develop products to support IEEE 802.16e, the next standard for WiMAX, the breed of service offered by Clearwire. (The coverage area of Wi-Fi is measured in feet; WiMAX serves an area measured in miles.)

The practice of cutting a ribbon composed of coaxial cable and telephone cord occurred two more times in 2004. On December 9, Clearwire added two more markets to its nascent service network. More than 20,000 homes in St. Cloud, Minnesota, became part of Clearwire's service area, the first step in plans to offer its wireless service in the central Minnesota area. The other launch occurred in Abilene, Texas, where 40,000 homes were made part of the Clearwire network. Next on the company's list of targeted U.S. markets was Daytona Beach, Florida, a system launch that was to be the first of 20 deployments scheduled for 2005. The success of McCaw's venture hinged on the achievements made during 2005, as the reclusive billionaire tested the worth of his business strategy in the public spotlight.

Principal Subsidiaries

NextNet Wireless, Inc.

Principal Competitors

Earthlink, Inc.; America Online, Inc.; Yahoo! Inc.; Microsoft Corporation.

Further Reading

Bajaj, Vikas, "Cellular Billionaire to Offer Wireless Broadband Service," *Dallas Morning News,* June 3, 2004, p. B4.
Bounds, Jeff, "Clearwire Halts Service, Cuts 55% of Work Force," *Dallas Business Journal,* October 12, 2001, p. 20.
Chen, Christine Y., "Craig McCaw's Private Life," *Fortune,* June 28, 2004, p. 36.
"Clearwire Secures $97 Million for Expansion," *123Jump,* April 24, 2001.
"Clearwire to Offer Voice, Data Over Wireless," *eWeek,* June 4, 2004, p. 32.
Cook, John, "Clearwire Is Involved in WiMax," *Seattle Post-Intelligencer,* October 26, 2004, p. E1.
Duryee, Tricia, "Intel Joins McCaw's New Tech Venture Investment in Clearwire," *Seattle Times,* October 26, 2004, p. C1.
——, "Stock Sale Raises $160 Million for Kirkland, Wash.-Based Broadband Venture," *Seattle Times,* August 28, 2004, p. B2.
Fryer, Alex, "Clearwire Chairman, CEO Tackles Wireless Broadband," *Seattle Times,* June 3, 2004, p. B1.
Gibbons, Timothy J., "Wireless Internet Firm Clearwire to Hire 100 in Jacksonville, Fla.," *Florida Times-Union,* June 26, 2004, p. 43.
Semilof, Margie, "ISPs Look to New Wireless Technology," *Computer Reseller News,* March 15, 1999, p. 1.
Williams, Fred O., "Clearwire Holdings Spins Off Equipment-Making Unit in Buffalo," *Buffalo News,* December 9, 2001, p. B3.
——, "New Wireless Internet Service Has Ties to Sierra Research," *Buffalo News,* August 1, 1999, p. B10.

—Jeffrey L. Covell

Cold Stone Creamery

<table>
<tr><td>

16101 North 82nd Street, Suite A4
Scottsdale, Arizona 85260
U.S.A.
Telephone: (480) 348-1704
Toll Free: (866) 464-9467
Fax: (480) 348-1718
Web site: http://www.coldstonecreamery.com

Private Company
Incorporated: 1988
Employees: 200
Sales: $285 million (2004 est.)
NAIC: 311520 Ice Cream and Frozen Desert
Manufacturing; 722213 Snack and Nonalcoholic
Beverage Bars

</td></tr>
</table>

Cold Stone Creamery operates on an independently owned franchise system of ice creameries headquartered in Scottsdale, Arizona. There are more than 900 Cold Stone Creamery stores in 47 states, including Alaska and Hawaii, and in the Caribbean and Guam. At each location, Cold Stone Creamery "crew" members handcraft ice cream fresh daily. Customers choose their "creations" from an assortment of flavors and mix-ins, which the crew blends to order on a granite stone chilled to 16 degrees Fahrenheit. Serving sizes range from the size of a tennis ball to the size of a softball and are called "Like It," "Love It," and "Gotta Have It."

1988–95: Creating the Perfect Ice Cream Experience

In the 1980s, Donald and Susan Sutherland, ice cream lovers, searched everywhere for ice cream that was smooth and creamy, rather than hard-packed or soft-serve. After years of finding nothing that met their standards of quality, flavor, consistency, and variety, they opened the first Cold Stone Creamery in Tempe, Arizona, in 1988. Cold Stone Creamery's ice cream was premium quality, containing 14 percent milk fat or butterfat—2 to 3 percent above the industry average—and had low "overrun," the amount of air pumped into the product during manufacture.

Cold Stone Creamery sold not just ice cream, but a concept: Customers designed their own personalized "dessert creations," choosing from basic ice cream, yogurt, and sorbet flavors and adding in fruit, candy, nuts, syrups, and other ingredients. Cold Stone Creamery staff, called crew members, mixed these ingredients together using spatula-like utensils on a frozen granite slab. The idea of add-ins was not new, having been first introduced in 1973 by Steve Herrell of Steve's Ice Cream of Somerville, Massachusetts, but Cold Stone Creamery took the add-in concept one-step further. The company aimed to deliver the "Ultimate Ice Cream Experience" by selling entertainment along with its super-premium ice cream. According to the company's web site, a visit to a Cold Stone Creamery store should be "a community event" as in the "good old days" of ice cream parlors. Aided by the aroma of fresh baked waffle cones and brownies and the warm reception of crew members, it would "transform the simple pleasure of eating ice cream into a memorable, one-of-a-kind experience . . . where people could create their own happiness."

Cold Stone Creamery was a hit, and, in 1990, the Sutherlands opened a second store in the Phoenix metropolitan area. Third and fourth stores followed during the next five years, during which time the company added partners as well: Ken Burk as chief executive officer in charge of establishing the foundation of the fast-growing company in 1994, and Doug Ducey as president responsible for business development and direction in 1995. Ducey was an Ohio native and a graduate of Arizona State University with a history in executive sales; he had held marketing positions with Procter & Gamble and Anheuser Busch before arriving at Cold Stone Creamery.

1995–2000: A Regional Success Goes National

Ducey began to build Cold Stone Creamery from a regional ice cream company into a national brand through adding franchises. The company's initial franchise fee of $42,000 was relatively low, and the typical store's footprint of about 1,100 square feet was small. These factors, combined with start-up costs of only about $300,000 per operation, opened many site opportunities for new creameries and helped generate a large number of prospective franchisees. In 1995, the first Cold Stone

Company Perspectives:

With every creation and every customer, the Cold Stone Creamery community is committed to delivering more than ice cream to the legions of ice cream lovers worldwide. They will deliver their passion for quality, their passion for variety, and their passion for choice. That passion is delivering the ultimate indulgence in ice cream.

Key Dates:

1988: The first Cold Stone Creamery store opens in Tempe, Arizona.
1990: The company opens a second store in the Phoenix metro area.
1995: Doug Ducey becomes a partner and president of the company; the company's first franchise store opens in Tucson, Arizona.
1997: Cold Stone Creamery's headquarters double in size and move to Scottsdale, Arizona.
2000: Doug Ducey becomes chief executive officer.

Creamery franchise opened in Tucson, Arizona, across the street from the University of Arizona. Between 1995 and 1999, the number of franchises increased dramatically and, by August 2000, the year in which Ducey became chief executive officer as well as president, the company had 100 stores in 16 states and placed 94th on *Entrepreneur* magazine's list entitled the "101 Fastest-Growing Franchises in America." In addition, Cold Stone Creamery doubled the size of its headquarters and moved to Scottsdale in 1997.

Cold Stone Creamery also began in-store promotions to raise interest in its products. Adopting the motto "Create Your Own Happiness," and claiming the title of "the nation's fastest-growing franchiser of gourmet ice cream and frozen yogurt stores," the company held a contest in 2000 in which customers submitted their own recipes for ice cream creations to compete for the chance to become an honorary partner of the company. One participant from each of the company's stores won an ice cream party for 25, $1,100 per month, and free ice cream every day for a year for family and friends.

Cold Stone Creamery also began to actively seek promotional partners in the sports and food industries. In January 2001, it became the official ice cream of the Phoenix Open golf tournament and joined with other businesses throughout the Phoenix community to contribute support to local charities. In February, it joined with the Colorado Avalanche hockey team to raise money for a community fund by sponsoring a contest in which participants competed to create a new "Hockey Road" flavor. Cold Stone Creamery had earlier enjoyed a partnership with the Phoenix Coyotes.

By 2001, Cold Stone Creamery, with some 225 stores in 25 states and the Virgin Islands, had expanded upon the entertainment aspect of its business, auditioning and hiring crew members based on their performance skills and personalities. Crew members began to sing and dance while serving customers and to enlist customer participation in games. In addition to creating a show-biz atmosphere, the singing and dancing distracted patrons from the fact that obtaining a Cold Stone Creamery cone could require a longer wait than at a less popular ice cream store. Some objected to Cold Stone Creamery's attempt to grab media attention when it added chocolate-covered crickets as a mix-in as part of a promotion linking it to the *Survivor* reality show in 2001; however, the crickets disappeared in record time.

2001–04: Steady and Widespread Expansion Through Franchising

In 2001, Cold Stone Creamery, then 90th on *Entrepreneur* magazine's list of the Fastest Growing Franchises in the nation,

began launching stores in northern California. Rapid expansion throughout the United States continued in 2002 with a focus on Chicago, and northeastern and southeastern states. The company was receiving almost 1,000 applications for new franchises per month in mid-2002 as opposed to 100 per month just the year before. As the number of Cold Stone Creamery stores edged up toward 300 units in 31 states, the company won the Spirit of Enterprise Award from the Center for Advancement of Small Business at Arizona State University's College of Business for its growth, enthusiastic approach, display of leadership, community service, and unique adventurous spirit and ranked 54th on the Fastest Growing Franchises list.

Domestic sales of ice cream amounted to $20.5 billion in 2002, of which $12.5 billion was spent on frozen confections consumed away-from-home. With the popularity of ice cream and frozen desserts increasing throughout the United States, Cold Stone Creamery began what would become an ongoing collaboration with Make-A-Wish Foundation, holding its first World's Largest Ice Cream Social in 2002. Guests at the event were treated to a free cone of ice cream and encouraged to make a donation to the foundation that fulfilled the wishes of children with life-threatening medical conditions. By 2004, the company's annual socials had raised $1.1 million combined for Make-A-Wish.

In mid-2003, there were Cold Stone Creamery stores in 32 states, and the company was opening about six new creameries per week, including one in New York City's Times Square, which a company news release described as "an important phase in the development of Cold Stone Creamery's aggressive growth strategy." In deference to the nation's skyrocketing obesity crisis and awareness, the company added its fat-free, sugar-free "Sinless Ice Cream." Even with the nation's increased health-consciousness, revenues continued to increase, and Cold Stone Creamery ranked 35th on *Entrepreneur* magazine's fastest growing list in 2003.

While Dairy Queen and Baskin-Robbins saw sales and units stagnate, Cold Stone Creamery's outlets rose by about 60 percent to 541. Boasting about $380,000 in annual revenue per store, Cold Stone Creamery's 2003 revenues exceeded $156 million, up 77 percent from $88 million in 2002 and more than triple 2001 sales. By mid-year 2004, the company had more than 700 units in 44 states and 250 more stores slated to open. Cold Stone Creamery had reached 25th on *Entrepreneur* magazine's "101 Fastest-Growing Franchises" list and came in fourth in *Restaurant Business* magazine's "Top 50 Growth Chains." Increased milk prices coupled with vanilla shortages bumped up the company's costs by double digits in the first half of the year; still the company went ahead with plans to add 12 ice cream cakes to its menu.

The manufacture and sale of ice cream appeared to remain big business despite the nation's obsession with low-carb diets. The company entered 2005 with more than 900 stores in 47 states, another 1,000 units in some stage of development, and ranked 12th on *Entrepreneur* magazine's "101 Fastest-Growing Franchises" list. Shortly after the start of the year, it launched its new vision statement: "The world will know us as the ultimate ice cream experience by making us the #1 best-selling ice cream brand in America by December 31, 2009."

Principal Competitors

Ben & Jerry's Homemade Inc.; Bruster's Real Ice Cream, Inc.; Carvel Corporation; CoolBrands International, Inc.; Dippin' Dots, Incorporated; Friendly Ice Cream Corp.; International Dairy Queen, Inc.; Marble Slab Creamery, Inc.; YoCream International, Inc.

Further Reading

Chandler, Michelle, "Arizona-Based Cold Stone Creamery Plans New California Branches," *San Jose Mercury News*, May 27, 2004.

Hogan, Donna, "Scottsdale, Arizona-Based Ice Cream Company Searches for Expansion Sites," *East Valley Tribune*, May 26, 2002.

"Ice Cream Is Fattening, CSPI Reveals," *Restaurant Business*, July 24, 2003.

Jardine, Jeff, "Modesto, California, Ice Cream Parlor to Offer Customers Songs with Their Scoops," *Modesto Bee*, June 26, 2001.

"Mix-in Masters," *Restaurant Business*, November 15, 2003.

Pringle, Bruce, "Cold Stone Rolls into Midway," *Delaware Coast Press*, December 15, 2004.

Reingold, Jennifer, and Ryan Underwood, "Was *Built to Last* Built to Last?" *Fast Company*, November 2004, p. 103.

Tasker, Greg, "Food and Fun: Cold Stone Scoops Hot Sales, Rapidly Growing Franchise Entertains Customers While It Serves Premium Ice Cream," *Detroit Free Press*, October 4, 2004.

—Carrie Rothburd

Columbia House Company

1221 Avenue of the Americas
New York, New York 10020
U.S.A.
Telephone: (212) 596-2000
Fax: (212) 596-2213
Web site: http://www.columbiahouse.com

Subsidiary of Blackstone Group L.P.
Incorporated: 1955 as Columbia Record Club
Employees: 2,200
Sales: $1.0 billion (2003 est.)
NAIC: 454390 Other Direct Selling Establishments

Columbia House Company is the leading club-based, direct-to-consumer marketer of music and movies in North America, conducting its mail-order business in the United States, Canada, and Mexico. Columbia House boasts approximately 8.5 million members who can choose from approximately 9,000 music selections and 5,000 DVD titles. The company operates three clubs: The Music Club, The DVD Club, and Video Library. The company also distributes video games through its music and DVD clubs. The Blackstone Group L.P., a New York-based investment firm, owns 85 percent of Columbia House, with the balance split between Sony Corporation and Time Warner Inc.

Origins

Columbia House began as an experiment, a venture whose quick success and sustained growth throughout the 20th century most likely surprised its creator. In 1955, an executive at CBS Records formed a new division of Columbia Records, one of the record labels owned by CBS. The purpose of the new division, which was named the Columbia Record Club, was to test the idea of marketing music through the mail. To attract interest in the concept, Columbia Record Club offered one free monophonic record to those who joined the club, offering its new members a wide selection of jazz, easy-listening, and Broadway show titles from which to choose. The response from the public confirmed the legitimacy of club membership and direct-mail marketing as an effective means of selling music.

By the end of 1955, the Columbia Record Club boasted 128,000 members who purchased 700,000 records.

The quick success of the marketing experiment forced management at CBS and Columbia Records to treat the division more seriously. Initially, when executives were testing the waters of selling to customers directly through the mail, the fulfillment operations of the division were housed in Manhattan in part of a building on Fifth Avenue. The public's embrace of the record club concept rendered the New York City facility obsolete by Columbia Record Club's second year in existence. To provide sufficient space for the warehouse and shipping functions of the division, a sprawling distribution center, staffed with more than 100 employees, was established in Terre Haute, Indiana, in 1956. The Terre Haute facility, the principal physical presence of an enterprise that lacked, in many consumers' minds, any physical dimension, served as the hub of operations throughout the 20th century. The city was chosen for its access to railways—of vital importance to a mail-order company at the time—and, equally important, because Columbia Records manufactured its vinyl discs in Terre Haute. The synergy achieved in Terre Haute established a pattern, later leading to the establishment of distribution centers near Columbia Records' other manufacturing facilities in Connecticut and California.

Within a decade of its formation, Columbia Record Club changed the profile of the retail music industry. A new dimension to the business of selling music emerged, a new way of placing music in the listener's hands that was created in large part by the advances made by Columbia Record Club. By 1957, two years after starting out, Columbia Record Club was using its Terre Haute facility to ship seven million records to its members, the ranks of which were swelling by the month. The club's success in signing new members was underpinned by its ability to tap into the growth of the industry it served. The music industry was expanding substantially during the latter half of the 1950s, its growth fueled by the emergence of a new genre, rock 'n' roll, and, to a lesser extent, by technological advances in the recording of music and the equipment used to listen to music. Columbia Record Club rode the wave of the popularity, introducing rock 'n' roll records, listed under the less controversial "Teen Hits" category, in 1958. The following year, the

Company Perspectives:

Throughout the company's rich history, an enthusiastic embrace of emerging technology has become an enduring corporate trademark. From CDs to videos and DVDs, Columbia House has created a club that has consistently met the public's demand for the latest advancement in entertainment products.

Columbia Records division began offering its members stereophonic records and it offered a small assortment of stereo equipment to help spark interest in the new format.

Columbia Record Club stood as a recognizable force in the U.S. music industry within a decade of its formation. By 1963, the division accounted for 10 percent of all the money spent on recorded music, achieving market share that forced traditional retailers to take notice. The club managed to capture a sizable portion of the market by offering a broad selection of music whose range would only be matched by the massive, national retail chains that emerged decades later. The division also tried to remain on the vanguard of technology that would improve the operation of its business, and it tried to anticipate the changing needs and tastes of its membership. The company, in a bid to attract audiophiles, introduced the Reel-To-Reel Club in 1960, offering recordings that could be played on reel-to-reel players. In 1962, Columbia Record Club became one of the national leaders in the use of data processing equipment after investing in computers, one of the first companies of any kind that embraced the new technology. To offer its membership the types of recording format that were being developed and proving popular, the company started the Columbia Cartridge Club, which targeted the 8-track market, in 1965, and four years later launched the Cassette Club, giving its members another recording format to stimulate their purchasing activity.

Columbia Record Club celebrated its 20th anniversary in 1975 having surpassed the three-million-member mark. The company, generating millions of dollars in sales from albums such as Simon and Garfunkel's *Bridge Over Troubled Water* and The Eagles' *One of These Nights,* was enjoying a decade of business that would be its last as a company exclusively devoted to marketing and distributing vinyl records. The 1980s and 1990s brought change, both welcomed and not welcomed, making the last years of the 20th century an era of defining significance for the music club.

Diversification in the 1980s

Columbia Record Club entered its new era of existence as an international enterprise. In 1979, the Canadian Music Club was formed, adding more than 100,000 new members by the end of the year. In 1981, the period of profound change began, touched off by the introduction of the CBS Video Library, which offered videos of old television shows and special interest programs to customers through the mail. The following year, the CBS Video Club was formed, moving Columbia Record Club into a business line that later would account for more than half of its sales. Another important addition to the club's selection of merchan-

dise occurred in 1986, when the company began offering compact discs (CDs), embracing a format that soon rendered vinyl discs obsolete.

During the late 1980s, Columbia House's parent company became part of an industrywide trend. The U.S. recording industry was controlled in large part by foreign companies during the 1980s, with the Dutch owning Polygram, the Germans owning RCA, and the British owning Capitol. The Japanese joined the fray in 1987, when Sony Corporation acquired CBS Records and its various labels, including Columbia, for $2 billion. The transaction ranked as the largest-ever Japanese purchase of a U.S. company.

With a new parent company, Columbia House entered the 1990s and reached an impressive milestone. The company shipped its one billionth record in 1990. The following year control over the company was divided between Sony and Time Warner Inc., with Columbia House organized as a joint venture company. Each company owned half of Columbia House, with all of the assets of Sony Music Entertainment—formerly CBS Records—and the Time-Life Home Video Club combined to form the new version of Columbia House. As part of the deal that made Columbia House a joint venture between Sony and Time Warner, the CBS Video Club changed its name to the Columbia House Video Club and the CBS Video Library was renamed the Columbia House Video Library. Membership in Columbia House exceeded ten million by the end of 1991.

Columbia House continued to demonstrate its ability to adapt to change during the 1990s. The more mainstream appeal of Latin pop music, which gained widespread popularity from singers such as Gloria Estefan and Ricky Martin, prompted the company to introduce Club Musica Latina in 1992. In 1995, the company fleshed out its North American presence and increased its commitment to Latin artists and customers by establishing Columbia House Mexico. The following year, Columbia House launched its web site, giving its customers the opportunity to peruse music and video catalogs and to purchase their selections online. In 1997, after establishing its online presence, Columbia House formed its DVD club, which proved to be a vital contributor to the company's revenue volume, helping, along with other video sales, to account for approximately half of the company's revenues.

As Columbia House prepared to exit the 1990s, it was beginning to suffer from the advances made by other retailers. Nationwide, record club sales declined during much of the 1990s, reaching their peak in 1994 when clubs of Columbia House's ilk accounted for 15.1 percent of all CD sales. By 2001, record clubs accounted for less than 8 percent of all CD sales, as the success of Internet-based retailers such as Amazon.com coupled with the sharply discounted prices offered by massive retail chains such as Wal-Mart Stores, Inc. hobbled Columbia House's progress. To combat the causes of its flagging business, the company sought a partnership with one of the pioneers of online music sales, CDNow.com Inc., which maintained a base of 2.3 million online customers. The two companies agreed to merge in mid-1999, recruiting a new chief executive officer, Scott Flanders, to lead the new company. An initial public offering of Columbia House was included as part of the merger plan, but in March 2000 the deal collapsed. Columbia House,

Key Dates:

1955: Columbia Record Club, a division of Columbia Records, is formed.
1963: The division accounts for 10 percent of the recorded music retail market.
1975: Membership in the club exceeds three million.
1979: The Canadian Music Club is formed.
1987: Sony Corporation acquires CBS Records, its various labels, and Columbia House.
1991: Time Warner Inc. and Sony organize Columbia House as a joint venture company.
1995: Columbia House Mexico is formed.
2000: A proposed merger with CDNow.com, Inc. collapses.
2002: Blackstone Group acquires a majority stake in Columbia House.

according to several industry observers, carried too much debt and lacked sufficient cash flow to support CDNow's operation.

In the wake of the scuttled merger agreement, Flanders, who had cofounded an e-commerce company, Telstreet.com, before being recruited by Sony and Time Warner, remained in charge of Columbia House. Sony and Time Warner executives wanted Flanders to resolve Columbia House's financial problems. Flanders responded by initiating a restructuring program in 2000 that produced positive cash flow by the end of 2000. In 2001, he closed the company's distribution center in Colorado City, Colorado, which was operating at 60 percent of the level of 1999.

Acquisition by Blackstone Group in 2002

Flanders succeeded in restoring some of Columbia House's luster. Despite the strides achieved, there was speculation that Sony and Time Warner were looking to sell Columbia House, a theory that became reality in 2002. In May, a New York-based private investment firm, Blackstone Group, acquired a majority stake in Columbia House, paying $410 million to take control of the company. After the deal was concluded, Sony and Time Warner each held a minority stake in Columbia House.

As Columbia House prepared for its 50th anniversary, another potential merger grabbed the headlines. In late 2003, rumors were circulating that Columbia House might merge with Blockbuster, Inc. The proposed merger promised to combine the largest video rental chain in the United States with the largest direct marketer of music and videos in the United States, joining Blockbuster's 48 million members with Columbia

House's more than eight million members. Blockbuster dominated the movie rental business, controlling 40 percent of the U.S. market, but the massive retail chain lagged behind in the DVD retail market, controlling only 3 percent of the U.S. market. The company announced that it intended to increase its market share to 9 percent by 2006. Columbia House, with between 7 percent and 8 percent of the DVD retail sales market, offered Blockbuster an expedient way to surpass its goal. As Columbia House entered the mid-2000s, speculation about its union with Blockbuster dominated news about the company, offering, in some analysts' minds, a new way for the company to approach its business in the future.

Principal Subsidiaries

ColumbiaHouse.com, Inc.

Principal Competitors

Amazon.com, Inc.; Bertelsmann AG; The Musicland Group, Inc.

Further Reading

Bawden, Tom, "Columbia House in Talks on Merger," *Financial Times,* September 20, 2003, p. 57.

Beard, Alison, "International: Blockbuster and Columbia House Discuss Merger," *Financial Times,* September 20, 2003, p. 9.

"Blackstone Buys Majority Stake in Columbia," *New York Times,* May 15, 2002, p. C4.

"Blackstone Confirms," *New York Post,* May 15, 2002, p. 31.

"Blackstone Nears Columbia House Deal," *Cincinnati Post,* May 14, 2002, p. 9C.

"Blockbuster May Merge with Columbia House," *Houston Chronicle,* September 20, 2003, p. 1.

Emery, Erin, "Record-Club Company Columbia House Set to Close Center in Colorado City, Colo.," *Knight Ridder/Tribune Business News,* April 3, 2001.

Garrity, Brian, "What Now for Col. House," *Billboard,* March 25, 2000, p. 1.

Grimes, Christopher, "International: CDNow and Columbia House End Merger Plans," *Financial Times,* March 14, 2000, p. 23.

Halkias, Maria, "Columbia House-Blockbuster Merger Rumor Entices Wall Street," *Knight Ridder/Tribune Business News,* September 20, 2003.

Hopkins, Marjorie, "Columbia House," *Indiana Business Magazine,* October 1993, p. 54.

Li, Kenneth, "Sony, Time Warner Merge Music Club with Online Music Firm," *Knight Ridder/Tribune Business News,* July 13, 1999.

Nye, Doug, "What's Old Is New," *Record,* June 6, 1997, p. 31.

Richtel, Matt, "CDNow Deal with Sony and Time Warner Is Called Off," *New York Times,* March 14, 2000, p. C1.

—Jeffrey L. Covell

Conair Corporation

150 Milford Rd.
East Windsor, New Jersey 08520
U.S.A.
Telephone: (609) 426-1300
Fax: (609) 426-9475
Web site: http://www.conair.com

Private Company
Incorporated: 1959 as Continental Hair Products, Inc.
Employees: 4,000
Sales: $1.27 billion (2003 est.)
NAIC: 335211 Electric Housewares Manufacturing

Conair Corporation is one of the world's largest privately held health and beauty and small appliance companies. Conair manufactures products under the Cuisinart, Interplak, ConairPro, Conair, Jheri Redding, Pollenex, Thinner, BaByliss, Waring, and Rusk names.

Continental Hair Products: 1959–75

Continental Hair Products, Inc., established and incorporated in 1959, was founded by Julian Rizzuto and his son Leandro (Lee). Julian had invented the "machineless permanent wave," a chemical process that replaced electric hair curlers for a time. He ran a beauty parlor on Manhattan's East 42nd Street with his wife, but this business collapsed in the late 1950s. This left him with only an improved, fast-drying hair roller he had invented. Continental Hair was launched in a Brooklyn basement to produce these premium-quality, premium-priced hair curlers for sale to the beauty salon business. The start-up capital was $100, raised from the $5,000 sale of Lee's Cadillac, with the rest of the money going to pay off family debt. The business was an instant success, requiring the Rizzutos to expand their assembly capacity nine times in four years. Within a few years the firm was selling curlers and Japanese-made hair clips at the rate of ten million per month.

Continental Hair suffered a setback when a fire in 1965 destroyed its underinsured Brooklyn quarters. Julian Rizzuto

died two years later. The company began recording remarkable and uninterrupted progress during 1968–69, however, when it developed and introduced hot combs, curling irons, and the first of a line of pistol-grip hair styler-dryers, which helped to popularize blow-dried hair styles. Initially made exclusively for the professional beauty care market, the hair dryers were immediately embraced as superior to the conventional bonnet-type, salon-type dryers. Continental Hair also began selling retail lines of electric hair appliances in late 1971, when it introduced the "Conair Pro-Style" dryer. Sales grew from $1.1 million in 1968 to $12.6 million in 1973. Net income rose from $52,000 to $910,000 in the same period.

Continental Hair was also designing and marketing a wide variety of electric appliances by 1974, including other hand-held dryers under the Conair name, and hot combs, curling irons, shampoos, conditioners, and other hair-care accessories. It was manufacturing the Vidal Sassoon line of hand-held dryers, brushes, and cutlery, as well as producing a number of private-label products. In 1973 it acquired Ethical Personal Care Products, Ltd., which became a subsidiary selling a line of hair dryers to mass-merchandise chains under the brand name "Superstars." Also in 1973, the company entered the liquid end of the business by acquiring Jheri Redding Products, Inc., whose product line, including shampoos, conditioners, and other hair care products, had a strong and wide following among hair stylists and beauticians throughout the United States.

Continental Hair's first venture into manufacturing as well as marketing its products occurred in 1972, when it purchased a one-third interest in a Hong Kong company. In 1973, 85 percent of the hair dryers sold by Continental Hair were produced by this firm, but the company remained substantially dependent on independent Japanese suppliers who could not sufficiently meet its demands for stepped-up production. Continental Hair, therefore, built a combination warehouse/manufacturing facility in Arizona in 1974 and moved its headquarters in 1975 from Brooklyn to a newly purchased assembly plant in Edison, New Jersey. Also in 1975, the company added personal care products to its line. The principal items were two shower massage units manufactured in Edison and marketed under the trade name "Waterfingers."

Public Company: 1972–85

Continental Hair made its first public offering of stock in 1972 to raise funds for working capital and expansion, but the majority of the shares remained in management hands. Net sales reached $24.7 million in 1975, and net income was $1.9 million. The company's name became Conair Corporation in 1976, when net sales reached $36.4 million and net income $2.2 million. The following year sales increased to $53 million and net income rose to $3.5 million.

In 1977 Conair's principal product line remained its electrical hair care products, headed by eight basic models of pistol-grip hair dryers plus variations of these models. It commanded the nation's largest overall share of this market. The Conair appliance line also included five models of curling irons, an air-styling hot comb, and an infrared standing model lamp sold exclusively to the professional market and used for hair drying, permanents, and coloring. In the shower massage market, Waterfingers was second only to Teledyne's Water-Pik. These and other Conair hair-care and personal care products were being sold in thousands of stores. The company also was conducting hundreds of "seminars" a year to demonstrate its products to professional customers.

The company's growth, which had been averaging an annual 32 percent on equity, came to a screeching halt in 1978, when it lost $2.1 million on sharply reduced sales of $40 million. A 1977 strike at the Edison plant had set the target dates on some Conair products behind by six months to a year—a virtual lifetime in the hotly competitive market for personal care appliances. Because of the delay, the company's new "Pro Baby" yellow, curved, freestanding hair dryers were released hastily, untested; they proved to be costly flops. Waterfingers sales also dropped sharply. In addition, a new IBM database system proved so complex that it took a year and a half to become operational.

Conair was able to unload its huge unsold Pro Baby inventory by using its component parts for the Pistol Power 1200, which by mid-1979 had become the hottest compact dryer on the market. To make itself less dependent on hair dryers (which were accounting for 80 percent of Conair's sales), the company introduced an affordable espresso/cappuccino coffeemaker and two new lines of liquid hair products for retail distribution: Royal Persian Henna shampoos, conditioners, and sprays; and "nucleic" hair-care products, so called because they contained nucleic acids, which were thought to benefit hair. Sal DiMascio, an experienced corporate controller, was hired as chief financial officer to impose more sophisticated financial controls and procedures. The manufacturing of appliances was shifted from Edison to Hong Kong and Taiwan.

The most lasting consequence of the Pro Baby debacle was Conair's decision to shift its emphasis from hard goods to toiletries, specifically to the Jheri Redding line of liquid hair-care products. Originally geared to the professional market, this line was renamed "Milk 'n Honee" for 1981 retail distribution. Bottles that sold for $3.50 to hairdressers were doubled in size and sold for $1.99, yet Conair still made money, partly because of economies of scale, partly because the salons had been selling these products to their customers for an exorbitant profit. By 1982 some 70 percent of company sales (85 percent by 1983) were being made directly by Conair through its own sales force and representatives, instead of 70 percent by distributors.

Conair's sales rose to $50.8 million in 1979, $64.7 million in 1980, and $87 million in 1981, and net income was $1.25 million, $2 million, and $3.1 million, respectively. In late 1982 the company held 30 percent of market share in hair dryers, almost twice that of its nearest competitor. This business accounted for 40 percent of its 1981 sales. Other personal care appliance lines, including curling irons and brushes, hairsetters, lighted makeup mirrors, and muscle relaxers, accounted for 45 percent. "Milk 'n Honee" products accounted for about 10 percent of company sales in its first year of distribution. The company's short-term debt of $10.6 million was liquidated completely in 1981, and long-term debt as a percentage of total capitalization was a modest 16 percent in late 1982.

Conair entered consumer electronics in 1983, when it began selling a line of telephones under the Conair Phone brand name. The new consumer electronics division's other products included telephone answering devices and cordless telephones.

1985 Leveraged Buyout

In June 1985 Conair arranged what was called the first leveraged buyout to be financed through the public sale of debt securities (in this case junk bonds), rather than a privately arranged bank loan. The financing called for Rizzuto to sell $190 million of debt securities through a new company that he wholly owned, Conair Acquisitions Corp., which then merged into Conair Corporation. Proceeds of the debt sale were used to buy $169 million of common stock from Conair shareholders.

The buyout was a windfall for Rizzuto, who had owned 40 percent of Conair's stock and emerged with $25 million in cash as well as complete ownership of the new, private Conair and a ten-year employment contract as chairman and president at $750,000 per year, not counting bonuses. Conair's shareholders also were well rewarded, receiving the highest price level in the company's history for their stock. An investor putting $8,750 into Conair's initial public offering of stock in 1972 would receive almost $300,000 before taxes. The new Conair's debt consisted of $80 million in zero coupon financing, with no cash payments required before 1990, and $110 million in interest-bearing debentures, due near the year 2000.

Private Company: 1985–95

Conair moved its headquarters to Stamford, Connecticut, and entered the kitchen appliance field, a market five times the size of personal care, in 1986. Launching a line called Conair Cuisine for delivery in 1987, the company introduced a downsized food processor, a countertop can opener, a five-speed hand mixer, and a two-slice toaster. The Conair Cuisine line, in late 1988, also included an automatic drip coffeemaker, microwave oven, shake and beverage maker, and three battery-powered gadgets. An Ultra line of more deluxe items also had been added, including an electric juicer, cordless can opener, programmable coffeemaker with automatic shutoff, and microwave oven that also baked, broiled, and toasted.

Conair's net sales rose from $235.4 million in 1986 to $256 million in 1987 and $282.2 million in 1988. Net income increased from $628,000 in 1986 to $6.3 million in 1987 and $118.4 million in 1988. The latter figure reflected the sale of the hair-care products division, a wholly owned subsidiary named Zotos International, Inc., to Japan's Shoseido Co. for more than $329 million. Conair had bought Zotos in 1983 for $71 million. In 1988 Conair had manufacturing facilities in Taiwan and Hong Kong and warehouses in Phoenix and East Windsor, New Jersey. The following year it also began to produce toiletry products in Rantoul, Illinois, and appliances in Costa Rica. Conair's long-term debt fell from $272.5 million at the end of 1987 to $145.6 million at the end of 1988 as the company used proceeds of the Zotos sale to pay off zero coupon notes.

Rizzuto had sought to buy Cuisinart Inc., manufacturers of the first food processor for home use in the United States, in 1986. After the company filed for bankruptcy in 1989, following a botched leveraged buyout, Conair paid about $17.7 million for the trademarks, patents, and assets of the $40- to $50-million-a-year company. It was not responsible for Cuisinart's debts, which eventually were settled for less than 50 cents on the dollar. In 1995 the Cuisinart product line included food processors, stainless steel cookware, accessories, and other kitchen appliances, such as pasta makers, hand mixers, chopper/grinders, toasters, blenders, and coffeemakers.

At the National Houseware Manufacturers Association's show in January 1990, Conair introduced, in the personal care segment of its business, three high-fashion hairstyling products for the home, two compact products for easy storage and travel, and a facial sauna. In the kitchen appliance segment, it introduced products with the Cuisinart label on them in two new categories: espresso makers and microwave ovens. Another

new Cuisinart product was a juice extractor/juicer. Contrary to speculation, the Cuisinart cookware line was retained. Conair also announced plans to enter a joint venture in Japan to market the Cuisinart line.

Conair's reputation for quality was underlined by *Discount Store News* surveys in 1989, 1990, and 1991 that found the company, in the opinion of both shoppers and store managers, to be tops in the field of personal care appliances. Twenty-three percent of discount shoppers rated Conair a preferred brand in 1991, compared with 14 percent for the runner-ups, Norelco, Clairol, and Vidal Sassoon. In 1994 Conair was still tops in this field among discount shoppers.

In 1995 Conair acquired Babyliss, S.A., a manufacturer and marketer of personal care appliances, principally in Western Europe, for about $38 million. During the early 1990s it signed long-term licensing and distribution agreements giving it exclusive rights to market telephones under the Southwestern Bell name and personal care products in Western Europe and Mexico under the Revlon name and in the Asia Pacific region under the Vidal Sassoon name.

Conair's net sales rose from $361.8 million in 1992 to $442.6 million in 1993 and $524.4 million in 1994. Net income rose from $1.2 million to $12 million and $20.5 million in these years, respectively. Of 1994 sales, personal care appliances accounted for 43 percent, consumer electronics for 29 percent, toiletries and professional salon products for 17 percent, and Cuisinart products for 11 percent. More than 5 percent of sales was international. The company's long-term debt was $100.4 million at the end of 1994.

At that time Conair entered the United Kingdom when it began selling hair-care items under the Revlon name. The company turned its sights to further expansion in Europe throughout the 1990s by buying the French personal care appliance company Babyliss SA in 1995.

Babyliss was the inventor of the first electric hair curling iron and topped the charts as the leading French manufacturer of personal care appliances. In addition to curling irons the company produced waxers, and facial saunas that were sold throughout the European market. Before acquiring Babyliss, Conair sales were approximately $500 million. With the addition of the French company sales for Conair rose to more than $650 million.

In 1996, Conair competitor Braun brought suit against Conair for patent infringement over a volumizing hair dryer attachment. Conair settled the suit and agreed to stop selling the attachment. This was the first of several patent infringement lawsuits that would plague the company over the next ten years.

The company continued to closely monitor consumer spending trends on personal care appliances and to develop products that followed shopper's interests. Throughout the late 1990s a trend for personal spa related items was growing and Conair introduced many new products that brought a spa-like experience into the home.

Conair developed a line of massagers that included a chair cushion massager in 1996, and a foot massager based on the

Japanese shiatsu method of pressure point massage, aptly named the Sole Doctor.

The company also produced a hand held type of shiatsu massager named the spin doctor, and a super reach massager, the Twist and Tone and the Infra Touch Plus Massager, for arthritic consumers.

By October 1996 the Cuisinart division of the Conair Corporation reported solid and growing sales. Cuisinart was responsible for approximately $100 million of the company's sales figures. Cuisinart had captured 70 percent of the small home electronics market.

Cuisinart helped sustain its higher end product reputation among gourmands by sponsoring the popular televised cooking show *The Cooking Secrets of the CIA*. The CIA referred to was the prestigious Cooking Institute of America.

Conair looked to an increasingly lucrative dental goods market in the latter part of 1996. At the time, 14 percent of all U.S. households were using power toothbrushes. That left 96 percent of the market share open to new buyers.

The end of the 1990s brought a string of consolidations in the housewares industry. Conair as one of the largest competitors joined in by buying Bausch & Lomb's oral care division. Interplak was its signature product and Conair capitalized on the Interplak name and introduced a series of new products. The company launched three new oral care appliances for the summer of 1998. The company planned further product development for its fourth quarter that year when it brought out its own fluoride toothpaste and antiseptic dental rinse.

In 1999 Conair continued to grow its personal spa equipment line by selling a runner bath mat that imitated a Jacuzzi action in an ordinary bath tub. The trend to develop goods that were therapeutic in nature was an attempt by the company to address the perceived needs of the aging baby boomer population, a demographic that retailers were eager to target.

In March 1999 Conair's Cuisinart division signed a licensing deal with kitchenware company Ekco to make higher end kitchen tools under the Cuisinart name. The kitchen tools were sold at department stores and select kitchen retailers.

In May 2000, Conair CEO Leandro Rizzuto and Arthur Taylor, head of Conair's importing and international shipping work, were charged in a $4 million tax fraud conspiracy. The alleged scheme for which they were subsequently indicted and convicted, involved overcharging on shipments from Hong Kong and then receiving kickbacks that were funneled into Swiss bank accounts.

There was further bad news for the company in November 2000. The Schawbel Corporation filed suit against Conair claiming it violated its patented Thermacell technology, a technology used for cordless hair curlers. Conair settled the suit and ceased manufacturing using a Thermacell type cartridge. The company eventually bought the Schawbel hair-care business in March 2003 and began producing cordless curlers.

While corporate wrongdoings hampered the company throughout the decade sales continued to grow and Conair

reached the billion dollar threshold in December 2000. It now had an array of recognized brands that were leading the industry, among them Cuisinart, Waring, Interplak, Rusk, ConairPro, Jheri Redding, Conair Shine, Forfex, BaByliss, Southwestern Bell Freedom Phone, and Conairphone.

In January 2002 Holmes sold the brand Pollenex and its water related showerheads, and massagers to Conair for an undisclosed amount of money.

The company continued its expansion in March 2004, buying Measurement Specialties Inc.'s Thinner brand bath-scales. Conair produced scales and body-fat monitors under the Thinner brand name.

Conair's patent infringement history took a turn for the better in April 2004 when on appeal, the company's $46 million judgment, resulting from a lawsuit brought by Dr. Harry Gaus, a German engineer, was reversed. Dr. Gaus attempted to further appeal the ruling by turning to the U.S. Supreme Court in August 2004, but Gaus's petition to the court was turned down.

In July 2004 Conair changed its distribution channels by opening a center in Southhaven, Mississippi. The facility was within the borders of a Foreign Trade Zone that operated outside the jurisdiction of U.S. Customs. The site was chosen in part to offset the cost of paying custom fees when shipping internationally.

The company continued to seek out consumer trends and produce products in anticipation of new markets into the mid-2000s with an emphasis on an aging baby boomer population and the needs it might perceive.

Principal Subsidiaries

Babyliss S.A. (France); Conair Consumer Products, Inc. (Canada); Conair Costa Rica, S.A. (Costa Rica); Conair UK, Ltd.; Continental Conair Ltd. (Hong Kong); Continental Products, S.A. (France; 50%); Cristal Gesellschaft fur Beteiligungen und Finanzierugen, S.A. (Switzerland); Cuisinart-Sanyei Co., Ltd. (Japan; 50%); HERC Consumer Products, LLC (50%); Rusk, Inc. (50%).

Principal Competitors

Braun GmbH; Helen of Troy Corporation; Rayovac Corporation.

Further Reading

"Acquiring to Thrive," *Business and Industry*, June 30, 1997, p. 19.

Belmont, David J., "Conair Stretching Its Line of Massagers," *Business and Industry,* August 5, 1996, p. 62.

Claffey, Mike, "Conair Head Charged in 4M Tax Fraud," *New York Daily News*, May 4, 2000, p. 42.

"Conair Buys into Europe," *Business and Industry*, January 30, 1995, p. 1.

"Cuisinart at 25: More in Store," *Business and Industry,* October, 14, 1996, p. 71.

Eckardt, Dorothy, "Conair Corporation," *Wall Street Transcript*, November 8, 1982, p. 67726.

Ellis, Beth R., "Conair's Commodity Savvy," *HFD,* November 16, 1987, pp. 141–43.

Gendron, Marie, ''Braun Settles Patent Suit Charging Rival Conair Corp.,'' *Boston Herald*, January 16, 1996, p. 23.

Gissen, Jay, ''Update Conair: 'Class to the Mass,' '' *Forbes*, February 1, 1982, p. 104.

Griffin, Marie, ''Conair Adds Novelty to Items in Kitchen Electrics Assortment,'' *HFD*, November 7, 1988, pp. 77, 80.

Mayer, Ted, ''Conair Corporation,'' *Wall Street Transcript*, April 11, 1977, pp. 46715-46716.

Monaghan, Jean, ''Electrical Hair Items Spur CONH's Growth,'' *Investment Dealers' Digest*, September 9, 1975, pp. 16–17.

''Power Seekers,'' *Business and Industry*, November 18, 1996, p. 53.

Purpura, Linda, ''Hair Trends Bring Versatility,'' *Business and Industry*, February 5, 1996, p. 64.

——, ''Smooth Sailing for Massagers,'' *Business and Industry*, March 18, 1996, p. 44.

Sample, Ann, ''Conair Unfolds Plan for the Millennium,'' *Business and Industry*, May 3, 1999, p. 32.

Smith, Geoffrey, ''You Don't Learn Anything from Success,'' *Forbes*, September 3, 1979, pp. 98 + .

Thau, Barbara, ''Ekco Housewares Licenses Cuisinart Name,'' *Business and Industry*, March 15, 1999, p. 46.

Trachtenberg, Jeffrey A., ''Make My Day,'' *Forbes*, July 29, 1985, p. 74.

—Robert Halasz
—update: Susan B. Culligan

Cranium, Inc.

2025 1st Avenue, Suite 600
Seattle, Washington 98121
U.S.A.
Telephone: (206) 652-9708
Fax: (206) 652-1483
Web site: http://www.playcranium.com

Private Company
Incorporated: 1998
Employees: 70
Sales: $40 million (2004 est.)
NAIC: 339932 Game, Toy, and Children's Vehicle
Manufacturing

Three-time winner of the Toy Industry Association's game of the year award, Cranium, Inc. creates board games designed to bring out the best in everyone. "Dedicated to restoring the brain to its rightful status as the body's most popular organ," the company has introduced a family of games, including Cranium, Cranium Turbo, Cadoo, Cariboo, Conga, Cosmo, Hoopla, Hullabaloo, Balloon Lagoon, and Zigity. The games are sold primarily in bookstores and Starbucks throughout the United States and in Target, Wizards of the Coast, and through Amazon.com. Cranium's games have won more than 50 industry awards and sell in 20 countries in ten languages.

1997–98: Developing a Game Allowing Everyone to Excel

Whit Alexander and Richard Tait met in the 1990s while working on the Encarta Encyclopedia at Microsoft and discovered that they shared a passion for entrepreneurship. In early 1997, Alexander, a native of Tucson, left his job of five years as developer of systems used in Encarta and other software, "ready to try something else," but uncertain of what that would be. Tait, a native of Scotland, resigned his job as senior manager for Microsoft's Encarta and World Atlas three months later. He had been an employee of Microsoft for the past ten years. Unemployed, the two men began to meet regularly for breakfast at Seattle's Jitterbug restaurant and to discuss starting their own business.

Tait and Alexander first toyed with the idea of starting a dot-com company, but "[i]t was already-been-done-dot-com time," as Alexander recalled in a 2001 *Arizona Daily Star* article. Soon thereafter, during a vacation with his wife and friends in the Hamptons, Tait came up with the idea that evolved into Cranium. After Tait and his wife easily defeated the other couple at Pictionary and then lost miserably at Scrabble, he began to dream up a board game that would allow everyone to shine and to have a great time.

Tait took his idea to Alexander, who at first laughed at it, then came around. Together Tait and Alexander began work on the board game with the goal of getting it into stores by Christmas 1998. Their first step was to embark on research on intellectual aptitudes, including the studies of Harvard University educator and psychologist Howard Gardner, whose theories explain that people learn and perform through a variety of intelligences. According to Gardner, people who excel spatially and verbally may do well at the game of Scrabble, but will not necessarily stand out at Trivial Pursuit, which rewards a good memory. Alexander and Tait also consulted numerous books about indoor activities, such as parlor games, published before television became commonplace in American households in the 1950s. In so doing, "[w]e were able to get a much richer framework to base the game on than just the left brain/right brain idea," explained Alexander in the 2001 *Arizona Daily Star*.

The men spent $100,000 of their own money to build and test the prototype Cranium game from 1997 to 1998. In its finished form, the game had four or more players, who moved clockwise around a board to reach Cranium Central. The winner was the player who reached Cranium Central first. To get to their next stop along the way, teams performed activities that were described in four decks of cards called Word Worm, Data Head, Star Performer, and Creative Cat. Activities ranged from spelling backward or forward, to playing Hangman, to defining words, sketching or acting out a clue, drawing blindfolded, impersonating a celebrity, whistling a song, or answering a question about an arcane fact.

Tait and Alexander founded Cranium in 1998. Tait assumed the role of the company's Grand Poohbah. Alexander became Cranium's Chief Noodler. By spring, they had assembled an editorial board of eight to work on questions for the game cards. They also hired Foundation Design of Seattle and illustrator Gary Baseman to help them design the game board, the cards, and the players' pieces, and Chuckerman Packaging Ltd. of Illinois to produce, package, and ship the Cranium game boxes. At each step along the way, Alexander and Tait showed their prototype game to potential consumers and solicited their opinions, a technique they had learned as software developers at Microsoft.

1998–2000: Word-of-Mouth Marketing for a Hot New Start-Up

By summer 1998, the Cranium team was ready to market its game. But the company had missed the window of opportunity for selling games to the big distributors for winter distribution. Thus, instead of getting their game onto the shelves of stores, such as Toys ''R'' Us, Wal-Mart, and Kmart, Tait and Alexander approached Barnes & Noble, Starbucks, and Amazon.com. These sellers also offered the added advantage of reaching Cranium's target audience of educated, affluent, 25- to 35-year old yuppies directly. Tapping into their network of friends who worked in the senior ranks at Starbucks, Tait and Alexander arranged a meeting that included a few rounds of their new game with Howard Schultz, chief executive of Starbucks. Schultz agreed to sell the game in 1,500 Starbucks coffeehouses. Barnes & Noble put the game in 150 stores. Virgin stores also agreed to carry it after Tait gave a gift copy of Cranium to Virgin founder Richard Branson.

Knowing that they could not afford a large-scale, ad-based launch, the company next hired Wham Communications, a public relations shop. Borrowing heavily from tactics employed in the launch of Trivial Pursuit, Wham embarked on a massive media relations program for Cranium. It persuaded radio jocks at 110 stations nationwide to read Cranium questions out loud over the air and give the game away to those who called in with the right answer. Celebrities received gift copies of the game, and there were game-playing events at Starbucks. For each Cranium game sold, the company donated one dollar to groups that provided visual or performing arts education to at-risk youth.

''Dedicated to restoring the brain to its rightful status as the body's most popular organ,'' as the company's web site put it, Cranium took hold. It was Amazon's best-selling game for the 1998 Christmas season. In fact, as the season wore on, Tait and Alexander had to fill their cars with boxes of Cranium which they delivered personally to Starbucks outlets after the coffee retailer sold out of the board game. Within four months, the company had turned a profit. After seven months on the market, 100,000 Cranium games had sold. In response to overwhelming demand, Cranium Booster Box was released the following year. By 2000, Cranium had become the number one-selling game on Amazon.com. In late 2000, the U.K. edition of Cranium, specially developed with British language, and indigenous cultural, historical, and popular references, made its debut. It sold nearly 30,000 copies in its first six weeks.

2001–04: Adding to Its Family of Games

By early February 2001, Cranium had amassed $18 million in sales. In 2001, Cranium Booster Box 2, with additional questions and activities, and sold exclusively at Starbucks, appeared, and in September 2001, Cranium Cadoo for Kids and Cranium Cosmo, an office version of the game, hit the market. Awards began to pile up: the Oppenheim Toy Portfolio's Platinum ''Best Toy Award'' and the Toy Industry Association's ''Game of the Year'' in 2002. Parents' Choice, the oldest nonprofit consumer guide in the United States, which reserves its seal of approval for products that meet or exceed standards set by educators, scientists, performing artists, librarians, parents, and kids gave Cadoo its Gold Award for helping kids to grow imaginatively, physically, morally, and mentally and for being fun, safe, and socially sound.

By early 2002, one million copies of Cranium had been sold, and the game had become the toy industry's first bona fide smash hit since Pictionary in 1985 and one of the best selling games for that year—the lone newcomer among the other bestsellers that included Trivial Pursuit, Monopoly, Scrabble, Life, and Ticket to Ride. In response to Cranium's success in Canada, two new editions, the Canadian edition in English and the Édition Québécoise, had been launched in Canada in 2001. These foreign editions were joined in 2002 by the German and Australian editions. In each case, the activities, questions, and references on cards were chosen specifically to suit the language and culture of the targeted nation.

Hoopla, a charade-based game that involved sketching, acting, or craft-making during a timed interval, was the company's new addition in 2003. Zigity debuted at Starbucks in 2004. By then, the total number of Cranium games sold worldwide had reached 2.5 million. Growth continued throughout 2004, with a 32 percent increase in unit sales despite the fact that the toy industry was down 34 percent that year. Between 2002 and 2004, the company had expanded into more than 18 international markets, and growth in its family of games had increased 60 percent overall. In 2003, Cranium had been named "Game of the Year" in Britain, Finland, and Denmark. It continued to be named "Game of the Year" in the United States in both 2003 and 2004.

Cranium also embarked on seven new promotional partnerships in 2003 and 2004 with Columbia Crest, Delta Song, KFC, Land O'Lakes, Pizza Hut, Dr. Pepper, and Regal Cinemas. The goal of the company that had already sold more than seven million games was to "reach consumers where they live, work and play, and not just where they shop," according to its spokeswoman in an October 2004 *Money* magazine. The company also partnered with Mobliss, a leading provider of mobile media and marketing services with more than 150 million registered wireless subscribers, to bring Cranium to mobile users.

Principal Competitors

Educational Insights, Inc.; Fundex Games, Ltd.; Hasbro, Inc.; Mattel, Inc.; Pressman Toy Corporation; Wizards of the Coast, Inc.; Zindart Limited.

Further Reading

Banchero, Paola, "Microsoft Dropouts' Brainchild Becomes Nation's Top-Selling Board Game," *Arizona Daily Star*, December 23, 2001.

Bhatnagar, Panja, "Price Wars in Toyland: Part 2," *CNNMoney.com*.

Bick, Julie, "Inside the Smartest Little Company in America," *Inc.*, January 2002, p. 54.

Broom, Jack, "Brain Trust: Local Inventors Bring an Array of Cerebral Elements to Hit Game Company," *Seattle Times*, August 30, 1999, p. E1.

Erb, George, "Brain Power: Cranium Inc.'s Founders Put Their Heads Together to Invent a Board Game That Requires Mental Dexterity," *Puget Sound Business Journal*, March 5, 1999, p. 11.

McNally, Shana, "Playing with Your Head: Former Microsoft Employees Develop a Breakthrough Game That's Headed for the Top," *Columbian*, November 26, 1999, p. C1.

—Carrie Rothburd

Cytyc Corporation

250 Campus Drive
Marlborough, Massachusetts 01752
U.S.A.
Telephone: (508) 263-2900
Toll Free: (800) 442-9892
Fax: (508) 635-1033
Web site: http://www.cytyc.com

Public Company
Incorporated: 1987
Employees: 723
Sales: $393.6 million (2004)
Stock Exchanges: NASDAQ
Ticker Symbol: CYTC
NAIC: 325413 In-Vitro Diagnostic Substance
    Manufacturing; 334516 Analytical Laboratory
    Instrument Manufacturing; 339112 Surgical &
    Medical Instrument Manufacturing

Cytyc Corporation designs, develops, manufactures, and markets innovative products that focus primarily on women's health applications, including cervical cancer screening, breast cancer risk assessment, and treatment of excessive menstrual bleeding. The company developed the ThinPrep System, an automated method for preparing microscope slides of cell specimens, which has become the most widely used method for cervical cancer screening in the United States. ThinPrep, which also relies on computer imaging technology to examine slides, can be used to perform cancer analysis on tissues from the breast, liver, lung, thyroid, and other organs.

1987 to Early 1990s:
Developing Better Screening for Cervical Cancer

Entrepreneur Stanley Lapidus founded Cytyc in 1987 to develop an improved alternative to the conventional Pap smear. The original Pap test, which was developed by Dr. George Papanicolaou in the late 1940s, could detect cervical cancer in its earliest stages and thus led to a 70 percent decrease in mortality from cervical cancer following its recommended adoption as an annual test for women by gynecologists. In fact, physicians credit the test with virtually eliminating death from cervical cancer among women who are screened yearly. Cervical cancer, when detected early, can be treated effectively and inexpensively.

In the classic Pap test, a doctor uses a swab to collect cervical cells and smears them onto a glass microscope slide for examination by a technician. This method invariably stacks cells one on top of the other. As a result, the traditional Pap test delivers a substantial number of inconclusive results and false negatives—in part because a technician who views scores of slides a day inspects each slide individually and in part because that technician has to hunt for as few as ten abnormal cells among the thousands in the smear. "The conventional test is like looking at a coin on the bottom of a swimming pool and trying to determine whether it's a nickel or a quarter or a dime," explained one doctor in a 1997 *Modern Healthcare* article.

Cytyc's alternative system aimed to reduce the Pap test's margin of error by introducing computer image analysis of Pap smear slides. However, the poor quality of Pap smear slides made computer imaging impossible; so, Cytyc's staff focused instead on developing a better way to prepare slides. The resulting ThinPrep technology puts the cervical cell sample that the doctor collects in liquid suspension. This solution is filtered in the lab, and a thin film of the sample is applied to a glass microscope slide. The technique results in a slide specimen that is one-cell layer thick and free of debris.

In 1990, Cytyc raised $8 million through a round of venture capital financing that it used to expand clinical trials of its technology at New England Medical Center, Brigham and Women's Hospital, and Salem Hospital, among others. It began marketing its ThinPrep Processor to cytology labs across the United States for use in examining non-gynecological cell samples in 1991. At the time, many other small companies were also banking on new medical technologies. Cytyc's product looked promising, but it had yet to receive Food and Drug Administration (FDA) approval, and insurers and doctors alike questioned its purported advances over the traditional Pap smear.

Company Perspectives:

We place significant emphasis on providing quality products and services to our customers. A major portion of our quality systems relate to the design and development, manufacturing, packaging, sterilization, handling, distribution and labeling of our products. These quality systems, including control procedures that are developed and implemented by technically trained professionals, result in rigid specifications for products design, raw materials, components, packaging materials, labels, sterilization procedures and overall manufacturing process control.

1994–2000: Increased Acceptance Among Healthcare Executives and Payers

In 1994, the year in which Patrick J. Sullivan became president and chief executive of Cytyc, the Food and Drug Administration granted its approval to market the ThinPrep System for cervical cancer screening. Later that same year, the FDA allowed Cytyc to label its product with the claim that it was "significantly more effective" in detecting low-grade and more severe cancer lesions than the conventional Pap in a variety of patient populations. United HealthCare Corporation, a Minneapolis-based managed-care company, began reimbursing for the ThinPrep test in November.

Cytyc completed trials of the ThinPrep System for gynecological testing in 1995. These tests proved the ThinPrep System to be five times more accurate than humans, lowering the need for repeat tests and more costly clinical examination. However, the cost of a conventional Pap smear ranged from $20 to $40, while the ThinPrep test cost about $60. More than 50 million women underwent Pap smears annually in the United States in the second half of the 1990s, and healthcare executives and payers remained unconvinced that Cytyc's new technology was worth the additional cost.

In 1996, Cytyc held an initial public offering of three million shares and used the proceeds from the sale to expand its marketing and sales efforts, to increase manufacturing capacity, and to fund additional research and development. Digene Corp., maker of gene-based medical tests that focused primarily on women's cancers and infectious diseases, asked for FDA approval in 1996 to test for the human papilloma virus—the virus that causes nearly all cervical cancer—using the residual solution left over from ThinPrep. Still Cytyc had yet to turn a profit, losing $11.9 million on revenues of $8.2 million in 1996.

Cytyc began a full-scale commercial launch of the ThinPrep System for cervical cancer screening in 1997. Early that year, Laboratory Corporation became the first national laboratory to offer the ThinPrep test to its physician clients. By mid-year, more than 400 laboratories used the ThinPrep System, and, by late 1997, about 500 systems were installed in labs worldwide. Also in 1997, Mead Johnson & Co., a division of Bristol-Myers Squibb, agreed to promote the ThinPrep test through its nationwide sales force. The company set up a subsidiary in Switzerland to launch the ThinPrep system in Europe.

Then, in 1998, the health insurance trade association delivered a blow to Cytyc's growth, issuing a report that questioned the benefits of ThinPrep's technology. In addition, a new insurance reimbursement code for the test which led to delay in payments to labs contributed to slowing demand for the test. By late 1998, only about 12 percent of the insurance companies in the United States were willing to pay for the ThinPrep pap test.

The situation began to reverse in 1999, when Aetna agreed to cover ThinPrep tests after independent studies showed it was better than the standard Pap exam in detecting cervical cancer. Aetna's decision increased Cytyc's market share from somewhere around 15 percent of the more than 50 million Pap tests performed annually in the United States to 19 or 20 percent. In a horizontal move, the company acquired Acu-pak, Inc., a contract packager specializing in the liquid reagent filling used in collecting ThinPrep samples in 2000.

2000–04: A Steadily Increasing Percentage of the Worldwide Market for Pap Tests

The year 2000 proved to be a watershed year for Cytyc. The company signed a renewed agreement with Quest Diagnostics, the nation's leading diagnostic testing company, which processed up to 40 million or 80 percent of the Pap tests performed each year in the United States. Also in 2000, the United Kingdom National Institute for Clinical Excellence recommended initiating a pilot implementation program for liquid-based cytology in its country. Cytyc's share of the domestic market for cervical cancer screening increased to 25 percent by midyear and reached 36 percent by year's end. More than 100 companies joined the ranks of insurers to cover the test throughout 2000. Revenues increased accordingly, from $81 million in 1999 to a little more than $140 million in 2000. In another boon for the company, Roche Diagnostics signed an agreement with Cytyc to couple ThinPrep cervical cancer testing with Roche's test for chlamydia.

By the end of 2001, ThinPrep had 57 percent of the domestic market for Pap tests and revenue had increased to $221 million. Digene Corp. and Cytyc agreed to promote each other's product in the United States, selling the medical community on the advantages of testing for human papilloma virus directly from the ThinPrep Pap test collection vial. In a move to expand its presence in the women's healthcare and cancer diagnostics markets, Cytyc, named to Deloitte & Touche's elite "Fast 50" high-tech growth list, started a venture capital firm, Cytyc Healthcare Ventures. The company's first acquisition along these lines was Pro-Duct Health, Inc., a company that developed a ductal lavage device that evaluated a woman's risk of breast cancer by detecting atypical cells lining her milk ducts. Cytyc began to market the test under the name FirstCyte.

In 2002, after Blue Cross Blue Shield agreed to cover ductal lavage and the FDA approved using combining Roche's tests for gonorrhea and chlamydia with ThinPrep's Pap test, Cytyc's revenue reached around $240 million. Cytyc began plans to acquire Digene Corp., a move that would bring with it tests for papilloma virus, chlamydia, gonorrhea, and blood viruses. However, federal regulators blocked the proposed merger on the grounds that it would eliminate competition, since Cytyc by then controlled 93 percent of the market for liquid Pap tests and 55 percent of the

Key Dates:

1987: Stanley Lapidus founds Cytyc.

1994: Patrick Sullivan becomes president and chief executive officer of Cytyc; the Food and Drug Administration (FDA) gives its approval to Cytyc to market its pap test.

1996: The FDA approves the ThinPrep Pap System as a replacement for the conventional Pap smear.

1997: The company enters into an agreement with Mead Johnson to co-promote the ThinPrep System across the United States; begins marketing its product in Europe.

1998: DIANON Systems begins to market ThinPrep to its client base of more than 50,000 physicians nationwide.

2000: The company acquires Acu-Pak, Inc.

2001: The company acquires Pro Duct Health, Inc.

2002: Plans to buy Digene are scuttled by the FDA.

2003: The FDA gives its approval to Cytyc's computer imaging system for ThinPrep slides.

2004: Cytyc moves its corporate headquarters to Marlborough, Massachusetts.

market for cervical cancer testing. Between 2000 and 2002, Cytyc's sales had grown on average 65 percent per year while profits increased an average of 50 percent per year.

The year 2003 proved to be a mixed one for the company. On the positive side, Cytyc won a five-year contract to supply cervical screening tests for all screening centers in Scotland and signed an agreement with Nastech Pharmaceutical Company to acquire worldwide patent rights to products that make use of Nastech's FDA-approved Mammary Aspirate Specimen Cytology Test, a test that draws nipple aspirate fluid from the breast. However, the company's main competitor, TriPath Imaging, whose liquid-based Pap tests cost $2 to $3 less than Cytyc's, won a contract to supply Quest Diagnostics with cervical screening tests. TriPath also gained FDA approval to say its liquid Pap test more accurately detected signs of cervical cancer than the traditional Pap smear.

Cytyc, which ranked eighth in the *Boston Globe's* Globe 100 in 2004, spent much of the year vigorously marketing its new computerized imaging system, which the Food and Drug Administration had approved in 2003. By mid-year, it had provided equipment at no charge to 51 laboratories, each of which tested on average 50,000 per year and would now rely on ThinPrep slides. The company also joined with the University of Massachusetts Medical School to fund research to develop a test to predict whether precancerous cells will progress to become aggressive cancer. By year's end, ThinPrep accounted for about 37 million Pap tests a year, about 70 percent of the U.S. market. Tripath, Cytyc's closest competitor and the only other company to market a product similar to the ThinPrep, controlled only 10 to 12 percent of the market.

Several 2004 agreements with laboratories promised to help maintain Cytyc's number one market position: LabOne, the largest volume, single-site testing laboratory in the United States, and LabCorp both adopted the ThinPrep Imaging System. The Department of Defense awarded Cytyc a sole source contract as the platform for cervical cancer screening at armed forces screening centers worldwide. In addition, the London Region of the National Health Service and the Strategic Health Authority of the United Kingdom announced their intention to convert all cervical screening between 2004 and 2009 to the ThinPrep test.

However, the company began to look to other products to keep its competitive edge in the face of price erosions. In 2004, Cytyc increased its presence in the women's healthcare field by purchasing Novacept, the company that marketed NovaSure, a device that performed uterine ablation to treat excessive menstrual bleeding. It also invested in Valeo Medical, a private company focused on developing a serum-based test for endometriosis. Late in 2004, Cytyc moved its headquarters to Marlborough, Massachusetts, in order to expand its facilities. The company continued with plans to offer a ThinPrep breast test to scan for breast cancer.

Principal Subsidiaries

Cruiser, Inc.; Cytyc (Australia) PTY LTD; Cytyc Canada, Limited; Cytyc Europe, S.A.; Cytyc S.a.r.l. (France); Cytyc Germany GmbH; Cytyc Health Corporation; Cytyc Healthcare Ventures, LLC; Cytyc Iberia S.L. (Spain); Cytyc Interim, Inc.; Cytyc International, Inc.; Cytyc Limited Liability Company; Cytyc Limited Partnership; Cytyc Securities Corporation; Cytyc (UK) Limited, Novacept, Inc.

Principal Competitors

ChromaVision Medical Systems, Inc.; Digene Corporation; Hemagen Diagnostics, Inc.; Molecular Diagnostics; Neoprobe Corporation; TriPath Imaging, Inc.

Further Reading

Aoki, Naomi, "Prevailing in a Test of Patience Cytyc Finally Finding Acceptance for Pap Smear Alternative," *Boston Globe*, April 6, 2001, p. D1.

Cooney, Elizabeth, "Predictive Cancer Test Pursued; UMass, Cytyc Reach Licensing Agreement," *Telegram & Gazette (Massachusetts)*, September 10, 2004, p. E1.

Day, Kathleen, "Build a Better Cancer Trap, But Will Anyone Buy It?; Lab in Laurel Offers Improved Pap Smear, But Costlier Test Is Out of Reach for Some," *Washington Post*, June 9, 1997, p. 5.

Hensley, Scott, "Technology: Improving the Benchmark: Makers of a Better, More Costly Pap Test Face a Tough Sell," *Modern Healthcare*, May 12, 1997, p. 52.

Kirchofer, Tom, "Cytyc Likes 2002 Look—Medical Tests Are Paying Off," *Boston Herald*, April 25, 2002, p. H7.

Miller-Medzon, Karyn, "New Test Gets Clear Results," *Boston Herald*, October 3, 1999, p. 57.

Stuart, Scott, "Blindsided Badly," *Corporate Control Alert*, September 28, 2002.

—Carrie Rothburd

 DePfa Group

DEPFA BANK PLC

International House, 3 Harbourma
Dublin
Ireland
Telephone: +353 1 607 1600
Fax: +353 1 829 0213
Web site: http://www.depfa.com

Public Company
Incorporated: 1922 as Preussische Landespfandbriefanstalt
Employees: 319
Total Assets: $218.36 billion (2003)
Stock Exchanges: Pink Sheets Frankfurt
Ticker Symbols: DPFHF; DEPF
NAIC: 522110 Commercial Banking

DEPFA BANK PLC (Depfa) is one of the world's leading public sector financing banks. Depfa is the result of the 2002 breakup of the former Deutsche Pfandbriefanstalt, owned by the German state, into its two primary operating sectors, public sector finance and property finance—the latter business, focused on the German market, was renamed Aareal. Following the split Depfa refocused its operation—including its registration and headquarters—to the International Financial Services Centre in tax-friendly Dublin, Ireland. The move also has permitted Depfa to shift its operations away from its core Pfandbriefe (Germany's asset-covered securities, or ACS) market to become a heavyweight in the international ACS market. As such, Depfa provides a range of financial products for the public sector, including financing for infrastructure projects, budget financing, and government investment banking needs. Depfa's embrace of the international market has enabled the company to reduce its reliance on the German market. Indeed, the company's primary market is now the United Kingdom, at 45 percent of revenues; Europe continues to generate 70 percent of the bank's business. Since the mid-2000s, Depfa has targeted the United States for growth and expects its U.S. operations to reach the size of its European business before the end of the decade. Depfa is also active in Japan and Hong Kong. The bank operates branches in Paris, Rome, Tokyo, and London, and representative offices in Madrid, Copenhagen, New York, Chicago, and San Francisco. In 2004 the bank's total assets reached more than $218 billion.

Prussia's Mortgage Credit Institution in the 1920s

The German "Pfandbriefe" represented the earliest example of covered bonds—that is, bonds backed by long-term assets as collateral—in Europe. Invented in the late 18th century, the Pfandbriefe were traditionally used in two ways: on the one hand, for funding property development by securing loans with mortgages, and on the other, for financing loans to the public sector. Used in Prussia and the Austria-Hamburg empire and into present-day Germany, the Pfandbriefe were traditionally small loans confined within the domestic market. The arrival of so-called "Jumbo" Pfandbriefe, suitable for the international market and representing bonds valued at more than EUR 500 million, came only in 1995. The Pfandbriefe were especially popular with Germany's investments, especially prized for their relative safety. By the mid-2000s, the Pfandbriefe market had grown into one of the world's largest, representing some EUR 1.5 trillion in all.

The rise of the Pfandbriefe market, particularly after the passage of legislation in 1900 codifying their usage, encouraged the creation of generally state-owned bodies specializing in this financial product. The Pfandbriefe segment became particularly important in the early decades of the 20th century. The rapid rise of industrialized production techniques had in turn created a surge in the urban population, stimulating a need for new and affordable housing for the growing working class. The economic and political upheavals of the post-World War I era made the Pfandbriefe and their relative safety particularly attractive.

In Prussia, in the future East German states, the Prussian government moved to set up a dedicated body for producing Pfandbriefe. In 1922, the Prussian State Parliament passed legislation calling for the creation of a new bank dedicated to financing the region's residential property development needs. The Prussian ministries of Finance, Public Welfare, and Justice joined together to create a nonprofit credit institution invested with Pfandbriefe-issuing rights.

The Preussische Landespfandbriefanstalt, as the new body was called, opened its first office in Berlin in December 1922. Given the economic turmoil of the time, and the impossibility of fixing the value of the hyper-inflating Germany currency, the new bank started out by issuing Pfandbriefe backed by gold, rather than the crippled mark. Despite the difficulties of the era, the bank grew quickly, moving to new and larger headquarters in 1927. In that year, the bank began operating as a property developer as well. Despite the advent of the Great Depression, the Preussische Landespfandbriefanstalt emerged as one of Germany's largest Pfandbriefe banks.

The Nazi hostility to the Pfandbriefe market spelled an end to the bank's growth. By the outbreak of World War II, the Prussian body's operations had come, in large part, to a standstill. The bombing of Berlin toward the end of the war partly destroyed the Preussische Landespfandbriefanstalt's offices. The bank opened a temporary office near Munich, but returned to Berlin following the end of the war. Unable to return to its original offices, the bank opened a new office in West Berlin.

Yet with Germany under control of the Allied military authorities, the Preussische Landespfandbriefanstalt was restricted from operating. In addition, much of the bank's loan activities had been in eastern regions of Berlin and Germany, which were now under control of the Soviets. In this way, the bank lost control of more than half of its assets.

Postwar Growth

The bank now decided to leave Berlin, moving to Wiesbaden, in West Germany. After setting up its office there, the bank shut down its Berlin office. Yet the bank had to wait until 1949 before it received permission to resume operations, and the state-owned bank began accepting new business in 1950. By 1952, however, the bank had succeeded in settling into two buildings provided by the Wiesbaden municipal government.

In 1954, the bank's ownership was transferred to the West German federal government, and the bank now became a federal corporation under public law. The new ownership led to the bank's adopting a new name, Deutsche Pfandbriefanstalt, or Depfa. Under its new structure, Depfa operated on a mostly nonprofit basis, with a mandate to grant loans to the residential property market.

As a government-owned banking institution carrying out the government's housing policies, Depfa had remained a tax-free operation as well. This status was taken away in 1976, which allowed Depfa to begin developing a new for-profit business side. The bank now began lending to the commercial property development market, and also entered the fast-growing public sector market, starting with the provision of long-term budget funding bonds.

Depfa's expanding interests in the commercial property sector led it to acquire majority control of Deutsche Bau- und Bodenbank AG in 1979. That Frankfurt-based bank had been founded in 1923 as Deutsche Wohnstättenbank AG (adopting its new name in 1926), a nonprofit provider of loans to the residential building sector. After lying dormant through World War II, Deutsche Bau- und Boden began offering bridge loans for home mortgages in the 1950s, then added loan financing for large-scale construction projects in the 1960s.

At the end of the 1980s, the German government began deregulating and privatizing the country's banking sector ahead of the lowering of European trade barriers in the early 1990s and the creation of a single currency at the end of that decade. Depfa's turn came in 1989, when the bank's status was converted to that of a joint-stock company, renamed Deutsche Pfandbrief- und Hypothekenbank Aktiengesellschaft. The bank then began preparations for its public offering, which came in 1991, with a listing on the Frankfurt Stock Exchange. The privatization of Depfa was to prove a strong success—from an initial market capitalization of the equivalent of EUR 400 million, the company's value soared, reaching EUR 3 billion by the early 2000s.

International Finance Specialist in the 2000s

While the bulk of Depfa's business remained in the domestic German market through the 1990s, the bank began developing an interest in the international market as well. One of the group's first moves was to open an office in Ireland in 1993, where the Irish government had enacted special legislation, including low tax rates, in order to attract the international banking community.

Depfa's interests in the public sector financing market grew through the late 1990s, while it continued to pursue its property business. Yet the bank's growth in public sector finance was hampered by restrictions in Germany's legislation governing mortgage banks. In 1998, the company launched a restructuring in part to remedy this conflict. After renaming itself Depfa Deutsche Pfandbriefbank AG, the bank placed its entire property operations into its subsidiary Deutsche Bau- und Bodenbank AG, which was then renamed as Depfa Bank AG. At the same time, the company launched a second subsidiary, based in Dublin, called Depfa Investment Bank Ltd., which targeted the public sector financing markets in the former Soviet bloc countries, as well as the Southeast Asian market.

This move proved the first step toward a breakup of Depfa itself. At the end of 2001, Depfa split its operations into two separate and independent businesses, a process completed only in 2002. The bank spun off its Depfa Bank property operations as a new, Germany-based company, Aareal Bank. The remaining Depfa, now composed of its public sector financing arm, then transferred its headquarters and registration to Dublin, Ireland, changing its name to Depfa Bank PLC. The bank retained its listing on the Frankfurt Stock Exchange, however.

Depfa now emerged as one of the world's leading specialist providers of public sector financing, with a full range of products and services. While its German operations, conducted through subsidiary DEPFA Deutsche Pfandbriefbank AG, re-

Key Dates:

1922: Preussische Landespfandbriefanstalt is founded by the Prussian government.

1923: Deutsche Wohnstättenbank Aktiengesellschaft is founded (renamed Deutsche Bau- und Bodenbank in 1926).

1949: Preussische Landespfandbriefanstalt reopens in Wiesbaden after losing half its loan portfolio following World War II.

1954: The bank is registered as a state-owned banking institution and it changes its name to Deutsche Pfandbriefanstalt (Depfa).

1976: The loss of its tax-free status enables Depfa to enter the commercial property market.

1979: Depfa acquires majority control in Deutsche Bau- und Boden.

1989: Depfa is privatized.

1991: Depfa is listed on the Frankfurt stock exchange.

1993: A representative office is opened in Dublin, Ireland.

1998: Subsidiary Depfa Investment Bank is launched in Dublin; the property business is restructured into Depfa Bank AG.

2002: Depfa hives off its property business (renamed as Aareal Bank) and transfers its public sector finance operations to Dublin, Ireland, as DEPFA BANK PLC.

2004: Operations are launched in the United States; a representative office is opened in Hong Kong as part of the expansion of business in the Asian region.

into the United States in 2004—with the expectation that its U.S. operation would equal its European business by the end of the decade. Depfa also stepped up its presence in the Asian market, where it already operated a branch in Tokyo, with the opening of a representative office in Tokyo. The new Depfa prepared to continue its history of banking success.

Principal Subsidiaries

DEPFA ACS BANK; DEPFA Capital Japan K.K.; DEPFA Deutsche Pfandbriefbank AG (Germany); DEPFA Investment Bank Ltd. (Cyprus); DEPFA UK Limited (U.K.); DEPFA-Finance N.V. (Netherlands).

Principal Competitors

Deutsche Bank AG; Dexia Group; IKB Deutsche Industriebank AG.

Further Reading

Chang, Helen, "Dublin-Based DEPFA Eyes U.S. Municipal Insurance Market," *Bond Buyer,* February 18, 2004, p. 4.

Day, Neil, "Bold Steps Are Rewarded," *Euroweek,* September 12, 2003, p. S38.

"Depfa Achieves 10 Year Success and 79% International Distribution with Eu3bn ACS," *Euroweek,* July 16, 2004.

"Depfa Reaches 100% Freefloat As Core Owners Sell Eur 1.3bn," *Euroweek,* November 7, 2003, p. 27.

"Depfa to Sell Pfandbriefbank As Base Shifts to Ireland," *Euroweek,* March 5, 2004, p. 5.

Fairlamb, David, "DEPFA: The Newcomer with Street Smarts," *Business Week,* April 14, 2003.

Hofer-Neder, Wally, "DEPFA As a Public Sector Refinancing Engine," *Euromoney,* September 2003.

"Hybrid Growth—The Split That Formed Depfa Bank Also Halved Its Capital Base," *Banker,* February 1, 2004.

"Plenty of Action at the EU's Edge," *Banker,* June 1, 2004.

—M.L. Cohen

mained strong, Depfa surprised the banking community in 2004 with its announcement that it intended to sell off that unit and focus its future growth on the global asset-covered securities (ACS) market. As part of this effort, the bank launched an entry

Developers Diversified Realty Corporation

3300 Enterprise Parkway
Beachwood, Ohio 44122
U.S.A.
Telephone: (216) 755-5500
Toll Free: (877) 225-5337
Fax: (216) 755-1500
Web site: http://www.ddrc.com

Public Company
Incorporated: 1992
Employees: 427
Sales: $602.9 million (2003)
Stock Exchanges: New York
Ticker Symbol: DDR
NAIC: 525930 Real Estate Investment Trusts

Developers Diversified Realty Corporation (DDR) is a real estate investment trust (REIT) based in Beachwood, Ohio. It primarily develops, acquires, leases, and owns open-air neighborhood shopping centers ranging in size from 250,000 square feet to one million square feet and featuring at least two major anchor tenants, such as national or regional supermarkets or big-box retailers Wal-Mart, Target, Home Depot, or Lowe's. To a lesser degree, the REIT also is involved in enclosed mini-malls, lifestyle centers, and business centers. DDR's portfolio consists of some 460 retail centers and 40 business centers for a total of more than 100 million square feet of real estate. DDR shares trade on the New York Stock Exchange.

Company Roots Dating to the Late 1950s

DDR grew out of the Developers Diversified group of companies founded by Bertram L. Wolstein. He was born during the 1920s in East Cleveland, the son of a cloth cutter who grew up under modest circumstances. When he was just 12 years old he went to work to help support his family. As a teenager he delivered newspapers, worked in a fruit market and drugstores, and was a concessionaire at Cleveland Indians baseball games. The United States was soon engaged in World War II and

Wolstein joined the Navy when he was just 16 years old. After being discharged he was at loose ends, uncertain what career to pursue. Taking advantage of the GI Bill, he studied accounting at Cleveland College of Western Reserve University. Then in 1953 he earned a law degree from Cleveland Marshall School of Law. He found legal work in the real estate field through an uncle and practiced law for a few years before deciding to become involved in property development. In 1959 he began building single-family homes, which were in great demand in the years after World War II when returning servicemen started families and fled to the country's new suburbs, including Wolstein's developments called Heritage and Heritage Hill. His first homes were priced at $17,000.

When the housing market collapsed, Wolstein in 1965 turned his attention to commercial real estate and the building of Kmart stores. His first Kmart was completed in Eastlake in 1967, and his new line of business took off. Wolstein was an old-school operator who relied on hunches as much as demographic studies. Known as a tough negotiator and difficult to work for, he was a man who prided himself on never asking someone to do something he would not do or had not already done. By the 1970s he was a wealthy real estate mogul and a Cleveland legend, at least in shopping center industry circles. In the late 1970s he bought the Cleveland Force professional indoor soccer team, which he ran successfully for a decade, and received far greater public recognition for his efforts than he had in real estate. He once told reporters, "I had been a successful developer for many years and all it got me was seven yawns."

Wolstein would be joined in his business ventures by his son, Scott Alan Wolstein, after he graduated from the University of Pennsylvania's Wharton School of Business in 1974 and earned a law degree from the University of Michigan in 1977, where he graduated cum laude. The Wolsteins expanded their real estate interests during the 1980s. By 1987 Developers Diversified owned shopping centers, mostly connected to Kmart stores, in 32 states, worth a total of $700 million. (At this stage the developer began switching over to Wal-Mart stores as the Kmart chain began to falter.) The company also spawned affiliates to become involved in residential, mixed-use, industrial, and hotel developments. But with the collapse of the real estate market in the early 1990s, Developers Diversified, like many real estate companies, found it difficult to fund new projects. After building ten shopping centers in 1990, the Wolsteins built just one in the next two years. Like a growing number of developers, they tapped into a new source of funding, the little-used REIT structure.

Development of the REIT Structure in the 1960s

REITs had been established by Congress in 1960 as a way for small investors to become involved in real estate in a manner similar to mutual funds. REITs could be taken public and their shares traded just like stock, and they were also subject to regulation by the Securities and Exchange Commission. Unlike other stocks, however, REITs were required by law to pay out at least 95 percent of their taxable income to shareholders each year, a provision that severely limited the ability of REITs to retain internally generated funds. During the first 25 years of existence, REITs were allowed to own real estate only, a situation that hindered their growth because third parties had to be contracted to manage the properties. Not until the Tax Reform Act of 1986 changed the nature of real estate investment did REITs begin to become truly viable. Limited partnership tax shelter schemes that had competed for potential investments were shut down by the Act: Interest and depreciation deductions were greatly reduced so that taxpayers could not generate paper losses in order to lower their tax liabilities. Separately, the Act also permitted REITs to provide customary services for property, in effect allowing the trusts to operate and manage the properties they owned. Despite these major changes in law, the REIT form was still not fully utilized. In the second half of the 1980s the banks, insurance companies, pension funds, and foreign investors (especially the Japanese) provided the lion's share of real estate investment funds. The resulting glutted marketplace led to a shakeout that hampered many real estate firms. With properties available at distressed prices in the early 1990s, REITs finally became an attractive mainstream investment option and many real estate firms, starting in 1993, now went public to become roll-up vehicles in different segments of the industry. Developers Diversified was one of a number of companies to take the plunge, electing to focus on its neighborhood shopping center portfolio.

In November 1992, Developers Diversified Realty Corporation was incorporated in Ohio. The new REIT then made an initial public offering (IPO) of shares, priced at $22 each, in February 1993, and on that same day they began trading on the New York Stock Exchange. The offering raised $176 million, which was then used to buy some 50 shopping centers owned by Developers Diversified Group. Almost all of them were anchored by the likes of Wal-Mart, Kmart, or a J.C Penney store, and 95 percent of their space was leased. Bert Wolstein served as chairman of the board and Scott Wolstein took over as CEO.

Their plan was to build the REIT through acquisitions, targeting shopping centers across the country that were new and well located, but lacked access to the financing the developers needed to pay off their expiring construction loans. There was no lack of candidates that fit this description, as DDR would begin the process of reviewing more than 200 shopping centers.

Within a matter of weeks of its IPO, DDR made its first acquisitions, paying $15.7 million to add a shopping center in Virginia and another in North Carolina. The REIT completed another 15 acquisitions in 1992, altogether spending about $150 million on acquisitions for the year. In 1993 the REIT posted revenues of $54.6 million and net income of $13.6 million. DDR continued to roll up shopping centers in 1994, adding another 14 properties at a cost of $183.1 million, thereby adding 3.2 million square feet of space. The company also was expanding some of its properties and engaged in development projects in Ohio and Pennsylvania. When 1994 came to a close, DDR saw its revenues improve to $82 million and net income to $21.1 million.

DDR enjoyed a solid 1995, acquiring another 20 properties. The major deal of the year was the $500 million purchase of the Homart Community Center Division of Sears Roebuck & Company. DDR picked up ten power centers plus 19 adjacent parcels of land. DDR spent another $81.6 million in 1995 to add ten shopping centers in South Carolina, Florida, Alabama, and Michigan. In addition, DDR completed expansion projects on 12 of its shopping centers and concluded a handful of development projects. As a result, the REIT finished the year with 19.3 million square feet of leasable space and revenues topped the $100 million mark, reaching $107.8 million. Net income for the year totaled $25.5 million.

DDR's expansion pace dropped off significantly in 1996. The REIT spent almost $100 million to acquire five shopping centers located in Arizona, Minnesota, Indiana, Texas, and Oregon. DDR continued to expand some properties and to develop projects in Canton and Aurora, Ohio, and also commenced development on three more shopping centers in Ohio and a fourth in Kansas. Also of note, in 1995 DDR completed a secondary stock offering, netting $75.4 million, used mostly to pay down debt. For the year, DDR posted revenues of nearly $131 million, while net income almost doubled the previous year's total, approaching $50 million.

In February 1997, 70-year-old Bert Wolstein decided to step down as DDR's chairman, turning over the title to his son. It was not a matter of retirement, more a dissatisfaction with the nature of running a public company, which he explained was "too structured, too bureaucratic" for his taste. As he told the *Cleveland Plain Dealer* at the time of his leaving, "In a public company, you can't buy land and put it on the shelf because every dollar you invest has to make a return. . . . I was a bit of a speculator. Finding the right piece of land at the right time at the right price has always been my forte." He also chafed at catering to shareholders and Wall Street analysts, once telling a reporter, "Working and meeting with analysts and having them tell you how to run a business they know nothing about didn't fit with my personality." Instead, to remain active in real estate, he formed Heritage Development Company to buy and develop golf courses. In 1998 he also attempted to return to professional sports, heading an investment group interested in landing a new

Key Dates:

1965: Bertram Wolstein begins building shopping centers.
1992: The company is incorporated as a real estate investment trust.
1993: An initial public offering of shares is made.
1997: Wolstein retires.
2002: JDN Realty Corp. is acquired.
2004: Benderson Development Company is acquired.

Cleveland National Football League franchise, but that attempt failed. In 2004 Wolstein died of a heart attack at the age of 77.

Scott Wolstein carried on with the travails of running a public company. In 1997 DDR expanded 13 of its properties and spent $281.6 million to acquire eight shopping centers in Arizona, Ohio, Minnesota, Maine, Colorado, Arkansas, and New Jersey. The company also arranged $800 million in financing for additional acquisitions in a joint venture with Prudential Real Estate Investors. Some of that money was put to use in 1998 when DDR acquired 41 properties. Of note was the purchase of the shopping center portfolio of the Sansone Group of St. Louis, Missouri, a deal that added 15 properties and strengthened DDR's position in the St. Louis market, where 13 of the properties were located. DDR also picked up Sansone shopping centers located in Cedar Rapids, Iowa, and Springfield, Missouri. Later in the year, DDR entered the Salt Lake City market by purchasing the nine-shopping center portfolio owned by Hermes Associates of Salt Lake City. Furthermore, in 1998 DDR made an investment in American Industrial Properties (AIP), a REIT that specialized in industrial properties, and DDR also transferred five light industrial properties it had picked up along the way to AIP.

Structural Changes in the Late 1990s

As DDR grew into a large operation, Scott Wolstein had to make some changes to run it effectively. He established a human resources department and hired someone to head it, and also brought in other executive talent. In addition, he formed an asset management group, with regional asset managers, to pay closer attention to each property in the portfolio, which at this point numbered 159 shopping centers. The task of monitoring the assets had simply grown beyond the capability of DDR's 11-member executive committee. Although the REIT completed just one acquisition in 1999, a 50 percent interest in a Phoenix shopping center, it spent another $46.6 million expanding 14 properties and completed construction on five shopping centers.

DDR entered the new century as a prosperous concern, yet the price of its stock was sluggish, primarily due to the unglamorous nature of strip shopping centers. Regardless, the REIT continued to grow on a number of fronts. In 2000 it was especially active in California, establishing a permanent office there in August, then a month later announced it was spending $355 million to acquire 15 West Coast properties from Burnham Pacific Properties, Inc. DDR expanded its holdings in the Southeast in 2002 by acquiring JDN Realty Corp., in a $1 billion transaction adding 81 properties in 19 states as well as projects under development by JDN. DDR completed an even larger acquisition in 2004, paying $1.5 billion plus the assumption of $800 million in debt for Benderson Development Company, a Florida-based firm with 110 shopping centers located in 11 states. Most of the properties, however, were in New Jersey and New York. The deal was of strategic importance because it greatly expanded DDR's limited presence in the New York market.

DDR's portfolio now exceeded 450 shopping centers located in 44 states. But the REIT also was looking beyond the United States for future growth. In November 2004 it made its first deal outside of the United States, agreeing to pay $1.15 billion to acquire 15 shopping centers in Puerto Rico from Caribbean Property Group. DDR also began looking at acquisition opportunities in Mexico and Canada, where many of its major tenants had stores and had plans for further expansion. Although some of the REIT's chief competitors also were interested in these emerging markets, there was every reason to expect DDR to land its fair share of properties and continue its steady growth.

Principal Subsidiaries

DDR Management L.L.C.; DDR Realty Company; JDN Development Company, Inc.

Principal Competitors

CBL & Associates Properties, Inc.; General Growth Properties, Inc.; New Plan Excel Realty Trust, Inc.

Further Reading

Bullard, Stan, "Baby REIT Embarks on Hunt for Properties," *Crain's Cleveland Business,* March 29, 1992, p. 3.
——, "DDR Turns an Eye to Mexico," *Crain's Cleveland Business,* November 15, 2004, p. 4.
——, "Diversified, Indeed! Wolstein Firm Travels New Avenues," *Crain's Cleveland Business,* June 8, 1987, p. 1.
Frango, Alex, "Cleveland REIT Plans to Purchase 110 Retail Centers," *Wall Street Journal,* April 1, 2001, p. B6.
Lubinger, Bill, " 'Aces Are in Their Places' for Real Estate Trust DDR," *Plain Dealer,* September 14, 1999, p. 1C.
——, "Departing on a Successful Note," *Plain Dealer,* February 26, 1997, p. 1C.
Lubinger, Bill, and Alana Baranick, "Bert Wolstein, Shopping Center Magnate, Dies at 77," *Plain Dealer,* May 18, 2004.

—Ed Dinger

DHL Worldwide Network S.A./N.V.

De Kleetlaan 1
B-1831 Diegem
Belgium
Telephone: (2) 713-4000
Fax: (2) 713-5000
Web site: http://www.dhl.com

Wholly Owned Subsidiary of Deutsche Post AG
Incorporated: 1969
Employees: 160,754
Sales: EUR 22.32 billion ($28.12 billion) (2003)
NAIC: 492110 Couriers; 488510 Freight Transportation
Arrangement; 541614 Process, Physical Distribution,
and Logistics Consulting Services

DHL Worldwide Network S.A./N.V., wholly owned by Deutsche Post AG (the German post office) since December 2002, is the world's leading cross-border express delivery service. Its global network encompasses over 4,000 offices and more than 120,000 destinations in more than 220 countries. DHL handles in excess of one billion shipments per year using more than 450 hubs, warehouses, and terminals and 75,000 vehicles. Within the United States, where the company began as an air-courier service from California to Hawaii, DHL has gained the number three position in express delivery, trailing only FedEx Corporation and United Parcel Service, Inc., since acquiring Airborne, Inc. in August 2003. The Airborne deal also provided DHL with a base for expanding its U.S. ground delivery operations. Under the Deutsche Post umbrella, DHL has additional operations in overland freight, air, and ocean transport, and logistics.

Three Men and a Purpose: 1969–79

DHL was founded in 1969 by three young shipping executives, Adrian Dalsey, Larry Hillblom, and Robert Lynn, who were casting about for a way to increase turnaround speed for ships at ports. They reasoned that if the shipping documents could be flown from port to port, they could be examined and processed before the ships arrived, and that speeding up the

process would decrease port costs for shippers. With this in mind, the trio combined the first letters of their last names to form the acronym DHL, thus beginning an air-courier company that revolutionized the delivery industry.

DHL rapidly developed into an express delivery service between California and Hawaii, then quickly expanded to points east. The company's primary customer was the Bank of America, which needed a single company to carry its letters of credit and other documents. DHL branched into the international market in the early 1970s when it began flying routes to the Far East. In addition, while competitor Federal Express was developing its domestic overnight delivery network, DHL focused on further developing its international service.

In 1972 the three original investors recruited Po Chung, a Hong Kong entrepreneur, to help them build a global network. Chung started DHL's sister company, DHL International Ltd., headquartered in Brussels, Belgium. Beginning then, DHL Worldwide Express functioned as two separate companies, DHL Airways, Inc. based in Redwood City, California, and DHL International. While each company acted as the exclusive agent for the other, by 1983 DHL International had grown to be five times larger than its domestic counterpart. DHL International's rapid expansion continued throughout the 1970s, adding destinations in Europe in 1974, the Middle East in 1976, Latin America in 1977, and Africa in 1978.

FedEx and UPS Up the Ante: 1980–88

The 1980s would bring the firm increased growth as well as greater competition. During this time DHL continued to expand, by turns cooperating with competitors and warring with them. The company also sought new outlets for service, working out an arrangement with Hilton International Co. in 1980, agreeing to provide daily pickup of documents at 49 Hilton Hotels, arranging for international delivery—its couriers moving the packages through customs—then delivering them locally. It was a win-win situation as Hilton was able to offer its patrons a high-class delivery service and DHL was guaranteed new outlets for its business. The next year, 1981, DHL flew ten million shipments between 268 cities and had approximately

Company Perspectives:

Our task as a global logistics provider is to network the world. Our aim is to provide excellent service quality to our customers at attractive prices, in the most environment-friendly way possible, embracing our social responsibilities.

$100 million in sales. The following year, Lawrence Roberts, who had founded Telenet Communications Corp. and headed GTE, joined DHL as president.

Although DHL had a strong international presence, business was occasionally made difficult because it was necessary for the company to negotiate with foreign governments. In 1982, for example, the French post office sought to reassert a monopoly dating back to the 15th century, and DHL, possessing 80 percent of the French market, was ordered to halt operations outside Paris. What could have been a potential crisis for the company was, however, favorably resolved.

DHL continued to expand its horizons, though, adding Eastern bloc nations in 1983. Prior to 1983, DHL had not pursued much business in the United States, leaving the field to Federal Express and United Parcel Service (UPS). Despite counting 97 percent of the nation's 500 largest companies among its customers, DHL still held only a minuscule share of the overall domestic market. To bolster its share of the American market, DHL installed two major hubs at airports in Cincinnati and Salt Lake City, and added nine mini-hubs in major cities across the country. The company also bought three Boeing 727s and seven Learjets, as well as new sorting equipment. In addition, in 1983 DHL Worldwide started using helicopters in New York and Houston to expedite documents during rush hour and the following year initiated helicopter service in Los Angeles as well.

Once the hubs had been installed, DHL Airways began offering point-to-point overnight service between 126 American cities. Still, for the year ending in 1983, DHL reached only 2 or 3 percent of the domestic market—yet had more than 5,000 employees with 400 offices in over 90 countries. As in its earliest days, banks accounted for a large portion of its business; other common shipments consisted of computer tapes, spare parts, and shipping papers. That year, DHL estimated it carried 80 percent of the bank material traveling by courier from Europe to the United States. Revenues were approximated at $600 million. In 1984, as former courier-driver Joseph Waechter became president of DHL Airways, DHL provided service to more than 125 countries, and its 500 stations were handling 15 million international and domestic shipments annually.

Yet just as DHL was looking to cut into the business of its domestic competitors, those same companies were aiming to siphon off portions of DHL's international business. In 1985 both Federal Express and UPS entered the international express market. As competition became more intense, DHL increasingly began to cooperate with businesses in similar areas. The company teamed up with Western Union to deliver documents generated on Western Union's EasyLink electronic mails, allowing people to send documents via courier without having to hand-deliver material to the courier's office. The next year,

1986, as DHL International formed its first joint venture in the People's Republic of China, known as DHL Sinotrans, Charles A. Lynch was named chairman and chief executive of DHL Airways, replacing Roberts. Lynch remained with the company just two years and was replaced by Patrick Foley, the former chairman of Hyatt Hotels. Meanwhile, FedEx and UPS were eroding DHL's market share, which fell from 54 percent in 1985 to 50 percent in 1987. An important competitive battleground existed in Japan, however, and while FedEx and UPS gained footholds in that country in the 1980s, by 1988 DHL still controlled 80 percent of the Japanese overseas market.

As the world economy boomed in the 1980s, DHL followed suit, even breaking new ground in the Communist-bloc countries. The company had first cracked the eastern bloc in 1983, when it began delivering packages to Hungary, East Germany, and several other countries. DHL Airways was not slouching either, reporting that between 1986 and 1987 alone, its volume rose 34 percent; in 1987 it was the 318th largest private company in the United States, with 5,000 employees and estimated sales of $375 million. Revenues for the entire DHL network, in 1988, were calculated to be between $1.2 billion and $1.5 billion, helped in part by another joint venture with a Hungarian company to create DHL Budapest Ltd. That year, DHL controlled 91 percent of the packages bound for Eastern Europe from the West and 98 percent of all outbound shipments.

Holding and Increasing Market Share: 1989–93

In 1989 DHL Worldwide was the 84th largest company in the United States with 18,000 employees, more than 50 million shipments, and service to 184 countries. Nevertheless, though DHL's international success was becoming firmly established, the company was not making the headway it had planned in the United States. As of 1989, DHL had only 5 percent of the domestic market. To bolster its name recognition in the United States, the company turned to innovative advertising techniques, including the use of humor. Cartoonist Gary Larson, creator of the wildly popular comic "The Far Side," was employed to draw cartoons for use in DHL advertising, and in 1990 the company introduced a campaign featuring flying DHL vans whizzing past competitors' planes. DHL also took an unusual approach to air delivery. Although the company used its own fleet of planes within Europe and on some major routes, DHL often used scheduled airlines to carry its shipments. Federal Express, in contrast, maintained its own fleet and seldom used other airlines. Rather than purchase its own planes, DHL chose instead to invest its capital in technology and ground-handling equipment, spending some $250 million on those areas in 1990 and 1991 alone.

In 1990, in order to infuse the company with fresh capital and take advantage of the resources of larger airlines, DHL International sold parts of its business to three companies. Japan Airlines Company, Limited (JAL) and the German airline Deutsche Lufthansa AG each purchased 5 percent, while Nissho Iwai K.K., a Japanese trading company, purchased 2.5 percent. Each firm also had the option of buying greater shares. In addition, the three companies also purchased a combined stake of 2.5 percent in the U.S.-based DHL Airways. The sale of these closely held interests brought $500 million in capital into the firm. The same year, despite a 60 percent share of the international overnight delivery

Key Dates:

1969: Adrian Dalsey, Larry Hillblom, and Robert Lynn form DHL, which quickly develops into an express delivery service between California and Hawaii.

1970s: Service to and from Far Eastern markets begins.

1972: With aid from Po Chung, DHL Worldwide Express forms DHL International Ltd., based in Brussels, Belgium, as international arm; DHL Airways, Inc., California-based, is the domestic counterpart.

1983: DHL begins offering expanded express service from point to point within the United States.

1990: To raise fresh capital, DHL International sells small stakes in itself to Japan Airlines, Lufthansa, and Nissho Iwai; DHL Worldwide enters the freight transport business.

1992: JAL and Lufthansa increase their stakes in DHL International to 25 percent, Nissho Iwai, to 7.5 percent.

1998: Deutsche Post AG purchases a 25 percent stake in DHL International.

2001: Deutsche Post increases its stake in DHL International to 51 percent; through a restructuring, DHL International now has full ownership of DHL Worldwide Express Inc. and a 25 percent stake in DHL Airways.

2002: Deutsche Post takes full ownership of DHL International.

2003: Danzas and Deutsche Post Euro Express are merged into DHL, and DHL becomes the single, global brand for all express delivery and logistics operations within the Deutsche Post group; DHL divests its remaining stake in DHL Airways and acquires Airborne, Inc.

market, the company began to expand into new areas of business. To keep up in an increasingly competitive industry, DHL Worldwide entered the freight services industry and began carrying heavier cargo. In the company's 20-year history of carrying small packages—generally under 70 pounds—this was DHL's first major departure from its core business. In 1991 DHL Worldwide had revenues of $2.3 billion, and was the 59th largest private company in the United States, its 21,000 employees handling more than 80 million shipments.

In June 1992, all three of DHL's major shareholders exercised their option to increase their shares in DHL International; JAL and Lufthansa each increased their stake to 25 percent, while Nissho Iwai's holdings grew to 7.5 percent. This was also the year DHL began service to Albania, Estonia, Latvia, and Greenland, and reestablished ties with Kuwait. In addition, in an unusual move DHL signed an agreement to share transatlantic and European aircraft operations with one of its competitors, Emery Worldwide. The economic recession and an overcrowded North Atlantic airway were cited as the reasons behind these cooperative measures, which would allow greater operating efficiency and expanded service. The arrangement represented the first of several alliances between integrated carriers, due to increasing pressure from other competitors, including Airborne Express and TNT Limited. In 1993 as reve-

nues hit $3 billion, DHL commenced a four-year $1.25 billion capital spending program to step up its technological capabilities, automation, and communications.

Mid-1990s Growth Initiatives

By 1994, DHL Worldwide's 25-year anniversary, the company controlled 52 percent of the Asian express shipment marketplace, with FedEx and UPS garnering a 24 percent slice each. The next year, DHL poured over $700 million into expansion of its Pacific Rim operations. DHL was not only shoring up facilities in Hong Kong and Australia, but also venturing into 16 new cities in China, India, and Vietnam. A new $60 million hub at Manila's Ninoy Aquino International Airport was scheduled to open in late 1995, with additional facilities slated for Bangkok, Tokyo, Auckland, and Sydney. In the midst of its ambitious expansion, DHL was rocked by the news of founder and majority shareholder Larry Lee Hillblom's death. Known as an avid though reckless pilot (he had survived a previous crash and had his pilot's license suspended), Hillblom, who had withdrawn from DHL's daily operations in 1980, was killed in a seaplane accident near Saipan where he lived.

The management at DHL was soon embroiled in an ugly controversy after Hillblom's 1982 will was released, as a spate of paternity claims and lawsuits were filed. Lurid details of Hillblom's penchant for young island girls reached the press, including an in-depth exposé in the generally staid *Wall Street Journal*. Since Hillblom had retained a mighty 60 percent of DHL Airways and 23 percent of DHL International (valued conservatively at the time at around $300 million), the company's officers scrambled to exercise an option to repurchase his shares. Yet financing and a host of complications held up the buyback and soon the entire estate was a miasma of lawsuits, bad judgment calls, and island politics.

Yet 1995 was still a good year for DHL Worldwide, as the company debuted its web site (www.dhl.com) and experienced an overall 23 percent growth in revenue to $3.8 billion, with an incredible 40 percent surge in volume in its Middle East operations. In response to the encouraging numbers, DHL broke ground on a new $4 million state-of-the-art express facility at the Dubai International Airport in the United Arab Emirates in 1996. The new 42,000-square-foot hub was to complement DHL's existing facilities in Bahrain. Over on the Asian continent, DHL broke with its longstanding tradition of leasing planes to buy its own cargo fleet. Though DHL International's previous strategy of leasing out cargo space had proved both successful and prudent, Chairman and CEO Foley told the *San Francisco Business Times* the company needed to control its own destiny, and having its own fleet would help alleviate the space limitations and scheduling snafus of commercial flights.

In 1996 DHL was looking to the future again by announcing plans for a $100 million hub in the Midwest to carry the company through the next two decades. While its Cincinnati "superhub" handled around 45 incoming flights every night, and sorted over 135,000 pieces at a rate of 60,000 per hour— DHL believed its growth would soon outpace the facility. The same was true for the San Francisco area, where Silicon Valley shipments represented 40 percent of DHL Airways' business in the Bay Area. Internationally, DHL was still growing at the speed of sound with expansion in the former Soviet Union to 37 branches, a new facility at Ferihegy Airport in Budapest, and the acquisition of Shigur Express in Israel. Though DHL had worked with Shigur for years, the $3.5 million purchase gave DHL a firmer presence in the country's emerging market. By 1998, DHL served 227 countries with 2,381 stations in cities from Paris and Prague to Bombay and Bangkok with over 53,200 employees. Stateside, however, DHL Airways still represented less than 2 percent of the market, though the California-based company got a boost from the August 1997 Teamsters' strike against UPS.

Late 1990s and Early 2000s: Gradual Beginning of the Deutsche Post Era

A new era began for DHL in 1998 when Deutsche Post AG, the German postal service, then still wholly government owned, bought a 25 percent stake in DHL International—essentially buying the interest formerly held by Hillblom. For DHL, the deal provided it with additional funds for expansion as well as greater access to the German market through Deutsche Post's 15,000 branches. For its part, Deutsche Post was looking for opportunities to expand beyond its domestic market as the integration of Europe continued apace. Toward this same end, Deutsche Post Euro Express was set up in 1998 as a ground-based parcel and distribution network for both Germany and Europe.

As its ownership structure evolved, DHL was also continuing to diversify the range of services it offered to customers. Building on its entry into freight transport, DHL began to move into the market for logistics services, aiming to essentially become part of its customers' supply chains. By 1998 the company had set up eight regional logistics centers where subassembly work on personal computers and other products could be carried out, and 54 parts centers that warehoused spare parts for field engineers. Such services enabled manufacturers and suppliers to reduce their inventories while still having quick access to parts and assemblies.

At the same time, Deutsche Post was also moving aggressively into worldwide logistics. During 1999 it acquired Danzas Group, a Swiss logistics company with roots dating back to 1815. Then in 2000 Deutsche Post acquired Air Express International Corporation (AEI) for $1.1 billion. AEI, the largest airfreight forwarder in the United States, with a branch network in 125 countries, was subsequently integrated into Danzas. This made Danzas, now operating in 150 countries, the world's leading airfreight forwarder and one of the top five players in ocean freight. Also in 2000 the privatization of Deutsche Post began with a November initial public offering (IPO) that sold 29 percent of the firm's shares.

During 1999 DHL entered into an alliance with the United States Postal Service through which the two entities began offering two-day-delivery service between 11 U.S. cities and Europe. DHL also unveiled that year a $1.5 billion plan to buy more than 40 new cargo jets and to modernize cargo hubs and other facilities at airports in Germany, Singapore, and Japan. After JAL reduced its stake in DHL from 26 percent to 6 percent, DHL announced in late 1999 plans to sell as much as 23 percent of its equity to the public in an IPO. These plans were shelved during 2000, however, when the company entered into

a new agreement with Deutsche Post through which the latter boosted its stake in DHL to 51 percent by the end of 2001. By this time, the DHL Worldwide Express network encompassed 80,000 destinations, linking 635,000 cities in 228 countries.

As this increase in ownership of DHL unfolded—and was fought by rivals FedEx and UPS, fearful of a stronger competitor in the huge U.S. shipping market—DHL altered its corporate structure. It was the Brussels-based DHL International that Deutsche Post took majority control of, and DHL International created a new U.S. holding company that owned a 25 percent voting stake in DHL Airways and had full ownership of DHL Worldwide Express Inc.—the latter having been carved out of DHL Airways and consisting of that entity's ground-based delivery operations in the United States. FedEx and UPS claimed that Deutsche Post, in its convoluted relationship with DHL Airways, was in violation of U.S. federal laws prohibiting foreign control or ownership of more than 25 percent of a U.S. airline. The U.S. Department of Transportation, however, eventually ruled in favor of DHL and Deutsche Post. Furthermore, in mid-2003 DHL International divested its remaining stake in DHL Airways, which was simultaneously renamed Astar Air Cargo Inc.

In July 2002 Deutsche Post acquired Lufthansa's share of DHL International, increasing its stake to more than 75 percent. That same month, a DHL cargo jet collided with a Russian passenger jet, killing 71 people in Germany's worst postwar air disaster. In December of that year, Deutsche Post took full ownership of DHL, buying out the minority interests of JAL and two investment funds. This laid the ground for a comprehensive rebranding and reorganization of Deutsche Post's operations in 2003. That year, Danzas and Deutsche Post Euro Express were merged into DHL, still headquartered in Brussels, and DHL became the single, global brand for all express delivery and logistics operations within the Deutsche Post group. Not only did the new structure offer the possibility for comprehensive cost savings, but DHL Worldwide Network S.A./N.V. emerged as a Deutsche Post subsidiary offering customers ''one-stop shopping'' for delivery and logistics services.

DHL Worldwide grew even larger in August 2003 when it completed the acquisition of Airborne, Inc. for $1.05 billion. Based in Seattle, Airborne was the third largest express delivery company in the United States. By acquiring Airborne, whose name was eventually phased out in favor of DHL's, DHL augmented its air express operations within the United States but perhaps more importantly gained control of Airborne's nascent ground delivery network and thereby gained ground on its U.S. arch-rivals, FedEx and UPS. DHL now had about 21 percent of the U.S. air delivery market but still only 2 percent of the ground sector. Airborne's airline unit was spun off as the standalone company ABX Air to comply with U.S. airline ownership laws. As the combined U.S. operations of DHL and Airborne were merged, U.S. headquarters were consolidated at DHL's offices in Plantation, Florida. In June 2004 DHL announced that it was stepping up its push into the U.S. market by committing to spend $1.2 billion over a three-year period to build or upgrade shipment-sorting operations and otherwise bolster its delivery network throughout the country. A key component of this expansion was the establishment of a West Coast air and ground hub, and in December 2004 DHL tentatively selected March Air Reserve Base in southern California as the location for this hub. As this buildup continued, DHL was losing hundreds of millions of dollars in North America, and this red ink was expected to flow well into 2005 and even 2006.

In the meantime, DHL was not standing still in its core markets of Asia and Europe. In 2003 the company earmarked $215 million for a five-year push into the rapidly growing express and logistics market of China. That year, DHL purchased a 5 percent stake in Sinotrans, the leading logistics firm in China. In mid-2004 DHL launched China Domestic, the mainland's first domestic express service operated by an international provider. India was another target of expansion, and in November 2004 DHL announced its acquisition of a majority stake in India's largest domestic courier, Blue Dart. This was followed one month later by the formation of a 50–50 joint venture with the express and logistics unit of New Zealand Post. Over in Europe, DHL had been planning to establish an intercontinental freight hub in its headquarters city of Brussels, but the move was scuttled by Belgian government noise-reduction requirements. Instead, DHL began laying the groundwork for a new European hub at Hall Airport in Leipzig, Germany, where operations could begin by 2008.

Principal Subsidiaries

Deutsche Post Euro Express Deutschland GmbH & Co. OHG (Germany); Air Express International USA, Inc.; Securicor Omega Holdings Ltd. (U.K.); Airborne, Inc. (U.S.A.); DHL Worldwide Express Inc. (U.S.A.); Danzas S.A. (France); Danzas ASG Eurocargo AB (Sweden); Danzas GmbH (Germany); DHL International (UK) Ltd.; Danzas S.p.A. (Italy); DHL Danzas Air & Ocean Germany GmbH (Germany); DHL Worldwide Express GmbH (Germany); Van Gend & Loos B.V. (Netherlands); Danzas AG (Switzerland); DHL International S.A. (France); Danzas Limited (U.K.); DANZAS Euronet GmbH (Germany); Danzas Limited (Hong Kong); DHL Japan Inc.

Principal Divisions

DHL Express; DHL Freight; DHL Danzas Air & Ocean; DHL Solutions; DHL Global Mail.

Principal Competitors

FedEx Corporation; United Parcel Service, Inc.; United States Postal Service; TPG N.V.

Further Reading

"Air-Express Firms Battle for Turf in Japan," *Wall Street Journal,* December 27, 1988.

Atkins, Ralph, "German Delivery for DHL: Change Is Forcing Deutsche Post to Act," *Financial Times,* March 26, 1998, p. 39.

Batchelor, Charles, "Deutsche Post's Stake Represents Coming of Age," *Financial Times,* June 18, 1998, p. 2.

"The Battle of Zaventem," *Forbes,* April 29, 1991.

Blackmon, Douglas A., "Transportation: Federal Express, UPS Battle for a Foothold in Asia," *Wall Street Journal,* January 22, 1997, p. B1.

Bole, Kristin, "DHL Gets Its Wings: Plans to Buy Own Jets in Asia Marks Change in Strategy," *San Francisco Business Times,* May 10, 1996, p. 1.

Boudette, Neal E., "Deutsche Post to Increase Stake in DHL International," *Wall Street Journal Europe,* September 18, 2000, p. 6.

Brady, Diane, "Delivery Giants Race to Set Up Hubs for Overnight Service to Asian Cities," *Wall Street Journal,* August 7, 1997, p. B6.

Brooks, Rick, "Airborne to Sell Ground Operations," *Wall Street Journal,* March 25, 2003, p. B4.

——, "Deutsche Post Gets a Victory over U.S. Rivals UPS, FedEx," *Wall Street Journal,* December 22, 2003, p. B2.

——, "DIIL Plans to Spend $1.2 Billion in Challenge of FedEx and UPS," *Wall Street Journal,* June 25, 2004, p. B2.

——, "Package Delivery Battle Hinges on DHL Ruling," *Wall Street Journal,* May 13, 2003, p. B1.

——, "U.S. Ruling Delivers Victory to Deutsche Post and DHL," *Wall Street Journal Europe,* May 14, 2001, p. 7.

"DHL Expands Its Domestic Operations," *H&SM,* July 1983.

"DHL International Stake to Be Bought by Three Concerns," *Wall Street Journal,* May 30, 1990.

"DHL International Will Sell 22.5% Stake to Deutsche Post AG," *Wall Street Journal,* March 27, 1998.

"DHL Ties Up East Europe Package," *Advertising Age,* August 29, 1988.

Ewing, Jack, Dean Foust, and Michael Eidam, "DHL's American Adventure," *Business Week,* November 29, 2004, pp. 126–27.

"An International Courier Takes on Federal Express," *Business Week,* May 9, 1983.

Johnson, Keith, and Victoria Knight, "DHL Shuns Brussels As Global Hub," *Wall Street Journal Europe,* October 22, 2004, p. A1.

Karnitschnig, Matthew, "Deutsche Post Girds for Battle: German Delivery Firm Asks EU to Impose Restrictions on Rivals UPS and FedEx," *Wall Street Journal,* October 6, 2003, p. A14.

Karp, Aaron, "Networking America: DHL Gets Down to the Ground Basics in Building a New Infrastructure in the United States," *Air Cargo World,* October 2004, pp. 10–11.

"Larson's Humor Flies for DHL," *Industry Week,* April 3, 1989.

McKenna, Ed, "Growth Is Costly for DHL," *Journal of Commerce,* November 15, 2004, p. 36.

Nelms, Douglas W., "Holding Its Own: A Massive Global Expansion Is Keeping DHL Well Ahead of Growing U.S. Competition," *Air Transport World,* June 1996, p. 151.

Orr, Deborah, "Delivering America," *Forbes,* October 4, 2004, pp. 78–80.

Ott, James, "Heavy-Weight Expansion Propels DHL Hub Growth," *Aviation Week and Space Technology,* March 4, 1997, p. 37.

Power, Stephen, and Rick Brooks, "Air-Cargo Fight Has Big Cast: FedEx and UPS, Backed by Legislators, Say Germans Run DHL," *Wall Street Journal,* July 18, 2003, p. A4.

Schwartz, Judith D., "DHL Puts Its Foot to the Floor As FedEx and UPS Pick Up Speed," *Adweek's Marketing Week,* January 1, 1990.

Shishkin, Philip, and Rick Brooks, "Deutsche Post to Split Up in Settlement That May Fan Battle over U.S. Market," *Wall Street Journal,* March 21, 2001, p. A3.

Solomon, Mark, "DHL, Japan Air, and Lufthansa Seek to Reshape Express Sector," *Traffic World,* May 21, 1990.

Tanzer, Andrew, "Warehouses That Fly," *Forbes,* October 18, 1999, pp. 120–22, 124.

Tausz, Andrew, "DHL Is Delivering on Courier Challenges," *Distribution,* September 1997, p. 22.

Waldman, Peter, "Heir Freight: How the Strange Life of a DHL Founder Left His Estate a Mess," *Wall Street Journal,* May 15, 1996, p. A1.

"We Go Anywhere," *Financial World,* January 25, 1984.

Wiebner, Mike, "Getting Grounded: For DHL Worldwide Express, the Road to Riches in the American Express Market Runs over the Ground," *Air Cargo World,* November 2002, pp. 22, 24.

—Daniel Gross
—updates: Taryn Benbow-Pfalzgraf; David E. Salamie

Dimension Data Holdings PLC

PO Box 56055
Pinegowrie 2123
South Africa
Telephone: +27 11 575 0000
Fax: +27 11 576 3631
Web site: http://www.didata.com

Public Company
Incorporated: 1987
Employees: 8,524
Sales: $2.36 billion (2004)
Stock Exchanges: London
Ticker Symbol: DDT
NAIC: 541513 Computer Facilities Management
Services; 518111 Internet Service Providers; 518210
Data Processing, Hosting, and Related Services;
541512 Computer Systems Design Services

Dimension Data Holdings PLC is South Africa's leading information technology services and solutions provider. The company is also one of the world's leading IT groups, with operations in more than 30 countries. Dimension Data operates in two core IT sectors: Networking Services, including high-speed Internet and Intranet installation, maintenance, and management, project engineering and management, and technical assistance; and Interactive Services, including e-commerce site development, hosting, and management, along with Customer Relationship Management services. Dimension Data's key markets include the United Kingdom, with 10 percent of revenues; the United States, accounting for 17 percent; Africa, at 18 percent; Asia/Pacific at 16 percent; and Europe at 29 percent. As it has approached the mid-2000s, Dimension Data has been actively reinventing itself, extending beyond its former capacity as a reseller and integrator of third-party technologies to become a "total solutions provider" with its own in-house and proprietary software and technologies. The shift toward higher-margin operations comes in part as a response to the company's losses during the high-tech slump of the early 2000s. Dimension

Data maintains its headquarters in Pinegowie, South Africa, and is led by founder Jeremy Ord.

Early 1980s Origins

Dimension Data was founded by Jeremy Ord in 1983 in order to provide information technology services to the South African market. Ord then merged his company with another company operated by two former Wit University schoolmates and fellow rugby fraternity members Richard Came and Bruce Watson. The company was then listed on the Johannesburg Securities Exchange in 1987, with Ord as company chairman. Dimension Data's expansion remained limited to South Africa into the early 1990s due to the embargo against South African apartheid laws.

The end of apartheid signaled new opportunity for Dimension Data. Into the mid-1990s, the company began to reposition itself, particularly by expanding beyond its former base as a systems integrator. By 1994, the company had launched a new Software and Services division. In that year, also, Dimension Data's importance in the South African market was highlighted by its being named one of Cisco's six internationally based Gold Partners. Next, the company added Internet and e-commerce capabilities, through the 1996 acquisition of 25 percent of Internet Solutions in South Africa. That purchase gave Dimension Data access to South Africa's leading internet service provider, as well as its experience developing infrastructures and services for the e-commerce sector.

By then, however, Dimension Data had begun preparing its drive into the international IT market. The company's first foreign move came in 1996 as well, when it bought a 45 percent stake in Com Tech Communications Ltd., based in Australia. The company subsequently increased its shareholding position in that company to 66 percent in 1997.

In the meantime, the company continued developing its software technologies, finding success on the international market for that division as well. In 1997, for example, the company reached a licensing agreement with the Deloitte & Touche Consulting Group for use of Dimension Data's proprietary software designed to help companies manage the so-called "millennium bug" ahead of the year 2000.

The year 1997 also marked a year of significant growth for the company. After buying up full control of Internet Solutions, the company returned to the global market, purchasing Australia's Datacraft Limited. That purchase helped transform Dimension Data into a major player in the Asian Pacific region's IT market, giving it some 25 percent of Australia's networking market. The acquisition of Datacraft also gave the company control of a 51 percent stake in Singapore-based Datacraft Asia, and a 20 percent share in the Asian region's networking market.

The company's attentions also turned to the United Kingdom. In 1997, the company acquired 75 percent of The Merchant Group. That company, founded in the early 1970s, had developed into one of the United Kingdom's leading IT outsourcing groups, with a specialty in the operations of customer contact call centers.

Global IT Leader in the 2000s

By the end of the decade, Dimension Data had clearly established its strategy of becoming one of the world's first truly global IT services and support companies. In 1999, Dimension Data moved to solidify its presence in Europe, acquiring GK Communications Ltd. That acquisition permitted the company to take a leading share of the United Kingdom's voice and data integration market. The company returned to England that year, buying up nearly 50 percent of Chernikeef Networks Ltd., which permitted Dimension Data to extend its own network integration operations.

Still more significant was the company's acquisition of the European operations of fellow South African Comparex Holdings. For a price of ZAR 8.1 billion, Dimension Data leapt to the top of the world's leading independent IT services companies. Next, Dimension Data went shopping for a stake in the United States. As Jeremy Ord explained to *Business Times:* "Didata wants to offer its customers service 24 hours a day, seven days a week, 365 days a year. That is why the U.S. has become an important point for us. Once we do, we will be the only global network service in the world. Our target market then becomes global players, multinationals. The sky is the limit in terms of market opportunities."

Dimension Data looked first to extend its network integration business as its entry to the United States. In 1999, the company located its first acquisition target, New Jersey-based RF/COM. Dimension Data paid $40 million to acquire 70 percent of that company.

To fuel its global ambitions, Dimension Data decided to switch its primary listing to the London Stock Exchange in 2000. The move permitted the company to raise its profile among international investors and generate a war chest for the next phase of its ambitious expansion drive.

By the end of 2000, Dimension Data had spent more than $1.2 billion in acquisitions, including the £200 ($350) million acquisition of the remaining shares of Chernikeef (renamed as DDUK), and the purchase of full control of Com Tech for $146 million. At the same time, the company stepped up its drive into the U.S. market, where it acquired Integrated Systems Group, based in New York, and Data Comm Systems Inc., expanding its network integration operations in the United States. Moving beyond New York, the company acquired TimeBridge Technologies, paying $135 million for the Maryland-based provider of network and e-business services. Dimension Data also boosted its presence in continental Europe, through the acquisition of Swiss network integration group Netpartner AG.

The company's buying spree continued into 2001, with the additions of Brussels-based Planet CTI, which brought Dimension Data expertise in the computer telephony integration sector, and Time Netbuilding B.V., one of The Netherlands' top network integration services companies. At the same time, in the United States, the company picked up two North Carolina-based companies, Premier Systems Integrators and Matrix Networking Group, for a total of more than $150 million. The company also outbid computer giant Compaq for Proxicom, a highly sought after e-services group based in Reston, Virginia. The purchase cost Dimension Data nearly $450 million. Also that year, the company entered Korea, paying $25 million to buy Dasan Electronics through its Datacraft Asia subsidiary.

The company also announced plans to expand into the United States' Midwest and West Coast markets, in addition to plans to enter Italy, Spain, and elsewhere in Europe. But the crash of the global high-tech markets quickly caught the company short. The company was seen as particularly vulnerable due to its heavy exposure to struggling Cisco Systems. By the end of the year, and after posting a profit warning in the summer, the group was forced to call a halt to further acquisitions. Indeed, by the end of its fiscal year in November, the company revealed losses mounting to $1.6 billion.

Chairman Ord put the best face possible on the group's difficulties, telling the *Times:* "We wanted to grow in the US, Europe and the UK. That is completed and we now intend to integrate the businesses." Dimension Data launched a cost-cutting effort through 2002, including shedding some 19 percent of its payroll. Yet that was seen as too little, too late, as the group's sales slumped to $2.2 billion that year, with pretax losses of $2.6 billion (a figure that included a $1.8 billion write-off of goodwill from its acquisition spree).

Losses continued to plague the company through 2003, and forced a management reorganization. Part of that reorganization involved the transformation of the company's chairman position—which previously had combined chairman and CEO

Key Dates:

1984: Jeremy Ord founds a network integration company in South Africa, then merges it with a company owned by two former schoolmates.

1987: Dimension Data goes public on the Johannesburg Securities Exchange.

1994: The company adds software development and services operations.

1996: Dimension Data acquires a stake in South Africa's Internet Solutions and makes its first international acquisition, of Australia's Com Tech Communications.

1997: The company acquires Datacraft Ltd. in Australia, and its Datacraft Asia subsidiary in Singapore; majority control of The Merchant Group in the United Kingdom is acquired.

1999: The company acquires GK Communications and Chernikeef Networks in the United Kingdom; Re/Com, its first U.S. acquisition; and the European holdings of Comparex.

2000: The company switches its primary listing to the London Stock Exchange, and launches an ambitious acquisition drive.

2001: Proxicom, an e-services provider in the United States, is acquired; the company posts losses of $1.6 billion for the year.

2004: The company reorganizes its management structure; Dasan Electronics in Korea is acquired.

roles—into a non-executive position. The company then moved former COO Brett Dawson into the new CEO spot, while Ord became the group's non-executive chairman. The company also continued its restructuring, selling off its cash-hungry, but profitable Proxicom subsidiary at the end of 2004.

The slow return to growth of the global IT market caught up with Dimension Data in 2004. By the end of its fiscal year, the company's sales had begun to grow again, topping $2.36 billion. The company also had significantly reduced its pretax losses, which dropped to just $4.4 million. In celebration, Dimension Data immediately returned to the acquisition trail, announcing its agreement to acquire Australia's SecureData, and its New Zealand SQL Services arm, in December 2004. Dimension Data prepared to resume its expansion as one of the world's global IT leaders into the new century.

Principal Subsidiaries

Comtech Holdings S.A. (Belgium); Conscripti (Pty.) Ltd.; Core People (Pty.) Ltd.; Datacraft Asia Limited (Singapore; 51.49%); Diginet AG (Switzerland); Dimension Data (Pty.) Ltd.; Dimension Data (US) Inc. (U.S.A.); Dimension Data Advanced Infrastructure Ltd. (U.K.); Dimension Data Algeria S.p.A.; Dimension Data Australia Pty. Ltd.; Dimension Data Belgium S.A.; Dimension Data Botswana (Pty.) Ltd.; Dimension Data Deutschland Holdings GmbH; Dimension Data España SL; Dimension Data France S.A.; Dimension Data Germany AG & Co.; Dimension Data Holdings Nederland B.V.; Dimension Data Italia S.R.L.; Dimension Data Luxembourg S.A.; Dimension Data Nederland B.V.; Dimension Data Network Services Ltd. (U.K.); Dimension Data North America Inc. (U.S.A.); Dimension Data Sverige AB; Dimension Data Switzerland S.A.; GK Communications Group Ltd. (U.K.); Internet Solutions (Pty.) Ltd.; Linx Holdings (Pty.) Ltd.; Merchants S.A. (Pty.) Ltd.; Planet CTI (Belgium).

Principal Competitors

New Africa Investments Ltd.; Electronic Data Systems Corporation; Computer Sciences Corporation; Sun Microsystems Inc.; Hewlett-Packard France; Singapore Technologies Private Ltd.; Oracle Corporation Ireland Ltd.; Fujitsu Services Holdings PLC; Sema S.A.; Convergys Corporation.

Further Reading

Aldrick, Philip, "Extra Dimension Is Revealed," *Daily Telegraph,* November 18, 2004.

"DiData Aims to Become Global Service Network," *Business Times,* March 7, 1999.

Foley, Stephen, "Dimension Data Looks Programmed for Growth," May 13, 2004, p. 42.

Hall, Dominic, "DiData to Focus Efforts on Returning to Profit," *MicroScope,* May 20, 2003, p. 6.

Jivkov, Michael, "DiData Tumbles Again As U.S. Connections Add to Its Woes," *Independent,* September 21, 2001, p. 22.

Kavanagh, Michael, "Dimension Agrees Sale of DDSA Stake," *Financial Times,* September 2, 2004, p. 20.

Pesola, Maija, "Tech Spending Increase Helps Dimension Data," *Financial Times,* November 18, 2004, p. 27.

Pullar-Strecker, Tom, "SQL Services Changes Hands Again," *Dominion Post,* December 6, 2004.

Wendlandt, Astrid, "Demand Pickup Helps DiData," *Financial Times,* May 13, 2004, p. 25.

White, Dominic, "Dimension Falls £480m into Red," *Daily Telegraph,* May 17, 2002.

—M.L. Cohen

ⅢDIXON

Dixon Ticonderoga Company

195 International Parkway
Heathrow, Florida 32746-5007
U.S.A.
Telephone: (407) 829-9000
Toll Free: (800) 824-9430
Fax: (800) 232-9396
Web site: http://www.dixonticonderoga.com

Public Company
Incorporated: 1868 as The Joseph Dixon Crucible
    Company
Employees: 1,403
Sales: $88.2 million (2004)
Stock Exchanges: American
Ticker Symbol: DXT
NAIC: 339942 Lead Pencil and Art Good Manufacturing;
    339941 Pen and Mechanical Pencil Manufacturing

One of the oldest companies in the United States, Dixon Ticonderoga Company for many years was known predominantly for its yellow and green pencils, but, after nearly two centuries of growth, Dixon's product line expanded substantially, comprising a diverse assortment of writing instruments and art supplies by the early 2000s. In addition to its flagship Ticonderoga brand, the company also markets products under the Dixon, Wearever, Prang, and Vinci brands. Its main manufacturing facilities are in Versailles, Missouri; Acton Vale, Quebec; Mexico City; and Beijing, China. Although Dixon Ticonderoga stood as the primary player in the history of the pencil in the United States, it was poised in late 2004 to gain an Italian parent. In December of that year, Dixon agreed to be acquired by Fila–Fabbrica Italiana Lapis ed Affini S.p.A., a producer of design and writing instruments, art materials, and modeling paste based in Milan.

Early History: An Entrepreneur
in Search of a Market

For Joseph Dixon, the bustle of commerce along the waterfront in his native Marblehead, Massachusetts, provided the inspiration for his lifelong work, an inspiration that was remarkable for two reasons: it came from a sight seen nearly every day by the residents of Marblehead and it came to Dixon when he was only 13 years old. Born in 1799, Dixon was the son of a local ship owner and, naturally, spent a considerable amount of time at the harbor watching ships arrive and depart from Marblehead's busy port. Bound for destinations along the Eastern Seaboard, to ports in Europe, and to as far away as the Orient, the ships left loaded with goods, the weight of which functioned as a ballast to keep the vessels upright. When ships returned without any goods, ship owners filled their hulls with sand or stones to give their ships the necessary ballast to counteract the weight of the ship's sails. Ship owners, like Dixon's father, who sailed between the Orient and Marblehead, used Ceylonese graphite as ballast for their ships, then dumped the graphite once back home. This wasted substance, which generally was discarded in the bay, was the source of Dixon's inspiration, the common occurrence he noticed one fateful day in 1812 that led to the creation of Dixon Ticonderoga and the country's dependence on the ubiquitous and indispensable pencil.

With the help of a local chemist named Francis Peabody and a cabinetmaker named Ebenezer Martin, Dixon was able to make a crude pencil, certainly not the first such writing instrument, but an item that was regarded nevertheless as somewhat of an oddity by Americans at the time. Pencils first appeared shortly after 1564, when a storm in Cumberland, England, uprooted a large tree and exposed a rich deposit of plumbago, or "black lead," the purest form of graphite yet discovered. Shepherds used chunks of this graphite to mark their sheep. These early versions—sticks of graphite known as "marking stones"—were considerably more primitive than Dixon's first attempts, but after several centuries of gradual improvements, pencils began to rival goose quills as the writing instruments of choice, the most noteworthy among the pencil's adherents being Napoleon Bonaparte, who reportedly became upset when his campaign to overrun Europe led to a paucity of graphite pencils. Accordingly, it was not so much the originality of Dixon's work with pencils, but his persistence in marketing the products that earned him the distinction as one of the pioneers of the U.S. pencil industry.

The same year in which Dixon's waterfront observations led him to make his first pencil, the War of 1812 broke out,

Company Perspectives:

More than a writing and art products company, Dixon Ticonderoga is a company that empowers people to take conscious and subliminal thoughts—facts, ideas, and dreams—and preserve them using tools that are simply extensions of themselves.

stanching the flow of British graphite into the United States, but dwindling supply did not spark increased demand. Americans, in contrast to Europeans, still had not developed an affinity for pencils. That relationship would be engendered later, by another war; Dixon, meanwhile, moved on to other interests, maintaining through his teenage years his fascination with pencils while pursuing an education in printing, medicine, and chemistry.

Ten years after his first introduction to pencil fabrication, Dixon, age 23, married the daughter of the cabinetmaker who had helped him construct his first pencil. Together, Dixon and Hannah Martin—who established a company in 1827 that would eventually be called the Joseph Dixon Crucible Company—began experimenting with different ways to make pencils, a process that accidentally led to considerable success with another product, one of several innovative successes credited to Dixon. Through their experimentation with graphite, the Dixons discovered the substance could be used as an effective stove polish, which they marketed, to widespread demand, as Dixon's Stove Polish. The product sold exceptionally well throughout the country, giving the couple sufficient profits to develop and refine their pencil business. The result of their labor and monetary investment were pencils they could produce and sell for ten cents apiece, but demand for their products still eluded them.

Dixon, however, did not go the route of a penniless entrepreneur selling his product to an unreceptive audience. Instead, he continued to find other, more marketable uses for graphite that met with considerable success. With the start of the Mexican-American War in 1846, iron and steel production in the United States increased substantially, and Dixon, producing a heat-resistant graphite crucible (a vessel used for melting iron and steel at high temperatures) shared in the profits spawned by increased military spending. He built a crucible factory in Jersey City, New Jersey, and moved the Joseph Dixon Crucible Company there in 1847, manufacturing crucibles, stove polish, and, of course, pencils. Dixon's crucibles sold well, but as before his attempt to generate profits from producing pencils met with disappointing results. After his first year of business, Dixon pocketed $60,000 from the sale of crucibles and lost $5,000 from selling pencils, financial results indicative of his more than 20-year history in the pencil business and his almost begrudging success with other products.

Success in Selling Pencils, Later 1800s

The country's next war finally engendered Dixon's long-awaited dream, as more and more Americans began buying and using pencils. More easily carried than quills and ink, pencils became popular with Union and Confederate soldiers during the Civil War, and their use spread throughout the country. By 1866, Dixon had invented a wood planing machine that churned out 132 pencils per minute, enabling him to meet the rising demand for his four-inch long, cedar pencils. Three years later, however, just as the pencil segment of the Joseph Dixon Crucible Company began to perform on an equal level with his stove polish and crucible segments, Dixon died, 57 years after his work with pencils had begun. In addition to his accomplishments with stove polish and graphite crucibles, Dixon had also designed a camera with a mirror—the precursor to the modern photographic viewfinder—and had patented a double-crank steam engine. He had also invented a new method for tunneling underwater, developed a photolithography process used in printing banknotes that was designed to thwart counterfeiters, and attracted the prestigious company of fellow American inventors Robert Fulton, Samuel Morse, and Alexander Graham Bell. None of these achievements, however, ranked in Dixon's mind as equal to his lifelong achievements with pencils.

After Dixon's death, his son-in-law took control of the company and presided over the first decade of genuine success in selling vast numbers of pencils. By 1872, the factory in Jersey City was making 86,000 pencils a day, which was roughly one-third of American consumption at the time. The following year, the company purchased the Ticonderoga, New York-based American Graphite Company. The addition of American Graphite and the city in which it was located (near a fort of the same name that passed between British and American control during the American Revolution) eventually—in 1913—led to a brand name change in the company's pencils. Dixon pencils became Dixon Ticonderoga pencils, although the company continued to be known as the Joseph Dixon Crucible Company. Meantime, leadership of the company devolved into receivership in 1883, when a bank president named Edward F.C. Young assumed control of the company, which he then passed to his son-in-law, George T. Smith.

By World War I, competition in the pencil market had intensified. European manufacturers had joined the fray, led by German and Japanese pencil producers, while in the United States, four pencil manufacturers, the "Big Four," battled for market share. Along with Eberhard Faber, American, and Eagle, Dixon was one of the four pencil manufacturers in the country that wielded overwhelming control over the market, together accounting for 90 percent of the pencil sales in the United States. Despite their enviable position, Dixon and the other three dominant pencil manufacturers began clamoring for increased tariffs in the early 1920s to staunch the flow of cheaper German and Japanese pencils entering the United States. A decade later, as foreign competition mounted and the Great Depression tapered demand, the Big Four's market share slipped to 75 percent.

World War II resuscitated the American economy and along with it the demand for pencils. By 1942, despite shortages of graphite, clay, metal, and rubber, 1.5 billion pencils were being produced annually, and Dixon, as one of the largest in the industry, captured a lion's share of the booming market. After the war, demand slipped slightly to 1.3 billion pencils a year, but whatever the annual volume of demand, the industry's Big Four, almost exclusively, continued to supply it. By 1954, however, the Big Four's 30-year dominance of the industry had

Key Dates:

1812: Joseph Dixon makes his first pencil.

1827: Dixon establishes a firm that will eventually be known as the Joseph Dixon Crucible Company, which finds initial success marketing graphite as a stove polish, and later a heat-resistant graphite crucible.

1847: Dixon builds a crucible factory in Jersey City, New Jersey, and moves his company there.

1866: Rising demand prompts Dixon to invent a machine that can produce 132 pencils per minute.

1869: Dixon dies, and his son-in-law takes control of the company.

1872: Company commences mass production of pencils— 86,000 a day.

1873: Ticonderoga, New York-based American Graphite Company is acquired.

1913: The Dixon Ticonderoga pencil makes its debut.

1954: Along with its three main U.S. pencil-making rivals, Dixon pleads no contest to charges of violating the Sherman Antitrust Act, including allegations of price-fixing; a manufacturing subsidiary is established in Mexico.

1957: Dixon merges with American Crayon Company, gaining "Old Faithful" pencils, Prang crayons, and Tempera art products.

1982: Wallace Pencil Company, along with its production facility in Versailles, Missouri, is acquired.

1983: Joseph Dixon Crucible Company merges with Bryn Mawr Corporation, forming Dixon Ticonderoga Company; Gino N. Pala becomes CEO; headquarters are in Vero Beach, Florida.

1986: Dixon acquires David Kahn Inc., gaining the Wearever brand of writing instruments.

1990: Headquarters are moved to Maitland, Florida.

1996: Company moves its headquarters to Heathrow, Florida.

1997: Prang Soybean Crayons are introduced; Vinci de Mexico is acquired.

2000: A manufacturing subsidiary is established in China.

2003: Dixon divests the last of its industrial businesses, making it strictly a consumer products firm.

2004: Dixon Ticonderoga agrees to be acquired by the Italian firm Fila–Fabbrica Italiana Lapis ed Affini S.p.A.

drawn the attention of federal officials and each was charged with violating the Sherman Antitrust Act. Together, Dixon, Eberhard Faber, American, and Eagle generated $15 million in annual sales, accounted for 50 percent of domestic sales and 75 percent of export sales, and controlled all aspects of pencil production, which, as the U.S. government alleged, included price-fixing. Each entered pleas of no contest, agreed in a consent decree to desist from further illegal practices, and paid a nominal $5,000 fine apiece. Also in 1954, Joseph Dixon Crucible Company de Mexico S.A. was established to manufacture pencils and color pencils for the Mexican and U.S. markets.

Following the company's legal turmoil, Dixon began to feel pressure from the pencil industry's fifth largest competitor, Empire, which prompted Dixon to redesign the packaging of its products and effect a merger, in 1957, with the American Crayon Company. Based in Sandusky, Ohio, American Crayon manufactured "Old Faithful" pencils, Prang school and marking crayons, and Tempera colors and art materials, which were then added to the Dixon product line, giving the company a broader supply of graphite lead pencils and valuable connections with the nation's school system, one of American Crayon's primary customers.

Gino Pala, Bryn Mawr, and the Creation of Dixon Ticonderoga in the Early 1980s

While for Dixon the next two decades passed without any major developments, significant events were occurring elsewhere that would result in a change in ownership for the venerable pencil and crucible manufacturer. Several years after Dixon merged with American Crayon, a series of events began unfolding in a small, family-owned bar and restaurant. The restaurant was Pala's Café in Wilmington, Delaware, run by Gino N. Pala, who left school in the 11th grade and began working in his father's fruit market in 1944. Shortly after his 21st birthday, Pala began running the family restaurant and bar in Wilmington, which by the mid-1960s had become a meeting place for the city's lawyers and real estate developers. During this time, some of the executives who frequented Pala's Café began inviting Pala to join them in their investments. Pala, who had been running the café for roughly 20 years by this time and had profited from a furniture business he and his brother had opened in 1954, had the cash and began investing it with some of his customers. One customer with whom Pala became particularly involved was David K. Brewster, a former deputy attorney general and securities commissioner of Delaware. In 1975 Pala and Brewster bought 20 percent of the shares in a company called Electric Hose & Rubber for $1.6 million, then initiated a proxy fight to gain control of the company. They lost the battle, but the company's management ended up buying the shares back for $2.4 million, giving each investor a healthy profit.

Pala and Brewster combined forces again in 1978, paying $1.5 million for a 51 percent stake in a failing real estate, restaurant, and bus company named Bryn Mawr Corporation. With $9 million of debt, Bryn Mawr needed much attention, so Pala ceded control of his restaurant to a younger brother, then moved to Florida and began selling off Bryn Mawr's assets. Several years and $25 million in assets later, Pala had revived Bryn Mawr, enabling the company to net $10 million in pretax profits. Pala and Brewster then began looking for another acquisition, and in 1981 found one: the Joseph Dixon Crucible Company.

Dixon had since become a lackluster performer, earning $1 million in 1981 on revenues of $64 million, then recording a $1 million loss the following year as revenues slipped to $57 million. After acquiring 13 percent of Dixon's stock, Pala and Brewster convinced the company's management to approve a merger between Bryn Mawr and Dixon, which was concluded in 1983. Concurrent with the merger, the Joseph Dixon Crucible Company became Dixon Ticonderoga Company, adding the brand name of its famous yellow and green pencils to its corporate title. Headquarters were shifted to Vero Beach, Florida, where Bryn Mawr had been based. Shortly thereafter, the company exited the crucible business entirely. In 1982, meantime, as this merger was being effected, Dixon acquired Wallace Pencil Company and its production facility in Versailles, Missouri. Subsequently, Dixon's pencil-making operations were gradually shifted from Jersey City to this Versailles (pronounced ver-SALES) plant.

Once in control, Pala sold off some of the company's assets, consolidated operations, revamped some of the company's manufacturing plants, and by 1985 had paid off $5.4 million of debt. Under Pala's stewardship, Dixon prospered for the next three years, expanding the scope of its operations and the breadth of its product line along the way. In 1986 Dixon purchased David Kahn Inc., a manufacturer of writing instruments marketed under the Wearever brand name, then two years later acquired Ruwe Pencil, National Pen & Pencil, and St. Louis Pencil. By 1988, the company's net income had eclipsed $3 million on revenues of nearly $80 million. Shortly thereafter, however, problems began to surface as the company's three-year period of financial growth turned into a retrogressive slide.

Early 1990s Difficulties Followed by a Brief Resurgence

In an effort to explain Dixon's anemic financial performance, Pala later related to the *Orlando Business Journal* that "I hired guys that I thought could run the company, [but] they didn't know how to run a business," an imputation that was evident in the precipitous drop in Dixon's net income. Now based in Maitland, Florida (near Orlando), the company lost $5 million in 1990, halfway through an injurious earnings drought that left Dixon without a profit in 1989, 1990, and 1991. To effect a recovery, Pala reorganized Dixon's sales, marketing, and customer service operations, closed down two inefficient manufacturing plants in Ontario and Shelbyville, Tennessee, and trimmed superfluous layers of middle management. By virtue of such measures, Dixon once again returned to the black in 1992, when the company reported a modest yet reassuring $327,000 in net income.

After recording a meager $3,000 gain in net income in 1993, the company plotted its course for the mid-1990s and beyond, revitalized but yet to capitalize financially on the steps its management had taken to provide for a more profitable future. By reformulating the company's marketing strategy to embrace national office wholesalers and streamlining its manufacturing operations in the early 1990s, Pala and Dixon's management had repositioned the company for such a future.

The strategic initiatives implemented by Pala did indeed prove largely successful for most of the 1990s. Results for 1994 were strong: $3.3 million in profits on revenues of $92.1 million, the latter up 12 percent from the previous year. In September 1994, in an unintentionally well-timed move, Dixon sold 49.9 percent of its formerly wholly owned Mexican subsidiary through an initial public offering (IPO) on the Mexican stock market. The IPO provided the company with about $5 million in proceeds, which helped it reduce its total debt by $7.5 million, or nearly 20 percent. It also insulated Dixon from the Mexican peso devaluation of December 1994, which put severe strains

on the Mexican economy and engendered a sharp drop in sales at the company's Mexican subsidiary.

By 1996, with direct sales to consumers via mass-market retailers continuing to increase, Dixon Ticonderoga achieved revenues in excess of $100 million for the first time. That same year, the firm moved its headquarters yet again, this time to Heathrow, Florida (north of Orlando). One year later it introduced what it claimed was the first new crayon in 100 years. Prang Soybean Crayons debuted in 1997, made not from paraffin wax, an oil-drilling byproduct, as other crayons were, but from soybeans, touted by Dixon as "a renewable resource" and "environmentally friendly." Dixon further contended that the new crayons did not flake and offered smoother application and brighter color than petroleum-based crayons. Packaging for the entire Prang line was concurrently overhauled, featuring black boxes adorned with animals and a new logo. Backed by a major marketing campaign, the new crayon line graced the shelves of such national retailers as Wal-Mart, Target, Staples, Office Depot, and OfficeMax. Also in 1997, Dixon acquired Vinci de Mexico, S.A. de C.V., a manufacturer of paints, chalks, and crayons for the Mexican and South American markets.

During the late 1990s, revenues at Dixon Ticonderoga peaked in 1998 at $124.7 million, while profits reached a height of $6.7 million the following year. The latter figure was aided in great measure by the sale that year of the firm's graphite division to Asbury Carbons Inc. for $23.5 million. The divestment was intended both to improve Dixon's balance sheet and to heighten its focus on its growing consumer products business, which now accounted for 80 percent of overall revenue. As sales began falling in 1999, Dixon reduced its workforce of 1,550 by about 150 employees and further consolidated its U.S. manufacturing operations as cost-saving measures.

Early 2000s: Return to Red Ink, Possible End to Independence

In March 1999 Richard F. Joyce, Pala's son-in-law, was named president and co-CEO, with Pala remaining chairman (a position he had held since February 1989) and co-CEO. Joyce had joined Dixon as corporate counsel in July 1990 and had also served as vice-chairman of the board since January 1990. The new management team had to immediately contend with declining sales, a return to red ink, and mounting cash-flow problems. One of the key factors sparking this latest challenge to the venerable firm was increasing competition from overseas pencil makers, particularly from China. Although demand for pencils in the United States grew in the 1990s, American pencil makers actually shipped fewer pencils at the end of the decade than at the beginning. The main reason was that cheap imports from China helped increase foreign manufacturers' share of the U.S. market from 16 percent to more than 50 percent—despite the U.S. government's imposition in 1994 of heavy antidumping duties on Chinese pencils. Throughout the 1990s, Dixon pursued various ways to cut its pencil manufacturing costs, such as shifting from California incense cedar to lower-priced Indonesian jelutong wood, for all but its premium Ticonderoga brand; and buying erasers from a Korean rather than its traditional U.S. supplier.

Although the pencil industry won renewed duties on pencil imports from China in mid-2000, Dixon reached the conclusion that it had to shift more of its own manufacturing outside of the United States in order to survive. During 2000 it moved some production to Mexico and also established a wholly owned production subsidiary in China. The Chinese plant began producing wooden slats, which were shipped to Mexico for assembly along with U.S.-produced graphite and erasers from Korea. Its Mexican manufacturing operations were also overhauled: Three plants were closed, 125 workers were terminated, and manufacturing operations were consolidated in a single, 300,000-square-foot facility. A restructuring charge of $1.6 million resulted in a loss of nearly $800,000 for 2000 on sales of $102.9 million.

Revenues fell to $90.5 million in 2001, and then stagnated at around $89 million over the following three years. The red ink continued through 2003 in part because of restructuring, debt refinancing, and other costs. During 2002 the company closed its crayon plant in Sandusky, Ohio (making the Versailles plant its only U.S. manufacturing facility), shifting the production to Mexico and eliminating an additional 115 jobs. A restructuring charge of $1.6 million was taken that year. In addition, Dixon divested its last remaining industrial division, selling New Castle Refractories to local management in late 2003. Dixon Ticonderoga was now focused exclusively on consumer products. Special items led to a net loss of $1.4 million for 2003, but Dixon managed to turn a profit on its continuing operations, a hopeful sign for the future.

Early in 2004 Dixon entered into talks with Jarden Corp. about being acquired by the Rye, New York-based company. Jarden had been growing rapidly during the early 2000s by acquiring a series of consumer product manufacturers. But Jarden, which had been considering a $5 per share bid for Dixon—for a total of $16.5 million—pulled out of the potential deal in March. Dixon, meanwhile, went on to post its best annual results since 1999 for the fiscal year ending in September 2004, finally reaping the benefits of its years-long consolidation, cost-containment, and debt-reduction efforts. Profits totaled $1.7 million on revenues of $88.2 million. It appeared, however, that the newly resurgent firm founded nearly two centuries earlier by Joseph Dixon would finally lose its independent status. In December 2004 Dixon Ticonderoga entered into an agreement to be acquired by Fila–Fabbrica Italiana Lapis ed Affini S.p.A., a producer of design and writing instruments, art materials, and modeling paste based in Milan. The Italian firm's brands included Giotto, Tratto, Pongo, Das, and Dido. Fila agreed to pay $7 per share in cash for Dixon's stock, or $22.4 million. Fila's tender offer was expected to commence in early January 2005.

Principal Subsidiaries

Dixon Ticonderoga, Inc. (Canada); Grupo Dixon, S.A. de C.V. (Mexico; 98%); Dixon Ticonderoga de Mexico, S.A. de C.V. (Mexico; 98%); Dixon Comercializadora Dixon, S.A. de C.V. (Mexico; 98%); Servidix, S.A. de C.V. (Mexico; 98%); Beijing Dixon Ticonderoga Stationery Company, Ltd. (China); Dixon Europe, Limited (U.K.).

Principal Competitors

Faber-Castell AG; Newell Rubbermaid Inc.; Binney & Smith, Inc.; RoseArt Industries, Inc.; Société BIC; JAKKS Pacific, Inc.

Further Reading

Boyd, Christopher, "Pencil Maker Strikes Deal: Dixon Ticonderoga OK's Its Sale to an Italian Maker of Writing Instruments," *Orlando Sentinel,* December 18, 2004, p. C1.

Bromfield, Jerome, "Everything Begins with a Pencil," *Kiwanis Magazine,* 1976, pp. 25–33.

Burnett, Richard, "Dixon Closes Three Mexican Pencil Plants," *Orlando Sentinel,* January 13, 2001, p. B9.

——, "Rewriting the Future: Lake Mary's Dixon Ticonderoga Has Turned to First Union Securities to Help It Figure New Strategies," *Orlando Sentinel,* September 12, 2000, p. B1.

Carns, Ann, "Point Taken: Hit Hard by Imports, American Pencil Icon Tries to Get a Grip," *Wall Street Journal,* November 24, 2000, p. A1.

Elliott, Brenda J., *Best of Its Kind: "Since 1795," the Incredible American Heritage of the Dixon Ticonderoga Company,* Heathrow, Fla.: Dixon Ticonderoga, 1996.

Erskine, Helen Worden, "Joe Dixon and His Writing Stick," *Reader's Digest,* November 1958, pp. 186–88, 190.

"Growing Sharper, Dixon Ticonderoga Points to Earnings of $2 a Share This Year," *Barron's,* April 16, 1987, p. 64.

Hagstrom, Suzy, "Becoming the Chief Pencil Pusher: Dixon Ticonderoga CEO Cultivated Business Savvy During Early Childhood," *Orlando Sentinel,* June 24, 1991.

——, "Sharpening Its Prospects: Maker of Writing Instruments Dixon Ticonderoga Restructures for Success," *Orlando Sentinel,* March 21, 1988.

——, "Vaulting Back: Dixon Ticonderoga Attempts to Overcome Financial Hurdles, Focus on Pencil-Making" *Orlando Sentinel,* June 24, 1991.

"How Dixon Made Its Mark," *New York Times,* January 27, 1974, p. 74.

Hubbard, Elbert, *Joseph Dixon: One of the World-Makers,* East Aurora, N.Y.: Roycrofters, 1912, 24 p.

Jackson, Jerry W., "Jarden May Acquire Dixon Ticonderoga," *Orlando Sentinel,* January 13, 2004, p. C1.

——, "Pencil Maker Sharpens Strategy: Pala, New Team Give Products Fresh Look at Dixon Ticonderoga," *Orlando Sentinel,* February 1, 1993, p. 13.

——, "Timing Write on Dixon Sale," *Orlando Sentinel,* March 13, 1995, p. 10.

"Lowly Pencil Involved in Global Controversy," *Wall Street Journal,* October 19, 1990, p. B1.

Lubove, Seth H., "Erasing Dixon's Me-Too Image," *Florida Trend,* September 1988, pp. 34+.

Marcial, Gene G., "This Penmaker Has Written Itself a Hot New Script," *Business Week,* May 9, 1988, p. 134.

Meeks, Fleming, "Better Than an M.B.A.," *Forbes,* June 26, 1989, pp. 88–94.

——, "Easier Does It," *Forbes,* October 29, 1990, p. 10.

Perrault, Mike, "Pencil in Profits: Dixon Ticonderoga to Erase Losses," *Orlando Business Journal,* June 26, 1992, pp. 1+.

Petroski, Henry, *The Pencil: A History of Design and Circumstance,* New York: Knopf, 1990, 434 p.

Tahmincioglu, Eve, "Making the No. 2 No. 1," *St. Peterburg (Fla.) Times,* August 22, 1999, p. 1H.

Vogel, Mike, "Pencil Pusher: Competition from Foreign Pencil Makers Has Worn Dixon Ticonderoga Down to a Nub," *Florida Trend,* December 2003, pp. 72–75.

Yasuda, Gene, "Not Just a Pencil-Pusher," *Orlando Sentinel,* July 14, 1997, p. 16.

—Jeffrey L. Covell
—update: David E. Salamie

Dot Foods, Inc.

Route 99 South
Mt. Sterling, Illinois 62353
U.S.A.
Telephone: (217) 773-4411
Toll Free: (800) 366-3687
Fax: (217) 773-3321
Web site: http://www.dotfoods.com

Private Company
Founded: 1960 as Associated Dairy Products
Employees: 2,000
Sales: $1.9 billion (2004 est.)
NAIC: 424410 General Line Grocery Merchant
 Wholesalers

Dot Foods, Inc. is the largest food redistributor in the United States, serving more than 3,000 food distributors with coast-to-coast deliveries from 480 manufacturers. With headquarters in Mt. Sterling, Illinois, this family-owned and operated business has experienced strong and steady growth since its inception in 1960. From a one-man operation delivering 15 different products from the back of a station wagon, to a thriving national corporation employing over 2,000 people and delivering goods from an inventory list of over 40,000 products, Dots Foods is the quintessential American success story. Despite its tremendous growth as a company, Dot Foods remains the "family business" it always was, operating on values of innovation, integrity, hard work, and respect for others.

Robert Tracy founded the company, and today seven of his 12 children are involved full time in the operation of the business. Dot Foods transports food and related products from manufacturers to food processors and foodservice distributors. The company has distribution Centers in Ardmore, Oklahoma; Liverpool, New York; Modesto, California; Vidalia, Georgia; and Williamsport, Maryland, and a fleet of 500 multi-temperature tractor-trailers, operated under Dot Transportation, Inc. Dot Foods also owns and operates Principal Resource, a company that performs telesales, telemarketing, and database management for foodservice clients.

1960s Roots in Dairy Delivery

Fueled by a passion to operate his own business, Robert Tracy founded Associated Dairy Products with his wife Dorothy in 1960. Initially, Robert worked out of his home, delivering three kinds of milk powders, cocoa, and other ingredients to ice cream manufacturers. He used the family station wagon for deliveries. Business grew enough that he soon switched to a pickup truck and then leased a delivery truck to handle larger orders. After just a year in business, Tracy invested in a small fleet of trucks and hired drivers to transport products.

Early on, Tracy set a precedent for exceptional customer service, and as a result his business grew steadily and was profitable each year. The company's increasing business volume had rapidly outgrown the rented warehouse space in Mt. Sterling, so in 1962 Tracy built Quonset hut warehouses to better handle his burgeoning business. By 1977 volume had increased so much that the company invested in building larger and more permanent warehouse facilities at the Mt. Sterling location.

Through 1978, Associated Dairy Products' focus had remained primarily in the product areas of dairy and ice cream-related items. Principal customers included dairy, bakery, and meat packing businesses. In 1981, Tracy renamed the company Dot Foods, Inc., in honor of his wife and partner, Dorothy. After two decades, Dot Foods had all the markings of a successful regional business. Sales had doubled every four years since 1961. By 1982 Dot Foods' employee roster had grown to 67 employees. The company now had a fleet of 24 trucks, and made deliveries to nearly 30 states. A second generation joined in company leadership in 1985, when Tracy's son Pat became president of Dot Foods. Robert Tracy was CEO.

Business Shifting to Foodservice Side: 1980s

According to company estimates, until 1980 about 80 percent of its service was to food manufacturers, and 20 percent was to foodservice distributors. Dot Foods reversed those statistics by 1990, resulting in a new and more lucrative direction for the business. In the company published book *Dot Foods: Redistributors to the Nation,* "this shift in business direction changed the future of Dot Foods. They foresaw the consolidation in the food manufacturing industry and slowly converted to food-service distribution. In so doing, they started on a new avenue of growth and prosperity.''

Dot Foods soon became the dependable middleman in the foodservice food chain. As a ''re-distributor,'' Dot delivered products directly from manufacturers to wholesale distributors, who in turn, delivered the products to retail foodservice, convenience stores, retail grocery stores, vending suppliers, and more.

The shift in service focus was a wise one. Dot Foods was poised to benefit from the significant growth in the foodservice industry nationwide. In 1988 Dot erected a state-of-the-art corporate office headquarters and began laying the groundwork for use of computers that would keep the company on the cutting edge technologically within the food distribution industry.

Seeking to expand Dot's product offerings into new areas, in 1990 Tracy created Arctic Foods, to specialize in frozen food distribution. Dot and Arctic operated concurrently until Tracy merged the two business entities in 1994 as a result of customer feedback. That same year Dot began a 40,000-square-foot addition to the Mt. Sterling warehouse which further enabled expansion to new markets.

Significant Nationwide Expansion: 1990s

By 1994 Dot Foods had grown larger than its founder had originally envisioned. Dot employed more than 600 people nationwide, with two-thirds of them working from the Mt. Sterling headquarters. Tracy established Dot Transportation, Inc. to efficiently operate and manage the fleet of specialized delivery trucks. At that time Dot was an industry innovator, using special trucks built to handle multi-temperature shipments of products. The multi-temp trucks made it possible to transport frozen, refrigerated, and room temperature dry products all in one truck. This capability helped Dot's smaller distributor customers to compete and operate more effectively in the marketplace.

Dot solidified its presence on the East Coast by opening a distribution center in Williamsport, Maryland, in 1994. The eastern region warehouse featured a multi-temperature facility which company literature stated was ''the prototype that signifies our commitment to future growth and to technological innovation.'' Following a long-range goal of expanding to the West Coast, Dot established a second regional distribution center in Modesto, California, in 1995 (though the company had used warehouse space in Stockton, California, since 1989). Burgeoning business volume pushed Dot to add on to that center in 1998.

By 1996 the company's product offerings numbered 21,000, gleaned from 215 suppliers, and Dot Foods employed more than 900 people. That year Dot expanded warehouse space for the eastern market by purchasing a 30,000-square-foot facility near the existing Williamsport distribution center. Already heavily

invested in the dry and frozen food distribution business, Dot took steps to grow in the refrigerated product area. An $8 million expansion to the Mt. Sterling facility increased storage space for perishables, doubling the distribution center's storage capacity. At that time Dot was the only company using the multi-temperature trucks and the only business of its kind providing service to all 50 states.

Gaining a Competitive Edge Through Technology

Also in the 1990s, Dot Foods made technology a company priority as a means of maximizing business efficiency and customer service. Dot utilized the Internet as a means of communicating with customers before most of its competitors were on board.

In 1996 the company installed and began implementing a technologically sophisticated warehouse management system designed by MARC Global (Material and Resource Control). The system resulted in improved management and accuracy of inventory and greater efficiency in moving products in and out of the warehouse. Within two years Dot implemented the computer system at all of its warehouse distribution centers.

Early on, Dot Foods had made technology part of its plan, using EDI, or electronic data interchange, when others were managing product movement on paper. A 1998 article in *Voice of Foodservice Distribution* cited Dot as one of three industry role models because it was ''striving for world-class status in logistics in an effort to create both a competitive advantage and to reduce costs.'' According to the article, Dot boasted the fastest lead time in the industry because of the company's ability to deliver product anywhere in the United States within two days. A big reason for that efficiency was that Dot owned and managed its own fleet for distribution. But Dot's underlying management information system and the multi-temperature trailers helped Dot maximize use of storage space and efficiency throughout the process.

Throughout its four-decade history, Dot Foods demonstrated a commitment to the personal and professional development and well being of its employees. Dot established an employee retirement plan in the 1970s, which was unusual for a small family business. During the 1990s the company created a program to offer employees with five years of service or more no-interest home loans for up to $50,000. Further illustrating a commitment to its employee satisfaction in the workplace as well as in their personal lives, the company created Dot Foods Learning Center in 1997, serving both the educational needs of Dot employees and the community. Dot's project partners were the local community college and the school district.

Dedicated Employees Show Gratitude

The Tracy family's employee focus did not go unnoticed. In 1999 Dot Foods' personnel responded with a very tangible and public show of gratitude. Many of the company's 1,200 employees donated to raise $25,000 among themselves to purchase a 53-foot trailer as a way to say thanks to company founders Robert and Dorothy Tracy. The trailer featured the Dot logo displayed in silver and gold mirrors, and the message ''The employees at Dot Foods/Dot Transportation, Inc. give this trailer in honor of our company founders Robert and Dorothy Tracy, whose commitment to a dream enriches the lives of many.'' Among the many things employees appreciated was that despite financially tempting offers to relocate company headquarters to a larger town or city, the Tracys remained committed to staying in Mt. Sterling and making Dot Foods an involved and vital member of that community.

In 1999 Dot Foods reinforced service to the southeastern United States by opening a distribution center in Vidalia, Georgia. By 2000 Dot employees numbered 1,500 nationwide. Founder Robert Tracy said employees were Dot Foods' ''single greatest asset.'' The company projected that business would continue to double every five years.

To accommodate growth, Dot's Mt. Sterling distribution center got a 126,000-square-foot addition, increasing dry capacity storage space and bringing the facility to nearly 650,000 square feet. Thanks to the warehouse addition, Dot was able to maintain more dry groceries as well as have additional capacity for a new area of business, light equipment and supplies. Dot made approximately 5,000 new products available to customers in the equipment and supplies area. Those items included glassware, flatware, servingware, china, and janitorial supplies.

First Billion-Dollar Year: 2001

In 2001 Dot Foods recorded its first billion-dollar year with $1.25 billion in sales. To expand its reach to become more of a full-service player to its distributors, Dot Foods acquired Principal Resource, of Dallas, Texas, that year. Principal Resource provided telemarketing, data analysis, and direct-mail campaigns to many of Dot's existing customers.

Reinforcing distribution to the northeastern region, Dot Foods purchased the Drescher Corporation in Liverpool, New York, in 2002. A subsidiary of US Foodservice, Drescher was a food redistribution company with $400 million in annual sales and a customer base of 1,200. The acquisition resulted in no immediate changes for employees of either company. At the time Drescher had about 250 employees.

By 2002 Dot offered its customer base a selection of 40,000 foodservice-related items and employed 1,800 people company-wide. Dot leaders recognized recent and future potential growth in the convenience store market which was influenced by the on-the-go lifestyle of so many consumers. As a result, the company focused more on expanding opportunities to serve the convenience store market, their ''c-store distribution channel.'' Dot reinforced how the company's extensive product selection, coupled with minimal and flexible ordering requirements, could benefit c-store distributors, helping increase inventory turns, decreasing inventory investment, and improving customer service. The c-store market responded with business growth.

Factors in Dot's Formula for Success

The list of factors contributing to Dot Foods' success was lengthy. Companywide use of technology was certainly one factor. The Dot Expressway, part of the company's edotfoods arm, facilitated customer access to information and ordering capability, and minimized duplicate data entry. This ''Virtual Store Front'' concept, gave distributors easy online access by linking them directly to the warehouse to purchase products or view what was available. The company also maximized efficiency in the distribution process through Dot Transportation Services, Inc., which boasted a very high rate for on-time delivery.

Dot Foods served a board range of customers, from huge companies such as SYSCO to small, local distributors; the company treated them all as valued members of the Dot family. Customers, especially smaller distributors, who appreciated Dot's minimal ordering requirements, ordering flexibility, and delivery frequency. The company was also able to pass on manufacturers' specials and discounts directly to the customers. Distributors could do business with multiple suppliers on one order, with one delivery, and one bill.

In 2004 Dot Foods' sales reached 1.9 billion, and there were no signs of waning growth. Serving 3,300 distributors and working with 480 manufacturers, Dot's leadership was poised to find the best ways to meet the needs of its diverse clientele. The company estimated that it gained 200 new customers each year. A new Dot Foods distribution center opened in early 2005 in Ardmore, Oklahoma. It enabled the company to better serve customers in Texas, New Mexico, and Oklahoma. The company planned to double that facility's storage capacity in 2006.

Dot Foods' Mt. Sterling headquarters and distribution center remained on the cutting edge in the industry with the latest freezer cooler scheduled for installation. The company also had plans to further refine efficiency by automating some warehouse operations. Dot leaders did not rule out additional acquisitions or expansion into new business territories as they guided their father's company into what looked to be a profitable and successful future.

Principal Subsidiaries

edotfoods; Dot Transportation, Inc.; Principal Resource.

Principal Competitors

Regional Redistributors; Purity Wholesale Grocers, Inc.

Further Reading

Bochme, Natalie, "Dot Foods Workers Say Thanks to Founders," *State Journal Register*, February 16, 1999, p. 20.

"Dot Adds E & S," *Foodservice Equipment & Supplies*, June 2000, p. 14.

"Dot Foods Inc.," Business Briefs, *State Journal Register*, May 11, 2001, p. 41.

"Dot Foods Inc.," Business Briefs, *State Journal Register*, May 24, 2002, p. 29.

"Dot Foods: Redistributors to the Nation," Heritage Publishers, Inc., Copyright - Dot Foods, 1998.

"Dot's Tracy: Boost Distributor's Value to Operators; Redistributor Focuses on Supply Chain Benefits of 'Cyber Warehouse,'" *ID Access* [internet source], January 14, 2005.

Gertz, Deborah, "Dot Expansion Lifts Mount Sterling," *Quincy Herald B Whig*, March 27, 1994, p. 1A.

——, "Dot Foods Reconfirms Commitment to Area," *Quincy Herald B Whig*, March 30, 1997, p. 17.

Hayes Madden, Kelly, "Making Foodservice Easy to Digest," *Distribution Channels*, June 2002, p. 44.

Husar, Edward, "Businessman to Receive Scout Award," *Quincy Herald B Whig*, February 25, 1996, p. B1.

Margulis, Ronald, "When It Absolutely, Positively Has to Get There," *ID: The Voice of Foodservice Distribution*, July 1998, p. 40.

Salkin, Stephanie, "Dot Expansion Sets Stage for E & S," *ID: Information Source for Managers & DSRS*, June 2000, p. 24.

—Mary Heer-Forsberg

El Pollo Loco, Inc.

3333 Michelson Drive, Suite 550
Irvine, California 92612
U.S.A.
Telephone: (949) 399-2000
Fax: (949) 399-2025
Web site: http://www.elpolloloco.com

Private Company
Incorporated: 1983
Employees: 3,600
Sales: $396.0 million (2003)
NAIC: 722110 Full-Service Restaurants; 533110 Owners
and Lessors of Other Non-Financial Assets

El Pollo Loco, Inc. (EPL) describes itself as the nation's leading quick-service chain specializing in flame-grilled chicken. EPL owns and operates nearly 140 El Pollo Loco restaurants while franchisees control nearly 180 restaurants. The restaurants are located in California, Arizona, Nevada, and Texas. A majority of the units—roughly 80 percent—are located in California. The restaurants offer a variety of Mexican entrees and side dishes, including chicken burritos, chicken quesadillas, tacos al carbon, and EPL's signature dish, the Pollo Bowl. The company's majority owner is a New York-based equity investment firm, American Securities Capital Partners, L.P.

Origins

During EPL's first 25 years of development, it experienced several periods of powerful growth, recording surges of expansion that stood in sharp contrast with long stretches of time in which the company languished. The company was started in 1975, when Juan Francisco "Pancho" Ochoa opened his first roadside chicken stand in Guasave, Mexico, a small town on Mexico's Pacific Coast whose residents first experienced Ochoa's "El Pollo Loco," as his dining concept was called from the start.

To the residents of Guasave, Ochoa's style of cooking was not novel, but it was enormously popular. Using a recipe he learned from his mother, Ochoa marinated his chicken in a combination of herbs, spices, and citrus juices before flame-grilling it. The result became a local favorite, fueling the rapid growth of the El Pollo Loco concept. By the end of the decade—four years after the first chicken stand opened—Ochoa and his family and friends had established 85 restaurants in 20 northern Mexico cities, making full use of the opportunity before them. El Pollo Loco demonstrated enviable strength as a dining concept, encouraging Ochoa to make a bold geographic leap into the United States.

In later years, EPL experienced considerable difficulties when it attempted to export its restaurant concept into new geographic regions, but the company's initial foray proved to be an unmitigated success. In 1980, Ochoa opened an El Pollo Loco on Alvarado Street in Los Angeles and enjoyed greater success than he had with the first unit in Guasave. The Los Angeles restaurant, which had seating for 38 diners, drew crowds of patrons, collecting $2 million in revenues during its first year. The initial success fueled aggressive expansion, much as it had five years earlier in northern Mexico. Ochoa opened an average of four new restaurants a year in Los Angeles for the next three years, by which time the performance of the El Pollo Loco concept had attracted the attention of a U.S. corporate suitor.

1983 Acquisition by Denny's, Inc.

EPL never faltered under the stewardship of Ochoa. The chain began to experience its first difficulties when under the control of corporate parent companies, the first being Denny's, Inc. The operator of a massive chain of inexpensive family restaurants, Denny's acquired Ochoa's 12 El Pollo Locos in Los Angeles in 1983 for $11.3 million. Ochoa and his family retained control of the concept in Mexico. The transaction marked the beginning of a new era for EPL, one that would see the company benefit and suffer from the tutelage of much larger parent companies. The homespun business that began in Guasave had matured, for better or for worse, and now faced a future of great expectations in a decidedly corporate world.

EPL existed as a division within Irvine, California-based Denny's throughout the mid-1980s. In 1987, the company was swept up in corporate maneuverings beyond its control when TW Services, Inc., one of the largest restaurant companies in the world, acquired Denny's and EPL. The transaction gave EPL a new parent, one that, like Denny's, saw the concept as a growth vehicle. From 1983 to the end of the decade, EPL, under the control of Denny's and TW Services, grew to be a nearly 200-unit restaurant chain. The growth was impressive, but it was achieved almost entirely in California. Under TW Services' control, an attempt to greatly broaden the chain's geographic presence had scored only moderate success in Arizona, Nevada, and Texas. Elsewhere, the efforts to export the concept failed, leading to the closure of units in Florida, Hawaii, and as far away as Japan, by the beginning of the 1990s.

EPL opened its 200th restaurant in 1991, but celebrations for the milestone were muted. The failed forays into markets outside California aside, the chain was beginning to perform sluggishly as it exited the 1980s. The onset of a national recession in the early 1990s only served to exacerbate the company's woes. Some members of the business press at that time observed that TW Services was willing to sell EPL, but the restaurant conglomerate was unable to find an interested buyer. EPL's fortunes did not improve until Raymond Perry took control of the chain in 1993, the same year TW Services changed its name to Flagstar Corporation. Perry, a foodservice veteran who served for years as the day-to-day operations chief of the Carl Jr.'s burger chain, added an important new dimension to EPL's business. Since its inception, EPL had operated almost exclusively as a dinner establishment, attracting only a limited lunchtime crowd. Perry changed that, introducing an expanded menu featuring barbecued chicken, new varieties of burritos, and tacos al carbon that attracted lunchtime patrons.

Its business invigorated by soaring lunch sales, EPL began to exude strength again as it entered the mid-1990s. Perry used the opportunity to start an ambitious remodeling program in 1994. The restaurants' exteriors were refurbished and salsa bars were added, among several other alterations that cost between $60,000 and $100,000 for each location. When Perry left the chain in mid-1995, his efforts to broaden EPL's appeal beyond a narrow ethnic niche created a vibrant enterprise that represented the jewel of Flagstar's holdings.

EPL was performing admirably by the mid-1990s, but the company had recorded only negligible physical growth since the start of the decade. The chain increased from 12 units to 200 units between 1983 and 1991. During the next five years, only 16 units were added to the chain. Flagstar's management, which had viewed EPL as a hindrance earlier in the decade, now looked at the chain as one of its primary growth vehicles. The parent company's executives declared their intention in 1996 to make EPL a 600-unit chain by the end of the decade. To give

themselves an opportunity for international growth, they acquired the foreign development rights for the El Pollo Loco concept from Ochoa, who retreated again, this time retaining the rights for only two small territories in Mexico. Flagstar's grand plans never materialized, however. Within months the company found itself in a severe financial crisis, leaving its well-performing subsidiary, EPL, to suffer from its parent company's malaise.

Flagstar had the desire to expand EPL, but not the capabilities to follow through on its goal. The company's other foodservice holdings—family dining chains Quincy's Family Steakhouse, Denny's, Carrows, and Coco's—were producing lackluster results. Further, the company itself was awash in debt, occupying a precarious position as it entered the late 1990s. Roughly a year after proclaiming its intention to triple the size of EPL, Flagstar filed for bankruptcy, leaving the thriving EPL chain to wait for its parent company's attempt to recover. Flagstar emerged from bankruptcy in 1998 under a new name, Advantica Restaurant Group, Inc., and with a revamped strategic focus, one that did not include EPL within its scope.

A Change in Owners in 1999

In 1999, Advantica's management began to sharpen its focus on its restaurant brands. EPL, as the only quick-service holding within its portfolio, no longer fit within the parameters of the conglomerate's operating strategy. Midway through the year, Advantica, in dire need of cash to aid in the redevelopment of its full-service restaurant chains, hired an investment banking firm to find a buyer for the 268-unit EPL chain. There was no shortage of interested buyers. The chain continued to perform well despite the financial troubles of its parent company. In May 1999, at approximately the same time Advantica decided to divest the chain, EPL announced that it intended to open 32 new restaurants during the year, its most aggressive expansion in a decade. More than 100 suitors inquired about acquiring the chain before a deal was struck. In November 1999, a New York-based equity investment firm named American Securities Capital Partners, L.P. acquired EPL, paying $128 million for the chain. American Securities, whose only other foodservice holding was a 132-unit Burger King franchise in Puerto Rico, managed a $350 million fund that included six companies.

EPL entered the 21st century with a new sense of confidence. Under the stewardship of Advantica and its predecessors, the chain's development had been stunted. The menu, aside from incorporating lunchtime items early in the 1990s, changed little during the decade. Physically, the chain had not expanded as much as it could have, particularly into new regions. The beginning of the new century and its new freedom as a relatively independent company marked the beginning of a new era, one that would take its direction from a new leader. In 2001, Stephen Carley was appointed EPL's new president and chief executive officer. Under his leadership, the chain pressed forward during the first half of the new decade, attempting to seize opportunities that it previously had been unable to exploit.

Carley, a Chicago native and graduate of Northwestern University's Kellogg School of Management, made several important contributions to EPL during his first years in control. Carley was in his late 40s when he took the helm at EPL, leaving his

Key Dates:

1975: Juan Francisco Ochoa opens the first El Pollo Loco in Guasave, Mexico.

1980: Ochoa opens an El Pollo Loco in Los Angeles, the first unit in the United States.

1983: Denny's, Inc. acquires Ochoa's restaurants in Los Angeles.

1987: TW Services, Inc. acquires Denny's and El Pollo Loco.

1993: TW Services changes its name to Flagstar Corporation.

1998: TW Services emerges from bankruptcy with a new name, Advantica Restaurant Group, Inc.

1999: American Securities Capital Partners, L.P. acquires the El Pollo Loco chain from Advantica.

2001: Stephen Carley is appointed president and chief executive officer of El Pollo Loco.

2004: Carley signs an agreement to expand the chain in Chicago.

post as president of a digital photography company named PhotoPoint Corp. to join the restaurant chain. Although Carley also spent three years as the head of Universal City theme park in Los Angeles, the bulk of his professional experience corresponded with the duties he assumed at EPL. Carley spent more than a decade as an executive at Taco Bell and its parent company, PepsiCo, Inc., gaining the experience he would rely on in running EPL.

Carley inherited a profitable enterprise when he joined EPL. His challenge was not to restore a troubled company's fortunes, but to help EPL realize its potential. One of his first actions was to initiate a remodeling program in 2001, an extensive program that took two years to complete. Once the remodeling program was underway, Carley turned his attention to the chain's menu. Between June 2002 and June 2004, eight new items were added to EPL's menu, including the Chicken Quesadilla, Caesar Pollo Salad, and Twice Grilled Chicken Burrito. Sales rose as a result of the new product offerings and the remodeling program, increasing more than 4 percent in 2003.

Carley injected EPL with new vitality during his first years in command, but his most challenging objective remained unfilled as the company entered the mid-2000s. For years, EPL had struggled to establish a meaningful presence outside California. Carley was determined to complete such a geographic leap, and he turned to his hometown as the proving ground for EPL's ability to thrive outside the West. In January 2004, Carley signed an agreement with a pair of operators in Chicago that called for the establishment of ten El Pollo Loco restaurants in Chicago during the ensuing ten years. If Carley achieved success in exporting the concept outside California, the development of a national chain was likely, but much remained to be determined as EPL prepared for its future.

Principal Subsidiaries

B D M Enterprises; Arizona Colorado Enterprises LLC; Cal-Sin Enterprises, Inc.; Lilend International Inc.; Minovitz Enterprises Inc.

Principal Competitors

Boston Market Corporation; Del Taco, Inc.; KFC Corporation.

Further Reading

Alva, Marilyn, "Crazy for Chicken," *Restaurant Business,* March 1, 1996, p. 84.

Bluth, Andrew, "Mexican Fast-Food Chain in Irvine, Calif., Gets New CEO," *Knight Ridder/Tribune Business News,* April 11, 2001.

Cebrzynski, Gregg, "El Pollo Loco Changes Course with New Food-Focused Campaigns," *Nation's Restaurant News,* May 19, 2003, p. 12.

Farkas, David, "Crazy Like a Fox," *Chain Leader,* June 2004, p. 45.

Hardesty, Greg, "New York Firm Buys Irvine, Calif.-Based Fast-Food Chain," *Knight Ridder/Tribune Business News,* November 9, 1999.

——, "Parent Firm Looks to Sell Irvine, Calif.-Based Fast-Food Chain," *Knight Ridder/Tribune Business News,* June 7, 1999.

Keegan, Peter O., "El Pollo Loco Hops on Home-Delivery Bandwagon," *Nation's Restaurant News,* January 28, 1991, p. 4.

Martin, Richard, "El Pollo Loco Chain Crows: 'We Drive Our Rivals Nuts,'" *Nation's Restaurant News,* December 5, 1994, p. 3.

Spector, Amy, "Advantica Sells El Pollo Loco for $128M to Aid Core Brands," *Nation's Restaurant News,* November 22, 1999, p. 1.

Walkup, Carolyn, "El Pollo Loco Set to Cross State Borders, Offer Mexican-Chicken Brand in Midwest," *Nation's Restaurant News,* February 9, 2004, p. 4.

—Jeffrey L. Covell

Empresas Copec S.A.

Agustinas 1382
Casilla 9391
Santiago 6500586
Chile
Telephone: (56) (2) 690-7000
Toll Free: (56) (800) 200-220
Fax: (56) (2) 672-5119 or 696-5063
Web site: http://www.copec.cl

Public Company
Incorporated: 1934 as Compania de Petroleos de Chile
    S.A.
Employees: 8,137
Sales: CLP 2.66 trillion ($4.48 billion) (2003)
Stock Exchanges: Borsa de Comercio de Santiago
Ticker Symbol: COPEC
NAIC: 113110 Timber Tract Operations; 113310
    Logging; 114111 Finfish Fishing; 212299 Other Metal
    Ore Mining; 311712 Fresh and Frozen Seafood
    Processing; 322110 Pulp Mills; 321212 Softwood
    Veneer and Pulpwood Manufacturing; 447110 Gasoline
    Stations with Convenience Stores; 454312 Liquefied
    Petroleum Gas (Bottled Gas) Dealers; 454319 Other
    Fuel Dealers; 522210 Credit Card Issuing

Empresas Copec S.A. is the largest privately owned company in Chile, and its consolidated sales represent no less than 5 percent of the nation's domestic production. It leads all Chilean companies in the distribution of all types of fuels and owns several hundred gasoline stations operating under the Copec name. Its Arauco subsidiaries make it the leading producer of forestry products in the country and, indeed, the largest forestry enterprise in South America, and its fishery subsidiaries are located in one of the world's most important fishing zones. Copec also has a substantial stake in other economic sectors: services, mining, and electricity. The company is majority-owned by AntarChile S.A., which functions as the holding company for the interests of the Angelini group.

Big Fuel Distributor: 1934–64

Compania de Petróleos de Chile S.A. was founded in 1934 by a team of Chilean entrepreneurs with the goal of importing and distributing fuels in the national territory. The objective was to assure the flow of these supplies, which had been undermined by the scarcity of Chilean currency that occurred with the onset of the Great Depression. Although faced by competition from the major world oil companies, Copec was able to establish a national distribution network, with service stations and storage tanks, and to make itself the national leader in its field.

Copec's first venture outside its original business started in 1941, when it began selling vehicles, machinery, and tires and accessories. In 1943, when fuel supply shortages began to bite again due to World War II, the company created Sociedad de Navegación Petrolera (Sonap), which acquired an oil tanker, the first to sail under the national flag. In 1956, in collaboration with two other oil companies, it formed the pipeline company Sonacol. The following year Copec joined with Mobil Oil Corp. to construct a modern plant for the manufacture of lubricants, with the purpose of producing and distributing a complete line of fats and oils under the Mobil name. In 1961 the company took a stake in Abastible S.A., an enterprise distributing liquid natural gas to homes and industry. It gradually took control of this company, which eventually became ABC Comercial Ltda., through successive augmentations of capital. Copec, in 1964, joined with the Chilean subsidiaries of Esso—that is, Standard Oil Co. of New Jersey—and Shell Oil (the Royal Dutch/Shell Group) to establish Sociedad de Inversiones de Aviacion Ltda. (Siav), dedicated to the supply of fuels, lubricants, and other aviation products. By this time Copec was by far the richest commercial company in Chile.

Forestry Foremost: 1977–96

In 1939 the government of Chile had established the Corporación de Fomento de la Producción (Corfo), a state body, to plan and direct the nation's industrial development. Aside from providing subsidies to private companies and protecting them from foreign competition with high tariffs, Corfo took a considerable stake in many enterprises, especially in sectors such as electricity, steel, and petroleum. Following the military coup that overthrew the left-wing socialist government of 1970–73, a wide program of privatizing state enterprises was instituted. The nation's largest holding company of this period, representing the Cruzat and Larraín families, took control of Copec. They put the company into the forestry business by purchasing government-owned Empresa Forestal Arauco Ltda. and Industrias de Celulosa Arauco S.A. in 1977 for $90.63 million. This network of forest tracts, sawmills, and cellulose (wood-pulp) plants was augmented in 1979 by the purchase from Corfo of Celulosa Constitución S.A., which was merged with Celulosa Arauco to form Celulosa Arauco y Constitución S.A. At the same time, four new forestry subsidiaries were established to develop forestry resources in southern Chile for parent Copec, which was now the largest privately owned enterprise in the nation.

The Chilean forestry industry was being aided by climatic conditions that were thought to foster the rapid growth of the radiata pine, which was introduced into the country from the Monterey Peninsula of California. These conditions included large shifts in temperature each day, nutrient-rich soil, an environment relatively free from disease, steady and reliable rainfall, and proximity to the sea. A government forestry official told Shirley Christian of the *New York Times*, "Here, the radiata pine has found a better place to grow than its place of origin." In addition, the forestry industry was diversifying its roster of customers. Once heavily dependent on Argentina, Chile was selling forestry products to more than 70 countries in 1988.

By 1980 Copec also had branched out into computation, tourism, and durable goods. In that year it purchased a fishery, Pesquera Guanaye Ltda., and two electricity suppliers and distributors, Sociedad Austral de Electricidad S.A. (Saesa) and Empresa Eléctrica de la Frontera S.A. (Frontel). The following year it invested in coal deposits in far-southern Chile, a joint venture with British investors that gave rise to Compania de Carbones de Chile (Cocar S.A.). But the severe financial crisis that ensued and that affected all of Latin America found Copec hobbled by bad financial investments and high foreign-currency debt in the wake of the virtual collapse of the Chilean peso. The Cruzat-Larraín group could not pay its debts and had to surrender the enterprise. Anacleto Angelini Fabbri, owner of the fourth largest group in Chile, acquired 41 percent of the company's shares in 1985–86, including Corfo's 14 percent holding.

Angelini was an Italian immigrant who, after arriving in Chile in 1948, founded a paint factory with a few machines and $100,000 in capital, and later established a construction firm. In collaboration with Chilean associates, he acquired, in 1956, a fishery, Pesquera Eperva S.A. In 1975 this company bought, for only $1.14 million, the state's controlling interest in Pesquera Indo S.A., which became the first modern enterprise in Chile for

the large-scale production of fishmeal and fish oil. In 1977 Eperva and Indo bought the government's 76 percent share of Pesquera Iquique, a fish processor dating from 1945. Iquique became the second largest company in its field and grew sevenfold between 1977 and 1987. The largest was Pesquera Chilemar S.A., a fishing fleet that dated from 1961 and also was owned by Angelini. Angelini entered the forest products business in 1958 by means of an investment in the company Sociedad Maderas Prensadas Cholguán S.A. Twenty years later, Forestal Cholguán S.A. was split off from this company to take charge of the strictly forestry end, including 9,114 hectares (22,512 acres) of pine plantations.

Angelini was financially prudent and thus in a position to acquire the interests of the debt-ridden conglomerates such as Cruzat-Larraín that emerged in the privatizations of the 1970s but failed in the 1980s. He was allowed to do so even in basic resource industries, although (as of 1985) he had not taken Chilean citizenship, not wanting to renounce his Italian nationality. His partner in Copec was Carter Holt Harvey Holdings Ltd., a New Zealand conglomerate that converted $160 million of Chilean debt that it held into equity and added $50 million of its own cash. Angelini and Carter Holt Harvey jointly held 60 percent of Copec through a holding company, Inversiones y Desarrollo Los Andes S.A. With 26 affiliates, Copec was the major holding company in Chile at the end of 1989. Angelini was chosen as the entrepreneur of the decade by the business magazine *Gestion*.

Angelini more or less ignored the petroleum-distributing aspects of Copec to concentrate on export growth in the forestry and fishing sectors. To provide more raw material for paper, Copec opened the most modern cellulose plant in Chile in 1991, and it united two fisheries in 1992 to form Pescuera Iquique-Guanaye S.A. (Igemar), the largest in Chile. Eperva acquired Chilemar in 1992 and Indo in 1994, subsequently absorbing both companies. Copec established Aserradores Arauco S.A. in 1993 to consolidate its sawmill activities and added Paneles Arauco S.A. in 1995 to produce wood strips and panels. Celulosa Arauco y Constitución bought Argentina's largest wood-pulp producer and its only wood-pulp exporter, Alto Paraná S.A., in 1996. That year Copec entered gas distribution in Santiago by taking a stake in Metrogas S.A., which had become the principal company in this field. The conglomerate's holdings in electricity distribution became larger with the acquisition in 1996 of Empresa Energía Río Negro S.A., which was active in southern Argentina. From 1991 to 92, Copec had entered mining by organizing a company to explore hydrocarbon deposits in Colombia and by taking a majority share of Compania Minera Can-Can S.A., which began mining metals in 1994.

Raising the Stakes: 1997–2003

By 1997 Copec was valued on Chile's stock market at more than $5 billion. It held nearly half of the fuel distribution market in Chile, with about 1,500 service stations, which included cafeterias, stores, and minimarkets, and its own credit card, TCT. But the chief enterprise in importance was Celulosa Arauco y Constitución, representing 70 percent of its profit and exporting to 70 countries. In 1998 it was Chile's largest exporter outside of the mining sector. Despite low prices for wood pulp, Arauco, as the lowest-cost producer in the world, was earning a profit. Perfectly

Key Dates:

1934: Compania de Petróleos de Chile S.A. (Copec) is founded.
1964: Copec is the biggest commercial company in Chile.
1977: Copec enters the forestry business with the purchase of two companies.
1980: Copec acquires a fishing company and two electricity suppliers and distributors.
1985–86: Anacleto Angelini Fabbri buys a controlling interest in Copec.
1989: With 26 affiliates, Copec is Chile's largest holding company.
1992: Copec's Igemar is the biggest fishing and fish-processing company in Chile.
1995: Forest products account for 70 percent of Copec's sales.
2000: Angelini buys International Paper Co.'s 30 percent stake in Copec for $1.23 billion.
2002: Copec is the world's sixth largest producer of cellulose.
2003: Following reorganization, Copec becomes Empresas Copec S.A.

symmetrical rows of fast-growing pine trees from the company's more than one million acres of forest were being sent to sawmills and factories for conversion to bleached pulp, and eventually into paper products, particle board, and furniture.

Relations with Carter Holt Harvey had deteriorated after International Paper Co. purchased majority control of the New Zealand firm in 1995. In 2000 International Paper's stake in Copec was purchased by AntarChile—Angelini's holding company—for $1.23 billion. To pay for this, AntarChile raised $613 million by a public offering of stock and also took out a five-year, $525 million loan. Also in 2000, Copec purchased Angelini's Forestal Cholguan for $300 million. This brought the company 63,000 acres (155,610 acres) of forest, a sawmill, and two processing plants, one of them making a highly sought-after wood-and-fiber panel called Trupán. In 2001 Copec earmarked $1.2 billion for a second huge cellulose plant in Valdivia, and the following year it opened two wood-panel plants, one in Chile and one in Argentina. To help pay down the debts it had incurred, Copec shed its electricity distribution interests in 2000–01, including the sale of its longtime distributors Saesa and Frontel for some $250 million.

By 2002 Copec—chosen company of the year by the Chilean business magazine *Capital*—was the world's sixth largest producer of cellulose, turning out more than 1.5 million metric tons of pulp a year. Its 12 sawmills had a capacity of almost 2.2 million cubic meters per year. The five wood-panel plants had a combined capacity of nearly one million cubic meters. The Valdivia cellulose plant, scheduled to come on line in 2004 with capacity to produce 600,000 metric tons a year, was to be accompanied by sawmills and other works. Copec already had in mind still another cellulose plant, in Itata, that could be operating at the end of 2010. Wood pulp had become Chile's second largest export, after copper, but commodity prices often

fluctuated, as, for example, when the 1998 financial crisis in Asia seriously reduced demand from some of the product's chief customers. Copec and its Chilean competitors had by then begun focusing on turning out wood products of greater added value and less price volatility. Copec's wood panels and moldings, for example, were strips of pine highly prized for their clear, knot-free wood.

Despite strong results, Copec was finding that investing in the forestry sector was expensive, given that new plantings of trees were continuously required but could not be harvested for at least 20 years. Copec's purchase of Alto Paraná was attractive because land was cheaper in Argentina, trees grew faster, there were fewer environmental regulations, and no problems—as in Chile—of conflicts with Indians who lived in the most heavily forested zones. Chilean forestry companies also were being courted by Uruguay. In 2004 Copec owned 930,000 hectares (2.3 million acres) of forests in Chile, 233,000 hectares (575,000 acres) in Argentina, and 28,000 hectares (69,000 acres) in Uruguay. About two-thirds of these holdings in Chile and about half in Argentina and Uruguay were in plantations, chiefly of radiata pine or eucalyptus.

Copec's fuel distribution business had 613 service stations in 2002, plus an industrial channel that was supplying fuel to 3,039 construction, electrical, fishing, forestry, and mining customers. The company also held 40 percent of Metrogas and, through Abastible, remained in the business of distributing liquid natural gas. Fishing was a poor-performing sector of Copec's holdings, although it held 8 percent of the world fishmeal market, but in 2002 Igemar returned to the black after years of incurring losses. In all, Copec earned CLP 332.9 billion ($560.6 million) on revenues of CLP 2.66 trillion ($4.48 billion) in 2003. Fuels accounted for 63.3 percent of sales but only 22.6 percent of profit; forestry for only 32.5 percent of sales but 73.1 percent of profit. The company's long-term debt at the end of the year was CLP 1.15 trillion ($1.94 billion). At 89 years of age in 2003, Anacleto Angelini, rated the fourth richest man in Latin America, was still in charge of Copec, with his nephew Robert Angelini waiting in the wings to succeed him as head of an experienced managerial team. Following a reorganization of the enterprise, Copec became Empresas Copec S.A. in 2003.

Principal Subsidiaries

ABC Comercial Ltda.; Abastecedora en Combustibles S.A.; Alto Parana S.A. (Argentina); Celulosa Arauco y Constitución S.A.; Compania Minera Can-Can S.A. (51%); Pesquera Iquique-Guanaye S.A. (82%).

Principal Competitors

Empresa CMPC S.A.; Esso Chile Petrolera Ltd.; Shell Chile S.A.C.

Further Reading

"Anacleto Angelini Fabbri," *Gestión,* December 1985, pp. 14–16.
Brown, Greg, "Green with Envy," *Latin Trade,* July 2001, p. 70.
Castillo, Nancy, "La amenaza extranjera," *Capital,* May 18–31, 2001, pp. 56–59.
Christian, Shirley, "Chile Promotes Forestry Industry," *New York Times,* October 31, 1988, p. D8.

''Desde una caja a un piano,'' *Gestión,* April 1990, pp. 15–16.

''El empresario de la decada,'' *Gestión,* January 1990, p. 38.

García de la Herta, Carolina, ''Big Money,'' *Capital,* January 1997, pp. 46–48.

''Los Hombres Clave en las Decisiones del Grupo Angelini,'' *Gestión,* June 2002, pp. 32, 34, 36, 38.

''Liderazgo obliga,'' *Capital,* August 1996, p. 73.

Medel, Lorena, ''Salto cuántico,'' *Capital,* December 20–29, 2002, pp. 84–86.

Pérez R., Soledad, ''El nuevo imperatore,'' *Capital,* October 10–23, 2003, pp. 22, 24, 26, 28.

Torres, Craig, ''Chile Squeezes Last Drop from Factories,'' *Wall Street Journal,* November 24, 1999, p. A15.

—Robert Halasz

ENI S.p.A.

Piazzale Enrico Mattei 1
Roma
I-00144
Italy
Telephone: +39 06 59821
Fax: +39 06 59822141
Web site: http://www.eni.it

Public Company
Incorporated: 1953
Employees: 76,521
Sales: EUR 51 billion ($64.72 billion) (2003)
Stock Exchanges: Borsa Italiana New York
Ticker Symbol: ENI
NAIC: 211111 Crude Petroleum and Natural Gas
Extraction; 211112 Natural Gas Liquid Extraction;
221210 Natural Gas Distribution; 324110 Petroleum
Refineries; 447110 Gasoline Stations with
Convenience Stores

ENI S.p.A., the former Italian state-owned Ente Nazionale Idrocarburi, is one of the world's top ten oil and natural gas companies, with revenues of EUR 51 billion ($65 billion) in 2004. ENI focuses on three core businesses: Exploration & Production; Gas & Power; and Refining and Marketing. The Exploration & Production division produces some 1.6 million barrels of oil equivalent (boc) per day and expects to top 1.8 million boe by 2006. That division, however, accounts for less than 10 percent of the company's total sales. More lucrative is its natural gas and power operations, including the supply and transportation (primarily from fields in Algeria and Russia), and the distribution and marketing of gas, as well as the production of electricity. The company distributes more than 69 billion cubic meters of gas each year, primarily in Italy and elsewhere in Europe. That division supplies approximately 30 percent of ENI's sales. The company's largest division is its Refining and Marketing division, at 42 percent of sales through a network of 7,300 Agip and Ip service stations in Italy and nearly 3,500 service stations located in Europe. The company also produces a number of petrochemicals

as part of its other operations. Italy remains ENI's primary market, at more than 49 percent of sales, and the extended European market, including Italy, accounts for 77 percent of group sales. Nonetheless, ENI is present in Africa (11.5 percent), the Asia Pacific (6 percent), and the Americas (5 percent). ENI is listed on the Borsa Italiana and the New York Stock Exchange. The Italian government maintains a 30 percent stake in the company.

Beginnings in the 1920s

ENI has its origins in the 1920s when the Italian government formed Azienda Generale Italiana Petroli (Agip) to pursue exploration for petroleum and natural gas in Italy. In the restructuring of Italian industry that followed World War II, Agip and related state-owned energy companies were grouped together to form ENI. Today Agip remains the principal oil company in the ENI group.

State participation in Italian industry dates from the stock market crash of 1929. In 1933, when many of the country's important banks were threatened by the collapse of industries in which they were heavily invested, the government established the Istituto per la Ricostruzione Industriale (IRI), a public agency that reorganized the banking system and acquired the banks' extensive industrial shareholdings in the process. In the petroleum industry, state participation also took the form of investment and joint ventures with foreign or private companies intended to boost Italy's refining capacity and exploration of new indigenous energy sources.

In addition to creating Agip, the state joined with private industries to establish other energy-related companies that would eventually become part of ENI. The Azienda Nazionale Idrogenazione Combustibili (ANIC) was formed to operate in the refinery sector in 1936, as was Industria Raffinazione Oli Minerali (IROM), a joint venture with the Anglo-Iranian Oil Company. A later joint venture with Standard Oil of New Jersey resulted in the formation of STANIC, when Italy could not afford to update ANIC's three large refineries after the war. In 1941, government investment created Società Nazionale Metanodotti (Snam) to build and run methane pipelines, and Società Azionaria Imprese Perforazioni (Saip), a state-owned consortium of drilling companies.

Company Perspectives:

Mission: Eni is one of the most important integrated energy companies in the world operating in the oil and gas, power generation, petrochemicals, oilfield services construction and engineering industries. In these businesses it has a strong edge and leading international market positions.

Eni's objective is to create new value to meet its shareholders' expectations through the continuous improvement of cost efficiency and the quality of its products and services and through the attention to the needs of its employees and the commitment to a sustainable growth pattern also encompassing the careful assessment of the environmental impact of its activities and the development of innovative and efficient technologies.

To achieve this objective Eni relies on the managerial and technical capabilities as well as the continuous development of its workforce, and on an increasingly lean and entrepreneurial organization.

The creation of ENI, a single holding company that integrated all of Italy's activities in the hydrocarbons sector, was in large part the work of its first president, Enrico Mattei. An able manager and entrepreneur with a nationalist, collectivist, and egalitarian ideology, Mattei campaigned to have the company established, and directed the course of ENI's growth and activities in its first decade. His aggressive promotion of Italy's self-reliance in energy won him wide popularity; it also set ENI on a collision course with large foreign and private oil companies.

Mattei, a former partisan commander with some experience as an industrial manager in the private sector, was appointed commissioner of Agip for upper Italy in 1945. The years immediately following the Allied liberation were a pivotal period for the nascent petroleum industry in Italy. Discovery of Middle East petroleum deposits during the war and the arrival of powerful international oil companies held major implications for a successful postwar recovery in Italy. The peninsula's strategic location in the Mediterranean made it a logical point for low-cost refining and shipment of petroleum products to the West European market.

Agip, like most of Italian industry, had been devastated during the war. Refineries and pipelines lay in ruins and Agip's tanker fleet was virtually eliminated. The apparent lack of indigenous energy resources and a desire to accommodate foreign and private investment in the petroleum industry led the postwar government in Rome to order the liquidation of Agip's bankrupt mining and prospecting activities.

Mattei delayed the liquidation, however, alerted by reports of considerable methane deposits in the Po Valley located during the war and by the haste of the foreign companies to buy Agip's outdated and apparently worthless prospecting operations. Instead of proceeding with the sell-off, Mattei disobeyed his instructions and ordered that exploration in the Po Valley be continued.

In 1946, Agip's team at the Caviaga gas field made a successful methane strike. Two years later, the state company was reorganized with Professor Marcello Boldrini as its presi-

dent and Enrico Mattei as vice-president. In 1949, Agip acquired full control of the state-owned pipeline company Snam, which enabled Mattei to begin to establish a network of methane pipelines to communities and industry in northern Italy.

In the absence of laws tying exploitation rights to successful exploration, the widely publicized Po Valley methane and oil strikes triggered three years of parliamentary debate, legislative proposals, and intensive lobbying by international and private oil companies, all revolving around the issue of state control versus free competition in hydrocarbons exploration.

National Oil Company in the 1950s

On February 10, 1953, two years after its introduction in the Italian parliament, a bill was approved that established ENI as the national hydrocarbons company. All corporations through which the state was operating in the hydrocarbons sector at that time were grouped to form a single entity, through a complex system of outright acquisitions and government investments. A clause in the bill guaranteed ENI exclusive rights to exploration in the Po Valley, while allowing private companies to compete in other areas of Italy. Four years later, Mattei helped pass a second law that extended ENI's exclusive rights to all of mainland Italy.

The new company was constituted with ITL 15 billion in capital and another ITL 15 billion consisting of the nominal value of the assets of its constituent companies. ENI was authorized to trade in shares, and to carry on its activities through subsidiaries, associated companies, and investments in other companies and joint ventures. Mattei was appointed president, with Marcello Boldrini as vice-president.

Mattei's first task was to integrate ENI's constituent companies into a single enterprise, by grouping ENI's shareholdings into manageable units along functional lines and liquidating or converting any irrelevant assets. A series of mergers and diversifications during ENI's first ten years resulted in the group's present structure. Mattei and his successors followed a policy of vertical integration, so as to render ENI invulnerable in its supplies of raw and semifinished materials, as well as in services and transportation.

At first, ENI focused on production and distribution of natural gas, the only considerable source of energy available in mainland Italy. A subsidiary called Agip Mineraria was formed by the merger of Agip and the Ente Nazionale Metano. The new company in turn controlled the Saip consortium of drilling companies and La Società Ravennate Metano, a methane gas producer.

The pipeline company Snam was reconstituted to include the natural gas network of Azienda Metanodotti Padani in the Po Valley, and promptly set about expanding its system of trunk provincial and interprovincial gas lines. Snam operated as the sector head of ENI's engineering activities, which later included international construction of refineries, pipelines, and chemical plants. In the refining and petrochemicals sector, ENI companies or subsidiaries were headed by ANIC.

ENI entered the machinery manufacturing sector in 1954, when it acquired the failing Pignone industrial equipment company in Florence. Reconstituted as Nuovo Pignone, the new

Key Dates:

1953: ENI is created under Enrico Mattei, incorporating the Italian government's oil interests.

1957: ENI gains a monopoly over all oil and gas exploration and production in Italy.

1975: ENI begins acquiring struggling and failing state-owned companies.

1992: The company converts to a joint-stock corporation as the government agrees to privatize ENI; the company begins a restructuring drive, selling off more than EUR 5 billion in assets and cutting 42,000 jobs by the early 2000s.

1995: ENI lists its first tranche of shares on the Borsa Italiana and New York Stock Exchange.

1998: The Italian government relinquishes majority control of ENI, dropping its stake to 38 percent.

2000: The United Kingdom's British Borneo is acquired for $1.2 billion.

2001: Lasmo, in the United Kingdom, is acquired for $4 billion.

2002: ENI acquires 50 percent of Union Fenosa's natural gas business.

2004: ENI announces plans to sell off petrochemicals unit Polimeri Europe; the Italian government's stake is reduced to 50 percent.

company provided pipeline pumps, motor compressors, valves, and other equipment for new refineries and petrochemical plants. Later it built floating platforms for offshore oil exploration.

Fresh capital from the rapidly expanding natural gas production and distribution helped launch ENI's program of international expansion. In negotiating oil concessions with producer states, Mattei introduced an innovative formula for joint investment that deliberately sought to eliminate the middleman role previously played by the major oil companies. Instead of simply paying a fixed fee for oil concessions and then assuming all of the burden of development, as the majors did, Mattei offered producer states a partnership in the exploitation of their natural resources.

Initially, ENI assumed all of the risk in exploration, as did the big multinational oil companies. If the search revealed commercially viable deposits of hydrocarbons, however, the host country earned 50 percent of all profits, and in addition could choose to join in the production, by sharing half of all the development costs. Since the host country gained 50 percent of net profits, above the 50 percent already received as taxes and royalties, ENI's program came to be called "the 75/25 plan."

Following a more conventional joint venture with the Egyptian government in 1955, the ENI plan was subsequently applied in Iran in 1957, and in Morocco in 1958. In 1959, ENI formed similar partnerships with the governments of Libya and Sudan, and with Tunisia and Nigeria in 1961 and 1962.

The joint ventures had the effect of establishing the terms for subsequent concessions that producer states made to other foreign oil companies. By introducing his system of partnerships with producer states, Mattei effectively stimulated creation of state oil enterprises abroad, thus disrupting the institutional profile of the international oil industry. In negotiations and public statements, he asserted Italy's acceptability as a country less tainted by colonialism, and openly sought a reduction in the power, profits, and autonomy of the so-called Seven Sisters—the handful of Western oil companies that had until then dominated the international market.

Mattei successfully applied the same strategy when Agip sought concessions to build refineries and distribute its refined products in the developing countries. ENI formed joint ventures in refining with Morocco in 1958, and in Ghana and Tunisia in 1960. In the 1960s ENI companies undertook refinery construction projects in the Congo, south Asia, and Latin America.

Meanwhile, the reorganization of ENI that created Agip Mineraria and Snam at the same time divested Agip of its exploration and pipeline companies, leaving it to operate as head of ENI's activities in distribution and marketing of gasoline, lubricants, and other petroleum products both at home in Italy and abroad.

ENI contributed to Italy's swift recovery after the war as a part of the Sviluppo Iniziative Stradali Italiane (SISI) industrial consortium. SISI, which included Fiat automobile manufacturers, Pirelli rubber products, Agip, and the road building group Italcementi, virtually created an automobile culture in a newly urbanized Italy. Affordable cars, a new network of superhighways, and Agip's gasoline and oil products combined to set Italy's postwar economic "miracle" in motion.

To help build the automotive market, Mattei promoted Agip's products and image by providing new, brightly colored service stations throughout Italy and offered amenities previously unknown at service stations such as coffee shops, restaurants, and motels. By 1962, ENI's roadside outlets in Italy included some 30 Agip motels and more than 400 Agip restaurants or coffee shops. During this period Agip introduced its Supercortemaggiore high-octane gasoline and the symbol of the six-legged dog, which later came to stand for the ENI group as a whole, as well as all Agip products.

Between 1956 and 1960 Agip formed companies for foreign distribution of gasoline and lubricants throughout most of Africa, in Greece, Austria, Switzerland, West Germany, Argentina, and—through a joint venture—with the Anglo-Italian financier Charles Forte in the United Kingdom.

In the same period, Mattei effected a series of mergers designed to rationalize the group's various activities. ENI's subsidiary Snam came to head two subholdings: Snam Montaggi, created in 1955 to build pipelines and drilling platforms, and Snam Progetti in 1956, specializing in tankers. In 1957, Agip Mineraria's Saip subsidiary was merged with Snam Montaggi to create Saipem. The new industrial groups allowed ENI to increase its gas and petroleum transportation activities at an accelerated rate. Saipem was a pioneer in offshore drilling for hydrocarbons in Europe, and in the 1960s allowed Mattei to initiate a central European pipeline project running from the port of Genoa north to Pavia before forking off to Switzerland and to West Germany where ENI's Südpetrol subsidiary was building refineries at Ingolstadt and Stuttgart. This gave Mattei an important advantage in his dealings with the majors, in particular Esso and Gulf, ENI's chief competitors in the market.

ENI activities in the petrochemicals field started to expand in 1954 following the discovery of considerable natural gas deposits near Ravenna. ANIC built three petrochemical plants there in 1957 to produce Buna-S, a synthetic rubber; fertilizers; and later, acetates and polyvinyl chlorides. In 1959 a joint venture with the U.S. chemicals firm Phillips Carbon Black expanded the Ravenna operations to include production of carbon black.

In 1956, the Italian parliament established a Ministry of State Participation in Industry, to integrate the activities of state-controlled companies with economic and development policies. New legislation was passed requiring state-controlled companies to direct 40 percent of all new investment to Italy's poorer southern regions. Following discovery of deposits of petroleum and natural gas at Gela, Sicily, in 1956 ENI initiated construction of a giant refinery and tanker terminal on the Sicilian coast and created a regional petrochemicals subsidiary, ANIC Gela. The Nuovo Pignone manufacturing company carried out an expansion in southern Italy with construction of Pignone Sud in 1960.

Mattei also effected several major horizontal expansions for ENI, beginning with the establishment of Agip Nucleare in 1956. Two years later the Nuovo Pignone company began producing components for a large nuclear generator to be built at Latina, south of Rome. In 1963, however, Mattei's ambition of building a complete single energy group consisting of electric generating and hydrocarbons was defeated by the creation of Ente Nazionale Elettricità (ENEL). The separate state-run utility absorbed ENI's nuclear program, leaving uranium prospecting and nuclear fuel activities to Agip Nucleare.

Also in 1956, ENI established a financial company, the Società Finanziaria Idrocarburi (Sofid) to organize financing for ENI's bigger projects, and handle all of the group's financial activities and investments. Other enterprises included a center for research in hydrocarbons and petrochemicals and a school for postgraduate studies in hydrocarbons at the group's Milan headquarters. In 1959, ENI began publication of *Il Giorno*, a Milan-area daily paper.

ENI's expansions outside its original mandate continued in the 1960s. A joint venture with the U.S. firm Libbey-Owens Sheet Glass established Società Italiana Vetro in 1962. At the same time, Sofid and ANIC bought a controlling interest in one of Italy's oldest and largest woolen textiles companies, Lane Rossi. The move strengthened ENI's position in the burgeoning synthetic textiles sector, looming acrylic and polyester fibers produced by already existing ANIC plants.

In 1962, as ENI neared its tenth anniversary, Enrico Mattei died when his executive jet crashed en route from Sicily to Milan. Reports of a plot against ENI's entrepreneur-hero went unproven but provided the basis for several books and a 1970 feature movie, *Il Caso Mattei*. Mattei was succeeded by his 72-year-old Vice-President Boldrini.

The loss hastened a reorganization of management structure begun by ENI in the late 1950s. For several years, managerial

responsibilities had been concentrated in the person of Mattei, who acted as chief executive of most of the group's sector head companies, including Agip Mineraria, Agip Nucleare, Snam, Saipem, ANIC, STANIC, Sofid, and the first joint venture in Egypt. By contrast, the group's new executive structure greatly extended the autonomy of mid-level managers.

ENI had grown spectacularly. In 1961 the group boasted total assets of ITL 955 billion and operated as one of the top international companies in hydrocarbons. Expansion continued in the following decade as projects that originated under Mattei came into fruition: a 1958 agreement for importation of Soviet crude oil to ENI refineries; the Latina nuclear power plant and plants for manufacturing of processed uranium for nuclear generators; the completion of the central European pipeline connection with northern Italy; new textile manufacturing. Most important of all was a long-term reciprocal agreement with Esso that entailed provision of crude petroleum to Agip refineries and purchase of equipment from Nuovo Pignone.

Until the Esso agreement, importation of Soviet crude had been essential to ENI's development: In 1962 Italy was the Soviet Union's largest single market for crude oil, and the imports allowed Agip to offer the lowest gasoline prices in Europe. Meanwhile, trade pacts with the Soviets provided markets for industrial expansion undertaken by ENI in Italy's underdeveloped south.

Diversification in the 1970s

Although the 1960s were a period of growth for ENI, the decade also brought changes in the oil industry and in the world economy that had a negative effect. Throughout the decade ENI subsidiaries won important contracts to build pipelines and refineries and explore for hydrocarbons in south Asia, South America, and Australia. At the same time, regional conflicts and a phase of sharper nationalism in the independence movements in Africa and the Middle East frequently brought Agip's operations to a halt or else forced renegotiation of its previous agreements with producer states. In 1967, the Arab-Israeli Six Day War interrupted Agip's joint venture with Egypt. In 1969 the Biafran secession disrupted Agip refining activities in Nigeria.

Growth in the 1960s brought changes at home as well. Italy's two leading private-sector chemical companies, Montecatini and Edison, merged in 1965, creating a single giant called Montedison. Two years later, to offset the competition from Montedison, the Italian parliament approved modifications in ENI's institutional law, providing the state company financing and freedom to develop its nuclear and chemical activities more aggressively.

After Boldrini's death in 1967, ENI Vice-President Eugenio Cefis was appointed president. A junior colleague of Mattei who had served under him in the Resistance, Cefis shared Mattei's unwavering commitment to ENI and to the mixed economy in Italy.

The formation of OPEC and the issuing of its Declaration of Member Countries' Petroleum Policy in 1968 marked the emergence of oil producing states as a decisive force in the world economy. It was followed by increases in the price of crude petroleum and by the nationalization of the Libyan and So-

Italian oil industries in 1970 and those of Iraq and Saudi Arabia in 1974. In 1973, following the Yom Kippur War, crude prices tripled. Italy's economic situation, already experiencing a slow-down, grew worse.

ENI's expansion in the chemicals sector was accompanied by new efforts to control industrial waste and damage to the environment. At ANIC's Sannazzaro refinery, a wastewater treatment facility was installed for the first time in 1970, and in 1971 ENI formed Tecneco, a company devoted to environmental research and protection. In the same year, Eugenio Cefis was replaced as president by Raffaele Girotti.

Development of new petrochemicals plants and acquisitions in the chemical sector led to difficulties at ENI. Conflict with Montedison increased, aggravated by sectorwide economic trouble, and in 1972 the government mediated an accord between the two companies that favored ENI with the larger share of an ITL 4 trillion program of investments.

In 1975 Girotti was succeeded by Pietro Sette, who presided over the beginning of a period of crisis at ENI. Government efforts to rescue other ailing industries by having ENI acquire the worst performers added huge burdens to the group, already pressed by increases in the price of crude oil.

In 1977, ENI acquired 33 metallurgic companies from the troubled EGAM group, which were reconstituted to create a new ENI division called Samim. The following year, ANIC reported losses of ITL 247 billion, mostly in its petrochemical activities. Giorgio Mazzanti, a former vice-president at ENI, replaced Sette as president and ENI started trying to turn itself around.

Mazzanti was replaced after one year by Alberto Grandi. ENI established a new textile machinery division called Savio, separate from Nuovo Pignone, and began to see a slight narrowing of its losses. But the losses continued into the 1980s, as ENI again had to rescue failing chemical companies in the private sector. These were reconstituted separately from ANIC as a new subholding called EniChem. At the same time a comissario straordinario, or special commissioner, Dr. Enrico Gandolfi, was appointed to replace ENI's president, when Grandi resigned before his term as president had expired.

In 1982, ENI named a new president, Franco Reviglio, and a new board of directors who would oversee the group's program of recovery. ENI's sector head ANIC was reconstituted as EniChimica, following further acquisitions in the troubled Italian chemicals industry. The overhaul of ENI's fragile new empire of chemicals companies moved forward in 1984 with the absorption of EniChimica by EniChem and in 1986 the state-controlled chemicals industries showed a profit for the first time in ten years.

During the same period in the private sector, Italian financier Raul Gardini had assumed control of the company Montedison, a debt-ridden giant with wide holdings in chemical derivatives, pharmaceuticals, and services. Almost immediately plans were laid for a merger of EniChem with Montedison, to create an international presence for Italy among the top ten chemicals companies in the world. The new company, Enimont, was formed early in 1989, with 40 percent owned by ENI, 40 percent by Montedison, and the remaining 20 percent to be traded publicly.

Gabriele Cagliari replaced Franco Reviglio in 1989, to preside over ENI's experiment in a large-scale partnership with the private sector. But the joint venture was short-lived, marred by conflict between its two partners, and was finally threatened by an attempted takeover by Gardini. Late in 1990 Gardini sold Montedison's 40 percent share to ENI, and the chemicals conglomerate was renamed EniChem in 1991 after two unproductive years.

Joining the Global Leaders for the 2000s

ENI achieved a sound financial position as it entered its fifth decade. Sales continued to increase in most sectors at the end of 1990, with higher oil prices pushing up profits in the energy sector. With the addition of former Enimont activities in base and secondary chemicals, derivatives, and pharmaceuticals, ENI would complete its transition from a petroleum company to a global energy business, with materials, engineering, and financial resources capable of resolving energy and environmental problems anywhere in the world.

ENI became a joint-stock corporation in 1992 as the Italian government prepared a five-stage privatization program for the company. The first tranche of the company's shares was listed on the Borsa Italiana and the New York Stock Exchange in 1995. By 1998, the Italian government had relinquished its majority, dropped its holding to just 38 percent. In that year, the company officially changed its name to ENI S.p.A. The government continued selling down its stake, and by 2005 held just 30 percent of ENI.

Through the 1990s, ENI continued expanding, gaining exploration agreements for fields in Kazakhstan, China, and Russia in 1993 and launching production of natural gas at the Port Fouad, Egypt offshore gas field in 1996. In 1997, ENI reached agreements for two new sites in Kazakhstan, followed by an exploration, development, and production agreement in the Caspian Sea offshore field in Azerbaijan in 1998.

In the late 1990s and early 2000s, ENI launched a widescale restructuring that saw it sell off more than $5 billion in assets and slash some 42,000 jobs. The company also sold off many of the diversified operations that it had bought over time, which included newspaper and production of flowers, among others. By the early 2000s, ENI had clearly refocused itself around a core of oil and gas production and distribution. As part of that process, ENI regrouped its Agip distribution business as a separate, publicly listed subsidiary in 1998.

ENI sat out, in large part, the mega-mergers that shook up the global oil and gas industries in the 1990s and early 2000s, despite having made a halfhearted attempt at a merger with French counterpart Elf (which ended up absorbed into Total). Instead, ENI targeted the midsized market, buying British Borneo in 2000 and Lasmo in 2001. The two U.K.-based companies helped strengthen ENI's geographic spread, boosting its exploration and production interests in the North Sea, while also boosting operations in South America and the Asian Pacific.

In 2002, ENI acquired full control of Italgas, the leading gas distributor in Italy, paying some EUR 2.5 billion to shore up its gas business ahead of the opening of the EU countries' gas markets to full competition in 2007. By the end of that year, ENI had positioned itself in the larger European market as well, with the purchase of 50 percent of the gas operations of Spain's Union Fenosa.

In the early 2000s, ENI began selling off much of its petrochemicals business, divesting its polyurethane operations in 2001 and parts of its elastomers business in 2003. In 2004, the company announced its plan to put its entire Polimeri Europe petrochemicals business up for sale.

By the end of 2004, ENI market capitalization had swelled to some EUR 75 billion, positioning the company at sixth place among the world's oil and gas giants. Yet the government's reduction of its shareholding to just 30 percent left ENI vulnerable to a potential takeover attempt by one of its still larger competitors. For this reason, ENI CEO Vittorio Mincato announced his intention to lead ENI on a new growth phase, setting a market capitalization of EUR 150 billion before the end of the decade as a target. The company, now freed to raise capital on the open market, expected much of its growth to come through acquisition. At the end of 2004, ENI suggested part of Russian oil giant Yukos as a possible acquisition target. ENI remained Italy's jewel in the crown—one of the world's largest oil companies, and one of the largest corporations of any kind in Europe.

Principal Subsidiaries

American Agip Company, Inc. (U.S.A.); Eni Lasmo PLC (U.K.); Italgas - Società Italiana per il Gas S.p.A.; Società Azionaria per la Condotta di Acque Potabili S.p.A.; Saipem S.p.A.; Sonsub Inc.; Snam Rete Gas S.p.A.

Principal Competitors

Exxon Mobil Corporation; Shell Transport and Trading Company PLC; BP PLC; Royal Dutch/Shell Group; ChevronTexaco Corporation; RWE AG; Total S.A.; Sumitomo Corporation.

Further Reading

Barker, Thorold, David Buchan, and Matthew Jones, "Italians Aim for Place in Major League," *Financial Times,* January 10, 2002, p. 22.

Betts, Paul, "Eni 'Needs to Double to Shut Out Predators,' " *Financial Times,* October 11, 2004, p. 25.

——, "A Quiet Baritone on Italy's Oil and Gas Stage," *Financial Times,* May 28, 2001, p. 9.

Crawford, Leslie, Fred Kapner, and Joshua Levitt, "Eni in Euros 440m Gas Unit Deal with Fenosa," *Financial Times,* December 6, 2002, p. 31.

Lane, David, "Remote Reserves in Reach," *Financial Times,* February 18, 2002, p. 20.

O'Flynn, Kevin, "ENI SpA's Chief Hints at Possible Acquisitions in Russia," *Times,* November 11, 2004, p. 65.

—M.L. Cohen

Enterprise Rent-A-Car Company

600 Corporate Park Drive
St. Louis, Missouri 63105-4204
U.S.A.
Telephone: (314) 512-5000
Fax: (314) 512-4706
Web site: http://www.enterprise.com

Private Company
Incorporated: 1957 as Executive Leasing Company
Employees: 57,300
Sales: $7.4 billion (2004 est.)
NAIC: 532111 Passenger Car Rental; 532112 Passenger
   Car Leasing

Enterprise Rent-A-Car Company is the largest rental car company in North America. The firm has more than 5,400 offices in the United States; these offices are located within 15 miles of 90 percent of the U.S. population. More than 600 additional offices operate in Canada, the United Kingdom, Germany, and Ireland. Worldwide, Enterprise's rental fleet exceeds 700,000 vehicles, and its fleet services unit serving corporate clients includes an additional 135,000 vehicles. Largely avoiding the higher margin, highly competitive travel segment dominated by such companies as Hertz Corporation, Enterprise dominates the "local" segment of the automobile rental market, catering largely to those consumers who need to rent cars temporarily: to replace ones that have been stolen, have been in an accident, or are in need of a mechanical repair; or for a special occasion, such as a brief business or leisure trip; or to conduct business in-town. The replacement car niche tends to be resilient in times of recession, and its traditionally fragmented nature has allowed Enterprise plenty of room for growth. In addition to its rental car and fleet services businesses, Enterprise also has a car sales unit and a nascent rental truck operation, the latter largely offering trucks for replacement and supplemental purposes to commercial businesses.

Finding a Successful Rental Niche

Enterprise was founded in 1957 by Jack Crawford Taylor. An unlikely candidate to father such an ambitious company,

Taylor had struggled to finish high school and drifted through two colleges in one year. During World War II he served in the U.S. Navy, becoming a fighter pilot in the Pacific and eventually witnessing the loss of one-third of his squadron. When he returned home he found enjoyable work and financial security as a Cadillac salesman for a dealership owned by Arthur Lindburg in St. Louis, Missouri. But before long he discovered that he had a desire to be an entrepreneur. Like Taylor the fighter pilot, Taylor the businessman enjoyed a little risk.

In his position at Lindburg's dealership, Taylor occasionally came into contact with Cadillacs leased out of Chicago by a Greyhound subsidiary. Struck by the apparent ease and convenience of leasing an automobile, he investigated the business, and found that the numbers looked promising. Taylor persuaded his boss to set up a leasing business, taking a 50 percent pay cut for a 25 percent share in the new business known as Executive Leasing Company. In a walled-off section of a body shop at one of Arthur Lindburg's Cadillac dealerships in St. Louis, the company that would later be called Enterprise was born, with a fleet of seven vehicles.

The company initially focused on long-term leasing, but Taylor began to examine the potential for car rentals, entering this field in 1962. At first the short-term rental business seemed more of a nuisance than a profitable business, but Taylor handed operations over to an energetic assistant, Don Holtzman, to see what he could do. Taylor asked how many cars would be needed to get started; Holtzman replied 17, a number that remains a mystery to Taylor. Holtzman took his 17 cars and, realizing that the small company was no match for Hertz and Avis, looked for a niche away from the airports to settle into. He soon discovered that insurance adjusters had a need for rental cars for clients whose cars had been damaged or stolen, and Enterprise directed its efforts at this market, offering more competitive rates than the bigger rental companies. After Holtzman left the company in 1965, Taylor nurtured this "home city" segment.

Branching Out in the 1970s As Enterprise

In 1969 the company branched out of St. Louis, opening an office in Atlanta, Georgia. Offices in Florida and Texas soon followed. To do so, however, a name change was in order

Company Perspectives:

Enterprise's mission is to fulfill the automobile and commercial truck rental, leasing, and car sales needs of our customers while exceeding their expectations for service, quality and value.

We strive to earn our customers' long-term loyalty by delivering more than promised, being honest and fair, and "going the extra mile" to provide exceptional personalized service that creates a pleasing business experience.

We must motivate our employees to provide exceptional service to our customers. We do this by supporting our employees' development, providing opportunities for personal growth, and providing fair compensation for successes and achievements.

We believe that it is critical to our success that we promote managers from within who will serve as examples of success for others to follow.

It is our goal to be the best—not necessarily the biggest or most profitable—company of our kind. Our success at satisfying customers and motivating employees will bring growth and long-term profitability.

because the Executive name was not available for use in some markets. Taylor therefore changed the company name to Enterprise Leasing Company in 1969, a name that honored the U.S.S. *Enterprise,* one of the aircraft carriers on which he had served during World War II. Taylor's national expansion got off to an excellent start in the early 1970s by targeting garage and body shop owners and persuading them to send their customers to Enterprise while their cars were in the shop. Motorists in the 1970s were so accustomed to freedom of movement that they could hardly live a day without a car, and drivers stranded while a car was being repaired were often happy to pay Enterprise's relatively low daily rate. Business improved in the early 1970s when a judicial precedent was set requiring casualty insurers to compensate insured motorists for economic loss due to being without a car. Another key development of the early 1970s came from a branch manager in Orlando, who began offering customers a free ride to the rental office. This service was quickly introduced throughout the growing Enterprise system, beginning the tradition that would be immortalized in the well-known company slogan, "We'll pick you up."

The energy crisis of 1974 hampered rent-a-car expansion for a short period. Although Enterprise continued to show a profit, the difficult economic conditions inspired the company to diversify. The purchase of Keefe Coffee Company, which provided in-room coffee service to hotel guest rooms, started what became Enterprise Capital Group, which expanded through acquisitions during the 1970s. The next acquisition was Monogramme Confections, a candy maker selling hotels and businesses candies with customized wrappers bearing their own logo. Other additions to the Non-Automotive Group included another coffee service, Courtesy Coffee, and Crawford Supply, a service provider to correctional facilities.

A key ingredient of Enterprise's success in all business segments was its emphasis on customer service. The "Cus-

tomer Giveaway Account" was set up to allow any Enterprise Rent-A-Car employee to charge off items up to a certain limit in order to satisfy a customer. A motivated workforce was crucial to the operation, and Enterprise instituted a variety of bonus plans that provided incentives to everyone from assistant branch managers on up. Customer service was further enhanced in 1980 with the opening of the National Reservation Center, which enabled customers to call a toll-free number to rent Enterprise vehicles nationwide.

Accelerating Growth in the 1980s

Enterprise's growth, meanwhile, continued throughout the 1970s and accelerated in the 1980s, averaging 27 percent annually between 1984 and 1990. A new threat was presented in the 1980s, when Hertz and National entered the home-city rental market. The business was vastly different from business and leisure travel rentals, and Hertz quickly found the profit margins to be too low. Hertz decided to pull out of the market by the end of the decade, and National's operations struggled to stay afloat. Enterprise, meanwhile, began cultivating a market called "discretionary rentals" in the late 1980s. Aimed at families visiting relatives, or kids coming home for the holidays, "discretionary rentals" offered cars at low prices.

In 1987 Enterprise Capital Group purchased a cellular telephone company. Enterprise Cellular added millions of dollars in revenues. The group's experience with an unprofitable frozen Mexican food subsidiary in the 1980s convinced Enterprise that its success was more closely related to giving superior customer service than to the quality of any specific product they handled. Future diversifications would be made with this in mind. By the early 1990s, the Enterprise Capital Group represented about 10 percent of Enterprise's revenues. Meantime, in 1989, the company changed its name to Enterprise Rent-A-Car Company to reflect what had become by far its largest business, with more than 500 offices and a fleet of more than 50,000 rental vehicles.

In 1989 Enterprise began advertising with an eye toward creating brand recognition of its service. With an initial television advertising budget of only about $5 million, Enterprise decided to strategically place its messages so that they would be seen by a demographically favorable group. The company limited its television sponsorship to one network—CBS—hoping to reach the older upper-income audience watching *60 Minutes* and *Murder She Wrote.* The practice seemed to work for the company as Enterprise's revenues hit $800 million in 1990.

Reaching the Industry Top in the 1990s

By the early 1990s, Enterprise's second generation of leadership was looking optimistically to the future. The company was the fifth largest car rental chain—behind Hertz, Avis, Budget, and National—but was the leader in the still fragmented home-city car market, where faster growth was expected. Though successful competitors such as Action, Agency, and Chrysler's Snappy Car Rentals had crept into Enterprise's domain, none had the foothold in the market enjoyed by Enterprise.

Jack Taylor's son Andrew, president of the company since the early 1980s and chief executive officer since 1991, picked

Key Dates:

1957: Jack Crawford Taylor founds Executive Leasing Company in St. Louis, Missouri, with a seven-vehicle fleet.

1962: Company expands into the rental car business with a fleet of 17 vehicles, focusing on the replacement vehicle niche.

1969: As expansion outside St. Louis begins, company changes its name to Enterprise Leasing Company.

Early 1970s: A branch manager in Orlando begins offering customers a free ride to the rental office, beginning the firm's "We'll pick you up" tradition.

1974: A diversification drive begins with the purchase of Keefe Coffee Company.

1989: Firm changes its name to Enterprise Rent-A-Car Company; rental fleet surpasses 50,000 vehicles.

1993: Company opens its first international office, in Windsor, Ontario.

1994: First European office opens in Reading, England.

1995: First Enterprise on-airport rental location opens.

1996: Enterprise surpasses Hertz as the number one rental car company in the United States.

1999: Taylor family splits off Enterprise's nonautomotive businesses into a separate company, Centric Group.

2002: Company opens its 5,000th rental office.

up where his father had left off. Under Andrew Taylor's guidance, Enterprise's level of customer service was not allowed to suffer through overly ambitious expansion, with growth proceeding at a pace dictated by the number of qualified managers available. Enterprise already operated in nearly all of the nation's top 100 market centers by 1992, and the company's successful recruitment and training programs promised no delays in growth. That year, revenues surpassed $1 billion for the first time. The company's leasing division took on the name Enterprise Fleet Services as it focused on serving business with small to midsized fleets.

Enterprise's growth accelerated in the mid- to late 1990s. Revenues jumped to $2.46 billion by fiscal 1995 and then to $4.73 billion by 1999. By decade's end the rental fleet had reached half a million vehicles, which were offered through 4,000 offices worldwide. This growth was aided by an international push that saw the company open its first international office in Windsor, Ontario, in 1993 and then open its first office in Europe the following year in Reading, England. While the off-airport market remained Enterprise's core business—a sector in which it held as much as a 50 percent share of the U.S. market in the 1990s—the firm began encroaching on the sector still dominated by Hertz and Avis, opening its first on-airport location at the Denver International Airport in 1995. By the end of the 1990s Enterprise was renting vehicles at 95 of the top 100 airports in the United States; at about half of these it had counters in the airport terminal, while the remainder were served by nearby offices.

Meantime, Enterprise reached a milestone in 1996: it surpassed Hertz as the number one car rental company in the

United States in terms of fleet size and number of offices. Enterprise also battled Hertz and other car rental companies over the use of the "We'll pick you up" line, which Enterprise had trademarked and had been using in advertising since 1994. The company reached an out-of-court settlement with Hertz over the matter in 1998. International expansion had continued in 1997 with the opening of offices in Ireland, Scotland, Wales, and Germany. In 1999 Enterprise launched its Rent-A-Truck business, which rented trucks for replacement and supplemental purposes to commercial businesses. That same year, the Taylor family split off Enterprise's nonautomotive businesses into a separate company, Centric Group.

Early 2000s and Beyond

Late in 2001 Jack Taylor became chairman emeritus, and Andrew Taylor took over as chairman while remaining CEO. The presidency, however, was bestowed upon Donald Ross, a 37-year company veteran who had most recently served as chief operating officer and who became the first non-Taylor to serve as president. Revenues stagnated in the post-9/11 travel downturn, but Enterprise fared better than its rivals, who saw their sales drop, because Enterprise continued to specialize more in the replacement car market, which held up better than the business and leisure travel markets. Revenues for fiscal 2002 were up just 3 percent, reaching $6.5 billion. Also in 2002 Enterprise agreed to a $2.3 million settlement of a class-action lawsuit alleging that Enterprise Leasing had discriminated against African American employees. By the end of 2002, Enterprise had 115 on-airport locations and had captured 3.3 percent of that market. Its 5,000th rental location opened that year, and its rental fleet included more than 533,000 vehicles.

Over the next two years, Enterprise added another thousand offices to its growing network, bringing the total to more than 6,000. The company expanded into Alaska for the first time, giving it a presence in all 50 states, and significantly stepped up its international growth. During 2004 more than $500 million in revenues was generated outside the United States, an increase of 20 percent over the previous year. Enterprise now had 63,000 rental vehicles in Canada, the United Kingdom, Ireland, and Germany. In the United States, another 27 airport outlets debuted, boosting the total to 170. The company's share of the airport market reached 7 percent. Worldwide, the company's rental fleet increased by more than 7 percent, reaching 600,000, and revenues of $7.4 billion also represented a jump in excess of 7 percent. The ongoing success of Enterprise, which remained a privately held company controlled by the Taylor family, meant that there was little need for change. Enterprise continued focusing particularly on two crucial ingredients for this success: customer service and hiring outstanding employees, treating them with respect and giving them opportunities to advance.

Principal Operating Units

Enterprise Rent-A-Car; Enterprise Fleet Services; Enterprise Car Sales; Enterprise Rent-A-Truck.

Principal Competitors

The Hertz Corporation; Budget Rent A Car System, Inc.; Alamo Rent A Car, LLC; Avis Group Holdings, Inc.

Further Reading

Baker, Amy, "Enterprise Revs Up: New Branches Tap Market for 'Virtual Car,'" *Kansas City Business Journal,* January 12, 1996, pp. 1, 30.

Burns, Stan, *Exceeding Expectations: The Enterprise Rent-A-Car Story,* Lyme, Conn.: Greenwich Publishing, 1997.

Carey, Christopher, "Enterprise Rent-A-Car Keeps on Growing," *St. Louis Post-Dispatch,* September 17, 2004, p. C1.

——, "$5 Billion IPO Was Enterprise Goal, Ousted Executive Says," *St. Louis Post-Dispatch,* March 20, 2003, p. E1.

Carpenter, Jason, "Enterprise Carves Corp. Car Rental Discount-Tier Path," *Business Travel News,* August 2, 2004, pp. 24+.

DeMatteo, John, "The Company That Jack Built," *Forbes,* October 15, 1990.

"Enterprising Growth with a Hometown Flavor," *St. Louis Commerce,* June 1, 1996, p. 10.

Faust, Fred, "Enterprise Is Independent, at the Top," *St. Louis Post-Dispatch,* January 25, 1998, p. E1.

Flowers, Grant, "The Big Green Machine," *Travel Agent,* August 24, 1998, p. 72.

Goldman, Kevin, "Why Firms Put Ads on One TV Network," *Wall Street Journal,* December 27, 1989.

Jacobson, Gianna, "Enterprise's Unconventional Path," *New York Times,* January 23, 1997, p. D1.

Kroll, Luisa, "Hard Drive," *Forbes,* November 26, 2001, p. 160.

Limone, Jerry, "Enterprise Expansion Paying Off," *Travel Weekly,* December 9, 2002, p. 48.

London, Simon, "Driving Home the Service Ethic," *Financial Times,* June 3, 2003.

Newman, John F., "Motorist's Friend in Need: Enterprise Rent-A-Car Succeeds As a Good Neighbor," *Detroit News,* October 5, 1990.

O'Reilly, Brian, "The Rent-a-Car Jocks Who Made Enterprise #1," *Fortune,* October 28, 1996, pp. 125+.

Scott, Mac, "Taylor's Goal: $1 Billion by 1991," *St. Louis Business Journal,* January 8, 1990.

Stern, Gabriella, "If You Don't Feel Like Fetching the Rental Car, It Fetches You," *Wall Street Journal,* June 9, 1995, p. B1.

—Thomas Tucker
—update: David E. Salamie

Erste Bank der Osterreichischen Sparkassen AG

Graben 21
Wien
A-1010
Austria
Telephone: +43 50 100 10100
Fax: +43 50 100 910100
Web site: http://www.erstebank.at

Public Company
Incorporated: 1819 as Ersten österreichischen Spar-Casse
Employees: 37,650
Total Assets: $167.89 billion (2003)
Stock Exchanges: Vienna
Ticker Symbol: EBS
NAIC: 522110 Commercial Banking

Erste Bank der Osterreichischen Sparkassen AG has broken out of the tiny Austrian banking market to become one of Central Europe's retail banking leaders. Since 1997, Erste Bank has built an impressive regional presence, with operations extending into the Czech Republic, Hungary, Croatia, and Slovakia. In each of these countries, Erste Bank has positioned itself among the top three. In the Czech Republic, for example, Erste Bank controls Ceská Sporitelna, that market's leading retail bank with a 32 percent share. Erste Bank's acquisition of Hungary's Postabank in 2003 gave it the number two position there. In Croatia, Erste Bank owns Erste & Steiermärkische Bank, which, following the 2003 acquisition of Rijecka bank, has become that country's third largest bank. At home, meanwhile, Erste Bank remains Austria's number three bank, with a 20 percent share of the market. By the end of 2004, Erste Bank counted nearly 12 million customers—up from just 600,000 in 1997—banking at almost 2,200 branches in the region. Erste Bank's strategy relies on the cultural and economic proximity of the Central European region, and the bank provides transparent cross-border banking services in its operating region. Erste Bank also has been lifted by the expansion of the European Union to include most of its area of operation.

Pioneering Austrian Banking in the 19th Century

The creation of the European banking system occurred in large part at the end of the 18th and the beginning of the 19th centuries. The first European savings bank, the Ersparniskasse, was developed in Hamburg, Germany, in 1778. England followed later, with the creation of the Rothwell Savings Bank in 1810. By the end of the decade, and following the economic upheaval caused by the Napoleonic Wars, Austro-Hungarian emperor Franz I called for the creation of a banking system in Austria as well.

In 1819, Johann Baptist Weber, minister of Leopoldstadt, founded Austria's first savings bank in Vienna. The bank, called Ersten österreichischen Spar-Casse, soon became a model for the development of the savings bank system throughout the Austro-Hungarian empire and the European continent as a whole. Savings banks quickly appeared in Trieste, Laibach, Innsbruck, Bregenz, Split, Graz, Hollabrunn, Prague, Görz, Klagenfurt, and many other markets in Austria and elsewhere in the empire. Many of these banks were established by the local aristocracy and wealthy citizens, and often were operated as nonprofit organizations. Others were established or otherwise owned by local governments. By the end of World War I and the breakup of the empire, Austria alone counted more than 200 savings banks.

Many of these became grouped together within a union of savings banks, with Erste Bank emerging as a central coordinating bank. Yet Erste Bank appeared in this position as early as 1825, when it founded the Allgemeinen Versorgungsanstalt für die Unterthanen des österreichischen Kaiserstaats. This body became the first privately held bank in Central Europe to offer social security-like services. In 1873, Erste Bank became instrumental in establishing the region's first mortgage and credit-lending services, a factor that led directly to the rise of a middle class in Austria.

The ownership structure of the many Sparkasse, coupled with restrictive Austrian banking rules that limited the number of branches each bank was allowed to operate, contributed to the fragmentation of the Austrian savings bank sector. As such, by the early 1970s, the country featured just 400 branches in all.

This situation began to change at the end of that decade, however, with the passage of new banking regulations that liberalized the opening of new branches. By the mid-1990s, the number of branches operating in Austria had nearly quadrupled.

Yet the number of banks had fallen dramatically. The 1980s saw a first wave of consolidation in the Austrian banking sector. Much of the consolidation occurred on a regional level, as the country's local sparkasse joined together to form larger, regionally focused banking unions. Meanwhile, Erste Bank expanded its function as a central umbrella bank, overseeing a number of mergers among the new regional banks.

Central European Leader in the New Century

The passage of new legislation deregulating Austria's banking industry in 1986 paved the way for the emergence of the modern Erste Bank. The bank began preparations for its conversion into a public corporation, which it carried out in 1993. With support from the Austrian government, Erste Bank then began consolidating the country's savings bank market. Between 1993 and 1997, Erste Bank absorbed some 17 of the country's regional savings banks.

Despite being one of Austria's larger banks, Erste Bank remained tiny in comparison to its Western European competitors. With just 600,000 customers, Erste Bank required scale in order to survive the increasingly competitive European market. The appointment of Andreas Treichl as CEO of the bank marked a new beginning.

In March 1997, Treichl pushed through a complex deal that enabled Erste Bank to acquire majority control of GiroCredit Bank. That bank had been formed in a three-way merger in 1992, combining Girozentrale, Bank der Osterreichischen Sparkassen, and Osterrichisches Credit-Institut. The addition of GiroCredit, allied with Austria's political left, doubled Erste Bank's total assets, to the equivalent of EUR 54 billion. Erste Bank then became Austria's third largest bank. In December 1997, Erste Bank launched a public offering of some 30 percent of its shares.

While its larger competitors, and much of Europe's banking sector, turned their focus to the fast-growing corporate finance

market, Erste Bank, because of its smaller size, had no choice but to concentrate on its core retail banking operations. The bank soon turned this limitation to its advantage.

Treichl now began a de facto consolidation of Austria's savings banks. By 1999, he had reached agreements to exchange 77 of Erste Bank's branches for equity stakes in nine of Austria's savings banks. In this way, Erste Bank established equity positions in these banks and, in many cases, acquired majority control. At the same time, the entire Austrian savings bank federation agreed to begin carrying Erste Bank products, such as insurance and investment products, and other services, and rebrand themselves as Erste Bank. In this way, Erste Bank stepped up its domestic customer base to more than two million.

Yet Treichl had spotted an opportunity for international growth. While the corporate market captured competitors' attention, the rapidly privatizing retail markets in the Central European countries were in large part overlooked. In 1997, Treichl led the company into its first foreign acquisition, with the purchase of nearly 84 percent of Hungary's Mezobank. Yet that acquisition proved a disappointment for Erste Bank. As only the tenth largest bank in Hungary, and with a market share of just 4 percent, Mezobank did not provide Erste Bank with the leverage it needed to compete in the Hungarian market. Nonetheless, Treichl learned an important lesson from the Mezobank acquisition. As he told *Institutional Investor,* "It taught me that you had to be big if you wanted to be a success in Central European retail banking."

The Mezobank acquisition merely whetted Erste Bank's appetite for future foreign expansion. The bank now identified a target region—what it called its "extended home market"—consisting of the Czech Republic, Slovakia, Croatia, and Hungary. The bank now began preparing for the next acquisition opportunity as these countries planned for the sell-off of most of the region's formerly state-owned banks.

Erste Bank's moment came in 2000, when it won its bid to acquire 52 percent of Ceska Sporitelna, the Czech Republic's largest bank. Ceska Sporitelna had been founded in 1953 as the country's consumer banking monopoly under Soviet domination. In 1993, after the fall of Communism, the bank went public, listing its shares on the Prague exchange. Nonetheless, the bank remained under government control, and weighed down by a huge, underperforming portfolio of loans to state-owned companies. The Czech government decided to put the majority of Ceska Sporitelna up for sale after it was forced to underwrite a CZK 7.6 billion bailout of the bank.

Erste Bank now turned its attention to the nearby Croatian market. In June 2000, the bank reached an agreement with Graz-based Steiermärkische Bank to form the Erste & Steiermärkische Bank joint venture. That bank then acquired three other Croatian banks, Bjelovarska banka d.d., Cakovecka banka d.d., and Trgovacka banka d.d., in September 2000. The merger of these operations enabled Erste & Steiermärkische Bank to claim a position among the top banks in that market.

Next, Erste Bank entered Slovakia, buying more than 87 percent of that country's leading bank, Slovenská Sporitelna, which had previously been controlled by the Slovakian government. The addition of Slovenska boosted Erste Bank's total

Key Dates:

1819: Johann Baptist Weber, minister of Leopoldstadt, founds Austria's first savings bank in Vienna, the Ersten österreichischen Spar-Casse (Erste Bank).

1993: Erste Bank converts to a public corporation and begins acquiring regional savings banks.

1997: The bank acquires GiroCredit; Mezobank of Hungary is acquired.

2000: The bank acquires Ceská Sporitelna; the Erste & Steiermarkische joint venture forms, which then acquires Bjelovarska banka, Cakovecka bankam, and Trgovacka banka.

2001: Slovenská Sporitelna is acquired.

2002: Rijecka banka in Croatia is acquired.

2003: A merger of Erste & Steiermarkische and Rijecka is formed; Postabank in Hungary is acquired.

2004: Postabank and Erste Bank Hungary merge.

2005: Erste Bank acquires 100 percent control of Slovenská Sporitelna.

customer base to more than eight million, and placed it among the top ten retail banks in all of Europe. By the end of the year, also, Erste Bank gained full control of Ceská Sporitelna.

Back in Austria, the bank also reached an agreement to acquire majority control of Tiroler Sparkasse. By the beginning of 2002, however, Erste Bank had organized the Haftungsverbund, or cross-guarantee arrangement, among 55 of Austria's banks, which placed these banks' assets under Erste Bank's central control. The agreement effectively boosted Erste Bank's total assets to EUR 124.8 billion, without requiring the bank to launch outright acquisitions of these banks.

Erste Bank continued building in Croatia as well. In April 2002, the bank acquired 85 percent of Croatia's fifth largest bank, Rijecka banka d.d. That purchase boosted Erste Bank's standing in Croatia to a 10 percent stake. The merger of Rijecka into Erste & Steiermärkische Bank in 2003 created Croatia's third largest bank.

Soon after, Erste Bank returned to Hungary, snapping up former state-owned bank Postabank. The purchase doubled Erste Bank's presence in Hungary and boosted its market share to 8 percent. Then in September 2004, Postabank and Erste Bank Hungary were merged, boosting Erste Bank's presence in that market to 11 percent. Following the Postabank acquisition, the company completed its takeover of Slovenská Sporitelna, boosting its share to 100 percent in January 2005.

Thus Erste Bank's initial Central European expansion strategy was completed. Yet the company continued to eye further growth in the region. The bank acknowledged its interest in expanding into Romania when that country begins its own bank privatization process. In the meantime, Erste Bank turned its focus on increasing the operating efficiencies of its international subsidiaries, while stepping up its presence as a cross-border financial services provider. Erste Bank also began building a strong presence in Internet banking, with more than 800,000 online customers at the end of 2004. Erste Bank had become a powerhouse in the Central European retail banking market.

Principal Subsidiaries

Allgemeine Sparkasse Oberösterreich; Bankaktiengesellschaft, Linz (Group); Bausparkasse der österreichischen; Česká Spořitelna a.s. (Czech Republic); Die Erste & Constantia Beteiligungsfonds Aktiengesellschaft; Erste & Steiermärkische banka d.d., Rijeka (Croatia); Erste Bank Hungary Rt.; Erste Financial Products Ltd. (U.K.); ERSTE-SPARINVEST Kapital anlagegesellschaft GmbH; Europay Austria Zahlungsverkehrssysteme GmbH; Postabank és Takarékpénztár Rt. (Hungary); Sparkassen Aktiengesellschaft.

Principal Competitors

Deutsche Bank AG; UBS AG; ABN AMRO Holding N.V.; DZ BANK AG; Westdeutsche Landesbank Girozentrale; Bayerische Landesbank Girozentrale; Kreditanstalt fur Wiederaufbau KfW; Landesbank Baden-Wurttemberg AG; KBC; Unicredito S.p.A.; Bank Austria AG; Raiffcisen International.

Further Reading

Bansal, Parveen, "Going for Grassroots Growth," *Banker,* June 1, 2004.

Falush, Peter, "Erste's High-Growth Eastern Strategy," *European Banker,* November 2002, p. 11.

Frazer, Patrick, and Peter Falush, "Erste Bank Wins Postabank," *European Banker,* October 2003, p. 1.

Galbraith, Robert, "Coming First Where It Counts," *European Banker,* September 2004, p. 12.

Lanchner, David, "Banking on the East," *Institutional Investor* (International Edition), January 2003, p. 17.

—M.L. Cohen

Eye Care Centers of America, Inc.

11103 West Avenue
San Antonio, Texas 78213
U.S.A.
Telephone: (210) 340-3531
Toll Free: (800) 669-1183
Fax: (210) 524-6996
Web site: http://www.ecca.com

Private Company
Incorporated: 1988
Employees: 4,200
Sales: $369.9 million (2003)
NAIC: 446130 Optical Goods Stores; 621320 Offices of
    Optometrists

Eye Care Centers of America, Inc. is one of the largest optical retail chains in the United States. It operates or manages more than 375 retail stores in 32 states and the District of Columbia using 11 stores names, including EyeMasters, Visionworks, Vision World, Doctor's VisionWorks, Dr. Bizer's VisionWorld, Dr. Bizer's ValuVision, Doctor's ValuVision, Hour Eyes, Stein Optical, Eye DRx, and Binyon's. Each is a leader in eye care service in its respective market. Stores are located primarily in the Southwest, Midwest, and Southeast, along the Gulf Coast and Atlantic Coasts, and in the Pacific Northwest regions of the United States.

Growing to National Proportions: 1984–88

In 1984, an investment group headed by Robert Schumacher founded the San Antonio-based Eye Care Centers of America. By 1986, Eye Care Centers of America operated 13 optical department stores in Texas and Louisiana under the name EYE PRO Express, Jack V. Gunion serving as president and chief executive officer. After an initial public offering of 1.1 million shares mid-year, the company began trading as IPRO on the NASDAQ.

Proceeds from the sale of Eye Care Centers' stock went toward acquiring or opening additional stores, and in the early fall of 1986 Eye Care Centers purchased a second chain of stores, 20/20 Eye Care Inc. of Phoenix, Arizona. With the addition of 20/20 and the opening of several new EYE PRO stores, Eye Care Centers became a chain of close to 30 stores. When it acquired EyeMasters of Baton Rouge around the close of the year, the company's properties exceeded 40 stores located in Arizona, California, Louisiana, New Mexico, and Texas.

Then, in a turn of events, Eye Care Centers was itself purchased by Chicago-based Sears, Roebuck & Co. in late 1987 as part of the larger company's strategy of shoring up its mature merchandising operations by buying fast-growing specialty stores. At the time of the purchase, Sears already had optical departments in about 600 of its 813 department stores. Over objections and lawsuits filed by two of Eye Care Centers' stockholders, Sears bought the optical chain for $52.5 million. The company no longer traded publicly after the purchase.

In purchasing Eye Care Centers, Sears opted to take advantage of the move toward growth throughout the 1980s for optical superstores nationwide. In 1974, two rulings had led to significant change in the nation's eye care industry. In the first, the U.S. Supreme Court decided that professionals had the freedom to advertise their practices. In the second, the Federal Trade Commission stated that optometrists had to give patients copies of their eyeglass prescriptions, allowing patients the freedom to shop for frames wherever they chose. Coupled with a variety of new trends, such as advances in eyewear technology, the increased popularity of fashion eyeglass frames, and the fact that baby boomers were beginning to turn 40—the age at which many people began requiring glasses for reading and driving—the optical superstore was born. What once was a quasi-medical enterprise, the prescribing, grinding, and fitting of eyeglasses, became a service and product-oriented business almost overnight. The merchandising phenomenon went from ground zero at the start of the decade to become the fastest growing segment of the $8-billion-plus retail eye care industry by the late 1980s.

By 1988, Eye Care Centers, along with LensCrafters and Pearle Vision, had become one of the largest optical superchains in the nation. Each of its stores had up to three doctors working at any time, examination rooms, a frame selection area,

Company Perspectives:

We offer our customers high-quality frames, lenses, accessories, and sunglasses—including designer and private label frames, at competitive prices. All of our stores offer lenses at great prices and the leading technology in vision correction. In addition, most of our stores provide one-hour service on most prescriptions by utilizing on-site laboratories.

Key Dates:

1984: Eye Care Centers of America (ECCA) is founded in San Antonio, Texas.
1986: The company holds an initial public offering (IPO); acquires 20/20 Eye Care Inc. of Phoenix, Arizona, and EyeMasters of Baton Rouge, Louisiana.
1987: Sears, Roebuck & Co. purchases Eye Care Centers.
1988: ECCA purchases Eye Co., Inc.; rebrands its stores under the EyeMasters brand.
1993: Desai Capital Management and ECCA executives buy the company from Sears.
1996: The company acquires Visionworks.
1997: The company acquires Hour Eyes.
1998: The company acquires Dr. Bizer's Vision World; Thomas H. Lee Company buys out Desai.
1999: The company acquires World Vision, Stein Optical, and Eye DRx.
2001: David E. McComas becomes chief executive officer.
2004: The company announces its acquisition by Moulin International Holdings Ltd. and Golden Gate Capital.

and a lens grinding laboratory. While optical retail chains accounted for only about 19 percent of the market, which was still dominated by independent optometrists, they were becoming some of the most successful businesses in the country thanks to advertising via television, radio, newspaper, and direct mail; competitive service; and the convenience they offered. Their large selection of eyewear, merchandising specials, and the promise of new glasses without a long wait both shaped and catered to consumer demand.

By the late 1980s, a growing number of new optometrists were opting not to start their own private practice. A 1988 *New Orleans City Business* article cited *Optical Index* magazine's national statistics showing that the " 'chain' segment of the eye care industry—optical centers with four or more retail locations—represent[ed] about 165 optical companies that operated a total of 6,250 outlets'' and that these centers garnered ''almost 30 cents out of every dollar spent in the industry.'' According to *Optical Index*, the eye care chains brought in a combined total of more than $2 billion in annual revenues.

The growth and convenience of the eye care business meant that people were going for eye exams and buying new glasses more frequently than in the past, predictors of better optical health nationwide. However, critics opined that the big business approach to optical care could mean that people would become less rather than more informed. ''The public's concept of an eye examination has become so that it is like buying a pack of cigarettes—it's all the same regardless of who does it,'' voiced the president of the New Orleans Academy of Ophthalmology in the 1988 *New Orleans CityBusiness* article.

1988–97: Ongoing Growth Through Acquisitions

The debate about the relative benefits of the optical superchain did nothing to slow the growth of Eye Care Centers. By 1988, it had more than doubled its size since having been purchased by Sears. In 1988, 20/20 Eye Care Centers acquired five Phoenix-area optical stores from Eye Co., Inc. and another 20 stores from Binyon's of Portland, Oregon. This acquisition brought Eye Care Centers' total to 88 stores nationwide doing business under the names Eye Co., EyeMasters, EyePro Express, and 20/20 Eyecare. Late in the year, it decided to rebrand all of its stores under the EyeMasters name. Immediately following this decision, it began expansion plans to build another ten EyeMasters stores in the state of Texas.

Growth continued for the company throughout the 1990s. In 1993, Sears sold Eye Care Centers to Desai Capital Management and a group of the company's executives. By 1996, with

stores operating under EyeMasters and Binyon's trade names, Eye Care Centers acquired Visionworks Inc. of Clearwater, Florida, an optical retailer with 60 stores in the southeastern United States. With annual sales of $61 million, Visionworks brought the company's number of stores to 204 and its revenues to about $158 million a year.

A year later, with revenues of $220 million and 243 optical stores in 21 states, the District of Columbia, and Mexico, Eye Care Centers acquired the Hour Eyes chain and relocated its distribution, equipment, repair, and some manufacturing operations to larger quarters to consolidate its facilities scattered around the San Antonio area and to accommodate its ongoing growth.

1998–2004: Future Growth Plans Based on a Strategic Market Focus

In 1998, Boston-based Thomas H. Lee Co. acquired about 90 percent of Eye Care Centers for $325 million. The money, which the company put toward expansion, provided ''. . . the perfect opportunity to bring new capital into the company and position it for future growth, both through new store openings and through acquisitions,'' according to Bernie Andrews, Eye Care Center's chief executive officer, in a company release. Eye Care Centers used the money obtained through the sale to blanket the market with outlets: five new stores in Utah under the EyeMasters name in the first phase of expansion with more stores to follow. These stores followed the typical EyeMasters format; they were about 3,000 square feet, located in a retail strip center, open seven days a week, and had a complete lab and doctor on site as well as a staff of 15 to 20 people.

More acquisitions followed as Thomas H. Lee Co. moved to revamp Eye Care Centers as a value provider of eyewear. In 1998, the company bought Dr. Bizer's Vision World and in 1999 it purchased 76 VisionWorld, Stein Optical, and Eye DRx stores, most of them in Minnesota, Wisconsin, and New Jersey. These acquisitions brought its total to 351 stores in 32 states. From 2000 to 2003, Eye Care Centers averaged ten new stores each year until in 2004 it had about 375 stores in more than 30 states selling under 11 brand names.

Revenues increased accordingly. In 1998, the company's sales totaled almost $238 million. In 2001, David E. McComas assumed the role of the company's chief executive, and by 2003, that number had reached $370 million. In 2004, it was approaching $400 million. In December 2004, a Hong Kong-based global leader in the manufacture, distribution, and retailing of eyewear, Moulin International Holdings Ltd., along with the San Francisco equity firm Golden Gate Capital, announced plans to purchase Eye Care Centers, and the company recommitted itself to its focus on the eyewear value segment. With nearly 88 percent of people over the age of 55 requiring some form of corrective eyewear and that segment of the population destined to grow, the company seemed well-positioned to maximize future growth.

Principal Competitors

1-800 CONTACTS, Inc.; Costco Wholesale Corporation; Emerging Vision, Inc.; J.C. Penney Company, Inc.; Lens-Crafters, Inc.; National Vision, Inc.; OptiCareHealth Systems, Inc.; Sears, Roebuck and Co.; U.S. Vision, Inc.; Wal-Mart Stores, Inc.

Further Reading

Daly, Brenon, "Eye Care Centers Files $375 Million IPO," *TheDeal.com*, May 10, 2004, p. 1.

Larroque, Nicole, "Optical Chains See Bright Future in Vision Business," *New Orleans CityBusiness*, March 14, 1988, p. 14.

MacFadyen, Kenneth, "T. H. Lee Opts for Sale of Eye Care Centers," *Buyouts*, December 13, 2004, p. 1.

Schwadel, Francine, "Sears to Buy Chain of Stores in Specialty Line," *Wall Street Journal*, December 16, 1987, p. 1.

Sheron, Don, "Eye Care Centers to Unload 90 Percent Stake," *San Antonio Express-News*, March 10, 1998, p. 1F.

Talmadge, Candace, "Pearie Frames Future with Optical Adjustments," *ADWEEK*, February 8, 1988.

Poling, Travis E., "San Antonio-Based Eye Care Centers Sold Again for $450 Million," *Knight Ridder Tribune Business News*, December 4, 2004, p. 1.

——, "San Antonio-Based Eye Care Company to Be Sold for Third Time in 10 Years," *Knight Ridder Tribune Business News*, November 12, 2004, p. 1.

—Carrie Rothburd

Fairmont Hotels & Resorts Inc.

100 Wellington Street West, Suite 1600
Toronto M5K 1B7
Canada
Telephone: (416) 874-2600
Fax: (416) 874-2601
Web site: http://www.fairmont.com

Public Company
Incorporated: 1907
Employees: 30,000
Sales: $771.0 million (2004)
Stock Exchanges: Toronto New York
Ticker Symbol: FHR
NAIC: 525930 Real Estate Investment Trusts; 721110
    Hotels (Except Casino Hotels) and Motels; 722211
    Limited Service Restaurants

Fairmont Hotels & Resorts Inc. is a leading owner and operator of luxury and first-class hotels and resorts, with more then 80 properties operated under the Fairmont and Delta banners. The hotels, located in Canada, the United States, Mexico, Bermuda, Barbados, Monaco, and the United Arab Emirates, rely mostly on business travelers. The company also holds real estate interests in some 50 properties through FHR Real Estate Corporation and its share in Legacy Hotels Real Estate Investment Trust.

1886–1999: Fairmont Hotels and Canadian Pacific Hotels & Resorts Intersect

In 1886, William Cornelius Van Horne built and began welcoming guests to Mount Stephen House high in the wilds of the Canadian Rocky Mountains. The guest house was part of Van Horne's vision of creating rest stops along the Canadian Pacific Railway. Considered by some to be a 19th-century visionary, Van Horne declared, according to company literature, "If we can't export the scenery, we'll import the tourists."

Van Horne's business, which, in time, came to be called Canadian Pacific Hotels & Resorts, built or acquired other

hotels in the years that followed: Banff Springs in 1888, Chateau Lake Louise in 1890, and Le Chateau Frontenac in 1893. During the next century, his company continued to expand across Canada and, by 1997, Canadian Pacific Limited, under the direction of CEO Bill Fatt, either owned or managed 25 properties with approximately 11,000 guestrooms under its luxury brand, Canadian Pacific Hotels. In 1998, it bought the Canadian National Railway Company's hotel chain. This purchase brought with it ownership of seven hotels, including the Chateau Laurier in Ottawa and the Jasper Park Lodge in Alberta, and made Canadian Pacific the largest owner-operated hotel company in Canada. The company had hotels as far west as Victoria, British Columbia, and as far east as St. John's, Newfoundland.

The company moved outside of Canada in 1998 with the purchase of Princess Hotels, which had properties in Mexico, Arizona, Bermuda, and Barbados. A year later, motivated to expand internationally, Canadian Pacific entered into a second international purchase agreement with Kingdom Hotels (USA) Ltd. and Maritz Wolff & Co. to acquire Fairmont Hotel Management L.P. (Fairmont L.P.). Owned by Prince al-Waleed bin Talal bin Abdulaziz Alsaud of Saudi Arabia and Lewis Wolff, Fairmont L.P.'s revenues had reached more than $400 million in the late 1990s.

Fairmont L.P. dated back to the early 1900s. Located in San Francisco, the original Fairmont Hotel had been started by two San Francisco natives, sisters Tessie and Virginia Fair in 1906. The opening was delayed by the San Francisco earthquake but finally, in 1907, the Fairmont began receiving guests for the first time. Benjamin H. Swig bought the Fairmont in 1945 and began building a portfolio of hotels as well as purchasing existing hotels, changing the name of each of his properties to "Fairmont" in honor of his company's California flagship. Under Swig, the Fairmont Hotels grew to include seven properties in key U.S. gateway cities and became a social hub for the rich and famous. These included the Grunewald in New Orleans, the renowned Plaza in New York City, and luxury hotels in San Jose, Chicago, Boston, and Dallas. In 1997, Fairmont L.P. acquired an interest in Legacy Hotels Real Estate Investment Trust.

1999–2001: Growth As a Subsidiary of Canadian Pacific Limited

The merger between Canadian Pacific Hotels and Fairmont L.P. yielded Fairmont Hotels & Resorts in 1999, the largest hotel management company in North America (as measured by the number of rooms). The new company had 29,400 rooms, 73 hotels, 26,400 employees, and two brands: Fairmont Hotels globally and Canadian Pacific Hotels in Canada. After the merger, six of Canadian Pacific's smaller properties were rebranded under the Delta Hotels name. These included hotels in Calgary, Toronto, Moncton, Halifax, and Charlottetown in Canada.

Fairmont Hotels & Resorts' parent company, Calgary-based Canadian Pacific Limited, was a diversified operating company, active in transportation, energy, and hotels at the time of the merger. The Canadian Pacific group of companies, which had grown into a Canadian icon after it built the transcontinental railway in the 1880s, also included Canadian Pacific Railway, CP Ships, PanCanadian Petroleum Ltd., and Fording Coal Ltd. Canadian Pacific's Fatt and Fairmont L.P.'s Wolff became co-chairmen of the new hotel management company. Following the merger, Fairmont Hotels & Resorts' strategy was to focus mainly on hotel management rather than hotel ownership because management of hotel properties offered a more stable income. Management fees are calculated as a percentage of hotel revenue streams whereas hotel ownership depends upon the more volatile bottom-line profit.

A year after the merger, in 2000, Fairmont Hotels & Resorts was attracting companywide acclaim with revenues of more than $150 million. The merger had brought awareness of the Fairmont name and created opportunities for global expansion. In 1999, Canada's largest owner-operated hotel corporation began expansion in Hawaii, purchasing the Kea Lani Maui from investors. In 2001, after Canadian Pacific Limited underwent restructuring with the creation of a holding company, it entered into a joint venture to manage the Fairmont Dubai, a 400-room hotel opposite the Dubai World Trade Center. At the time, its total number of hotels was 38. In its second deal with Arab royalty that year, Canadian Pacific also bought a 50 percent stake in the Fairmont Copley Plaza in Boston, which it had managed since 1996. Meanwhile, Delta's holdings had increased to 40, primarily in Canada.

2001–04: An Increasing Focus on Management and International Presence

Canadian Pacific spun off all five of its operating subsidiaries in 2001. Hours after the spinoff, Fairmont Hotels & Resorts launched a buyback of its yet-to-be-issued stock, which would trade on the Toronto stock exchange. Earlier in the year, it had sold two of its Canadian properties while retaining long-term management contracts for each. The timing, given the fallout of the September 11th attacks, made it difficult for the hotel chain to go public, and the Fairmont struggled to keep its share price strong so that it was not at risk of being bought out by one of the larger U.S.-based hotel chains. CEO Fatt went on a cross-country road show in 2001 to convince investors of the company's solidity and changed its reporting currency to the U.S. dollar. New hotel construction stopped. However, when the Fairmont Dubai opened for business in the summer of 2002, Fairmont was stronger than ever.

In fact, Fairmont actually benefited from some of the changes brought about following September 11th. Fairmont's controlling interest in its real estate investment trust (REIT), Legacy Hotels, enabled it to take advantage of depressed markets. Canadian law allowed the company to sell some of its more mature hotels to the REIT in order to free up assets to buy less productive hotels with potential for expansion.

By 2002, Fairmont was actively pursuing the goal of becoming an operator of premier resorts and hotels with elite city-center locations. It began managing the 75-year-old Sonoma Mission Inn & Spa in California, the Legacy-acquired Monarch Hotel in Washington, D.C., and The Orchid at Mauna Lani on Hawaii, named to Condé Nast Traveler's Gold List. Other management agreements followed in 2003 and 2004: in Puerto Rico, Florida, and near Playa del Carmen, Mexico. Fairmont also sold off some of its properties—the Kea Lani Maui and the Glitter

Bay in Barbados—but signed on to continue to manage these properties.

At the same time, Fairmont began to strengthen its international presence with agreements to manage unopened hotels and resorts in Abu Dhabi and Dubai in the United Arab Emirates and in Cairo and by investing in luxury hotels in key European markets. In 2004, in a joint venture with Kingdom Hotels and Bank of Scotland Corporate, it agreed to manage the Savoy in London and to purchase the Monte Carlo Grand Hotel in Monaco.

At the close of 2004, Fairmont sold off part of its share in Legacy Hotels Real Estate Investment Trust. Its portfolio at the time consisted of more than 80 luxury or first-class hotels and more than 40 city center and resort hotels in Canada, the United States, Mexico, Bermuda, Barbados, and the United Arab Emirates. As published in its annual report, its goal was to increase the number of hotels under its management through management agreements, strategic partnerships for development, the acquisition of new properties, and the expansion of existing properties.

Principal Subsidiaries

FHR Holdings Inc.; FHR Properties Inc.; Fairmont Hotels Inc.; Delta Hotels Limited; FHR Real Estate Corporation.

Principal Competitors

Four Seasons Hotels Inc.; Hilton Hotels Corporation; Global Hyatt Corporation; Marriott International, Inc.; Radisson Hotels & Resorts; Ritz-Carlton Hotel Company, L.L.C.; Starwood Hotels & Resorts Worldwide, Inc.; Wyndham International, Inc.

Further Reading

Bagnell, Paul, "CP in Deal to Run Seven U.S. Luxury Inns," *National Post (Canada)*, April 20, 1999, p. C4.

Benjamin, Jeff, "Street Wise: Canadian Hotel Chain's REIT Stake Provides Buying Power," *Investment News,* August 12, 2002, p. 25.

Binkley, Christine, "Fairmont Teams Up with Porsche: Hotels' Cross-Marketing Offers a Luxury Va-Room! and a Picnic Boxter Lunch," *Wall Street Journal*, October 8, 2002, p. B9.

Janah, Monua, "San Francisco-Based Hotel Firm to Team with Canadian Firm in Expansion," *San Jose Mercury News*, April 20, 1999.

King, Laura, "CP Shareholders Approve Spinoffs," *Daily Deal*, September 26, 2001.

Rosenwald, Michael, "Fairmont Buys 50 Percent Stake in Copley Hotel," *Boston Globe*, July 25, 2001, p. F3.

Youn, Jacy, "Top Wealthiest Landowners: It's Quality, Not Quantity," *Hawaii Business*, November 1, 2003, p. 30.

—Carrie Rothburd

Federico Paternina S.A.

Avda Santo Domingo 11, Apartado
Haro La Rioja
E-26200
Spain
Telephone: +34 941 31 05 50
Fax: 34 941 31 27 78
Web site: http://www.paternina.com

Public Company
Incorporated: 1896
Employees: 93
Sales: EUR 40 million ($45.9 million) (2003)
Stock Exchanges: Bolsa de Madrid
Ticker Symbol: PAT
NAIC: 312130 Wineries; 311423 Dried and Dehydrated
Food Manufacturing; 424490 Other Grocery and
Related Product Merchant Wholesalers; 424820 Wine
and Distilled Alcoholic Beverage Merchant
Wholesalers

Federico Paternina S.A. is one of Spain's leading Rioja-region wine producers. The Haro La Rioja-based company produces Rioja wines, including the Banda Oro, Reserva, and Gran Reserva labels and the flagship brandy, Conde de los Andes Solera Gran Reserva. Paternina is also present in Spain's two other principal wine appellations, producing Ribera del Duero wines and Jerez (sherry) brandy, including its flagship brandy. The company also produces and markets a range of spirits and liqueurs, including the Otaola brand line. Paternina operates several wineries, the oldest of which is the Conde de los Andes located at Ollauri, which features four 16th-century wine cellars with a total capacity of four million bottles. Paternina operates more modern facilities at Haro, where the company has built one of Europe's largest wine and brandy production and aging facilities, covering an area of 87,000 square meters; the El Cuadro bodega (winery) in Jerez, producing wines and brandies; and the company's most recent winery, Marques de Valparaiso, producing Ribera del Duero wines. While sourcing grapes from the region's farmers, Paternina also has acquired its own vine-yards, including 41 hectares in Pesquera de Duero. The company expects to expand its holdings to more than 100 hectares, in order to become self-sufficient and ensure the quality of its wines. Paternina is one of the only Spanish wine producers listed on the stock market; 80 percent of the company remains controlled by the Eguizábal family, which acquired Paternina in the early 1980s and is credited with reviving the reputation of not only the winery, but also the Rioja appellation itself. In 2003, Paternina's revenues reached EUR 40 million ($45 million).

16th-Century Cellars

The cellars at Ollauri, on the top of the hill overlooking the town itself, were built in the late 16th century. Cut into some 40 meters of rock, the cellars, each about 150 meters long, provided constant temperatures for the maturing of the region's well-known wines and brandies. The site remained a wine-making center for the next centuries.

In 1896, Federico Paternina bought the three bodegas (Spanish for wineries) in Ollauri, and merged them to form the company that took on his name. Paternina started out with three cellars, and some 1,000 oak casks, with a total storage capacity of about 500,000 liters.

Paternina set about boosting production, but also developing the quality of his wines, soon earning a reputation as one of the region's leading Rioja producers. In 1920, the Paternina company expanded, buying up the Catholic Farmers' Union Co-operative in nearby Haro. This purchase permitted the company to greatly expand its production, while retaining its commitment to developing quality wines. By the 1940s, the Paternina name was respected not only throughout Spain, but also had begun to gain international renown. The company began exporting its wines to other European markets and to the American market. Attesting to Paternina's renown were the frequent visits from well-known visitors, such as Ernest Hemingway, into the 1950s.

The period proved something of a peak for Paternina. By the 1960s, the company, and Spanish wines in general, faced growing competition from a new breed of ''new world'' winemak-ers, such as in the United States, Australia, South Africa, and

Chile. Consumer tastes began to shift away from the relatively heavy, oak-aged Rioja wines to new lighter, sweeter, and fruitier wine types.

Adapting to the new market proved difficult for Paternina. Part of the reason for this was the adoption of regulations governing the Rioja appellation varieties. The top Gran Reserva required at least five years of cellar time, including at least two years of aging in oak casks for red wines, and four and a half years for white wines. The next level, Reserva, required three years in the cellar, with at least one year in the cask for red wines, and two and a half for white wines. Even the entry-grade Crianza required at least two years in the cellar with at least one year in the cask. Although these methods helped ensure the quality and character of the Rioja appellation, it made it more difficult for the company to adapt its wines to the new market preferences.

Its fortunes slipping, Federico Paternina was acquired in 1974 by fast-growing Spanish conglomerate Rumasa, owned by Jose Marea Ruiz Mateos. Yet Rumasa's financial foundations proved fragile, and, as the conglomerate slipped toward collapse at the beginning of the 1980s, Rumasa, including Paternina, was taken over by the Spanish government. In the meantime, Paternina had seen little investment under Rumasa, and the winery, once one of the region's most important brands, had sunk into disrepute.

The winery might have faded altogether, if not for Marcos Eguizábal Ramirez. A native of Rioja, and already owner of another winery, Bodega Franco-Espanolas, Eguizábal agreed to purchase the Paternina company from the government for just one peseta. Eguizábal quickly developed plans to restore Paternina to its former glory.

Equizábal had to fight against Paternina's poor reputation among restaurant owners and other former Paternina customers. Throughout the 1980s, Equizábal worked to restore Paternina's image, including offering to replace much of the stock the company had sold. In all, Equizábal threw away some 40,000 cases of wine.

At the same time, Equizábal led Paternina in developing a new generation of wines more suited to the modern wine-drinking tastes. In the early 1990s, Paternina began a modernization effort, renovating its existing winery. Paternina also revamped its cellars, raising the ceilings to accommodate a new shipment of larger, 225-liter American white oak casks—replacing the company's 180-liter casks, which had been used for producing sherry as well.

Revitalized for the New Century

Paternina's investment program went still further. In the early 1990s, the company built a state-of-the-art facility at Haro, installing modern winemaking and bottling equipment. The company installed a new bottling line capable of processing 12,000 bottles per hour. The new line also was equipped to detect defects in the bottles, and to reject bottles that had not been completely filled. The new facility, at 87,000 square meters, became one of the largest and most modern winemaking facilities in Europe.

By the mid-1990s, Paternina had succeeded in restoring both the high quality of its wines as well as its brand image. The company, now joined by Eguizábal's son Carlos, began to diversify its portfolio. In 1994, the company acquired Bodegas Internacionales, based in Jerez, which included a number of traditional sherry brands, such as Marqués de Mérito, Díez Hermanos, Bertola, and José Pemartín y Cía. These were merged, creating Paternina's Sherry Division. The company began producing fortified wines under the Jerez-Xérès-Sherry y Manzanilla de Sanlúcar de Barrameda appellation.

Throughout this period, Paternina and the Eguizábals faced an ongoing challenge from Jose Marea Ruiz Mateos, who attempted to regain control of the winery. In 1997, however, the Spanish Supreme Court at last came down on the side of the Eguizábals. Freed from concerns for the company's ownership and eager to continue investing in Paternina's growing operations, the Eguizábals turned to the stock market, launching Paternina as a public company on the Bolsa de Madrid in 1998.

In 1999, Paternina extended its winemaking operations into the Pesquera de Duero region, buying up its first vineyards there and establishing a new wine label, Marquess de Valparaiso. The company then began construction of a ESP 630 million winery complex in Quintana del Pidio, completed in 2001. At the same time, Paternina bought more vineyards in the Duero appellation region.

By 2004, the company had acquired some 40 hectares of vineyards. Yet the company had become determined to achieve self-sufficiency in order to gain tighter control over the quality of its wines, with plans to increase its vineyard holdings to at least 100 hectares in the new century. The year 2004 saw the release of the company's acclaimed 1994 vintage. The wine sported a new label as Federico Paternina turned with fresh confidence into its second century.

Principal Subsidiaries

Conde de los Andes; El Cuadro; Ribero del Duero.

Principal Competitors

Larios Pernod Ricard S.A.; Bacardi Espana S.A.; Osborne Compania S.A.; Freixenet S.A. Grupo; J Garcia Carrion S.A.; Grupo Codorniu; Bodegas y Bebidas S.A.; Gonzalez Byass S.A.; Miguel Torres S.A.

Further Reading

Boland, Vincent, ''Bodegas Paternina Issue Tests Investor Appetite,'' *Financial Times,* September 8, 1998, p. 40.
Rose, Anthony, ''Spanish Practices,'' *Independent,* November 8, 1997, p. 67.
Tremlett, Giles, ''Spain to Offer Winery to Institutional Investors,'' *European,* September 15, 1998.

—M.L. Cohen

Finning International Inc.

666 Burrard Street, Suite 1000
Vancouver, British Columbia V6C 2X8
Canada
Telephone: (604) 691-6444
Fax: (604) 331-4899
Web site: http://www.finning.com

Public Company
Incorporated: 1933 as Finning Tractor & Equipment
   Company Ltd.
Employees: 11,409
Sales: CAD 3.59 billion (2003)
Stock Exchanges: Toronto
Ticker Symbol: FTT
NAIC: 333120 Construction Machinery Manufacturing

Finning International Inc. is a dealer for Caterpillar Inc. on a global scale. Finning International sells, rents, finances, and provides customer support services for equipment and engines made by Caterpillar, the world's leading manufacturer of heavy equipment. Finning International operates on three continents, serving customers in North America, Europe, and South America. The company's North American operations are conducted through Finning (Canada), an Edmonton, Alberta-based entity that operates as the Caterpillar dealer at 41 branch locations in Alberta, British Columbia, Yukon, and the Northwest Territories. Finning (UK) Ltd. operates as the national Caterpillar dealer for Great Britain, serving customers at 22 branch locations in England, Scotland, and Wales. In South America, Finning International operates 34 branch locations in Argentina, Bolivia, Chile, and Uruguay. Through a subsidiary named Hewden Stuart PLC, Finning International operates one of the largest rental companies in the United Kingdom. Hewden Stuart, with more than 300 offices, rents a full range of equipment, including small- and medium-sized construction equipment, tools, and cranes and self-propelled powered access platforms.

Origins

Finning International developed out of its founder's ties with Caterpillar Tractor Co., a relationship that began shortly after the heavy equipment maker was established in 1925. Earl B. Finning was working in California, employed as a salesman for Caterpillar's distributor for the region, when he began to dream of living elsewhere. In 1928, when he was in his 30s, Finning moved north, opting for the mostly undeveloped area of Canada's Pacific Coast. Finning settled in Vancouver, British Columbia, where he set up a small business selling and servicing heavy equipment. Before his first year in Vancouver was over, Finning formed a partnership with a man named Morrison, who had founded his own company, Morrison Tractor & Equipment Ltd., two years earlier. The pair worked together during the first years of the Great Depression, but Finning would have to endure much of the century's most devastating economic crisis on his own. In 1932, Morrison relinquished his interests in the company, leaving to Finning the daunting challenge of keeping a business afloat during the deleterious times.

Finning was awarded the Caterpillar dealership for most of British Columbia when he started out. He succeeded in staving off collapse, but his first years on his own offered little enjoyment. Incorporating the company as Finning Tractor & Equipment Company Ltd. at the beginning of 1933, he applied his own business philosophy to its operation. Finning, unlike most of his competitors, believed strongly that success depended on the availability of parts and reliable repair service. His mantra, according to company historians, was "We service what we sell," a mindset that distinguished Finning Tractor from others and won the loyalty of customers who depended heavily on their Caterpillar equipment in the rugged and isolated country of western Canada. Perhaps because of Finning's emphasis on stocking parts and providing repair service, the company stayed in business during the desperate years of the Great Depression, enjoying enough financial stability to open its first branch location in Nelson, British Columbia, in 1937. The satellite office in Nelson was the first branch office of what would become a network of Finning Tractor locations scattered throughout British Columbia, Alberta, the Yukon, and the Northwest Territories.

Post-World War II Expansion

Following World War II, the sparsely populated, mostly undeveloped province of British Columbia experienced a tremendous surge in growth. The growth was industrial, as the province's

Company Perspectives:

The Finning Formula: Leverage the CAT brand; Command strong regional market shares; Maximize parts, service and rental revenue; Solve difficult customer problems; Establish clear financial expectations throughout the organization; Transfer the formula to other geographies.

industries expanded at a robust pace, finding the financial resources to fund such expansion relatively easy to come by in the fertile economic climate present throughout North America following the war. The highly favorable economic conditions provided the impetus for British Columbia's mining, forestry, hydroelectric, and oil pipeline concerns to push forward with expansion plans, the execution of which would require the equipment sold by Finning Tractor. The company flourished in the decades following World War II, becoming one of the most successful companies on Canada's west coast.

Finning leveraged his company's success to create his vision of what a Caterpillar dealership should be. He placed a high priority on establishing a network of Finning Tractor branch locations, consistently opening new satellite offices once he had begun to do so in 1937. Finning also directed that branch locations be opened in the most remote areas, creating a comprehensive network that left few potential customers without the ability to turn to Finning Tractor for their heavy equipment needs. When major government highway, hydroelectric, and defense contracts materialized during the 1950s and 1960s, Finning Tractor was there to serve, maintaining a presence in areas eschewed by his competitors.

Finning presided over his company's defining era of growth, turning what could have been a one-location Caterpillar dealership into a network of offices that aided in the industrialization and modernization of British Columbia. His three-decade-long reign of command ended with his retirement in 1962, when Maury Young was appointed president and general manager of Finning Tractor. In 1965, Finning passed away, leaving his family to take control of the company. The Finning family would hold a sizable interest in the company for the next several decades, but Finning Tractor was essentially Young's company from the late 1960s forward. Young was appointed chief executive officer in 1967, a position from which he would exert considerable influence over Finning Tractor's development. Earl Finning's contribution to the development of Finning Tractor was immense and not to be forgotten, but Young's influence over the company rivaled that of his mentor's. Earl Finning created Finning Tractor, but Maury Young turned Finning Tractor into Finning International.

Using the foundation created by Finning, Young took the company to a higher plateau. His seminal contribution to Finning Tractor occurred roughly 20 years after he was named president of the company, but in the interim his achievements were not to be ignored. Finning Tractor was generating nearly CAD 80 million in revenue when Young took control of the company. In 1969, he presided over the company's initial public offering of stock and used the proceeds to finance expansion during the

1970s. Finning Tractor began manufacturing its own line of equipment during the decade, equipment that was designed primarily for use by the forestry industry. In 1971, GM Phillpot Co. was acquired, an acquisition that later led to the formation of the Allied Products division, which was organized into three separate operations: Materials Handling, Drills and Compressors, and Non Cat (Caterpillar) Forestry. The company recorded phenomenal growth during the decade, doubling its sales and profits twice over. By the end of the decade, after becoming the Caterpillar dealer in the Yukon in 1977, Finning Tractor stood as an imposing force, controlling much of western Canada. The fertile economic conditions that had supported the company's growth since the end of World War II evaporated as the new decade began, but the company responded to the anemic economic conditions by executing the boldest move in its history.

Going Abroad in 1983

During the early 1980s, a recessive Canadian economy delivered a stinging blow to Finning Tractor's markets. The resource industries of western Canada fell into a slump, causing a lull in the bustling mining, forestry, and construction activity that had underpinned Finning Tractor's growth. Young, and the company's newly appointed president, Vin Sood, responded to the bleak market conditions by taking the greatest geographic leap in Finning Tractor's history. Young and Sood decided to find growing markets elsewhere, choosing the United Kingdom as the company's new proving ground. In 1983, they acquired two U.K. Caterpillar dealerships, Bowmaker (Plant) Ltd. and Caledonian Tractor and Equipment Co. Ltd., which gave the company the right to represent Caterpillar in western England, Scotland, and Wales. The two acquisitions were merged in 1984, creating Finning Limited, the U.K. arm of Finning Tractor.

The foray into the United Kingdom marked the beginning of Finning Tractor's transformation into a multinational corporation. The company did not forsake its Canadian business, however. Following the acquisition of the two U.K. dealerships, Finning Tractor was generating roughly CAD 450 million in sales annually. The company's revenue volume represented a dramatic increase from the less than CAD 100 million it was collecting 15 years earlier. In the years to come, the company's revenue totals would increase at an even more vigorous rate, as management demonstrated an eagerness to broaden Finning Tractor's geographic scope. In 1989, the company directed its attention toward its Canadian operations, acquiring the R. Angus Caterpillar dealership in Alberta. The acquisition gave the company the right to represent Caterpillar in all of Alberta and in the Northwest Territories west of the Saskatchewan-Alberta border.

During the 1990s, Finning Tractor again began to look at foreign markets for growth opportunities. Management searched for markets that were showing increasing activity in the sectors that Finning Tractor served—mining, forestry, construction, and other industries that needed Caterpillar's heavy equipment and diesel engines. During the early 1990s, the company saw rapid growth in such sectors in Chile, which led to the acquisition of Gildemeister S.A.C. in 1993. Gildemeister had served as Chile's only Caterpillar dealer since 1940. The acquisition, renamed Finning Chile S.A. four years later, gave Finning Tractor the right to serve all of Chile. The company's

<table>
<tr><td colspan="2">Key Dates:</td></tr>
<tr><td>1928:</td><td>Earl B. Finning moves to Vancouver, British Columbia, and becomes a partner in Morrison Tractor & Equipment Ltd.</td></tr>
<tr><td>1932:</td><td>Morrison divests his interests, making Finning the sole owner of the company, which he incorporates as Finning Tractor & Equipment Company, Ltd. the following year.</td></tr>
<tr><td>1937:</td><td>Finning Tractor opens its first branch location in Nelson, British Columbia.</td></tr>
<tr><td>1967:</td><td>Two years after Earl Finning's death, Maury Young is appointed chief executive officer.</td></tr>
<tr><td>1969:</td><td>Finning Tractor completes its initial public offering of stock.</td></tr>
<tr><td>1983:</td><td>Finning Tractor enters the United Kingdom through the acquisition of two Caterpillar dealerships.</td></tr>
<tr><td>1986:</td><td>The Finning family divests its controlling stake in the company.</td></tr>
<tr><td>1987:</td><td>Finning Tractor changes its name to Finning Ltd.</td></tr>
<tr><td>1993:</td><td>Finning Ltd. acquires the Caterpillar dealership in Chile.</td></tr>
<tr><td>1997:</td><td>Finning International Inc. is adopted as the company's corporate title.</td></tr>
<tr><td>2001:</td><td>Finning International acquires Hewden Stuart PLC.</td></tr>
<tr><td>2003:</td><td>Caterpillar dealerships are acquired in Argentina, Bolivia, and Uruguay.</td></tr>
</table>

60th anniversary also marked an increased involvement in the United Kingdom. Leverton, the only other Caterpillar dealer in England, was acquired, giving Finning Tractor control over all of England, Scotland, and Wales.

Finning Tractor recorded enormous revenue growth during the 1990s. The company entered the decade with approximately CAD 1 billion in sales and it exited the decade with sales in excess of CAD 2.2 billion. Finning Tractor's international expansion played a large role in fueling the sales growth, a contribution the company formally acknowledged in 1997, when the name Finning International Inc. was adopted as the corporate title for all of the company's operations.

Finning International in the 21st Century

The company's expansion continued as it entered the 21st century, an era in the company's development that was led by a new president and chief executive officer. Doug Whitehead was appointed to both posts in 2000, joining Finning International after serving as chief executive officer of Fletcher Challenge Canada Ltd., a unit of a massive New Zealand-controlled forestry conglomerate.

Under Whitehead's guidance, Finning International assumed an aggressive acquisitive posture during the first years of the new century. In 2001, the company acquired Hewden Stuart PLC, one of the largest rental companies in the United Kingdom. Through three divisions—general hire, tool hire, and lifting hire—Hewden rented a broad range of equipment at more than 300 locations scattered throughout the United Kingdom. In 2002, the company's Chilean entity, Finning Chile, acquired Distribuidora Perkins S.A.C., the exclusive distributor of the product lines for Perkins Engines and FG Wilson in Chile. The following year, Whitehead led the company's charge into South America, where during a four-month period he secured control over nearly the entire continent. In January 2003, the company acquired Macrosa Del Plata S.A., the Caterpillar dealer in Argentina, and General Machinery Co., S.A., the Caterpillar dealer in Uruguay. In April 2003, Finning International acquired Matreq Ferreyros S.A., the Caterpillar dealer in Bolivia.

As Finning International planned for the future, the company's first 70 years in business offered compelling evidence that success would continue. The company never posted an annual loss during its first seven decades of business. Although Whitehead faced a formidable task to match the contributions of his two most notable predecessors, Finning and Young, his move to entrench the company's presence in South America offered proof that he, too, held lofty ambitions for Finning International. The company entered the mid-2000s as the largest Caterpillar franchise in the world, with annual sales climbing toward CAD 4 billion. In the years ahead, the company was expected to strengthen its presence globally and hold sway as one of Canada's largest companies.

Principal Subsidiaries

Hewden Stuart PLC; Macrosa Del Plata S.A. (Argentina); Matreq Ferreyros S.A. (Bolivia); General Machinery Co. S.A. (Uruguay); Finning Chile S.A.; Finning (UK) Ltd. (U.K.); Finning (Canada) Ltd.

Principal Divisions

Finning (Canada); Finning (UK) Ltd.; Finning South America; Hewden Stuart.

Principal Competitors

AGCO Corporation; CNH Global N.V.; Western Power & Equipment Corp.

Further Reading

"Finning Acquires Caterpillar Dealerships in Three South American Countries," *Canadian Corporate News,* November 27, 2002.
"Finning Acquires the Largest Independent Materials Handling Company in the U.K.," *Canadian Corporate News,* April 28, 2003.
"Finning Closes Acquisition of the Caterpillar Dealership in Bolivia," *Canadian Corporate News,* April 8, 2003.
"Finning Closes Acquisitions of Caterpillar Dealerships in Argentina and Uruguay," *Canadian Corporate News,* January 13, 2003.
"Finning International Inc.," *Market News Publishing,* June 11, 2001.
Francis, Diane, "Weekend Hippie in a Boy's Paradise," *National Post,* June 1, 2002, p. FP1.

—Jeffrey L. Covell

FLIR Systems, Inc.

16505 Southwest 72nd Avenue
Portland, Oregon 97224
U.S.A.
Telephone: (503) 684-3731
Toll Free: (800) 322-3731
Fax: (503) 684-3207
Web site: http://www.flir.com

Public Company
Incorporated: 1978
Employees: 885
Sales: $311.97 million (2003)
Stock Exchanges: NASDAQ
Ticker Symbol: FLIR
NAIC: 334511 Search, Detection, Navigation, Guidance,
    Aeronautical, and Nautical System and Instrument
    Manufacturing; 541511 Custom Computer
    Programming Services

FLIR Systems, Inc. (Flir) designs and manufactures thermal imaging systems and infrared camera systems. Flir's products are used in a variety of applications in commercial, industrial, and government markets. The company is the market leader in providing airborne imaging systems used by television and radio broadcast stations and in providing airborne systems used by law enforcement agencies. In industrial settings, the company's products are used to detect heat loss, which often foretells equipment failure. Flir generates more than 40 percent of its revenues from international customers. The company operates manufacturing facilities in Boston, Massachusetts; Portland, Oregon; Santa Clara, California; London, England; and Stockholm, Sweden.

Origins

Flir's founding in 1978 marked the birth of one of the world's pioneers in infrared technology. Although the company's contributions to advancing thermal imaging technology began almost immediately after its inception, Flir's commercial success took years to arrive, as the company struggled to find its place in the industry. Initially, Flir provided infrared imaging systems that were installed on vehicles. The vehicles, able to detect the infrared radiation, or heat, emitted by all people, objects, and materials, were used to conduct energy audits of residential areas. By using Flir's thermal imaging systems, the vehicles were able to identify abnormal leakage of heat emanating from the doors, windows, walls, and roofs of individual houses.

Flir's initial business lacked the muscle to support the company's growth. The demand for equipment to conduct residential energy audits was never very strong, and, not long after the company entered the market, what little demand existed soon dissipated. Flir discovered a far more robust market for its technology by serving law enforcement agencies. The company developed stabilized thermal imaging systems for use in aircraft used by law enforcement agencies, who used infrared radiation to track suspects.

Airborne applications for thermal imaging systems represented a viable market for Flir, one that the company would come to dominate and one that remained part of its business into the 21st century. Relying on the needs of law enforcement agencies, however, resulted in problems similar to those presented by the company's reliance on the demand for conducting residential energy audits. The market for airborne thermal imaging systems was not big enough to drive the growth of Flir, not to the scale of the company's stature in the 21st century. The central challenge facing the company involved the dynamics of its industry, a challenge Flir began to address in the late 1980s.

Historically, Flir's industry had struggled to attract widespread demand for its technology. The early applications for thermal imaging technology were developed for use in combat situations such as weapons targeting, a use that demanded exceptional performance no matter the cost. Basic forms of the technology were applied to other uses, such as in limited industrial applications to detect heat loss from buildings, which, in contrast to the systems used by the military, emphasized cost over performance. The result was an industry that only met the needs of users with virtually unlimited financial resources who required high-performance systems and users with little capital at their disposal who needed only basic thermal imaging systems. The industry was split between providing high-cost, high-

performance systems and low-cost, low-performance systems,
leaving the gulf between the two extremes—a large group of
potential users in the public safety sector and in commercial
markets—for the most part ignored. For long-term growth, Flir
needed to tap the unexploited middle area of the market, and the
company did so, becoming one of the first companies to bridge
the gap separating the two poles of the thermal imaging market.
Flir, particularly after its 1990 acquisition of Hughes Aircraft
Co.'s industrial infrared imaging group, began developing products with a combination of price and performance that met the
needs of a much broader customer base, enabling it to record
substantial gains in revenues for the first time in its history.

During the mid-1980s, Flir was a roughly $4 million-in-
sales company. A decade later, the company was generating
more than $30 million in annual sales. The increase was signifi-
cant, confirming the thermal imaging market's capability to
support meaningful financial growth, but the revenues generated during the mid-1990s represented only one-tenth of the
total Flir collected ten years later. Much transpired during this
signal decade of exponential growth, as Flir experienced both
the joys of establishing itself as one of the premier thermal
imaging concerns in the world and the despair of watching its
success evaporate within several months. The source of both the
joy and the despair were two acquisitions completed in the late
1990s, acquisitions that greatly enhanced the company's capabilities and nearly caused its ruin.

Faltering in the Late 1990s

Flir gained the right to claim a pioneering status in the
thermal imaging industry in large part through the acquisition of
a Swedish company. In December 1997, the company purchased Stockholm-based Agema Infrared Systems AB, a company that was recognized as the world leader in the design,
manufacture, and marketing of handheld infrared cameras for
detecting and measuring temperature differences for a wide
variety of commercial and research applications. Agema, in
1965, had developed the first commercial infrared scanner, a
device designed for inspecting power lines. In March 1999, a
little more than a year after purchasing Agema, Flir acquired the
legacy of another industry pioneer, merging in a stock-for-stock
transaction with Boston-based Inframetrics, Inc., a company
that developed the first television-compatible infrared system in
1975. Inframetrics was known for producing thermal imaging
equipment used to find potential failures in industrial manufacturing and utilities systems.

When Flir announced its intention to acquire Inframetrics in
December 1998, the company appeared headed for a much
brighter future. The acquisition of Agema and the imminent
arrival of Inframetrics greatly increased its expertise and capabilities in serving nonmilitary customers. At the end of 1998,
when the company's chief operating officer, Kenneth Stringer,
was promoted to chief executive officer, Flir passed an important turning point, obtaining, for the first time in its history,
more revenues from commercial contracts than government
contracts. The addition of Inframetrics promised to increase the
company's advances in the commercial sector, but within a year
of completing the deal, Flir found itself embroiled in a devastating scandal.

The acquisitions of 1997 and 1999 more than doubled Flir's
size. Their addition to the company's fold made sound strategic
sense—an assessment that did not change even as the company
appeared destined for bankruptcy in large part because the
acquisitions were completed. The problems did not stem from
the price paid for the acquisitions, but in how management dealt
with its finances in general. In March 2000, the company
announced that its fourth quarter results would be materially
below expectations, with the cause stated as errors made when
the company consolidated entries for subsidiaries in the United
States and Europe. Around this time, the company's chief
financial officer, J. Mark Stamper, left the company. In May
2000, Flir announced that Stringer was no longer chief executive officer of the company. As it was alleged after numerous
investigations, Stringer, Stamper, and a senior vice-president,
William Martin, had inflated Flir's revenues and hidden millions of dollars in expenses to present a false image of the
company's health to shareholders.

Flir's stock value plummeted during 2000, falling to $1.50
per share by the end of the year. Shareholders reacted with fury,
resulting in more than ten class-action lawsuits filed against
Flir. Flir's difficulties quickly mounted, creating a litany of
woes that afflicted the company. Flir's accountants quit, the
company's bank pulled its line of credit, the Securities and
Exchange Commission launched an investigation, and so did
the Federal Bureau of Investigation, which, three years later,
issued a 47-count indictment against Stringer, Stamper, and
Martin. The situation was disastrous, but the exposure of the
company's faults only exposed more faults. Flir was awash in
high-yield debt, which stood in default, and hobbled by excess
inventory, leaving the company precariously close to filing for
bankruptcy. "Flir is a classic story of what happens when many
things go wrong," an analyst commented in an August 2001
interview with *Oregon Business*. "Management was hanging
onto a story of growth and momentum and created pressure to
keep it going. They didn't recognize the problems until they
became a scandal."

Arrival of New Leadership in 2000

Flir was a severely troubled company at the start of the 21st
century. The individual who inherited the company's numerous
problems was Earl Lewis, who was appointed president and
chief executive officer in November 2000. Lewis joined Flir
from Thermo Instrument Systems, Inc., an instruments manufacturer he took public in 1986. When Lewis completed the
company's initial public offering it had a market capitalization

of $70 million. During the next 14 years, Lewis substantially increased the company's market capitalization by purchasing troubled companies and improving their performance, an acquisition strategy he applied 110 times over the course of 14 years, eventually raising Thermo Instrument's market capitalization to $3 billion. One of the acquisitions completed during Lewis's tenure was that of a Swedish laser instrumentation manufacturer named Spectra-Physics AB, which owned 28 percent of Flir. The acquisition was made in 1999. In the months that followed, Lewis gained a seat on Flir's board of directors. Not long afterward, Thermo Instrument's former parent company, Thermo Electron Corp., bought back its former subsidiary and began appointing its own management team. Lewis was being eased out just as Flir needed a new leader.

"This company was very close to bankruptcy," Lewis said in a March 8, 2004 interview with the *Daily Deal,* remembering the state of Flir in the fall of 2000. Lewis moved quickly to rid the company of its ills, spending $20 million to realign its operations. He focused on products with higher profit margins, eliminated lower profit margin products, improved manufacturing efficiencies, and reduced production and distribution costs. "We made cash king," Lewis explained in an August 2001 interview with *Oregon Business.* "We started reporting cash flow daily to make sure we wouldn't run out of funds. We curtailed procurements of inventory, stopped acquisitions of capital equipment."

The measures put in place by Lewis quickly reversed Flir's fortunes. By mid-2001, the company was generating positive cash flow consistently and its stock had rebounded, trading for nearly $20 per share. Both industry observers and Lewis credited the success of the turnaround program to the quality of Flir's products and the dominant market share enjoyed by the company. Flir controlled 70 percent of the market for airborne imaging systems used by television and radio broadcast stations and 85 percent of the market for airborne law enforcement systems. Aside from those mainstay product lines, management also envisioned a number of other markets for the company, an outlook embraced by Lewis, who foresaw a future in which infrared technology would play an important role in the commercial sector.

During the early years of the 21st century, Flir's thermal imaging cameras were used for a number of purposes. Professionals used the company's cameras to scan refineries for heat leaks, a preventive maintenance niche Flir dominated. Flir also developed a thermographic flashlight for use by law enforcement agencies, a device that enabled an officer to locate a suspect hiding in a dark alley and determine whether the suspect possessed a weapon, for instance. In Asia, when the sudden acute respiratory syndrome (SARS) crisis erupted, government officials purchased more than 100 Flir devices, paying $15,000 apiece, to detect travelers with high fevers, one of the earliest symptoms of SARS. Lewis predicted many more uses for the company's technology, foreseeing a time when homeowners could go to their local construction supply store and rent a thermographic camera to check their home for heat leaks. Lewis claimed that in the future all electricians would carry an infrared camera. He also saw the automobile manufacturing industry as a big potential customer, touting the incorporation of the company's night-vision technology into automobiles as inevitable.

The central problem in widening the use of Flir's technology in the commercial sector was the price of its products. The roughly 50 camera systems made by Flir ranged in price from $10,000 to $1 million, far too expensive for most of the potential customers envisioned by Lewis. One of his primary objectives after restoring Flir's financial health was to try to lower the price of the company's products, a goal that he made a stride toward achieving with an acquisition. In 2003, Lewis approached a Santa Clara, California-based manufacturer of infrared technology components named Indigo Systems Corp. Lewis offered to buy the company, but Indigo officials rejected his offer. "They didn't quite understand how they might value the business so they decided to go to an auction," Lewis explained in a March 8, 2004 interview with the *Daily Deal.* "Quite frankly, I was disappointed," Lewis added, "I was hoping we could just do a negotiation." An auction was held in October 2003, with Flir emerging as the winner. Flir paid $165.5 million in cash and roughly $25 million in stock for Indigo, completing the deal in January 2004.

Indigo's integration into Flir's operations provided Lewis with the opportunity to lower the cost of his products. By having control over the manufacture of components the company previously acquired from third parties, Flir was expected to save money, savings that would be used to reduce prices primarily on the company's thermography products. "There are a number of markets for infrared detection that will only be satisfied when the price of those cameras is significantly lower than it is today," Lewis explained in his March 8, 2004 interview with the *Daily Deal.* As Lewis set himself to the task of making Flir's products more widely used in the commercial sector, there were more than 30,000 of the company's cameras in use throughout the world. In the years ahead, with the help of Indigo and other attempts to drive down the cost of thermography products, Lewis hoped to increase that figure exponentially.

Principal Subsidiaries

FLIR Systems International Ltd. (U.K.); FLIR Systems AB (Sweden); FLIR Systems Ltd. (Canada).

Principal Competitors

Raytheon Company; Nippon Avionics Co., Ltd.; DRS Corporation; Lockheed Martin Corporation; The Boeing Company.

Further Reading

Alva, Marilyn, ''Flir Systems Inc.,'' *Investor's Business Daily,* September 7, 2001, p. A8.

Colwell, Janet, ''Serving the Almighty Market,'' *Oregon Business,* August 2001, p. 25.

Earnshaw, Aliza, ''Flir's Stock Comes Around After Long Run of Bad News,'' *Business Journal-Portland,* June 29, 2001, p. 1.

——, ''Flir Turnaround Gains Steam with New Niches,'' *Business Journal-Portland,* July 13, 2001, p. 14.

Henry, David, ''Not So Dark at Flir,'' *Business Week,* September 1, 2003, p. 101.

Kincade, Kathy, ''Flir Systems Survives SEC Investigation,'' *Opto-electronics Report,* December 1, 2002, p. 6.

Manning, Jeff, ''New Public Companies Find Stock Market Capricious,'' *Business Journal-Portland,* September 20, 1993, p. 1.

McMillan, Dan, ''Flir Systems Board Dismisses CEO Stringer,'' *Business Journal-Portland,* May 26, 2000, p. 9.

Miller, Matt, ''Beyond Night Vision,'' *Daily Deal,* March 8, 2004 13.

Shinkle, Kirk, ''Flir Systems Inc.,'' *Investor's Business Daily,* August 12, 2004, p. A7.

Yim, Su-jin, ''Portland, Ore., Infrared Imaging Firm Signs Pact to Acquire Rival,'' *Knight Ridder/Tribunes Business News,* December 17, 1998.

—Jeffrey L. Covell

Florida Public Utilities Company

401 S. Dixie Highway
West Palm Beach, Florida 33401
U.S.A.
Telephone: (561) 832-0872
Fax: (561) 833-8562
Web site: http://www.fpuc.com

Public Company
Incorporated: 1924 as Palm Beach Company
Employees: 337
Sales: $102.7 million (2003)
Stock Exchanges: American
Ticker Symbol: FPU
NAIC: 221112 Fossil Fuel Electric Power Generation;
    221210 Natural Gas Distribution

Florida Public Utilities Company (FPU) is a small but growing publicly traded energy company, providing electricity, natural gas, and propane to some 91,000 customers in a number of Florida communities. Traditionally FPU has been a conservatively run company, an approach that has allowed it to pay a dividend for more than 50 consecutive years, but has also led to only modest growth over the past half-century. In recent years, however, a new management team led by CEO John "Jack" T. English has launched an expansion effort, especially in the propane business. The West Palm Beach, Florida-based company is listed on the American Stock Exchange.

Formation of Company: 1920s

FPU was founded in 1924 as Palm Beach Gas Company. With 14 miles of gas mains, the company served 1,300 customers located in Palm Beach, West Palm Beach, and Lake Worth, Florida. While gas companies in the 1800s had focused on lighting, with the rise of electricity in the early years of the 20th century, gas companies turned to cooking and heating applications. Early in the 1900s, gas ranges began replacing coal ranges because gas was a more efficient fuel that resulted in less waste. Moreover, gas required no hauling or clean-up like coal. Gas used to heat homes offered these same advantages and

more: Units were smaller, quicker to heat a room, and required far less maintenance. Palm Beach Gas was just one of a multitude of small gas companies that cropped up to meet a community's cooking and heating needs, producing its product in local plants. Typically, gas was made by reducing coal to coke in a retort house, which was then piped to another facility where it was purified by lime. The gas was then piped to an immense tank called a gasholder or "gasometer," from which it would be delivered to customers through the company's network of mains. This method of producing gas would remain essentially unchanged and predominant until natural gas provided by wells in the southwestern United States began to be distributed throughout the country by a vast network of pipelines.

In 1926 Palm Beach Gas became part of Consolidated Electric and Gas Company, a public utility holding company. A year later Palm Beach Gas acquired Gas Service Co. of Key West and added its gas manufacturing plant, prompting a change in name to Florida Public Utilities Company. FPU made another purchase in 1929, picking up Pensacola Gas Company and another gas-making facility.

During the 1930s FPU adjusted its business mix. In 1931 it shut down the Pensacola plant and three years later sold the Pensacola Gas business to Gulf Power Co. The Key West operation was then divested in 1938. On the other hand, FPU expanded beyond gas during this period. In 1935 it acquired Southern States Power Company, operating in Marianna and Fernandina Beach, Florida. The deal brought with it electric and water utilities, as well as ice assets. While FPU would remain in the electricity and water businesses, ice would be phased out as electric refrigerators replaced iceboxes.

Post-World War II Move into Propane

In April 1945 FPU underwent a change of ownership when Jesse L. Terry bought the company from Consolidated Electric and Gas Company. In July 1946 he took FPU public. Another major development during the post-World War II period was the 1949 creation of Flo-Gas Corporation, which supplied bottled propane gas to customers who lived too far from FPU mains. But a much bigger development in the gas industry was beginning to take place during this time: the rise of natural gas.

Natural gas, which is found like other petroleum products trapped within Earth's strata, became a viable product in the Southwest in the 1930s, and in fact had been used for centuries. But natural gas was no better than manufactured gas because it was only available in its immediate area, limited to a local network of mains. That situation changed with the improvement of pipeline technology made necessary with the advent of World War II. Even before the United States entered the war, the government began preparing the country for its participation. A vital consideration was the protection of the petroleum products that a modern army, and economy, depended on. Given the success German submarines enjoyed during World War I in disrupting shipping, it was deemed essential that the country build a pipeline system to deliver fuels underground. The idea of establishing a pipeline system in the southeastern United States had been in the exploratory stages during the 1930s, but the prospect of war was the key factor in making the concept a reality. After the war the pipeline system was expanded, and in the 1950s natural gas provided by wells in the southwestern United States began to be distributed throughout the country. In Florida the primary reason for the introduction of natural gas during the 1950s was to fuel electric power plants. But eventually, residential gas customers were also converted from "town gas" to natural gas. FPU made the transition in 1959, when it began selling natural gas in Palm Beach County. Local gas plants now became obsolete and were gradually closed in the 1960s. But the property on which the plants had been located became a matter of concern for gas companies as local governments began forcing them to clean up leftover contaminants, a problem that FPU would face as well.

Although it held onto its water company operating in Fernandina Beach, FPU concentrated on building its natural gas assets during the 1960s. In 1965 it acquired Sanford Gas Company and inherited some cleanup problems that would only come to the surface years later. In 1967 it added Deland-based Florida Home Gas Company and its natural gas system. In addition, FPU sold off its Marianna water business to North Florida Water Company in 1967. The company now settled into a long stretch of conservative management, a period of more than 30 years in which FPU made no acquisitions and simply operated the assets in hand. It was generally the lowest cost provider in Florida and consistently turned a profit, maintaining an uninterrupted string of years in which it paid a dividend.

FPU also benefited from having consistent management, with only four presidents heading the company from its founding until 1998. Leading them through the critical years of the 1980s and 1990s, when the gas industry moved toward deregulation, was Franklin Charles Cressman, Jr., who spent his entire working career at FPU. Even before he graduated from the University of Florida's School of Engineering in 1960,

Cressman worked part-time as a meter reader and serviceman during summers and vacations. He worked his way up through the company and in 1985 was named president and chief operating officer. He became CEO in 1991. In addition, Cressman served as a member of the Florida Natural Gas Association for over 20 years, including a stint as president. He retired in 1998 at the age of 65 and died three years later from lung cancer.

Aggressive New Leadership in Late 1990s

Replacing Cressman as CEO was 54-year-old Jack English, who also enjoyed a long tenure at FPU. A native of Long Island, English earned undergraduate and graduate degrees in electrical engineering from Georgia Institute of Technology before joining the company in 1973 as division superintendent in the Northeast Division. He was named vice-president of the company in 1991, made senior vice-president in 1993, and a year before Cressman retired, English took over as president and COO. Although on one level English maintained the company's continuity in management, he recognized that FPU would have to become more aggressive in order to remain successful. In 2000 the company expanded its propane business to its northeast Florida territories, but more importantly it began to map plans for the future. FPU hired consultant Decision Processes International and created a 13-person management team that by the end of the year determined a corporate strategy for the next five to seven years. Initially the team planned to build upon its infrastructure to offer additional products, but it soon became apparent that FPU was simply too small and lacked the capital required to launch major new products and services. Instead, FPU elected to expand on its customer base: Rather than sell more products, it would sell more of the same products to more energy customers, whether they be residential, commercial, or industrial. In the end, FPU planned to become a total energy company instead of a mere supplier of gas and electricity.

While management was developing its new strategy in 2000, FPU played an unwitting role in a hostile corporate takeover attempt. The United States' largest power plant developer, AES Corp., was attempting to gain control of CA Electricidad de Caracas, Venezuela's largest power company, which was caught off guard by the unsolicited bid. In an attempt to ward off AES, Electricidad bought a 9.9 percent interest in FPU at a cost of $7 million. Because the Venezuelan company now owned more than a 5 percent stake in a U.S. power company, the maneuver hindered AES, which would now have to gain SEC approval before completing the deal. Electricidad made it clear that it had no intention of seeking control of FPU. Despite this clever ploy, however, Electricidad eventually succumbed to the inevitable and was swallowed up by AES, and FPU returned to relative obscurity.

A major part of FPU's new business strategy was to grow its propane business, to become in the words of its CEO the "Publix of propane." The goal was to acquire one propane company each year. English's first move in this effort was the 2001 purchase of Z-Gas Company, Inc., which had 1,100 customers in Nassau County in northeast Florida. A few months later, FPU also added the Nassau County propane business of Atlantic Utilities. In 2002 FPU acquired another propane business, purchasing Nature Coast Gas, Inc., an Inglis, Florida-based company with more than 1,300 customers. After completing the acquisition,

Key Dates:

1924: Company is formed as Palm Beach Gas Company.
1927: Name is changed to Florida Public Utilities Company.
1946: Company is taken public.
1949: Flo-Gas Corporation is formed to supply propane.
1959: Company moves from manufactured gas to natural gas.
1998: Jack English is named CEO.
2002: Nature Coast Gas, Inc. is acquired.
2003: Water interests are sold.

FPU folded its Dunnellon, Florida, operation and its 1,200 customers into the Nature Coast unit, which would continue to use the Nature Coast Gas name.

As FPU formulated its new growth strategy, it had no intention of expanding on its water business, which was generating close to $3 million in annual revenues. When the City of Fernandina Beach in 2002 offered to buy the water division, management jumped at the opportunity to focus its efforts on energy while at the same time gaining more money to make further acquisitions. The two parties reached an agreement in December 2002 and closed the deal in March 2003. FPU received a total of $25 million, of which $19.2 million was in cash and the balance in future considerations.

FPU held off making any further acquisitions in 2003, instead devoting its energies to reorganizing the Nature Coast Gas unit. The company also sought state approval to combine its two electric divisions, a precursor to a rate increase request. In addition, FPU took a number of steps in 2003 to cut costs. It established a customer payment processing center in its Northwest Florida Division to better automate the customer payment process, a system that not only saved money but freed up customer service representatives to spend more time with customers, in keeping with the goal of improving customer service to help facilitate internal growth. Also to this end, the company introduced new customer service training programs. Other cost-saving efforts in 2003 included a switch in medical insurance brokers and the company's auditing firm.

FPU also began to display a more aggressive posture under English. In 2002 the company came into conflict with Peoples Gas System. In 1991 the two companies had established a territorial agreement that divided Palm Beach County between them, but 11 years later Peoples Gas became upset when FPU built a gas line extension into Juno Beach, an area that Peoples Gas believed was its territory. They reworked their agreement, but found themselves in conflict again in 2004, as both vied to supply gas to a 6,000-acre site in Palm Beach County, the future home of The Scripps Research Institutes' Florida expansion, where thousands of potential customers would be found in the form of new biotechnology companies, other businesses, and homes. The research center was not scheduled to open until 2006 at the earliest, and no matter how state regulators ruled on which gas company was to serve the area, it was clear that the days of FPU simply minding its own knitting were well in the past. In 2004 *Fortune* magazine named FPU as one of the 100 fastest growing small companies in the United States, slotted at number 77, as revenues grew from $88.5 million in 2002 to $102.7 million in 2003. There was every reason to believe that FPU's management team was taking steps to continue moving up in the rankings.

Principal Subsidiaries

Flo-Gas Corporation.

Principal Competitors

Chesapeake Utilities Corporation; JEA; TECO Energy, Inc.

Further Reading

Circelli, Deborah, "Ex-Utility Chairman Franklin Cressman, Utility CEO (obituary), *Palm Beach Post,* September 8, 2001, p. 4B.
——, "Florida Public Utilities Sells Water Business to Fernandina Beach," *Palm Beach Post,* December 5, 2002, p. 1.
——, "FPU Aim: 'Publix of Propane,' " *Palm Beach Post,* February 11, 2002, p. 1D.
——, "Fla. Utility Company Tangled in Takeover," *Palm Beach Post,* June 6, 2000, p. 5B.
Swartz, Kristi E., "Fuel Fight," *Palm Beach Post,* June 6, 2004.

—Ed Dinger

FöreningsSparbanken AB

Brunkebergstorg 8
Stockholm
S-105 34
Sweden
Telephone: +46 8 5859 0000
Fax: +46 8 796 80 92
Web site: http://www.foreningssparbanken.se

Public Company
Incorporated: 1997
Employees: 16,366
Total Assets: SEK 1.0 trillion ($146 billion) (2003)
Stock Exchanges: Pink Sheets Berlin
Ticker Symbols: FGSKY; FSPBA
NAIC: 522110 Commercial Banking

FöreningsSparbanken AB (FS-banken) is one of Sweden's leading banks and one of the largest banking groups in the Nordic (Scandinavia and the Baltic states) region. FS-banken's total assets of more than SEK 1 trillion (nearly $150 billion) also places it among the top 50 banks in Europe. FS-banken offers a full range of banking services, and is especially present on the local level—the group's 785 branches are operated through 93 local banks, but also include 80 independently owned banks that operate under the FS-banken umbrella. Altogether these branches serve more than six million private customers, nearly 350,000 corporate customers, and nearly 350 city councils and municipalities. FS-banken also has taken advantage of the technological savvy of the Scandinavian and Baltic markets, operating a highly successful Internet banking service with nearly three million active customers, and a telephone banking service with more than 1.5 million customers. The company's 1,200-strong ATM network accommodates more than two million "self-service" customers as well. FS-banken's failed 2001 merger with rival Swedish bank SEB—which would have placed it among Europe's top 20 banks—has forced FS-banken to focus on building a Nordic presence, instead of a pan-European presence. As such, FS-banken has expanded throughout the Nordic region, primarily through alliances, including SpareBank 1 in Norway and Aktia

Sparbank in Finland, in which FS-banken holds 19.5 percent and 24.4 percent stakes, respectively. The company also controls Estonia's Hansapank, active throughout the Baltic region, Norway's First Securities, and Denmark's FIH, a corporate finance specialist. The company markets its products through its alliance partners, with additional markets including Poland and Austria. The company also operates a number of specialist subsidiaries, including Robur (fund management products), Spintab (mortgages), Swedbank Markets (investments and asset management), and FöreningsSparbanken Finans. In 2005, the company expects to open the first foreign branch under its direct control, in Copenhagen. FS-banken was formed in 1997 through the merger of Föreningsbanken and Swedbank (known as Sparbanken Sverige inside Sweden). FS-banken is listed on the Stockholm Stock Exchange.

Merging Swedish Banking History in the 1990s

The merger of cooperative banking group Föreningsbanken and the savings bank-based Sparbanken Sverige (known as Swedbank internationally) brought together two concurrent streams of Swedish banking history. The earliest savings bank in Sweden was established in Gothenburg in 1820, emulating a trend that had begun in Europe earlier in the century. The new bank format responded to the rising demand for banking facilities suited to the growing middle-class and worker populations that appeared in force during the Industrial Revolution.

The savings bank format proved extremely popular in Sweden, and by the end of World War I, the country boasted nearly 500 separate and independent savings banks. A significant feature of the savings banks was their decidedly local focus—most had been set up to serve a single community and were, in large part, owned and operated by the "notables" of a community, that is, judges, industrialists, elected officials, and the like. These bank owners remained fiercely independent.

Nonetheless, the Depression Era put a stop to the growth in the savings bank sector and forced the merger of a number of banks in a first wave of consolidation. While the remaining banks continued to assert their independence, they were nonetheless forced to recognize the need—and benefits—of cooperating more closely. In 1942, the savings banks established Sparbankernas Bank, which literally meant "The Savings Banks' Bank." The new bank provided a number of centralized services to the savings banks, including foreign exchange operations and securities issuing. Sparbankernas's operations ended there for the most part, however, as its savings banks' owners refused to allow it to develop into a full-fledged bank capable of competing with their own banks.

While Sparbankernas Bank and the savings banks tended to the financial needs of Sweden's towns and cities, another branch of the country's banking system had developed specifically oriented toward the country's agricultural sector. The first banking cooperatives had appeared in Europe in the 19th century—many, such as the United Kingdom's mutual aid societies—had been formed initially as temporary cooperatives with a specific end purpose, such as the building of homes for each member, for example. The cooperative movement took off throughout Europe in the second half of the 19th century and evolved into permanent rivals to the growing savings banks and established commercial banks.

Sweden's first cooperative bank was founded in Västerhaninge in 1915. The cooperative credit society soon inspired the creation of new cooperative banks. From the outset, Sweden's cooperative banking movement was oriented toward the country's agricultural communities. The early decades of the century were a time of rapid technological development in the farming and other agricultural industries. With the advent of industrialized agricultural techniques, farmers required new means of raising the capital to invest in the new methods, equipment, and machinery.

By 1958, the cooperative movement had matured enough to require its own centralized banking facility. In that year, the country's farming cooperatives founded Jordbrukets Bank (Swedish for Agricultural Bank). The new entity enabled its credit society owners to compete on more equal terms, and encouraged continued growth of the movement. The cooperative societies became known collectively as Jordbrukskassan, or Farming Cooperative Credit Society.

Into the 1970s, however, the Jordbrukskassan—like the country's savings banks—operated under legislation that restricted their range of activities. Because of this, the cooperative banks operated at a disadvantage to the country's larger commercial banks. This situation was changed in 1969 when the financial sector was liberalized and the cooperatives and savings banks achieved parity with the commercial banks.

One result of this was continued growth of the cooperative movement, which by the early 1990s boasted more than 350 members. To underscore this change in status, the Jordbrukskassan changed its name, to Föreningsbanken, in 1974. The savings bank sector, meanwhile, also had begun to evolve. While

Sparbankernas Bank continued to act as a central savings bank, the sector had consolidated into more than ten regionally active savings banks, 100 local savings banks, as well as another unit, the Swedish Savings Bank Association. These banks not only competed with the commercial, cooperative, and other financial entities, they also came into competition with each other.

Emerging from Crisis in the 1990s

The Swedish banking industry was deregulated in the 1980s, introducing a new era of competition—including the entry of foreign banks into Sweden for the first time. The deregulation, coupled with the country's buoyant economy, sparked a huge expansion of the country's credit market—by the late 1980s private borrowing had increased from 85 percent to more than 135 percent of the country's gross domestic product.

Sparbankernas Bank faced a number of challenges during this time. For one thing, operating as a central bank for the many local banks had become overly expensive in an era when competition turned cutthroat. Worse for Sparbankernas Bank, it also faced a revolt from within its own ranks. In the early 1980s, two of the larger savings banks behind Sparbankernas Bank, those in Stockholm and Gothenburg, had merged to form Sparbanken Forsa. The new bank began developing its own centralized services during the 1980s, coming into direct competition with Sparbankernas Bank. By the late 1980s, the competition had intensified, leading to Sparbanken Forsa's exit from the Sparbankernas Bank union.

At Sparbankernas Bank, meanwhile, Chief Executive Goran Collert had been struggling to transform the bank into a more directly active financial player in order to allow the savings bank sector to compete more effectively with the other banking sectors. By 1990, Collert began advocating the consolidation of the savings bank movement into a single unit, with the Sparbankernas Bank taking over as the head banking operation. Yet Collert met extreme resistance from the sector's many independently minded "notables."

Collert had his way, however, thanks to the crisis that rocked the Swedish financial industry at the beginning of the 1990s. Years of unbridled credit had come to a crashing halt with the collapse of the global economy and especially the property markets. Sweden's banks found themselves forced to foreclose on vast portfolios of defaulted loans as the country's real estate developers went bankrupt. Many of the country's banks teetered on the edge of bankruptcy themselves and were forced to turn to the Swedish government for a massive bailout.

Reeling from the crisis, the savings bank sector agreed to the reform led by Collert. In 1991, 11 of the country's largest regional savings banks, which converted themselves into limited banking companies, joined with the Savings Bank Association and Sparbankernas Bank to create a single cohesive entity, Sparbanksgruppen. Some 100 local banks chose not to join the new union outright, but instead agreed to continue to operate under its umbrella. Upstart Sparbanken Forsa was left out of the initial merger—then was absorbed by Sparbanksgruppen in a government-backed bailout in 1992.

As the financial crisis worsened, Collert finally gained the upper hand, and the country's savings banks were merged

Key Dates:

1820: The first Swedish savings bank is founded in Gothenburg.

1915: The first farmer's cooperative credit society is formed in Västerhanige.

1942: A central savings bank, Sparbankernas, is created, providing support services to the larger savings bank industry.

1958: Jordbrukets Bank is created as a central bank for farmers' cooperative banks.

1974: The cooperative bank changes its name to Föreningsbanken.

1991: A banking crisis leads to the creation of a single savings bank entity, Sparbankgruppen.

1992: A full-scale merger of savings banks creates Swedbank; 350 cooperative banks merge to form Föreningsbanken AB.

1994: Föreningsbanken AB goes public on the Stockholm Stock Exchange.

1995: Swedbank goes public on the Stockholm Stock Exchange.

1997: Föreningsbanken AB and Swedbank merge to form FöreningsSparbanken (FS-banken).

1998: Expansion into the Nordic region begins through alliances with Sparebank 1 (Norway), Aktia Spar-Bank (Finland), and acquisitions of majority stakes in Hansapank (Estonia) and FIH (Denmark).

2001: A merger with SEB is attempted, but is abandoned after EU monopolies scrutiny.

2004: The company announces plans to open its first international branch in Copenhagen in 2005.

outright into a single banking structure, Sparbank Sverige, or Swedbank, as it came to be known internationally. Swedbank's début hardly seemed auspicious—between 1991 and 1993, the bank lost some SEK 20 billion ($3 billion). Yet the creation of Swedbank enabled Collert to lead a massive restructuring of the bloated savings bank industry, closing a number of underperforming branches and cutting nearly 25 percent of its payroll in just two years. By 1994, Swedbank had lowered its operating costs by some 20 percent and the company prepared to launch a public offering.

Regional Force in the New Century

Swedbank was beaten to the market by Föreningsbanken. Emerging from its own difficulties during the banking crisis, Föreningsbanken too had restructured, merging its 350 former cooperative members into a single banking entity to become Föreningsbanken AB in 1992. By 1994, Föreningsbanken had returned to growth, and in that year listed its stock on the Stockholm Stock Exchange. Swedbank's listing came the following year.

By 1996, Sweden's banks had not only staged a comeback from the crisis at the beginning of the decade, they had emerged as some of the most profitable banks in all of Europe. The banking sector now began looking forward to a new era, as the

European banking industry began preparing for the full deregulation of the sector and the arrival of the single European currency at the end of the decade. The later 1990s were marked by a wave of consolidations within the various domestic markets, creating a smaller number of national powerhouse banks capable of competing on a European—and global—scale.

In 1997, Föreningsbanken and Swedbank joined the consolidation drive, announcing their agreement to merge to form FöreningsSparbanken (FS-banken). The new bank now became one of Sweden's top four banks—and one of the largest in the Scandinavian and wider Nordic regions.

FS-banken quickly began to assert itself as a major player in the Nordic region—which combined the Scandinavian and Baltic markets. In order to expand internationally, the bank developed a strategy of forming alliances with local partners. Such was the case in Finland, when the company acquired a minority stake in that country's Aktia. In 1998, the bank forged a similar alliance with Norway's Sparebank 1, in which FS-banken agreed to pay NOK 720 million ($90 million) for a 25 percent share of Sparebank 1 Gruppen. That organization, which controlled four regional savings banks as well as 16 local savings banks in Norway, agreed to market FS-banken's financial products to its customers.

Elsewhere, FS-banken moved into Estonia, acquiring majority control of that country's Hansapank. The purchase enabled FS-banken to expand throughout the Baltic states. The bank returned to Norway the following year with the purchase of 60 percent of that country's FIH, a major corporate finance specialist. FS-banken also formed an alliance with Erste Bank in Austria, and began marketing its products in Poland as well.

FS-banken next attempted to enter the European big leagues. In 2001, the bank announced its agreement with rival Swedish bank SEB—the Wallenberg family's banking vehicle—to merge to form one of Europe's top 25 banks. The merger would have given FS-banken the critical mass needed to extend its reach beyond the Nordic region in order to establish a truly pan-European operation.

The merger quickly foundered, however, when the initial review of the European Commission raised monopoly objections—the proposed merger would have created an entity controlling more than 50 percent of the Swedish market. Observers criticized the commission for not recognizing the special conditions of the smaller market countries, such as Sweden, and their need to create larger, more internationally competitive banking structures. Yet FS-banken and SEB surprised observers as well by calling off the merger without challenging the review—or even allowing it to reach a conclusion.

Thwarted in its ambition of becoming a pan-European bank, FS-banken contented itself with solidifying its Nordic region presence in the 2000s. The bank made a highly successful entry into the Internet banking market, attracting nearly three million customers by late 2004, including more than 1.3 million Baltic region customers. FS-banken, which previously operated in the larger Scandinavian market through its alliances, then began plans to establish its own international operations. In December 2004, FS-banken announced its intention to launch its own banking network in Denmark, with the first branch expected to open in Cophenhagen by mid-2005. FS-banken prepared to build on its position as a major Nordic region banking player in the new century.

Principal Subsidiaries

AB Spintab; Aktia Sparbank Abp (24.39%); Allround AB (67%); AS Hansapank (59.71%); Babs Paylink AB (49%); Bergslagens Sparbank AB (48%); Entercard AS; Eskilstuna Rekarne Sparbank AB (50%); Färs & Frosta Sparbank AB (30%); FI-Holding A/S (74.7%); First Securities ASA (33.3%); Förenings-Sparbanken Administration AB; Förenings-Sparbanken Fastighetsbyrå AB; Förenings-Sparbanken Finans AB; Förenings-Sparbanken Jordbrukskredit AB; Förenings-Sparbanken Juristbyrå AB; Förenings-Sparbanken Öland AB (60%); Förenings-Sparbanken Sjuhärad AB (47.5%); Förenings-Sparbanken Söderhamn AB (40%); HSB Bank AB; Kundinkasso AB K.I.A.B.; Robur AB; Robur Fonder AB; Robur Försäkring AB; Robur Kapitalförvaltning AB; Spare-Bank 1 Gruppen ASb (25%); Sparia Försäkrings AB; Swedbank Luxembourg S.A.; Vimmerby Sparbank AB (40%).

Principal Competitors

Nordea Group; Svenska Handelsbanken; Skandinaviska Enskilda Banken.

Further Reading

''Advantages in Abundance: Swedish Banks Lead the Field on Many Fronts—Customer Satisfaction, NPL Ratios and IT Among,'' *Banker,* December 2002, p. 38.

Brown, Jonathan, ''A Rude Shock to Domestic Bliss,'' *Euromoney,* November 2001, p. 74.

Burt, Tim, ''Swedish Bank Lifts Estonian Stake,'' *Financial Times,* September 11, 1998, p. 32.

''FöreningsSparbanken to Launch Operations in Denmark,'' *Nordic Business Report,* December 15, 2004.

George, Nicholas, ''Turbulence Hits Fsbanken,'' *Financial Times,* August 26, 2002, p. 6.

George, Nicholas, and Christopher Brown-Humes, ''FSB and SEB Come to Terms with Life on Their Own,'' *Financial Times,* September 20, 2001, p. 30.

''Saved: Swedish Banking,'' *Economist,* December 17, 1994, p. 78.

''Swedbank Divests Holding in Erste Bank for SEK 1,564m,'' *Nordic Business Report,* June 19, 2003.

—M.L. Cohen

The Franklin Mint

U.S. Route 1
Franklin Center, Pennsylvania 19091
U.S.A.
Telephone: (610) 459-6000
Fax: (610) 459-6880
Web site: http://www.franklinmint.com

*Wholly Owned Subsidiary of Roll International
   Corporation*
Incorporated: 1964 as General Numismatics Corporation
NAIC: 327112 Vitreous China, Fine Earthenware and
   Other Pottery Product Manufacturing; 339911 Jewelry
   (Including Precious Metal) Manufacturing; 339914
   Costume Jewelry and Novelty Manufacturing

The Franklin Mint is a subsidiary of Roll International Corporation, owned by Stewart and Lynda Resnick, and based in Franklin Center, Pennsylvania, a Philadelphia suburb. Although it portrays itself as a company devoted to producing quality one-of-a-kind art objects, to many The Franklin Mint is little more than a mass purveyor of kitsch. Nevertheless, the company is a pioneer of the collectibles industry, starting with coins, which the company minted itself, and branching out to include such items as limited edition paintings and books, commemorative plates, figurines, celebrity likeness dolls, jewelry, seasonal giftware, and die-cast model airplanes and automobiles. But as the collectibles industry has faltered with the rise of the Internet and the emergence of Ebay, The Franklin Mint has steadily lost business, forcing a major restructuring. The company now concentrates on its die-cast automobile and airplane models and Harley-Davidson motorcycle branded items, although it continues to offer dolls, jewelry, and a variety of gift items.

Company Founder: 1940s Whiz Kid Entrepreneur

The Franklin Mint was founded by Joseph M. Segel, a legendary entrepreneur, who launched a number of businesses in his career, including the QVC television shopping channel. He was born in Philadelphia, Pennsylvania, in 1931. When he was 13 he started a printing business and in 1947, at the age of 16, he entered the University of Pennsylvania's Wharton School of Business to major in accounting. As an underaged graduate student he also taught marketing classes at Wharton, while earning money on the side by selling promotional items, such as postcards with messages written in invisible ink. The recipient had to dip the card in water in order to reveal the message. It was a brilliant marketing gimmick, inducing the target to invest time by creating a desire to read the promotion. Because it was difficult to find a company to make the postcards, Segel compiled a list of suppliers as well as promotional products. In 1950 he published the *Advertising Specialty Directory* and launched a company he called the Advertising Specialty Institute. He ran the business until selling it in the early 1960s.

Segel's inspiration for creating The Franklin Mint was the result of the cross-pollination of two events. On March 25, 1964, the U.S. Treasury ceased to sell silver dollars, a decision that led to long lines of people at the Treasury building eager to buy the remaining silver dollars, and packs of photographers taking pictures of them for the newspapers and magazines, including *Time,* which published a photograph that caught Segel's attention. He was already very much aware that as silver coins became scarce there was a growing number of people interested in collecting them. He sensed a business opportunity, which would come to fruition after another event took place that received widespread media attention that year: the funeral of General Douglas MacArthur. As Segel explained to *Direct Marketing* in 1988, "My idea was to issue a series of solid sterling silver medals, a little larger than the silver dollar, of the highest quality of limited edition and each designed by a different famous sculptor." The first coin was to commemorate General MacArthur.

In 1964, with an investment of $10,000, Segel formed the National Commemorative Society to issue the medals, which would be numbered and sold only to members. The die would then be destroyed to ensure exclusivity. The Society also would publish a monthly newsletter to promote new offerings and provide a historical perspective on the pieces. Members would vote monthly to determine the people or events to commemorate. Once again Segel displayed his marketing acumen in

---

Company Perspectives:

Sharing your passion for collecting.

---

attracting members. He ran an ad simultaneously in several coin magazines to announce the formation of the society, which would sell memberships for just eight weeks. To heighten the sense of urgency, Segel added a sliding scale for membership fees: early birds paid just $10 during the first two weeks, while latecomers were charged $40 during the final two weeks. He hoped to sign up 1,000, maybe 2,000 members, but far surpassed his own expectations. After eight weeks the Society signed up 5,250 members.

Starting a Private Mint in the Mid-1960s

Segel sold his initial "coins" for $6.50, and although the Society members were satisfied with the quality, he was far from pleased. He had promised to produce proof-quality coins, but such coins featured a reflective background and a satin or frosted finish on the area in relief. Even the U.S. mint had difficulty in striking such quality coins, making them a rarity that collectors call a "gem proof" or "frosted proof." To complicate the matter, Segel wanted to strike larger coins, the size of a British crown, but they required stronger dies to withstand the required pressure. Unfortunately, tougher dies led to reduced surface quality. Segel tried two different companies, but neither could meet his high standards. That is when he decided to start his own private mint. He approached Gilroy Roberts, the chief sculptor-engraver of the U.S. Mint, who was about to retire, and convinced him to join him in the venture. Roberts agreed, and in late 1964 they established General Numismatics Corporation, with Segel serving as president and Roberts as chairman. Roberts soon solved the problem in producing large proof-quality coins by employing different alloys in the die. The business changed its name to The Franklin Mint in 1965, and what started with a $10,000 investment now earned $10,000 in profits each month. Segel took The Franklin Mint public in 1965 and completed a $4 million initial offering of stock. Although scoffed at in the beginning, the private mint soon had experts from around the world paying visits to learn how it produced such quality proofs.

In addition to striking coins for the National Commemorative Society, The Franklin Mint began doing work for foreign countries, such as the Bahamas, Jamaica, Trinidad, Panama, and Tunisia. It also added other collector items. The Franklin Mint produced aluminum coins bearing the likenesses of U.S. presidents (which were given away at gas stations as a sales incentive), Christmas plates, commemorative ingots, and fine art plaques. Business was so strong that sales grew from $392,000 in 1965 to $45.8 million in 1970. But the collectibles industry was just beginning to take off, as an increasing number of items were now being produced simply to be collected, and The Franklin Mint was at the forefront. In 1973 The Franklin Mint posted sales of nearly $113 million and a net profit of more than $9 million. However, the company would have to continue on without its founder, because in 1973 Segel stepped away from the business, as would be the case with so many of the companies he started. He told *Direct Marketing* in 1988, "I may have a short span of attention, but the businesses I create tend to have a long life." Over the next 20 years he started eight more companies, including the QVC television shopping channel.

Segel left The Franklin Mint in the experienced hands of Charles Lovett Andes, another native Philadelphian, whom Segel hired as the company's president in 1969. He would become chief executive officer and chairman of the board, titles he held until 1985. Under his leadership, The Franklin Mint continued to expand its offerings of collectibles. The company's first gold coins were struck in 1974. The Franklin Mint also began offering items such as paintings, leatherbound books, records, etched crystal, porcelain, historic arms, and chess sets. In addition, he acquired Eastern Mountain Sports Inc., not only picking up a sports equipment and clothing retail chain, but a mail-order operation as well. By the end of the 1970s Franklin Mint sales grew to $360 million. But success did not come without missteps or controversy. The company's claims that its silver coins were a solid investment were contradicted by *Forbes,* and the story was picked up by CBS's *60 Minutes.* The Franklin Mint saw its earnings tail off in the late 1970s and also had to contend with a stockholder's lawsuit. Andes responded by cutting back on the company's original commemorative coin business and adding other collectibles, such as furniture, jewelry, and figurines. The company also looked to move beyond direct marketing and began opening retail shops.

In 1980 The Franklin Mint generated sales of $360 million and net income of $21.8 million. At the close of the year, Andes arranged a sale of the company to Warner Communications Inc. for about $225 million in cash, stock, and warrants. By becoming part of Warner, The Franklin Mint gained the deep pockets of a corporate parent that Andes hoped would fuel future growth. Warner, on the other hand, bolstered its consumer products division. The arrangement was short-lived, however. The Franklin Mint added its Precision Models unit, which produced a popular line of miniature cars, but after two years under Warner ownership Franklin Mint experienced a drop in sales. Moreover, Warner had money problems of its own. It owned video game company Atari, and when its market collapsed in the early 1980s, the price of Warner's stock fell, making it susceptible to a hostile takeover. The company suffered massive losses and was forced into a restructuring program, which resulted in Warner selling off Atari in 1984. Late in that year The Franklin Mint also was put on the block and a buyer was found in the form of American Protection Industries Inc. (API), which completed the $167.5 million purchase in 1985, at which point Andes left the company. Warner retained a 15 percent stake in Franklin Mint and elected to keep Eastern Mountain Sports as well as The Franklin Mint center, which it would lease back to API.

Based in Los Angeles, API was owned by Stewart A. and Lynda Rae Resnick. It was a holding company for a central-station alarm company, Teleflora Inc. (a flowers-by-wire service that the Resnicks acquired in 1979), and three agricultural subsidiaries. When they took over The Franklin Mint, the company's annual sales had dipped to $250 million. The Resnicks took steps to revitalize the business, which was then divided among four major product groups: jewelry, porcelain dolls,

Key Dates:

1964: Joseph Segel establishes General Numismatics Corporation to mint coins for the National Commemorative Society.
1965: General Numismatics is renamed Franklin Mint and taken public.
1973: Segel retires.
1980: Warner Communications acquires the company.
1985: Lynda and Stewart Resnick acquire the company.
1992: Efforts to complete a stock offering fail.
1998: The company is sued by the Princess Diana Memorial Fund.
2004: A major restructuring effort begins.

tableware, and the male division, which produced miniature cars and items such as a Civil War chess set. The company also changed its marketing approach somewhat, putting more money into television.

The Franklin Mint showed some initial improvement, growing net income to $22.5 million in 1987, but the following three years brought losses. The company returned to profitability in 1991, and a year later it filed to make a public offering of stock at $16 a share, in the hope of raising about $180 million for the Resnicks and the company. A large share of the money was earmarked to pay down debt. But the response on Wall Street was cool and the offering was soon withdrawn.

Overall, the 1990s brought mixed results for The Franklin Mint. The company continued to bring out distinctive collectibles. For example, Lynda Resnick bought the faux pearl necklace owned by Jackie Onassis, estimated to be worth $700, for $211,500, and then had Franklin Mint make thousands of replicas. Costume jewelry in general was a strong product category for the company during this period, as overall sales grew to more than $700 million. But the company also received unwanted notoriety in 1998 when the Diana, Princess of Wales, Memorial Fund sued Franklin Mint in California to stop it from producing items bearing her image. The doll in question showed the late princess dressed in the outfit she wore during her campaign in Angola to ban landmines. Franklin Mint had been selling Diana dolls since the late 1980s without comment by the royal family, but it now became the focal point of the Memorial Fund's efforts to see that the proceeds from any items bearing her likeness went to charitable causes. The Franklin Mint was vilified openly by Fund officials, who called the Resnicks "vultures feeding on the dead." The matter was dismissed by a district court, which held that Diana had to have been born in California in order for her representatives to hold rights over her image in that state. The Memorial Fund appealed the case, and the Resnicks countersued for $25 million, claiming that the Fund and executors of the estate had acted "maliciously, wantonly . . . and with the intent to oppress" Franklin Mint. In 2002 the U.S. Court of Appeals for the 9th Circuit upheld the lower court ruling, and in November 2004 the Memorial Fund and The Franklin Mint reached an out-of-court settlement just before jury selection on the suit filed by Franklin Mint. Neither the company nor the Resnicks received any money. Rather, the

Fund pledged to spend $25 million over the next five years on jointly agreed-upon charitable causes, such as HIV-Aids, landmines, and caring for the terminally ill. It was clearly a face-saving arrangement for both sides, who after six years of bitter discord were ready to let the matter rest.

Sales Peak in the 1990s

During the years the Resnicks and The Franklin Mint were involved in litigation, they saw a change in the collectibles industry. The market peaked in 1998 with sales of $10 billion, but the bottom soon fell out as sales plummeted to $6.5 million by 2001. Part of the reason for this collapse was generational, as fewer young people were interested in collecting limited edition items but some of it was inherent in the nature of the collectibles industry itself. Because the items were made to be collected, people held onto them, often believing that they would increase in value. But rising prices had been based on scarcity and although the collectibles were limited in edition they were still mass produced. People who thought they were making an investment quickly learned that anyone who would want the item most likely already owned one. Scarcity was delivered a further blow by the emergence of the Internet and the Ebay online auction site in particular. The sense of urgency that Joe Segel played on when he first started Franklin Mint, the need to buy an item if you stumbled upon it at a garage sale or antique shop, was gone. Every day dozens of that special something were put up for bid on Ebay, including thousands of Franklin Mint items, once highly prized but now available at a steep discount. Virtually every kind of collectible and antique dropped in value, not only the kind of collectibles in which Franklin Mint specialized. The entire dynamic of the industry changed, so that people who counted on the prices found in collectible guides were sorely disappointed when they sold their collections, often receiving just a fraction of what they invested. Thus, virtually overnight, countless collectibles had turned into mere dustables.

The Franklin Mint also made strategic errors along the way. As reported by *Catalog Age* in a 2004 article, "According to one anonymous source, Franklin Mint spent too much money on acquiring customers via space ads. And when the company started ramping up its catalog business in the mid-'90s, it discovered that the buyers of less-expensive collectibles didn't always convert into repeat buyers of higher-end gifts. 'The plan was to sell consumers a commemorative plate for $19.95, then get them to buy a $195 sculpture of Marilyn Monroe or Jackie Onassis,' the source says, 'It just never worked.'" Clearly, some major retooling of the business model was in order. In 2004 the company drastically cut back on its catalog mailings, closed its 30 retail stores and its museum in Franklin Center, and laid off some 200 employees. The downsizing also extended to the company's product offerings, as Franklin Mint decided to focus on its miniature airplanes and cars and Harley-Davidson branded items. Hence, the long-term health of The Franklin Mint, and the collectibles industry that it spawned, was very much in doubt.

Principal Competitors

The Boyds Collection, Ltd.; The Bradford Group; Lenox, Incorporated; Enesco Group, Inc.; Russ Berrie and Company, Inc.

Further Reading

Eckstein, Sandra, "Bear Market Collectibles," *Atlanta Journal-Constitution,* August 7, 2002, p. E1.

"The Franklin Mint," *Nation's Business,* December 1971, p. 74.

Halford, Quinn, "Collectibles at a Crossroads," *Gifts & Decorative Accessories,* February 2004, p. 16.

Hazelton, Lynette, "More of the Same Bolsters Franklin Mint Marketing," *Philadelphia Business Journal,* April 7, 1986, p. 20.

Jardine, Cassandra, "No One's Going to Make a Mint Now," *Daily Telegraph (London, England),* November 9, 2004, p. 16.

Lubove, Seth, "King of the Startups," *Forbes,* November 8, 1993, p. 186.

—Ed Dinger

GameStop

GameStop Corp.

2250 William D. Tate Avenue
Grapevine, Texas 76051-3978
U.S.A.
Telephone: (817) 424-2000
Fax: (817) 424-2002
Web site: http://www.gamestop.com

Public Company
Incorporated: 2001
Employees: 15,600
Sales: $1.58 billion (2003)
Stock Exchanges: New York
Ticker Symbol: GME
NAIC: 451120 Hobby, Toy, and Game Stores

GameStop Corp. is the largest U.S. player in the retail sector specializing in video game and PC entertainment software, and also ranks in the top five in the broader toy retailing sector. In addition to new and used software, GameStop's stores also sell new and used video game equipment. The company operates approximately 1,750 retail stores located in 49 states (the exception being Wyoming), the District of Columbia, Puerto Rico, and Ireland, primarily under the GameStop brand. Nearly two-thirds of the stores are located in strip shopping centers, and these average about 1,500 square feet in size. Most of the remainder are located in shopping malls and are smaller on average, approximately 1,200 square feet. GameStop also operates an e-commerce web site at www.gamestop.com and publishes *Game Informer,* one of the leading multiplatform video game magazines, with more than 1.5 million subscribers.

Early Years of Babbage's

GameStop has a lineage that includes several retailing names now relegated to the historical graveyard. One of the key predecessors was Babbage's, Inc., named for Charles Babbage, the 19th-century British mathematician generally credited with inventing the first major forerunner of a computer. Babbage's traces its roots to two Harvard Business School classmates, James B. McCurry and Gary M. Kusin. At Harvard during the

mid-1970s, McCurry and Kusin discussed going into business together but went in separate directions after graduation. McCurry became a consultant for Bain & Company's San Francisco office, while Kusin became a Dallas-based general merchandise manager for the Sanger-Harris division of Federated Department Stores. In 1982 McCurry approached Kusin with a business proposal to establish a chain of software stores that would capitalize on the burgeoning computer and home video game industries. His idea was based on the expectation that increasing consumer interest in computer equipment and games would make the specialty store the ideal marketing outlet. Kusin, who had been watching such specialty stores gradually take over department store business, liked the idea, and, at the end of the year, both men quit their jobs and began seeking startup financing for a software business.

McCurry and Kusin's business plan met with little interest among venture capitalists until February 1983, when businessman Ross Perot—who knew Kusin's family in Texarkana—offered to provide a $3 million credit line in exchange for one-third ownership in the company. Perot also advised the entrepreneurs to shelve their plan for immediately opening 20 stores in favor of establishing one outlet, which they would manage themselves until they knew the business inside and out. McCurry and Kusin took Perot's money and advice, and, on Memorial Day 1983, they opened the first Babbage's store in a Dallas regional mall. McCurry, the company's chairperson, managed the company's finances, while Kusin, the company's president, acquired software products from local distributors. Both partners took turns opening and closing the store and seeing to other administrative details.

During this time, McCurry and Kusin tested their business strategy, which involved four key provisions: a constantly updated mix of products, a competitive pricing system, a flexible store design with sections devoted to various computer and entertainment system platforms and software categories, and an enthusiastic, noncommissioned sales staff that would not intimidate customers with technical jargon. Two months after opening the first Babbage's store, McCurry and Kusin met their sales projections and hired their first full-time employee, Mary Evans, who later became vice-president of stores. Between Labor Day and Thanksgiving of 1983, Evans helped open and manage four more Dallas-area stores.

Babbage's set a precedent of selling entertainment software for the most popular computer and video game systems. At the time, the dominant home video game system was the Atari 2600, which featured four-color graphics. Eventually Atari was superseded by Nintendo and Sega of America systems, and Babbage's redirected its product line accordingly.

In 1984, Babbage's first full year of operations, the company lost $560,000 on sales of $3 million. Two years later, it broke even after generating nearly $10 million in revenues from an expanded chain of 23 stores, financed through the private sales of company stock. In 1987 Babbage's added another 35 stores and began selling software for the then-dominant eight-bit Nintendo Entertainment System with 16-color graphics. For fiscal 1987, the company earned $1.16 million on sales of $29 million.

In July 1988 Babbage's took its software specialty store concept public, offering 30 percent of the company's equity for $20 million, or $13 a share. Following the public offering, Perot tendered his stake in the company, and Babbage's continued accelerating its expansion drive with the proceeds of stock sales, opening 50 new stores that year to give the company 108 retail outlets. This expansion resulted in rising sales; in 1988, Babbage's annual revenues doubled to $58 million, while earnings shot up 136 percent to $2.7 million.

In 1989, Babbage's began losing business because of severe allocations of video games. Struck by a string of losses in the first three quarters of the year, the company responded by reducing prices on leading computer software titles and adding new cartridge-based video games to its line. Moreover, in the fall, Babbage's helped introduce the new 16-bit, 64-color Sega Genesis entertainment system, which quickly changed the landscape of the video game industry. Because of its superior capabilities, Sega Genesis generated a renewed interest in home video game systems. Rising sales of entertainment systems and software contributed to a strong 1989 holiday sales season for Babbage's, as the company managed a $2.3 million profit on annual sales that increased 62 percent to $95 million.

Early 1990s: Rising Revenues from New Game Systems

Fifty-three new store openings in 1989 (bringing the company's total to 160) and a barrage of new low-profit-margin products pushed the company's earnings and its stock's trading value down. By early 1990, Babbage's stock, which had debuted at $13, had plummeted to less than $5. Babbage's responded to its financial troubles by scaling back the company's expansion program—opening only 19 stores in 1990—and focusing on cost-control measures and improved inventory turnover. Moreover, a new computerized point-of-sale inventory system was established, tracking sales and inventory after each business day and automatically generating orders for shipment from the company's Dallas warehouse the following morning. Powered by a surge in video game systems and software—including Sega's 16-bit Genesis and Nintendo's handheld Game Boy player—the company's revenues rose 39 percent to $132.8 million in 1990 as earnings increased to $4.1 million.

Opal P. Ferraro, who joined Baggage's in 1986 as controller, was named chief financial officer in 1991, and, two years later, Ferraro joined McCurry and Kusin as the only other company officer on Babbage's board of directors. With the company in improved financial shape, Babbage's boosted its number of stores from 178 to 204 and reported 1991 earnings of $5.58 million on sales of $168.3 million.

In 1992 Babbage's added more than 40 new stores and began selling a CD-ROM peripheral attachment for the Sega 16-bit system that allowed interaction with digitized video footage. Sparked by a price war in the computer industry, sales of IBM-compatible software and 16-bit video systems and software rose substantially, and the company's stock value increased accordingly, climbing to more than $24 per share. The company's earnings also increased 21 percent to $6.78 million, and sales jumped 24 percent to $209.1 million.

In the fall of 1993, Babbage's began selling Panasonic's 32-bit game system, which operated through compact discs. This new technology threatened to render the 16-bit systems obsolete, and Babbage's experienced rapid declines in its sales of video game systems and software during the Christmas season, with the average Babbage's store posting 5 percent lower sales than a year earlier. Realizing that the market for 16-bit technology had matured, Babbage's slashed prices on hundreds of video game titles early the following year in an effort to unload its inventory of the increasingly dated software.

In 1993 Babbage's opened 56 new stores. The company, however, generated only a 12 percent increase in sales, and, for the first time since 1989, increased revenues did not translate into higher earnings for the company. Earnings fell 36 percent to $4.3 million that year as entertainment software continued to comprise about two-thirds of Babbage's business. Education and productivity software, along with computer supplies and accessories, cumulatively accounted for the remaining third.

1994 Merger with Software Etc., Creating NeoStar Retail Group

Babbage's entered 1994 with a 300-store chain and plans to open between 30 and 40 more stores that year. As a result of holiday season price reductions, Babbage's stores had substantially reduced their inventory. The company was in a stronger financial position, however, as it had no long-term debt and maintained a cash surplus of $10.5 million. Babbage's entered

Key Dates:

1983: James B. McCurry and Gary M. Kusin found Babbage's, Inc., opening the first Babbage's software store in a Dallas regional mall.

1984: B. Dalton Bookseller Inc. creates a division called Software Etc. to open software stores within B. Dalton bookstores.

1986: Dayton Hudson Corporation sells B. Dalton to Barnes & Noble, Inc. (B&N) and partners.

1987: Software Etc. is split off from B. Dalton, begins operating as Software Etc. Stores, Inc., and starts shift to standalone locations.

1988: Babbage's is taken public to accelerate an expansion drive.

1992: Software Etc. Stores is taken public.

1994: Babbage's merges with Software Etc., forming NeoStar Retail Group, Inc.

1996: NeoStar files for Chapter 11 bankruptcy protection; an investor group led by Leonard Riggio buys the Babbage's and Software Etc. chains, operating them within the newly formed Babbage's Etc. LLC.

1999: New strip-mall-based chain, GameStop, is launched; e-commerce web site, later called gamestop.com, begins operations; Babbage's Etc. is sold to Barnes & Noble for $215 million.

2000: B&N acquires Funco, Inc., operator of 400 FuncoLand video game stores, mainly in strip malls; Babbage's Etc. becomes a wholly owned subsidiary of Funco, which changes its name to GameStop, Inc.

2001: GameStop Corp. is incorporated in anticipation of an initial public offering (IPO).

2002: B&N completes a partial IPO of GameStop stock; it retains a 67 percent stake in GameStop.

2004: B&N distributes its remaining stake in GameStop to B&N shareholders, making GameStop a fully independent corporation.

the mid-1990s facing increasing competition from other software specialty stores, mass merchandisers (such as Wal-Mart Stores, Inc.), computers centers and superstores, electronics stores (particularly Best Buy Co., Inc. and Circuit City Stores, Inc.), toy stores, and mail-order outlets, many of which were larger operations and had greater resources at their disposal. In order to better position itself within this increasingly competitive environment, Babbage's elected to merge with another specialty software retailer.

Software Etc. Stores, Inc., Babbage's merger partner, began in 1984 as a division of B. Dalton Bookseller Inc., then owned by Dayton Hudson Corporation. That year, B. Dalton began adding Software Etc. ''stores-within-a-store'' to its bookstores. Late in 1986, however, Dayton Hudson sold B. Dalton to Barnes & Noble, Inc. (B&N), Leonard Riggio (the chairman and founder of B&N), and Dutch retailer Vendex International N.V. Riggio played a key role in separating Software Etc. from B. Dalton, and the former began operating as Software Etc. Stores, Inc. in 1987. A gradual physical separation began as well, as Software Etc.

units moved out of B. Dalton bookstores and into their own, largely mall-based, standalone stores. The chain was also expanded to nearly 200 units by the end of 1988, and its product mix was altered, away from entertainment software toward higher-end PC and Mac software applications. Software Etc. then broadened its product line in 1990, once again selling video game software. The company's timing was excellent as it was able to ride the latest crest in the video game sector in the early 1990s, registering 20 to 30 percent annual increases in same-store sales (that is, sales at stores open at least one year). Revenues for the fiscal year ending in October 1991 reached $152 million, up $35 million from the previous year. Early in 1992, operating about 230 stores in 37 states and the District of Columbia, Software Etc. Stores completed an initial public offering of 2.3 million shares of common stock at $11 per share.

By the completion of the merger with Babbage's in December 1994, Software Etc. was operating about 380 stores and had annual revenues of about $240 million. Babbage's had about 335 stores and revenues of $230 million. There was little overlap between the two chains: the two operated stores in fewer than 50 of the same malls. Combined, the chains fielded stores in more than half of the 1,200 malls in the Unites States—making it the largest consumer software specialty retailer in the country. The deal was structured as a stock swap in which both Babbage's and Software Etc. shareholders received shares in a newly formed holding company, NeoStar Retail Group, Inc. Babbage's, Inc. and Software Etc. Stores, Inc. became subsidiaries of NeoStar, and each chain retained their separate identities. Riggio was named chairman of NeoStar's executive committee; Babbage's chairman, McCurry, became board chairman and CEO of NeoStar; and Kusin, president of Babbage's, and Daniel DeMatteo, president of Software Etc., continued in those same roles. In February 1995, however, Kusin left the company, and DeMatteo was named president and COO of NeoStar. Headquarters for NeoStar were established in Dallas, where Babbage's had been based.

The 1995 introductions of a new generation of video game systems, the Sega Saturn and Sony Playstation, both 32-bit systems, failed to provide the boost to NeoStar that the previous new waves of hardware had given to the company's predecessors. One key reason was competition. Previously, Babbage's and Software Etc. stores were two of the few places where the latest systems and games were available early on. By the mid-1990s, mass-market retailers such as Wal-Mart, Best Buy, Target, and Toys ''R'' Us, Inc. had stepped strongly into the market. As a result, sales began declining, and NeoStar managed to post only a minuscule profit of $120,000 for the fiscal year ending in January 1996 on sales of $513.5 million. In the first quarter of the following year, same-store sales fell 9 percent and the loss of $8.3 million was more than double that of the previous year. This prompted management and organizational changes. DeMatteo resigned and McCurry took on the additional post of president. NeoStar's three retail units (the third operating leased software departments within Barnes & Noble bookstores) were combined into one organization, and Alan C. Bush was brought onboard as its head. Bush was the former president of Tandy Corporation's Computer City division. Soon thereafter, in July 1996, Barnes & Noble took over management of the software departments at its stores.

1996–2002: The Riggio/B&N Era Involving Babbage's Etc., Funco, and GameStop

Not able to stem the decline in sales nor to secure enough financing to stock its shelves for the coming holiday season, NeoStar filed for Chapter 11 bankruptcy protection in September 1996. Board member Thomas G. Plaskett was named chairman and charged with leading the reorganization, while Mc-Curry continued to handle day-to-day operations as CEO and president. Plaskett had gained a reputation as a turnaround expert from his failed but valiant attempt to rescue Pan Am Corp. in the late 1980s and early 1990s and from his success at saving Greyhound Lines, Inc. in the mid-1990s. In October 1996 NeoStar announced it would close 42 of its stores, all of which were located near other company stores. When the company could not secure the additional financing it needed in order to reorganize, the stores were placed up for sale. Finally, in November, a group of investors led by Riggio bought the chains for $58.5 million, beating out a rival bid from Electronics Boutique Holdings Corp., Babbage's and Software Etc.'s biggest competitor.

Riggio created a new holding company called Babbage's Etc. LLC, which took over the operation of 467 Babbage's and Software Etc. outlets. The remaining 200 or so stores were shut down. Riggio served as chairman, and he brought R. Richard "Dick" Fontaine back onboard as CEO. Fontaine had been the chief executive of Software Etc. during the late 1980s and early 1990s. Likewise, DeMatteo returned as president and chief operating officer. The two chains began keeping a similar mix of video game and software titles, with an increasing emphasis on the former. Improved operational strategies and the introduction of a new 64-bit Nintendo system helped Babbage's Etc. return to double-digit growth in the late 1990s.

By 1999 Babbage's Etc. had recovered sufficiently to begin growing again. Plans were set for opening 50 new stores that year, and a significant portion of this growth was aimed at expanding the company into the field of strip malls. A new name, GameStop, was selected for the 20 new strip mall outlets. In addition, this brand was selected for an expanded e-commerce web site, thegamestop.com (later shortened to gamestop.com). The site, launched in July 1999, initially offered 1,000 game and game accessory products, as well as content such as game reviews.

In October 1999, shortly after the launch of GameStop and the web site, Riggio and company sold Babbage's Etc. to Barnes & Noble for $215 million. Although some analysts raised their eyebrows at the price B&N paid for Babbage's—more than three times what Riggio's group had paid for it three years earlier—a spate of new game systems augured well for the timing. Sega's Dreamcast and Nintendo's handheld Game Boy Color machines were released in the latter months of 1999 and Sony's 128-bit PlayStation 2 system made a spectacular debut in the fall of 2000.

B&N wasted little time bolstering its new subsidiary. In the spring of 2000 it entered into a bidding war with Electronic Boutique Holdings over Funco, Inc., operator of about 400 FuncoLand video and computer games stores, mainly located in strip malls, with revenues for the fiscal year ending in March

1999 of $206.7 million. B&N emerged victorious, completing a $161.5 million acquisition of Eden Prairie, Minnesota-based Funco in June 2000. The deal was noteworthy both for the significant boost it gave to Babbage's nascent move into strip mall centers and for FuncoLand's major business in used video games. About 40 percent of its revenues came from the sale of used games, which were bought from customers and then resold—with a much higher markup than what was typical for new games. Funco also published *Game Informer,* one of the industry's leading multiplatform video game magazines. In the structure of this latest deal, B&N acquired Funco, and Babbage's Etc. became a wholly owned subsidiary of Funco. Then in December 2000 Funco changed its name to GameStop, Inc., marking the beginning of what would be a gradual shift to the GameStop name.

As GameStop increased its store count past the 1,000-unit mark during 2001, it received a lift from several more new game system releases: Nintendo's Game Boy Advance, which debuted during the summer, and Microsoft Corporation's long-awaited Xbox console and Nintendo's GameCube system, both launched in November. The industry was clearly on another uptrend: The number of installed video game systems in the United States jumped from 26 million in 2000 to 65.1 million in 2002. The time seemed right for B&N to partially cash in on its foray into gaming, and GameStop Corp. was incorporated in August 2001 in anticipation of an initial public offering.

The first attempt at an initial public offering (IPO), however, failed. B&N had intended to take GameStop public on the NASDAQ in the fall of 2001, but an adverse IPO market thwarted that attempt. Instead, GameStop Corp. was listed on the New York Stock Exchange in February 2002 through the sale of 20.8 million shares at $18 per share. Just prior to the listing, B&N transferred all of its interest in GameStop, Inc. to GameStop Corp. Following the IPO, B&N retained a controlling 67 percent interest in GameStop.

Independent GameStop Corp., 2002 and Beyond

Under the continued leadership of Fontaine as chairman and CEO, and DeMatteo as president and COO, GameStop expanded smartly in 2002 and 2003, opening 210 and 300 new stores, respectively. During this period the company rebranded more and more of its stores under the GameStop name, until by 2004 nearly all of the units used that moniker. Two-thirds of the stores were now located in strip malls which were considered more convenient than enclosed shopping malls by most consumers. The company had its best year ever in 2003, posting record sales ($1.58 billion) and record profits ($63.5 million). Perhaps most impressive, GameStop was profitable every quarter. In all of its various past incarnations, it had made money only during the last, holidays-inclusive quarter. GameStop also ventured overseas during 2003, spending $3.3 million to acquire a controlling interest in Gamesworld Group Limited, which ran 16 electronic games stores in Ireland.

Through the first nine months of 2004, GameStop opened another 230 stores. Longer term, the company's executives estimated that it could open several thousand more outlets before having saturated the U.S. market. The rapidly expanding company was quickly outgrowing its headquarters in Grapevine, Texas, and in May 2004 announced that it would move into a larger building in the spring of 2005. Late in the year, GameStop gained its full independence from Barnes & Noble. In October it spent $111.5 million to buy back 6.1 million shares of its stock from B&N. One month later, B&N distributed its remaining 59 percent GameStop stake to B&N shareholders as a tax-free dividend. The newly independent company appeared to have a bright future as the video game industry seemed to be less cyclical than in the past because of the ever-increasing installed hardware base (which reached 86.9 million units in 2003), although the competitive environment continued to loom as a threat to GameStop's long-term prospects.

Principal Subsidiaries

GameStop, Inc.; GameStop.com, Inc.; Marketing Control Services, Inc.; Sunrise Publications, Inc.; Babbage's Etc. LLC; Gamesworld Group Limited (Ireland; 51%).

Principal Competitors

Electronics Boutique Holdings Corp.; Best Buy Co., Inc.; Circuit City Stores, Inc.; Wal-Mart Stores, Inc.; Toys ''R'' Us, Inc.; Target Corporation; Kmart Corporation; Amazon.com, Inc.

Further Reading

Ahles, Andrea, ''Babbage's Offers Web Site with GameStop Brand,'' *Fort Worth Star-Telegram,* July 9, 1999.

Deener, Bill, ''Hired Gun Makes a Stop at NeoStar,'' *Dallas Morning News,* October 13, 1996, p. 1H.

——, ''NeoStar Plans Overhaul As Sales Decline,'' *Dallas Morning News,* May 24, 1996, p. 1D.

Halkias, Maria, ''Babbage's, Software Etc. Sold to One of Founders,'' *Dallas Morning News,* November 27, 1996, p. 1D.

——, ''NeoStar Retail Seeks Chapter 11 Protection,'' *Dallas Morning News,* September 17, 1996, p. 1D.

Howatt, Glenn, ''Two of the Biggest Software Retailers Agree on Merger,'' *Minneapolis Star Tribune,* August 26, 1994, p. 1D.

LaHood, Lila, ''Ahead of the Game: With Its Recent IPO, GameStop Says It's Primed to Pick Up Even More Market Share,'' *Fort Worth Star-Telegram,* April 1, 2002.

Landy, Heather, ''Winning the Gaming Game: GameStop, a Video-Game Retailer, Plans to Open Almost 300 Stores This Year and Next,'' *Fort Worth Star-Telegram,* December 21, 2003, p. 1F.

McCartney, Scott, ''Babbage's, Software Etc. Stores to Merge in Bid to Compete with Bigger Concerns,'' *Wall Street Journal,* August 26, 1994, p. B2.

McConville, James A., ''Software 'R' Us,'' *HFD–The Weekly Home Furnishings Newspaper,* February 24, 1992, pp. 83+.

McMullen, John, ''New Attitude Spurring Software Etc. Growth,'' *Computer and Software News,* October 17, 1988, pp. 48+.

——, ''Software Etc. Solving Identity Crisis,'' *Computer and Software News,* July 4, 1988, pp. 1+.

Moore, Janet, ''Funco Suitor Drops Chase: Electronics Boutique Won't Match B&N Bid,'' *Minneapolis Star Tribune,* May 3, 2000, p. 1D.

Opdyke, Jeff D., ''This Time, Neostar May Not Get Big Lift from New Game Systems,'' *Wall Street Journal (Texas Journal),* p. T2.

Poole, Claire, ''Learn to Walk Before You Try to Run,'' *Forbes,* December 21, 1992, pp. 96–98.

Quick, Rebecca, ''Barnes & Noble Agrees to Acquire Babbage's Etc. LLC,'' *Wall Street Journal,* October 7, 1999.

——, ''Barnes & Noble Makes Another Play in Video Games,'' *Wall Street Journal,* May 8, 2000, p. B6.

Seitz, Patrick, ''GameStop, EB Games Playing with Big Boys,'' *Investor's Business Daily,* November 29, 2004, p. A20.

Steinert-Threlkeld, Tom, ''Babbage's Plans Merger with Software Etc.,'' *Dallas Morning News,* August 26, 1994, p. 1D.

Trachtenberg, Jeffrey A., ''Barnes & Noble Pares GameStop,'' *Wall Street Journal,* October 5, 2004, p. B6.

——, ''Book Chain to Take a Video-Game Retailer Public,'' *Wall Street Journal,* February 12, 2002, p. B1.

——, ''Investors Brace for Barnes & Noble Plot Twist,'' *Wall Street Journal,* May 27, 2004, p. C1.

—Roger W. Rouland
—update: David E. Salamie

Gas Natural SDG S.A.

Avda Portal de l'Angel 22
Barcelona
E-08002
Spain
Telephone: +34 902 199 199
Fax: +34 93 402 58 70
Web site: http://www.gasnatural.com

Public Company
Incorporated: 1992
Employees: 6,150
Sales: EUR 5.63 billion ($7.35 billion) (2003)
Stock Exchanges: Bolsa de Madrid
Ticker Symbol: GAS
NAIC: 221210 Natural Gas Distribution; 221122 Electric
    Power Distribution; 238210 Electrical Contractors;
    532310 General Rental Centers

Spain's Gas Natural SDG S.A. is one of the three largest natural gas companies in Europe, and the largest in South America. The former state-owned natural gas monopoly remains a leader at home—with more than 72 percent of Spain's natural gas market—although legislation has forced the company to begin reducing its market share to 60 percent before the end of the 2000s. Yet that same legislation, which liberalized Spain's utility market, has provided Gas Natural with the opportunity to expand into new areas of business, including electrical generation. The company expects to have more than 6,000 MW of power generation capacity online by 2008. Gas Natural is the leading supplier of natural gas to the Latin American market, with operations focused on Argentina, Colombia, and Brazil, as well as to Mexico and Puerto Rico. Since the beginning of the 2000s, Gas Natural has begun an expansion into the European market as well, with Italy as its first target market. In December 2004, the company reached an agreement to purchase 35 percent of Greece's state-owned gas company, Depa. The company also joined with its major shareholder Repsol-YPF in acquiring the construction and operation contract for Algeria's Gassi Touil integrated gas production and pipeline project, strength-

ening Gas Natural's supply base. Gas Natural also has invested in alternative energy sources, including buying some 50 percent of five wind farms in Spain at the beginning of 2005. In addition to its gas production and distribution operations, Gas Natural operates a fleet of ten methane tankers, making it one of the world's leading transporters of natural gas. Gas Natural is listed on the Bolsa de Madrid and produces revenues of more than EUR 5.6 billion ($7.3 billion) per year.

Gas Beginnings in the 19th Century

Spain's interest in natural gas as an energy source began in the first half of the 19th century, when in 1826 professor Josep Roura became the first in Europe to succeed in producing a gas light using gas from coal. Roura was commissioned by then King Ferdinand VII to provide lighting for the Queen's procession during a celebration in Madrid in 1832. Roura built the country's first gas plant in Madrid and built a temporary grid of 100 gas-powered streetlights. Following that display, Roura was asked by the royal family to build a gas-powered lighting facility for the royal palace in Oriente.

The first wide-scale use of gas in Spain came in the 1840s when a group of investors, including Frenchman Charles Lebon, established Sociedad Catalana para ele Alubrado por Gas (SCAG) in order to build a public lighting grid in the city of Barcelona. SCAG quickly attracted investors and by 1845 had become one of Spain's largest companies. SCAG listed its shares on the Bolsa de Madrid as early as 1853.

In Madrid, meanwhile, another group of investors, backed by British capital, launched Madrilena por Gas (Gas Madrid) in order to install a gas lighting network in that city as well. That business started up in 1846 and remained one of Spain's major gas producers and distributors. In 1864, it was joined by another company, Gas Lebon, founded by Charles Lebon.

The advent of electrical lighting put an end to the growth of the coal gas-based networks by the dawn of the 20th century. As Spain phased out its gas-light networks, SCAG and the other gas distributors reacted by investing in electrical power generation. In 1896, for example, SCAG and Gas Lebon joined together to build the Central Catalana de Electricidad. In 1911,

SCAG founded Sociedad General de Fuerwas Hidroelectricas and built its first hydroelectric plants in the Pyrenees mountains. The following year, SCAG bought Central Catalana de Electricidad. The company's growing interest in electrical power generation was reflected in its name change to Catalana de Gas y Electricidad (CGE). That company continued to grow until the Spanish Civil War. Acquisitions remained a part of the company's growth, and included La Energia de Sabadell and Propagadora del Gas.

The bombing of the company's Barcelona gasworks reduced CGE's production capacity during and after the war. Shortages of raw materials, exacerbated by the outbreak of World War II, made it difficult for CGE to rebuild. The lack of coke also hampered CGE's ability to produce gas into the late 1950s.

Gassing Up in the 1960s

CGE began investigating new sources of gas in the early 1960s, and in 1963 the company began producing gas based on naphtha, rather than coal, for the first time. More important for the company, however, was the discovery of vast natural gas fields, including off the coast in nearby Algeria. The promise of producing gas more easily and less expensively encouraged CGE to abandon its electricity wing in the early 1960s and refocus itself entirely as a gas business. The company then began an extensive modernization effort in order to adapt its distribution network for the reception of natural gas.

The first shipments of natural gas arrived in Spain via methane tankers in 1969 for treatment in a purpose-built re-gasification plant in Barcelona. Meanwhile CGE had begun to expand beyond the Catalan region, buying Compania Espanola de Gas, a distributor of gas to the Valencia region.

Over the next decades, CGE continued to construct a national network. The company also began building a fleet of methane tankers, and later became one of the world's leading transporters of natural gas. Limited supply (as Spain had no natural gas fields of its own) meant that the use of natural gas was slow to spread in Spain, however. In Madrid, for example, Gas Madrid continued to rely on its production of naphtha gas until the late 1980s.

The 1990s marked a new era for CGE and for Spain's natural gas sector. In 1991, the Spanish government led a restructuring of the domestic gas industry, merging CGE with Gas Madrid to form a new company, Gas Natural. To this business was added the gas distribution pipeline operated by Spanish petroleum giant Repsol. That company then became one of Gas Natural's major shareholders.

Gas Natural's relationship with Repsol (later Repsol-YPF) brought it to Repsol's primary expansion market in South America. In 1992, Gas Natural joined Repsol in Argentina, taking 50 percent of Gas Natural BAN. That company became primarily active in service to the area around Buenos Aires.

Back at home, Gas Natural strengthened its grip on the Spanish natural gas market when the government pushed through a merger between it and far larger competitor Enagas. The absorption of Enagas gave Gas Natural control of the country's gasification plants, as well as its transport network. The merged group now not only controlled the Spanish natural gas market, but also had become Europe's third largest natural gas company.

The acquisition of Enagas also gave Gas Natural control of Sagane, which owned more than 72 percent of Metragaz, a joint venture created in 1992 to build and operate the Mahgreb-Europe natural gas pipeline linking Algeria and Spain across the Gibraltar Strait. By 1996, Metragaz had completed the pipeline. With this new supply of natural gas, Gas Natural was able to extend its natural gas operations across Spain for the first time. In 1999, Gas Natural created a dedicated subsidiary for its natural gas purchasing needs. Natural Gas Aprovisionamientos, as the subsidiary was called, supported Gas Natural's operations not only through Metragaz pipeline-based purchases, but also through supply contracts with natural gas producers in Norway, Qatar, Nigeria, and elsewhere.

Latin American Expansion in the 1990s

Gas Natural expanded rapidly in the Latin American market in the late 1990s, and by the end of the century had become the single largest provider of natural gas to these markets. The company entered Brazil in 1997, joining a consortium that acquired gas distribution rights to the state of Rio and the Rio de Janeiro market and gaining control of newly privatized CEG and CEG Rio. In 2000, Gas Natural formed a new wholly owned subsidiary, Gas Natural SPS, which was awarded a gas distribution concession in Sao Paulo State. In that year, the company also formed Serviconfort Brasil to lend support services to its distribution businesses in Brazil.

Gas Natural also entered the Colombian market in 1997, acquiring 59 percent of the privatized ESP group of companies, renamed as Gas Natural ESP. Gas Natural then began expanding across Colombia, acquiring another ESP company, Gasoriente ESP, operating in Santander, Bucaramanga, and elsewhere. The company also was awarded a distribution concession for Cundiboyacense plateau in 1998. The company extended its Serviconfort operations into Colombia the following year.

Key Dates:

1826: The first successful gas lighting experiment in Spain is conducted.

1843: Sociedad Catalana para ele Alubrado por Gas, the predecessor to Gas Natural, is created.

1896: The company enters electricity production, building Central Catalana de Electricidad in partnership with Gas Lebon (founded in 1864).

1911: The company founds Sociedad General de Fuerwas Hidroelectricas, and builds its first hydroelectric plants in the Pyrenees mountains.

1912: Central Catalana de Electricidad is acquired and its name is changed to Catalana de Gas y Electricidad (CGE).

1963: Gas Natural spins off its electricity generation operations to focus on the gas market.

1965: Compania Espanola de Gas is acquired.

1969: The company receives its first natural gas imports.

1991: Gas Natural is merged with Enagas.

1992: The company enters Argentina's natural gas market.

1996: The company opens the first pipeline linking Spain and natural gas fields in Algeria.

1997: Operations are launched in Brazil, Colombia, and Mexico.

2000: The Spanish government begins liberalizing the Spanish market, breaking up Gas Natural's monopoly; Gas Natural expands into electricity generation, sales, and distribution.

2002: The company launches its first 800 MW of electricity generation, with expansion plans to 6,000 MW; company expands into Italy with the creation of Gas Natural Vendida.

2004: The company acquires Brancato Group, Smedigas, and Nettis in Italy.

2005: The company acquires stakes in five Spanish wind farms.

Mexico was also a Gas Natural expansion target, with the company acquiring the concession for the Toluca region in 1997. The company extended its Mexico operations to the Monterrey region and into the Bajio market in 1998, and then added businesses in San Luis Potosi, Bajio Norte, and Aguascalientes in 1999. A big boost for the company's Mexico operations came in 2000 with the purchase of Metrogas, which enabled it to penetrate the Mexico City market. The Metrogas acquisition also transformed Gas Natural Mexico into the leading natural gas supplier in that country. Gas Natural continued to seek out other Latin American expansion opportunities, including the purchase of failed energy conglomerate Enron's Puerto Rican natural gas assets in 2003.

The Spanish government began breaking up Gas Natural's domestic monopoly in 2000. Under terms governing the liberalization of the Spanish market and in line with European Union directives, Gas Natural was required to reduce its position in the Spanish market to just 60 percent by the end of the decade. By 2004, the company had made progress toward that goal, dropping its market share to 72 percent.

Diversified for the 2000s

Gas Natural's response to the liberalization of the Spanish market took two approaches. On the one hand, the company decided to return to the electricity market, launching an ambitious construction program designed to boost the company's production capacity to nearly 6,000 MW by the end of the 2000s. By 2004, the company's first plants were already producing some 800 MW, with another 800 MW in testing and 1,200 MW more under construction. In 2003, Gas Natural launched an ambitious takeover offer for Iberdrola, Spain's second largest electricity producer. The offer quickly met with refusal from Iberdrola and then was struck down by the mergers and monopolies commission.

In the meantime, Gas Natural had put into place the second prong of its expansion strategy, that of expanding its energy distribution business onto the European continent. For this, the company chose Italy as its first target, creating Gas Natural Vendida in 2002 to take advantage of the deregulation of the Italian gas market. Gas Natural Vendida became operational in 2003. The following year, the company acquired Sicily's Brancato Group, that region's leading privately held gas business. That purchase was followed up by another Sicily-based company, Smedigas, which operated in the natural gas distribution sector. Then in September 2004, Gas Natural bought Nettis, extending its gas operations to the Publia and Calabria regions of Italy as well.

Gas Natural boosted its access to the North African natural gas fields in November 2004 with its 40 percent stake in a consortium with Repsol-YPF that won a bid to construct and operate the $3 billion Gassi Touil integrated gas project in Algeria. The company then returned its attention to its European expansion. In December 2004, the company agreed to purchase a 35 percent stake in Greek government-owned Depa. The purchase was to be completed in 2005.

As it continued construction of its energy generation capacity, Gas Natural turned toward the renewable energy field as well. In January 2005, the company acquired stakes in five Spanish wind farms. As it turned into the mid-decade, Gas Natural had successfully built a geographically diversified energy empire.

Principal Subsidiaries

Companhia Distribuidora de Gas do Rio de Janeiro (Brazil); Gas Natural Aprovisionamientos; Gas Natural BAN (Argentina; 50.4%); Gas Natural Comercializadora; Gas Natural ESP (Colombia); Gas Natural Internacional; Gas Natural Mexico; Gas Natural Servicios; Gas Natural SPS (Brazil); Gas Natural Trading; Gas Natural Vendita (Italy); Grupo Brancato (Italy); Metragaz.

Principal Competitors

Royal Dutch/Shell Group; ENI S.p.A.; Repsol-YPF S.A.; TRACTEBEL S.A.; SONATRACH; Galp Energia SGPS S.A.; Union Fenosa S.A.

Further Reading

Crawford, Leslie, "Spain Starts to Break Up Gas Natural Monopoly," *Financial Times,* October 23, 2001, p. 37.

"Gas Natural Plans Italian Boost," *Gas Connections,* September 30, 2004, p. 5.

"Gas Natural's Depa Purchase Awaits Greek Ratification," *Gas Connections,* December 9, 2004, p. 8.

"Gas Natural Sets Out Expansion Plan," *Gas Connections,* April 29, 2004, p. 6.

Hawkins, Nigel, "Gas Natural," *Utility Week,* October 3, 2003, p. 29.

Mollet, Paul, "Merger Creates Europe's Third-Largest Gas Company," *Petroleum Economist,* March 1995, p. VIII.

"Spain Triumphs in Gassi Touil Contest," *Gas Connections,* November 25, 2004, p. 3.

Webb, Tim, "Spain's Largest Gas Company Faces New Challenges," *Sunday Business,* June 29, 2003.

—M.L. Cohen

Great Lakes Dredge & Dock Company

2122 York Road
Oak Brook, Illinois 60523
U.S.A.
Telephone: (630) 574-3000
Fax: (630) 574-2909
Web site: http://www.gldd.com

Private Company
Incorporated: 1905
Employees: 850
Sales: $398.8 million (2003)
NAIC: 234990 All Other Heavy Construction

Great Lakes Dredge & Dock Company has been in the dredging business for 115 years and has made major contributions to the nation's ports and shorelines. Its dredging operations generally fall into three different categories: capital dredging (involving ports), beach nourishment (replenishing or fortifying eroded areas), and maintenance (redredging and improvements). In addition to dredging in its namesake waters, Great Lakes also builds lighthouses, bridges, piers, and docks. Famous landmarks constructed with the aid and expertise of Great Lakes include Chicago's Navy Pier and Michigan Avenue Bridge; MacArthur Lock in Sault Ste. Marie; the St. Lawrence Seaway between the United States and Canada; the Mackinac Bridge in upper Michigan; and coastal port and pier work in Africa, the Caribbean, Europe, the Middle East, and South America.

In the Beginning: The 1890s

The story of Great Lakes Dredge & Dock Company begins at the end of the 19th century in Chicago, Illinois. William A. Lydon and Fred C. Drews founded Lydon & Drews as a marine construction company. Formed in 1890, the firm described itself as "Contractors for Dredging, Docking and General Pile Driving," and was adept at building bridges, piers, lighthouses, and tunnels. Lydon served as the firm's engineer and first president while Drews, who had worked in marine construction, served as general superintendent. The partners opened an office in the Unity Building on Dearborn Street, which later became the Chicago Chamber of Commerce building.

The marine construction company's first job was to dig a brick-lined water tunnel under Lake Michigan from an offshore water intake at Chicago Avenue to a new "crib" under the lake. The project came to be known as the "Two Mile Crib," and was vital to the growing water works of Chicago. The contract could make or break the fledgling company, especially since the work was set to begin on Friday the 13th of February. Fortunately, neither Lydon nor Drews was particularly superstitious and the Two Mile Crib was completed without incident.

Two years after the company's founding, Lydon & Drews worked on one of Chicago's most amazing undertakings, the 1892 Columbian Exposition. The immense World Fair was to celebrate the 400th anniversary of Columbus's discovery of America and to top the festivities of the Paris Exposition when the Eiffel Tower was unveiled. The reputation of the entire United States rested with the Chicago Exposition, and leading architects and engineers from around the country contributed to the immense undertaking. Lydon & Drews was tapped to fortify the lake's shoreline where numerous buildings were under construction for the Exposition. Some of what was constructed on Lake Michigan's coastline became the foundation for Navy Pier.

Over the next decade Lydon & Drews finished several successful marine projects, including another water intake tunnel and crib for the city's water supply. In 1894 the firm built its first rig, appropriately named "Dredge No. 1," a huge dredging machine with a four-yard dipper or bucket. A second dredger was built in 1896, followed by a third in 1898. By the end of the 1890s Lydon & Drews had earned a reputation for excellence and timely completion. With a major portion of Chicago's livelihood tied to its waterways, Lydon & Drews became instrumental in the city's growth as a pivotal midwestern port. The company's success also allowed it to expand operations to other nearby ports.

A New Century and New Name: The 1900s–20s

In the 20th century, Lydon & Drews had grown substantially through the acquisition of four Chicago companies (Chicago Dredge & Dock Company, Green Dredging Company, Hausler & Lutz, and McMahon & Montgomery). This growth prompted Lydon and Drews to change the firm's name to the somewhat cumbersome Chicago & Great Lakes Dredge & Dock Company

Company Perspectives:

Dredging is a specialized field that can include handling a full range of natural underwater materials—silts, clays, sands and rock formations. Great Lakes applies its dredging expertise to deepen and maintain waterways, shipping channels, and ports; create and maintain beaches; excavate harbors and build docks, terminals, and piers; reclaim land; restore aquatic and wetland habitats; and excavate pipeline, cable, and tunnel trenches.

in 1903 and then to its present incarnation, Great Lakes Dredge & Dock Company. The latter was incorporated in 1905 in New Jersey because of that state's favorable corporate laws.

At the time of its creation Great Lakes Dredge & Dock (Great Lakes) owned equipment valued at more than $1.7 million, including 13 dredges (11 with dipper-buckets and two with clamshell-shaped equipment), ten tug boats (with one named for Lydon and another for Drews), dozens of scows (flat-bottomed, squared boats often pulled by tugs), and six derricks (sturdily constructed towers for lifting and moving heavy items). Great Lakes also owned and operated two machine shops and had expanded operations into Indiana, Michigan, Ohio, and Wisconsin.

The new Great Lakes had eight board members and 21 stockholders. Lydon and his wife owned 29 percent of the company and Drews, who was not on the board and no longer an officer, held 9 percent. Other Chicagoans who had joined Great Lakes included Harry Wild (Lydon's brother-in-law) as treasurer and a board member, as well as John P. Hopkins (a former mayor of Chicago) and Roger C. Sullivan (a prominent Democrat), movers and shakers in Chicago's tumultuous political arena.

Great Lakes bought Duluth Dredge & Dock Company in 1905 and by 1908 had additional offices in Duluth (Minnesota), Cleveland and Toledo (Ohio), and Sault Ste. Marie (Michigan's Upper Peninsula/Ontario). In 1912 Great Lakes undertook a major project for the U.S. Army Corps of Engineers in the Boston Harbor area, which served two very important functions: not only did the Boston project bring the company substantial work along the East Coast (prompting the formation of an Atlantic Division headquartered in lower Manhattan), but began its long and lucrative association with the Army Corps of Engineers. By 1917 Great Lakes had acquired six more companies, including two in Buffalo (New York) and two in Milwaukee (Wisconsin), to conquer all of the Great Lakes ports. The acquisitions brought the company's assets to more than $6 million.

Great Lakes suffered a shock in 1918 with the loss of its cofounder and president, William Lydon. After a brief illness, the 55-year-old Lydon was dead. He was succeeded as president by Roger Sullivan until 1920, when Harry Wild took the reins as the firm's third president. Despite the loss of Lydon's guidance, Great Lakes maintained solid growth and finished several pivotal projects in Chicago, helping the city become the Midwest's leading cultural and business center. Among the company's contributions were the Franklin-Orleans Street Bridge (1919), the Michigan Avenue Bridge (1922), and the foundations for the Adler Planetarium, Shedd Aquarium, Soldier Field, and the Field Museum (1923). Additional work included building lighthouses and breakwaters, and dredging for construction of the Great Lakes Naval Training Station. In 1924 John Cushing became the fourth president of Great Lakes. The following year revenues topped $13.8 million and earnings were $1.5 million.

Wartime Prominence: The 1930s and 1940s

In the 1930s, as the United States was in the grip of the Great Depression, Great Lakes managed relatively well working in and around its namesake waters. Projects included the Naval Armory in Chicago in 1933, the Inland Steel complex at Indiana Harbor (1935), and breakwater for Calumet Harbor (1935), with stone provided by a Lemont, Illinois quarry the company had purchased. Great Lakes lost Cushing in a plane crash in 1935, and he was replaced as president by John R. Williams, the company's top engineer, who succumbed to illness months later. Williams was replaced by Major General Edward Markham, who had served as chief of the Army Corps of Engineers during the first presidency of Franklin Roosevelt. Markham became the sixth president of Great Lakes in August 1938, and the company finished the year with robust revenues of $20.1 million and earnings of $2.2 million.

Markham's tenure was filled with militaristic discipline and bad blood as many executives left or were fired. During his seven years heading the company, accomplishments were overshadowed by increasing tension in the boardroom. In 1939 Great Lakes undertook a huge dredging job at Lake Charles, Louisiana, and bought a competing dredge company. The early 1940s brought Great Lakes into war production as the country entered World War II. Several of the company's tug boats were commandeered by the Navy, and dredgers were busy digging out docks for battleship construction. Another significant project involved the replacement of the small Sault Ste. Marie lock with the much larger and modernized MacArthur Lock. A round-the-clock project for Great Lakes, the MacArthur Lock ran ahead of schedule and opened in 1943 to much acclaim from the U.S. Navy. Great Lakes was awarded the prestigious Navy E-Flag for its contributions to the war effort.

Markham, the only outsider ever appointed president of Great Lakes, resigned in 1945 to the relief of many. A longtime engineer of the firm, William Freeley, was named president. In the immediate postwar years, Great Lakes shored up its inventory, since a number of tugs and dredgers had been damaged or lost during the war. The company bought two tugs from the Navy and installed two floating drydocks, one in Chicago and the second in Buffalo. The floating drydocks meant Great Lakes no longer had to pay to dock its tugs; they also translated into reduced downtime, such as waiting in line at commercial docks.

Booming: The 1950s–70s

In the 1950s Great Lakes was involved in many projects in and around Lake Michigan. One of the more unusual was the delivery of a captured World War II German submarine, the *U-505,* to Chicago's Museum of Science and Industry in 1954. The sub arrived at the company's floating drydock where it was spruced up and then towed along with the entire drydock through a dredged canal to the shore near the museum. The sub was then dragged over rail tracks to its home adjacent to the world-renowned museum (where it remains to this day). Great Lakes also was involved in the construction of the famous Mackinac Bridge between the upper and lower peninsulas of Michigan in 1954. The Mackinac Bridge was an engineering feat at five miles in length and 552 feet in height. Also in 1954, Freeley retired, and William Lydon's son, Eugene, was named president of Great Lakes.

Great Lakes was a major participant in the huge 60-nautical mile St. Lawrence Seaway project jointly undertaken by the United States and Canada in the mid-1950s, while also working on Brookley Air Force Base in Mobile, Alabama, and a host of dredging and digging jobs in Florida, Indiana, Kentucky, Massachusetts, Michigan, New York, Wisconsin, and international jobs in Colombia, Kenya, Puerto Rico, Saudi Arabia, and Venezuela. Gene Lydon was felled by a massive heart attack on November 22, 1963, just hours before President John F. Kennedy was assassinated. Great Lakes mourned its own leader and the country's Commander-in-Chief at the same time. Langdon Hardwicke was installed as the firm's new president. Revenues for 1963 reached an all-time high of just less than $33.4 million, with earnings climbing to $3.36 million.

Hardwicke served Great Lakes a little more than two years before retiring and was replaced in 1966. By this time Great Lakes had expanded its operations to include jobs on the West Coast and soon found its primary form of business, dredging, under fire. The growing environmental movement in the United States hit marine construction hard, with a variety of developments stymied by ecological concerns, including the federal

government's own waterworks projects. It fell on the new president, John (Jack) Downs, to steer Great Lakes in an increasingly difficult era. Ecological concerns were not the only problems facing dredgers: work was hard to find and most private firms could not compete with the better equipped and funded Army Corps of Engineers. The loss of smaller competitors to bankruptcy may have given Great Lakes pause, yet the dredging giant thrived. Revenues for 1975 hit more than $56.9 million and earnings were $4.5 million. The following year revenues were steady at $57.0 million but earnings nearly doubled to $8.1 million in 1976.

Great Lakes teamed with industry leaders and the National Association of Dredging Contractors (NADC) to take on the Army Corps. The Corps' primary advantage was its line of hopper-dredges, which no private firm owned due to their immense cost. Great Lakes tapped into this exclusive market by building its own self-propelled hoppers, which seemed the future of dredging since they were huge, sturdy, and capable of carrying vast amounts of material. The company's first hopper was completed in 1977, quickly followed by a second and third. At this time the company also segued into huge international projects, with domestic dredging jobs at all-time lows. Great Lakes took its expertise to the Persian Gulf, where it completed a series of jobs, and worked on projects in Latin America. Foreign work constituted more than three-quarters of the company's revenues in 1977 alone, a trend it would repeat in the next decade. Revenues for the year climbed to $87.8 million, while earnings had nearly doubled from the previous year to $15.3 million. At the end of the decade, in 1979, Great Lakes International, Inc. was created as a holding company for the firm's growing assets.

International Expansion: The 1980s and 1990s

After its recent success abroad, Great Lakes continued its emphasis on international projects and branched into another sideline, beach refurbishment or "nourishment." Jack Downs, who had led the company for 17 years, retired in 1980 and was replaced by William Colnon, who stepped down in 1986 in the midst of antitrust lawsuits against the United States' largest dredging companies. Great Lakes was caught in the fray but survived unscathed. Another development in 1986 was passage of the Water Resources Development Act (WRDA), which allocated federal and municipal funding for constructing "super-ports" or upgrading and expanding the country's highest traffic ports. As the number one dredging firm in the nation, Great Lakes not only secured a large slice of the resulting work, but it also had gained the unflinching notice of the Chicago-based Itel Corporation.

Itel Corporation first bought stock in Great Lakes in 1985 from a New Jersey group that pulled out of a possible takeover attempt. Itel originally acquired a 5.4 percent stake in the company and increased it over the next few months to 20 percent. Great Lakes agreed to Itel's friendly takeover, selling the entirety of its stock at $62.50 per share in November 1985. DeWitt Barlow, a third-generation Great Lakes dredger, was named president in 1987; revenues for the year came in at $156.7 million with earnings of $13.3 million.

Despite a decline in domestic dredging contracts, Great Lakes stayed busy with projects like the deepening of Curtis

Bay and the Port of Baltimore's 42-mile long channel in 1990, the year of its centennial. The firm also looked into further international expansion. With the resources of parent company Itel behind it, Great Lakes formed a foreign division to capitalize on global possibilities as domestic dredging jobs became harder to find. Late in the following year, however, Great Lakes was sold by Itel to Blackstone Dredging Partners LP, part of the massive Blackstone empire.

In 1992 Great Lakes became embroiled in a series of lawsuits due to repair work on a bridge in Chicago. While replacing wooden pilings, Great Lakes had inadvertently weakened an underground tunnel system built in the early 1900s. The tunnel began leaking and later collapsed, flooding the basements and lower levels of hundreds of Chicago buildings in April 1992. Lawsuits over the damage mounted into the millions, many of them naming Great Lakes along with the city of Chicago. Although initially found liable, Great Lakes was later cleared because the city had not properly maintained the tunnel system and had been aware of leaking and damage well before the flood. Despite the flood imbroglio in 1992, by 1993 Great Lakes had made great strides in its international expansion plans with projects in Africa, the Middle East, South America, Mexico, Denmark, and Sweden.

At the same time Great Lakes had pursued international growth, the company had segued into "beach nourishment" projects along American coastlines. Rebuilding and reshaping beaches and shorelines became an integral part of the company's business. A new president and chief executive also brought a new perspective to Great Lakes as Doug B. Mackie, who had joined the firm as corporate counsel in 1978, took the reins. By 1998 some of the long-awaited WDRA contracts had come to fruition, with Great Lakes securing a number of capital ("Deep Port") improvements from the Army Corps of Engineers, including port deepening in New York, New Jersey, Boston Harbor, and San Juan (Puerto Rico), as well as the construction of a massive pier in Los Angeles. During the same year Great Lakes was sold by Blackstone Dredging to Vectura Holding Company L.L.C., an affiliate of Citicorp (later Citigroup) Venture Capital. Great Lakes brought in revenues of $289 million for 1998 and $302.3 million the following year.

Another Century: The 2000s

By the year 2000 Great Lakes maintained its status as the United States' top dredging firm, with an ever increasing fleet of dredging and digging equipment. Revenues for the year were robust, due in part to WDRA contracts, at $339.1 million. In 2001 Great Lakes entered a related business segment, demolitions, with the purchase of 80 percent of the Boston-based North American Site Developers, Inc. Great Lakes increased its ownership by another 5 percent in 2003. Deep Ports projects continued to bring in the majority of the company's revenues, with projects in California, Georgia, Florida, Kentucky, Mississippi, New York, North Carolina, Pennsylvania, Rhode Island, and Texas. In 2003 Great Lakes was the first American firm to

begin work in war-torn Iraq, at the Umm Qasr Port. The Iraq work was dangerous, due to ongoing hostility against Westerners, as was a construction project in the Middle East, in Bahrain. In December 2003 Great Lakes was sold for the third time in 12 years to Madison-Dearborn Partners, a Chicago-based private capital firm. Revenues for 2002 had reached $362.6 million and leapt to $398.8 million for 2003.

In 2004 Great Lakes continued reaping the rewards of the WDRA's Deep Ports contracts, winning bids for work in Louisiana, New Jersey, North Carolina, and several different dredging projects in California. International contracts included further work in Bahrain along the Persian Gulf, and a new airport in neighboring Qatar. Entering 2005 Great Lakes was on solid ground: its revenues continued to climb annually despite being bought and sold a number of times in the previous two decades. Great Lakes continued to maintain the largest and most diverse dredging fleet in the United States with 24 dredges, 27 material transportation barges, two drillboats, and numerous other specialized support vessels, valued in excess of $1 billion.

Principal Subsidiaries

Amboy Aggregates (50%); Great Lakes Caribbean Dredging, Inc. (Puerto Rico); Lydon Dredging and Construction Company, Ltd. (Canada); North American Site Developers, Inc. (85%).

Principal Competitors

Penta-Ocean Construction Co., Ltd.; Koninklijke BAM Groep nv; Weeks Marine, Inc.

Further Reading

"Contract Near on Durrat al-Bahrain," *MEED (Middle East Economic Digest),* June 22, 2001, p. 14.

Dickinson, Paul R., *Great Lakes Dredge & Dock Company: A Century of Experience, 1890–1990,* Oak Brook, Ill.: Great Lakes Dredge & Dock Company, 1990.

"Great Lakes Mobilised for Umm Qasr Dredging," *MEED (Middle East Economic Digest),* May 2, 2003, p. 7.

Hattori, April, "Chicago, Contractor Sued by Contractors Over Flood," *Bond Buyer,* March 3, 1993, p. 4.

Holman, Kelly, "Madison Dearborn Gets U.S. Dredger," *Daily Deal,* November 14, 2003.

Lenckus, Dave, "Review Sought on Decision Limiting Chicago Flood Cover," *Business Insurance,* August 20, 2001, p. 3.

McManus, Terry, "Local Company Opening Beachhead in Africa," *Crain's Chicago Business,* August 23, 1999, p. 14.

Pierog, Karen, "Flood-Related Lawsuit Against Chicago Settled for $36 Million," *Bond Buyer,* August 15, 1995, p. 4.

Richards, Don, "Plans to Widen Houston Ship Channel Move Ahead," *Chemical Market Reporter,* September 28, 1998, p. 7.

Strong, Michael, "Piling It On: Local Sandwich Chains Face Onslaught of Competition from National Companies," *Crain's Detroit Business,* November 10, 2003, p. 3.

—Nelson Rhodes

Gymboree Corporation

500 Howard Street
San Francisco, California 94105
U.S.A.
Telephone: (415) 278-7000
Toll Free: (877) 449-6932
Fax: (415) 278-7100
Web site: http://www.gymboree.com

Public Company
Incorporated: 1979
Employees: 9,345
Sales: $578.0 million (2004)
Stock Exchanges: NASDAQ
Ticker Symbol: GYMB
NAIC: 448130 Children's and Infants' Clothing Stores

Based in San Francisco, California, Gymboree Corporation designs, manufactures, and retails unique, high quality apparel and accessories for children and women. The company has retail businesses under the Gymboree, Janie and Jack, and Janeville names. Gymboree operates more than 600 stores in the United States and Canada as well as an online business. The company also operates parent-child developmental play programs for infants through age five. There are more than 530 play and music centers in the United States and 24 other countries, many of which are franchises.

Origins

Gymboree's children's recreation and exercise operation represented a relatively meager portion of its income by the 1990s, but it was that business that launched the venture in the 1970s and established a foundation for its future success in the retail industry. The concept of a commercial children's exercise program was inspired by Joan Barnes. Barnes, in her early 20s, had taught modern dance to children in New York City before organizing a children's recreation program for the Jewish Community Center in San Rafael, California. She was serving as the recreation administrator at that center when, in 1975, she came up with the notion of offering exercise classes for babies with their parents. The idea stemmed partly from her personal desire to share physical fitness playtime with her own daughter.

The baby exercise classes were an instant hit. Parents lined up to bring their babies and toddlers to Barnes's exercise sessions. Recognizing the commercial potential of her idea, Barnes left her job with the Jewish Community Center and opened her first commercial children's workout center in 1976. She had little trouble filling her classes with enthusiastic parents. She knew that she was dealing with a viable business concept, moreover, when some of those parents started asking her about opening their own children's exercise centers. After polishing her concept, Barnes did start opening other centers in the late 1970s.

Barnes recognized that her expertise was working with parents and children, not in building a sprawling franchise business. To help her take the concept cross-country, she hired franchise specialist Robert Jacob, who was best known for developing the hugely successful Midas International car-service franchise system. Jacob helped Barnes set up a successful licensing program for Gymboree centers that focused on low start-up costs. Franchisees typically paid Barnes a $20,000 start-up fee, which included about $8,000 worth of equipment and enough money to get the center moving. The franchisees also agreed to pay Barnes 6 percent of their revenue. To help fund the expansion effort, Barnes turned to venture-capital firm Venture Partners, of Menlo, California.

The Gymboree franchise effort was a triumph. By 1984, 125 Gymboree franchises were operating in 20 states and were bringing in more than $1 million in revenue annually. The franchises were typically operated by women, many of whom had training in occupational therapy or education. Classes were usually held in church halls and community buildings, and parents were charged only $4 to $8 per 45-minute session. Classes varied to accommodate children ranging from three months to four years in age, but a typical session included the children hanging from bars to build up arm muscles, popping soap bubbles to develop eye-hand coordination, or walking on inflated logs to improve balance. In addition, the tots could exercise on brightly colored tunnels, slides, and other apparatus, and no class was complete without a visit from a clown-puppet named ''Gymbo.''

By 1985 Barnes's net worth had sailed past $1 million. As important to her as the financial gain, though, was the success of her idea: ''It's a neat feeling to know the same scene is going on in scores of centers at the same time,'' she said in the May 1984 *Money*. ''It feels like I've given birth to a new experience.'' Barnes had, indeed, given birth to a viable concept, as evidenced by Gymboree's rapid expansion during the mid-1980s. By 1987, in fact, the Gymboree chain had grown to include more than 350 centers throughout the United States and in ten foreign countries. Those units were generating over $10 million in annual sales. Importantly, the Gymboree name had become known and respected by parents.

Barnes decided in 1986 to start capitalizing on the goodwill that Gymboree had accrued since she had opened the first exercise center in 1976. To that end, she opened the first few Gymboree retail stores: ''. . . because we recognized that we have a unique marketing platform,'' she said in the November 1987 *Chain Store Age Executive*. ''No one could approach our authenticity, no one could knock off what we do because of the number of children already participating in our Gymboree programs.'' The first Gymboree stores piggy-backed off of the original Gymboree concept. Approximately 1,000-square-feet in size, they were designed similar to a children's gym, incorporated displays that looked like bleachers, had video screens showing tapes of Gymboree exercise classes, and had pictures of Gymbo the clown throughout.

The first Gymboree store, opened in 1986, was a success. With financial backing from Venture Partners, Barnes opened an additional 15 stores by the end of 1987. The initial idea was to open the stores in areas where Gymboree centers were established (although the company eventually determined that the concept could work in areas without an established customer base). The outlets stocked about 60 percent apparel and 40 percent hard goods and targeted a price range that attracted buyers between the upscale and middle-income markets. Gymboree sustained its unique image and increased profit margins by designing and manufacturing many of its own products, which could not be found in other stores.

New Management: 1989

By 1989 Gymboree was operating 32 retail stores, mostly in malls, in addition to its base of 350 Gymboree franchises. Sales rose to nearly $17 million, although the company posted a net loss of nearly $1 million. It was clear that Gymboree's future was in retailing, rather than in children's fitness. Barnes's influence in operations had steadily declined in proportion to the amount of money infused by her investment partner, U.S. Venture Partners. U.S. Venture Partners believed that the company was failing to reach its potential, so the investment company began installing a new management team that it hoped would take Gymboree to new heights.

In 1989 U.S. Venture Partners brought in Don Cohn to serve as chairman and chief executive of Gymboree. Cohn was the founder of the successful New England Clothing Co. and had served stints with such venerable retailers as Mervyn's, Laura Ashley, I. Magnin, and Ross Stores. Among other moves, Cohn adopted an incentive-based approach to sales by allocating work hours to store employees based on a sliding scale influenced by their performance. He also fired several managers and brought in more experienced retail executives. Cohn also received much of the credit for the company's successful initial public offering in March 1993 that brought $43 million into Gymboree's coffers.

Partly as a result of Cohn's efforts, Gymboree's sales increased to $48.5 million in 1991 and then to a lofty $68 million in 1992 (fiscal year ended January 31, 1993), while net income rose to a healthy $6.9 million. The total number of retail outlets increased to 120 in late 1993, by which time Gymboree was employing more than 2,100 workers. Despite impressive gains, however, Cohn was forced to resign in 1993 to make way for new chief executive Nancy Pedot. In fact, it was Pedot, as the manager of Gymboree's merchandising strategy, who had been largely responsible for the chain's rapid rise during the early 1990s.

Pedot had been hired by Gymboree in 1989 to serve as a general merchandise manager. Previously, she had worked at Mervyn's Inc. as a division merchandise manager. She was effectively handed Gymboree's 32 retail stores and told to fill them with products. She quickly revamped the stores' entire product line and introduced brightly colored, high-quality jumpers, dresses, pants, and tops for newborns to six-year-olds. The Gymboree-brand apparel was a hit and per-store sales surged. She augmented that effort by reducing the number of toys in the product mix and shifting the focus to high-margin clothing items. The change moved Gymboree into a higher price bracket, which paid off in some of the highest profit margins in the industry.

Pedot's appointment as the president and chief executive cemented a near matriarchy at Gymboree, where the six vice-presidents for production, real estate, human resources, stores, merchandising, and franchise operations were all women. Only the chief financial officer of the company, James Curley, was male. Under the direction of that management team, Gymboree sustained the aggressive growth it had achieved in the early 1990s, opening a stream of new Gymboree retail outlets and pushing both sales and profits to record levels. Indeed, revenues in 1993 rose to $130 million and net income doubled to $14.1 million. By late 1994 the Gymboree chain had grown to more than 200 stores throughout the United States.

Gymboree continued to expand during 1995, adding more than 50 new outlets to its chain. At the same time, management began intensifying efforts to whip the sprawling distribution and inventory operations into line. To that end, new purchasing, planning, and distribution managers were hired, and new information systems were implemented. In addition, the company launched a Gymboree mail-order catalog and introduced larger goods including furniture into many of its stores. After posting an average annual growth rate of 63 percent over five years, Gymboree increased revenues in 1994 (fiscal year ended January 31, 1995) to $188 million, about $22.2 million of which was netted as income.

To sustain future growth, in 1995 Gymboree began exploring the possibility of overseas retail expansion. Its exercise franchises were already operating in Taiwan, Mexico, and eight other countries. Pedot identified potential areas for expansion in Europe and announced plans to open overseas retail units in late 1995 or 1996. In addition, the company planned to increase the size of new stores in the United States and to add more merchandise, in keeping with the superstore concept sweeping the retail industry in the mid-1990s. Gymboree was also working to develop its own educational toys and products and to extend its targeted age range to seven year olds. The company hoped to have as many as 500 Gymboree retail outlets operating by 1998.

Facing Challenges: Late 1990s

The late 1990s were turbulent years for retailers in the clothing sector and Gymboree posted a rollercoasteresque earnings chart that led to high turnover rates among corporate leaders.

In 1997 Nancy Pedot was replaced as CEO and president by Gary White, who had been the former COO. Shortly thereafter, James P. Curley stepped down as senior vice-president and CFO. Curley had also served on the board of directors. Under White, the company initiated a stockholder rights plan in March that was meant as protection against hostile takeover. Stock share prices had been on a decline and Gymboree began a $30 million stock buyback in November. The buyback was designed to boost company share prices. White reported that the board's decision to buy back some of its stock, "is consistent with our objectives of enhancing shareholder value and reflects its continuing confidence in Gymboree's business and prospects."

It had become apparent to management that some restructuring of the company was in order and in January 1998, with a new year underway and some lagging holiday sales, Gymboree added four top management positions. The positions were chief information officer, senior vice-president in sourcing and logistics, vice-president–logistics, and a managing directorship based in Hong Kong for sourcing and production. New sales figures in March showed a significant increase, with sales up 20 percent from the prior quarter.

Gymboree entered the Japanese market by adding a new concept store for older children called Kid Cool in the spring of 1998. It remained to be seen whether the concept would prove successful in the Asian market. That summer Gymboree also relocated its distribution center to Dixon, California. The 285,000-square-foot facility was opened in June.

In January 1999 Director of Design and Merchandising Lisa Harper was named vice-president, design. Harper was largely responsible for the creative designs that brought the company record sales. Harper later continued her success at Gymboree and eventually went on to become the company's CEO.

Plagued by erratic sales performance, Gymboree continued to replace its leadership. In February 1999 the company hired Melanie Cox, who had a marketing background, as president. Gary White continued in his post as CEO. Cox began a remerchandising effort in an attempt to boost the chain's image. Changes were made to the interior of the company's retail spaces, and Gymboree closed 12 poorly performing stores. The most notable change was in following style trends in children's apparel rather than relying on Gymboree signature bright color separates.

Despite its recurrent woes, Gymboree was named one of the most family friendly companies by *Working Mother* magazine. Ken Meyers, vice-president of human resources, commented on the award by saying, "Our policies foster an environment which provides challenge, fun and flexibility in the workplace."

The end of the 1990s also saw company expansion of play and music programs worldwide. Master franchisees were opened in the United Kingdom, Puerto Rico, and Ireland. The company had already established a presence in Australia, Canada, Colombia, France, Indonesia, South Korea, Mexico, Singapore, and Taiwan. In addition, Gymboree had play and music programs pending in Central America, the Middle East, and the Philippines.

Renewed Focus: 2000s

In January 2001 Gymboree sold its Zutopia store chain to the retail outlet The Wet Seal, Inc. The company cited its focus on building shareholder value and expanding its Gymboree brand as the reason for unloading Zutopia.

After a tumultuous series of corporation leaders, the company named Lisa Harper, a longtime Gymboree employee, its CEO and vice-chair. Sales began to rise by November 2001. Other retailers that quarter were not as fortunate and this was noted and rewarded with Gymboree shares gaining on the NASDAQ.

The company had been based in Burlingame, California, since 1980 but considered a move in November 2003. The following spring the company chose a 160,000-square-foot facility on Howard Street in San Francisco as its new home.

Gymboree took a departure from its kidware and considered catering to the mother instead in 2004 when it launched its Janeville concept stores. The stores focused on women in their late 30s. The stores featured a cottage-like atmosphere reminiscent of the Hamptons or Sonoma, California. The company opened ten stores its first year with more to follow at upscale shopping complexes.

Sales at moderate to higher end retail establishments were stagnant during the recession of the early 2000s and Gymboree posted its share of flat sales. Nonetheless, the public demand for quality baby clothes remained, and with further expansion of its other store concepts in Janie and Jack, and Janeville, Gymboree seemed poised for renewed growth in the coming years.

Principal Divisions

Janie and Jack, Inc.; Janeville Stores, Inc.; Gymboree and Play and Music.

Principal Competitors

The Gap, Inc.; Target Corporation; The Children's Place Retail Stores, Inc.; Hanna Anderson Corp.

Further Reading

"As Sales Jump, Gymboree Predicts Profit," *San Francisco Chronicle*, November, 17, 2000.

Bary, Andrew, "Kid Stuff," *Barron's,* July 18, 1994, p. 17.

Burstiner, Marcy, "Retailing's Child Prodigy," *San Francisco Business Times,* August 20, 1993, p. 4A.

Carlsen, Clifford, "Gymboree Toys with Catalog Sales, Overseas Expansion," *San Francisco Business Times,* October 21, 1994, p. 1.

——, "Shakeup Time in Gymboree's Executive Suite," *San Francisco Business Times,* January 21, 1994, p. 3.

Emert, Carol, "CEO, President Flee Staggering Gymboree," *San Francisco Chronicle,* February, 16, 2000, p. D1.

——, "Gymboree Hires Marketing Whiz to Balance out Seesawing Sales," *San Francisco Chronicle,* February 3, 1999, p. D2.

——, "Gymboree Plans Big Makeover," *San Francisco Chronicle,* July 8, 1999, p. B1.

——, "Gymboree's Pivotal CEO Decides to Step Down," *San Francisco Chronicle,* February 14, 1997, p. B1.

Eng, Sherri, "Market Share of California's Gymboree Rises on Merchandising Strategy," *Knight-Ridder/Tribune Business News,* February 13, 1994.

"Gymboree," *Fortune,* February 7, 1994, p. 137.

"Gymboree Is More Than Just Child's Play; Toddler Activity Classes Grow into Lifestyle Concept Retail Stores," *Chain Store Age Executive,* November 1987, p. 115.

"Gymboree Shares Rise 18% on Revised Sales Forecast, *New York Times,* August 24, 2001, p. 4.

Martin, Michael B., and Leslie Laurence, "Joan Barnes's Workout Centers Help 12-Pound Weaklings Pump Iron," *Money,* May 1984, p. 21.

Mitchell, Russell, "A Children's Retailer That's Growing Up Fast," *Business Week,* May 23, 1994, p. 95.

—Dave Mote
— update: Susan B. Culligan

H.M. Payson & Co.

One Portland Square
Portland, Maine 04101
U.S.A.
Telephone: (207) 772-2761
Web site: http://www.hmpayson.com

Private Company
Incorporated: 1854
NAIC: 523100 Securities and Commodity Contracts
Intermediation and Brokerage

H.M. Payson & Co., based in Portland, Maine, is one of the oldest independent investment firms in the United States. Primarily providing investment advice and trust management services, Payson has a well-earned reputation for honesty and prudence. Although small, the firm maintains its own research staff and as a result has avoided the herd mentality of Wall Street and avoided such pitfalls as the technology bubble of the late 1990s. Payson has more than $1.6 billion in assets under management and serves more than 1,100 individuals, trusts, endowments, and foundations.

Corporate Beginnings: Mid-1800s

The man behind the founding of H.M. Payson was Henry Martyn Payson, born in Portland, Maine, in 1821, the son of a minister who moved his family to the area after graduating from Harvard. The life of the younger Payson was beset with tragedy. When he was just six years old his father died, followed 20 years later by even worse misfortune. He married and had a son, but the child was sickly and died when he was only six months old. Payson's grief was then deepened by the subsequent death of his wife, who had never recovered from the loss of her child. At the time, the hardware store he co-owned failed, forcing him into bankruptcy. The year was 1849 and across the country in California gold had been discovered, prompting a wide swath of society to make their way to the goldfields of northern California in hopes of realizing their fortune. With no family or business to keep him in New Hampshire, Payson became part of the gold rush that made its way to the nation's untamed West Coast.

He traveled by ship, arriving in San Francisco in January 1850. He soon learned that prospecting for gold was backbreaking work that made few people wealthy. He shoveled dirt into a sluice and screened for minute particles of gold during every daylight hour, yet he only made enough money to sustain himself. After four years of witnessing folly and suffering misery, he returned to Portland, but during his wilderness years he learned something of the way in which financial agents worked. He also brought back a hard-earned knowledge about the foolishness of get-rich-quick schemes, and an appreciation for a cautious approach to doing business. Perhaps of more importance, he returned to a growing city, whose population in the past 20 years had doubled to 25,000. Portland had eight banks, a thriving timber trade, and was also involved in sugar refining and rail stock manufacturing. Moreover, Maine's economy in general was improving at a steady clip, spurred by railroad construction that linked the once isolated state to Canada and the larger U.S. cities to the south, as did the Magnetic Telegraph Company, whose lines provided communication direct to Boston and beyond.

In 1854, to take advantage of the increased need for financial middlemen to continue Maine's development, Payson set himself as a stock and bond broker and a dealer in paper money, this at a time when state banks printed their own currency to supplement the limited amount of gold and silver coins that the federal government was able to mint. Nevertheless, a great deal of Payson's business for the first 20 years involved transactions in gold, as he cashed drafts and acceptances from California and London institutions.

Because banking and investment firms were so unreliable during this time, and government regulations all but nonexistent, a businessman's reputation for honesty was of great value. Payson built up a reservoir of trust in the community, which was bolstered by his decision to pay off his old creditors even though he was not legally required to. He was also known to be a careful investor of clients' money, preferring blue chip investments over speculative ventures. His prudent, circumspect nature became part of the firm's culture, passed down through succeeding generations. During the boom times of the early 1870s, when stock speculation ran rampant, Payson stayed the course, refusing to

---

Company Perspectives:

Through the years, we have acquired a deep appreciation of the timeless fundamentals of investing. We know that while times change, the basic characteristics of a good investment do not.

---

buy stock on margin and concentrating his investments on reliable utility bonds, particularly municipal water companies. He also helped to build Maine's economy by becoming involved in the funding of railroads serving the state, including the Leeds and Farmington Railroad and the Eastern Railroad.

Involvement in Water Bonds Dating to 1860s

Payson first became involved in water bonds when the Portland Water Company was formed in 1866, the same year that a great fire destroyed more than 200 acres in the heart of Portland, including Payson's own offices. It was a major blow to the local economy, given that an estimated $10 million in property was destroyed and only a third was insured. Payson helped to buoy the city's confidence by immediately making a public declaration that he would rebuild his office on the old site and vowed to be back in business there within six months. In many respects, a reliable water supply available to combat fires was of even greater importance during this period than healthy drinking water. New York City, for example, was in great need of unpolluted water, but it was only due to the threat of large-scale fires that the leading American city saw fit to build a modern water works.

In Portland the idea to tap into nearby Sebago Lake was first suggested in 1854, due to a drought that led to a short supply of water, but it was not until February 1866 that the Portland Water Company was incorporated. The fire that devastated the city on July 4 helped to spur the actual launch of the company. Water from Sebago finally began serving Portland in November 1869. Unfortunately, the company was poorly funded and managed. The main had not been properly laid, significantly hampering the flow of water. After the company twice succumbed to bankruptcy, Payson in the early 1870s was induced to join the board and help place the company on a solid financial footing. He was instrumental in securing the funds necessary to improve the infrastructure and turn Portland Water into a profitable business. It also marked Payson's entry into the water business, which became a main interest of the company for several decades.

As a result of his conservative approach, Paysons' clients were not wiped out like so many investors when the panic of 1873 hit the country, leading to a harsh five-year depression. During this time, in 1874, Payson took on his first partner, George F. Thurston, whom he had groomed since Thurston had graduated from high school and went to work for him as a clerk. A third partner joined the firm in 1879: Payson's nephew, Charles H. Payson, who like Thurston had no more than a high school education and worked his way up, also starting out as his uncle's clerk. Charles Payson's tenure would last more than 50 years and his influence on the firm's growth, both nationally and internationally, was so pronounced that he was considered H.M. Payson & Co.'s second founder.

Seven years after becoming a partner he became president when Payson chose to retire. Under Charles Payson's leadership the firm became even more committed to the water business. In 1888 he traveled to London to sell $1 million worth of bonds in the Portland Water Company to help shore up the utility's finances. Moreover, he represented another $1 million in water for nine other water companies, including ventures in Elmira, New York; East Greenwich, Connecticut; Kokomo, Indiana; Sheboygan, Wisconsin; Wichita, Kansas; Fort Smith, Arkansas; Huntington, West Virginia; Meridian, Mississippi; and Merrill, Wisconsin. On that trip he also sold securities for the Marion (Indiana) Gaslight Company. In addition to selling bonds, Charles Payson became involved in running several water companies that he helped to found or acquired. The firm also underwrote any number of utility bonds during the final decades of the 1800s. The firm's interests spread from coast to coast, touching more than 100 utilities and leading Payson to become known as "The Water Bond House."

Charles Payson and several outside partners in 1886 created the American Water Works and Guarantee Company, which built and developed water companies across the country. Soon joining him would be two Payson partners: George S. Payson, the founder's son, who became a partner in 1883 and Herbert Payson, who became a partner in 1889. The three men acted as American Water Work's financial agents. When the firm formed American Water Supply Co. in 1888, the Payson partners added operational responsibilities as well. Payson now acquired control of water companies as far away as Kansas and ran them out of the Portland office. Even after American Water Supply was liquidated, the investment firm remained involved in the water business. In 1926 two Payson partners—Herbert Payson and Harold C. Payson, who became partner in 1919—and five outside partners formed a utility holding company called Consumer's Water Company, which not only housed some of the partners' water assets but also acquired companies, so that by the early 1930s the venture controlled ten subsidiaries in seven states. Payson maintained a connection to the company until 1999 when Philadelphia Suburban Water Company acquired it. Also of note, was Payson's acquisition of Lewiston Gas Light Co. in 1899. The firm developed the utility, which became a highly successful New England company, now part of Northern Utilities Inc.

Limiting the Effects of the Great Depression

Although the firm was willing to risk its own money on some speculative utility ventures, when it came to investing clients' money, Payson continued to follow a cautious approach, sticking to blue chip securities. When the country was once again gripped by an economic panic, this time in 1893 leading to a three-year depression, Payson proved to be as reliable a firm for individuals to entrust their money as could be found. Payson's prudence would be put to the test in the next century during the stock market delirium of the 1920s, as masses of small-time investors began playing the market by buying stock on margin, and the firm's continued recommendation to invest in water bonds was considered quaint and out of step with the times. Nevertheless, Payson refused to succumb to pressure and establish margin accounts, so that in 1928 the firm lost half of its brokerage business, which was cut in half again

Key Dates:

1854: Henry Martyn Payson founds company.
1874: Payson takes his first partner.
1886: Charles H. Payson assumes presidency.
1926: Payson partners and other investors form Consumer's Water Company.
1987: Business is incorporated.
2000: Charter is granted to serve as non-depository trust company.

in 1929. The firm lost $100,000 in 1929, forcing the partners to make up the shortfall. But after the stock market crashed in October 1929 and countless investors were ruined because they were unable to pay their margin calls, Payson was well positioned for a rebound and its customers were able to weather one of the worst patches in the nation's economic history.

The firm also underwrote a large number of municipal bonds in Maine for sewage and school districts, while it continued to underwrite water bond issues until 1981, when it took on the Houlton Water Co., after which the firm referred its underwriting clients to the Maine Municipal Bond Bank, which was better suited to perform the business at less expense. It was during this time that Payson switched from managing trust portfolios on a commission basis, opting instead to do the work for a fee. In this way, Payson was better able to fulfill its fiduciary responsibility to clients without the taint of self-interest. The trust business grew at a strong clip, so that in 2000 the firm sought and received a charter from the Maine Bureau of Financial Institutions to serve as a non-depository trust company.

Payson changed its ownership structure in 1987, when the business was incorporated, but little changed in terms of culture. The firm continued to resist overexposure to bull markets and proved to be a safe haven when good times invariably turned to bad. While other investors became over-exuberant about technology stocks in the late 1990s, Payson continued to take a balanced approach, which once again paid off for clients when the tech bubble burst. There was every reason to expect that in the new century the longtime Yankee firm would continue to pursue its successful, prudent approach to investing.

Further Reading

Gormley, John H., ''Yankee Frugality Thriving,'' *Portland Press Herald,* May 10, 1998, p. 1F.
H.M. Payson & Co: Partnership for 100 Years, Portland, Maine: H.M. Payson & Co., 1954.
Walker, John H., and Peter E. Robbins, ''H.M. Payson & Co.,'' Exton, Pa.: Newcomen Society of the United States, 2004, 24 p.

—Ed Dinger

Héroux-Devtek Inc.

Suite 658, East Tower
Complexe Saint-Charles
1111 Saint-Charles Street Ouest
Longueuil, Québec J4K 5G4
Canada
Telephone: (450) 679-3330
Fax: (450) 679-3666
Web site: http://www.herouxdevtek.com

Public Company
Incorporated: 1942 as Héroux Machine Parts Limited
Employees: 1,100
Sales: CAD 213.21 million ($163.0 million) (2004)
Stock Exchanges: Toronto
Ticker Symbol: HRX
NAIC: 333611 Turbine and Turbine Generator Set Units
    Manufacturing; 334511 Search, Detection, Navigation,
    Guidance, Aeronautical, and Nautical System and
    Instrument Manufacturing; 336412 Aircraft Engine
    and Engine Parts Manufacturing; 336413 Other
    Aircraft Parts and Auxiliary Equipment Manufacturing

Héroux-Devtek Inc. primarily produces landing gear, structural components, and other parts for a variety of commercial and military aircraft. It also makes industrial gas turbine parts and small arms. The company was formed by the 2000 merger of Héroux and Devtek. It has landing gear plants in Kitchener, Ontario, and Montreal, Québec, and an industrial turbine component plant in Cincinnati, Ohio.

Origins

Héroux Inc. was incorporated in Québec on March 17, 1942, as Héroux Machine Parts Ltd. Located in Longueuil, a suburb of Montreal, Héroux's small factory turned out machined components for military equipment. The workforce originally numbered fewer than 15 people.

The company began to specialize in aerospace in the mid-1950s. The company moved to a new site in Longueuil in 1954.

Early projects included producing servos and landing gear for the Canadair CL-215 water bomber and de Havilland's DCH-6 Twin Otter. A high point in the company's history was providing landing gear for the Apollo space program's lunar module.

The United States was beginning to account for much of Héroux's business. Héroux won a contract to overhaul landing gear for the U.S. Air Force in 1970. This would be an enduring business. The company soon established a second maintenance base at Saint-Jean-sur-Richelieu Airport to the southeast of Montreal. This facility, however, would be closed in 1982. Bombardier Inc. acquired Héroux in 1973.

Sales were about CAD 14 million a year by 1985. In that year, corporate parent Bombardier Inc. sold Héroux to two of its managers, Gilles Labbe and Sarto Richer, who had joined the company three years earlier. Citibank Canada financed the CAD 10 million purchase. Labbe, then 29, had joined the company in 1982 as director of finance. According to the *Globe and Mail,* Labbe and Richer were able to pay off the bank loan in 18 months, while sales more than tripled to CAD 49 million in three years. One-fifth of shares were floated in a 1986 stock offering on the Montreal Stock Exchange.

Héroux acquired McSwain Manufacturing Corporation of Cincinnati, Ohio, in November 1987. McSwain produced precision machined parts for a variety of industries.

Héroux specialized in building and overhauling landing gear for heavy U.S. military transport aircraft, including the colossal C-5. In 1989, Héroux paid $18.5 million for 80 percent of ABA Industries Inc., a Florida company that produced engine parts. ABA had 270 employees. It had originally been founded in Connecticut in 1944 and went public in 1969 before being acquired by General Defense Corp. in 1983 for $20.4 million. It had undergone a management buyout in 1987. The ABA acquisition made Héroux a certified supplier for engine giants General Electric and Pratt & Whitney.

Civil Focus in the 1990s

Héroux started the 1990s with sales of $73.5 million a year, 70 percent of it from military business. The Soviet Union's

Company Perspectives:

Corporate Mission: To optimize our precision manufacturing engineering capabilities in order to produce highly reliable products and related services for customers with growth potential in the aerospace and industrial sectors in North America and rapidly growing markets. Héroux-Devtek will grow as a leader in our industry by exceeding customers expectations through the participation, dedication and commitment of our people.

Cold War threat to the West was waning, and Héroux steered its efforts toward the commercial, rather than military, side of the aviation industry. The company began producing after-market parts for Boeing in early 1990. It also overhauled planes for Canadian Airlines International Ltd. and U.S. Air.

Seeking to diversify into industrial products, Héroux acquired a 60 percent holding in FRE Composites Inc. in 1992. FRE was a Canadian manufacturer of composite products for the aerospace and mass transit industries.

Military downsizing continued throughout the 1990s, but it produced some additional business for Héroux. For example, in September 1996 the U.S. Navy opted to have Héroux overhaul landing gear for its S-3 Viking surveillance aircraft, work that had previously been done in-house. Still, defense accounted for just 30 percent of revenues in the mid-1990s.

In 1998, Héroux announced that it was partnering with Messier-Dowty Inc. to produce landing gear for a civilian derivative of the V-22 Osprey tiltrotor. Two other contractors for Bombardier regional jets were acquired in June 1999. Metro Machining Corp. and Les Industries C.A.T. Inc. together had sales of CAD 11.6 million in 1998, and specialized in structural aircraft components. Héroux sold off FRE Composites for CAD 5.3 million in January 2000 to concentrate on its aerospace and power generation businesses. FRE had accounted for less than 10 percent of Héroux's sales.

Acquisition of Devtek in 2000

Héroux Inc. acquired Devtek Corporation in 2000. Devtek's origins went back to 1981, when auto parts manufacturer Magna International Inc. spun off 80 percent of its aerospace and defense business to a group led by Helmut Hofmann. Hofmann had emigrated from West Germany in 1951, when he was a tool-and-die maker by trade.

The spinoff was named Devtek Corporation. It specialized in electronics. Its Diemaco Inc. division, based in Kitchener, Ontario, produced rifles for the Canadian Armed Forces. About 90 percent of Devtek's sales were to the military.

Devtek acquired two companies in early 1986. Hochelaga Workshops—renamed Hochelaga Aerospace Inc.—was a Montreal-based manufacturer of flight control and landing gear assemblies. General Manufacturing of Fort Lauderdale, Florida, produced precision machined components. Devtek also owned Magna Electronics and Verral Metal Fabricators, both based in

Scarborough, Ontario. Unit Hermes Electronics Ltd. of Halifax, Nova Scotia, produced sonar buoys for detecting submarines.

Devtek Corporation, based in Markham, Ontario, went public on the Toronto Stock Exchange in November 1986 when sales were about CAD 75 million a year. Its initial public offering raised CAD 14 million.

Devtek bought a 50 percent share of Interfast Inc., a high-tech aerospace fastener company based in Toronto, in April 1988. A seven-year noncompete agreement with Magna International expired that year, and Devtek returned to its roots by investing CAD 6 million plus shares worth CAD 1 million in privately owned auto parts supplier Tridon Ltd. Tridon employed about 900 people and was best known for its windshield wiper blades. Annual sales were about CAD 100 million. In December 1989, Devtek raised its stake in Tridon from 27 percent to 51 percent. It acquired the remainder within a few years.

Devtek had about 2,000 employees in three units in the early 1990s. A falloff in defense business prompted Devtek to shift to commercial aircraft such as the Boeing 747 and de Havilland Dash-8. The civil air business, however, also was entering a slump. Devtek posted losses for the fiscal years 1991 to 1993. In late 1994 Devtek announced that it was focusing on the auto industry.

Devtek was profitable again by 1994, posting net income of $3.3 million. Operating revenues were $261.6 million in 1995, with net income of $4.6 million. By this time, noted the *Financial Post,* the automotive industry was accounting for 60 percent to 70 percent of Devtek's revenues. Britain's Automotive Components Dunstable Ltd. was acquired for CAD 22.4 million in February 1996. This purchase made Devtek a global leader in integrated wiper systems. Devtek's revenues were CAD 320 million in 1996.

In August 1997, a joint venture of Devtek won a CAD 100 million contract from Ford Motor Co. to provide bi-fuel systems for pickups and vans. These allowed vehicles to operate with either gasoline or natural gas or propane. Devtek's equal partner in the venture, Kitchener-based GFI Control Systems Inc., was Stewart & Stevenson Services Inc. of Houston.

Sales were about CAD 400 million a year in the late 1990s. Devtek had 13 plants in North America and Europe. ACD Tridon Inc. employed 1,550 people and had sales of $296 million in 1998. Nevertheless, Devtek moved to quickly unload Tridon when it began to show quarterly losses. In April 1999, Tomkins PLC bought the unit for $55 million, plus the assumption of $100 million in debt. GRI Controls Systems was not included in the deal.

New Challenges After 2000

Héroux Inc. changed its name to Héroux-Devtek Inc. in September 2000 after acquiring Devtek. The combined company was organized into four divisions: Landing Gear, Gas Turbine Components, Aerostructure, and Logistics and Defence.

Héroux-Devtek had to deal with a shifting business climate again after the September 11, 2001 terrorist attacks on the United States, which plunged the commercial aviation industry

Inc.; McSwain Manufacturing Corporation (U.S.A.); Metro Machining Corporation; Progressive Incorporated (U.S.A.).

Key Dates:

1942: Héroux is formed as a small machined components manufacturer.
1954: The company moves to Longueuil, focuses on aeronautic industry.
1969: Apollo Lunar Module features landing gear by Héroux.
1973: Bombardier Inc. acquires Héroux.
1981: Devtek Corporation is spun off from Magna International Inc.
1985: Héroux is acquired by two managers.
2000: Devtek Corporation is acquired; company is renamed Héroux-Devtek Inc.
2004: Progressive Incorporated is acquired.

into a crisis while increasing the demand for defense-related hardware. Héroux supplied components for the new generation of unmanned aerial vehicles (UAVs) being deployed in Afghanistan.

Noted *Investors Digest,* when such commercial aircraft manufacturers as Bombardier reduced their workforces, they tended to shift more work to contractors. Nevertheless, in 2002 the company laid off 100 people from two plants in the United States that made jet engine parts, as the demand for turbines fell. Other divisions pushed the company to record sales and income for the 2001–02 fiscal year. Net income was up 40 percent to CAD 17.4 million on revenues of CAD 316.3 million, up 22 percent from the previous year.

ABA Industries, a Héroux-Devtek subsidiary in Pinellas Park, Florida, was closed in 2003. The shutdown was attributed to a weak economy in the United States and a falloff in demand for industrial gas turbines.

Sales for the fiscal year ended March 2004 were up 8 percent to CAD 213.21 million ($163.0 million). After breaking even the previous year, the company posted a CAD 2.2 million ($1.7 million) loss.

A $34 million offer for bankrupt NMF Canada Inc., a producer of wing panels, failed to go through. Héroux-Devtek was able to acquire Texas-based Progressive Incorporated, however, which produced structural components for military aircraft, paying $57.6 million in April 2004. The buy brought the military-related share of Héroux-Devtek's revenues to 60 percent, noted the *Financial Post.* Progressive had sales of more than $37 million (CAD 50 million) a year and had been founded in 1971.

Principal Subsidiaries

Devtek Aerospace Inc.; Devtek Corporation; Héroux Corporation; Héroux-Devtek Aerostructure Inc.; Les Industries C.A.T.

Principal Divisions

Landing Gear; Aerostructure; Gas Turbine Components; Logistics and Defence.

Principal Competitors

Goodrich Landing Gear Division; Hawker Pacific Aerospace; Honeywell Aerospace; Messier-Dowty International.

Further Reading

Daly, Kieran, "Heroux Plans Civilian Widebody Programme," *Flight International,* October 23, 1991, p. 16.

Daw, James, "Tridon Takes 550 Jobs to U.S.," *Toronto Star,* Bus. Sec., September 21, 1990, p. C1.

"Devtek Sells Automotive Business," *Plant,* April 26, 1999, p. 2.

"Entrepreneur of the Year; Profile of Gilles Labbe," *National Post* (Canada), December 1, 2001, p. 88.

Fitzpatrick, Peter, "Defence Industry Dons Civvies in Bid for Profits," *Financial Post* (Toronto), Sec. 2, October 30, 1996, p. 28.

——, "Devtek Shifts Gears from Aerospace to Automotive," *Financial Post* (Toronto), Sec. 2, July 31, 1996, p. 21.

——, "Landmark $100M Deal with Ford Fuels Surge in Devtek Share Price," *Financial Post* (Toronto), Sec. 1, August 26, 1997, p. 1.

Gibbens, Robert, "Heroux Sees More Business from Takeover: Company Trumpets Its Acquisition of Progressive Inc.," *National Post's Financial Post & FP Investing* (Canada), September 3, 2004, p. FP6.

——, "Héroux's Flight Plan Increases the Emphasis on Civil Aircraft," *Financial Post* (Toronto), Sec. 1, August 1, 1990, p. 4.

"Heroux-Devtek May Add to Earlier Layoffs," *National Post's Financial Post & FP Investing* (Canada), November 19, 2002, p. FP9.

"Heroux-Devtek to Do Well Despite Airline Slump," *Investors Digest,* November 1, 2002.

Languedoc, Colin, "Devtek Buys a Stake in Tridon," *Financial Post* (Toronto), Sec. 2, December 14, 1988, p. 23.

Lindberg, Anne, "Canadian Company to Close Local Plant," *St. Petersburg Times,* March 2, 2003, p. 3.

Lowman, Ron, "Devtek Decides to Go Public After Creating 8 Companies," *Toronto Star,* October 3, 1986, p. E7.

——, "Toronto-Based Weapons Maker Buys Two Firms," *Toronto Star,* January 29, 1986, p. C4.

"The Making of a Magnate," *Globe and Mail,* September 16, 1988, p. 77.

Romain, Ken, "Devtek Increases Tridon Stake to Offset Lagging Defence Thrust," *Globe and Mail,* December 13, 1989, p. B6.

——, "Devtek Takes First Loss in 10 Years; Company Attributes Setback to Reduction in Defence Spending, Recession," *Globe and Mail,* December 11, 1991, p. B10.

Roper, Akil Salim, "Devtek Looks South for U.S. Private Placement," *Private Placement Letter,* April 6, 1998.

Sokol, Marlene, "Canadian Firm Buys 80 Per Cent of ABA Stock," *St. Petersburg Times,* April 11, 1989, p. 2E.

Surtees, Lawrence, "Submarine Detection Buoys Profits for Expansionist-Minded Devtek," *Globe and Mail,* December 11, 1986, p. B16.

—Frederick C. Ingram

Hexal AG

Industriestrasse 25
Holzkirchen
D-83607
Germany
Telephone: +49 8024 9 08 0
Fax: +49 8024 9 08 2 90
Web site: http://www.hexal.de

Private Company
Incorporated: 1986
Employees: 7,000
Sales: EUR 1.11 billion ($1.5 billion) (2003)
NAIC: 325412 Pharmaceutical Preparation
    Manufacturing; 424210 Drugs and Druggists'
    Sundries Merchant Wholesalers

Hexal AG is Germany's second largest producer of generic drugs, and also claims the number four position in the worldwide generics market. Based in Holzkirchen, Hexal produces some 1,000 pharmaceutical products based on more than 250 active ingredients. The company specializes in developing new delivery methods and dosages for its generics, including tablets, capsules, transdermal patches, ampoules, and aerosols. Since 2004, Hexal also has launched production of its active ingredients, becoming the only independent manufacturer of active ingredients in Germany. Hexal operates five production plants in Germany, which continues to account for more than 60 percent of Hexal's EUR 1.1 billion ($1.5 billion) in 2003 revenues. Yet the company also has established a strong global presence, with production sites and production joint ventures in Canada, Denmark, China, Indonesia, Brazil, Argentina, Portugal, Japan, and elsewhere. The company also operates a number of international sales and marketing subsidiaries. Europe remains the group's largest market, adding 29 percent to annual sales, while the company has a growing presence in the Americas and in the Asian Pacific region. In addition to production of active ingredients, Hexal's research and development budget routinely accounts for as much as 15 percent of its sales. Hexal also has begun raising its profile, launching a marketing drive to establish its brand name. Hexal is led by cofounders and twin brothers Thomas and Andreas Strüngmann and remains a privately owned company.

Generics Opportunities in the 1980s

Hexal was founded by twin brothers Thomas and Andreas Strüngmann. The Strüngmann brothers were no strangers to pharmaceuticals: father Ernst Strüngmann had earlier founded the Frankfurt-based company Durachemie. While Andreas pursued his medical studies, Thomas received a doctorate in business administration from the University of Augsburg in 1977. He then went to work for Schering-Plough as a product manager, at first in Lucerne, before being transferred to that company's New Jersey branch in 1978. Strüngmann's encounter with American "can-do" optimism was to have a lasting impact, and became a driving force behind Hexal's success. Thomas Strüngmann then returned to Germany, becoming Durachemie's CEO in 1979. In the meantime, Andreas had completed his studies and gone to work as a physician in the South African bush where he was directly confronted with the urgent need for more affordable medicines.

By the mid-1980s, the German government had actively begun encouraging the substitution of generic medicines for their branded equivalents in order to help control rising healthcare costs. The Strüngmanns quickly recognized an opportunity to combine both brothers' experiences. In 1985, the family spun off one of Durachemie's subsidiaries, then sold Durachemie itself to Cyanamid in 1986. That year, the brothers set up shop in a house in Tegernsee, in Germany's Bavaria region, in order to produce low-cost, generic drugs.

Hexal Chemie GmbH & Co. KG, as the company was called, started off with five drug preparations and just 22 employees. Instead of producing copycat generics, Hexal recognized the market potential for developing new formulations and delivery methods of existing drugs. Among the company's first successes was its lower-dosage formulation of a popular kidney medicine.

Hexal hit the ground running. In its first month, it posted sales equivalent to EUR 220,000. By 1988, the company's revenues had topped the equivalent of EUR 28 million. In that year, the company finished construction of a full-fledged headquarters and production facility, in the picturesque town of Holzkirchen. A major feature of that complex was its research and development laboratory. Hexal's commitment to research and development and its willingness to plow its profits back into the company played a major role in the company's success.

Foreign Expansion in the 1990s

Hexal's Holzkirchen production unit was completed in 1990, and enabled the company to begin large-scale production of its formulations. In that year, also, Hexal made its first acquisition, buying up former DDR chemical giant Fahlberg-List's pharmaceutical division, located in Barleben, outside of Magdeburg. This marked the first of several company production sites, highlighting Hexal's commitment to maintaining its manufacturing presence in the newly unified Germany. In 1992, the company began construction of a new production facility in Magdeburg. Known as Salutas and completed in 1996, the new facility was one of the most modern in all of Europe and positioned Hexal as a major generics producer in Germany. Between 1992 and 1995, the company's sales soared from the equivalent of EUR 89 million to nearly EUR 260 million.

A key factor in Hexal's growth was its decision early on to expand production and distribution into the global market. The company's first foreign move came in 1990, when it opened a marketing subsidiary in South Africa, with an office in the Durban suburb of Pinetown.

Closer to home, Hexal entered Portugal in 1991, establishing a joint venture with a local pharmaceutical maker to introduce Hexal's drugs in that market. The company later bought out its partner, establishing Bexal S.A. there in 2002. Partnerships continued to play an important role in Hexal's international expansion. In 1993, the company joined with fellow German Rowa Pharmaceutical's Irish subsidiary to form the Rowex joint venture in Bantry, County Cork. In that year, also, Hexal entered Poland, setting up HEXAL POLSKA Sp. z o.o. in Warsaw, as a sales and marketing subsidiary. In 2002, however, the company began building a new headquarters and production facility, including a blistering facility, in Poland. The following year, Hexal entered Russia, establishing a representative office in Moscow.

Hexal converted its structure to a limited liability company in 1995, changing its name to Hexal AG that year. The company continued seeking out new international markets, creating subsidiaries in the Czech Republic and Australia, as well as a representative office in Vietnam. The following year was a busy one for the company, with new production subsidiaries

launched in China and Argentina, and new marketing subsidiaries introduced to The Netherlands and the Baltic states. The completion of the Salutas plant, at a cost of EUR 260 million, added production capacity of more than five billion capsules and tablets per year in order to support the company's steady growth. The year also marked the launch of the company's ACC acut, one of its most successful drug formulations.

In 1997, Hexal formed RhoxalPharma Inc. in a joint venture with Rhodiapharm, the generics subsidiary of Rhône Poulenc Rorer. The new subsidiary gave Hexal access to the North American market, as well as new production capacity. In 1999, Hexal took full control of the Canadian operation. Also in 1997, Hexal established a marketing subsidiary in Austria.

By the end of 1998, Hexal's sales neared EUR 450 million. That year marked another major milestone for the group, as it began research operations in biotechnology, molecular medicine, and genetics in order to develop its own in-house drugs. In 1998, the company founded two new subsidiaries, Hexal Biotech and Hexal Gentech.

At the same time, Hexal stepped up its international expansion. The company turned to Scandinavia, buying up Denmark's GEA, founded in 1927. The GEA acquisition also enabled the company to enter Sweden and Finland. The company launched a new production facility in Mexico that year, then added sales subsidiaries in Ukraine and Romania. Hexal also moved into Japan, acquiring Hoescht subsidiary Cox Japan that year. That company was then renamed as Nippon Hexal in 1999. New markets that year included Spain, through subsidiary Bexal Farmacéutica S.A., and Turkey, through the acquisition of Ilsan Iltas. The company's international production portfolio took a major step forward that year as well, with the acquisition of a controlling stake in Indonesia's PT Prima.

Branded Generics Leader in the 2000s

Hexal scored a new success in 2000, when its research and development efforts paid off in the form of OncoQuick. That product offered a breakthrough in cancer testing and tumor detection techniques. The company became a leading innovator in transdermal delivery techniques as well. Also in 2000, Hexal entered the United States for the first time, buying up Eon Labs, which was subsequently launched as a public company in 2002.

By the end of 2001, Hexal's sales had topped EUR 750 million. In that year, the company launched a new German production subsidiary, Jenahexal Pharma, which opened an ampoule-filling facility in the town of Jena. That year, the company boosted its presence in Turkey with the takeover of Koz Pharmaceuticals / Biokem through its subsidiary there. Meanwhile, the company entered Greece, establishing Novexal.

Continued expansion brought Hexal into Egypt, Guatemala, and the Philippines in 2002, boosting the group's presence in the Middle East, Central America and the Caribbean, and in Southeast Asia, respectively. In 2003, Hexal added sales subsidiaries in Italy and South Korea. A trend toward new legislation requiring or encouraging substitutions of generic products had been building steam, reaching such markets as Finland and France, and boosting Hexal's future prospects. By the end of that year, the company's annual sales had topped the EUR 1 billion mark for the first time.

Key Dates:

1979: Thomas Strüngmann joins his father's company, Durachemie, as CEO.

1985: Strüngmann spins off the Durachemie subsidiary in order to launch a new company with his twin brother Andreas.

1986: Durachemie is sold to Cyanamid; Hexal Chemie GmbH & Co. KG is launched.

1988: Revenues reach the equivalent of EUR 28 million.

1990: The first production facility is completed; the first international subsidiary is established in South Africa.

1992: Construction of a new state-of-the-art production facility is launched at Salutas.

1996: Production at Salutas begins.

1995: The company's name is changed to Hexal AG.

1998: New biotech research subsidiaries Hexal Biotech and Hexal Gentech are established.

2000: The company acquires Eon Labs in the United States.

2002: Eon is spun off as a separate, publicly listed company.

2004: The company acquires a production facility in Dresden and launches the Hexal Synthese active ingredients production unit.

2005: The company announces plans for a possible initial public offering.

Despite its success, and its growth into Germany's number two generics manufacturer and a position among the world's top five, Hexal itself remained, in large part, unknown. The company took steps to counter that in 2004, launching its first marketing campaign in Germany, which remained the group's core market at more than 60 percent of sales. The company made another important move that year in order to heighten its profile when in July 2004, Hexal acquired Arzneimittel Werk Dresden (AWD), which permitted the company to launch production of its own active ingredients for the first time.

Hexal began making preparations for its next growth phase. While remaining committed to its private, family-controlled status in the short term, Hexal recognized the need to change its status in the long term. As Thomas Strüngmann told *Reuters:* "In the long run—in the next 10 years—we could see Hexal merge or acquire another big generic company and establish a stronger presence worldwide. For the moment, we have made the decision that there will be no family member of the next generation in the company. We want to de Strüngmannize Hexal." As part of that process, the company announced its intention to launch a public offering, possibly as early as 2005. Given the company's success in building on its generics base, Hexal appeared poised for fresh expansion in the new century.

Principal Subsidiaries

Bexal Farmacéutica S.A. (Spain); GEA (Denmark); HEXAL AB (Sweden); HEXAL ARGENTINA S.A.; Hexal Australia; HEXAL Centroamericana S.A. (Guatemala); Hexal Korea Corporation; HEXAL Pharma; HEXAL Pharma (S.A.); HEXAL POLSKA Sp. z.o.o. (Poland); HEXAL S.p.A. (Italy); HEXAL Syntech GmbH; Hexanel S.R.O. (Czech Republic); ILSAN HEXAL (Turkey); JENAHEXAL Pharma GmbH; Laboratories Hexal México; Nippon Hexal (Japan); RhoxalPharma Inc. (Canada); Rowex Ltd. (Ireland); Salutas Pharma GmbH.

Principal Competitors

PG Enterprises; Celesio AG; HOLDPHAC S.p.A.; Degussa AG; Solvay S.A.; Boots Group PLC; Boehringer Ingelheim Group; Fresenius AG.

Further Reading

Beyer, Stefan, "Die Tabletten-Twins vom Tergernsee," *Wirtschaft,* February 2004.

"Degussa's Radebeul Site Sold to Hexal," *Manufacturing Chemist,* April 2004, p. 11.

"Europe's Hot Growth Companies," *Business Week Online,* October 24, 2004.

"German Drugmaker Hexal Sees Growth Through M&A," *Pharma News Bulletin,* January 5, 2005.

McIntosh, Bill, "Bioglan Acquires Hexal Skin Treatment Products for Pounds 16m," *Independent,* January 4, 2001, p. 19.

—M.L. Cohen

Hooters of America, Inc.

1815 The Exchange
Atlanta, Georgia 30339
U.S.A.
Telephone: (770) 951-2040
Fax: (770) 618-7032
Web site: http://www.hootersofamerica.com

Private Company
Incorporated: 1984
Employees: 25,000 (systemwide)
Sales: $275 million (2002 est.)
NAIC: 533110 Lessors of Non-Financial Tangible Assets;
541613 Marketing Consulting Services; 722110 Full-
Service Restaurants

Hooters of America, Inc. operates and franchises a chain of casual restaurants that feature waitresses known as Hooters Girls. The first Hooters Restaurant opened in Clearwater, Florida, in 1983. The concept was licensed in 1984 to Hooters of America. The franchiser bought the trademark from Hooters Inc. in 2001.

Free Publicity Launches the Concept: 1983–89

The first Hooters restaurant was opened on April Fools' Day in 1983 in Clearwater, Florida, by six friends, all businessmen who had no experience in the restaurant industry. As Gil DiGiannantonio, one of the partners, told *Florida Trend* magazine three years later, after Hooters had become a roaring success, they were "a bunch of guys who got tired of going to fern bars." Apocryphally, the six combed Clearwater Beach searching for attractive young women who were interested in becoming the first Hooters Girls.

In addition to DiGiannantonio, a sales representative for a liquor distributor, the other founding partners were: L.D Stewart and Dennis Johnson, also partners in a general contracting business; Kenneth Wimmer, who had worked for Stewart and Johnson before starting his own paint business; Ed Droste, owner and chief executive of a resort development business;

and William Ranieri, a former service-station owner who had retired to Florida. Stewart was the majority owner.

The restaurant struggled for almost a year before receiving a fortuitous break in the form of free publicity. In January 1984, Tampa hosted the NFL Super Bowl between the Los Angeles Raiders and the Washington Redskins. John Riggens, then a star running back for the Redskins, ate lunch at Hooters the day before the game. After the Super Bowl, he returned with several teammates for a midnight snack. With the resulting media attention, Hooters quickly went from grossing $2,000 a night to nearly $4,000.

In 1984 the original owners, who had formed Hooters of Clearwater, Inc., sold expansion and franchise rights to Neighborhood Restaurants of America, a group of Atlanta investors, who formed Hooters of America, Inc. Hooters of Clearwater received 10 percent of Hooters of America and 3 percent royalties on all Hooters sales. Hooters of Clearwater also retained the final say on restaurant design and menu, and the right to build Hooters restaurants in Pinellas and Hillsborough counties in Florida.

Hooters vs. EEOC: 1991–96

Within two years, Hooters had become a $16 million chain with nine restaurants in Florida and two in Atlanta. By 1991, there were some 50 Hooters restaurants and Hooters of America had revenues of more than $100 million. The chain had reached 100 restaurants and $200 million in revenues by the end of 1993.

Hooters continued to thrive on free publicity. When the Soviet national boxing team was in Tampa to fight the Americans in the summer of 1986, the Soviets ate dinner at Hooters. The next day, the *Tampa Tribune* ran a full color picture of a Russian boxer eating chicken wings with a Hooters Girl, wearing a tight-fitting Hooters T-shirt, standing next to him. In July 1986, Hooters girl Lynne Austin was *Playboy* magazine's Playmate of the Month. The men's magazine also included a small article about Hooters and some of the pictures showed Austin in a Hooters outfit. Droste told *Florida Trend,* "We were already doing well at that point, but (the *Playboy* article) was important because it gave us our first national exposure."

But probably the greatest marketing coup came in 1995 when Hooters of America hired a hairy male actor and dressed him in a Hooters waitress outfit to poke fun at allegations that Hooters restaurants discriminated against men. Hooters of America ran full-page advertisements showing ''Vince'' in *USA Today* and the *Washington Post*. But more importantly, according to then vice-president of marketing Michael McNeil, television camera crews showed up at every Hooters restaurant in the United States the same day to do local stories.

Hooters of America liked to boast that ''Hooters is to chicken wings what McDonald's is to hamburgers.'' But the Hooters Girls, not the restaurants' food or drink, were always the essence of the Hooters concept. Hooters restaurants hired young, attractive women as waitresses and dressed them in orange running shorts—''sized to fit comfortably,'' according to corporate literature—and white tank tops or T-shirts. Hooters of America readily acknowledged that ''the concept relies on natural female sex appeal'' and the waitresses were encouraged to sit down and chat with the predominantly male clientele.

Hooters Girls also made celebrity appearances at sporting events and charity functions, and were pictured on billboards, trading cards, and calendars. Hooters of America published a glossy *Hooters Magazine* that featured Hooters Girls in everything from swimsuits to evening wear. According to the corporate literature, Hooters Girls were expected to ''always maintain a prom-like appearance with hair, make-up and nails done neatly. Hooters Girls should project a positive attitude with a bubbling personality and the prettiest smile in the world.''

Although the founders of the original Hooters in Clearwater always insisted the name referred to an owl in the restaurant's logo, they did so tongue-in-cheek, and it was a claim that few people accepted. ''Obviously the name is a double entendre,'' McNeil told *Business First,* a Columbus, Ohio, business newspaper in 1994. ''Hooters is an innocuous slang expression for a part of the female anatomy. We don't deny that. We also realize that most people believe that that is the case.'' Critics of the name and concept dubbed Hooters the nation's first ''breastaurant.''

In 1996, the *American Spectator* noted that Hooters featured ''socially adept and lightly dressed young women who delight a generally beefier crowd of male patrons by simply feeding them from a reasonably priced menu. It is a simple but successful concept, one that would offend only the worst sort of prig.'' But offend it did.

Women's groups expressed outrage at the skimpy Hooters Girls uniforms. Hooters restaurants were also forced with some regularity to defend themselves against allegations of sexual harassment. In the most high profile case, three former wait-

resses at a Hooters franchise operated by Bloomington Hooters Inc. at the Mall of America in Minnesota filed suit in 1993, claiming they had been fondled and verbally abused by male employees at the restaurant. Representing the waitresses, attorney Lori C. Peterson, who also sued the Stroh Brewery Co. over its controversial Swedish Bikini Team commercials, went on television talk shows to denounce the Hooters concept. Among her demands were that Hooters change its name and uniforms.

But in an interview with *Corporate Report Minnesota,* attorney Lisa A. Gray, hired by the restaurant, countered, ''For me to deny that sex appeal is part of the concept, part of what's happening at Hooters, would be ludicrous. But I've always thought feminism is all about choice. If people are offended by Hooters, they should vote with their feet. Don't go to the restaurant to eat. Don't apply to work at it.'' Hooters of America also denied that Hooters restaurants fostered a ''hostile environment'' for women and publicly stressed a strict corporate policy against any form of sexual harassment. The suit was eventually settled out of court.

Hooters restaurants also attracted the attention of the Equal Employment Opportunity Commission (EEOC), which launched an investigation in 1991 into alleged discrimination because Hooters refused to hire male waiters. In an 80-page finding released in 1994, the EEOC determined that ''no physical trait unique to women is required to service food and drink to customers in a restaurant.'' The EEOC demanded that Hooters of America pay $22 million to men who could show they had been denied jobs because of their gender. The agency also demanded that Hooters establish a scholastic fund ''to enhance the skills, employment opportunities or education of males.''

The EEOC findings were generally ridiculed by the news media and a public that had grown skeptical of government interference, especially since the EEOC had a backlog of seemingly more serious cases. Bureaucracy watchdog James Bovard, writing in the *Washington Post,* responded, ''What sort of education program did the EEOC have in mind? Teaching the new male hirees how to flirt with burly construction workers without getting punched in the nose?''

Hooters of America argued that Hooters Girls, in addition to foodservice, provided entertainment, which entitled the restaurants to an exemption from equal employment laws under the ''Bona Fide Occupational Qualification'' section of the Civil Rights Act. Forcing Hooters to hire men as waiters, the restaurant chain said, would be like forcing Radio City Music Hall to hire male Rockettes for its famed chorus line.

In a more serious vein, McNeil explained that ''Hooters Girls have been the essence of our business since the first store opened in 1983,'' and pointed out that Hooters employed men as cooks and in management positions. Hooters fought back with a $1 million publicity campaign, featuring ''Vince,'' the hirsute waiter in a skimpy Hooter's outfit, designed to ridicule the EEOC. Under the headline ''What's wrong with this picture,'' the newspaper ads complained, ''The Equal Employment Opportunity Commission is wasting taxpayers dollars, ignoring its mission, and setting aside the interests of individuals with real discrimination claims in an effort to force Hooters Restaurants to hire men to be Hooters Girls. This excessive government interference threatens Hooters business and the jobs of more than 13,000 employees. Taking away jobs from Hooters gals to hire men is unfair and it's just plain ridiculous.''

Tad Dixon, then public relations manager for Hooters of America, told *Nation's Restaurant News* that his office received more than 500 telephone calls the day the campaign broke. Hooters of America also coordinated a ''March on Washington'' with a rally at Freedom Park in Washington, D.C., where more than a hundred Hooters Girls carried placards with such slogans as ''Men as Hooters Guys—What a Drag.''

In addition to the newspaper ads, Hooters used ''Vince'' on billboards, other print materials, and even on its radio commercials. In a brief statement, the EEOC called the public relations campaign an effort ''to intimidate a federal law enforcement agency, and, more importantly, individuals whose rights may have been violated.'' But, eventually, the EEOC dropped its demands and the investigation. In 1996 Gilbert F. Casellas, then chairman of the EEOC, sent a letter to the U.S. House subcommittee on employment in which he concluded ''it is wiser for the EEOC to devote its scarce litigation resources to other cases.''

In 1996 the privately owned Hooters of America operated 57 Hooters restaurants and franchised 135. Of the more than $300 million in revenue generated systemwide, Hooters of America said 65 percent came from the sale of food, 30 percent from the sale of beer and wine, and 5 percent from Hooters merchandise, including Hooters Girls trading cards. *Restaurant & Institutions* ranked Hooters as the 75th largest foodservice chain in the United States, and 11th among casual, dinner-house restaurant concepts.

Controversy Continues: 1997–99

While the company was waging battle with outsiders an internal struggle ensued in the Hooters system. Hooters of America CEO Robert H. Brooks had bristled against the constraints of the franchise agreements with Hooters Inc. from the outset. Mickey H. Gramig wrote for the *Atlanta Journal/The Atlanta Constitution* in 1997, ''They've repeatedly lawyered the licensing agreement, altering it twice in 1984, three times in 1986, and again in 1990 and 1995.'' Hooters Inc. filed a lawsuit against Hooters of America in 1997 claiming franchise violations, including requiring franchisees to buy products from a Brooks-owned company.

Brooks's first experience with the food industry came on his family farm in South Carolina, followed by a dairy science

degree in 1960, then a seven-year stint with a food company. He founded Eastern Foods Inc. in the late 1960s, introducing the Naturally Fresh line in 1980. In 1984, while recovering from a stroke, he put up money for an associate's purchase of a Hooters franchise. Brooks took possession of the endeavor when his partner was unable to pay him back.

By 1997, the Hooters of America owned or franchised restaurants outnumbered Hooters Inc. 192 to 12. Brooks's Hooters restaurants were bringing in an average of $2 million in annual sales. Part of his profits went to buying out Hooters shareholders, purchasing a country club, and donating to charity. Among his donations was an art center at Clemson University, honoring Mark Brooks. His son had been killed in a 1993 plane crash along with Hooters of America sponsored NASCAR driver Alan Kulwicki. The company had entered into sports sponsorships to build loyalty among members of its target market.

Hooters Girls would remain all female with the settlement of a class-action lawsuit in 1997. The $3 million-plus out of court agreement compensated men denied employment as waiters because of gender. Hooters would continue to hire only women as Hooters waitresses but would consider men on an equal basis for other more visible positions, such as manager or bar assistant, according to *Time*.

The company's ability to garner controversy was not limited to the states. In Mexico, where Hooters had begun opening restaurants, they faced the challenge of translating its name and sexy image in another culture. On a broader scale, American companies were seen by some as ''corrupting Mexican values,'' according to the *Chicago Times*, especially since 1994 when the North American Free Trade Agreement went into effect. North of the border, Miss Canada International lost her crown when she became a Hooters Girl. Two years later, an Edmonton lawyer moved to keep Hooters Inc. from gaining a Canadian trademark.

The Hooters management maintained its sense of humor and even facilitated the negative product placement in the 1999 box office hit *The Spy Who Shagged Me*. ''Some might say that [Big Daddy's depiction of Hooters] was disparaging in some way,'' Ed Droste, one of the founders, told *Fortune*. ''But we're very much tongue-in-cheek; we make fun of ourselves.''

Trademark Changes Hands: 2001–05

Hooters of America purchased the Hooters trademark from Hooters Inc. in 2001. Brooks said of the $60 million deal in a *PR Newswire* release: ''As the Hooters system expands throughout the United States and internationally, we at Hooters of America felt that it was important that we own the trademark and have complete control of the Hooters concept and thus our own destiny.''

Hooters of America operated 80 company owned restaurants and had agreements with 25 domestic and 12 international franchisees, operating, respectively, 170 restaurants in the United States and 20 restaurants in countries including Canada, Mexico, Argentina, England, Singapore, Switzerland, Austria, Puerto Rico, and Aruba. Hooters Inc. would continue to operate in Tampa Bay, Chicago, and New York and gain rights of development elsewhere.

The groundwork for the trademark sale was laid in 1999. Hooters Inc. won the legal dispute over contractual agreements but Hooters of America was granted the option of acquiring all trademarks.

Hooters Air was launched in March 2003. An attempt by Brooks to buy the belly-up Vanguard line in 2002 failed, but he was able to purchase charter air carrier Pace. The company began with flights between Atlanta and Myrtle Beach where its golf course was located. The going price for tickets exceeded that of discount flights, but two Hooter Girls aboard each flight, in addition to the professional crew, were the promised perks. Other routes were in the works.

Hooters of America was highlighting its plans for international expansion during the later half of 2004 and into very early in 2005. Thailand, India, Trinidad, Shanghai, Croatia, and Australia were the locales on the docket.

Principal Competitors

Buffalo Wild Wings; Carlson Restaurants Worldwide; Metromedia Restaurant Group.

Further Reading

Baker, Ryan, "Hooters No Stranger to Controversy," *Ottawa Citizen,* June 8, 2000, p. A4,

Brovard, James, "The EEOC's War on Hooters," *Wall Street Journal,* November 17, 1995, p. A18.

Cebrzynski, Gregg, "Move Over Xena: Halle the Hooters Girl Makes Her Comic Book Debut," *Nation's Restaurant News,* February 23, 1998, pp. 106+.

de la Garza, Paul, "Opening of Hooters Exposes Nerves of Some in Mexico City," *Chicago Tribune,* November 25, 1997, p. 10.

"EEOC's Politically Correct Crusade Against Hooters a Wasted Effort," *Nation's Restaurant News,* December 4, 1995.

Farkas, David, "Hooters of America Expects Systemwide Sales to Increase from $500 Mil in 2000 to Around $570 Mil in 2001," *Chain Leader,* June 2001.

Gramig, Mickey H., "Hooters vs. Hooters: Fighting for Control," *Atlanta Journal/ Atlanta Constitution,* September 21, 1997, p. G1.

Grimsley, Kristin Downey, "Hooters Plays Hardball with the EEOC," *Washington Post,* December 10, 1995, p. H1.

Goto, Shihoko, "GoTo Shop: Hooters' Family Fun," *United Press International,* March 13, 2003.

Hagy, James, "How Big Can Hooters Get?," *Florida Trend,* September 1987, p. 80.

Hayes, Jack, "Hooters Comes Out Against EEOC's Sex-Bias Suit," *Nation's Restaurant News,* November 27, 1995, p. 3.

——, "Hooters Eyes Franchise, Int'l. Growth in 2001," *Nation's Restaurant News,* April 16, 2001, pp. 4+.

——, "Hooters Founding Group Hits Road with Pete & Shorty's 'Joints,' " *Nation's Restaurant News,* April 1, 2002.

"Hooters of America, Inc. Acquires Hooters Trademark," *PR Newswire,* March 23, 2001.

"Hooters vs. the EEOC," *Seattle Times,* May 6, 1996, p. B4.

"Hostess with the Mostest," *Economist,* June 28, 2003, p. 65US.

Huettel, Steve, "Hooters Wings, Aisle 2, Servers Not Included," *St. Petersburg Times,* October 14, 2003, p. 6E.

Mckay, Rich, "Hooters Celebrates 20 Years," *Orlando Sentinel,* May 25, 2003, p. H1.

Prewitt, Milford, "Hooters Unit Sued for Harassment," *Nation's Restaurant News,* May 3, 1993, p. 3.

Segal, David, "Hooters Vows to Decide Where the Boys Aren't," *Washington Post,* November 16, 1995, p. B11.

Shiflett, Dave, "Hooters Gals," *American Spectator,* July 1996, p. 48.

Wheat, Alynda, "One Man's Insult Is Another Man's Publicity," *Fortune,* August 16, 1999, p. 38.

Wieffering, Eric J., "Defending Hooters," *Corporate Report Minnesota,* September 1991, p. 52.

Wright, J. Nils, "Hooters Eatery Is Coming to Town with Controversial Fare," *Business Journal* (Sacramento, Calif.), April 25, 1994, p. 8.

Zagorin, Adam, "Sexism Will Be Served," *Time,* October 13, 1997, p.65.

—Dean Boyer
—update: Kathleen Peippo

Israel Aircraft Industries Ltd.

Ben Gurion International Airport
Lod 70100
Israel
Telephone: +972-3-935-3111
Fax: +972-3-935-8278
Web site: http://www.iai.co.il

State-Owned Company
Incorporated: 1953 as Bedek Aviation Company
Employees: 14,500
Sales: $2.06 billion (2002)
NAIC: 336411 Aircraft Manufacturing; 336413 Other
   Aircraft Parts and Auxiliary Equipment Manufactur-
   ing; 336414 Guided Missile and Space Vehicle Manu-
   facturing; 541614 Process, Physical Distribution, and
   Logistics Consulting Services; 811310 Commercial
   and Industrial Machinery and Equipment (Except
   Automotive and Electronic) Repair and Maintenance;
   927110 Space Research and Technology

Israel Aircraft Industries Ltd. (IAI) is a state-owned aero-space manufacturer. IAI has accounted for about 9 percent of Israel's exports and is the country's largest employer. The company's strengths include overhauling and converting jet fighters and large commercial transports, and manufacturing UAVs (un-manned aerial vehicles).

Origins

Israel has had armed conflicts with its neighbors dating back to the country's founding in 1948. The development of a domestic defense industry would become even more of a priority after France embargoed arms sales to the country after the Six Day War in 1967.

In 1953, the Ministry of Defense formed Bedek Aviation Company to maintain Israel Defense Forces (IDF) aircraft. Based at Lod Airport, the enterprise originally had 70 employees. American expatriate Al Schwimmer was the company's founder and first president.

Bedek began manufacturing aircraft six years later. The first, a V-tailed twinjet trainer of French design, was the Fouga-Magister or Snunit ("swallow"). The Arava STOL (short take-off and landing) transport aircraft followed as the first aircraft to be designed and built by IAI. It first flew in 1969 after three years of development.

Fighters and Business Jets for the 1970s and 1980s

In response to the French embargo, IAI began developing its own fighter aircraft, a derivative of the Mirage 5 called the Nesher ("eagle"), in 1968. In the same year, IAI acquired Rockwell's Jet Commander series of business aircraft. Renamed the Commodore Jet, this became the basis for the Westwind line. IAI also developed the Gabriel anti-ship missile in the mid-1960s. In the late 1960s, the Elta electronics unit developed an inexpensive aircraft radar which would become a successful export item.

The Nesher entered service in 1971, in time for the Yom Kippur War. It was followed by the Kfir ("lion cub"), which was delivered in 1975.

According to the history on IAI's web site, the number of employees had grown from 4,000 in 1968 to 14,000 in 1970. IAI was already conducting extensive overhauls on dozens of different aircraft types. Since it worked on engines as well as airframes and interiors, IAI could provide more comprehensive refurbishments than even the aircraft manufacturers themselves, noted a *New York Times* profile in 1973. In 1972, the company had bought 13 Boeing 707 airliners from TWA to refurbish and resell.

During the 1970s, IAI developed relationships with companies in the United States, which replaced France as Israel's main foreign arms supplier. Exports grew to account for 50 percent of sales in 1976. IAI accompanied its success in the military market with the Westwind business jet. Civilian products accounted for just 10 percent of sales at the beginning of the 1980s.

IAI created another line of business jets, called the Astra, by stretching the fuselage and designing a new swept wing. IAI began manufacturing the mid-sized, long range Astra business jet in 1986. It was originally marketed in the United States, the world's largest executive jet market, by a distributor and after 1988 by an IAI subsidiary, Astra Jet.

Company Perspectives:

Israel Aircraft Industries is globally recognized as a leader in developing military and commercial aerospace technology. This distinction is the result of nearly a half-century of designing, engineering and manufacturing, for customers throughout the world.

From a relatively small operation to become an industry leader, a company must be versatile and highly motivated, innovative and competitive. IAI was built around these qualities, and has improved upon them with its years of acquired experience.

The Company's ambition is to continue to initiate and achieve technological breakthroughs that characterize the best in the industry.

The Bedek maintenance unit had 4,000 employees in the mid-1980s and overhauled a huge range of aircraft, from propeller-driven trainers to airliners. In 1984, IAI formed a joint venture with rival Tadiran to market both companies' remotely piloted vehicles (RPVs).

Former air force commander General Mordechai Hod became IAI's head in 1986. Hod had directed the 1967 air strikes that destroyed neighboring air forces in the Six Day War.

Expensive aircraft development programs such as the Lavi struggled and a number of employees were laid off in the mid-1980s. Some IAI businesses were thriving, though, noted the *Financial Times,* particularly the Elta electronic warfare unit and the Bedek MRO (maintenance, repair and overhaul) division. Elta was then specializing in high-tech intelligence tools, and its sales had grown from $70 million in 1981 to about $182 million a year. Clients included Hughes and Westinghouse of the United States. Another division, Ramta, was doing a brisk business supplying armored vehicles and missile boats to third world countries. Israel exported $950 million worth of military goods in 1986, according to the *Financial Times,* and IAI accounted for two-thirds of the total. IAI was the largest company in Israel.

Lavi Canceled 1987

IAI's biggest setback was the government's cancellation (by one vote in Parliament) of the Lavi program in August 1987. IAI had invested $1.6 million in the Lavi, producing two prototypes (much of the funding was from U.S. military aid credits). The Lavi ("young lion") was designed to handle multiple missions, with strengths in the ground attack role. It first flew in 1986.

Moshe Keret, who became IAI's CEO in 1985 (he had first joined the company in 1959 as a mechanical engineer), told the *Jerusalem Post* that due to the increasing costs of developing aircraft, Israel had little hope of producing its own fighter in the foreseeable future. However, the Lavi project was credited with developing a number of advanced technologies that IAI was able to market.

By the end of the 1980s, IAI was established as a world leader in upgrading aircraft. Planes such as the Vietnam-era McDonnell Douglas Phantom II were modernized with ad-

vanced avionics and weaponry to keep them from obsolescence. The Lahav Division carried out this work.

IAI's annual sales were about $1 billion at the time. The enterprise employed more than 22,000 people, but this was cut by 5,500 in 1988 as the company lost $21 million. IAI posted a profit of $11.8 million on sales of $1.28 billion in 1989. The company had four divisions—Aircraft, Aviation, Electronics, and Technologies—and 17 factories.

Shifting Markets in the 1990s

Sales were $1.42 billion in 1990; exports were worth $1.1 billion. IAI was selling about a dozen Astra jets a year. In 1990, the Astra SP was unveiled; it featured advanced avionics and aerodynamics as well as a new interior (which was installed at the Fort Worth, Texas facility). The more powerful Astra SPX was developed a few years later. Another big civil aviation program was conversion of Boeing 747s to freighters by the Bedek Aviation division. IAI was working on a variety of aerospace projects in the 1990s, including the AMOS communications satellite and Ofeq observation satellite and Barak naval defense missile systems.

Global military spending fell dramatically as the Soviet Cold War threat dissolved. IAI posted losses from 1992 to 1996, finally breaking the slump with net income of $24.3 million on sales of $1.7 billion in 1997. The staff was reduced to 13,500 employees as part of the recovery program.

The Galaxy, a business jet with an intercontinental range, made its first flight in December 1997 and entered service in 2000. In 1999, IAI signed an agreement to have Gulfstream of the U.S. market the Astra SPX and the Galaxy under the designations G-100 and G-200.

IAI's revenues were $2 billion in 1999. The group had 14,600 employees. While annual sales had risen 7 percent, net profits of $70 million were up 71 percent from the previous year. According to the *Jerusalem Post,* IAI accounted for 9 percent of Israel's exports.

Domestically, IAI provided the IDF with the Arrow Weapon System, the first operational system able to destroy tactical ballistic missiles. It was built by IAI's MLM Division. Two of IAI's divisions, MBT and Malat, were producing UAVs.

Exports Booming After 2000

Keret told the *Jerusalem Post* he favored an eventual privatization of the company as a way to bolster its financial structure. However, the company was holding its own. Revenues rose 9 percent to $2.2 billion in 2000; exports accounted for more than three-quarters of sales. Net profit was up 26 percent to $84 million.

In May 2001, General Dynamics—Gulfstream's corporate parent—bought IAI's Galaxy Aerospace Co. L.P. unit for $330 million plus a potential performance-based bonus of up to $315 million. IAI had launched Galaxy in 1997 in a joint venture with the Hyatt Corporation to keep the Galaxy executive jet program alive. Galaxy Aerospace was based in Fort Worth, Texas, and had 3,000 employees. It had recently won a

Key Dates:

1953: Israel's Ministry of Defense forms Bedek Aviation Company to maintain Air Force planes.
1959: IAI begins manufacturing its own aircraft.
1968: IAI begins building Nesher fighter; Westwind business jet line is acquired.
1976: Exports account for 50 percent of sales.
1987: Lavi fighter program is canceled.
1999: Annual revenues reach $2 billion.
2001: Galaxy business jets are marketed by Gulfstream.
2004: India awards IAI colossal $1 billion contract for AWACS planes.
2005: New G-150 business jet is unveiled.

$2 billion order from Executive Jet Inc. for 50 aircraft. The company also maintained existing IAI business jets including the Westwind. IAI continued to manufacture the Galaxy jets and a widebody version of the G100 called the G150 was added to the lineup.

IAI's Bedek Aviation unit did a brisk business in converting passenger airlines into freighters due to growth in the air cargo industry. Bedek had sales of $500 million in 2003, according to *Globes*. An IAI source stated that the company had done 40 of the 60 Boeing 747 conversions completed since 1998.

IAI's revenues were $2.2 billion in 2000 and about $2.1 billion in 2001 and 2002. The company had about 14,500 employees. In 2002, IAI invested $99 million in a 30 percent share of Koor Industries subsidiary Elisra, which specialized in defense electronics.

IAI landed a huge $1.1 billion contract from India in March 2004. The deal called for the Elta unit to install three Phalcon AWACS planes, using radars modified from the Lavi project on Russian-made Ilyushin Il-76 transports. IAI had previously sold a shipment of Phalcons to China, but undid the deal under pressure from the United States.

The company was back in the aircraft design business. IAI was teaming with Aviation Technologies Group (ATG) of the United States to develop a low cost light jet called the Javelin for the civil and military markets. In 2005, IAI introduced its first new business jet since 1987, the six-to-eight-passenger G-150.

Principal Divisions

Military Aircraft Group; Systems Missiles & Space Group; Elta Systems LTD; Bedek Aviation Group; Commercial Aircraft Group.

Principal Operating Units

Commercial Aircraft; MRO and Conversion; Military Aircraft Upgrade; Unmanned Air Vehicles; ISR Systems; Space Systems; Theater Defense; Naval Attack and Defense Systems; Ground Systems; Homeland Defense.

Principal Competitors

Elbit Systems Ltd.; BAE SYSTEMS; The Boeing Company; Dassault Aviation; Raytheon Company.

Further Reading

"After the Lavi," *ICEN*, November 9, 1990, p. 22.
Blackburn, Nicky, and Arieh O'Sullivan, "The Sky Is the Limit," *Jerusalem Post*, Econ. Sec., May 23, 1999, p. 10.
Carnegy, Hugh, "Waging a War on Cut-Backs—The Defence Industry Is Combating the Fall in Military Spending," *Financial Times* (London), Survey, April 17, 1990, p. 31.
Egozi, Arie, "Survival Strategy," *Flight International*, November 30, 1994, p. 21.
——, "The Uncertain Arrow," *Flight International*, September 18, 1991, p. 27.
"Enduring Value," *Flight International*, September 30, 1998, p. 70.
Faber, Harold, "Big Israeli Aircraft Plant Is a Supermarket of Planes," *New York Times*, January 7, 1973, p. 64.
Frisch, Felix, "IAI Signs Phalcon Deal with India; The Supply Contract Is the Largest Ever for Israel's Defense Industries," *Israel's Business Arena*, March 7, 2004.
——, "Moshe Keret to Continue As IAI CEO," *Israel Business Arena*, February 15, 2004.
"General Dynamics Acquires IAI's Galaxy Aerospace," *Ha'aretz* (Tel Aviv), May 2, 2001.
Goldman, Marvin G., *El Al: Star in the Sky*, Miami: World Transport Press, 1990.
"Israeli High-Tech 50 Years Review," http://www.infochina.co.il/israeltech/news/review.htm.
Kestine, Hesh, "A $640 Hammer Is a Bargain," *Forbes*, June 30, 1986, pp. 46+.
Krivine, David, "Striving for Excellence," *Jerusalem Post*, Econ. Sec., May 3, 1991.
Lennon, David, "Export Sales Pick Up As Industry Adapts," *Financial Times* (London), Sec. III, Survey, Aerospace, Israel, August 28, 1984, p. XVIII.
Marom, Dror, "IAI First to Convert Boeing 747-400s to Carry Cargo," *Globes—Israel's Business Arena*, September 23, 2003.
Muscal, Tal, "Government to Float 20%–30% of Israel Aircraft Industries on TASE," *Jerusalem Post*, Econ. Sec., August 11, 2003, p. 16.
Osborne, Graeme, "IAI Sees Strength in Consolidation," *Flight International*, December 31, 2002, p. 18.
O'Sullivan, Arieh, "IAI Unveils Newest Business Jet," *Jerusalem Post*, January 18, 2005, p. 18.
"Waiting for Change," *Flight International*, December 7, 2004, p. 34.
Whitley, Andrew, "Painful Change Towards Exports," *Financial Times* (London), Survey, June 1, 1987, p. 21.
——, "Worries of a Fragile Industry," *Financial Times* (London), Survey, June 9, 1987, p. XIII.

—Frederick C. Ingram

JONES
SODA CO.®

Jones Soda Co.

234 9th Avenue North
Seattle, Washington 98109
U.S.A.
Telephone: (206) 624-3357
Toll Free: (800) 656-6050
Fax: (206) 624-6857
Web site: http://www.jonessoda.com

Public Company
Incorporated: 1987 as Urban Hand Limited
Employees: 38
Sales: $20.1 million (2003)
Stock Exchanges: Over the Counter
Ticker Symbol: JSDA
NAIC: 311421 Fruit and Vegetable Canning; 312111 Soft
Drink Manufacturing

Jones Soda Co. develops and markets alternative beverages under the Jones Soda Co. and WhoopAss labels. The company's Jones Soda Co. brand constitutes its main product line, composed of its selection of 15 Jones Soda Co. flavors and several product extensions of its Jones Soda Co. line, including sugar-free versions of its Jones Soda Co. line, Jones Naturals, a selection of noncarbonated juices and teas, and Jones Energy, citrus drinks competing in the energy category of the alternative beverage market. The company's WhoopAss brand, operated through a subsidiary company, also competes in the energy category of the alternative beverage market. Jones Soda Co.'s products are sold in 39 states in the United States and in seven provinces in Canada. The beverages are sold primarily through independent distributors to convenience stores, delicatessens, and supermarkets, but the company also employs a "direct to retail" business strategy, selling its beverages directly to retailers. Toward this end, Jones Soda Co. has reached agreements to sell its beverages in stores operated by Barnes & Noble, Panera Bread Company, CostPlus World Markets, and Starbucks Coffee Company.

Origins

The irreverent, visionary architect of Jones Soda's development has been its founder, an Edmonton, Alberta, native named Peter van Stolk. Van Stolk attended Grant McKewan College in his hometown, but he never completed his studies. His attention was focused elsewhere, specifically on his two chief interests: skiing and business. Van Stolk was an adept skier and spent the winter months in the Canadian Rockies, a passion he paid for by working as a ski instructor. When the snow melted, he turned to his other area of interest, business. Van Stolk's entrepreneurial bent found expression in a number of ventures, but his most resounding success was realized in his early 20s with the March 1987 establishment of Urban Hand Limited, Jones Soda's predecessor.

Founded in Edmonton, Urban Hand represented van Stolk's entry into the beverage distribution business. The business began modestly, involving not much more than van Stolk hawking beverages in Edmonton as an alternative to his job as a ski instructor. In September 1987, the business received a considerable boost to its stature when van Stolk brokered a deal with Just Pik't Juices. He obtained the rights to market and distribute the company's patented line of fresh squeezed juices throughout western Canada. As van Stolk devoted more and more of his time to running his distribution business, his efforts were rewarded with a fast-growing business, one that cemented his standing as an able entrepreneur in Canada's beverage distribution industry.

After spending roughly two years in Edmonton, van Stolk moved Urban Hand to Calgary, Alberta, in 1989. The following year, another move established the company's headquarters in Vancouver, British Columbia, putting van Stolk and Urban Hand a three-hour drive away from their future home in Seattle. His distribution business by this point was far more than a sideline venture. By 1991, the company ranked, on a per capita basis, as the largest distributor of Just Pik't Juices in North America, a distinction that fueled van Stolk's desire to greatly expand his business. He set out to acquire the distribution rights for other alternative, or "New Age," beverages, intent on developing a range of complementary product lines in the fast-growing sector of the beverage industry. In 1992, he acquired

Company Perspectives:

There's a lot more to the beverage industry than simply creating a product. At Jones Soda Co. we cover the categories with a full line of unique beverages, and the manufacturing, distribution and marketing knowledge to deliver the alternative to the mainstream. We are pioneers in the youth-oriented, New Age Beverage industry—an industry that generates almost $10 billion in annual sales—with the proven ability to develop and market products that resonate with today's image-conscious consumer. All of our unique products focus on the fast-growing 12- to 24-year-old market segment. With a current population of over 50 million people, this decidedly individualistic group spends more than $300 billion annually, and influences the spending of an even greater amount. At Jones Soda Co. we understand our customer. We share common beliefs, attitudes and vision with our target audience. Our products create an immediate connection with our consumer and allow them to play a part in everything Jones.

the exclusive rights to distribute Thomas Kemper Sodas throughout all of Canada. In September 1993, he acquired the exclusive rights to distribute AriZona Iced Teas for all of western Canada. Several months later, in early 1994, van Stolk secured the distribution rights for the West End Soda Brew line of products in every Canadian province except Quebec.

From Distributor to Brand Creator in 1994

By 1994, van Stolk had established Urban Hand as a comprehensive alternative beverage distributor, but just as he completed his objective he began to pursue a new goal. He wanted to develop his own brands rather than distribute the creations of others, a desire that signaled the end of Urban Hand, the distributor, and its transformation into what eventually became Jones Soda Co. For a short period of time in the mid-1990s, van Stolk split his energies between his two areas of interest, expanding his distribution business while he worked on creating his own brands. He began working on developing his own brands in 1994, which led to the introduction of the company's first internally developed brand in March 1995, a brand of bottled water marketed as WAZU. In January 1996, van Stolk introduced his second brand, Jones Soda Co.

Although van Stolk was determined to make internally developed brands the sole focus of his business efforts, his company increased its involvement in the distribution side of the alternative beverage industry while the WAZU and Jones Soda Co. labels tested their market worth. In April 1995, the company acquired the rights to Lahaina Iced Teas and Lemonades. The following month, the company acquired the rights to distribute Odwalla's line of fresh fruit and vegetable-based beverages. After these transactions were concluded, van Stolk began to terminate the distribution agreements he had made, freeing his company to focus exclusively on creating and marketing its own brands. The company discontinued the distribution of Odwalla in February 1996, Lahaina Iced Teas and Lemonades in May 1996, Thomas Kemper Sodas in September 1996, West

End Soda Brews in October 1996, and its mainstay line, Just Pik't Juices, in December 1996. By the beginning of 1997, the company, operating as Urban Juice & Soda Company Ltd., was exclusively focused on developing its own brands.

As van Stolk's career as a distributor was coming to an end, his brand-development career showed encouraging promise. The stronger of his two initial brands was Jones Soda Co., which debuted in six traditional flavors in western Canada, Massachusetts, and Washington State. Van Stolk employed unusual marketing methods to bring recognition to his sodas, putting his own coolers, each decorated with distinctive flames, in venues such as snowboarding shops, tattoo and body-piercing studios, clothing stores, and music stores. "I wanted to create a brand," van Stolk remarked in a March 2, 2001 interview with *Puget Sound Business Journal,* "realizing the world doesn't need another soda. I wanted to create a product that would make an emotional connection." To help make such a connection, van Stolk offered consumers the opportunity to design the labels affixed to Jones Soda Co. bottles, a marketing ploy that created a stir of interest in the new brand.

The Jones Soda Co. brand quickly caught the interest of both consumers and the press, helping van Stolk gain entry into more conventional distribution channels. The company's sodas were the subject of several *New York Times* articles in 1996 and 1997 and featured on the national television program *NBC News Today* at the end of 1997. The media attention gave van Stolk the leverage to negotiate deals with national retail chains, which greatly increased the availability of his sodas. To take full advantage of the exposure his brand was receiving, van Stolk began developing product extensions, creating spinoff brands of the Jones Soda Co. line. In June 1998, the company introduced Natural Jones Soda, a natural soda formulation that debuted in three flavors. In January 1999, the company launched Slim Jones, a line of diet sodas. Later in the year, in October, the company introduced Jones Soda WhoopAss, a citrus drink containing riboflavin, niacin, vitamin B6, and thiamin that was developed to compete in the energy category of the New Age beverage industry. (The word "Jones" was dropped from the name of the brand several months after its debut, abbreviating the brand name to "WhoopAss.")

Van Stolk's unconventional marketing tactics reached a new level in 1999, as he enhanced the interactive quality of the relationship between Jones Soda Co. and its customers. During the year, the company launched a new web site, www.myjones.com, that allowed consumers to create personalized 12-packs of Jones Soda Co. beverages. Instead of submitting a label design and hoping it would be selected by the company's staff, customers could scan their photographs through www.myjones.com and crop and create their own labels, which were downloaded at the company's head office, packed, and shipped to the consumer.

By the end of 1999, van Stolk's business was a recognizable, national force in the alternative beverage industry. The company's products were available in 41 states and in eight provinces in Canada. By this point, the Jones Soda Co. brand consisted of 15 flavors ranging from conventional formulations such as Orange Soda and Grape Soda to peculiar, eye-catching formulations such as Blue Bubblegum Soda and Pineapple Upside-Down

Key Dates:

1987: Peter van Stolk founds Urban Hand Limited.
1994: Van Stolk begins to develop his own beverage brands.
1996: Jones Soda Co. is launched, debuting in six flavors.
1998: Natural Jones Soda is introduced.
1999: WhoopAss, a citrus drink developed to compete in the energy category of the alternative beverage industry, is introduced.
2000: Van Stolk moves his company from Vancouver, British Columbia, to Seattle, Washington, and renames it Jones Soda Co.
2001: Jones Juice debuts.
2002: Jones Juice is renamed Jones Naturals.
2003: Jones Soda Co. begins to negotiate distribution agreements with national retailers, securing deals with Barnes & Noble, Panera Bread Company, and CostPlus World Markets.
2004: Jones Soda Co. signs an agreement with Starbucks Coffee Company to carry two flavors of soda in all of the chain's U.S. stores.

Soda. In July 1999, the company forged an important relationship with Starbucks Coffee Company that put Jones Soda Co. beverages in all of the chain's stores in western Canada, an agreement that paved the way for a later agreement with Starbucks for distribution in the chain's stores in the United States.

As van Stolk's Urban Juice & Soda entered the 21st century, the company began to contend with issues stemming from its success. The early years of the new decade were devoted to reorganization and re-branding initiatives, beginning with the relocation of the company in January 2000. Urban Juice & Soda exited the 1990s deriving 84 percent of its sales from the United States, which prompted van Stolk to move the company's headquarters from Vancouver to Seattle at the start of 2000. In another move that acknowledged the primary forces that underpinned its success, the company changed its name. The Jones Soda Co. brand, including the product extensions of the company's carbonated line, generated more than 85 percent of Urban Juice & Soda's total revenues. Accordingly, Jones Soda Co. was adopted as the official corporate title of the company in August 2000.

Jones Soda Co. in the 21st Century

With a new name and a new home base, the company began working on a new product extension. In November 2000, work began on developing a new line of products to be marketed as Jones Juice. The development efforts were made public in February 2001, when the company announced that it was preparing to introduce a line of Jones Juice products in April 2001. The product line debuted with two varieties of teas and four varieties of juices that were sold in 20-ounce bottles. Featuring all natural flavors, Jones Juice beverages contained ingredients such as ginseng, royal jelly, kava kava, zinc, and valerian root.

Jones Soda Co.'s reorganization efforts were underway in the spring of 2002. One of the changes implemented involved

re-branding the Jones Juice line. The name Jones Juice was dropped and replaced with Jones Naturals (the company stopped producing its original line of Natural Jones in June 2000). The change was part of a comprehensive reorganization of the company's structure that divided its operations along its two separate brands, Jones Soda Co. and WhoopAss. In March 2002, the same month Jones Juice was renamed Jones Naturals, the operation of WhoopAss became the responsibility of a subsidiary named WhoopAss USA Inc.

In 2003, Jones Soda Co. recorded a number of notable accomplishments that pointed to a promising future for the company. It recorded its first annual profit during the year, ending a string of consecutive annual losses. The company also continued to realize success in introducing new products. Jones Soda Co. introduced three new sugar-free products in September 2003—Sugar-Free Black Cherry, Sugar-Free Root Beer, and Sugar-Free Ginger Ale—but the year's most noteworthy product launch was the debut of its Turkey & Gravy Soda in the weeks leading up to Thanksgiving. The offering sold out online almost immediately after attracting attention from coast to coast. Although the interest generated by the debut of Turkey & Gravy Soda did much for Jones Soda Co.'s visibility, it overshadowed a more meaningful development during 2003, one whose contribution to the company's growth promised a Jones Soda Co. of a much larger scale.

Van Stolk and his small group of executives began looking at a new way to distribute the company's products. They began to negotiate directly with large national retailers to carry the company's products, employing a "direct to retail" strategy. In April 2003, the company secured its first such agreement, signing a three-year deal with Barnes & Noble to carry Jones Naturals in Barnes & Noble Cafes throughout the United States. In June 2003, the company signed another lucrative contract, reaching an agreement with Panera Bread Company to sell six flavors of Jones Soda and three flavors of Jones Naturals in more than 500 of the chain's bakery-cafes. In November 2003, Jones Soda Co. signed an agreement with the 201-store CostPlus chain to carry six flavors of Jones Soda in all of the company's stores.

As Jones Soda Co. entered the mid-2000s, the increasing exposure of the company's beverages promised to deliver substantial growth in the years ahead. In March 2004, the company signed an agreement with Starbucks to carry two flavors of Jones Soda in the all of the chain's U.S. stores. In August 2004, the company completed two big deals, signing agreements with Target Corporation to carry Jones Soda in the chain's 1,275 stores and with Winn-Dixie Stores Inc. to carry seven flavors of Jones Soda in more than 1,000 stores. With these direct-to-retail agreements bringing the flavors of the company closer to a much larger percentage of the population, considerable growth seemed inevitable, particularly given the public's fascination with the concoctions dreamed up by van Stolk and his employees. The company's holiday offering at the end of 2004 did not disappoint those consumers intrigued by the introduction of Turkey & Gravy Soda. At select locations in November 2004, Jones Soda Co. offered a $15.95 six-pack containing Turkey & Gravy Soda, Cranberry Soda, Mashed Potato & Butter Soda, Fruitcake Soda, and Green Bean Casserole Soda.

Principal Subsidiaries

WhoopAss USA Inc.

Principal Competitors

Cadbury Schweppes PLC; The Coca-Cola Company; PepsiCo, Inc.; Hansen Natural Corporation; Pyramid Breweries Inc.

Further Reading

Blake, Judith, "Pop Psychology Jones Soda Founder Peter Van Stolk Makes His Young Customers Feel Like the Quirky Specialty Soft-Drink Brand Belongs to Them," *Seattle Times,* March 10, 2004, p. C1.

Ennen, Steve, "Jones'n Hard," *Food Processing,* August 2001, p. 52.

"Jones Soda Co. Announces Reorganization of Brand Groups," *PrimeZone Media Network,* March 7, 2002.

"Jones Soda Co. Launches Five New Holiday Flavors," *Canadian Corporate News,* November 8, 2004, p. 32.

"Jones Soda Listed in 1,022 Winn-Dixie Stores," *Canadian Corporate News,* August 10, 2004, 13.

"Jones Soda Signed a Distribution Agreement Deal with Target," *Brandweek,* August 9, 2004, p. 5.

"Jones Soda Swamped with Requests for Turkey & Gravy Soda," *Canadian Corporate News,* November 20, 2003, p. 21.

Kaplan, Andrew, "Oh My, My Jones," *Beverage World,* December 15, 2002, p. 12.

King, Paul, "Sodas Bring New Meaning to 'Turkey in the Straw,'" *Nation's Restaurant News,* November 29, 2004, p. 20.

—Jeffrey L. Covell

Kerzner International Limited

Coral Towers
Paradise Island
Bahamas
Telephone: (242) 363-6000
Fax: (242) 363-5401
Web site: http://www.kerzner.com

Public Company
Incorporated: 1993 as Sun International Hotels Ltd.
Employees: 11,485
Sales: $561.3 million (2003)
Stock Exchanges: New York
Ticker Symbol: KZL
NAIC: 713290 Other Gambling Industries

Based in the Bahamas, Kerzner International Limited is a publicly traded premiere resort operator listed on the New York Stock Exchange and named after its famous founder and chairman, Solomon "Sol" Kerzner—the one-time vilified builder of South Africa's Sun City resort. Although all but one of the company's properties features a casino, Kerzner relies less on gaming income than does his competitors, focusing his attention instead on income derived from rooms and the sale of food and beverages. The company's flagship property is the Atlantis, Paradise Island resort complex in the Bahamas. Taking the legend of Atlantis as its theme, the resort offers 2,300 rooms, 35 restaurants and lounges, a 100,000-square-foot casino entertainment complex, an 88,000-square-foot convention center, and a full-service marina. Kerzner also operates a string of smaller, luxury five-star resorts under the One&Only brand. On Paradise Island, the company operates the Ocean Club, which has been catering to Hollywood celebrities and royalty since the 1940s. In addition, the One&Only label has been applied to resorts located in the Maldives, Mexico, Dubai, and Mauritius. Kerzner also has attempted to crack the U.S. market, resulting in setbacks in Atlantic City and Las Vegas. The one success is the company's 50 percent interest in the Mohegan Sun, a Connecticut tribal gaming resort. Howard Kerzner, the founder's son, now serves as the company's chief executive officer.

Company Founder: A 1950s Accountant

Sol Kerzner was born in 1935 in a poor section of Johannesburg, South Africa, the child of Russian Jewish immigrants. As a youngster he worked in the family's small hotel, peddling potato chips and chewing gum. He proved to be ambitious and aggressive and went on to college at the University of Witwatersrand in Johannesburg, where he earned a degree in accounting and became a welterweight boxing champion. After graduating in 1958, Kerzner took a position at one of South Africa's leading accounting firms. Although he became a junior partner by the age of 25, he found the work less than stimulating and decided to become involved in the hotel business, but in a manner decidedly different from his family's kosher hotel. He told *Hotels* in a 2004 profile, "I always thought a hotel should be more than a bed factory. It should have good restaurants, nice pubs, good entertainment." Kerzner convinced his family to buy a second hotel—described by some as a fleabag hotel or a "dockside dive"—that had a liquor license. He leased the hotel and managed it at night and on weekends while continuing to hold down his accounting job. Kerzner's concept of adding entertainment to a hotel was novel in South Africa and proved very popular.

The taste of success only whetted Kerzner's appetite, inspiring him to build South Africa's first five-star hotel, despite never having seen a five-star hotel or having been out of the country in his life. Nevertheless, in 1963 he was able to raise $200,000 from a former accounting client and forged ahead. He acquired some beachfront property in a small fishing village near Durban, South Africa, and then did some belated homework. As he told *Hotels,* "I decided I should probably get on a plane and see that I wasn't building something stupid." Kerzner spent several days in the United States visiting hotels in New York City and Miami Beach. Although he would not visit California, when it came time to name his new 80-room five-star hotel, he chose Beverly Hills, "because it sounded glamorous, and I knew it was going to be a glamorous hotel and that all the glamorous people in South Africa were going to want to be there." He was proven right, and he followed this success with another luxury hotel in Durban, the 450-room Elangeni, turning to South African Breweries (SAB) for financing. Because SAB wanted to make the transition from the beer business to the hotel business, Kerzner now had the financial backing to become a hotel magnate. Over the next several years he built the Southern Sun chain of more than 30 high-end hotels in South Africa.

The crown jewel of the Southern Sun chain was the Sun City resort. South Africa at the time was both segregationist, practicing the notorious apartheid system that kept blacks and whites separate, and puritanical. With the exception of horse racing, gambling was illegal. When the government established black homeland states, which were allowed to make their own laws, Kerzner took advantage of the situation and in 1977 he struck a deal with Bophuthatswana—a state with a population of 1.4 million and an average annual income of less than $500—to gain exclusive gaming rights. Here he built the legendary resort Sun City, which opened in 1979. It featured a man-made lake, a 148,000-acre wildlife park, four hotels, casino, two golf courses, and a 6,000-seat arena. To open the arena in 1981, Kerzner paid Frank Sinatra $2 million for nine performances over a week.

Guilt by Association Hindering 1980s Growth

Because South Africa's apartheid system was receiving increased condemnation from around the world, Sun City had to pay entertainers a premium. Kerzner maintained that Sun City was unfairly targeted by anti-apartheid forces, arguing that Bophuthatswana allowed blacks and whites to mix openly, and that the resort provided thousands of jobs to blacks and brought in tax revenue to the homeland state. Nevertheless, Sun City became a symbol of apartheid to many, its reputation firmly established in 1985 by the protest song "Sun City," in which such celebrity singers as Bruce Springsteen, Bono, and Bob Dylan chanted a pledge, "I ain't gonna play Sun City." In 1983 Kerzner broke away from SAB, retaining Sun City and four other casino hotels located in the independent homelands. His company was called Sun International South Africa. Although he harbored international ambitions, Kerzner found it difficult to transcend his association with South Africa and apartheid. In the early 1980s he failed to convince Atlantic City to allow him to build a $250 million hotel casino. Investments in France and Australia were also rebuffed. It was not until the release from prison of Nelson Mandela, the longtime black opponent of apartheid, that Kerzner began to see business pick up at Sun City and he was able to expand internationally.

Kerzner's first order of business was to upgrade the Sun City complex. In 1992 he opened The Lost City, a $300 million resort designed to look like a city buried by a volcano and rediscovered centuries later. In addition to a 338-room hotel called The Palace, The Lost City included a man-made jungle complete with rivers and waterfalls. While The Lost City helped to renew interest in Sun City, it also served as a trial run for

Kerzner's next project, the Atlantis resort on the Paradise Island stretch of beach near Nassau, in the Bahamas.

During the 1980s and early 1990s both Donald Trump and Merv Griffin failed to turn Paradise Island Resort & Casino into a gambling mecca in the Caribbean. The property fell into disrepair and eventually filed for bankruptcy under Griffin. In 1993 Kerzner incorporated Sun International Hotels Ltd. in the Bahamas in order to purchase the Paradise Island complex from Griffin's Resorts International, Inc., paying $125 million for the property in 1994—Kerzner's first major acquisition outside of South Africa. He picked up three hotels, a golf course, a small airline and airport, and acres of undeveloped beachfront property. He also took over a complex that was in woeful condition, both in terms of the operation and the physical condition. Most of the buildings leaked and the famous Ocean Club had been virtually destroyed by termites. Not only would Kerzner have to rebuild Paradise Island's structures, he also faced the daunting task of repairing the marketing damage done to the resort, as many people who had once vacationed in the Bahamas now traveled to resorts elsewhere in the Caribbean, Puerto Rico, and Mexico. Kerzner quickly took steps to integrate the Paradise Island properties into a massive resort and get it opened for business, essentially designing while building. As he explained to *Hotels*, "When we started Atlantis my idea was to bring the ocean into the resort and create these fish habitats. I again felt that if we were really going to do it, it really had to be the right scale." During this first phase, Kerzner spent $100 million to build a themed hotel tower and add a water park that offered raft rides, water slides, and an outdoor aquarium with live sharks. The resort reopened in December 1994 as the Atlantis Paradise Island, occupancy quickly increased by 16 percent, and the resort essentially revitalized the Bahamas' tourism industry. But Kerzner was only beginning to realize his dream for Paradise Island. Construction on phase II of Atlantis, costing nearly $500 million, was already underway.

Even as Kerzner was dedicating a great deal of his resources to the Bahamas, he also was turning his attention to the United States. In the early 1990s he became involved in the rapidly growing tribal gaming industry. The Indian Gaming Regulatory Act of 1988 gave Native American tribes the right to conduct gaming on tribal lands, including casinos with state permission. One of the most successful of the Native American casinos was the Foxwoods resort, located near North Stonington, Connecticut. It was run by the Mashantucket Pequot Indians, which as a matter of historical fact were virtually eradicated by English settlers and rival tribes in 1637. Members of the reconstituted tribe had to be one-sixteenth Pequot, but these requirements were soon loosened so that anyone who could trace his or her lineage to a Pequot listed in the 1900 or 1910 census was eligible to apply for tribal membership. Foxwoods, located close to New York and Boston, was an immediate success, attracting the attention of another branch of the Mashantucket Pequot family tree, the Mohegans, who broke away before the 1600s and moved to Connecticut. For years a group of about 1,000 people claiming Mohegan lineage petitioned the U.S. Bureau of Indian Affairs to be recognized as a sovereign tribe. Helping them through the process that would lead to a highly coveted gaming license was hotel developer Len Wolman. After the Mohegans gained their recognition, Wolman, who had never run a casino, turned to Kerzner for

Key Dates:

1979: Sol Kerzner opens Sun City resort in South Africa.
1993: Kerzner forms Sun International Hotels Ltd. to acquire Paradise Island resort.
1996: Mohegan Sun resort opens.
1998: Phase II of the Paradise Island complex is completed.
2002: The Kerzner International name is adopted.
2003: Ground is broken on phase III development of Paradise Island.

help. Sun International and Wolman's group of investors formed Trading Cove Associates, which built Mohegan Sun, a casino resort located just ten miles away from Foxwoods in Montville, Connecticut, opening in October 1996. Trading Cove would operate the resort for several years, taking 40 percent of the profits, and after the Mohegans assumed control, the venture would continue to receive a cut of the profits.

Disappointment in the U.S. Market in the 1990s

Flush with successes in the Bahamas and Connecticut, Kerzner tried once more to become involved in Atlantic City, as well as Las Vegas. Again he looked to pick up the pieces left behind by Merv Griffin. After selling his interest in Sun City in 1996, he bought Merv Griffin's Griffin Gaming & Entertainment, acquiring an older 644-room casino. He promised to bring something special to Atlantic City, but the venture proved to be one of the few failures in Kerzner's career. Atlantic City was too mature a market and he was simply unable to compete on price. Eventually Sun International Hotels sold the property, altogether losing $1 billion on the venture. During the late 1990s Kerzner also cast his eye on Las Vegas. He was on the verge of buying the Desert Inn casino located in the heart of the city's Strip and famous for housing the reclusive Howard Hughes. In the end, Kerzner backed out of the deal, concluding that he could spend $2 billion and still have difficulty standing out in a market like Las Vegas. Chastened by his experience in Atlantic City and Las Vegas, Kerzner chose to concentrate on what he did best, developing one-of-a-kind theme resorts where he was able to operate as a virtual monopoly.

Phase II of Atlantis Paradise Island opened in 1998, adding the 1,200-room Royal Towers hotel, which featured a six-story "Hall of Waters" lobby and 50,000-square-foot casino. Despite the slump that hit the tourist industry in the aftermath of the September 11, 2001, terrorist attacks on the United States, business at Atlantis remained strong and the resort continued to contribute the lion's share of revenues and profits for Sun International. However, Kerzner, although well into his 60s, continued to harbor big dreams. He was now aided by his son, Butch Kerzner, who, after earning an M.B.A. from Stanford University, spent several years on Wall Street involved in mergers and acquisitions. Although he would not officially become chief executive officer until 2003, several years earlier he took over the day-to-day responsibilities of running Sun International Hotels, which in 2002 changed its name to Kerzner International Limited.

The younger Kerzner brought a new aggressive spirit to the company, launching a number of initiatives. In 2002 the company unveiled its One&Only brand of luxury resorts, a label applied to its collection of luxury resorts to serve as a marketing umbrella. One&Only started out with five properties, including the Ocean Club in the Bahamas and properties in Mauritius and Dubai. Soon the collection was supplemented by the addition of a resort in the Maldives and the reopening of a resort in Mauritius. The company also bought a half-interest and took over the management of the Palmilla Resort in Los Cabos, Mexico, and the Royal Mirage in Dubai was doubled in size. Kerzner International also looked to brand its Atlantis concept. In 2003 it struck a deal to develop a $650 million Arabian-inspired resort on man-made Palm Island located off the coast of Dubai, to be called Atlantis, The Palm. In much the same way that Disney transplanted its theme parks around the world, The Palm was Kerzner's first step in making the Atlantis brand global, perhaps one day taking it to Europe and Asia.

In the meantime, the company had not forgotten about its flagship Paradise Island resort. After negotiating about $93 million in concessions from the Bahamian government in 2003, it launched a $600 million expansion project, immediately breaking ground on three luxury villas at the One&Only Ocean Club. The plan also called for the construction of a 1,200-room Pirate's Cove hotel, new water-entertainment features, new restaurants, retail shops, expansion of the convention space, and a new 18-hole golf course. The company owned a considerable number of acres of Paradise Island, more than enough to accommodate its ultimate goal of 5,000 rooms in the complex. Kerzner International, along with American competitors, also began pursuing opportunities in the United Kingdom, which was in the midst of deregulating its gaming industry to allow Las Vegas-style gambling. With a second generation of the Kerzner family well established in a leadership role, there was every reason to expect the resort operator to continue to pursue an aggressive growth strategy for many years to come.

Principal Subsidiaries

Trading Cove Associates (50%); Harborside at Atlantis (50%); Sun Hotels International (Bermuda) Limited; Sun International Management (UK) Ltd.

Principal Competitors

Caesars Entertainment, Inc.; Harrah's Entertainment, Inc.; Trump Hotels & Casinos, Inc.

Further Reading

Arellano, Luisa Esquiroz, "One-Man Brand," *Travel Agent,* April 14, 2003, p. 36.
"King Sol," *Time,* September 12, 1983, p. 53.
Lubove, Seth, "Atlantis Rising," *Forbes,* November 1, 2004, p. 108.
Schuman, Michael, "Here Comes the Sun," *Forbes,* September 26, 1994, p. 62.
Strauss, Karyn, "Hoteliers of the World," *Hotels,* November 2004, p. 38.
Watkins, Ed, "High-End Gold," *Lodging Hospitality,* June 2003, p. 24.

—Ed Dinger

Krung Thai Bank Public Company Ltd.

35 Sukhumvit Road, Khlong Toei Nu
Bangkok 10110
Thailand
Telephone: +66 2 255 2222
Fax: +66 2 255 9391
Web site: http://www.ktb.co.th

Public Company
Incorporated: 1966
Employees: 15,000
Total Assets: $27.47 billion (2003)
Stock Exchanges: Thailand
Ticker Symbol: KTB
NAIC: 522110 Commercial Banking

Krung Thai Bank Public Company Ltd. is Thailand's largest bank and also one of four banks controlled by the Thai government. Krung Thai boasts the largest banking network in Thailand, with more than 500 branches, including nearly 100 in Bangkok. The bank also operates nearly a dozen branch offices overseas, including in Hanoi, Vietnam; Mumbai, India; Phnom Penh, Cambodia; Vientiane, Laos; Rangoon, Burma; Singapore; the Cayman Islands; Los Angeles; New York City; and Kunming, China. Krung Thai also operates the largest network of automated teller machines in Thailand. Since 2004, Krung Thai has stepped up its expansion of its automated teller network, adding more than 250 machines that year, and launching plans to add more than 600 ATMs in 2005. Krung Thai offers a full range of private and corporate banking services and products, including deposit services, loan and mortgage products, credit cards, and other services. The bank is a major lender to Thailand's business sector, especially to small and medium-sized businesses, and also provides lending for the country's municipal and national governments. The bank's lending policies are often dictated by the Thai government. For example, Krung Thai has been given the objective of providing grants of up to THB 1 million ($24,000) to every Thai village. The bank also has been given a directive to provide loans to the country's poor rural population. Following another government directive,

Krung Thai set up a separate Islamic Bank with features specifically tailored to the religious needs of the country's southern Muslim population. These government-inspired lending imperatives have often brought Krung Thai into difficulty, however, saddling the bank with higher-than-average bad debt ratios. Krung Thai underwent a partial privatization in 2004, listing 27 percent of its stock on the Thailand Stock Exchange. The Thai government controls the remainder of the company.

Political Banking Tool in the 1960s

Banking remained, in large part, unknown in Thailand, then known as Siam, through the mid-19th century. Pawnshops, often run by Chinese immigrants, which appeared in the 1860s, remained the country's only financial institutions until much later in the century.

The first full-fledged bank to be set up in Thailand was a branch of the British-owned Hong Kong and Shanghai Bank, which opened in Bangkok in 1888. The country's banking sector remained driven by foreign interests into the beginning of the 20th century, with the arrival of Chartered Bank in 1884, and France's Banque de l'Indochine, established in 1897. Foreign banks dominated the country's financial scene into the mid-20th century; by then there were a dozen foreign banks operating in the country. These banks focused primarily on financing trade between their home countries and Thailand, however.

In 1904, a group of Chinese immigrants came together to form their own bank. Initially called the "Book Club," the bank was renamed as Siam Commercial Bank in 1906. Other banks followed over the next several decades, including the Providence Bank, Wang Lee Bank, established in 1933, the Tan Peng Chuan Bank, formed in 1934, and the Bank of Asia, in 1939. Most of the country's banking sector remained privately controlled, and for the most part were owned by Chinese groups and families, or by the country's noble class.

The rise of a domestic banking industry brought the need to create a central banking organization. The creation of the National Banking Bureau in 1939 provided an initial effort toward providing centralized banking functions. A formal central bank, the Bank of Thailand, was then established in 1942.

Company Perspectives:

Strategic Intent: Krung Thai Bank intends to be a "Convenience Bank."

A center of wide variety of quality financial products that meet people's needs by providing core banking business in accepting deposits, lending, accepting payments and collaborating with other businesses in offering the best products for sale through the Bank.

Located in suitable areas, convenient to buy, easy to pay, no wasted time. Open daily at any hour.

Mission: Presenting financial services that reach the target customer segments with speedy and accurate services at competitive prices through branch network covering all areas nationwide by adhering to good management principle.

The Bank of Thailand and the Thai government began to assert their sovereignty over the Thai financial market in the mid-1950s. The passage of new legislation in 1955 restricting foreign banks' entry into Thailand encouraged the growth of the domestic sector.

Yet the Thai government itself became an active participant in the country's business and financial sectors. The passage of the Government Organization Bill in 1953 gave the Thai government the right to set up its own businesses as a means of stimulating the country's economic development, providing jobs as well as public services. These businesses were provided with funding from the country's budget, and spurred the creation of a number of important Thai companies. Among these were the Thai Playing Cards Manufacturing Factory, the Thailand Tobacco Monopoly, the Liquor Distillery Organization, and, later, the Government Lottery Office.

The bill also inspired the government to create a number of banks targeting different areas of the nation's economy. For example, the government set up the Government Housing Bank, the Export-Import Bank of Thailand, and the Government Savings Bank. Another early government-owned banking initiative was the creation of the Agricultural Bank.

In 1966, the Thai government took over a private bank, the Providence Bank Limited, and merged it with the Agricultural Bank, forming a new major national bank, Krung Thai Bank. Krung Thai was created as a state-owned enterprise, placed under control of the Ministry of Finance. As such, and in order to emphasize the government's intention to transform Krung Thai into one of its primary financial arms, Krung Thai adopted the Ministry of Finance's symbol—the mythical Wayupak bird—as its own logo.

Krung Thai launched operations with assets of more than THB 4.5 billion and deposits of THB 4.2 billion. The bank began opening new branches throughout Thailand, and by the late 1980s had established the largest banking network, with more than 288 branches operating in every one of the country's provinces. By then, too, Krung Thai had added international operations, opening its first foreign branch in New York in 1982. Other branches were to follow over the next two decades, and by 2004 the bank had branches in Vietnam, India, Cambo-

dia, Laos, Burma, Singapore, the Cayman Islands, and China, as well as a second U.S. office in Los Angeles.

Krung Thai and the government's other banks enabled the Thai government to take control of the domestic banking market during the 1970s. By the beginning of the 1980s, the country's financial market was dominated by a handful of primary government-owned banks, which in turn were closely guided by the Bank of Thailand. Although a number of foreign banks remained present in Thailand, they had become only marginal players.

Thailand's banks, meanwhile, played an important role in financing the country's strong economic growth during the period. Yet the banks' lending policies more often reflected political interests rather than financial sense. By the middle of the decade, the banking sector had slumped into crisis and a number of the country's banks were on the verge of collapse. In 1987, Krung Thai's role evolved to include the rescue of the failed Thai banks. One of these was the Asia Trust Bank, which had been rocked by a financial scandal earlier in the decade. After that bank, in the interim renamed as Sayam Bank, collapsed in August of 1987, its assets were transferred to Krung Thai. As a result, Krung Thai emerged as the country's leading bank, with the largest branch office network.

Government Cleanup Vehicle in the 2000s

Krung Thai grew steadily through the 1990s. In 1989, the bank's shares were first listed on the Thailand Stock Exchange, although Krung Thai remained under government control. In that year, also, Krung Thai was the first of Thailand's banks to be given the right to roll out an automated teller network. In 1994, the company was reincorporated as a public limited company, with its English name changed to Krung Thai Bank Public Company Ltd. The following year, Krung Thai was given the new status as a Group 1 State Enterprise, acknowledging its position as the country's largest bank.

During this period, the bank was led by Sirin Nimmanahaeminda, brother of Thai Finance Minister Tarrin Nimmanahaeminda. Appointed in 1992, Nimmanahaeminda led Krung Thai into a period in which, on paper at least, Krung Thai emerged as one of Thailand's most profitable banks.

Yet the economic crisis that began in Thailand in 1997 and swept through the Asian region exposed the extreme vulnerability of the Thai banking sector. Unsound lending policies, and particularly unbridled lending during Thailand's property boom in the early part of the decade, brought Thailand's banking sector to its knees.

The government tapped Krung Thai, with its reputation for profitability, to play a central role in the restructuring of the Thai banking sector. Over the next two years, Krung Thai absorbed several of the country's teetering banks, including First Bangkok City Bank, which was merged into Krung Thai in 1998.

By 1999, however, Krung Thai's true financial position was revealed with the leak of an internal audit—fully 84 percent of the bank's loans were, in fact, nonperforming. The resulting scandal led to the departure of Sirin Nimmanahaeminda. By September 2000, the Thai government was forced to come to

Key Dates:

1966: Krung Thai Bank is formed from the merger of government-owned Agriculture Bank and privately held Providence Bank as a state-owned enterprise.
1982: The bank opens its first foreign office in New York City.
1987: Krung Thai absorbs the assets of failed Sayam Bank (Asia Trust Bank).
1989: Krung Thai introduces its first ATM machines in Thailand; the bank lists stock on the Thailand Stock Exchange.
1994: The bank is registered as a public corporation; the English name is changed to Krung Thai Bank Public Company Ltd.
1997: Krung Thai absorbs the failed First Bangkok City bank along with several other banks during the Thai banking crisis.
1999: The Thai government takes over $12 billion in non-performing loans from Krung Thai.
2004: Krung Thai begins developing a new plan as a convenience bank, planning to open 40 new branches and 850 new ATMs by the end of 2005.

Krung Thai's rescue, taking over THB 520 billion ($12.22 billion) of Krung Thai's worst performing loans, essentially cleaning the bank's balance sheet. In exchange, the Thai government took greater control of Krung Thai's stock, holding more than 92 percent by the end of the decade.

Krung Thai began a restructuring, including cutting back a payroll that had grown to more than 15,000. The bank also introduced computer-driven information systems for the first time. The bank remained a central part of Thailand's redevelopment plans, now led by new prime minister and tycoon, Thaksin Shinawatra. Under Shinawatra, Krung Thai was encouraged to underwrite the growth of the country's business sector. Into the mid-2000s, Krung Thai gained a great deal of new business, although much of that came from picking up defaulted business loans from other banks.

On a positive side, Krung Thai enacted another government initiative, that of bringing so-called Islam banks to the country's predominantly Muslim population in the south. The move, seen as a means of easing tensions in the regions, provided banking facilities adapted to Islamic law for the first time. Krung Thai set up the first branch of its new Islamic banking service at the end of 2001. By the end of 2002, the service had opened several more branches and had attracted deposits of more than THB 100 billion.

Krung Thai continued to expand its loan portfolio, which had grown 70 percent by 2004. The bank's role as financial backer for the country's small businesses and poor was underscored by a series of television commercials portraying it as a white knight come to rescue small businessmen. Into mid-decade, Krung Thai's aggressive lending policies had given it control of some 17 percent of Thailand's total commercial lending.

In October 2004, Krung Thai was partially privatized again, with a new listing of 27 percent of its shares on the Thailand Stock Exchange. The share offering was highly successful, yet quickly ran into trouble. At the end of 2004, the bank revealed that its nonperforming loan rate had risen to 12 percent, sparking fears of a new lending crisis. Nonetheless, most analysts considered the bank financially sound, despite the higher-than-expected bad loan rate.

Krung Thai had begun to reinvent itself as it moved toward mid-decade. Under bank President Viroj Nualkhair, and his successor, Apisak Tantivorawong, who took over in December 2004, Krung Thai began repositioning itself as a convenience bank, with plans to step up its fee income revenues. As part of that plan, the bank began expanding its bank network, with 40 new branches to open through 2005, and its ATM network. In 2004, the bank added 250 new ATMs and expected to add as many as 600 through 2005. As Thailand's largest bank, Krung Thai remained an essential component in the country's economy.

Principal Competitors

Sumitomo Mitsui Banking Corporation; Bank of Tokyo-Mitsubishi Ltd.; Industrial and Commercial Bank of China; Mizuho Corporate Bank Ltd.; China Construction Bank; Bank of China Ltd.; Agricultural Bank of China; Hongkong and Shanghai Banking Corporation Ltd.; Japan Bank for International Cooperation; Mitsubishi Trust and Banking Corporation; Kookmin Bank.

Further Reading

Arnold, Wayne, ''Investors Worried and Angry Over Thai Bank's Risky Loans,'' *New York Times,* August 25, 2004, p. W1.
Cholada, Ingrisawang, ''Thai Bank to Expand Its China Base,'' *Bangkok Post,* September 17, 2001.
Chudasri, Darana, ''Thai Bank Hopes to Wrap Up Its Privatization Plans in Fourth Quarter,'' *Bangkok Post,* January 17, 2002.
Hamlin, Kevin, and Robert Horn, ''Chatu Mongol Took the High Road,'' *Institutional Investor International Edition,* February 2000, p. 13.
Kazmin, Amy, ''Krung Thai Cleans Up Its Balance Sheet,'' *Financial Times,* September 22, 2000, p. 34.
——, ''Rush to Lend Backfires on Krung Thai,'' *Financial Times,* August 9, 2004, p. 18.
''Krung Thai Privatization Next Test for Thailand's Markets,'' *Euroweek,* July 26, 2002, p. 16.
''Picking Up the Pieces: After the Furor, Krung Thai Bank Moves On,'' *AsiaWeek,* March 13, 2000.
Somruedi, Banchongduang, ''KTB Aims to Boost Fee Income,'' *Nation,* December 17, 2004.

—M.L. Cohen

Lazy Days RV Center, Inc.

6130 Lazy Days Boulevard
Seffner, Florida 33584-2968
U.S.A.
Telephone: (813) 246-4999
Toll Free: (888) 500-4408
Fax: (813) 246-4408
Web site: http://www.lazydays.com

Private Company
Incorporated: 1976
Sales: $750 million (2003 est.)
NAIC: 441210 Recreational Vehicle Dealers

Based in Seffner, Florida, ten miles north of Tampa Bay, Lazy Days RV Center, Inc. has mixed aspects of Wal-Mart and Disney World to become the world's largest seller of recreational vehicles. The dealership's "SuperCenter" occupies 150 acres and has available for sale more than 1,200 RVs, covering 150 models from 18 manufacturers and ranging in price from less than $10,000 for basic units to more than $1 million for luxury coaches. Units are presented in a park-like setting, unlocked and open for customer inspection. Each year Lazy Days serves more than 300,000 complimentary breakfasts and lunches to customers and prospects. The SuperCenter also includes an RV park capable of accommodating 300 RVs, a 12,000-square-foot RallyCenter, banquet kitchen, screened-in swimming pool, tennis courts, a Camping World store, Flying J RV Travel Plaza, and a Cracker Barrel restaurant. The Super-Center is so large that Lazy Days maintains a fleet of some 170 six-passenger golf carts to transport employees and customers around the lot. In addition, the site includes some 275 service bays, with 24 service bays making up the largest RV collision center in the country. The company also maintains three massive paint booths capable of handling three 45-foot RVs simultaneously. For customers who buy luxury motor homes costing more than $250,000, Lazy Days also provides Crown Club membership. In addition to first-class check-in for RV service, members have access to an exclusive clubhouse on the Super-Center grounds, where they are served free meals and cocktails in an opulent setting. Because of all that Lazy Days has to offer, its SuperCenter has become a major RV tourist attraction in itself, each year attracting more than 1.25 million visitors from all over the world. Although the New York City private equity firm of Bruckmann, Rosser, Sherrill & Co. bought the company in 2004, it continues to be run by Don Wallace, whose family founded Lazy Days.

Patriarch of Wallace Family
a Product of the Depression

Although Don Wallace is the man most responsible for the creation of Lazy Days, it was his father, Herman Kemper "H.K." Wallace, who became the public face of the business in the early years. The elder Wallace was born in the mountains of Virginia, close to the Tennessee border, one of 12 children. When Wallace was just six years old his father died after losing his grocery store, forcing the youngster to drop out of school after the second grade to help his mother scrape by during the difficult years of the Depression. He helped farmers, he shined shoes—anything to make some money. He also followed in his father's footsteps and became involved in the grocery business, eventually running a few stores in Tennessee, where he raised his family. He uprooted his two sons and daughter when they were teenagers and moved them to Florida. Wallace became an auto parts jobber, starting out by selling parts to repair shops and garages from the back of his truck. He remained in this line of work until his son Don enlisted him and another son, Ron, to join him in selling RVs.

Don Wallace graduated from high school in Tampa, Florida, married, then returned to northeastern Tennessee to farm tomatoes and corn. Although it was a challenge at first, after nine years of farming Wallace became bored. In the mid-1970s he decided to move back to Florida to start a landscaping business with his brother-in-law. After selling the farm he bought a tractor and 16-foot travel trailer to make the move and provide a place to live when he got to Florida. He soon decided to trade up and sold the trailer, making a $500 profit. He bought a bigger unit, but even before he moved in he sold it as well at a profit. His success in these transactions prompted him to buy two used trailers, one damaged by fire which he rebuilt with the help of his mother. After he sold these units, he abandoned the idea of getting involved in the landscaping business. Instead, he approached his father and brother, and they agreed to go into the RV business together.

Starting an RV dealership in Tampa, Florida, was a bit of luck that in hindsight could be mistaken for a stroke of genius. Not only was the local market virtually untapped, Tampa was also a popular winter home for many people who were potential RV customers. After the Wallaces found 1.75 acres of land along North Florida Avenue in Tampa available to lease, they studied trailer and RV manufacturers in order to acquire inventory. They decided they wanted to sell Prowler Trailers, only to learn that the manufacturer already had a Tampa dealer. They contacted Fleetwood and were told that it too had an area dealer, but the company also suggested that the Wallaces talk to the dealer, who might be interested in cashing out. The Fleetwood dealer sold them his stock of two trailers and Lazy Days was in business. Don Wallace then traveled to Pennsylvania to acquire another trailer, a mini motorhome, as well as a tent trailer on consignment. With this meager inventory and $500 in the till, Lazy Days was launched in 1976.

Turning Point in the 1980s

The initial sales goal for Lazy Days was two new and two used trailers each month. To drum up business the Wallaces visited area campgrounds and even went door-to-door. Their efforts paid off and by the end of the first year in business they were able to buy the lot they had been leasing. During the first five years Lazy Days limited itself to travel trailers and mini motorhomes, growing sales to $13 million in 1980. Then, in 1981, they expanded into Class A units by taking on the Fleetwood Pace Arrow line of motorhomes. It proved to be a turning point for the company, which then saw its sales grow exponentially. In 1983 sales reached the $50 million mark.

Much of Lazy Days' early growth was the result of television commercials that featured H.K Wallace, who became something of an area celebrity. His Tennessee drawl, quick-fire delivery, and down-home personality appealed to customers. "Come on in," he told them, before adding his signature tag line: "Tell them H.K sent you." By the mid-1980s he and his children had become millionaires selling RVs, so that when he was recognized in restaurants by satisfied customers, H.K was more than happy to pick up the check. By this time his daughter, Connie, also had joined Lazy Days. She would prove instrumental in aligning the service department with sales. Each service manager was assigned several salespeople and together they worked in teams.

Lazy Days expanded beyond Tampa in the 1980s, opening dealerships elsewhere in Florida. By 1986 the company was operating seven stores on Florida's west coast. The Wallace family dreamed about operating hundreds of lots spread across the country, but Don Wallace began to have misgivings about this approach. Sales growth was slowing and he suspected that rather than adding business the new stores were actually taking it from each other. Moreover, he was exhausted from traveling store to store. According to a 2002 *Florida Trend* company profile, "On Christmas Eve 1986, during a miserable drive from Bradenton to Tampa, Wallace decided to try to convince his dad and brother that a single RV super center in the Tampa Bay area was the way to go. 'It was raining like hell outside,' he recalls, 'and I decided I didn't want to do this anymore.'"

The family would ultimately agree to the super center concept but another ten years passed before Don Wallace's idea became a reality. In the meantime, the family was struck by tragedy. Ron Wallace, who served as Lazy Days' general manager and secretary-treasurer, was killed in February 1989 when his car ran into the back of a bus in Tampa's Ybor City. H.K Wallace took the death of his son hard and began to ease out of the business. He soon retired and Don Wallace bought out his father in 1993. After a long illness H.K Wallace died in June 2002 at the age of 83.

Lazy Days also was threatened by scandal in the early 1990s. A former employee, William M. Jones, who had been fired by Don Wallace, went to the state attorney's office and accused Lazy Days of fraud, which led to a well publicized state investigation. The company was accused of engaging in a practice known as "bumping," in which Lazy Days allegedly sold vehicles on consignment, then pressured the customers into accepting a lower price while selling the RV for the full price and pocketing the difference. In addition, Lazy Days was accused of telling customers that their RVs needed expensive repairs before they could be sold on consignment, but the repairs were not actually done. Don Wallace vehemently denied these charges, maintaining that Jones was providing misinformation to the state attorney's office. After several months of reviewing files, investigators found Lazy Days had not conducted any criminal wrongdoing and the attorney general's office exonerated the company. Jones, on the other hand, was arrested and charged with extortion after sheriff's investigators caught him on tape telling Don Wallace that for $250,000 he would refuse to help investigators and urge other employees not to cooperate as well.

In 1992 Don Wallace promised Lazy Days employees that they would gain a stake in the tremendous growth the company had enjoyed over the past decade. In 1995 he launched a stock ownership plan in addition to the company's profit-sharing retirement plan. The Employee Stock Ownership Plan (ESOP) went into effect in 1996 and began to buy out Don Wallace's stake in the business. Not only did the employees gain ownership in the company, Wallace was able to cash out and take advantage of tax provisions allowing him to defer capital gains tax if he invested the proceeds in stock and bonds within a year. By 1997 employees owned about 10 percent of Lazy Days. Then in 1999 Wallace sold a majority interest in the business to the ESOP.

Opening Crown Club in the Early 21st Century

It was also in 1995 that Don Wallace announced that after several years of planning, Lazy Days was finally ready to begin construction on its SuperCenter located ten miles south in the

Key Dates:

1976: The company is founded by the Wallace family.
1989: Ron Wallace is killed in an auto accident.
1993: Don Wallace buys out his father.
1996: RV SuperCenter opens in a Tampa suburb.
1999: The Employee Stock Owner Plan gains majority control.
2004: A New York investment firm buys a controlling interest.

Tampa suburb of Seffner. The Lazy Days SuperCenter opened on Memorial Day weekend in 1996 and Tuesday of the following week the original North Florida Avenue location, which over the years had grown to 14 acres, was officially closed. The new location was 110 acres in size, selling 110 models from 14 manufacturers and 800 units in inventory. The campground could accommodate 164 RVs and there was a separate 72-site area where buyers could stay free while changing over to their new RVs. Despite the scale of the facility, Don Wallace was far from satisfied. In 1998 he was asked at a rally if Lazy Days had any plans to cater to the customer who bought the luxury coaches. From that question the seeds for Crown Club were planted. Not only did it make sense to provide a higher level of service to RV high rollers, thus keeping them coming back to buy even more expensive motor homes, but it also created further excitement about the Lazy Days SuperCenter. As Wallace told the *Tampa Tribune* in 2004, "We're kind of like Disney World. Every couple of years you've got to build a new roller coaster." The RV equivalent of a new roller coaster was the $2.3 million Crown Club that opened in 2001. The opulent clubhouse featured a British West Indies look, with antique elm floor, maple paneling, and a granite bar. A three-year membership to the club was granted to anyone purchasing a new RV costing $250,000 or more, or two years for buying a used RV in that price range. Memberships could be renewed only by making an additional purchase.

Lazy Days also expanded the rest of the SuperCenter, adding service bays and camp sites. Sales grew at a rapid clip, topping $500 million by 1999, prompting Wallace to set a goal of reaching the $1 billion level by 2003. But sales began to stall industrywide in 1999 and in 2000 Lazy Days only achieved 2 percent growth to $556 million. In 2001 Lazy Days posted sales of $584 million and Wallace pushed back his target date for reaching $1 billion to 2005. Nevertheless, the company was still trending upward. One of its greatest challenges was keeping up with the demand for service. Although Lazy Days remained committed to providing emergency service, wait times for routine service reached two months.

Lazy Days sold 8,842 RVs in 2003 and generated sales of $750 million and an estimated net profit of $36.4 million. Several months later, in June 2004, a majority interest in the company was sold for $206 million to the New York private investment firm of Bruckmann, Rosser, Sherrill & Co. LLC (BRS). Wallace retained a 10.6 percent stake in the business. The employees figured to be major beneficiaries of the deal, as each one was slated to receive a share of the ESOP buyout, depending on their length of service. Employees were also in line to earn more common stock as it was issued from the new owners. BRS was known to take a hands-off approach if a company was performing well, so that there was little reason to believe that Lazy Days would see any major changes in the years to come. It would soon face increased competition, however, in the form of La Mesa RV Center, one of the largest RV dealers in the country with 12 dealerships located in five Western states, generating about $700 million in annual sales. La Mesa announced in late 2004 that it planned to open a sales center in the Tampa market. But Lazy Days remained well positioned for continued growth. The demographics were on the company's side, as the nation's graying population entered its prime RV-buying years. Moreover, the average age of the RV buyer was dropping. Although Lazy Days had closed its other dealerships to focus on a single location, there was a good chance that in the years to come it might open super centers in other locations, such as Texas and Arizona.

Principal Competitors

Cruise America, Inc.; Earnhardt's Auto Centers; La Mesa RV Center, Inc.

Further Reading

"Big Wheel," *Florida Trend,* July 1, 2002, p. 51.
Johnston, Jo-Ann, "New York Firm Pays $206 Million for Tampa, Fla.-Area RV Dealer," *Tampa Tribune,* May 21, 2004, p. 1.
Longsdorf, Robert, Jr., "Old Promise Provides Impetus for Sterling Success at Lazy Days," *RV Business,* July 1995, p. 32.
Miracle, Barbara, "Road to Riches," *Florida Trend,* July 1, 2002, p. 48.
Nelson, Brett, "Twenty-Ton Cult," *Forbes,* November 29, 2004, p. 192.

—Ed Dinger

Leap Wireless International, Inc.

10307 Pacific Center Court
San Diego, California 92121
U.S.A.
Telephone: (858) 882-6000
Fax: (858) 882-6010
Web site: http://www.leapwireless.com

Public Company
Incorporated: 1998
Employees: 1,400
Sales: $751.3 million (2003)
Stock Exchanges: Over the Counter (OTC)
Ticker Symbol: LEAP
NAIC: 425110 Business to Business Electronic
Markets

Leap Wireless International, Inc. is a QUALCOMM Incorporated spinoff that started off quickly, fizzled with the meltdown of the telecom industry, filed for Chapter 11 bankruptcy protection, and is struggling to find its place in an industry that appears to have rendered its business model obsolete. The San Diego company, whose stock trades on an over-the-counter basis, markets Cricket, which originated as a flat-rate wireless telephone service for local calls only (no roaming) with no long-term commitment, essentially sold as an alternative to traditional landline service. Relying on an all-digital CDMA (code division multiple access) network, Cricket is offered in 39 markets in 20 states. The idea of no-frills, flat-rate wireless service was appealing at first, and many people turned to it because they did little traveling and did not require roaming capabilities. With major wireless companies now offering cheaper plans, Cricket has begun adding new services, such as the addition of long-distance calling capabilities, unlimited text messaging, voicemail, caller ID, call waiting, three-way calling, and family plans. As a result, there is now little distinction between Cricket and other wireless providers, aside from price, making the company highly dependent on its cost-effective CDMA system.

Parent Company a Pioneer in the Late 20th-Century Mobile Telecom Industry

Leap Wireless started out as a collection of wireless assets owned by QUALCOMM, which was founded in 1985 by seven men. One of them was Harvey White, who would become Leap's CEO. QUALCOMM was interested in applying mobile satellite communications technology, initially for military purposes, but soon turned its attention to the transportation industry. In 1988 QUALCOMM introduced a satellite-based data messaging service used to manage trucking fleets. The company then looked to the fledgling cellular telephone business, convinced that its analog transmission technology would one day give way to digital signals. It was in the hope of creating a new wireless digital standard that QUALCOMM began work on CDMA technology, which the company successfully demonstrated in 1990. In the meantime, however, the Cellular Telecommunications Industries Association had adopted time division multiple access (TDMA) as the new digital cell phone standard. The CDMA approach made more efficient use of the cellular frequencies, resulting in higher voice quality over greater distances, fewer antennas to provide coverage, and the ability to carry twice as many calls as a TDMA system—and ten times as many as analog. Despite the obvious advantages of CDMA over TDMA, it took years of persistent effort from QUALCOMM to gain industry acceptance. Finally in 1993 CDMA was adopted as the cellular standard by the U.S. Telecommunications Industry Association and the company began to pick up business rapidly.

While QUALCOMM continued to lobby for global acceptance of CDMA, it made acquisitions and launched a number of joint ventures around the world in an effort to drum up demand for the technology, so that by the late 1990s the company was doing business in such diverse countries as Australia, Chile, Mexico, and Russia. This grab bag of assets consisted mostly of licenses, which QUALCOMM believed were valuable; to investors, however, they were a distraction and potentially harmful to earnings because they would require a great deal of capital to unlock their potential. Thus QUALCOMM decided to package these assets into a new company called Leap International, Inc., which was incorporated in June 1998. It was then spun off

231

Company Perspectives:

Leap Wireless International, Inc. is a leading provider of innovative and value-driven wireless communications services.

in September 1998 to shareholders, who received one share of Leap for every four shares of QUALCOMM they owned. Heading the new venture was Harvey White, who had championed the idea of spinning off Leap.

Leap began deploying CDMA networks overseas and in the United States. Early in 1999 the company's Mexican subsidiary launched that country's first all digital wireless network, but it was domestic subsidiary Cricket Communications that quickly attracted most of the attention. Cricket offered what it called ''comfortable wireless,'' a wireless telephone plan that provided unlimited local calls for $29.95 a month. The idea was considered a bold move for several reasons: the price was cheap enough to persuade some landline customers to give up their traditional telephones; most cell phone customers only used their cell phones to make local calls; and the flat rate made billing simple for customers, who did not have to worry about going over their allotted minutes, and the provider, which did not have to devote resources to keeping track of customer activity. The service was first rolled out in March 1999 in Chattanooga, Tennessee. Earlier in the year, Leap picked up the wireless license to Chattanooga by acquiring Chase Telecommunications Holdings, Inc. The company also added licenses to the Nashville, Memphis, and Knoxville metropolitan areas and contiguous territory in six adjacent states.

Early Success in 1999

Leap enjoyed early success with Cricket. During the first three months it was able to capture 2.8 percent of the Chattanooga cell phone market and plans were made to expand into Nashville. The company also added 36 markets by making the winning $18.7 million bid in a federal government re-auction of licenses. Moreover, a Mexican venture was off to a strong start, and in Chile Leap acquired a 100 percent interest in a joint venture, Chilesat PCS, which had shown steady growth since its wireless network was launched in September 1998. A joint venture in Russia also launched wireless services in the early months of 1999, but by the end of the year Leap pulled out of the arrangement after its operating partner defaulted on loan agreements. Leap also sold an Australian subsidiary in 1999 when it was offered a good price for the business. The promise of Leap was such that seasoned telecommunications executives quit their jobs to join the start-up, including 22-year industry veteran Sue Swenson, the president and CEO of Cellular One.

As Leap marked its first anniversary in September 1999, management could point to a number of achievements. Not only had the company launched wireless networks in Mexico, Chile, Russia, and the United States, it had also acquired a number of licenses in the United States. These markets included Albuquerque, New Mexico; Charlotte, North Carolina; Dayton, Ohio; Little Rock, Arkansas; Salt Lake City, Utah; Spokane, Wash-

ington; Tucson, Arizona; Tulsa, Oklahoma; and Wichita, Kansas. Altogether, these communities contained 24 million potential subscribers. If Chattanooga was used as a measuring stick, the company's prospects appeared bright. By the end of the fiscal year, Cricket had captured 4 percent of that city's market.

In late 1999 Leap filed to make an initial public offering (IPO) of stock and investor interest was so great that the offering was increased from three million to four million shares. During the months leading up to the IPO, Leap continued to add licenses in markets such as Denver; Pittsburgh; Charlotte and Greensboro, North Carolina; Macon, Columbus, and Albany, Georgia; and Dayton, Ohio. The company then raised the funds it needed to launch service in these markets with a highly successful securities sale in February 2000. The sale of stock and private placement of ten-year notes resulted in $1.24 billion for the young company. The company's stock was priced at $88 and after it began trading on the NASDAQ, investors continued to bid up the price, which reached a high-water mark of $111 a share a few weeks later.

Cricket began servicing the Nashville market in 2000 and continued to buy licenses in additional markets, including Phoenix, Arizona; Reno, Nevada; Roswell, New Mexico; Buffalo and Syracuse, New York; Omaha and Lincoln, Nebraska; Birmingham, Alabama; Daytona, Florida; Honolulu, Hawaii; Jackson, Mississippi; Eugene, Oregon; Lakeland-Winterhaven, Florida; Greeley, Colorado; and Visalia, California. Cricket soon began servicing several of these communities, so that by the end of the year Cricket was offered in ten markets and the customer base reached 190,000. Increasingly Leap focused on Cricket and severed its ties to overseas ventures. In May 2000, Leap received an attractive cash buyout offer from its Chilean partner and management decided it was in the interests of shareholders to accept. Leap's lone remaining foreign investment was in Mexico.

In January 2001 Leap participated in a federal spectrum auction and won wireless operating licenses for 22 markets at a cost of $350 million. The new communities included Columbus, Ohio; Providence, Rhode Island; Houston and San Antonio, Texas; New London, Connecticut; Jacksonville and Melbourne, Florida; Columbus and Indianapolis, Indiana; Lexington and Louisville, Kentucky; Worcester, Massachusetts; Asheville, North Carolina; Las Cruces, New Mexico; Albany and Poughkeepsie, New York; Scranton, Pennsylvania; and Austin, Brownsville, Bryan, El Paso and McAllen, Texas. With the addition of these licenses, Cricket now had the potential of reaching more than 70 million customers in 36 states. As Cricket continued its rollout during the course of 2001, it began to service 39 markets in 20 states and cracked the one million mark in number of customers.

Setbacks Mounting in 2002

Yet Leap had essentially reached its high-water mark, as early enthusiasm now began to give way to cold reality. Some of the company's winning license bids in 2001 were challenged by NextWave Communications, which took the matter all the way to the U.S. Supreme Court. Moreover, Leap had taken on $1.9 billion in debt, mostly to equipment makers Nortel Networks, Lucent Technologies, and Ericsson, but it was a long

Key Dates:

1998: The company is spun off from QUALCOMM Incorporated.
1999: The first Cricket service is launched in Chattanooga, Tennessee.
2000: The company makes an initial public offering of stock.
2003: The company files for Chapter 11 bankruptcy protection.

way from becoming a profitable business. Investors were beginning to lose faith, as they did with all of the telecom sector, so that by early 2002, Leap shares dipped below $8. In February 2002 Cricket began serving Buffalo, New York, its 40th market, but by early May, Leap announced a reorganization effort that would put a halt to further expansion in favor of focusing on improving operations in existing markets. A poor quarterly report and an analyst downgrade combined to drive down the price of Leap stock to $2.60, and matters worsened when the company announced that it needed an infusion of $225 million in cash by the end of the year. Bad news continued to snowball in 2002. Leap had to reveal that about 5 percent of its subscribers, or 69,000 customers, obtained Cricket service through fraudulent means: through stolen credit cards, or by signing up with false information to get a free month of service. The company implemented more stringent anti-fraud measures, but its reputation in the investor community was already damaged.

In August Leap received an unfavorable arbitration decision regarding the purchase of licenses covering Buffalo and Syracuse, and was ordered to pay an additional $41 million in cash or issue 21.5 million additional shares of stock to the seller, MCG PCS Inc. It was money that Leap simply did not have, and Wall Street reacted harshly. The price of Leap stock dipped well below $1, to 65 cents a share. White continued to express faith in Cricket's flat-rate, no-frills model, but conditions had changed since the heady days of September 1998. Competing wireless carriers cut prices, added minutes, and sweetened their prepaid offerings, making the Cricket plan less distinctive. Leap responded by offering a $39.99 option that included unlimited local service, 500 minutes of long-distance calls, along with voice mail, call waiting, caller ID, and three-way calling. To many observers, this new approach cut against the message that Cricket was different from other wireless carriers. Some simply concluded that the original concept was fundamentally flawed. Cricket was supposed to be so different from the competition that it would not need to spend as much to add customers. In truth, Leap's marketing costs continued to rise as did customer turnover, known as "churn" in the industry. As one analyst told the *San Diego Union-Tribune,* "If their product is so great, why is churn so high?"

In September 2002, Leap announced that it was in violation of its credit facility agreements and also faced delisting by the NASDAQ. The company sold its Mexican interests and cut its workforce, while key executives began to depart as well. In December 2002 Leap shares, now trading below 25 cents, were delisted by the NASDAQ, and relegated to over-the-counter status. By the time the company filed for Chapter 11 bankruptcy protection in April 2003, Leap stock was worth less than a dime. The company had debt of nearly $2.5 billion and listed assets of $2.2 billion.

Leap's bankruptcy reorganization was contentious, as MCG in particular maintained that Leap was undervaluing its assets and that its plan unfairly enriched some creditors at the expense of other creditors and shareholders. Finally, in October 2003, the court accepted the plan, which called for the debt of Leap and its subsidiaries to be replaced by a $350 million secured note, which would be held by the investors who had purchased the debt of Leap's equipment suppliers: Lucent, Nortel, and Ericcson. The company now changed the top ranks of leadership, as White retired and Swenson resigned to "pursue other interests." Taking over as CEO was William M. Freeman, a 30-year veteran in telecommunications who came to Leap from Verizon Communications. He expressed optimism that there was still a place for the Cricket service in the current wireless climate, even as critics were eager to pronounce the patient all but dead. Nevertheless, the company, free of its crushing debt load, reissued stock, reorganized its board, and began offering a variety of products to attract customers, including unlimited text messaging for $4.99 a month and prepaid plans. It also began on a trial basis data services such as ring tone, wallpapers, games, weather reports, and an English-Spanish dictionary. In addition, in a complete departure from its origins, Leap considered offering roaming to customers. The company's future remained very much in doubt. Unable to compete with major carriers in large markets, Leap's best hope appeared to reside in small cities.

Principal Subsidiaries

Cricket Communications, Inc.

Principal Competitors

Cellco Partnership; Cingular Wireless LLC: Sprint PCS Group.

Further Reading

Allen, Mike, "Qualcomm Spinoff's Cricket Growing by Leaps and Bounds," *San Diego Business Journal,* October 2, 2000, p. 1.

Balint, Kathryn, "Leader of Leap Wireless Optimistic Despite Post-Bankruptcy Losses," *San Diego Union-Tribune,* November 19, 2004.

Beach, Tarre, "Leap of Faith," *Wireless Review,* August 1, 2000, p. 16.

Davies, Jennifer, "San Diego-Based Leap Wireless Faces Times of Turmoil," *San Diego Union-Tribune,* August 18, 2002.

Harris, Nicole, and Stephanie N. Mehta, "Leap Wireless Plans Flat Rate for Cell Calls," *Wall Street Journal,* March 17, 1999, p. 1.

Luna, Lynnette, "Leap Wireless Comes Tumbling Down," *Telephony,* September 9, 2002, p. 8.

—Ed Dinger

LIFEPOINT
HOSPITALS, INC.

LifePoint Hospitals, Inc.

---

103 Powell Court, Suite 200
Brentwood, Tennessee 37027
U.S.A.
Telephone: (615) 372-8500
Fax: (615) 372-8575
Web site: http://www.lifepointhospitals.com

Public Company
Incorporated: 1999
Employees: 9,300
Sales: $907.1 million (2003)
Stock Exchanges: NASDAQ
Ticker Symbol: LPNT
NAIC: 622110 General Medical and Surgical Hospitals

LifePoint Hospitals, Inc. of Brentwood, Tennessee, a suburb of Nashville, came into existence when healthcare giant Columbia/HCA spun off a number of hospitals in 1999. LifePoint was initially comprised of 23 rural hospitals in the Southeast, while sibling spinoff Triad Hospitals was made up of 34 hospitals. Since its formation, LifePoint has suffered major setbacks yet managed to garner the respect and praise of the healthcare industry through consistent earnings, renovating its properties, and luring top physicians to its hospitals. In 2005 LifePoint merged with rival Province Healthcare Company to become one of the country's leading for-profit healthcare providers with 50 hospitals nationwide and revenues of more than $1.5 billion annually.

The Birth of LifePoint: Late 1990s

There were many factors prompting the formation of LifePoint Hospitals, Inc. The firm was the result of its parent company, Columbia/HCA, spinning off a number of its holdings after the federal government began investigating the hospital conglomerate's aggressive business practices. Columbia Hospital Corporation was founded back in 1987 by two Texans, lawyer Rick Scott and financier Richard Rainwater, to purchase two hospitals in El Paso. Columbia expanded rapidly into other states and merged with Smith Laboratories; next came a series

of healthcare acquisitions until the advent of HMOs (health management organizations) and a crackdown of Medicare and Medicaid fraud that put many competing providers in jeopardy.

The end of 1980s' merger mania and the arrival of the sobering 1990s found Columbia in disarray. The company had been at the mercy of its executives. Firms were bought then sold, the firm went public, then private, and public again as its management changed hands. Columbia, fortunately, was able to weather the storms and went back on the acquisitions trail. In 1994 the company purchased the Tennessee-based Hospital Corporation of America (HCA) and merged operations. The new Columbia/HCA then went on a seemingly endless acquisitions spree, gobbling up dozens of healthcare providers over the next two years. The company's actions attracted the attention of the federal government, however, which initiated inquiries into Columbia/HCA's acquisitions and business tactics in 1997. In the ensuing investigation, several executives were indicted and/or fired and a chastened Columbia/HCA, still the country's largest for-profit hospital corporation, began selling off some of its holdings.

In 1998 Columbia/HCA filed a lawsuit of its own against a former financier for fraud; by the following year, the company was still selling assets, including two regional units christened LifePoint Hospitals, Inc. and Triad Hospitals. LifePoint Hospitals was made up of 23 nonurban hospitals in predominantly southeastern states, headquartered in Brentwood, Tennessee. Most of the hospitals spun off to become LifePoint were not sterling moneymakers, but could certainly benefit from corporate independence. Up and coming maverick Scott Mercy, who had originally worked at HCA since the 1980s and had become a senior vice-president at the merged Columbia/HCA, was appointed LifePoint's chairman and chief executive with James Fleetwood, Jr., who had served as Columbia/HCA's head of operations for Florida, named president and chief operating officer.

LifePoint seemed poised to make a splash in the healthcare industry, yet Wall Street was not impressed. With financing tight, top LifePoint executives were offered stock in the new company. All bought into the new venture, including Mercy, who commented to *Modern Healthcare* (December 6, 1999), ''This management team is willing to bet their house basically on the success of the operating strategy. . . . I'm willing to put my money where my mouth is.'' Mercy initially invested almost $3 million of his own funds, then spent an additional $200,000 on stock before the year was out.

By the end of its maiden year, LifePoint opened its first new facility, the $32 million Bartow Memorial Hospital, replacing a 74-year-old property in Bartow, Florida. At over 120,000 square feet, the new hospital was a dream come true for the under-15,000 population of Bartow in Polk County. LifePoint had also shed two underperforming hospitals, began renovating its other 20 hospitals (excluding Bartow), and finished the year with revenues of $515.2 million.

Tragedy Striking Twice: 2000–01

Under Mercy and Fleetwood, LifePoint's *raison d'être* was to invigorate its properties and make them the most desirable medical facilities in their region. Underperforming hospitals were sold in favor of others poised to outperform in their sectors, like the Putnam Community Medical Center in Palatka, Florida, which LifePoint bought from former parent Columbia/HCA (renamed HCA—The Healthcare Company). With a number of its hospitals the only major facility in rural or small towns, LifePoint was determined to keep patients in the area, to not feel compelled to drive to major cities, sometimes hours away, for better treatment. Millions were poured into replacing outdated equipment, remodeling, and hiring physicians away from competitors. New labor/delivery and intensive care units were built, operating rooms were refurbished and enlarged, and more outpatient services and procedures were added.

By 2000 LifePoint was comfortable in its independence; the company continued upgrading its properties and hired more doctors and support staff, bringing the total number of affiliated medical professionals to 6,000. Mercy and Fleetwood had achieved solid success in fighting migration to larger, better equipped metropolitan hospitals. It all came to a sudden halt, however, in May 2000 when Scott Mercy was killed in a plane crash. Mercy had been piloting the small plane, and a flight instructor also died in the crash near Smyrna, Tennessee.

Fleetwood was immediately given the duties of chief executive with longtime board member DeWitt Ezell becoming interim chairman. As if the loss of the 38-year-old Mercy was not enough, LifePoint's rating was downgraded and its stock plummeted nearly 6 percent when news of Mercy's death was reported. Robert Mains, an analyst with the Connecticut-based Advest, commented to *Modern Healthcare* (June 5, 2000) about Mercy's death and LifePoint's future: ''When somebody of that stature dies suddenly, it raises questions about both continuity and succession.''

Fleetwood easily stepped into wunderkind Mercy's shoes, officially becoming chief executive and chairman in June, two weeks after his predecessor's demise. Fleetwood, along with Kenneth Donahey, executive vice-president and COO, redoubled efforts to fight LifePoint's biggest problem: keeping both patients and doctors from migrating to better equipped facilities. While Mercy and Fleetwood had been able to staunch the flow the previous year, the new millennium would set the stage for years to come. LifePoint continued to put millions into state-of-the-art medical equipment and upgrading facilities. Revenues for 2000, despite the year's difficulties, were strong at $557.1 million, with net income of $17.9 million.

In March 2001 LifePoint made a secondary public offering of common stock, raising over $100 million to pay off debt, sending share prices upward despite weakness in the healthcare industry itself. The company had rebounded after Mercy's untimely death and Fleetwood had maintained both steady growth and revenues. Yet tragedy struck LifePoint again: in May Fleetwood suffered a massive heart attack and died a year and three days after Mercy's death. The 54-year-old Fleetwood had been sailing with his wife off the coast of Florida. The impact of Fleetwood's death sent shockwaves through the company; upon Mercy's death there was a likely successor since Fleetwood had been his right-hand man. LifePoint's board was now in a quandary since Fleetwood had served as chief executive, president, and chairman.

DeWitt Ezell was again appointed interim chairman as rumors circulated over whether executive vice-president and COO Kenneth Donahey would take the reins of the company. Some believed the board would look to an outsider. Business, however, went on as usual at LifePoint despite the loss of Fleetwood. Donahey ran the company until he was officially named chief executive and chairman less than a month after Fleetwood's death.

Setting a Stable Course: 2002–05

LifePoint proceeded cautiously in early 2002 after its own tragedies and the national crisis caused by the terrorist attacks of September 11, 2001, affected the entire nation. The company had been buying select hospitals to bolster its presence in the Southeast, especially in Georgia and Louisiana, then bought three Alabama hospitals in 2002. LifePoint also completed the acquisition of the Kansas-based Dodge City Healthcare Group, the majority of which had been bought by HCA in 1995, before LifePoint's formation. Additionally, LifePoint submitted the winning bid for a bankrupt hospital in Logan, West Virginia, in November 2002. By the end of 2002 LifePoint owned and operated 28 hospitals with a workforce of over 7,000 and had generated revenues of $743.6 million, a healthy 20 percent increase over 2001's $619.4 million.

In early 2003 Wall Street was atwitter with rumors of a merger between LifePoint and Province Healthcare. LifePoint's stock

---

Key Dates:

1987: Columbia Hospital Corporation is founded.
1994: Columbia buys Hospital Corporation of America; the new company is called Columbia/HCA.
1995: Columbia/HCA buys a majority stake in Dodge City Healthcare Group.
1999: LifePoint Hospitals Inc. is formed following the spinoff of 23 hospitals from Columbia/HCA.
2000: LifePoint's chief executive is killed in a plane crash.
2001: LifePoint's second chief executive dies of a heart attack.
2002: The company buys the remaining interest in Dodge City Healthcare Group.
2003: Stock plummets after LifePoint denies merger talks with Province Healthcare Company.
2004: LifePoint announces its intention to acquire Province and merge operations.
2005: Province Healthcare's holdings are merged into LifePoint.

---

fell sharply, by over 9 percent, when Donahey denied any deal. Instead, LifePoint continued to buy smaller facilities, like Lebanon, Kentucky's Norton Spring View Hospital (which also included a nursing home and pediatrics practice), bringing its total hospital count to 29. The company received good publicity late in the year when four of its hospitals were named to *Modern Healthcare*'s annual listing of the nation's "100 Top Hospitals." The four facilities, selected from more than 5,600 hospitals nationwide, were Meadowview Regional Hospital (Maysville, Kentucky), Georgetown Community Hospital (Georgetown, Kentucky), Crockett Hospital (Lawrenceburg, Tennessee), and Ashley Valley Medical Center (Vernal, Utah). LifePoint finished 2003 with robust revenues of $907.1 million, a 22 percent climb from the previous year, and net income of $68.5 million.

Five years after its creation, LifePoint had survived the deaths of two chief executives and a tumultuous healthcare industry. The company had proven resilient and its chief executive, Donahey, steered a well-plotted course to expand LifePoint's holdings. In 2004, like previous years, the company sought small- to medium-sized hospitals to add to its growing roster. River Parishes Hospital in LaPlace, Louisiana, met the

necessary requirements to join the LifePoint family in May. LifePoint then stunned many with its agreement to acquire rival Province Healthcare Company for $1.7 billion. Although LifePoint had strenuously denied rumors of a buy or merger with Province back in 2003, the two companies had since worked out the details. The merger would give LifePoint a total of 50 hospitals in 19 states and estimated annual revenues in excess of $1.5 billion.

By the second quarter of 2005 LifePoint and Province had completed their merger. Prospects for the new and improved LifePoint were bright and the company had become far more successful than imagined when spun off from Columbia/HCA only six years earlier. In the wake of tragedy, Donahey had proved a stalwart leader, guiding the company to soaring stock prices and continually climbing revenues.

Principal Competitors

Catholic Healthcare Partners; Community Health Systems, Inc.; HCA, Inc.; Health Management Associates, Inc.; Tenet Healthcare Corporation; Triad Hospitals, Inc.

Further Reading

Dixon, Lisa, "LifePoint Hospitals: A Good Prognosis," http://www.kiplinger.com/columns/picks/archive/2005/pick0104.htm, January 30, 2004.

Kirchheimer, Barbara, "Executives Take Leap of Faith," *Modern Healthcare,* December 6, 1999, p. 54.

——, "Plane Crash Kills One of Nashville's Elite," *Modern Healthcare,* June 5, 2000, p. 3.

——, "LifePoint Rocked by Second CEO Death," *Modern Healthcare,* June 11, 2000, p. 18.

Lau, Gloria, "LifePoint Hospitals Inc.: Brentwood, Tennessee Hospital Chain Finds a Cure for Bear Market," *Investor's Business Daily,* April 12, 2001, p. A12.

"LifePoint Acquires Hospitals in Alabama and Dodge City, Kansas," *Health Care Strategic Management,* November 2002, p. 4.

"LifePoint Continues on Successful Path by Improving Services, Recruiting Docs," *Health Care Strategic Management,* February 2000, p. 15.

"LifePoint to Buy Province Healthcare for $1 Billion," *New York Times,* August 17, 2004, p. C4.

"LifePoint Wins Logan General," *Daily Deal,* November 15, 2002.

—Nelson Rhodes

Lincoln Center for the Performing Arts, Inc.

70 Lincoln Center Plaza
New York, New York 10023
U.S.A.
Telephone: (212) 875-5000
Fax: (212) 875-5275
Web site: http://www.lincolncenter.org

Nonprofit Company
Incorporated: 1956
Employees: 9,000
Operating Revenues: $79.6 million (2004)
NAIC: 711310 Promoters of Performing Arts, Sports, and
    Similar Events, with Facilities

Lincoln Center for the Performing Arts, Inc. runs a huge performing arts complex in the center of New York City. The organization is both the landlord and administrator for the 12 resident organizations housed within Lincoln Center, and also a concert organizer and producer. Lincoln Center sits on over 16 acres of land in midtown Manhattan. Lincoln Center's concert halls include the Metropolitan Opera House, Avery Fisher Hall, the New York State Theater, and the Vivian Beaumont Theater. Lincoln Center's resident organizations include the New York Philharmonic, the Metropolitan Opera, the New York City Opera, the Film Society of Lincoln Center, Jazz at Lincoln Center, the Chamber Music Society of Lincoln Center, the New York City Ballet, the School of American Ballet, the Juilliard School, the New York Public Library for the Performing Arts, and the Lincoln Center Theater. While the resident organizations retain their own autonomous management, the groups do share the funds Lincoln Center raises, and are represented on Lincoln Center's board of directors. Lincoln Center's financial support comes from concert revenue, rental fees, and gifts from individuals, private foundations, and corporations. Lincoln Center's constituent groups present some 5,000 concerts and performances annually, and the Center serves as many as five million visitors and concertgoers. Lincoln Center serves an additional 200,000 students each year through its educational outreach programs. Lincoln Center is also the home of many free outdoor events such as Lincoln Center Out of Doors and Midsummer Night Swing. Lincoln Center also reaches an audience of an estimated 35 million television viewers through its ongoing *Live from Lincoln Center* series of broadcast performances.

From Vision to Reality in the 1950s

When Lincoln Center was conceived in the mid-1950s, it was the first such massive arts complex in the nation. Alan Rich, in *The Lincoln Center Story*, declared that one would have "to run the clock back to a Medici palace in Renaissance Florence" to find anything comparable in the world at the time Lincoln Center was being designed. Lincoln Center came about as the confluence of a trio of needs and circumstances. First, the Metropolitan Opera, New York's venerable opera company, had decided to leave its inadequate concert hall and was looking for space to build a new one. Second, the New York Philharmonic, the city's leading orchestra, was also looking for a new home as the hall it rented, Carnegie Hall, was slated to be torn down in 1959. The third crucial element that brought Lincoln Center to life was the planned razing of several blocks of midtown Manhattan tenements. The area, known as Lincoln Square, was a four-block stretch between 62nd and 66th Streets, bounded by Broadway, Columbus, and Amsterdam Avenues. Home to more than 1,600 families, the area was considered blighted, and had attracted the eye of New York's "master builder," urban renewal chief Robert Moses. Leaders of the Philharmonic and the Met, as the opera company is called, got together with philanthropist John D. Rockefeller III, who was interested in doing something for the arts, for exploratory talks in 1955. Rockefeller and others involved in the project toured Europe in 1956, visiting other cultural capitals, and when they returned, they decided that building a large combined performing arts complex that would house both the opera company, the Philharmonic, and possibly other arts groups, was a feasible plan.

Lincoln Center for the Performing Arts, Inc. was incorporated in 1956 as a nonprofit corporation. At its incorporation, the group was essentially only a name as it had no cash, no staff, and no real estate. In 1958, the group bought a four-block, 14-acre plot from the City of New York, using donated funds. Over the next year, Lincoln Square's residents were relocated, and in May 1959 the group held a lavish groundbreaking ceremony, with President Dwight Eisenhower wielding the shovel. By that time, Lincoln Center's member organizations included the Philharmonic and the Met, which would each get their own auditorium, the Juilliard School, and the New York Public Library, which was to have a special performing arts library. Lincoln Center also hoped to have a resident theater company and a ballet company.

Lincoln Center went through many design options. The corporation bought more land, expanding its parcel to more than 16 acres. The overall design of the complex was in the hands of architect Wallace K. Harrison, and Harrison also designed the Metropolitan Opera House. Philharmonic Hall (now Avery Fisher Hall) was designed by Max Abramovitz; Philip Johnson designed the hall for the ballet company, which became known as the New York State Theater; Pietro Belluschi designed the building for the Juilliard School and the chamber music auditorium Alice Tully Hall; and another iconic mid-century architect, Eero Saarinen, designed the Vivian Beaumont Theater. The architects managed to work together to produce an array of striking buildings arranged around a central plaza. The buildings were completed at different times, with Philharmonic Hall the first to open in 1962.

Finding Its Feet in the 1960s and 1970s

Philharmonic Hall opened with a grand concert led by Leonard Bernstein on September 23, 1962. The orchestra had marked its first season in its new home by commissioning new works by leading composers including Aaron Copland, Paul Hindemith, Samuel Barber, and conductor Bernstein himself. Yet in spite of the orchestra's obvious pride in its new home, it was not long before the mood dampened. Audiences and orchestra players alike found the acoustics of Philharmonic Hall dry and inconsistent, a poor comparison to the beloved Carnegie Hall. Over the next few years, Philharmonic Hall underwent several extensive overhauls in order to fix the acoustics. The hall's original cost had been projected at $5 million. This had risen to more than $14 million before the hall opened, and the subsequent work added substantially to the building's price tag.

The other buildings were completed one by one. Lincoln Center's landmark fountain was completed in 1964, a few weeks before the New York State Theater opened. The Vivian Beaumont Theater was completed in 1965, as was the New York Public Library and Museum of the Performing Arts. That year also saw the installation of two massive outdoor sculptures in the plaza, a figure by Henry Moore and a piece by Alexander Calder. The Metropolitan Opera House opened in 1966. Like

Philharmonic Hall, the Metropolitan Opera House had gone significantly over budget before it was done. First projected at $15 million, it took more than twice that amount of money, or $37.4 million, to complete, in part because the hall was built on a foundation with a tendency to flood. In 1969, Lincoln Center added Damrosch Park and the Guggenheim band shell. That year, the Juilliard School was finally completed.

The list of donors that made all this possible included many wealthy private citizens, major charitable foundations, and leading corporations. John D. Rockefeller, Jr., headed the list of individual donors, and many Rockefeller family members also contributed substantially to getting Lincoln Center built. Major foundation donors included the Ford Foundation, the Alfred P. Sloan Foundation, the New York Foundation, the Rockefeller Foundation, and dozens of others. Many of the nation's foremost corporations gave money to Lincoln Center in its early years, including General Motors Corporation, International Business Machines, Chase Manhattan Bank, Manufacturers Hanover Trust, Texaco, Shell Companies, Inc., and many more.

In 1970, Amyas Ames became Lincoln Center's new chairman of the board. Ames, who made his living at the investment firm Kidder, Peabody, had been involved in planning Lincoln Center from the very beginning, and he remained a strong advocate of the arts throughout his tenure as chairman, which ended in 1981. The Center continued to add new constituents in the 1970s and to expand its programming. In 1972, the Chamber Music Society became a Lincoln Center resident organization, adding to the variety of musical offerings already on hand with the Philharmonic and the Met. The Chamber Music Society's performance space was Alice Tully Hall, named for a generous patron. Two years later, the Film Society of Lincoln Center became a constituent. In 1976, Lincoln Center televised the first of its live broadcasts on the nation's Public Broadcasting System (PBS), the popular show *Live from Lincoln Center*. This television series continued into the 2000s, and drew millions of viewers into Lincoln Center's concert halls. Philharmonic Hall was renamed Avery Fisher Hall in 1973 in recognition of a major gift. Work continued on the hall's acoustics, and in 1976 the performance space closed for some time, to make way for a major reconstruction. This last re-do seemed to finally satisfy the hall's critics, at least for some time.

Travails of the Repertory Theater in the 1980s

Lincoln Center's constituent organizations seemed to flourish in the new performing arts complex despite some initial difficulties such as the ongoing acoustical tinkering in Avery Fisher Hall. The New York Philharmonic and the Metropolitan Opera had fulfilled longstanding dreams with permanent homes of their own. The New York City Ballet, an incubator for American dance, became a legendary corps under choreographer George Balanchine at Lincoln Center. Other groups, such as the Film Society, came to life in the new space, and were able to offer New York audiences more than might have been possible in a smaller or less central venue. The notable exception was Lincoln Center's theater company, which stumbled from the start, did not exist for several years, and did not really begin to flourish until the mid-1980s, long after the other Lincoln Center groups were established.

The Repertory Theater differed from the other Lincoln Center groups in that it was created to occupy the space, rather than being an existing organization that found a new home. It was conceived as a showcase for American playwrights, and it held its first season outdoors in Washington Square over 1963 and 1964 while its space, the Vivian Beaumont Theater, was under construction. This first season was led by a pair of directors, Robert Whitehead and Elia Kazan. Kazan, a noted movie director, and Whitehead, who worked on Broadway, had no experience running a repertory theater, and after disagreement with Lincoln Center's board, the pair departed. The next season, beginning in the fall of 1965, was led by another pair of directors, Jules Irving and Herbert Blau. Their efforts were not appreciated by New York's theater critics, and their season too ended in acrimonious departure, with Blau decamping back to California.

In 1973, Irving made way for Joseph Papp, who was renowned for his Public Theater and the New York Shakespeare Festival. Papp stayed until 1977, putting on new American plays in Lincoln Center's two theaters, the Vivian Beaumont and the smaller Mitzi Newhouse. However, Papp's vision was difficult to reconcile with Lincoln Center's more mainstream expectations. With no one very happy, Papp resigned. Having no other director in line to take Papp's place, the Repertory Theater "went dark" in theater parlance, or refrained from putting on plays. The theater reopened for one season in 1980, under director Richmond Crinkley. This season, like many before, was not a critical success. Crinkley remained on the job, though the Vivian Beaumont stayed dark for several more years. Crinkley wanted to renovate the playhouse, changing the configuration of the stage. This plan led to conflict with Lincoln Center's board, which wanted the theater company to formulate an artistic vision and a schedule of plays before worrying about the physical structure of the playhouse. All this came to a head in August 1983, when Lincoln Center's board moved to cut the theater company out of the general funds the Center disbursed, and to forbid the company from using the name Lincoln Center Theater Company. While Lincoln Center's board had allowed its constituent organizations autonomy regarding artistic decisions and day-to-day operations, it apparently felt compelled to step in at this point and take drastic action.

In 1985, Richmond Crinkley was replaced by Gregory Mosher, a veteran of Chicago's Goodman Theater. Mosher put aside what had been his predecessor's pressing issue, renovation, and produced a successful season of plays in 1986 under the auspices of Lincoln Center. By 1988, the theater was routinely selling out, and the theater company had made some $35 million in ticket sales. After a very slow start, the Lincoln Center Theater Company at last established itself with New York audiences.

New Developments in the 1990s

By the late 1980s, Lincoln Center for the Performing Arts, Inc. had come into a new role, far beyond what its creators had first envisioned. The nonprofit corporation was much more than the landlord and administrator of a performing arts complex. The corporation had become something of an arts producer itself, as it extended New York's concert season to a year-round affair. In 1964, Lincoln Center first produced its Great Performers series, with a schedule of 12 concerts. By the late 1980s, the Great Performers series had grown to 75 to 80 concerts annually, a tremendous increase. Lincoln Center also produced many summer concert events, such as its Mostly Mozart festival and Lincoln Center Out-of-Doors. The Center itself managed and promoted these series, and others such as its contemporary music program Serious Fun! and a Classical Jazz series. By the late 1990s, Lincoln Center was open 52 weeks a year, and its summer music and dance events attracted crowds of 10,000 to the outdoor plaza.

Though it seemed good business sense to keep its halls filled year-round, Lincoln Center still did not break even on the events. In 1990, for example, the corporation projected it would need $7.5 million to put on the concerts it produced, figuring in fees for artists, ticket-takers, and other personnel, advertising, and all the related costs of running its halls. Ticket sales only covered $4.5 million of the total. Even sold-out performances, with rave reviews might lose tens of thousands of dollars because ticket sales simply did not cover costs. Thus the corporation continued to depend heavily on donations. Lincoln Center raised money for what it called its Consolidated Corporate Fund. All the constituent organizations shared in this fund, in exchange for giving up their right to fund-raise on their own. Member groups could raise funds for particular projects, but general donations all went through the Consolidated Corporate Fund.

The corporation seemed to have little trouble raising great sums of money, however. In 1990, Lincoln Center spent some $180 million on its new Samuel B. and David Rose Building, which gave the Juilliard School space for dormitories as well as administrative offices. The Walter Reade Theater was completed the next year. This was a movie house, built to the specifications of the Film Society. In 1994, Lincoln Center chose a new chair of its board, the retired opera singer Beverly Sills. Sills had been one of the nation's most popular opera stars, well-known to television audiences. A key role of the chairperson was to raise money, and Sills's fame and outgoing personality made her ideal for the position.

Yet by the late 1990s, Lincoln Center and other arts organizations around the country were feeling somewhat pinched. Though this was a booming time for corporate America, waves of mergers and consolidations meant that overall, there were fewer companies giving out donations, and support for the arts tightened up. In early 1999, Lincoln Center announced that it was considering selling a painting by the American artist Jasper Johns that had hung in the New York State Theater lobby for the past 35 years. The painting was worth from $10 million to $15 million, so selling it was a very attractive option. Public outcry led Lincoln Center to take the Johns painting off the auction block. That the corporation would consider such a move dramatically underscored the Center's increasing need for fundraising.

Rebuilding in the 2000s

By the late 1990s, many of Lincoln Center's buildings were showing their age. Though there were many needed changes, one of the most pressing was the restoration of the white travertine marble that formed the buildings' facades. This material had eroded badly. The concert halls also needed interior updates to incorporate the latest sound and lighting technology. Lincoln Center commissioned studies on how best to accomplish a major fix-up. In 1999, the corporation spawned a group, the Lincoln Center Constituent Development Project, to coordinate plans for redevelopment of the entire arts complex. One of the early plans the group considered was submitted by one of the world's leading architects, Frank Gehry. Gehry envisioned a glass dome capping Lincoln Center's main plaza. Lincoln Center Chair Beverly Sills announced to the *New York Times* that she found the dome idea absurd, and that project was withdrawn.

The Constituent Development Project went through several changes of leadership before a new renovation plan was adopted, submitted by the architects Elizabeth Diller and Ricardo Scofidio. The whole renovation was expected to take ten years, with a budget of $1.5 billion. The City of New York was to contribute $240 million. After September 11, 2001, and a major decline in the stock market, the project was scaled back by almost half, to a projected $675 million. The expensive project had both its fans and its detractors. Paul Goldberger, writing for the *New Yorker* (July 7, 2003) noted, however, that Lincoln Center had become, tragically, the last of its kind: "With the World Trade Center gone, Lincoln Center is the one true temple of nineteen-sixties architecture on a grand scale that New York has left."

Overseeing and paying for its renovation was not the only problem Lincoln Center encountered in the early 2000s. Its constituent the New York City Opera threatened to leave Lincoln Center, unhappy with the nixing of its plans to build a new opera house. The longstanding summer Mostly Mozart series ran into trouble in its 2002 season, when contract negotiations between the musicians and Lincoln Center broke down. But everyone seemed cheered next summer, with the orchestra under a new conductor, Louis Langree. Yet around that same time, Lincoln Center's founding constituent, the New York Philharmonic, abruptly announced that it was leaving Avery Fisher Hall and returning to its old home, Carnegie Hall. The orchestra was apparently worried about the cost of the reconstruction of Avery Fisher Hall, and it came up with a new plan to merge its corporate umbrella with the nonprofit that ran Carnegie Hall. The negotiations between Carnegie Hall and the Philharmonic had gone on without Lincoln Center's participation, and though Lincoln Center promptly announced it would have no problem filling Avery Fisher on the 120 nights that had been set aside for the Philharmonic, the orchestra's departure

was obviously a heavy blow. Three months later, the Philharmonic and Carnegie realized they could not merge their organizations, and the orchestra agreed to stay in Avery Fisher.

During the same time, Lincoln Center went through several changes of personnel in top positions. Gordon Davis was named the new president of the organization in January 2001, but he only served through September of that year. He was succeeded by Reynold Levy. Beverly Sills stepped down as chairwoman of the board in 2002, and was succeeded by Bruce Crawford. Crawford had been president and general manager of the Met, and he was viewed as a calm negotiator who would be able to bring the sometimes fractious constituent member boards together so that the renovation could go forward. Crawford agreed to serve as chairman for three to five years. He announced his resignation in January 2005. Lincoln Center had raised roughly $60 million of the $320 million it was committed to raising for the first part of its renovation, which was expected to begin in 2006. Meanwhile, Jazz at Lincoln Center had built a new auditorium, Frederick P. Rose Hall, at a cost of $128 million. It opened in 2004. Crawford pointed to this as one of the achievements of his short tenure as chairman of Lincoln Center. Lincoln Center was still at the beginning of an enormous fundraising campaign and the many daunting challenges of renovating the arts complex in 2005, and the way seemed difficult. Yet Lincoln Center had accomplished the same time and again, planning, building, revising, raising money, expanding, and rebuilding through the 40-plus years since it first broke ground.

Principal Competitors

Carnegie Hall Society, Inc.; Brooklyn Academy of Music, Inc.

Further Reading

Brustein, Robert, "Cycles of Lincoln Center," *New Republic*, October 10, 1988, p. 28.

Davidson, Justin, "Mostly Mozart's Makeover," *Opera News*, June 2003, p. 36.

Freedman, Samuel G., "Gregory Mosher to Head Lincoln Center Theaters," *New York Times*, April 30, 1985, p. C13.

Goldberger, Paul, "West Side Fixer-Upper," *New Yorker*, July 7, 2003, p. 36.

Isherwood, Charles, "N.Y. Phil, Carnegie Hall Scuttle Wedding Plans," *Daily Variety*, October 8, 2003, p. 4.

Kay, Jane Holtz, "Robert Moses: The Master Builder," *Nation*, April 24, 1989, p. 569.

Kozinn, Allan, "Beverly Sills Is Named by Unanimous Vote to Head Lincoln Center," *New York Times*, January 25, 1994, p. C15.

——, "The Institution As Impresario," *New York Times*, July 23, 1989, p. H1.

Lawson, Carol, "$4 Million Grant Is Lost for Work at Beaumont," *New York Times*, November 20, 1982, p. 15.

"Lincoln Center Action Wins Cautious Support," *New York Times*, August 26, 1983, p. C3.

Lincoln Center for the Performing Arts, New York: Lincoln Center for the Performing Arts, Inc., 1964.

"Lincoln Center Recomposing Itself," *Crain's New York Business*, June 9, 2003, p. 3.

McBride, Murdoch, "Arts Coping with Downsized Support," *Back Stage*, January 15, 1999, p. 4.

Pogrebin, Robin, "Lincoln Center Chairman Is to Resign," *New York Times*, January 13, 2005, pp. B1, B7.

——, "Recasting Lincoln Center's Role, Then Bowing Out," *New York Times*, March 29, 2000, p. E1.

Pogrebin, Robin, and Blumenthal, Ralph, "Philharmonic Deal, Completed Quickly, Left Some in Dark," *New York Times*, June 3, 2003, pp. A1, B7.

Reiss, Alvin H., "An Unlikely Scenario for Future Arts Funding, or Then Again. . . ," *Fund Raising Management*, April 1999, p. 30.

Rich, Alan, *The Lincoln Center Story*, New York: American Heritage Publishing Co., 1984.

Rothstein, Mervyn, "A Theater Company Faces the Problems of Its Own Success," *New York Times*, August 25, 1988, p. C21.

Salinas, Mike, "$1.5B to Redo Lincoln Center," *Back Stage*, January 26, 2001, p. 4.

Schonberg, Harold C., "Lincoln Center Moves Against the Beaumont," *New York Times*, August 25, 1983, p. A1.

Shanet, Howard, *Philharmonic: A History of New York's Orchestra*, New York: Doubleday & Co., 1975.

Shepard, Richard F., "Lincoln Center—the First 20 Years," *New York Times*, May 20, 1979, p. D1.

Soucar, Miriam Kreinin, "Small Arts Groups Starving, Big Institutions Get Most Funding," *Crain's New York Business*, March 5, 2001, p. 1.

—A. Woodward

Logitech International S.A.

CH-1143 Apples
Switzerland
Telephone: (21) 863-51-11
Fax: (21) 863-53-11
Web site: http://www.logitech.com

Public Company
Incorporated: 1981 as Metaphor Inc.
Employees: 6,000
Sales: $1.27 billion (2004)
Stock Exchanges: Swiss NASDAQ
Ticker Symbol: LOGN (Swiss); LOGI (NASDAQ)
NAIC: 334119 Other Computer Peripheral Equipment
    Manufacturing; 334310 Audio and Video Equipment
    Manufacturing; 334290 Other Communications
    Equipment Manufacturing

Logitech International S.A. is one of the world's leading manufacturers of input and interface devices for personal computers (PCs) and other digital products. Best known as a producer of mice, the company has shipped more than 500 million of the essential devices in numerous models—including corded, cordless, optical, and laser. Building on its success with mice—its first product—Logitech by the early 2000s had branched out into a wide variety of interface devices, including trackballs, keyboards, web cameras, joysticks and other controllers for both PC and console games, multimedia speakers, PC and game console headsets and microphones, mobile phone headsets, three-dimensional (3D) motion controllers, and advanced remote controls. Although the company started out supplying original equipment manufacturer (OEM) products, Logitech has increasingly targeted the retail market, which now accounts for 80 percent of revenues. Logitech was incorporated in Switzerland, and its stock has its main listing on the Swiss Exchange; its worldwide headquarters, however, are in Fremont, California, providing it with access to Silicon Valley's talent base, and Logitech has a secondary stock listing on the NASDAQ. The firm's main research and development operations are in Fremont; Romanel, Switzerland; Hsinchu, Taiwan; Vancouver, Washington; and Toronto, Canada. Its primary manufacturing facilities are in Suzhou, China. Product distribution reaches more than 100 nations worldwide, with Europe generating 47 percent of net sales; North America, 37 percent; and the Asia-Pacific region, 16 percent.

Pointing the Way to the Future in the 1980s

One of the most important inventions for "personalizing" computers was that of the computer mouse. Developed by computer visionary and pioneer Douglas C. Engelbart, a new computer input device made its debut in 1963 at the Stanford Research Institute. Engelbart continued to refine the concept, and by 1968 Engelbart's team made the first public presentation of the device—by then dubbed the "mouse"—at the 1968 American Federation of Information Processing Societies' Fall Joint Computer Conference at San Francisco.

Engelbart's mouse would change the course of computing history and would launch Logitech as a company a decade later. The first commercial presentation of the mouse also would present the first "windows"-type graphical user interface, which, controlled by the mouse, would enable the computer to become accessible for individual and home use, and not the private domain of highly trained programmers. In conjunction with the mouse, Engelbart would introduce such basic computer concepts as the onscreen combining and manipulating of text and graphics, hypertext and hyperdocuments (which would become extremely important for later Internet development), and videoconferencing. Engelbart's place in the computer industry of the 1960s and 1970s was highlighted by his office's position as the second node of the ARPAnet, which would later become the Internet.

Engelbart also proved an inspiration for a new generation of engineers and computer industry developers, including two Stanford University engineering students, Daniel Borel, from Switzerland, and Pierluigi Zappacosta, from Italy. Inspired by the burgeoning Silicon Valley scene, Borel and Zappacosta decided to set up their own company to produce software products. The partners hoped to bring the same sense of entrepreneurship that they had found in California to the European computer industry.

In contrast to the United States, where high-tech companies could find a vast pool of venture capital and other financial

Company Perspectives:

Logitech's objective is to strengthen its leadership in the growing market for personal interface products, linking people to the digital world wherever and whenever they need to access digital information to communicate, learn and play. The Company has historically served the installed base of PCs by offering innovative personal interface devices to address the needs of the desktop. While PCs are being used more and more as the digital hub to access information and communicate, other platforms such as game consoles and cell phones are also becoming a rich resource for people to access information, communicate and enjoy an expanding offering of interactive games. Logitech believes that the Company is well positioned to take advantage of the many opportunities in this growing marketplace.

backing, especially for the development of computer technology and products, the European situation in the late 1970s remained fixed on an older corporate model. Unable to find the venture capital that they needed, and with no banks willing to risk a multimillion-dollar load, Borel and Zappacosta were forced to place their dream of starting their own software company on hold.

Engelbart's invention would change the pair's direction. As Zappacosta told *Fortune:* "We didn't want to be in mice. They seemed to be beneath our intelligence. We wanted to be a software company—like Microsoft." Nonetheless, it was with the computer mouse that Borel and Zappacosta finally would go into business. In 1981 the pair acquired the U.S. distribution rights for a mouse designed in Switzerland. Hardware proved an easier investment sell than the pair's software dream. With the backing of a number of Swiss investors, Borel and Zappacosta set up the company that would later become known as Logitech. (The name, which would not be adopted until 1988, was derived from the root of the French word for software, *logiciel,* plus the word *tech.*) Originally operating from a "garage" shop, the company was established with headquarters in Apples, Switzerland, but with a strong U.S. presence from the start.

Borel and Zappacosta's timing was fortuitous. In 1982 Steve Jobs, of the rising computer star Apple, made the decision to incorporate Engelbart's mouse in the company's computer systems. The decision would revolutionize the computer industry, paving the way for the first truly "personal" computers. Other computer designs would soon adopt the mouse as well. Borel and Zappacosta, originally scornful of the mouse, quickly discovered the device's interest, as well as its possibilities. They continued to make improvements in the design and manufacturing methods.

Logitech at first produced mice for the Apple computer system. As other manufacturers began producing mice-controlled computer interfaces, Logitech's mice were adapted for these systems, too. For the distribution of its products, Logitech was unable to afford the retail path. Instead, the company took out ads in the growing number of computer and other electronic technology magazines, newspapers, and trade journals.

Logitech also would find a new boost as an OEM. In 1984 the company was contracted by Hewlett-Packard (HP) to produce mice for that company's computer systems. The HP

contract placed Logitech—then known as Metaphor—on the computer peripherals map. Soon after, the company signed contracts with AT&T, Olivetti, Convergent Technologies, DEC, and others. Apple, which was in the process of launching the breakthrough Macintosh computer systems, soon would turn to Logitech for its computer mouse needs as well. Around this time, Logitech also introduced the first "cordless" mouse, a product that would forecast the growing demand for the wireless desktop in the late 1990s.

Logitech expanded rapidly. In the middle to late 1980s it began increasing its manufacturing capacity, with plants in California and new plants in Taiwan in 1986 and in Cork, Ireland, in 1988. The launch of production in the Taiwan facility enabled Logitech to take on its largest client to date: IBM and its personal computer range, which already had succeeded in defining an industry standard for personal computing. In 1988, when revenues had reached $40 million, Logitech incorporated under the name Logitech International S.A., listing its shares on the Bourse de Zurich through an initial public offering.

Going Beyond the Mouse in the Early to Mid-1990s

By then Logitech had moved into the retail channel, with the launch of its C7 mouse in December 1985. A square-shaped mouse in marked contrast to later "ergonomic" designs, the C7 nonetheless featured the three-button design that would become something of a Logitech hallmark. Throughout the late 1980s and early 1990s Logitech continued to build its position in the computer market. A 1991 joint venture agreement brought the company to mainland China, reinforcing its manufacturing position, while also bringing additional funding from both the Chinese government and from Hong Kong.

Logitech also was branching out. In 1988 the company produced its first non-mouse peripheral, a handheld scanner. A 1990 deal gave the company a share of Canada's Advanced Gravis, a maker of joysticks as well as pointing devices, including a Mouse Stick, for the variety of computer systems available at the time—including the Amiga, Atari, Tandy, and others. In 1991 Logitech increased its share in Advanced Gravis to 58 percent, giving Logitech seats on Advanced Gravis's board of directors. Also in 1991 Logitech introduced the industry's first radio-based cordless mouse, the MouseMan Cordless.

In that same year Logitech made another significant acquisition, buying up 50 percent of Gazelle Graphics Systems, of California. The company would acquire full ownership of Gazelle in 1993, giving Logitech control of Gazelle's innovative trackball technology, which soon would become an important feature of the growing portable computer market. The introduction of new 3D pointing technology, initially developed by NASA, brought Logitech into the high-end graphics market, with its Magellan 3D pointer for Silicon Graphics and other high-end CAD/CAM/CAE workstations. The Magellan, developed in conjunction with Germany's Space Control GmbH, would be dubbed the Space Mouse for the European market. Logitech later, in 1998, acquired a 49 percent equity stake in Space Control.

Not all of Logitech's investments were successful. In 1993, for example, the company joined with cable television giant TCI in an investment in Virtual I/O, a Seattle-based maker of a 3D computer display headset. This product, however, proved to be a bit ahead of its time. The company also attempted to enter the soundcard market, with, among other products, its SoundMan speaker system. The company's sound products failed to move the computer industry, which was just beginning to adopt another soundcard technology, the Soundblaster, as a de facto standard.

Meanwhile, Logitech continued to look beyond the pointing device and joystick market. In the mid-1990s the company targeted two other promising markets: scanners and digital cameras. Logitech would achieve some early success in the scanner market, with its handheld and sheetfed scanner designs. Yet Logitech was far from alone in entering this market, which soon was flooded with products from a large number of competing businesses. A price war broke out, severely cutting into Logitech's profit margins. Worse for Logitech, the market clearly shifted away from the sheetfed design to the flatbed design. By the late 1990s Logitech's scanner division was losing money heavily. The company faced a similar situation in the digital camera market. The entry of such major manufacturing names as Sony, Philips, and others into the digital camera market forced Logitech into the niche player position of that market.

The company's financial troubles, exacerbated by an extended economic crisis both in the United States and in Europe, forced Logitech to reorganize its operations in 1995. The company closed its U.S. and Ireland manufacturing facilities, moving production entirely to China and Taiwan, while cutting some 500 jobs. The center of manufacturing was now in Suzhou, China, where Logitech had opened a manufacturing facility in 1994.

Logitech, which had posted revenues of more than $300 million in 1994, also was facing new competition in its core product line and from the most fearsome competitor of all. In the mid-1990s the Microsoft Corporation was branching out into computer peripherals, launching its own mouse products and joysticks. Given its near-monopoly position in the worldwide personal computer market, Microsoft was able to impose itself quickly on the pointer market, taking some 40 percent of it. Logitech, which had been earning margins up to 50 percent on its pointing products, was forced to cut its prices to compete with the software giant. Nonetheless, Logitech was able to maintain its leadership position, particularly as the leading OEM mouse supplier, with customers including 18 of the world's 20 largest computer manufacturers.

Logitech's restructuring would cost the company some $20 million in 1995. By 1996, however, the company had once again been restored to profitability in time to celebrate the production of its 100 millionth mouse. Regrouped around its pointing devices, Logitech would quickly double that figure, announcing the production of its 200 millionth mouse in December 1998. The company's scanner division was sold off in 1997 to Storm Technology, a deal that also gave Storm a 10 percent investment in Logitech. In March 1997 Logitech listed its stock on the NASDAQ National Market, selling four million American Depository Shares.

New Leadership, Growth Through Acquisition in the Late 1990s and Early 2000s

Since its origins, Logitech had been headed by Daniel Borel and Pierluigi Zappacosta, who had shared CEO and other duties. In 1998, however, Borel retired to the position of company chairman. (Zappacosta had left Logitech in 1997 to become chairman of Digital Persona Inc., a firm specializing in biometrics.) Logitech brought in Guerrino De Luca, a former executive at Apple Computer and architect of Apple's Claris division's success. De Luca, who had served as CEO of Claris and had once been pegged for the top Apple spot as well, resigned from Apple with the return of company founder Steve Jobs to its leadership. De Luca moved quickly to enhance Logitech's image beyond that of a mouse and joystick maker to that of the leading computing interface company.

One of De Luca's first acts was the acquisition of the Quick-Cam PC video camera division from Connectix Corporation, a $26.2 million deal completed in September 1998. The QuickCam had been one of the first video cameras designed for easy incorporation into a personal computing system. Introduced in the mid-1990s, the distinctive QuickCam—shaped much like an eyeball—had captured the industry's lead. The rise of the Internet, and the appearance of faster modem and other data transfer technologies, including satellite and cable internet access, had made videoconferencing technology viable. This acquisition propelled Logitech into the top spot in PC video cameras.

In addition to the QuickCam purchase—which, by late 1998, resulted in three new Logitech-signed QuickCam products—Logitech purchased a 10 percent interest in Immersion Corporation, pioneer of "force feedback" technologies, designed to enhance user interactivity with games, Internet, and other computer applications. In early 1999 Logitech also debuted several new products, including its next-generation mouse designs, such as the Gaming Mouse, developed specifically for computer strategy and FPS (first-person shooter) games. Logitech continued to make revenue advancement, topping the $400 million mark for 1998. Although mouse sales continued to lead the way, Logitech was already generating 25 percent of its revenues from non-mouse interface devices.

Explosive demand for Internet video cameras (or webcams) helped reestablish Logitech as a computer industry growth stock. Revenues surged 31 percent for the year ending in March 2000, hitting $615.7 million, while net income jumped 73 percent, to $30 million. The company's shares rose an astounding 174 percent during the year, the peak year for the Internet bubble. During 2000 Logitech sold its 300 millionth mouse and captured a commanding 70 percent share of the world mouse market.

A key move under De Luca's leadership was a major shift away from OEM products to higher-margin, branded products for the retail market. By 2001, 80 percent of revenues were coming from the retail side. This helped buffer Logitech from the severe early 2000s slump in PC sales. The firm also continued to seek growth through new product lines. During fiscal 2001 Logitech introduced its first peripheral designed for a game console, the Driving Force racing wheel for the Sony PlayStation 2. Over the next few years, the company developed more than 15 more peripherals for consoles, two of the most popular being cordless controllers for the PlayStation and Microsoft's Xbox, both introduced in 2002. Logitech pioneered another new iteration of the mouse in 2001, introducing the Cordless MouseMan Optical, the first cordless optical mouse. The optical mouse, which used a light-based tracking system, began replacing the older type of ball-based mouse.

In March 2001 Logitech significantly strengthened its position in the audio peripheral sector by purchasing Vancouver, Washington-based Labtec Inc. for $73 million. Labtec produced PC speakers, headsets, and microphones, and Logitech greatly expanded this line in the next few years, extending into audio products for game consoles and entertainment as well as headsets for mobile phones. At the same time, Logitech was developing products based on the new Bluetooth wireless technology. In 2002 it introduced a pointing device that allowed a user to control presentations within 30 feet of a PC. The company the following year brought to market its first cordless headset for a mobile phone, the Mobile Freedom Headset, which featured wind-canceling technology. Among the numerous other new products introduced in 2002 was the io Personal Digital Pen, a pen with a built-in camera for electronically capturing written notes for transmittal into a PC document. Another mouse milestone was reached in September 2003 when Logitech shipped its 500 millionth mouse.

By the fiscal year ending in March 2004, Logitech had enjoyed a remarkable string of success during a down period for the personal computer industry. Both revenues and profits had grown for six straight years since De Luca came onboard: revenues jumping from $470.7 million to $1.27 billion, profits from $7.1 million to $132.2 million. Logitech launched more than 100 new products during fiscal 2004 and shipped more than 47 million units under the Logitech brand. Continuing to seek new niches within the human–machine interface sector, Logitech bought Intrigue Technologies, Inc. for $29 million in cash. Based in Mississauga, Ontario, Intrigue produced ad-

vanced remote control devices for entertainment products such as televisions, DVD players, and the like. Later in 2004 Logitech announced plans to build a new factory in Suzhou, China, with an initial capacity increase of 30 percent, and it also introduced the world's first laser cordless mouse. The company said that the laser tracking system, codeveloped with Palo Alto-based Agilent Technologies Inc., offered 20 times greater sensitivity than LED-based optical mice. By accelerating organic growth through aggressive new product development initiatives, seeking additional medium-sized acquisitions similar to that of Intrigue, and increasing manufacturing capacity, Logitech aimed to triple its revenues by around 2010.

Principal Subsidiaries

Logitech, Inc. (U.S.A.); Labtec, Inc. (U.S.A.); 3Dconnexion, Inc. (U.S.A.); Intrigue Technologies, Inc. (U.S.A.); Logitech Hong Kong, Ltd.; Logitech Europe S.A.; LogiCool Co. Ltd. (Japan); Logitech Far East, Ltd. (Taiwan); Suzhou Logitech Electronic Co. Ltd. (China).

Principal Competitors

Microsoft Corporation; Creative Technology Ltd.; Royal Philips Electronics N.V.; Altec Lansing Technologies, Inc.; Veo.

Further Reading

Brevetti, Francine, "Logitech Big Cheese in World of Mice," *Oakland (Calif.) Tribune,* February 3, 2003.

Buckler, Grant, "Advanced Gravis, Logitech Complete Deal," *Newsbytes News Network,* May 9, 1991.

Einstein, David, "Building a Better Mouse: Logitech Is Big Cheese of Input Devices," *San Francisco Chronicle,* August 12, 1997, p. C1.

Girard, Kim, "Lord of the Mice," *Chief Executive,* July 2003, pp. 42–44.

Hall, William, "Increased Sales Help Logitech Buck PC Trend," *Financial Times,* October 25, 2000.

——, "Logitech Proves No Mouse Among Men," *Financial Times,* January 6, 2003, p. 15.

Jolly, Vijay K., and Kimberly A. Bechler, "Logitech: The Mouse That Roared," *Planning Review,* November/December 1992, pp. 20+.

Joseph, Cliff, "De Luca's Peripheral Vision," *Independent,* September 21, 1998, p. 14.

Lillington, Karlin, "Mouse That Roared Forms Basis for Logitech's Ongoing Success Story," *Irish Times,* October 18, 2002, p. 56.

"Logitech: 40 million de mulots," *Les Echoes,* May 18, 1998, p. 67.

"Logitech Is Now Market Leader for Computer Mice," *Economist,* July 7, 1990, p. 81.

"Logitech Mice Reach 100 Million," *Newsbytes News Network,* April 15, 1996.

Nulty, Peter, "Logitech International," *Fortune,* November 11, 1994, p. 116.

Olenick, Doug, and Steve Koenig, "Connectix Opts Out of Videoconferencing Market—Logitech Moves to Acquire QuickCam Line for $25 Million," *Computer Retail Weekly,* August 17, 1998, p. 2.

Phillips, Tim, "If You Plug It into a Computer, Logitech Wants to Sell It to You," *International Herald Tribune,* July 30, 2001, p. 9.

Rodger, Ian, "Almost Caught in the Mouse Trap," *Financial Times,* August 22, 1994, p. 7.

Ward, Jennifer Inez, "Logitech Hits Mouse Milestone: Company Ships Its 500-Millionth Device," *Oakland (Calif.) Tribune,* September 11, 2003.

—M.L. Cohen
—update: David E. Salamie

MACQUARIE
BANK

Macquarie Bank Ltd.

Level 15, No. 1 Martin Pl.
Sydney
NSW 2000
Australia
Telephone: +61 2 8232 3333
Fax: +61 2 8232 7780
Web site: http://www.macquarie.com.au

Public Company
Incorporated: 1969 as Hill Samuel David Clarke
Employees: 5,716
Total Assets: $32.96 billion (2004)
Stock Exchanges: Australian
Ticker Symbol: MBL
NAIC: 522110 Commercial Banking; 522292 Real Estate
   Credit; 522320 Financial Transactions Processing,
   Reserve, and Clearing House Activities; 523120
   Securities Brokerage; 523130 Commodity Contracts
   Dealing; 523210 Securities and Commodity
   Exchanges; 523920 Portfolio Management; 523999
   Miscellaneous Financial Investment Activities

Macquarie Bank Ltd. is Australia's leading domestically owned investment bank, and also is one of the leading independent investment banks in the world. The company has more than 5,000 employees, with operations in 22 countries, and direct investments in a wide range of companies throughout the world. Macquarie operates through seven primary—and mostly autonomous—business groups. The group's Assets and Infrastructure Group controls some AUD 7 billion in global infrastructure assets, such as toll roads, airports (including the Sydney international airport), railroads, seaports, telecommunications networks, water supply and sewage pipelines, and energy transmission and other utilities. The Treasury and Commodities group is active in the markets for precious metals, foreign exchange, debt markets, agricultural commodities, and capital management markets in Australia, the United States, the United Kingdom, Brazil, Japan, Korea, and Hong Kong. The Corporate Finance Group provides mergers and acquisition and

other corporate advisory services, while its Equity Capital Markets division provides services ranging from initial public offering (IPO) advice and management to share buy-backs, securities issuing, and the like. Macquarie's Equity Group is one of the top equity brokerages in Australia, targeting the institutional and corporate segments. The group also operates an Equity Markets division providing financial services and products to the retail and wholesale markets for clients in Australia, Hong Kong, South Africa, and elsewhere. Macquarie's Investment Services Group manages a portfolio of more than AUD 20 billion, primarily for its Australian clients, but also through joint ventures in South Africa, Korea, and Malaysia. The Banking and Property Group operates through eight divisions worldwide, including property investment management, financing, banking, securitization, lending, and professional and business banking services. Last, the Financial Services Group, formed in 2000, is the company's retail financial services arm, with more than AUD 10 billion in funds under management. In 2004, Macquarie acquired the Asian equities operations of The Netherlands' ING, providing the bank with a distribution network in ten of the region's major markets. Macquarie was formed in 1985 as one of Australia's independent private banking groups. Led by CEO Alan Moss, the bank boasts total assets of nearly $33 billion.

Creating Australian Trading Bank in the 1980s

Macquarie Bank was founded in 1969 as the Australian subsidiary of British investment house Hill Samuel. That company stemmed from a small business founded by Marcus Samuel in London in 1832. Samuel started out as an importer, bringing in goods, such as shells, from the Far East. By the middle of the 19th century, M. Samuel & Co. had developed a significant export business, shipping goods throughout Europe and to North America as well. Toward the end of that century, Samuel had begun trading oil, at first shipping cases from Russia to Japan. The company quickly launched full-scale oil shipping operations, and its first ship, the *Murex*, earned the distinction of being the first to pass through the Suez Canal. While Samuel maintained its focus as an investment house, the oil division later developed into the Shell Oil company, taking its name from one of Samuel's early trading successes.

In 1965, Samuel merged with the investment firm Philip Hill, Higginson, Erlangers Ltd., becoming Hill Samuel. In 1969, the company spotted the rising opportunities to provide localized investment banking services to the fast-growing Australian market, and established a subsidiary there, Hill Samuel David Clarke. That office became operational at the beginning of 1970, located in Sydney, and boasting a staff of just three people. Hill Samuel itself remained an important force in the U.K. and global merchant banking markets, later merging with the TSB Group in the late 1980s, which in turn merged with Lloyds Bank in 1995.

Hill Samuel David Clarke, set up by former Hill Samuel executive Stuart David Clarke, grew strongly through the 1970s and changed its name to Hill Samuel Australia as it expanded its focus to include direct investments in 1982. By then, the company had hired David Moss, who later emerged as a driving force behind the group's development into a world-leading investment bank.

Moss had started his career at the Australian Industries Development Corporation, before attending Harvard Business School, where he attracted the attention of Hill Samuel's CEO Tony Berg, in Cambridge on a recruiting mission. Moss joined Hill Samuel Australia in 1977 and by 1984 had been put in charge of establishing and leading the bank's risk management business. That operation became a critical part of the group's later growth.

Focused on the Australian market into the mid-1980s, Hill Samuel Australia made its first international move in 1985, setting up a branch in New Zealand. By then, however, Hill Samuel Australia had begun to outgrow its position as a subsidiary of a foreign company which, under Australian banking rules, was not allowed to establish full commercial banking services in the country. The Australian government, at the same time, had begun instituting a deregulation of the country's banking industry, including a proposal to allow a limited number of foreign banks to establish operations in Australia.

In 1981, Hill Samuel Australia began preparations for its transformation into an independent operation capable of competing in the deregulated Australian market. Because Hill Samuel remained small compared with the major banks petitioning for an entry into the country, the subsidiary determined that its best chance of winning one of the coveted new commercial banking licenses was in re-establishing itself as an independent, Australian-based business. In 1985, therefore, Hill Samuel Australia approached the Australian federal government with a proposal to change its shareholding structure in order to qualify for a license to operate as an Australian trading bank.

The Federal Treasurer agreed, and granted Hill Samuel Australia its license that same year, marking only the second time a private trading bank had been created in the country since the end of the 19th century. As part of that process, Hill Samuel reduced its share of the new bank to less than 14 percent. Hill Samuel Australia then changed its name, becoming Macquarie Bank.

Inspiration for the group's new name came from Lachlan Macquarie, one of the first governors of the early Australian settlement, who was given much of the credit for enabling Australia to shed its original role as a penal colony and become one of the Asia-Pacific region's most vibrant economies. One of Macquarie's achievements had been resolving an early currency shortage at the colony by creating a new currency when Macquarie bought up a number of Spanish coins, then worth five shillings, and had holes punched into them, creating the "Holey Dollar," worth five shillings, and a second coin, "the Dump," valued at one shilling three pence. In recognition of that early and inspired move, Macquarie Bank adopted the Holey Dollar as its own logo.

International Investment Bank in the New Century

From the start, Macquarie adopted a relatively flat operating structure, with central management overseeing a number of autonomously operating groups and divisions. In this way, the company encouraged an entrepreneurial culture from the outset, with its operations becoming directly responsible for, and rewarded by, the success of their business. In 1988, the bank's growing interests in direct investments led to the creation of a dedicated unit, Macquarie Direct Investment. In support of that business, the company established a third-party investment fund, Macquarie Investment Trust, later succeeded by the larger Macquarie Investment Trust II in 1994.

In the meantime, the company had brought in consultants to help it determine its future strategy. The consultants recommended that Macquarie limit its operations to the Australian market, rather than go head to head with its far larger competitors on the global market.

Yet Macquarie found it difficult to heed this advice. In the early 1990s, for example, Macquarie headed to the United States, forming its Security Capital Markets Group joint venture, later renamed as the Macquarie Capital Partners (MCP). By the beginning of the 2000s, MCP had already been involved in transactions worth more than AUD 33 billion, and also had been instrumental in raising more than AUD 25 billion debt and equity capital. Macquarie also moved into the Canadian market in the early 1990s, where it emerged as a major infrastructure investment group, adding to its portfolio of toll roads, airports, and the like.

South Africa represented another early international market for Macquarie Bank, where, through a joint venture, the bank developed significant activity in the bullion and other treasury-related commodities markets. The company later boosted its South African operations, establishing an infrastructure equity joint venture with Old Mutual Asset Managers in 2000, as well as a portfolio funds management joint venture with Samlam

Key Dates:

1832: Marcus Samuel & Co. is established in London.

1965: Marcus Samuel merges to form Hill Samuel.

1969: The Hill Samuel David Clarke subsidiary is created in Australia, subsequently renamed as Hill Samuel Australia.

1982: Hill Samuel Australia begins direct investment operations in Australia.

1985: Hill Samuel Australia receives a license to function as a commercial trading bank in Australia and changes its name to Macquarie Bank Ltd.

1988: The bank establishes a dedicated direct investment division.

1991: Macquarie Bank enters the U.S. market.

1994: A German office is established in Frankfurt.

1995: Macquarie establishes its first office in China, in Tianjin.

1996: Macquarie goes public with a listing on the Australian Stock Exchange.

1999: A joint venture with Industrial Bank of Japan is established.

2000: An alliance with Banco do Brasil is established.

2004: Macquarie acquires ING's Asian equity offices, gaining a Pan-Asian distribution network with operations in ten Asian markets.

Ltd. In 2003, the company stepped up its South African presence again, forming an alliance with NedBank Ltd. to market equity derivatives products.

The fast-growing Asian markets became natural targets for Macquarie as well. The company opened an office in Hong Kong in 1994, then turned to the mainland, opening an office in Tianjin, China, in 1995, a property development operation. In 1996, the company opened a Shanghai office, managing an 88,000-square-meter residential complex in Pudong. As the Chinese market matured in the early 2000s, Macquarie added mortgage and securitization services in Shanghai, in 2002, then formed Macquarie Investment Advisory (Beijing) Co. in 2004 to offer investment and asset management for the Beijing and Chinese markets.

By the end of the century, Macquarie had added operations primarily through joint ventures with local partners in Malaysia and Korea. The company's Korean extension started in 1998, with an alliance with Kookmin Bank. Also in Korea, Macquarie formed a joint venture with Shinhan Bank targeting the investment banking market, and particularly the property development and infrastructure sectors. The company also formed a joint venture in 2000 with IMM Asset Management, which built a portfolio of nearly AUD 3 million in assets under management by 2003. In 2004 another Korean venture, Macquarie International Asset Management Company, successfully brought its Macquarie Central Office Corporate Restructuring REIT to the Korean stock exchange.

Macquarie also entered the Japanese market at the end of the 20th century. In 1999, the bank formed a joint venture with the Industrial Bank of Japan, in order to trade and issue equity derivatives for the Japanese market. That venture placed Macquarie as the first Australian bank to begin doing business in Japan's newly deregulated banking sector.

In 2004, Macquarie significantly boosted its presence in the Asian region when it agreed to acquire the ten offices of ING's Asian equity operation. The move was described as a crucial part of Macquarie's expansion in the region, giving it a Pan-Asian distribution network for the first time.

Macquarie had in the meantime continued to develop its interests elsewhere in the world. At home, for example, the company boosted its national presence through an extension into western Australia. The move, which included mergers with Nevitts, in Brisbane, and Day Cutten, in Adelaide, at the end of the 1990s, not only positioned Macquarie closer to the important natural resources region in Australia, but also moved its operations closer to its growing Asian interests. A key part of Macquarie's success was its ability to locate and dominate a number of niche markets, such as infrastructure holdings, overlooked by its larger competitors. Fueling the company's growth was its decision to go public, listing on the Australian Stock Exchange in 1996.

Macquarie extended its American interests south in 2000 with the creation of a partnership with Banco do Brazil to price risk protection to the country's agricultural sector, as well as derivative and other equity structured products.

Macquarie also had established a presence in Europe, with a strong focus on the German-speaking market. First established in 1994, Macquarie's operations grew to include offices in Frankfurt and Vienna. In these markets the company targeted cross-border leasing and project finance advisory services, in particular for the infrastructure and related markets. With more than 5,000 employees and nearly $33 billion in total assets, Macquarie had emerged as a major player in the global investment market.

Principal Subsidiaries

A-Train AB (Sweden); A-Train Invest AB (Sweden); The Falcon General Partnership (Hong Kong); Generator Bonds Limited (New Zealand); Hills Motorway Management Limited; Horizon Energy Investment Management Limited; ING International Holdings Limited (U.K.); Macquarie (HK) Financial Services Limited (Hong Kong); Macquarie Airports Management Limited; Macquarie Americas Corporation (U.S.A.); Macquarie Communications Infrastructure Management Limited; Macquarie CountryWide Management Limited; Macquarie Diversified Portfolio Investments Pty. Limited; Macquarie Equity Capital Markets Limited; Macquarie European Infrastructure Fund Limited Partnership; Macquarie Funds Management Holdings Pty. Limited; Macquarie Global Debt Investments No. 1 Pty. Limited; Macquarie Infrastructure Investment Management Limited; Macquarie International Asset Management Co. Limited (Korea); Macquarie Investment Management (UK) Limited; Macquarie Investment Trust; Macquarie Leisure Management Limited; Macquarie Marinas Management Limited; Macquarie Office Management Limited; Macquarie Specialised Asset Management Limited; Mongoose Pty. Limited; South East Water PLC (U.K.); SPAL Limited.

Principal Competitors

National Australia Bank Ltd.; Commonwealth Bank of Australia; Westpac Banking Corporation.

Further Reading

"Diversity Buoys Macquarie," *Australian Banking & Finance,* May 18, 2004, p. 7.

Irvins, Steven, "Macquarie's Winning Ways," *Euromoney,* April 1999, p. 34.

Leahy, Chris, "Macquarie Goes Mainstream," *Euromoney,* May 2004, p. 46.

"Macquarie Bank Australia Rakes in US$191 mln in Performance Fees," *AsiaPulse,* January 6, 2003.

"Macquaric Benefits from Transactions and Initiatives," *Australian Banking & Finance,* May 20, 2003, p. 5.

"Macquarie Enjoys Fruits of Selective Expansion," *Australian Banking & Finance,* May 17, 1999, p. 5.

"Macquarie Out to Stay No. 1," *Australian Banking & Finance,* January 31, 2004, p. 3.

Rae, Marion, "Macquarie to Focus on Medium-Term Growth," *Australian Banking & Finance,* June 14, 2001, p. 9.

"Secrets of Macquarie's Success Revealed," *Australian Banking & Finance,* October 31, 2001, p. 9.

"Serial Networker," *Economist,* September 11, 2004, p. 69.

—M.L. Cohen

Mediacom Communications Corporation

100 Crystal Run Road
Middleton, New York 10941
U.S.A.
Telephone: (845) 695-2600
Fax: (845) 695-2699
Web site: http://www.mediacom.com

Public Company
Incorporated: 1995 as Mediacom LLC
Employees: 3,899
Sales: $1.0 billion (2003)
Stock Exchanges: NASDAQ
Ticker Symbol: MCCC
NAIC: 517510 Cable and Other Program Distribution

Mediacom Communications Corporation is a cable television multiple system operator (MSO), the eighth largest in the United States. Based in Middletown, New York, the company concentrates on smaller markets that the larger MSOs avoid. All told, Mediacom serves more than 1.5 million subscribers in 23 states. In addition to providing basic cable television channels, Mediacom also offers digital television, video-on-demand, high-definition television, broadband Internet access, and telephone service. The latter is an important part of Mediacom's effort to fend off competition from satellite television providers, which have enjoyed a great deal of success in taking away customers by offering an increasing number of local channels. Although Mediacom is a public company trading on the NASDAQ, it is majority owned by its chairman and chief executive officer, Rocco B. Commisso, who controls nearly three-quarters of the voting stock.

The Bronx and Beyond: 1960s–70s

As a 13-year-old boy, Commisso moved with his family from Italy to the Bronx in 1962. The son of a carpenter, he had greater ambitions than to lead a life of manual labor, although he retained a strong work ethic. Early on he decided he wanted to attend Columbia University, despite his inability at the time to speak English. In 1971 he earned a degree in industrial engineering at Columbia. He then took a job as a production manager for Pfizer Pharmaceutical and after four years resumed his studies at Columbia, receiving an M.B.A. in 1975, at which point he began a successful, and somewhat hectic, business career. Not only did he take a job at Chase Manhattan Bank, he and his brother opened a Bronx disco where he learned some practical lessons about marketing and running a business. The young entrepreneurs quickly realized that patrons were prone to move on to the next trendy night spot. As Commisso told *Multichannel News* in a 1996 interview, "We segmented the market and set aside different nights for different clients. We had a Spanish night, an Italian night, and so on. It worked." At the bank, in the meantime, Commisso was initially put to work in the transportation unit, but in short order his superiors transferred him to the media group, realizing that his flamboyant personality was better suited to the entertainment industry. It was here that Commisso became involved in his first cable television loan, a deal that whetted his appetite for greater involvement in the field and led him to become a cable specialist.

Working at the bank during the day and the disco at night proved exhausting and he sold his share of the club to his brother in 1981. In that same year he took a position with the Royal Bank of Canada's U.S. subsidiary in New York, establishing the Media Industries Lending Group and becoming a senior vice-president. His five-year stint in this role then prepared him to become the chief financial officer for Liberty, New York-based Cablevision Industries Corporation, a position he would hold from 1986 to 1995. During his tenure at CVI, Commisso played a pivotal role in growing the company from the 25th largest MSO with 223,000 subscribers to the eighth largest with 1.3 million subscribers. He developed an innovative loan agreement, an industry first, that allowed CVI to borrow money on the number of homes the company served rather than cash flow. Altogether Commisso was able to assemble $5 billion in financing for CVI. But after nine years of service he became the victim of his own success when CVI's owner, Alan Gerry, decided to cash in, selling the company to Time Warner, Inc. for nearly $2.8 billion. Despite disagreeing with the decision, Commisso emerged a wealthy man.

Formation of Mediacom: 1985

Commisso could have easily retired at the age of 46, but instead the self-described workaholic decided to launch his own MSO, to become the captain of his own destiny. Thus, in July 1995 he formed Mediacom, LLC in Middleton, New York, to acquire undervalued cable television systems located in non-metropolitan markets, a plan out of keeping with the prevailing opinion that the days of the small companies were long past. He spent the first few months working out of his home and putting together his business plan. ''The hardest part,'' he told *Multichannel News,* ''was dealing with all kinds of details, from personnel to accounting to answering your own phones.'' Commisso was able to take advantage of his contacts and reputation to attract financial backers, including Waller Capital Corporation, First Union Bank's Communication and Media Finance Group, and his old boss at Chase, Tom Reifenheiser, group executive of the bank's global media, telecom, and technology group. In March 1996 Mediacom became operational following the acquisition of a 10,300-subscriber cable system located in Ridgecrest, California, a deal that was soon followed by the purchase of a 7,000-subscriber system in nearby Kern Valley. The company completed another four acquisitions by the end of 1997, at which point Mediacom had more than 60,000 basic subscribers in systems located in Arizona, California, Delaware, and Maryland.

In January 1998 Commisso added another 17,200 subscribers to the California operation by acquiring the Lake County business of Jones Intercable, Inc., and a deal he completed later in the month elevated Mediacom to the next level. At a cost of $308.7 million he acquired the U.S. Cable unit of Cablevision Systems Corporation, adding about 265,000 basic subscribers located in markets in such southeastern states as Alabama, Florida, Kentucky, North Carolina, as well as Missouri. Commisso was able to acquire the system at a very low price, just under $1,200 per subscriber, at a time when rural systems were priced as high as $1,600 per subscriber. Mediacom's bid, in fact, was the third highest, but Commisso won out because his deal was fully financed, with $100 million in equity and $215 million in bank loans. Cablevision was eager to divest itself of the properties to focus on its core clusters of New York City, Boston, and Cleveland, and was confident that it would have no problem in closing the deal with Mediacom. Commisso called it ''the defining acquisition'' for Mediacom, which he believed had now achieved the scale to become the kind of company he had envisioned when he founded it in 1995.

Mediacom completed a pair of acquisitions in 1999 similar to the ones in 1998, with a small purchase followed by a major, strategic transaction. The first was the $19.5 million addition of Zylstra Communications and its 14,000 cable subscribers in Iowa, Minnesota, and South Dakota. The second, costing more than $750 million, was the acquisition of Triax Midwest Associates L.P., the largest deal in Commisso's life—although that was due to change a year later. Triax brought 342,000 subscribers located in Arizona, Illinois, Indiana, Iowa, Michigan, Minnesota, and Wisconsin communities. The cost per subscriber was about $2,100, but it was the last available acquisition of this size available in a market where prices as high as $4,500 per subscriber were not surprising. In contrast to the Cablevision deal, the main advantage of which was simply its cheap price, the Triax deal provided scale. In one stroke, Mediacom doubled in size to about 700,000 subscribers and was now large enough to consolidate in some markets. The company used fiber optic lines to connect the small systems, reducing the number of headends (where satellite signals are prepared for distribution), and management functions for an area could be consolidated.

Not only was Mediacom growing in size, Commisso was investing to rebuild and upgrade his systems, in keeping with a strategy to squeeze further profit out of his assets by gaining the ability to offer digital cable and highspeed Internet access, and keeping open the possibility of offering telephony in the future. To pay down the debt incurred in growing the business and upgrades, Mediacom prepared to make an initial public offering (IPO) of stock. In a preliminary step, the business was reincorporated in Delaware in November 1999, assuming a new name: Mediacom Communications Corporation. With Credit Suisse First Boston acting as underwriter, Mediacom raised about $380 million when the IPO was completed in February 2000. The company had a market capitalization of more than $1.6 billion, with Commisso owning a stake worth around $550 million.

With cash from the offering and a $640 million line of credit, Mediacom returned to the acquisition trail in 2000, completing several deals before the end of the year. First, it paid $8 million for Rapid Communications Partners, L.P., adding 6,000 subscribers in Illinois and Kentucky, followed two weeks later by the $8 million purchase of MidAmerican Cable Systems, L.P., picking up another 5,000 customers in the Midwest. In May 2000 Mediacom completed the $1.8 million acquisition of Tri Cable, Inc., serving communities in Illinois and Wisconsin. A month later Mediacom paid $10.8 million for Spirit Lake Cable TV, Inc., adding more than 5,000 subscribers in Iowa. Mediacom then spent $2.1 million for the cable television assets of South Kentucky Services Corporation, followed by the $1.2 million purchase of Dowden Midwest Cable Partners, L.P., which bolstered Mediacom's Illinois subscriber base. In October 2000, Mediacom completed a pair of acquisitions, paying $15.6 million for the cable television systems, and their 8,000 subscribers, owned by Illinet Communications of Central Illinois, LLC for $15.6 million, and $27.5 million for the cable assets of Satellite Cable Services, Inc., adding 12,000 subscribers in South Dakota. Then, to cap off 2000, Mediacom spent $34 million to acquire the cable television systems of an AT&T Broadband subsidiary, adding 14,000 subscribers in the Fairhope, Alabama, area.

Triax Acquisition in 2001

Another defining moment in the history of Mediacom took place in June 2001, when Mediacom completed an acquisition that dwarfed the Triax deal, paying $2.2 billion to AT&T Broadband for cable television systems in Iowa, Illinois, Georgia, and Missouri. As a result of adding 840,000 subscribers, Mediacom doubled its subscriber base to 1.6 million, becoming the eighth largest MSO in the United States. Although Mediacom paid about $2,600 per subscriber, the deal was still lower than the $5,000 to $6,000 price range of other acquisitions made in recent years. Unloading the assets made sense for AT&T because they were located in non-strategic markets, but for Mediacom their addition added new markets and created clusters that allowed Mediacom to realize some economies of scale. The company also had greater leverage when negotiating with programmers and suppliers. Moreover, by surpassing the 1.5 million mark in subscribers, the company was better positioned to catch the attention of Wall Street investors, and hopefully prop up the price of the company's stock, which had experienced lukewarm success since the initial offering.

Mediacom embarked on a period of digestion as it incorporated all of the new assets into its system. By the end of 2001 the company was generating revenues of $923 million, a significant increase over the $585.2 million achieved in 2001. The company was still unprofitable, although the net losses dropped from $190.9 million in 2001 to $161.7 million in 2002. Aside from integration issues, Mediacom was also facing increased pressure from satellite television providers DirecTV and EchoStar. Previously, small market cable operators, despite their inability to offer as robust a package of cable networks and sports packages, had an advantage because the satellite services did not offer local channels. But with changes in laws and technology the situation changed, as local stations in smaller and smaller markets became available to satellite television customers. In 2002 satellite providers offered local channels in just 15 percent of Mediacom's markets, but by June 2003 that number increased to 34 percent and by the end of the year reached about 60 percent. Moreover, the satellite providers were extremely active in their efforts to drum up new business, saturating markets with discounts and aggressive price promotions. As a result, Mediacom experienced some deterioration in its subscriber base and was forced to take steps to protect its market share.

Like the larger MSOs who had to deal with satellite competition earlier, Mediacom began offering digital cable, which not only featured a comparable lineup of cable television channels and sports packages (minus Sunday Ticket, DirecTV's exclu-

sive National Football League programming) but also video-on-demand and high-speed Internet access. The company was also hopeful that many basic customers, who far outweighed the number willing to pay for digital cable, would come back once the temporary satellite offers expired. Another area that Mediacom hoped would provide a competitive edge was telephony services, taking advantage of high-speed Internet access to offer voice-over-Internet Protocol (VOIP) to provide unlimited local and long distance telephone calls at a set price. With cable television encroaching on the business of the telephone companies, new alliances began to emerge. As described by the *Wall Street Journal* in 2004, cable and telephone companies each lacked one vitally important offering: "Cable companies don't have wireless networks, while phone companies can't easily offer television on their networks. To make up for this, phone companies are forging deals with satellite providers to offer video services and deploying high-speed fiber-optic lines. However, cable operators generally have a cost advantage, since it is relatively cheap to offer voice service over a cable network, particularly for cable companies that use Internet-based technology to send the calls." In 2004 Mediacom struck a deal with Sprint to offer phone service using VOIP to all of its customers by the end of 2006. Sprint was also looking to make its cellular system available to cable operators to offer cellular service under their brand name to fill in another gap. Mediacom was a likely partner for this venture as well. In the meantime, Mediacom still had to contend with the loss of subscribers to satellite providers, even as it began to post the first profitable quarters in its history as revenues topped $1 billion in 2003. How the company would fare in the coming years was very much an open question.

Principal Subsidiaries

Mediacom LLC; Mediacom Broadband Corporation; Mediacom Capital Corporation.

Principal Competitors

The DirecTV Group. Inc.; EchoStar Communications Corporation.

Further Reading

Farrell, Mike, "Rocco Moves on Up," *Multichannel News,* March 5, 2001, p. 1.

Gardyasz, Joe, "Mediacom Begins to See Fruits of Investments," *Des Moines Business Record,* February 16, 2004, p. 1.

McAdams, Deborah A., "All in the Family," *Broadcasting & Cable,* September 20, 1999, p. 77.

Paikert, Charles, "CVI's Commisso Starts Over," *Multichannel News,* April 22, 1996, p. 6.

Sherman, Jay, "Satellite Growth Bigger Threat for Small Cablers," *TelevisionWeek,* January 12, 2004, p. 24.

Willoughby, Jack, "Offerings in the Offing: Rockin' Rocco," *Barron's,* January 31, 2000, p. 47.

—Ed Dinger

Merillat.

Merillat Industries, LLC

5353 West U.S. Highway 223
Adrian, Michigan 49221-9461
U.S.A.
Telephone: (517) 263-0771
Fax: (517) 265-3325
Web site: http://www.merillat.com

Wholly Owned Subsidiary of Masco Corporation
Incorporated: 1946 as Merillat Woodworking Company
Employees: 4,200
Sales: $564 million (2003 est.)
NAIC: 337110 Wood Kitchen Cabinets and Countertop Manufacturing

Merillat Industries, LLC, a wholly owned subsidiary of Masco Corporation, is the largest manufacturer of cabinetry for the kitchen, bath, and home in the United States. The company's main product lines, from high end to low end, include Merillat Masterpiece, Merillat Classic, and Merillat Essentials. Merillat, which operates 11 manufacturing plants located throughout the United States, is a key component of the MascoBuilder Cabinet Group, which in 2003 generated 28 percent of Masco's $10.94 billion in revenues.

Early History

Merillat was launched in 1946 as Merillat Woodworking Company by Orville and Ruth Merillat. In the early days, the company manufactured custom kitchen cabinetry at a 2,400-square-foot plant in Adrian, Michigan. Merillat's original product line, Merillat Kitchens of Birch, was sold mainly to local consumers. It was also available through two modular housing manufacturers based in nearby Toledo, Ohio.

By the mid-1950s, consumer demand for Merillat products was increasing significantly, as was Merillat's market share. To cope with increasing demand, the company moved to a new, 15,000-square-foot, modular kitchen cabinet manufacturing plant, also located in Adrian. The firm also implemented several new marketing strategies, including a two-step distribution sys-

tem designed to provide more efficient product delivery. Revenues surpassed the $1 million mark in 1959.

Throughout the years, Merillat continued to position itself as a leader in the manufacture of cabinetry. For example, the company instituted a mechanized assembly line that was able to manufacture its kitchen and bath cabinets—with self-closing hinges, high-pressure laminate construction, and aluminum drawer glides—more quickly. In 1962 Merillat received a patent for its self-closing hinges, which replaced magnetic catches, leading to a new level of industry awareness of the company's technological advances.

In the mid-1960s, Merillat introduced a product line with reversible doors and drawer fronts, featuring two different wood grain-designed Formica brand laminates. The company also developed a hollow core laminated door, moving away from birch and toward the lightweight, highly durable products that the market was demanding. To stay ahead of increasing demand for its products, Merillat expanded its Adrian plant to 76,000 square feet in 1964, and to 135,000 square feet in 1966.

In 1968 Richard Merillat, son of the company founders, obtained a design patent for the "Romance" cabinet line. "Romance" was awarded a patent for using injection-molded plastic doors—an industry first. Prestique, a styrene material used in "Romance" cabinet production, provided the look and feel of wood, while being resistant to moisture damage.

In 1971, the 25th anniversary of the founding of Merillat Woodworking, the company was renamed Merillat Industries, Inc. Soon after, the company introduced cabinets with solid oak, double-doweled front frames and vinyl-laminated particle board end panels. By the mid-1970s, Merillat had expanded its product line with the introduction of an oak raised-panel cabinet called Forest Oak. In 1976 the firm built a manufacturing facility in the town of Jackson, Ohio, for the production of solid oak front frames.

Taken Over by Masco in the 1980s

The opening of the Jackson plant signaled a growth period during which Merillat Industries became by 1985 the nation's

---

Company Perspectives:

Since Orville Merillat began custom-fabricating kitchen cabinets in 1946, Merillat has grown to become the nation's largest manufacturer of cabinets by focusing on the needs of our customers.

---

largest manufacturer of cabinetry for the kitchen, bath, and home. By the mid-1980s, the firm had more than 2,000 employees in seven plants throughout the country: Adrian, Michigan; Jackson, Ohio; Lakeville, Minnesota; Culpeper, Virginia; Atkins, Virginia; Rapid City, South Dakota; and Las Vegas, Nevada. In 1982 the company moved into a new 21,000-square-foot corporate headquarters in Adrian. Three years later, Richard Merillat assumed the position of president of Merillat Industries, while Orville Merillat was named chairman. Also in 1985 Masco Corporation purchased Merillat for $144 million.

The evolution of the company continued in 1986 with the opening of a door frame and veneering plant in Mt. Jackson, Virginia. In addition, the Jackson, Ohio, and Culpeper, Virginia, plants were expanded that year. In 1988 a 43,000-square-foot addition tripled the size of Merillat's headquarters, enabling the company to better meet the increasing demands of the market.

In 1991 Merillat opened two additional manufacturing plants. The 75,000-square-foot plant in Atkins, Virginia, was opened to manufacture door panels. A new 225,000-square-foot plant in Loudenville, Ohio, was built to manufacture the Amera cabinetry line. Amera was introduced to provide product alternatives in the expanding remodeling market, which was becoming increasingly populated by sophisticated and upscale consumers. The Atkins and Loudenville plants brought Merillat's total manufacturing plant count to ten facilities and more than 2.5 million square feet. Merillat also had distribution centers in Denver, Colorado; Orlando, Florida; and West Palm Beach, Florida. The company sold its product through a network of 100 distributors and specialists who worked directly with major building contractors and individual remodelers.

1990s New Product Introductions

In January 1992 Merillat introduced six new oak raised-panel cabinetry styles with full overlay design into its ready-to-install cabinetry lines. Alexis and Alexis Arch provided a light finish, Bristen and Bristen Arch provided a medium finish, and Cambric and Cambric Arch provided a pickled finish. The products were all available with optional mullion doors with glass inserts.

The following year, Merillat introduced four new frameless maple raised-panel cabinetry styles: Kingsley and Kingsley Arch with natural finishes, and Rockingham and Rockingham Arch with pickled finishes. Also introduced at this time was a new generation of Merillat's traditional overlay light, medium, and pickled-oak cabinetry with the addition of full-concealed hinges, a new edge profile on doors and drawer fronts, and Merillat's own dual captive WhisperGlide drawer and tray system.

In 1994 Merillat introduced the Premium Woods, a line of three new wood species in traditional overlay, raised-panel

cabinetry. The Premium Woods included Preston Cherry, which was available in Nutmeg finish and red-toned Paprika; Darlan Hickory, which was available in Nutmeg and honey-colored Cider; and Shetland Maple, which was available in natural finish and oatmeal pickled finish. At that time, Merillat offered more than 40 traditional and contemporary cabinet styles in cherry, maple, hickory, and oak. In addition, Merillat cabinets were offered in three oak finishes, two cherry finishes, two hickory finishes, and two maple finishes. They were also available in one vinyl and four melamine laminate colors. Cabinet doors in the ready-to-install line had a variety of style treatments, including raised center panels with square, arched, and cathedral styling, square recessed panels, mullion doors with glass inserts, and flush contemporary doors, some with sculptured oak pulls and trim.

Merillat also offered more than 100 "Customizers" accessories for the kitchen and bath. The Customizers program provided builders or remodelers with a wide range of accessories. For example, the Appliance Garage provided a convenient stowaway area for appliances, and the swing-out pantry helped make the homeowner's kitchen accessible but not cluttered. Other accessories included drawer dividers, tip-out hampers, and a hutch. The program was supported by a full package of marketing materials and trade publication advertising. William H. Ficken, Merillat's vice-president of marketing, told *Professional Builder and Remodeler* that he believed the customized package of accessories was very important to the builder as well as the buyer. "The Customizers Program addresses the fact that there is a need to properly accessorize the kitchen and other areas of the home," he said. "Builders who upsell will have a good sales margin opportunity in these option packages."

Amera was another Merillat cabinet product line that offered customization and attention to detail. Amera kitchen products came in more than 50,000 combinations, including traditional framed and European frameless construction, 21 traditional and contemporary door styles, four wood species, six wood finishes, five laminate colors, and a full range of storage features.

By the mid-1990s, Merillat was well established as an upscale manufacturer and marketer of high-quality products. An article that appeared in the *Detroit News* noted that Merillat kitchen products were used in the 1994 renovation of the Manoogian Mansion, the traditional home of Detroit's mayor. Merillat attributed its success to its focus on brand awareness, according to *Professional Builder and Remodeler*. "Our customers recognize that our name creates a quality impact and awareness."

Merillat continued to expand and otherwise tinker with its product line in the late 1990s. The Amera line was expanded in 1997 to encompass more than 300 combinations of door styles, wood species, and finishes. The following year the company began offering its customers a streamlined cabinet selection process that featured standard architecture, a uniform assortment of cabinet sizes and accessories, and a simplified naming system. Clay Kiefaber was named president of Merillat in 1998, having joined the company in 1989 as director of just-in-time planning. In 1999 Masco entered into a strategic alliance with Pulte Corporation whereby Merillat Industries and Quality Cabinets, a sister company of Merillat within the Masco empire, became the primary cabinet suppliers for Pulte through 2002. Pulte was one of the largest home builders in the country.

Key Dates:

1946: Orville and Ruth Merillat launch Merillat Woodworking Company in Adrian, Michigan.
1962: Merillat receives patent for self-closing hinges, which replace magnetic catches on cabinets.
1971: Company is renamed Merillat Industries, Inc.
1985: The same year that Merillat becomes the leading kitchen/bath cabinet manufacturer in the nation, Masco Corporation acquires Merillat for $144 million.
2001: Masco reorganizes Merillat as a limited liability company.
2002: Company introduces its Merillat Masterpiece, Merillat Classic, and Merillat Essentials lines.

Early 2000s and Beyond

By 2000 Merillat's 11 manufacturing plants were churning out the equivalent of 1,000 kitchens' worth of cabinets per day. The firm's 11th plant opened that year in Ocala, Florida. This state-of-the-art kitchen and bath cabinet facility encompassed 240,000 square feet of space. During 2001, Masco changed Merillat into a limited liability company (effecting a name change to Merillat Industries, LLC).

Merillat that same year introduced its Organomics concept, a word created from the combination of *organization* and *ergonomics*. The Organomics system was aimed both at eliminating clutter and disorganization and, according to Doug Austin, advanced design manager for Merillat, allowing ''homeowners to perform household tasks without excess bending, reaching and running around.'' A key aspect of the system was dividing rooms into zones for specific tasks; for example, in the kitchen, the zones might be the sink, food preparation, cooking, storage/display, planning, and eating. After identifying the different zones in a potential kitchen, a homeowner could then select the cabinetry best designed to meet the tasks that would be performed in each zone. Merillat simultaneously introduced lines of cabinets for home office and home entertainment use that also incorporated Organomics into their design.

In January 2002 Merillat closed its plant in Lakeville, Minnesota, shifting production to its plants in Adrian and Las Vegas and the new plant in Ocala. One factor in the closure was excess capacity in Merillat's system of manufacturing facilities, but the company was also in the process of realigning its production resources to meet the growing demand in the Southeast and Southwest. Keith Allman, vice-president of manufacturing for Merillat, noted that ''as construction in these areas continues to outpace national averages, it is vital for us to have significant manufacturing resources in those regions.'' The opening of the Ocala plant was part of this same realignment as was the closure in March 2002 of Merillat's plant in Loudenville, Ohio. The Amera line had been produced at the latter plant, but this line was discontinued and replaced with the Merillat Masterpiece semicustom, premium line of cabinetry. Masterpiece was part of a new three-tier line of products that also included two lower end offerings, Merillat Classic and Merillat Essentials. Production of the Masterpiece line began at a plant in Middlefield, Ohio, owned by KraftMaid Cabinetry, Inc., another Masco subsidiary. Masco had typically taken a hands-off approach to its array of subsidiaries, but poor financial performance had forced it to seek out new approaches, one of which was encouraging cross-subsidiary cooperation, such as that between Merillat and KraftMaid. Meantime, Merillat sales were estimated to have fallen from $650 million in 2001 to $550 million the following year as Masco eliminated distributors in order to sell more cabinets directly to builders. Continuing to seek business in the fast-growing Sunbelt, Merillat announced in December 2004 that it would build a new manufacturing plant in Los Lunas, New Mexico, located just south of Albuquerque. The $36 million, 260,000-square-foot facility was expected to begin production in the fall of 2006.

Principal Subsidiaries

Merillat Corporation; Merillat Transportation Company.

Principal Competitors

MasterBrand Cabinets, Inc.; American Woodmark Corporation; Elkay Manufacturing Company.

Further Reading

''Cabinetry Zones in on Users' Needs,'' *Professional Builder,* April 2001, p. 35.
Colborn, Marge, ''Masco Is Making the Most of the Manoogian Face-Lift,'' *Detroit News,* September 24, 1994, p. D20.
Ford, Susan, ''Hanson Designs Merillat Site to Be Fast, Intuitive, Informative,'' *Toledo Business Journal,* June 2004, p. 15.
Fracassa, Anne, ''Adrian Cabinet-Maker Merillat Inc. Builds Itself a Nationwide Business,'' *Detroit News,* October 7, 1991, p. F7.
Huber, Tim, ''Kitchen Cabinet Maker Closes Lakeville, Minn., Assembly Plant,'' *Saint Paul Pioneer Press,* January 5, 2002.
Kuhl, Helen, ''Introducing Merillat's First Frameless Line,'' *Wood and Wood Products,* November 1988, p. 68.
Merillat—America's Cabinetmaker Fact Sheet, Adrian, Michigan: Merillat Industries, 1994.
''Merillat Introduces New Semi-Custom Line,'' *Kitchen and Bath Business,* March 2002, p. 9.
''Merillat Means Cabinets and So Much More,'' *Professional Builder and Remodeler,* November 1, 1991, p. 121.

—Pamela Berry
—update: David E. Salamie

Monster Cable Products, Inc.

455 Valley Drive
Brisbane, California 94005
U.S.A.
Telephone: (415) 840-2000
Fax: (415) 468-0311
Web site: http://www.monstercable.com

Private Company
Founded: 1978
Employees: 330
Sales: $100 million (2003 est.)
NAIC: 335931 Current-Carrying Wiring Device Manufacturing

Based in Brisbane, California, privately owned Monster Cable Products, Inc. sells a wide range of mostly high-end electronic cabling products. The Monster Cable Home AV division sells speaker cable, video interconnect cables, connectors, splitters, and clamps, as well as in-wall and outdoor speakers and mounts. Monster Car Audio is devoted to speaker cable connectors, audio interconnects, and power delivery cables for automobile sound systems. Monster Power provides power cords for home theater systems, computers, and other electronic equipment. Monster Computer product offerings include printer cables, monitor cables, network cables, and digital and USB cables. Monster THX Products, licensed by Lucas Films Ltd., sells a variety of home theater audio and video interconnects, cables, and speakers. Monster Game focuses on cables made specifically for video gaming systems. Monster Mobile offers cell phone products, including chargers and cases, hand-free headsets, and other audio, video, and power solutions. Monster PowerCells offers rechargeable, alkaline, and lithium batteries. Monster Photo offers rechargeable powercells and lithium powercells, as well as photo cables and camera bags. In addition, Monster offers custom installation services. All told, the company offers more than 4,000 products, which are sold in about 80 countries.

Engineer's Passion for Music Leading to 1970s Business

Monster Cable was founded by Noel Lee, who was conceived in China but born in San Francisco on Christmas Day 1948, prompting his parents to name him Noel to mark the occasion. He attended San Francisco City College before earning a mechanical engineering degree at California Polytechnic State University. Like many second-generation children from Chinese families, Lee at first followed the career path selected by his parents, but he also possessed a rebellious streak. Dutifully he took a job at Lawrence Livermore National Laboratories in 1968, where he worked on laser-fusion experiments and after several years became the program head, no doubt making his parents proud. During his spare time, however, he pursued a musical career, and in 1971 he began playing drums for an all-Asian country rock band called Asian Wood, producing music in the vein of Crosby, Stills, Nash, and Young. In 1974 the band was given a chance to tour around the world, and to the shock and dismay of his family Lee decided to quit his comfortable prestigious job to pursue music full-time.

Lee and Asian Wood first traveled to Hawaii, where they soon learned that their producers were expecting a pure rock band and were disconcerted by their country rock edge. After getting fired from this engagement, Asian Wood responded by virtually overnight transforming itself into a top-40 cover band. It soon found work and played the islands for the next 18 months before breaking up. Lee continued to work for another six months in Hawaii, then decided to return to the mainland to find steadier work. But the time he spent as a professional musician paid dividends, providing Lee with a practical business education as he learned how to deal with some of the less-than-ethical business people that populated the music field.

Back in the San Francisco area, Lee was able to land an engineering position at Lawrence Berkley Laboratory, but he found his assignments unexciting, and directed much of his passion toward his music interests. In fact, he would have gladly taken a job in the audio business, but with his background in laser fusion he was considered far too qualified to hire. He was obsessive about his sound equipment, and because he lacked the

256

Company Perspectives:

Already holding over 200 US and international patents, Monster is continually striving to discover and develop new, advanced technologies and designs to meet the needs of the ever-advancing consumer electronics industry.

money to buy the best available components he looked for ways to improve the quality of what he already owned. He soon realized that speaker cable was the weak link in the system. At the time, cheap zip cords were used as speaker wire and stereo dealers provided as much as a customer needed.

Working at night on a pingpong table in the two-room garage apartment he shared with his wife and son, Lee began experimenting with cables using different grades of copper, methods of winding, and insulation materials. He also added gold-plated connectors to provide better transfer of power from the wire to the speaker. Using his ear as a guide, Lee found the right combination of elements to make a speaker cable vastly superior to typical zip cord, offering a more dynamic and crisper sound. Although he was convinced that he had developed a superior product and desired to launch a company to market it, he faced the daunting task of convincing people, who expected to get speaker wire for free, to pay a premium price for a product they did not think they needed. With a small amount of money drawn from his savings and nothing but a gut instinct for marketing, Lee launched a speaker cable business in 1978. For a name he chose something that he believed embodied the powerful sound that resulted from the use of his product: Monster Cable.

Lee set up a makeshift production line in his garage apartment, hiring three people to begin assembling cables while he worked the telephone to arrange demonstrations at area stereo stores. An important moment came at the Consumer Electronics Show held in Chicago in the summer of 1979. Lee barely had enough money to pay for the trip and was fortunate to convince a vendor to let him set up a demonstration on the edge of his booth. Because, as Lee believed, hearing was believing, Lee's Monster cables were well received by attendees, and he was encouraged to continue his efforts to market them.

Introducing Additional Products in the 1980s

Lee slowly built his business, heavily dependent in the early years on the number of demonstrations he was able to give to store owners, during which he performed a side-by-side comparison of the sound produced by zip cords and Monster cables. As more stores began to carry his products, word of mouth among audiophiles also began to grow, and the business built momentum. In 1980 Lee also introduced a second product, Interlink, an audio cable that moved Monster Cable beyond mere speaker cable. During that same year, Lee was able to move production out of his garage and into a San Francisco facility. In 1983 Lee received a patent on his Xterminator electrical connector. During this early period, Monster Cable also attempted to move into the car audio market but soon

abandoned the field to concentrate on home audio. Nevertheless, after five years of effort and exponential growth in annual sales, Monster Cable had established itself. Now Lee's major challenge was arranging the financing needed to buy enough raw materials for the company to produce cable in the quantities demanded by consumers.

Monster Cable developed something of a cult following among audiophiles and high-end retailers, who were a bit disconcerted in 1987 when the company launched a mass-market product. This move was just a hint at the ambitious plans Lee had in store for Monster Cable. Mostly he pursued product areas directly related to cable and connectors, but that did not prevent him in 1989 from starting Monster Music, a small music label. In the early 1990s Monster Cable returned to the car audio market to stay and it also introduced a new line of standard speaker cable as well as its first speaker product: the Persona One, a three-way speaker that could be plugged into a Walkman, television, or personal computer. This product was part of an effort to position Monster Cable in the home office and photography markets, to further move the brand outside of its traditional high-end audio store channels. During this period, the company began to enter the home theater market by acquiring a license from Lucas Films Ltd. to offer cables under the highly regarded THX label, which indicated that equipment met a high standard of quality. But the company did not neglect its original focus, in 1992 introducing the M series of high-end cables. Moreover, Monster Cable expanded globally, especially in Asia, where it entered markets such as Japan, Hong Kong, Singapore, Malaysia, Korea, and Taiwan. Taiwan proved to be a sore point for the company, however. It allowed its Taiwanese distributor to file the trademark, but after the agreement was terminated the distributor began making and selling cables under the Monster label. Only then did Monster Cable realize that under Taiwanese law the filing party owned a trademark. After a lengthy legal battle, the matter was finally settled out of court to the satisfaction of Monster Cable.

Launching the Dealer Program in the Early 1990s

A key element in the success of Monster Cable was the innovative dealer program Lee developed over the years and formalized in 1993 as the M4 Dealer Success Program. The four "Ms" were Mix, as in product mix; Merchandising, including displays; the "Monsterization" training program; and Management commitment. The roots of M4 grew out of Lee's efforts early on to view the selling of his product as if it were a machine. Just as he had done with his home sound system, he looked to enhance *throughput,* but instead of delivering more power to the speakers to achieve better sound, he now wanted to move more products to consumers in an effort to make more money for himself. Again, he looked to strengthen each link in the chain, to create greater throughput, and soon realized that he had to find a way to have a greater impact at the point of purchase. Unlike most marketers, he did not try to motivate the top 20 percent of salespeople who generated 80 percent of the sales. His idea was to motivate the 80 percent of salespeople whose performance was pedestrian, assuming that the top earners would take care of themselves. M4 consisted of simple concepts that even the worst of salespeople could use to drive up sales of Monster cables. The first M, Mix, simply meant that

---

Key Dates:

1978: Noel Lee founds the company.
1980: The company offers its second product.
1987: The company enters the mass market.
1994: The M4 Dealer Success Program is formalized.
1998: A new headquarters and manufacturing facility opens.
2001: The Monster Mobile division is launched.
2003: Monster Photo products are offered.

---

a retailer needed to have on hand the full range of Monster cables a customer might need. Merchandising was something the company aided by providing retailers with excellent displays. ''Monsterization'' was training provided to dealers and salespeople to maximize the sale of Monster products. At its most basic level, salespeople were directed to ask, ''Would you like us to show you how to get the best performance from your system?'' Because customers generally wanted to get their money's worth out of an expensive electronic product, they were more than willing to pay a premium on cable to achieve the best results. To motivate the salespeople, Monster Cable sent top producers on all-expense-paid trips. Finally, the Management component of M4 was little more than commitment to the program from retailers, who became believers after enjoying success. Given the tight margins found in electronic products, which usually dropped quickly in price after their introduction, the sale of high-margin Monster Cable products provided a significant share of a retailer's net income, making them even more committed to Lee's program.

In the early 1990s Monster Cable generated $20 million in annual sales, but by the end of the decade that number reached $100 million. One of the company's chief problems during this run-up was lack of production capacity, a situation remedied by the opening of a new manufacturing facility and distribution center in 1998. Growth also was achieved by continuing to add products. In 1998 Monster Cable introduced a line of power products, including heavy-duty power cords with gold connections and enhanced surge protectors.

The company continued to bring out new products during the 2000s. It began selling a line of cable dedicated to gaming systems such as XBOX, PS2, and Gamecube. In 2001 Monster Cable launched its Monster Mobile division, offering products for use with cell phones and digital cameras. In 2003 the company added its dedicated Monster Photo product line as well as its Monster Signature Series Power line. The company also ventured a little far afield in 2004 with the introduction of high-tech furniture, a spinoff called M-Design run by Lee's son, Kevin Lee. The furniture was designed to hide large subwoofers. It also made an $8,000 Action Couch, which vibrated the seat cushions in conjunction with a movie's sound effects.

In 2004 Monster Cable increased its profile somewhat by paying $6 million for the naming rights to Candlestick Park, where the San Francisco 49ers National Football League team played. The facility was renamed Monster Park, rather than Monster Cable Park. Although Monster.com, the online employment site, received some benefit as well, Lee explained that his main goal was to help bolster San Francisco's recreation and parks budget, which received $3 million from the deal. He was less tolerant, however, of Monster.com's use of the word Monster in its own name, although the two companies came to an accommodation. Lee's attorneys also filed trademark infringement suits across the country, taking on parties such as the *Monster Garage* television show produced by the Discovery Channel, and Walt Disney's movie, *Monsters, Inc.,* as well as obscure business ventures. Settlements were reached with the major companies, while many of the small players were allowed to pass after the company made a public display of taking action, more a warning to larger companies than anything else.

Offering 4,000 products and recognized as the gold standard in an industry it essentially invented, Monster Cable was well positioned to enjoy continued growth. Ironically, some of that growth would be achieved through the introduction of new wireless products, which were becoming increasingly popular and, because of digital technology, more viable. The health of the company's founder, however, was not as robust. Lee suffered from degenerative nerve damage, which he said was the result of radiation exposure from his days involved in laser-fusion research. Lee was unable to walk very fast and relied a great deal on a small fleet of Segway Human Transporters to move around his 700,000-square-foot headquarters and manufacturing facility.

Principal Divisions

Monster Power; Monster PowerCells; Monster Game; Monster Mobile; Monster Car Audio; Monster Photo; Monster Computer; Monster THX Products.

Principal Competitors

Belden Wire and Cable Company; Cobalt Cable; JPS Labs LLC; Liberty Wire & Cable, Inc.

Further Reading

Evangelista, Benny, '' 'Head Monster's' Winning Ways,'' *San Francisco Chronicle,* November 8, 2004, p. C1.
Goldberg, Ron, ''Monsterize the Industry!,'' *Dealerscope,* January 2004, p. 96.
La Franco, Robert, ''Selling Sizzle with Sizzle,'' *Forbes,* December 28, 1998, p. 66.
Nahm, H.Y, ''The Cable Guy's Monster Attitude,'' GoldSea.com, http://goldsea.com/Business/Leen/leen.html.
Warshaw, Michael, ''The Golden Key to Selling,'' *Success,* May 1996, p. 44.

—Ed Dinger

Nagasakiya Co., Ltd.

3-7-14 Higashi-Nihonbashi
Chuo-ku
Tokyo 103
Japan
Telephone: (03) 3661 3810
Fax: (03) 3664 3843
Web site: http://www.nagasakiya.co.jp

Private Company
Incorporated: 1948
Employees: 5,000
NAIC: 445110 Supermarkets; 445120 Convenience Food
   Stores

Nagasakiya Co., Ltd. is one of Japan's leading retail chains, with a nationwide network of large supermarkets. The main line of retail is apparel, but the Nagasakiya group, which includes all of the subsidiaries of Nagasakiya, covers a wide range of retail activities, including home appliances, restaurants, and convenience stores. The Nagasakiya group is also involved in leisure development, finance, and import/export. During the 2000s, faced with insurmountable debt, the company declared bankruptcy and underwent major restructuring.

Post-World War II Beginnings

Nagasakiya was founded early in 1948 by Kohachi Iwata. The original store consisted of a small refreshment stand in Hiratsuka in Kanagawa Prefecture, near Tokyo. Kohachi Iwata was the son of a local retailer, Chohachi Iwata, who in 1919, at the age of 22, opened a small Japanese bedding or futon store in Chigasaki. The store was moderately successful, and Chohachi hoped his son Kohachi would join him in the family business after graduating from university. The young Kohachi Iwata failed his entrance exams, however, and left school in 1940 at the age of 19 to work in his father's store. His first job was to stand in front of the store and try to attract customers, and for the next five years he worked extremely hard at this.

The store was destroyed in the bombing of the Kanto area in air raids in the summer of 1945, leaving the Iwata family with nothing but the land on which their store had stood. The young and ambitious Kohachi Iwata decided to start a venture of his own on a small plot of land owned by his family in Hiratsuka, near Chigasaki. The plot was in the ruins of Hiratsuka railway station in the town center, and it was here in 1946 that Kohachi Iwata and his new bride set about making a living. The initial venture, called Nagasakiya, was a small refreshment store of about 20 square meters, and the main product sold was crushed ice flavored with fruit juice. In the summer heat it was a cheap refreshment for the city dwellers, many of whom were still poverty-stricken and were rebuilding their homes following the end of World War II.

Iwata worked frantically to make ends meet and build a successful business. In the winter, when the demand for iced refreshments had fallen, Iwata expanded his store to offer cotton clothes as well as the bedding that was his family's traditional business. In Hiratsuka, a relatively depressed city in the Kanto plain, Iwata's store offered basic necessities at a cheap price. Business grew to such an extent that by 1948 Iwata formed a company called Nagasakiya Co., Ltd.; its sole purpose at that time was the operation of the store.

Japan was rapidly changing for the better, however, and in the early 1950s the economy experienced rapid growth. The city of Hiratsuka became a shopping center for consumers in the surrounding suburban areas. Iwata noted that people were coming from Odawara and Isogo to shop at his store, rather than traveling into the city of Yokohama. By 1950 Iwata had accumulated enough savings to open a second store in nearby Machida, which also was called Nagasakiya. Apparel was now the main product line of both stores. In 1953 Iwata bought the building containing his original Hiratsuka store and converted the complex into a larger store.

The success of Iwata's stores in the early 1950s can be attributed to the booming consumer demand for essential household items and also to Iwata's constant hard work. During this time, several of the largest retailing chains in Japan today were emerging. Iwata saw Daiei Co., Ltd. and Ito-Yokado Co., Ltd. as his main competitors. In 1954 he envisaged a ten-year plan to set up a national chain of large supermarkets. He pinpointed the 40 largest metropolitan areas as targets for his stores. In 1957 Iwata was one of 16 entrepreneurial retailers traveling to North

Key Dates:

1948: Kohachi Iwata opens a small refreshment stand in Hiratsuka, near Tokyo, and then founds the Nagasakiya Co. and opens the first store.
1950: A second store is opened in Machida.
1958: The company sets up the restaurant subsidiary Choeisha and launches the Oasis restaurant chain.
1959: The company opens the first seven-story "superstore" in Hiratsuka.
1961: A public offering is made on the Tokyo Stock Exchange.
1973: The company launches a specialist retail subsidiary, Babybird Co., Ltd., which sells babies' and children's clothing.
1974: Sunbird Finance Company is launched to engage in corporate and personal loans for customers of Nagasakiya.
1981: The company opens its 100th department store; the convenience store chain Sunkus Co. is launched; company begins ambitious expansion and diversification, launching new eyewear, home appliances, high-end fashion, computer services, and other retail chains.
1989: Kohachi Iwata retires as president of Nagasakiya.
2000: With debts of more than ¥380 billion ($3.5 billion), Nagasakiya collapses, the largest bankruptcy in Japanese retailing history.
2001: New York-based investment group Cerberus agrees to acquire control of Nagasakiya and help it to restructure; Nagasakiya de-lists from the Tokyo Stock Exchange and begins closing 30 of its 84 stores.
2002: Company creditors agree to a rescue plan, including a debt-repayment program spread out over 16 years.
2003: Nagasakiya continues cost-cutting operations, including taking proposals from employees.

America on a month-long fact-finding mission. The group traveled to Hawaii and Los Angeles and then on to New York. Iwata was fascinated by the U.S. retail market and the use of a single brand name, such as J.C. Penney, to cater to mass consumer shopping nationwide. He also noted the use of vending machines, a phenomenon that had yet to reach Japan. These observations helped form Iwata's vision of a retailing empire in Japan. On his return to Japan, Iwata arrived at the port of Ichikawa in Chiba Prefecture, where he happened to notice a restaurant catering to the servicemen of a nearby U.S. Navy base. Iwata thought that the Westernized aspects of the restaurant could be applied throughout Japan. He promptly hired the manager of the restaurant and set up a subsidiary called Choeisha, which would eventually become the restaurant chain Oasis, a subsidiary of Nagasakiya.

As the first step in the creation of what he termed "superstores," Iwata decided to construct a seven-story building on the Hiratsuka site. His main problem at the time was the lack of financing for the project, yet he succeeded in obtaining not only planning permission but also loans from a wealthy bureaucrat in the Kanagawa Prefectural government in charge of new con-

struction, who was anxious to promote development in the area. Construction began in mid-1959 and was completed by the end of the year. It was the first Nagasakiya superstore, with elevators, escalators, and refrigerated food display cabinets. In order to repay the loans, Iwata announced cut-price sales at his other stores in nearby Hachioji, Kamakura, and Machida.

During this time Iwata opened stores at the rate of about one a year, and by 1961 there were ten Nagasakiya stores in Kanagawa Prefecture. Nagasakiya was at this time still privately owned by Iwata. He was advised that, in order to achieve the kind of expansion he envisaged, it would be necessary to float the company. Iwata was initially reluctant, being fairly ignorant of the financial world. After looking into the advantages and workings of the stock market he agreed to float his company on the First Section of the Tokyo Stock Exchange. The company was initially capitalized at ¥480 million. Nagasakiya now possessed the foundations for building a nationwide retail empire. It had the capital in the form of publicly traded shares, the market in the form of a booming Japanese consumer market, and leadership in the form of Iwata and his team of able managers.

The 1960s was a dynamic time in Japanese retailing. Supermarket chains Daiei and Ito-Yokado were setting up their nationwide networks at a furious pace. These chains provided a full range of household items. Nagasakiya, on the other hand, concentrated on clothing retailing, although in 1960 food retailing commenced on the ground floor of many Nagasakiya stores.

By 1967 Nagasakiya consisted of 30 superstores, compared with 20 stores five years earlier, with combined sales of more than ¥3 billion. The period 1967 to 1968 saw massive expansion in the Nagasakiya chain, with more than ten new superstores added during this year. These included stores in Shizuoka and Omiya, both in the Kanto region, with floor space of more than 2,500 square meters. The policy was to concentrate on opening large stores in the key areas identified by Iwata ten years earlier. In 1967 Nagasakiya launched its in-house brand of clothing— Sunbird—to be sold exclusively in the stores. The Sunbird line was costlier than Nagasakiya's other clothing, and by 1980 the brand was a well-established name in the Japanese fashion world.

In the period 1970 to 1974 Nagasakiya continued to thrive, with sales and floor space doubling during this time. Nagasakiya achieved sales of ¥100 billion in 1973. In the same year Nagasakiya felt that specialty stores were going to be profitable in the future and established a subsidiary, Babybird Co., Ltd., which sold babies' and children's clothing. In 1974 Nagasakiya established Sunbird Finance Company to engage in corporate and personal loans for customers of Nagasakiya. Sunbird Finance Company sold its services through outlets at Nagasakiya stores, and by 1980 these outlets numbered 200.

Nagasakiya's rapid growth was slowed somewhat by the oil shock of 1973, when the OPEC member nations increased the price of crude oil threefold overnight. This had a devastating effect on the Japanese economy, which relied on Middle Eastern oil for 70 percent of its energy needs. For the first time in ten years the Japanese economy experienced negative monthly gross domestic product (GDP) growth. The effects were not as severe for Nagasakiya as they were for retailers selling high-class and luxury goods, and the chain continued to grow, albeit at a slower pace. By 1978 sales had reached ¥200 billion, with a total of 90 Nagasakiya stores. By 1981 there were 100 stores. Nagasakiya entered the convenience store market in 1980 with the establishment of Sunkus Co., Ltd. With 630 branches, Sunkus was a fairly large player in this market but did not compare with Seven Eleven Japan and Circle K Japan, which owned thousands of stores. The establishment of specialty stores was a policy of all the major retailing groups at this time. Nagasakiya started Sun Men's Shop Co., Ltd., selling men's clothes, and Sun Optical Co., Ltd., selling eyeglasses and watches, in 1981. Cymbal Co., Ltd., started in 1983, specialized in clothes for the 12 to 18 age group, and Sun Techno Services Co., Ltd. was established in 1984 to provide building services for the Nagasakiya stores and other clients. In 1985 Kanoko Co., Ltd. was established to sell woolen goods, Sun Kaden to sell electrical home appliances, and L & B Co., Ltd. to sell high-fashion women's wear. Sun Systems Development was begun in 1986 to provide computer services for Nagasakiya and other customers.

In 1987, with significantly more than 100 Nagasakiya stores open throughout Japan and more than a thousand stores operated by Nagasakiya subsidiary companies, the company had become one of the top ten retailing groups in Japan. Like most markets in Japan, the retail market was extremely competitive. Nagasakiya embarked on a large-scale store renewal program in 1987. Old, inefficient stores were rebuilt under the "scrap and build" policy. Maximum use was made of floor space, and extensive market research was undertaken to plan store layout and stock levels. In 1988 the company's founder, Kohachi Iwata, retired as president of Nagasakiya to allow his son Fumiaki to take over the day-to-day operations of the company. Kohachi assumed the position of chairman and remained the inspiration behind the company.

At the beginning of the 1990s the Nagasakiya group of companies consisted of 115 Nagasakiya superstores and 53 subsidiaries operating mainly in the retail sector. Other business areas in which group companies were involved included real estate development, leisure centers, import/export, advertising, and an overseas restaurant in Singapore.

Collapsing in the New Century

A major development was the opening in September 1990 of Fantasy Dome near a Nagasakiya store in Tomakomai in Hokkaido. With 30,000 square meters of floor space, it was one of the busiest amusement parks in Japan and, being completely enclosed, it was the first all-weather leisure center in Japan.

Nagasakiya's growth was hampered by a fire in its Nagasakiya store in May 1990, in which there were a number of casualties. As a result of the ensuing negative publicity, the company was forced to initiate a costly safety assessment program in all of its stores. Compensation to the victims and their families also tied up capital intended for expansion. The company feared that it could even be forced to sell assets, depending on the total cost of the disaster. In the long term, however, this setback was not expected to affect the company significantly and steady growth was predicted in the 1990s, with slower growth in the mature clothing retail markets contrasting with the high growth of the convenience stores and restaurants.

But Nagasakiya's ambitious expansion of the 1980s and early 1990s caught up with the company—as well as Japan's retail sector in general—by the end of the 1990s. The company's drive to expand, and to finance its expansion through debt, depended on the buoyancy of Japan's consumer spending. Yet by the end of the 1990s, years of recession had cut deeply into consumer spending. Consumer spending habits also had shifted, toward larger-scale stores. Nagasakiya's heavy debt load, however, made it impossible for the group to follow suit. From peak sales at the start of the 1990s, Nagasakiya's sales dropped rapidly. The company initiated a store-closing program, shutting more than 15 stores through the decade. By the middle of the decade, the company had slipped into the red. In 1999, after five straight years of losses, the company's ¥184 million loss pushed it over the edge. Fully one-third of the company's 84 stores were losing money.

Finally, by 2000, Nagasakiya found itself crushed by more than ¥280 billion ($3.4 billion) in debt. Unable to pay its obligations, the company was forced to declare bankruptcy in order to shield itself from its creditors. This action, accompanied by difficulties among many of the company's competitors, helped spark the collapse of Japan's banking sector as well.

New York-based Cerberus Group, an investment group set up by Stephen Feinberg and specialized in rescuing failed companies, stepped in to provide financial backing to aid in Nagasakiya's rehabilitation. The company promptly began a new store-closing program, shutting 30 of the company's unprofitable stores. By 2002, with its total debt load topping ¥420 billion (including two company affiliates) the company had presented its rehabilitation plan to its creditors—which included the forgiving of some 99.4 percent of its debt. A reduced version of the plan was agreed to by the company's main creditor, Mizuho Corporate Bank, in July 2002.

The company continued exploring plans to cut its costs, including sponsoring a contest for cost-cutting ideas among its employees in 2003. At the same time, Nagasakiya began looking for new business ventures, such as an agreement with Ninety-Nine Plus Inc., which operated ¥99 fixed-price stores, to cooperate in the creation of a new chain of convenience stores. With its rehabilitation plan in place, Nagasakiya could look forward to a fresh start in the new century.

Principal Subsidiaries

Sun Denka Co., Ltd.; Sun Bird Tour Co., Ltd. (88%); Kanoko Co., Ltd.; Nagasakiya Photo Service Co., Ltd.; L & B Co., Ltd.; Sun Advertising Co., Ltd.; Be Gol Co., Ltd.; Sun Planning Centre Co., Ltd.; Cymbal Co., Ltd. (60%); Sun Systems Development Co., Ltd. (70%); Hiroya Co., Ltd.; Sun Assort Co., Ltd.; Baby Bird Co., Ltd.; Sun East International Co., Ltd. (67%); Sun Men's Shop Co., Ltd.; Sunland Co., Ltd. (98%); Sun Optical Co., Ltd.; SunBird Finance Co., Ltd. (39%); Nagasakiya Home Centre Co., Ltd.; Sun Techno Services Co., Ltd.; Sunkus Co., Ltd. (95%); ODS Nagasakiya Co., Ltd. (Singapore; 75%); Oasis Co., Ltd. (80%); Sun Leisure Co., Ltd. (83%); Sun Fantasy Co., Ltd. (90%).

Principal Competitors

The Daiei, Inc.; Ito-Yokado Co., Ltd.

Further Reading

"Crippling Legacy of Over-Expansion," *Grocer,* February 19, 2000, p. 11.

"Failed Nagasakiya to Close Some 30 Stores," *Japan Weekly Monitor,* Nov 12, 2001.

"Japan's Nagasakiya Uses Cost-Cutting Plans Proposed by Employees," *AsiaPulse News,* February 19, 2003.

"Katokichi Chief's Family Business May Support Nagasakiya," *Japan Weekly Monitor,* March 11, 2002.

"Nagasakiya Rescue Plan Agreed, Mizuho May Waive 79 bil. Yen," *Japan Weekly Monitor,* July 1, 2002.

Nakamae, Naoke, and Gillian Tett, "Japanese Supermarket Operator Collapses," *Financial Times,* February 14, 2000, p. 29.

Seiki, Ikai, *Shorai no Gotoshi—Ino no Shonin, Kohachi Iwata,* Tokyo: T and T Co., Ltd., 1988.

Turesik, Richard, and Jenny Summerour, "Japanese Confectioner Nagasakiya Files for Court Protection," *AsiaPulse News,* July 10, 2000.

——, "Japanese Retailer Goes Bankrupt," *Progressive Grocer,* April 2000, p. 20.

—Dylan Tanner
—update: M.L. Cohen

Napster, Inc.

455 El Camino Real
Santa Clara, California 95050
U.S.A.
Telephone: (408) 367-3100
Toll Free: (866) 280-7694
Fax: (408) 367-3103
Web site: http://www.napster.com

Public Company
Incorporated: 2000 as Roxio Inc.
Employees: 360
Sales: $99.3 million (2004)
Stock Exchanges: NASDAQ
Ticker Symbol: NAPS
NAIC: 518210 Data Processing, Hosting, and Related
   Services

The one-time renegade provider of music file-sharing software, Napster, Inc. has been reborn as a legitimate Internet music subscription service that offers the work of more than 45,000 artists on an on-demand basis. All told, the Napster music library includes some 700,000 individual songs and 65,000 albums. The Santa Clara, California-based company offers two levels of service. Napster Light is designed for people who merely wish to purchase music, which costs 99 cents per track and $9.95 for an album. Users also are permitted to search for music and listen to 30-second clips. Purchased music can then be played on a computer, burned to a CD, or transferred to a portable device. In addition, Napster Light users have access to music library functions, allowing them to use Napster to play CDs, create custom play lists that can then be shared with other Napster subscribers, import nonsecure WMA and MP3 files into their library, import tracks into a Napster library, and organize the music collection using Napster software. In addition to these "lite" features, monthly subscribers can listen to the Napster library on demand and receive a discount on music purchases. They also receive 50 radio stations and the ability to build custom stations.

Founder Born to Single Mother in 1980s

The man who conceived of the original Napster program was a college freshman named Shawn Fanning. He was born in Brockton, Massachusetts, in 1980, the result of a teenage pregnancy. His mother, Coleen Fanning, was one of eight children raised in a working-class family in the Boston area. At a sibling's high school graduation party held at the family house, a local band played, and Coleen met the guitarist, Joe Rando, who would become Shawn's father. (It was also during this party that his uncle, John Fanning, 14 years old at the time, got his first taste of business by passing the hat to pay for the band and accumulating a few thousand dollars. He would become a self-styled entrepreneur and play a prominent role in Napster's rise and demise.) Just 18 years old and the product of a much wealthier family, Rando ended the relationship when he learned Coleen was pregnant. She decided to have the baby and attempted to raise Shawn herself.

Coleen Fanning eventually married a truck driver and with him came four more children. Money was tight, resulting in a great deal of tension at home. Nevertheless, as a teenager Shawn emerged as a good athlete and a solid student. It was during this time that John Fanning took his nephew under his wing, rewarding him with money for good grades and buying the youngster his first computer, an Apple Macintosh. Shawn became obsessed with programming and the Internet, spending a great deal of time conversing with likeminded teens via Internet Relay Chat (IRC). He taught himself how to write software programs in UNIX code and became an aspiring hacker (as opposed to a "cracker," who used programming knowledge for nefarious deeds). He further indulged his new passion during the summers while working for his uncle's Internet venture. Never able to complete his degree at Boston College, John Fanning had bought a struggling computer company that eventually dissolved. He then launched an Internet company called Chess.net, a site where players could meet and play online. For programmers, he relied on several Carnegie Mellon University students who had developed an Internet chess server. It was from these students that Shawn Fanning refined his programming knowledge. He became proficient enough as a hacker that he was invited to join an exclusive IRC

Company Perspectives:

Napster is back with the answer for both the music industry and music fans: safe, legal and reliable access to hundreds of thousands of songs.

channel called w00w00, home to hackers and crackers alike, where members could share their programming interests. For his nickname on the channel, Fanning used what he had been called on the basketball court, Napster, because of his short, nappy hair. It was to w00w00 that Fanning turned when he began developing a pet project that would allow people around the world to share each other's music files. It was also where he connected with the two young men who would cofound Napster.

Shawn Fanning Entering College in 1998

Shawn Fanning applied to Carnegie Mellon, but was turned down and instead enrolled at Northeastern University in Boston in 1998. He was soon bored by his computer classes, which were too elementary for his skill level, and he began spending an increasing amount of his time toying with an idea to make music sharing on the Web easier. By now the MP3 format for compressing CD-quality music into digital data had become the norm, and some sites offering music files had cropped up. But there were some serious shortcomings: the songs were often not available because the index was out of date or the link was broken. Some sites also required users to know File Transfer Protocol (FTP) commands, a relic of the pre-browser days of the Internet. Shawn Fanning began thinking about a better way to make music available on the Web and conceived of a real-time index of all the sites available at any given moment. To achieve this, users had to log on to a central server, which acted as a matchmaker. But in order to download music files, users had to make their own music files available to anyone else who wanted them. As a result, the amount of available music grew as the number of people using the system increased.

To help develop the program that would become known as Napster, Fanning turned to fellow hackers on w00w00, sending them an early version of the Napster application. One of them was Jordan Ritter, who was a couple years older and employed at BindView, a security software firm. He became increasingly more involved in refining the program and eventually was put in charge of the Napster server, becoming one of the company's cofounders. Another of Fanning's IRC friends was Sean Parker, who combined an interest in computers with an entrepreneurial spirit, and became Napster's other cofounder. During his freshman year at college, Fanning spent most of his time working on his file-sharing program and found it more productive to work at his uncle's offices on the weekends than in his dorm room. By early 1999 he decided to quit school and devote himself completely to Napster, working out of the Chess.net offices, where he was oblivious to the fact that the business was failing. According to Joseph Menn in his *All the Rave,* John Fanning took note of his nephew's project and, sensing an opportunity, had papers drawn to incorporate Napster Inc. He then convinced Shawn in May 1999 to assign 70 percent of the business to him, leaving 30 percent for his nephew, arguing that investors would only come on

board if an "experienced businessman" were in charge. More familiar with the ways of business than his friend, Parker was stunned that Shawn had agreed to such terms. On future occasions John Fanning introduced himself as Napster's founder, a claim that was true in the sense that he was the one who incorporated the business. But instead of attracting investors, he reportedly drove them away, and instead of building a business, one that forged a partnership with the music industry, his truculent nature led to costly litigation and ultimate disaster for the company.

Parker had already been busy lining up backers for Napster. The basic business model was to get as many people as possible to use the web site, then sell them ancillary merchandise, like T-shirts and concert tickets. As for the record companies, the hope was that they would eventually decide it was in their best interests to cut a deal. While John Fanning was meeting with interested investors, involved in negotiations that seemed like an end unto themselves, Napster went online. At first Shawn Fanning shared a test version with 30 friends he met through IRC, all of whom pledged not to tell anyone about the project. But Napster proved irresistible and within a matter of days the word had spread and some 15,000 people downloaded the program. Napster spread across the Internet world, especially among college students, who took advantage of their high-speed connections through their schools' computer center servers. Only slowly did administrators realize that their bandwidth was being consumed by a single Internet service they had never heard of. Traffic grew so heavy that servers were often clogged with Napster transfers, so that by the early months of 2000 schools began to block the service.

In the meantime, after alienating several potential investors, John Fanning finally managed to strike a deal with Napster's first outside investor, Yosi Amram, who insisted the company be located in northern California where he could keep an eye on it. He installed as interim chief executive a veteran Silicon Valley venture capitalist, Eileen Richardson. Shawn Fanning relocated to the West Coast, bringing with him Parker and Ritter. His uncle remained in the Boston area, but he was still the company's largest shareholder and continued to influence the future of the company, which would soon become caught up in a firestorm of publicity and litigation, because not only did young people become aware of the power of Napster, so too did the music industry, which quickly concluded that Napster was a serious threat. Napster was branded as little more than a site that facilitated music pirating, and the industry did not accept Richardson's argument that Napster did not violate the law because it did not actually host the music. Her contention that Napster would actually spur CD sales by exposing people to new music also fell on deaf ears. In December 1999 the Recording Industry Association of America sued Napster, contending copyright infringement. At first all the suit accomplished was to further publicize Napster, playing some part in the woes to be experienced by university computer centers.

Musicians were split about Napster, with unknown bands and those with poor-paying record deals supportive. Backing the industry, however, was the best-selling heavy metal group, Metallica, which dealt a serious blow to Napster's reputation by filing its own copyright infringement suit in April 2000. In the midst of legal maneuvering and publicity firefights, Napster also was attempting to secure more funding. Amram and Richardson

Key Dates:

1999: Napster goes online.
2000: The court orders Napster to shut down.
2002: Roxio, Inc. acquires Napster's assets in a bankruptcy sale.
2003: A new Napster web site is launched.
2004: Roxio assumes the Napster corporate name.

convinced venture capital (VC) firm Kleiner Perkins Caufield & Byers to invest in Napster, but John Fanning, who likely would have been ousted from the Napster board of directors, had enough shares of stock to scuttle the deal. Richardson approached other VC firms, but none could satisfy John Fanning. Finally, Hummer Winblad Venture Partners made an offer, at a time when Napster was becoming desperate for money. Instead of valuing the company at $100 million like previous deals, Hummer Winblad assigned a $65 million valuation, but it also agreed to let John Fanning retain his seat on the board. Fanning signed on, but was soon maneuvered off the board.

Bertelsmann Investing in 2000

Having stayed longer than expected, Richardson stepped down as CEO, replaced by venture capitalist Hank Barry, whose background as a corporate lawyer was a welcome addition. But even the addition of attorney David Boies (who would gain greater attention later in the year litigating the presidential election between George W. Bush and Al Gore) could not prevent a federal judge in July 2000 from ordering that Napster be closed. An appeals court stayed the injunction two days later. In dire need of funds, Napster now attempted to build a legitimate business, and in October 2000 it found an unlikely partner when the German publishing conglomerate Bertelsmann AG, owner of the BMG record label, agreed to lend Napster $50 million to develop a commercial music service. Although the third largest record label, BMG had been performing poorly, and Bertelsmann felt it was worth a chance to align itself with Napster in the hope that the addition of an online distribution system might revive BMG's fortunes. The company expected the other labels to fall in line and to sign up as well, but they were instead incensed that Bertelsmann had provided Napster the financial resources it needed to continue fighting them in court. The possibility of cutting a deal with the other labels was then given a crippling blow in February 2001 when an appeals court ordered Napster to stop allowing copyrighted material to be shared on its web site. Napster exacerbated the situation by Barry holding a press conference to make an offer to the record labels, promising $1 billion over five years, the money to come from a new subscription service Napster had in the works. Because that amount made little difference to the record companies, and on a per-song basis was a pittance, the public offer backfired. Nothing less than unconditional surrender and the shutting down of the Napster site would satisfy the labels. Only then would they be willing to discuss the possibility of negotiating a realistic licensing agreement.

Napster attempted to comply with the court order and developed a filtering system to prevent the copying of songs from lists provided by the labels. Napster's engineers and outside consultants cobbled together a system that worked reasonably well, but still allowed 1 or 2 percent of the banned songs to slip by, due in large part to problems with copyright infringement notices. Rather than be in contempt of court, Napster voluntarily shut down its site on July 1, 2001.

Although it vowed to be back online soon, Napster remained dormant and essentially dead. A new CEO, Konrad Hilbers, made a last-ditch effort to negotiate a compromise with the record labels but failed. Napster began laying off staff in the early months of 2002 and turned to Bertelsmann for more funding. Bertelsmann now decided that it would be better off simply buying Napster outright and take its chances in cutting a licensing deal with the major record labels. In May 2002 Bertelsmann made an offer for the company, but the deal was all but sabotaged by John Fanning, who attempted to stage a coup and wrest away control of the board by filing suit against the board of directors. The Bertelsmann offer lapsed but was revived later when Bertelsmann offered to acquire the Napster assets for $8 million as part of a bankruptcy proceeding. In June 2002 Napster filed for Chapter 11 bankruptcy protection. But Bertelsmann's attempt to position itself as Napster's largest creditor, and thus have the inside track to acquiring Napster's assets, failed because its infusion of cash was not considered a loan but, rather, a backdoor attempt to gain an equity stake in Napster, an arrangement that was intended to shield Bertelsmann from any liabilities Napster incurred in its litigation with the music industry.

In November 2002, Roxio Inc., maker of CD-creation and digital-media software, emerged the winner in bankruptcy court, paying $5 million for the Napster name and its intellectual property. Parker and Ritter were long gone, and Shawn Fanning served briefly as a paid consultant. It was the name that clearly had the most value, as Napster retained a high level of brand awareness, becoming what the *New York Times* called ''the Kleenex of downloadable music.'' Roxio began building a music subscription business, helped greatly by the May 2003 $40 million acquisition of Pressplay, a digital music service jointly created by Sony and Universal. As a result, Roxio was well stocked with licensing agreements when the new Napster went live later in 2003. Roxio sold its other assets and assumed the Napster name, fully committed to its new business. It faced competition from a score of other music services, but was betting that the power of the Napster brand would provide a competitive edge. Napster's founder, Shawn Fanning, in the meantime was busy developing a new project called Snocap, in effect a clearinghouse for legitimate online music file sharing. It would serve as an accountant to make sure that registered copyrights were not infringed. The record labels were impressed and began signing up to register their catalogs, more than willing to forgive the young man whose revolutionary idea had caused them so many headaches.

Principal Competitors

Apple Computer, Inc.; MusicNet, Inc.; RealNetworks, Inc.

Further Reading

Ante, Spencer, ''Shawn Fanning's Struggle,'' *Business Week,* May 1, 2000, p. 197.

Chmielewski, Dawn C., "Struggle Embroiling Napster Could Threaten Bertelsmann Deal," *Knight Ridder Tribune Business News,* March 29, 2002, p. 1

Kover, Amy, "It's Back, But Can the New Napster Survive?," *New York Times,* August 17, 2003, p. 3.

——, "Napster: The Hot Idea of the Year," *Fortune,* July 26, 2000, p. 128.

——, "Who's Afraid of This Kid?," *Fortune,* March 20, 2000, p. 129.

Levy, Steven, "The Man Can't Stop Our Music," *Newsweek,* March 27, 2000, p. 68.

Menn, Joseph, *All the Rave,* New York: Crown Business, 2003.

—Ed Dinger

The Sight & Sound of Information

National Semiconductor Corporation

2900 Semiconductor Drive
Santa Clara, California 95052
U.S.A.
Telephone: (408) 721-5000
Toll Free: (800) 272-9803
Fax: (408) 739-9803
Web site: http://www.national.com

Public Company
Incorporated: 1959
Employees: 9,700
Sales: $1.98 billion (2004)
Stock Exchanges: New York
Ticker Symbol: NSM
NAIC: 334413 Semiconductors and Related Device
   Manufacturing; 334419 Other Electronic Component
   Manufacturing

National Semiconductor Corporation is a leading U.S. manufacturer of semiconductors used in a broad range of electronics applications. During its rapid rise to prominence in the late 1970s, National Semiconductor gained a reputation as the most efficient producer of semiconductors in the world, turning out a wide array of standardized, reliable parts at very low cost. National's prosperity relied less on high-tech genius than on low-tech frugality and hard work, qualities instilled in the company by its longtime president and chief executive, Charles E. Sporck. In the increasingly crowded world of semiconductors, however, National suffered during the 1980s from Asian price competition, turned around in the 1990s under another chief executive, Brian Halla, and used its expertise in analog chips in the 2000s to stake its claim in the evolving consumer products market. National's microprocessing chips power a multitude of portable electronics, such as cellular phones with cameras and Internet access, personal digital assistants, global positioning systems, tiny handheld television screens, and MP3 and iPod music players.

Humble Beginnings: Late 1950s

"Semiconductor" is the name given to a group of elements that under normal conditions do not conduct electricity, but that when slightly modified can be used as conductors with great precision and reliability. The development of the modern electronics industry, beginning with the 1949 invention of the transistor, depended on the use of semiconductors to control and direct electricity in very small packages known as integrated circuits or "chips." In 1959 Dr. Bernard Rothlein, formerly of Sperry Rand Corporation, joined the burgeoning semiconductor industry by creating National Semiconductor in Danbury, Connecticut (the company moved to Santa Clara, California, in 1968). The firm was tiny by industry standards, with only $5.3 million in sales by 1965, but it offered a variety of fairly sophisticated semiconductors and was operating at a profit.

Dr. Rothlein's former employer filed a suit against National for patent infringement, however, and the case depressed the company's stock price when it reached the courts in the mid-1960s. The low stock price encouraged a substantial investment by East Coast financier Peter J. Sprague (son of the chairman of Sprague Electric Company), who became chairman of National in 1966 and set out to make the company a major player in the semiconductor industry. Sprague recognized that National needed an injection of strong management if it was to make the transition from small research lab to commercial manufacturer, and in the spring of 1967 he surprised the industry by hiring away five top executives from Fairchild Camera & Instrument Corporation, then the nation's second largest maker of semiconductors.

Sporck Taking Charge:
The Late 1960s and Early 1970s

Chief among the new recruits was Charles E. Sporck, 39-year-old head of Fairchild's semiconductor division, who accepted a 50 percent cut in pay to become National's president (and owner of a chunk of its stock). From then until 1991 National Semiconductor would remain, in large part, the creation of Peter Sprague and the hard-driving Charlie Sporck.

Sporck and National Semiconductor were ideally suited to each other. National had some excellent products but lacked management control, while Sporck was not a technical genius but knew how to run a tight ship, market his wares, and make money. With the full financial and moral backing of Sprague and the board of directors, Sporck turned National upside down in the year following his arrival. He marked down the value of

Key Dates:

1959: Dr. Bernard Rothlein forms National Semiconductor in Danbury, Connecticut.
1967: Charles Sporck joins the firm as president.
1968: The company moves to Santa Clara, California.
1969: Fierce price wars erupt in semiconductor manufacturing.
1970: National reaches sales of $42 million.
1976: Company sales top $365 million, and National enters the computer mainframe market.
1981: Sales top the $1 billion mark for the first time.
1987: National buys Fairchild Semiconductor.
1989: National's mainframe unit, Datachecker, is sold.
1991: Gilbert Amelio is named National's new president and the company reorganizes.
1996: Brian Halla comes on board as the firm's new president and chief executive.
1997: National buys Cyrix, a manufacturer of microprocessors, and sells Fairchild.
2000: National and Taiwan Semiconductor Manufacturing Corporation partner to produce chips in Maine.
2004: The company opens its first manufacturing facility in China.

National's inventory of transistors by $1.5 million (giving the company a $2 million loss in fiscal 1967) and focused its energies on selling large quantities of standard semiconductors in three different market areas: linear, Transistor-to-Transistor Logic (TTL), and metal-oxide semiconductors (MOS).

Sporck also kept a tight lid on corporate overhead, using outside sales representatives whenever possible, farming out basic engineering and accounting work to independent contractors, and generally promoting a corporate ethic of austerity. In an industry rapidly flooding with new competitors, Sporck's penny-pinching proved key to National's survival in the coming price wars. As he told *Business Week* in 1970, "We make money because we have to."

Although it might not have been apparent to the casual observer in 1967, National Semiconductor had assembled a trio of powerful business advantages. First, National was in an industry about to undergo tremendous growth, as the spread of computers made semiconductors critical to every aspect of modern life. Second, National was able to draw on the financial strength of its investors to raise the large amounts of money required for expansion, and third, the company was run by a man naturally inclined to efficiency and thrift. The combination of these elements allowed National to grow with amazing swiftness, from 1965 sales of $5.3 million to $42 million in 1970 and an incredible $365 million in 1976.

For less well-prepared companies, the same period was fatal as bitter price wars erupting in 1969 and 1970 drove even giants such as General Electric and Westinghouse out of the semiconductor business and kept profit levels minuscule. Silicon Valley was suddenly very crowded and from among its scores of visionary entrepreneurs only a few would survive to dominate the national scene.

Sporck brought a global awareness to National. It was one of the first semiconductor companies to move its assembly operations to the Far East, where labor was available at a fraction of its cost in the United States. The company also sold about 20 percent of its finished products overseas, much of it going to Europe at prices that stirred charges of unfair trade practices. On the other hand, Sporck appeared to have grossly underestimated the long-term potential for competition from the Far East, where the growth of an indigenous semiconductor industry drove prices ever lower on the kind of standardized semiconductors made by National. Sporck's preference for selling a high volume of standard items generated National's prodigious growth, so long as its competition was limited to American firms operating on similar cost bases.

When the Japanese made semiconductors a global business in the 1980s, this formula brought consistent losses and a desperate appeal from Sporck for federal trade protection. National was at the forefront of political pressure leading to the 1986 Semiconductor Trade Agreement.

Failed Diversification Efforts: The Middle and Late 1970s

Sporck was aware of National's vulnerability and beginning in the early 1970s he made a number of attempts to diversify the company's sales base by "integrating forward," making consumer products as well as the semiconductors that went inside them. National leapt into the manufacture of calculators, digital watches, and video games, enjoying initial success as the public responded to the novelty of these high-tech gadgets. Within a few years, however, National's emphasis on low-price mass merchandising again left it vulnerable to the crush of competitors entering these markets. National had no experience in retail manufacturing and before long its products were saddled with a reputation as low-end junk, without the style or cachet needed to survive in a maturing market. By the time every American was wearing a digital watch, National had been driven from the marketplace, suffering minor losses that, fortunately, were overshadowed by its roaring success in semiconductors.

Two other efforts by Sporck to widen National's product line had more complex histories, though both also ended in failure. In the mid-1970s National became interested in the possibility of electronic point-of-sale terminals for use in supermarkets. In association with a group of California supermarkets, National developed the "Datachecker" system for the scanning and recording of sales, with which it built a substantial and modestly profitable business over the following decade. Of greater potential was National's decision around 1976 to enter the computer business, originally as a producer of mainframe computers for sale by Itel Corporation, a San Francisco-based marketing and finance company. As many others had tried before, Itel and National hoped to cut into IBM's domination of the mainframe market by selling similar machines at a reduced price. At first, National was satisfied simply to make computers for the Itel name. In the late 1970s, however, National tried to push into the market with its own line of mainframes and minicomputers encouraged by the huge profits it was making on the Itel IBM-compatibles.

National's System 200 and 400 lines of large computers never got off the ground, due in part to renewed competition from the ever vigilant IBM. Itel had similar but more severe problems, forced by IBM price pressure in early 1979 to ask National for cheaper computers with which to compete. Sporck recognized a golden opportunity: He agreed to supply Itel with cheaper computers only if they agreed to buy more machines. Itel did so and when the market softened later in the year, Itel was stuck with computers it could not sell and an obligation to buy many more. Faced with a complete disaster, Itel essentially gave its inventory and sales force to National in exchange for a release from its contracts. As one former Itel executive told *Fortune,* ''National blackmailed us and then stole the business.''

Be that as it may, Sporck had ''stolen'' little more than a distraction and headache. National enjoyed sporadic success selling a line of mainframes made by Hitachi in Japan, but again its timing and approach were all wrong. During the 1980s National, aside from the inherent difficulties of competing with IBM, faced a general decline in the mainframe segment of the computer industry that even IBM was not able to withstand. The monolithic mainframe was being replaced by combinations of mini and microcomputers, and in a shrinking market National's chances of success against IBM fell from slim to none. The company eventually sold its National Advanced Systems division in 1989.

Buffeted by Asian Competition: The 1980s

Despite its mainframe difficulties, National's semiconductor business continued to boom. Sales for 1981 reached $1.1 billion—tripling in four years—and the company employed 40,000 workers, two-thirds of them in Southeast Asian assembly plants. Its strength continued to be the manufacture of linear and bipolar logic integrated circuits in large quantities and at low cost; as a competing executive told *Fortune,* National was the ''sweatshop of our industry—a pipe-rack, low-cost, survival-oriented company.'' National, however, soon faced a number of grave problems. In 1981 a handful of key National executives left the company to accept more lucrative offers elsewhere, among them Pierre Lamond, who had been National's chief designer and engineer.

While job hopping was common in the electronics industry, the defection of Lamond was a significant blow. National had never been particularly strong on technical ingenuity and the company had relied on its brightest designer. Worse yet, competition from the Far East had increased and National would soon feel its impact. National's line of staple items was easily reproducible, and although it was the cheapest semiconductors manufacturer in the United States, it was not the cheapest producer worldwide.

The recession of 1981–82 plunged National into the red. Its losses totaled only $25 million, but they set the tone for the coming decade. The company was solid in the following few years, suffered a sharp downturn in 1985 and 1986, and then recovered again in late 1987. At this point Sporck made a purchase that must have given him great personal satisfaction, whatever its permanent value to National Semiconductor. For $122 million National bought the semiconductor division of Fairchild Camera, the same Fairchild from which Sporck and his management team had emigrated back in 1967. Fairchild had been one of the pioneers in semiconductors, but since Sporck's departure it had staggered through many losing years and was now available

at what some observers thought was a bargain price. Sporck felt that Fairchild's strengths in chips for mainframes and supercomputers and its excellent military ties would complement National's relative weakness in these segments.

The timing of the Fairchild deal, however, was poor, as the mainframe market continued to shrink and military spending declined from its peak during the Reagan administration. Moreover, Fairchild had lost $265 million in the two years prior to its purchase by National, and the latter already had plenty of its own problems.

Changing Directions: The 1990s

From 1987 through 1992 National posted an aggregate loss exceeding $500 million. President Sporck and Chairman Sprague took vigorous measures to right their floundering ship, getting out of computers and point-of-sale equipment, dropping the two least profitable semiconductor lines, and in early 1991 replacing Sporck himself with Gilbert F. Amelio. Under the leadership of Amelio, a former Rockwell International executive who had a Ph.D. in physics from Georgia Institute of Technology, National turned more of its energies toward the market for analog semiconductors, used increasingly by the telecommunications industry. Analog chips not only made consumer products simpler, but lengthened battery life and powered audio and visual components. National was already a top producer of analog chips, which for years had been all but lost in the excitement over digital chips for computer applications, and Amelio hoped the changing demands of the market would make National's analog expertise far more valuable in the 1990s.

The immediate signs, unfortunately, were not encouraging. Even after writing off $144 million in the massive reorganization of the company in 1991, National came up with a $120 million loss in the following year. As the restructuring took hold, National began to post healthy profits and saw revenues increase with each year. In addition to selling off noncore assets, Amelio also divided the company's chip lines into two areas: lower-margin, more cyclical logic and memory chips (the so-called ''commodity chips'' upon which National gained prominence); and higher-margin, value-added analog and mixed-signal chips.

Amelio's divisional shift seemed to point toward the eventual divestment of the commodity chips but before he was able to make this dramatic move, Amelio left National in early 1996 to become CEO of Apple Computer Inc. and attempt another turnaround. Amelio's replacement was brought on board in May 1996. National's new CEO and president (soon chairman as well) was Brian Halla, a former executive vice-president at LSI Logic Corporation who also had spent 14 years in marketing at Intel Corporation. The month after Halla's arrival, National announced the consolidation of its commodity chip lines within a new unit, Fairchild Semiconductor, resurrecting the name of the pioneering Silicon Valley chip company National had bought nine years earlier. Within months, however, in March 1997, National sold the Fairchild unit to an investment company for $550 million, retaining a 15 percent stake.

Halla also gambled on the ''system-on-a-chip,'' new technology able to handle all functions, including processing, logic, and memory, on a single chip. National's initial plans for the system-on-a-chip was to drive down the costs of PCs, essentially creating a PC-on-a-chip. National was not the only company pursuing this technology, rivals Texas Instruments and the France-based SGS-Thomson also were developing their own versions. Although Texas Instruments was bigger and SGS-Thomson had the clout of the French and Italian governments behind it, National seemed to be the most aggressive. The company made a number of acquisitions designed to gain the combination of technologies needed to make the PC-on-a-chip a reality. In March 1997 National paid $74.5 million for Mediamatics, Inc., a Fremont, California-based maker of audiovisual chips for the PC market.

Cyrix Corporation was acquired in November 1997 for about $540 million. Cyrix specialized in lower-priced Intel-compatible microprocessors used in PCs under $1,000. Halla planned to use Cyrix chips as a base for the revolutionary new chip, telling *Electronic News* (April 6, 1998), "First the PC goes on a chip. Next, the PC becomes a plug-in behind the dashboard of your car, behind a flat-panel display in your kitchen, or inside a set-top box. The PC disappears just the way electric motors are invisible in our lives. We use them all day long, but we only think about the appliance, not the motor."

Even though Cyrix seemed the most valuable piece of the system-on-a-chip puzzle, National acquired several other firms to make the chips a reality. Unfortunately, the road to fruition was not smooth. Workforce reductions occurred in 1996, 1997, and 1998, along with the closure of a manufacturing plant in Scotland. While National was certainly pouring research and development dollars into the system-on-a-chip technology, the company also inked a deal with Three-Five Systems, Inc. to develop liquid crystal silicon microdisplays for electronics and initiated a $2.5 million program to give teachers free training on the Internet.

In May 1998 National paid $122 million for ComCore Semiconductor, Inc., a manufacturer of integrated circuits for computer networking and communications. Sufficient progress had been made on the PC-on-a-chip for several top companies including Compaq and IBM to sign on, but delays, a softening PC market, and Intel's highly functional, competitively priced Celeron chip sent National into a tailspin. National sank into the red for both 1997 and 1998 despite overall sales of $2.68 billion for 1997 and $2.54 billion in 1998.

In 1999 National left the PC-on-a-chip business by selling most of Cyrix's assets for less than $200 million, keeping only the firm's MediaGX microprocessing products. MediaGX technology was used in National's new Geode line of chips for the rapidly expanding "information appliance" market. Information appliances, such as PDAs (personal digital assistants), MP3 players, and phones with Internet capabilities, used Geode chips to share data and power their many functions. The first Geode products included tiny handheld television screens for Philips Electronics and AOL. Other National product launches included a miniscule analog amplifier in protective packaging called "micro SMD" and "Merlin," the industry's first high-performance single-chip color scanner.

The New Century: The Early 2000s

The new millennium brought National renewed focus and vigor in its core operations. Analog products, while less glamor-

ous than its sibling components, continued to be the mainstay of the company with new innovations in display screens, wireless technology, and interface capabilities. National also turned increasingly toward a wide array of information appliances, as well as informational infrastructure (Internet and related technology). In addition to finalizing a deal with Taiwan Semiconductor Manufacturing Corporation (TSMC) to produce chips, National unveiled a new slogan, deeming its mission to be the "sight and sound of information" to its many customers around the world.

National finished 2000 with fiscal sales topping $2.14 billion and net income of slightly less than $621 million. The next year, however, was particularly tough on chip manufacturers, despite strides made in technology such as National's joint venture with IBM for remote Internet access and the acquisition of Wireless Solutions Sweden AB, Vivid Semiconductor, and InnoCOMM Wireless. The cost of the acquisitions, ongoing research and development, and a weak chip market took its toll in 2001, forcing National to lay off about 10 percent of its workforce. The company finished the fiscal year with sales of $2.11 billion and income of $245.7 million.

In 2002 and 2003 National continued to hone its amazing technological breakthroughs, with its chips becoming smaller, more sophisticated, and more reliable as the demand for handheld consumer products swept the world. Cell phones with Internet access and cameras dominated the market, along with a new generation of PDAs and musical devices (such as MP3 players and Apple's new iPod). National seemed to be ahead of these trends, but fierce competition and a still struggling economy forced sales well below the $2 billion mark to $1.49 billion for 2002 with a loss of $121.9 million for the fiscal year ending in May.

In 2003 National fared only slightly better: Sales reached $1.67 billion and income was still a loss but at $33.3 million. By 2004, however, National had begun another turnaround, hitting its stride with new product introductions, the opening of its first manufacturing plant in China, and the sale of its imaging sensor unit for small handheld appliances and cellular phones to Eastman Kodak. Sales for 2004 climbed only to $1.98 billion, but income rose to just shy of $283 million, a healthy leap from the previous two years' losses.

For early 2005 National's sales continued to fluctuate, though earnings were strong. Worldwide economic woes, however, did not bode well for continued strength in the chip market. Despite National's strong showing at the end of 2004 and in the first quarter of fiscal 2005, a round of layoffs was announced in January to keep the firm on the straight and narrow. Although National's outlook for the future was somewhat shaky, the company had come though several years of repositioning itself as a worldwide leader in analog technology. National already owned the color display market, with the majority of the planet's half-billion cellular phones using its chips for sight and sound functions. The future of National Semiconductor continued to lie within the tiniest of possibilities: creating microscopic chips with ever more tremendous capabilities.

Principal Subsidiaries

National Semiconductor A.B. (Sweden); Semiconductor Asia Pacific Pte. Ltd. (Singapore); National Semiconductor (Australia) Pty. Ltd.; National Semiconductor B.V. Corporation; National Semiconductor Bangkok Ltd.; National Semiconductor Benelux B.V. (Netherlands); National Semiconductor Canada Inc.; National Semicondutores do Brazil Ltda.; National Semiconductor France S.A.R.L.; National Semiconductor GmbH (Germany); National Semiconductor Hong Kong Ltd.; National Semiconductor (Israel) Ltd.; National Semiconductor Japan Ltd.; National Semiconductor Korea Limited; National Semiconductor (Maine), Inc.; National Semiconductor S.R.L. (Italy); National Semiconductor Technology Limited (China; 95%); National Semiconductor (UK) Ltd.

Principal Competitors

Analog Devices, Inc.; Cirrus Logic Inc.; Intel Corporation; LSI Logic Corporation; STMicroelectronics N.V.; Texas Instruments Inc.

Further Reading

Amelio, Gil, and William L. Simon, *Profit from Experience: The National Semiconductor Story of Transformation Management,* New York: Van Nostrand Reinhold, 1996.

Brandt, Richard, "The Man National Is Putting Its Chips On," *Business Week,* February 18, 1981.

Carroll, Paul B., "For National Semiconductor, Revenue Is the Challenge," *Wall Street Journal,* February 8, 1996, p. B4.

——, "National Semi Resets Agenda with New CEO," *Wall Street Journal,* May 6, 1996, pp. A3, A9.

"Color LED Displays Synchronize Light and Audio," *Product News Network,* November 19, 2004, n.p.

"Confounding an Industry on Prices," *Business Week,* November 21, 1970.

Epstein, Joseph, "Semi Circle: National Semiconductor's Turnaround Isn't Quite Complete," *Financial World,* October 21, 1996, pp. 82+.

"Fast Footwork in an Industry Talent Hunt," *Business Week,* March 11, 1967.

"Geode IA Processor Hits the Streets," *ElectronicBuyers' News,* April 17, 2000, p. 28.

Gomes, Lee, "Chip Maker to Revamp Cheaper Lines," *Wall Street Journal,* June 21, 1996, p. B7.

"The Hot New Computer Company," *Business Week,* October 22, 1979.

Kenneally, Christopher, "New & Improved," *PC Week,* May 12, 1997, p. 21.

Kirkpatrick, David, "Three Promising (non-Intel) Chipmakers," *Fortune,* December 8, 1997, p. 211.

Levine, Bernard, "Betting on System-on-a-Chip," *Electronic News,* June 26, 2000, p. 22.

Lubove, Seth, "Deus ex machina," *Fortune,* November 30, 1998, p. 50.

Miles, Robert H., *Corporate Comeback: The Story of Renewal and Transformation at National Semiconductor,* San Francisco: Jossey-Bass, 1997.

Murray, Thomas J., "Live Wire at National Semi," *Dun's,* August 1972.

Reinhardt, Andy, "National Semiconductor's Silicon Dreams," *Business Week,* October 14, 1996, pp. 94, 97.

Richards, Bill, "Computer-Chip Plants Aren't As Safe and Clean As Billed," *Wall Street Journal,* October 5, 1998, pp. A1, A13.

Roberts, Bill, "Virgin Territory," *Electronic Business,* September 2000, p. 132.

Silverstein, Roberta, "Old Chipmakers Learn New Tricks," *Business Journal,* March 24, 2000, p. 22.

"Streetalker," *Forbes,* February 21, 2000, p. 166.

Takahashi, Dean, "National Semiconductor to Acquire Cyrix," *Wall Street Journal,* July 29, 1997, pp. A3, A4.

——, "New CEO Strives to Revitalize National Semiconductor," *Wall Street Journal,* January 3, 1997, p. B5.

——, "New Chip by National Semiconductor May Drive PC Prices to Less Than $400," *Wall Street Journal,* April 6, 1998, pp. A3, A6.

Uttal, Bro, "The Animals of Silicon Valley," *Fortune,* January 12, 1981.

—Jonathan Martin
—updates: David E. Salamie; Nelson Rhodes

NAVTEQ Corporation

222 Merchandise Mart, Suite 900
Chicago, Illinois 60654-1105
U.S.A.
Telephone: (312) 894-7000
Toll Free: (888) 628-6277
Fax: (312) 894-7050
Web site: http://www.navteq.com

Public Company
Incorporated: 1985 as Karlin & Collins, Inc.
Employees: 1,411
Sales: $272.6 million (2003)
Stock Exchanges: New York
Ticker Symbol: NVT
NAIC: 541370 Surveying and Mapping (Except
   Geophysical) Services

NAVTEQ Corporation (Navteq) is a Chicago-based company that provides the digital map information used by Internet mapping services, automotive navigation systems, and mobile navigation devices. Navteq builds its database from the streets up, rather than taking the approach tried by others reliant on government sources supplemented by geometric extrapolation. Navteq employs hundreds of field researchers to drive every street, back alley, and dead-end lane, keeping track of some 160 road attributes, including speed limits and turn restrictions. Territories are also periodically revisited to keep track of changes. All told, Navteq's database includes coverage of 40 countries on four continents, at different levels of detail, covering 8.7 million miles of roadways. In the United States and Canada, where the company offers the most detailed information, Navteq covers 5.4 million miles of roadways. Navteq is looking to move beyond mere digital maps to interfacing them with traffic information, which can then be delivered to vehicles using the XM Satellite Radio service, allowing drivers to avoid traffic jams. Navteq is a public company trading on the New York Stock Exchange.

Company Launched in Mid-1980s

Navteq was founded by Barry Karlin and Galen Collins, with the former supplying the inspiration for the company. Born and raised in South Africa, Karlin earned an engineering degree before immigrating to the United States in 1976. He continued his studies at Stanford University, earning a master's degree in 1978, followed by a 1981 doctorate in Engineering-Economics Systems. He stayed in the Bay Area, working as a consultant for Strategic Decisions Group, gaining valuable experience working with major corporations, but he was attracted to the entrepreneurial atmosphere of Silicon Valley and developed a desire to start his own business. Through mutual friends he was introduced to Collins, who like Karlin was in his 20s and eager to go into business. A Northern California native, Collins held an engineering degree from the University of California, Berkeley and had done work for several Silicon Valley companies. He was strong in all areas of engineering, making him a good partner for Karlin, who was more interested in management and marketing. The two men considered some ventures but no idea caught their imagination.

Then, one day in early 1984 Karlin got lost driving in the Bay Area. He had a paper map in the car, but spreading it out across the steering wheel while he attempted to drive proved to be more of a nuisance than a help. "That evening," he recalled in a 2005 interview, "I thought, 'Wouldn't it be nice if I had someone sitting next to me in the car who knew the way?'" He then wondered if it were technologically possible to create a navigational system that could emulate such human assistance and tell him in clear steps the turns he needed to make to reach his destination. The more he thought about it, the more obsolete he considered the traditional paper map. He began doing some research and was soon convinced that creating such a navigational tool using an electronic map was technologically feasible. Karlin shared his idea with Collins, who was excited by the idea as well, and the two men decided to develop the concept commercially.

Collins worked up a pilot system, essentially to show that writing navigational software was feasible. The major elements of the concept were simple enough: the system had to know where you were, it had to know how to get you to your

272

destination, and it had to be able to render that information in step-by-step instructions. When Karlin tried Collins's mockup system he was told by the computer to do something that was not feasible, such as making a left turn where one was not permitted, and he realized that the underlying database of information had to include far more than just the layout of streets and their names. As a marketer he also knew that customers would be unforgiving with a system that proved frustrating. As a result, from its inception Navteq became very much detail-oriented in its approach to digital mapmaking.

Everyone with whom Karlin and Collins shared their idea recognized its potential, but when Karlin began looking for seed money he faced some major obstacles. In essence they were attempting to create a new industry, this at a time when venture capitalists took fewer chances, preferring to fund people with more stellar credentials. Moreover, the technology involved in making a navigational system was complex at every level. A massive database had to be built; GPS was in its infancy and overly expensive; and the software, which would be required to make driving decisions, had some artificial intelligence elements to contend with as well. Over the course of a year Karlin was turned down by virtually every venture capital firm west of the Mississippi River, everyone invariably questioning whether there was a market for a navigational device and intimidated by the disparate elements involved in making the concept work. There was a general recognition, however, that the idea made sense in the long run, but Karlin was warned he was embarking on an extended journey.

Because rental car companies were a likely customer for a navigational system, Karlin met with Budget Rent A Car's president, who suggested he contact T. Russell Shields, who had done some work for Budget and was known to sometimes provide funding for companies involved in database work. Shields was a Chicago entrepreneur who in 1969 founded a computer consulting company called Shields Enterprises Incorporated, later known as SEI Information Technology. Among its many accomplishments, SEI in the 1970s developed a mainframe business system for the U.S. Veterans Administration and real-time fulfillment systems for Time-Life, TV Guide, National Geographic, and Guideposts Publishers. Karlin met with Shields, who agreed to supply $500,000 in seed money, enough to prove the concept with greater specificity.

Mapping of Bay Area Began in Mid-1980s

In August 1985 Karlin & Collins, Inc. was launched in Sunnyvale, California, and began mapping the six counties and more than 100 cities that comprised the San Francisco Bay area. The company received another $2.5 million in seed money from Prudential Bache. The mapping proved time consuming and expensive. Aside from copyright infringement issues, relying on paper maps was not an option, since they proved to be fraught

with errors and acceptable for their intended use but not suitable as a foundation for electronic navigation. Far more useful was the work done by the census bureau, which had begun to create a digital geographic network for demographic purposes. Karlin & Collins also took high resolution aerial photographs of the Bay Area, then developed technology to integrate the census information with the pictures. People were also hired to drive the entire road network, armed with a Dictaphone to describe in detail everything they observed. To keep track of a vehicle's location, a key element in a navigational device, a dead reckoning system was developed in lieu of the GPS satellite technology the company later adopted. In essence, the system relied on a gyro compass and a distance measuring device to keep track of where a vehicle was on an electronic map. Then the location was constantly matched to the map at certain markers, such as turns, so that the system updated itself.

Mapping the Bay Area took about two years to complete. Because the idea of digital mapping was so new, there was no initial market for Karlin & Collins's database. They had to create turnkey products, the first of which was called DriverGuide, a countertop kiosk, which was essentially a dedicated computer that could be used by customers in car rental offices and hotel lobbies to provide printed driving instructions. The company had two other products in development as well: Mobile DriverGuide, a vehicle navigation product, with backing from Ford Motor Company; and Dispatch DriverGuide for fleet operators. In the early months of 1987 DriverGuide was set up in a number of Bay Area locations on a test basis. By October 1987 the product was rolled out commercially, and after a year nearly 80 of the $12,000 machines were placed in car rental outlets, hotels, restaurants, and convenience stores. Users were charged 50 cents per set of instructions and the company received a 25 percent cut in the money they generated. The *Business Journal of San Jose* described the way the system made use of the database: "The algorithm that pieces that data together uses the information to construct two detailed maps that surround the starting point and the destination. The two maps are then incorporated into a map of the area as a whole, and the computer then sends out two 'cars' to explore all possible routes. The 'car' that achieves the best travel time is selected by the computer."

It had cost $3 million to $4 million to complete the mapping of the Bay Area. Shields, who was highly enthusiastic about the technology, offered to invest another $3 million, but on the condition that he also be named the chief operating officer. Given that he had experience managing large teams of engineers, which was not Collins's strong suit, Karlin agreed. Shields now spent part of each week in both Sunnyvale and Chicago. Moreover, the company changed its name, becoming Navigation Technologies Corporation in September 1987. Other companies were now looking to develop navigational devices. Most notably, in Silicon Valley, Etak Inc. was selling a product that used an onboard computer, compass, wheel sensors, and mapping software to show drivers their exact location on a display screen. But the Etak product did not offer driving directions, a fundamental shortcoming, and when the company tried to emulate Navigational Technologies it quickly came to realize that its underlying map was not up to the task and the company decided to seek other opportunities. Nevertheless, Etak at this stage was aligned with General Motors and looking for partners in both Japan and Europe. Virtually every major automaker in the world, in fact, was working on similar products. European giant Philips N.V. began investing in Navigation Technologies in 1989 as part of its own effort to develop an automobile navigation system.

Early in the 1990s Karlin came to better understand the expense involved in mapping the United States, as well as the time it would take. The company was mapping a handful of metropolitan areas, such as Los Angeles, Atlanta, Chicago, Detroit, and Miami, selecting them mostly on the basis of having potential customers. For instance, Miami was chosen because of ties to Ryder Trucks, and Chicago because of Hilton Hotels. The company's kiosk business was doing reasonably well, but Karlin had already shelved the Mobile DriverGuide idea, realizing that a vehicle navigational device was not yet a feasible idea. For one, there had to be a complete digital map of the country before anyone would really want to buy the product. Karlin now realized that the time and money involved in making kiosks could be better used in building the database. It was at this point that Navigational Technologies changed its business model, so that instead of selling hardware it now licensed its database, allowing others to develop products that made use of the digital mapping information. Karlin also came to realize that it would take a number of years before the company would come to fruition and that he was not interested in waiting. He decided instead to sell out to a corporation with the patience, and deep pockets, to nurture the company. He found a buyer in Philips, which had assumed from the start that a map database was a crucial element in any navigation system it developed. Collins also chose to leave around this time, as did most of the early employees who recognized the massive commitment involved and simply wanted to pursue other interests in their lives. Shields remained with the company, however, ultimately taking over as CEO and in 1996 moving the corporate headquarters to Chicago.

New Technologies Help Accelerate Mapping in 1990s

The emergence of satellite and other technologies in the 1990s helped to accelerate the mapping process but Navigation Technologies was still years away from turning a profit. All told, Philips invested about $600 million into the company, and in the end decided to scrap its plan to build an automotive navigation system. From the perspective of Navigation Technologies, however, it was a wise investment, given that there was clearly a future demand for mapping information, and that because of the high cost of entry into business, Navigation

Technologies would eventually be advantageously positioned to reap a reward.

In 1996 Philips, which was under pressure to divest money-losing ventures, tried to cash out by way of an initial public offering (IPO) in hopes of raising from $125 million to $150 million. But at this stage all Navigation Technologies had to sell to investors were prospects. In 1994 the company generated $1.7 million and lost $41.1 million, followed in 1995 with sales of $3.3 million and a loss of $56.9 million. Because of poor market conditions the IPO was postponed. Philips continued to maintain majority control and Shields, still a major shareholder, stayed on as CEO and chairman.

In late 1998 Philips sold about 20 percent of its 60 percent stake in Navigation Technologies to a consortium of Dutch financial institutions. Several months later, in October 1999, Philips again took steps to prepare Navigational Technologies to become a public company. Shields was replaced as chairman by Richard de Lange, chairman of Philips Electronics Netherlands B.V., and a search was launched to recruit a new CEO, one with significant executive experience with a public company. In April 2000 Philips hired Judson C. Green, a longtime executive at The Walt Disney Company, who was raised in the Chicago area. He joined Disney in 1981 and eight years later rose to the rank of chief financial officer. Two years later he was named president of the company's theme park and resort business, Walt Disney Attractions, eventually adding the title of chairman in 1998. He launched a major investment program that resulted in the launch of a cruise ship line, the Animal Kingdom park in Florida, permission to build a theme park in Hong Kong, and a second theme park in Anaheim, California.

Green took over at Navigation Technologies in May 2000, charged with readying the company for an initial public offering of stock. The timing proved less than ideal, however, as the bottom soon fell out of the technology sector and the offering had to be shelved once again. But the postponement allowed Navigation Technology to at least spruce up its balance sheet. With an increasing number of automakers offering navigational systems and Internet mapping applications gaining greater usage, the demand greatly increased for Navigation Technologies' digital mapping information. Sales stood at just $51 million in 1999 but reached $110.4 million in 2001, then grew to $165.9 million in 2002 and $272.6 million in 2003, an increase of more than 500 percent for the five-year period. Moreover, the company finally posted a profit, $8.2 million in 2002, followed by $235.8 million in 2003. Although $165.5 million of that amount in 2003 was the result of a tax benefit, the company was clearly moving in the right direction. Its prospects were also likely to improve because it continued to map new countries and add greater detail to countries it already entered. The company was especially active in mapping Europe as well as the Middle East. Work also remained to be done in the United States, as researchers expanded its coverage level of rural counties. In addition, Navigation Technologies began working on dynamic maps, combining traffic reports with display-screen maps to help drivers find the fastest routes to their destinations. As the research progressed, the company forged an alliance with XM Satellite Radio to disseminate the information to drivers.

In 2004 management felt conditions were right to finally conduct an IPO. In preparation, the company changed its name to Navteq Corporation in February 2004. Then, with Credit Suisse First Boston and Merrill Lynch & Co. acting as the lead underwriters, the company completed its offering in August 2004. Interest was strong enough that the company was able to price its shares in the upper range of its asking price, $22, resulting in proceeds of $880 million. Philips reduced its 83.5 percent stake to 41.2 percent, while garnering $783 million, an amount that justified the company's backing of the venture for more than 15 years. Philips was expected to sell the rest of its stake over the course of the next year. It was likely to fetch an attractive price for the stock, which topped $40 by November.

Navteq's prospects appeared bright as it embarked on the next phase of its history as a publicly traded company. There was a great deal of the earth left to map, and with Navteq's head start, it had become prohibitively expensive for a new company to enter the field. Only Dutch company Tele Atlas stood as a serious competitor, as Navteq boasted a market share in the 75 percent range. More than 80 percent of the company's business was tied to navigation systems, and that business was very much in the early stages. In 2003 only 3 percent of new cars sold in the United States featured navigation systems, and in Europe, where the technology saw greater penetration, the number was probably 10 percent or less. As these devices inevitably gained in popularity, economics of scale would kick in, so that an option costing in the range of $2,000 would quickly fall and one day likely become as ubiquitous in cars as air conditioning. Moreover, Navteq's dynamic mapping service offered promise

as an additional revenue stream, making the $376 million in revenues the company expected to generate in 2004 and $476 million in 2005 appear but a fraction of the numbers Navteq would likely post in the years to come.

Principal Subsidiaries

NAVTEQ North America, LLC; NAVTEQ International, LLC.

Principal Competitors

Tele Atlas NV; Intergraph Corporation.

Further Reading

Goldfisher, Alastair, ''Nav Tech Expects Record IPO Will Finally Put It on the Map,'' *San Jose Business Journal,* September 9, 1996.

Gurrero, Agustina, ''Digital Maps Need People Too,'' *Chicago Tribune,* August 29, 2001.

Hughlett, Mike, ''Chicago-Based Digital Mapping Firm Navteq Charts Successful Path,'' *Chicago Tribune,* November 9, 2004.

Koland, Cordell, ''Know the Way to San Jose?,'' *Business Journal – San Jose,* February 23, 1987, p. 2.

Meyer, Cheryl, ''Navteq Leads Map Tech Revival,'' *Daily Deal,* April 22, 2004.

Walsh, Robert, ''No Gas Station Needed,'' *Business Journal of San Jose,* October 24, 1988.

—Ed Dinger

NETĒZZA

Netezza Corporation

200 Crossing Boulevard, 5th Floor
Framington, Massachusetts 01702
U.S.A.
Telephone: (508) 665-6800
Fax: (508) 665-6811
Web site: http://www.netezza.com

Private Company
Incorporated: 2000
Employees: 90
Sales: $8.5 million (2003 est.)
NAIC: 341190 Other Computer Peripheral Equipment
    Manufacturing

Netezza Corporation is a private company based in Framington, Massachusetts, that makes enterprise-class data warehouse appliances. By integrating server, database, and storage in a single machine roughly the size of a refrigerator, Netezza has achieved a major improvement in the analysis of large amounts of data. What would take hours to accomplish by a general purpose computer system can be done in a matter of minutes by a specialized Netezza appliance. The least expensive of the company's products sells for $300,000, capable of holding 400 gigabytes of data, while the top-of-the-line model costs $10 million and accommodates 27 terabytes of data. A 100-terabyte machine is in the works, at which point Netezza will begin competing more directly with the major players in the data warehousing field: IBM, Oracle, and Teradata. The Netezza approach is so promising that the company has had its choice of venture capital firms through three rounds of funding.

Founders Gaining Diverse Experience During the 1980s

Netezza was founded in 2000 by its chief executive officer, Jit Saxena, and chief technology officer, Foster D. Hinshaw. Saxena was born in Bina, India, in 1945, the son of a doctor and the only one of four brothers not to choose medicine as a career. After earning degrees at St. John's College in Agra and Bombay's India Institute of Technology, he came to the United States for postgraduate work, earning a master's degree in electrical engineering at Michigan State University in 1968. He went to work in Honeywell's minicomputer division and then moved to Boston in the early 1970s to earn his M.B.A. at Boston University at company expense. He next took a position with Data General, heading the software development group. He stayed until 1983 when he struck out on his own, starting a Boston-area company named Applix Inc. to develop and sell word processing and spreadsheet software for corporate workstation computers using the Unix operating system. The company's eventual cash cow was a robust spreadsheet that could provide instant market data to financial traders.

Hinshaw, in the meantime, earned bachelor of science and master's degrees in Electrical Engineering from Cornell University, followed by an M.B.A. from Harvard University. He became involved in hardware and software development at the Department of Environmental Protection, Stone Associates, Design Marketing, and Maplewood Enterprises, and also developed on-screen TV guides at VideoGuide. He then went to work for Keane, Inc., a major software consulting firm, and became a Y2K consultant before becoming independent, handling such important clients as Staples and other Boston-area corporations. It was because of this work that Hinshaw came to understand how much time companies spent trying to merge databases and storage archives using software applications. The companies were accumulating data at a rapid clip and the only answer they had in dealing with this massive amount of information, to get some actual use out of it, was to keep the platform and try to speed up the hardware or the software. Hinshaw realized that this approach was losing the battle and a more radical solution was required. He began developing a parallel system for database analysis. In this way, a request could be reduced to a number of smaller, more manageable queries that could be addressed to the database simultaneously, then reassembled on the backside to provide a much quicker answer. He also realized that the bottleneck in most systems resulted from the transfer of files from the disk storage system to the processor. To solve this problem, he designed an appliance that put a microprocessor on each drive as well as a database program burned into the circuits. As a result, data requests were made at the drive itself, and instead of sending huge files to the main computer to be mined for information, the drives sent back pertinent data only, which could then be quickly organized and analyzed. Because so much needless activity was eliminated, Hinshaw's integrated, parallel approach was able to perform data warehousing chores at a much faster rate than traditional systems.

Saxena enjoyed a successful run at Applix, but as Unix workstations began to be superseded by the Microsoft platform in the 1990s, he had to switch gears and move Applix into business intelligence and customer relationship management. Realizing that he had done as much as he could with the company, he turned over the CEO position and became chairman. He also began looking around for new opportunities. One of the people he met with was Hinshaw, who was searching for a chief executive to run a company to develop his idea for a data warehousing appliance. Saxena was the only executive Hinshaw met who actually understood why his approach was so important. The two men agreed to team up, and in September 2000 they founded Netezza, which was Urdu for "results."

Initial Round of Funding in 2000

In December 2000, Saxena was able to raise $8 million in initial round start-up funds from venture capital firms Charles River Ventures and Matrix Partners. Matrix was already familiar with Saxena, having helped to fund Applix. Netezza may have had more difficulty hiring personnel than it did raising money. Hinshaw recruited at the Massachusetts Institute of Technology only to find students had little interest in the data warehousing field. Nevertheless, Hinshaw was able to build a staff of about 70 and Netezza set up shop in Framington and began developing the company's first product. Advance buzz about the company's technology was so strong that by late 2001, when the company was not yet generating a dime in revenues, Saxena was besieged by four venture capital firms eager to get a stake in the new company. After little activity in the previous year or so, due to a meltdown in the technology marketplace, venture capital firms had plenty of money to invest, an estimated $1 billion, and were now anxious to put it to work. But they were also cautious and only interested in the best available ideas. As a result, the right to invest in companies like Netezza was auctioned, leaving the vast majority of start-ups ignored. Netezza's second round of venture capital funding was completed in January 2002 after the venture capital firms bid up the company's valuation. Although the exact valuation figures were not revealed, it was understood to be a significant increase over the first round. All told, Netezza raised more than $25 million, with Battery Ventures leading round B, which also included the company's initial investors, Matrix and Charles River, along with Orange Ventures.

Other than venture capital firms, Netezza also received a vote of confidence in May 2002 when Ed Zander, who had recently announced his resignation as CEO of Sun Microsystems, agreed to join the Netezza board. Saxena had worked with

Zander during his days at Data General, and he first approached him about joining the Netezza board in 2001. His presence on a company's board was in high demand, and since the mid-1900s, when he began serving on boards, he became a director at SeeCommerce, Portal Software, and Multilink Technology Corporation. For a start-up like Netezza to land Zander was a major coup and validation in the marketplace. As he told reporters, "I don't pick just any old board." Zander also made himself available to Saxena to fine-tune Netezza's business plan, and to help zero in on the company's primary customers. Zander was immediately helpful by downplaying Netezza's position as a potential rival to the servers sold by Sun, IBM, or Hewlett-Packard. Instead, Zander maintained that Netezza's appliance could complement expensive servers already in place, fielding data requests so that the others' servers could more quickly perform a business-intelligence application. In this way, Netezza could sell alongside the much larger companies, in effect acting as a partner. Such a message delivered by someone with Zander's stature was a major plus for the young company, but his presence on the board was also something of a distraction, as Saxena had to contend with rumors that Zander was about to take his job. That talk finally subsided when Zander took the top job at Motorola Inc. He would remain a vital member of Netezza's board and according to the *Boston Business Journal,* he placed "the occasional call to assist a sale, particularly in his old stomping ground of Silicon Valley, to prospective buyers who have reservations about entrusting their systems to a small Massachusetts startup."

Introducing the First Product in 2002

In the fall of 2002, Netezza introduced its first product, the Netezza Performance Server 8000 line, which was priced from $622,000. It was well received in the marketplace, despite being panned by Stephen Brobst, an important figure in data warehousing who had taught at MIT before joining Teradata. According to the *Boston Business Journal,* Brobst said Netezza's "designs were based on the work of Michael Stonebraker and were never intended for decision support. Brobst said that Netezza has put back to work employees and ideas from two defunct supercomputer companies: Thinking Machines Corp. and Kendall Square Research Corp., a Waltham company that dissolved amid financial scandal in 1992." Saxena responded by saying, "He clearly didn't understand what it was we were doing."

The people who did understand were the people who bought Netezza appliances and became the company's reference customers, who in the beginning were involved in retailing and marketing. They included Epsilon, a junk mailer that used high-performance analytics to segment and target customers for large-scale marketing campaigns, and The TJX Companies, a major retailing operation that needed quick access to inventory and customer service customers. These early users were quite pleased with Netezza's performance. Epsilon claimed the new boxes ran 20 times faster than the company's IBM computers and cost half as much.

Netezza's investors were clearly satisfied with the company's progress, convinced that the company was on the verge of defining a new category and had the potential to become a major company. Its products were suitable for customers in a large number of industries, including financial services, healthcare,

Key Dates:

2000: The company is founded.
2002: The first product is launched.
2003: The third round of venture capital funding is completed.

pharmaceuticals, and telecommunications. A telephone company, for example, had to come to grips with billions of phone calls and the reality that the volume of data was just going to increase with time. The only company offering a data warehouse solution was Teradata, but it could not match Netezza on price. According to one analyst quoted by *Mass High Tech,* Netezza's "biggest challenge is finding customers who have tried to solve this big data management problem on their own and have failed. Because if you're talking to people who haven't tried to do it yet, they won't understand the benefits."

In July 2003 Netezza completed the C round of funding, raising another $20 million, this time led by California-based Sequoia Capital. Netezza's previous investors also participated. At this stage the company had just five customers. Nonetheless, its backers were excited by the company's potential.

In 2003 Netezza broadened its range of customers to include bioinformatics and the life sciences market. Several years earlier as life sciences companies raced to sequence the human genome, a number of start-up companies attempted to develop database tools to help pharmaceutical companies sift through the massive amounts of genetic information their researchers were producing, but in the end the drug companies elected to develop their own applications. Unlike earlier companies, Netezza did not sell prepackaged applications. Rather, it offered an infrastructure that allowed the custom applications developed by pharmaceuticals to run much faster.

By September 2004, Netezza had 15 customers and had shipped 35 systems. Some of those companies—TJX, AT&T Wireless, and Nextel—were return customers. As a result, Netezza was on track to become profitable at the end of the year. In November 2004, the company added a new product to the 8000 Series, the NPS 8025, capable of handling one terabyte of information, a far cry from the hundreds of terabytes that systems constructed by Teradata was building for such giant retailers as Wal-Mart, FedEx, and Dell. Netezza hoped to have a 100-terabyte unit ready for sale in the next year or so. With spending on data warehouse systems reaching $15.5 billion in 2003, there was ample market share available to Netezza, which combined an attractive price with excellent performance. Saxena told *Forbes* in 2004 that he was certain Netezza would become a $1 billion company. It was also a certainty that when the time was ripe, shareholders would either take Netezza public or engineer an exit strategy by selling the company to a giant rival.

Principal Competitors

Teradata; International Business Machines Corporation; Oracle Corporation.

Further Reading

Lelii, Sonia R., "Everyone's into Appliances—This Alternative to All-Purpose Machines Is Making Waves," *VARbusiness,* November 11, 2002, p. 95.

Lyons, Daniel, "Speed Demon," *Forbes,* December 13, 2004, p. 110.

Hibbard, Justin, "Outgoing Sun President Ed Zander Joins Startup's Board," *Red Herring,* May 13, 2002.

Miller, Jeff, "Four Term Sheets Later . . . ," *Mass High Tech,* March 11, 2002.

——, "Netezza Gets Tera-Size $20M Round for Its Appliance," *Mass High Tech,* July 28, 2003, p. 1.

Pickering, Mark, " 'Emerging' Netezza Latest Reward: $20M.," *Indian New England,* December 15, 2003.

Soule, Alexander, "Executive Profile: Jit Saxena, Data's David," *Boston Business Journal,* September 10, 2004, p. 3.

Torode, Christina, "Data Recovery Companies Well-Poised for Success," *Mass High Tech,* September 27, 2004, p. 7.

—Ed Dinger

O.C. Tanner Co.

1930 South State Street
Salt Lake City, Utah 84115
U.S.A.
Telephone: (801) 486-2430
Toll Free: (800) 453-7490
Fax: (801) 493-3013
Web site: http://www.octanner.com

Private Company
Incorporated: 1927
Employees: 2,000
Sales: $300 million (2003 est.)
NAIC: 541612 Human Resources and Executive Search
   Consulting Services

O.C. Tanner Co. provides employee recognition tools to many of the world's leading businesses, including many of the *Fortune* 100. The company designs and implements employee recognition programs in the areas of service, performance, sales, and safety. Along with an award line that includes more than 2,500 products, the company provides custom Internet and on-demand print communication tools, administration solutions for companies, and presentation training for managers. O.C. Tanner ships 2.5 million recognition awards per year, 81,000 of which are sent outside of North America.

1927–38: The Early Years

Obert C. Tanner was a 17-year-old student at the University of Utah in 1921 when he started in the jewelry business as an errand boy and clerk at a local jewelry store. In 1927, Tanner, then teacher and principal at the Latter Day Saints' seminary in Spanish Fork, Utah, expanded upon his experience by selling high school and seminary class pins. His immediate goal was to pay off a $500 debt he had incurred while traveling in the Near East and Europe after completing his missionary year as a Mormon.

Tanner purchased 10-karat gold pins consisting of block letters, numerals, and a chain for two dollars from a jewelry manufacturing shop in Salt Lake City and sold them for $2.25. On his first order of 50 pins, he made $12.50. After a run-in with the seminary board over his liberalism in teaching, which marked "a turning point in [his] life," as he explained in his autobiography, he "began to think more about becoming financially independent. I started to work harder in my business for I felt that, at some future time, my intellectual integrity might be at risk."

Although he had no background in business and no capital, Tanner was inventive as a salesman, an attribute he ascribed to his prior training as dairy farm hand, railroad worker, carpenter, missionary, and teacher. After losing several class contracts to representatives of other more established class ring companies, he began to design his own class rings, focusing on expert craftsmanship and designs that were "original, harmonious, and sharp in every detail." Soon he had secured sufficient orders from schools that he needed to find other manufacturers to fulfill his contracts. In 1929, he expanded his territory to include high schools in eastern Idaho and added other items to his line, such as high school awards, club pins, and more.

Tanner placed great emphasis on the quality of the items he sold, and when the companies from which he purchased rings and pins disappointed him with their late deliveries or inferior products, he became his own manufacturer, going into partnership with two former students. The trio set up a drop-hammer in Tanner's mother's garage, and several years later, moved their shop to a downtown Salt Lake City location where they remained for 19 years.

The company's first nine years were lean ones. When finally in 1938 the O.C. Tanner Co. began to turn a profit, Tanner took on other partners and began to give away shares of his company. But even as late as 1945, Tanner's company struggled with being undercapitalized. During the war, manufacturing was limited due to the nation's rationing of metals, and Tanner opened a chain of three jewelry stores in Utah to help make ends meet. He later sold all but one of his stores.

1945–80s: Building the Market for Employee Recognition

Then in 1945, came the change that would distinguish O.C. Tanner Co. After 18 years of selling school and organization jewelry, the company began to market emblematic awards for employee recognition. At the time, the use of recognition awards was a new idea. Only telephone and utility companies used them and those were mostly bronze, sterling and gold-filled. Tanner traveled throughout the United States, meeting with corporate executives to make his case that "recognizing and motivating employees with beautiful, quality emblems would promote better employer/employee relations."

Business continued to grow and in 1954, O.C. Tanner Co. bought land on which to build the company's first factory, an 8,100-square-foot structure that became O.C. Tanner Manufacturing Limited, a wholly owned subsidiary. With the opening of the plant, sales began to increase. They continued to increase every year throughout the 1960s and 1970s. O.C. Tanner Co., committed to giving back to the communities in which it did business, began to make a point of donating at least 10 percent of its gross profits annually to community, educational, and charitable organizations.

Reward programs finally took off solidly in the late 1970s when the workforce shifted from industrial to knowledge-based skills and companies, at the advice of compensation experts, began dressing up salary offers with "emotional compensation." Recognition came to be viewed as an important way to spread pride in an organization, according to a 2004 *Wall Street Journal* article. Kent Murdock, who became O.C. Tanner's president in 1993 and third chief executive officer in 1997, later asserted that a good recognition program brought employees in line with "the company's essential strategy, vision, and imperatives."

Several changes occurred in tax laws in the 1980s that helped promote O.C. Tanner's line of business. In 1981, an addition to the new tax bill allowed companies to take deductions of up to $400 (an increase from $300) per employee award and up to $1,600 if the average award in the company's recognition program stayed below $400. Then in 1986, another change in the tax law made corporate service awards tax free. Both changes were actively and publicly supported by the management of O.C. Tanner Co.

1990s–2004: Entering the International Recognition Market

By the late 1990s, a growing number of employers were aiming to improve employee satisfaction as a means of positively affecting corporate profit. Researchers ran mountains of data through elaborate computer models to measure the links between employee satisfaction, consumer satisfaction, and revenue. According to a Brookings report referred to in the *Wall Street Journal* on July 22, 1998, driving the effort was "the growing

role of 'human capital' in corporate wealth. As little as one-third to one-half of most companies' stock-market value is accounted for . . . by such hard assets as property, plant and equipment. . . . The growing share lies in 'soft' attributes . . . such as patents, processes and customer or employee satisfaction."

O.C. Tanner had customers in close to 170 countries and was producing thousands of customized awards per day, often in quantities of one as it reached the end of the 1900s. During this period, the company made innovations in short-lead, just-in-time manufacturing processes and automated distribution. It built its new state-of-the-art Automated Distribution Center, which improved inventory control and shipping accuracy and introduced an online ordering option to its customers. It also reorganized its workforce into cross-trained teams so that "everyone throughout the organization truly [understood] the goals of the company and [was] focused on exceeding customer expectations," according to a company press release.

The company's changes in distribution and workplace practices earned it the internationally recognized Shingo Prize for Excellence in Manufacturing in 1999. The Shingo prize, which promotes world-class manufacturing and recognizes companies that excel in productivity and process improvement, quality enhancement, and customer satisfaction, acknowledged what a 1999 survey of O.C. Tanner's clients attested: 99 percent of those surveyed responded that the company had met or exceeded their expectations.

The following year, O.C. Tanner was chosen to design and produce commemorative rings for all of the U.S. athletes who had participated in the 2000 games in Sydney. The company was also named the official Olympic victory and commemorative medal supplier for the 2002 Winter Games and the VIII Paralympic Winter Games in Salt Lake City. The company would also make U.S. Team Rings for the 2004 Summer Games in Athens.

O.C. Tanner also created a line of U.S. Olympic-related jewelry in 2000, with pieces ranging in price from $20 to $20,000 that it commissioned from designers such as Fabergé, David Yurman, Oscar Heyman, Christopher Radko, Peter Unger, Cunill Silver, Hoya Crystal, Wellendorf, Halcyon Days, and Native American artist Terry Wadsworth. The pins were displayed at the company's new retail store in Park City, Utah, which featured designer jewelry of all sorts.

The slowing economy of 2001 led to layoffs affecting 70 of O.C. Tanner's workforce of 2,000. With companies nationwide trimming their ranks, there was a reduced demand for service and sales awards, which led to cutbacks in the company's manufacturing teams. Partly in response to the need to run a tighter organization, the company's IT staff began the implementation of computer methodologies to improve productivity beginning in 2002, which won it *CIO* magazine's award as one of the "Agile 100."

On the occasion of its 75th birthday in 2002, O.C. Tanner Co. recognized ten "Everyday Heroes" with $75,000 in donations to ten community organizations of their choice in Utah. That same year, the company received the American Business Ethics Award from the Society of Financial Service Professionals, one of three companies chosen nationally for its dem-

Key Dates:

1927: Obert C. Tanner starts selling graduation class rings and pins.
1945: O.C. Tanner Co. starts selling corporate recognition awards.
1954: O.C. Tanner builds its first factory.
1993: Kent Murdock becomes president of the company.
1999: The company wins the Shingo Prize for Excellence in Manufacturing.
2000: The company begins to make Olympic-related jewelry.
2002: The company begins to manufacture Olympic medals.
2003: The company launches its European Distribution Center; acquires B2B Initiatives Ltd.

onstrated commitment to ethical business practices through management and employee behavior. Continuing its commitment to charity, the company also matched all contributions received by The Road Home, Utah's largest homeless shelter, during the 2002 Christmas season. For this generosity, the shelter awarded O.C. Tanner Co. its Pamela J. Atkinson Outstanding Humanitarian Service Award in 2003.

By 2004, O.C. Tanner, which by then produced 81,000 awards each year internationally, began a thrust to move into the European recognition market. After it opened its European Distribution center in the Netherlands in 2003, it began to provide its European clients with European-specific award selections. O.C. Tanner also acquired B2B Initiatives Ltd., a U.K.-based promotion management services and evaluation firm in London that offered multi-brand award redemption, warehousing, handling, and delivery.

According to the latest research in 2004, high performance workplaces had one thing in common—a culture of recognition.

Reports also showed that acknowledging strategic behavior on a consistent basis yielded tangible dividends in terms of improved company performance and satisfied employees. O.C. Tanner Co. had a solid history of being well ahead of the curve. As the pioneer in its market, it seemed ideally positioned to capitalize on the 90 percent of North American companies that then offered some sort of recognition program for employees and to convert the remaining 10 percent.

Principal Subsidiaries

B2B Initiatives; O.C. Tanner Recognition Company Ltd. (Canada); B2B Initiatives (U.K.); Fraser Hart Awards and Incentives (U.K.).

Principal Competitors

Maritz Inc.; Jostens, Inc.; The Tharpe Company; Carlson Marketing Group.

Further Reading

Abrahamsen, Lane, and Greg Boswell, "Nearly Nine in Ten Companies Offer Some Sort of Recognition Program for Employees," *Workspan*, December 2003, p. 25.

Crumpacker, John, "The Metal for the Medals," *San Francisco Chronicle*, February 7, 2002, p. 3.

Kovaleski, Dave, "Perception Problems," *Corporate Meetings & Incentives*, September 1, 2004, p. 9.

Mitchell, Lesley, "Salt Lake City-Based Employee-Award Firm Lays Off 70," *Salt Lake Tribune*, November 8, 2001.

Sandberg, Jared, "Been Here 25 Years and All I Got Was This Lousy T-Shirt," *Wall Street Journal*, January 28, 2004.

Shanker, Thom, "Fatter Deduction for the Gold Watch Handshake," *New York Times*, August 9, 1981, p. F21.

Tanner, Obert C., *One Man's Journey*, Salt Lake City: The Humanities Center at the University of Utah, 1994, pp. 153–84.

—Carrie Rothburd

Onion, Inc.

536 Broadway, 10th Floor
New York, New York 10012
U.S.A.
Telephone: (212) 627-1972
Fax: (212) 627-1711
Web site: http://www.onion.com

Private Company
Incorporated: 1988
Employees: 50
Sales: $7.0 million (2004 est.)
NAIC: 511110 Newspaper Publishers; 511130 Book
    Publishers; 511199 All Other Publishers

Onion, Inc. serves as the holding company for a number of ventures that developed out of the popularity of the satirical newspaper the *Onion*. The print edition of the newspaper is distributed in Madison, Wisconsin; Boulder and Denver, Colorado; Chicago; New York City; and Minneapolis-St. Paul, Minnesota. The electronic edition of the newspaper is updated every Wednesday on the company's web site, www.onion.com, which also sells merchandise and a series of best-selling books produced by the company. Onion, Inc. also broadcasts on the radio through the Onion Radio Network, syndicated by Westwood One. Approximately 320,000 copies of the *Onion* are distributed each week. The company's web site averages 3.6 million unique visitors and more than 30 million page views each month.

1988 Start-Up

From its start, the *Onion* offered its satirical perspective on events surrounding it, picking its birthplace as its first subject. The print edition of the *Onion*, the first of a handful of media that generated revenue for Onion, Inc., was started by two University of Wisconsin students, Tim Keck and Chris Johnson. In 1988, the pair, with the help of fellow students, printed the first edition of the *Onion* on notebook-sized paper and distributed it for free, offering their mocking view of campus life and the college town supporting it. Advertising in the newspaper consisted of coupons for the two staples of student life: draft beer and pizza. One year after its debut, the "newspaper," improbably, was acquired. "A bunch of college kids in Madison, Wisconsin, were putting out copies of what they thought was good satirical humor," the publisher of the *Onion* remembered in an October 23, 2002 interview with *ContentBiz*. "It was good enough that entrepreneur Scott Dikkers bought it from them to run as a formal publishing company. I'm not sure what the amount of the sale was, but I'm sure it wasn't much."

The intervention of Dikkers, whose financial resources were not revealed, did not lead to an immediate transformation of the *Onion* into a "formal publishing company." Dikkers's goal of having the *Onion* delivered to doorstops nationwide alongside issues of the *New York Times* was, like the *Onion* itself, tongue-in-cheek. The printed tabloid did develop, however, a small but loyal following, as Dikkers, with the help of Peter Haise, a 1990 graduate of the University of Wisconsin, developed a brand of topical, parodying humor, that proved to be exportable to markets outside Madison. In 1994, the Milwaukee edition of the printed tabloid debuted, distributed, like the Madison version, for free. The most important achievement during this early period in the *Onion*'s development, one only known to the enclaves of readership in Madison and Milwaukee, was the quality of work produced by Dikkers, Haise, and several other writers. The writing was humorous and well received, attracting a cult-like following that would find acceptance from a much larger audience not long after the expansion into Milwaukee. The catalyst for this transformation—the development from a cultish print tabloid into a publication known nationwide—was the emergence of the Internet.

1996 Debut on the Internet

The *Onion* was just the type of entity to benefit from the public's embrace of the Internet. Dikkers and Haise could never realistically hope to distribute the *Onion* nationwide alongside copies of the *New York Times*, but they potentially could reach the same readership base electronically through the Internet. The two editors launched their web site in 1996, producing an electronic version of the *Onion* at the address www.theonion .com (rights to www.onion.com were purchased in October 1999 to redirect misdirected attempts to locate the site). A

Company Perspectives:

Every week, three million readers turn to the world's most popular humor publication for a much-needed dose of Onion satire and entertainment coverage. In a history spanning 15 years, six popular books, and 10 Webby Awards, the Onion *has attracted legions of loyal fans drawn to its scathingly funny commentary on world events, human behavior, and journalistic convention.*

presence on the Internet meant everything for the irreverent, witty editors, giving them a soapbox neither could have dreamed of in 1989. Distribution of the printed version expanded into the Chicago market in 1998, but the effect on the *Onion*'s development paled in comparison to the benefits realized after the launch of the web site. "The Web site is the driving force for all our business now," Haise acknowledged in an October 11, 1999 interview with *Advertising Age.*

The Internet represented the lifeblood of Onion, Inc.; the reasoning for the move onto the World Wide Web represented the crucible of its success. Haise explained the thinking behind the launch of the web site: "We always found the most success [by] creating the shortest distance between our product and our customers," Haise explained in his October 11, 1999 interview with *Advertising Age.* "Our goal was to get the *Onion* in front of as many faces as we possibly could. We'd had challenges getting the *Onion* on already crowded newsstands, and the Internet presented an exciting opportunity for bucking the traditional distribution system." Haise explained the company's rationale and strategy further, saying, "We eschewed interactivity to begin with, and we in no way promoted the launch. We didn't want to be in your face. We wanted readers to feel as though they were discovering the product, which always makes them feel closer to it and, potentially, more loyal."

The *Onion*'s presence on the Internet gave the Madison-based writers exposure to the world. The capability to reach potentially billions of readers as opposed to hundreds or thousands of readers did much to solidify the *Onion*'s existence, but equally as important as the exposure to a vast readership was the exposure to potential advertisers. Onion, Inc., like any company, needed revenue to survive, and securing advertising dollars was the way the company survived. By 1999, there were 20 marketers advertising on www.theonion.com, paying between $10 and $30 per thousand impressions to put badges and text links on the web site's front page. Companies such as American Express Co., Warner Bros., and the publishers of *Rolling Stone* were paying Onion, Inc. to advertise on www.theonion.com, major corporate entities that would not have entertained marketing in an alternative publication distributed for free in markets such as Madison and Milwaukee. The revenue obtained from advertisers enabled Onion, Inc. to post $4.5 million in sales in 1999. Venture capitalists became interested in the band of Madison writers, inundating their company with offers of cash to greatly accelerate expansion.

The revenue generated by Onion, Inc. at the end of the 1990s owed its existence not only to advertising dollars, but also to the blossoming Onion brand. The company diversified, delivering its signature satire through other media. The ability of the writers to branch out and express their creativity through different channels was directly related to their presence on the Internet. In the first half of 1999, Onion, Inc. released its first book, *Our Dumb Century: The Onion Presents 100 Years of Headlines from America's Finest New Source.* The book, published by Crown Books, contained headlines created by nine writers at the *Onion* who offered their take on the events and mores that shaped the 20th century. A story dated July 28, 1953 carried the headline: "CIA Subdues Fruit-Hatted Peoples of Lesser Americas." An August 16, 1966 headline read: "Democracy Flowers Around Globe After Bombing of Vietnamese Village." A headline from 1960 announced: "Soviet Space Program Ahead in Dog-Killing Race." More than 80,000 copies of the book were sold in four days leading up to its release on April 1, 1999, forcing Crown Books to order a second emergency printing. *Our Dumb Century* quickly became a *New York Times* bestseller, becoming the first of a series of best-selling books written by the *Onion*'s staff. Several months after the release of *Our Dumb Century,* Westwood One began syndicating *Onion Radio News,* a feature that was aired on 45 radio stations nationwide.

A Move to Manhattan in 2000

The beginning of the 21st century brought significant change to Onion, Inc. In 2000, Michael Schafer, chairman of the $1 billion Schafer Cullen Capital Management fund, acquired a stake in the company, eventually becoming its majority owner. "For years," Schafer said in an August 7, 2004 interview with the *Chicago Tribune,* "they had done a great job using a little cash here and a little cash there to keep it running, but that's not a long-term strategy. It just needed some discipline on the business side." The year also marked the relocation of the editorial staff from Madison to New York City, where they occupied a former warehouse in the Chelsea section of Manhattan. The move, made at the end of 2000, put the writers near the site of the following year's catastrophe, an event that tested the boundaries of satire in the aftermath of devastation.

The terrorist attacks of September 11, 2001 silenced the comedy world. For painfully obvious reasons, those who normally applied a humorous slant to news events could find nothing humorous in the deaths of thousands and the losses suffered by thousands more. David Letterman and Jay Leno, the two comedic oracles of late-light television, did not refer to the attacks. *Saturday Night Live* and Jon Stewart's *The Daily Show* aired re-runs, as writers and producers pondered when, how, and if to touch the subject of the attacks. In the wake of the attacks, the writing staff at the *Onion* struggled with what their response, if any, should be. "At first, we were at a bit of a loss," Robert Siegel, the editor-in-chief at the *Onion,* said in an October 1, 2001 interview with the *New York Times.* Siegel explained that if he and his writers avoided the subject "we would have looked painfully irrelevant—it would make us ask why do we even exist if we would resist weighing in on the biggest news story since Pearl Harbor."

The *Onion,* the first of its ilk to do so, responded directly to the attacks in its September 26, 2001 edition. Instead of writing a single article about September 11th and its aftermath, the writers devoted the entire issue to the subject. Headlines in the issue

Key Dates:

1988: The *Onion* is first published in Madison, Wisconsin.
1994: The *Onion* begins distribution in Milwaukee, Wisconsin.
1996: The web site www.theonion.com is launched.
1998: The *Onion* begins distribution in Chicago.
1999: *Our Dumb Century,* a book compiled by the *Onion*'s writers, is released.
2000: The editorial staff relocates from Madison to Manhattan.
2004: The *Onion* begins distribution in Minneapolis-St. Paul, Minnesota.

included: "U.S. Vows to Defeat Whoever It Is We're at War Against," "Hijackers Surprised to Find Selves in Hell," "God Angrily Clarifies 'Don't Kill' Rule," and "Dinty-Moore Breaks Long Silence on Terrorism with Full-Page Ad." The public's response was overwhelmingly positive, drawing a deluge of e-mails from readers applauding the effort. The October 8, 2001 issue of the *Los Angeles Business Journal* hailed the issue, saying it "wildly succeeded, mixing irony and anger into a hilarious parody that validates the Internet's role as a breeding ground for brave content no traditional media outlet would touch."

The writing staff at the *Onion* distinguished themselves in 2001 and enjoyed themselves in 2002. For the *Onion*, a newspaper that mocked the practices and tone of traditional newspapers, nothing could deliver more pleasure than a legitimate newspaper using one of its fabricated stories as legitimate news. In its June 26, 2002 edition, the *Arkansas Democrat-Gazette* did just that, using a piece written by the *Onion* writers two weeks earlier. On the front page of its food section, the *Arkansas Democrat-Gazette* informed its readers that the U.S. Department of Agriculture (USDA) had added a new food group to the USDA Food Pyramid, a food group called "fixin's." The head of the USDA, Ann Veneman, was quoted, announcing, "We recommend five to eight servings from the fixin's group, which includes such hearty sides as coleslaw, mashed potatoes, steak fries, baked beans, and macaroni 'n' cheese." That same month, the *Beijing Evening News* took the bait as well, informing its readers that members of the U.S. Congress intended to quit unless the U.S. Capitol building was replaced with a newer, nicer building.

By 2004, Onion, Inc. presided over a fiefdom of satire. The company served as the corporate parent of the print edition of the *Onion*, its electronic version on the Internet, book publish-

ing, The Onion Radio Network, and merchandise sales conducted through the web site. Together, this quiver of businesses produced roughly $7 million in annual revenue, a total, according to majority owner Schafer, that was expected to increase 25 percent annually to reach $21 million by 2009.

Schafer's sanguine financial forecast was based, in part, on the company's plans for expansion. In 2004, the *Onion* entered the Minneapolis-St. Paul market, the first time the newspaper entered a new market since the editorial staff moved to New York City. Short-term expansion plans called for entry into the San Francisco, Boston, and Austin, Texas, markets by 2006, followed by debuts in Atlanta, Georgia, Washington, D.C., and Ann Arbor, Michigan.

Principal Subsidiaries

The Onion A.V. Club.

Principal Competitors

National Lampoon, Inc.; News Corporation; Yahoo! Inc.

Further Reading

"Big Apple Welcomes Cheeseheads," *St. Louis Post-Dispatch,* January 25, 2001, p. B6.

Gilbert, Jennifer, "The Onion Transforms Satire into Big Success," *Advertising Age,* October 11, 1999, p. 68.

Kirchen, Rich, "Hardly the Onion," *Business Journal-Milwaukee,* May 18, 2001, p. 2.

Lazaroff, Leon, "Satirical Weekly 'The Onion' Takes Root in Minneapolis/St. Paul," *Chicago Tribune,* August 7, 2004, p. C3.

Loftus, Peter, "Is It OK to Laugh Yet?," *Capital Times,* September 28, 2001, p. 8C.

"The Onion—How the Web's Most Beloved Humor Site Stays Profitable," *ContentBiz,* October 23, 2002, p. 32.

Owen, Rob, "The Onion Peels Back 100 Years of Media Pretensions," *Star-Ledger,* August 1, 1999, p. 4.

"Peeling Back the Century," *Capital Times,* June 4, 1999, p. 13A.

Porges, Seth, "Read It and Weep," *Editor & Publisher,* November 24, 2003, p. 18.

Romell, Rick, "The Onion Moves Its Newspaper Writers from Wisconsin to New York," *Milwaukee Journal Sentinel,* January 26, 2001, p. C3.

Salkowski, Joe, "Web Site Keeping Sense of Humor Throughout Tragedy," *Los Angeles Business Journal,* October 8, 2001, p. 19.

Schwartz, John, "Seriously, People Seem Ready for a Good Laugh," *New York Times,* October 1, 2001, p. C15.

Tatge, Mark, "A Funny Thing," *Forbes Small Business,* January 31, 2005.

Turner, Lance, "Goofing Up," *Arkansas Business,* July 8, 2002, p. 26.

—Jeffrey L. Covell

PALMER & CAY

Established 1868

Palmer & Cay, Inc.

25 Bull Street
Savannah, Georgia 31401-0847
U.S.A.
Telephone: (912) 234-6621
Toll Free: (800) 755-9594
Fax: (912) 234-5427
Web site: http://www.palmercay.com

Private Company
Incorporated: 1947
NAIC: 524210 Insurance Agencies and Brokerages

With co-headquarters located in Savannah and Atlanta, Georgia, Palmer & Cay, Inc. is the third largest privately held insurance brokerage in the United States. The firm offers a wide range of services, including insurance brokerage services, reinsurance services, retirement plan services, risk management consulting, risk control, surety bond services, compensation consulting, actuarial services, investment consulting services, and human resource consulting and outsourcing services. Long a regional company, Palmer & Cay has in recent years aggressively moved into new markets. The firm now has 38 offices located in 22 states and the District of Columbia. Serving as chief executive officer and chairman of Palmer & Cay is John E. Cay III, a member of the fourth generation of the family to head the firm.

Palmer & Cay's Heritage
Dating to Post-Civil War Era

The lineage of the firm can be traced back to the 1868 founding of The Carswell Insurance Group, which was a key acquisition for Palmer & Cay in 1985. Like Palmer & Cay, Carswell started in Savannah, established by Confederate General Joseph E. Johnston, who at the age of 58 went into business after a long career in the military. Representing Massachusetts Life Insurance and the Royal Globe Insurance Company of London, he succeeded in building a prosperous firm that within four short years was doing business throughout Georgia, Alabama, and Mississippi. Supposedly, the ex-General personally settled insurance claims in Savannah by dispensing gold coins

from the saddlebags of his horse. In 1876 Johnston retired to Virginia and left the business to others to run. John Devine Carswell, fresh out of the University of Georgia, joined the firm in 1888. By 1905 he was able to buy the company and he renamed it after himself. About ten years later the firm began to compete with an upstart Savannah agency, Palmer & Cay.

The Palmer family business began as a cotton and naval store brokerage in the 1800s. The business prospered until the end of the century, but as cotton grew less dominant in the Southern economy, Savannah became more of a shipping town and the firm was forced to adapt. In the early years of the 20th century, it focused increasingly on its naval stores as well as marine hardware. Marine insurance became a natural extension and in 1913 Armin B. Palmer, a member of the second generation to lead the family business, launched an agency to provide coverage. It was in that same year that his daughter married John Eugene "Gene" Cay, who worked as an underwriter for an Atlanta insurance company. Cay was induced to come work for his father-in-law two years later, so that in 1915 the Palmer & Cay partnership was begun.

Palmer & Cay prospered during World War I, which brought a great deal of shipping business to Savannah. After the war the firm moved beyond marine insurance, becoming involved in adding coverage to a number of industries, including railroad, construction, and manufacturing. Like the rest of the United States, Savannah enjoyed the boom times of the 1920s and when the stock market crashed in 1929, setting off the Great Depression of the 1930s, it suffered its share of bankruptcies and bank failures. Palmer & Cay scraped by until the economy recovered in the 1940s, spurred by military spending that resulted from the United States' participation in World War II. It was also during the Depression, in 1937, that a third generation went to work for the firm: John "Jack" Eugene Cay, Jr., a recent graduate of the University of North Carolina at Chapel Hill. As was the case during the first world war, the Savannah shipping industry boomed during the second world war. Not only were dozens of Liberty ships and other vessels built in the port, military installations including Fort Stewart and Hunter Field brought business to the area and Palmer & Cay benefited in equal measure.

Post-World War II Change in Leadership

Following the war, in 1947, the firm was incorporated as Palmer & Cay, Inc. Jack Cay now assumed leadership of the firm, which was dedicated to serving as a general insurance agency and brokerage, with a modicum of real estate interests. The firm now rounded out its personal and commercial insurance offerings, as well as adding employee benefits services. After a recession that immediately followed World War II, the United States enjoyed another boom time, especially in the housing market. With ex-servicemen getting married and having children at a record clip, giving rise to the Baby Boom generation, housing developments sprang up across the country to accommodate these new families. In 1951 Palmer & Cay looked to take advantage of the building explosion by launching a mortgage company. Four years later the firm added a consumer financing unit.

Starting in 1961 Palmer & Cay began to grow by external means as well. In that year it acquired a pair of area insurance agencies: the Lynes Insurance Agency and the Joseph S. Espy Insurance Agency. They would be just the first of many agency acquisitions Palmer & Cay completed over the next four decades.

The following year, 1962, brought the death of the firm's cofounder, Gene Cay, marking the end of an era. A few years later, in 1968, John Eugene Cay III graduated from the University of North Carolina at Chapel Hill and became the fourth generation of the family to join the firm. He was already well familiar with the business, having worked there during summers since he was ten years old. He would soon be called away, however, to serve in the military because of the Vietnam War. As part of the Army Reserve military intelligence unit, he served six months of active duty, then relocated to New York City, where he learned the underwriting business working for Home Insurance Company, and rounded out his education by taking graduate classes at the College of Insurance. He was just 27 years old when he returned to Savannah in 1970 and succeeded his father as Palmer & Cay's president and chief executive officer, while his father stayed on as chairman.

John Cay brought a new energy to the firm. He immediately eliminated the afternoon coffee break and named the firm's first woman vice-president, and then took steps to vigorously grow Palmer & Cay, both by opening new offices in nearby coastal Georgia and by acquiring additional agencies. But Palmer & Cay was not the only firm eager to expand: The insurance brokerage business underwent a period of consolidation, resulting in ever larger companies. By the end of the 1970s, Palmer & Cay changed course, and instead of trying to build up its business in the immediate area, it began to position itself as a regional concern. In the early 1980s Palmer & Cay moved deeper into Georgia. It opened an office in Vidalia and acquired a pair of leading agencies: the Brunswick-based Shelander-Cowden-Warwick Agency and the Robert Walton Insurance Agency in Augusta.

By 1985 Palmer & Cay reached a major turning point in its drive to become a larger player. In December of that year, the firm acquired its longtime Savannah competitor, The Carswell Insurance Group, which had eight offices in three states and annual revenues of $4.5 million. In one stroke, Palmer & Cay doubled in size and took on debt for the first time in its history. But with its increased size, Palmer & Cay was now able to enter larger markets, such as Atlanta and Jacksonville, Florida. In the second half of the 1980s, the firm strengthened its position in Jacksonville through acquisitions, and also expanded into North Carolina by opening an office in Charlotte. The decade ended on a sad note with the passing of Jack Cay. His son now assumed the chairmanship as well as chief executive responsibilities.

A key to Palmer & Cay's growth was the addition of executive talent. The Carswell acquisition brought with it a number of seasoned insurance professionals. Then in 1991 the firm was able to pry F. Michael Crowley away from Johnson & Higgins, an old-line New York company that was the leading privately held insurance services and employee benefits consulting firm in the world. Crowley brought his 17 years of experience at Johnson & Higgins to Palmer & Cay, where he now became president and took the lead in beefing up the middle management ranks to position the firm for winning and servicing larger regional and national accounts.

In the first half of the 1990s the firm continued to pursue its strategy of achieving growth through external and internal means. Palmer & Cay acquired Mitchell/Woolfolk Insurance to establish a presence in Columbus, Georgia, and later supplemented the business with the acquisition of The Jordan Agency. The following year, Palmer & Cay acquired Midyette-Moor Insurance Agency, the largest independent agency in Tallahassee, Florida, which became the firm's second Florida operation. Next, in 1994, Palmer & Cay moved into Charleston, South Carolina, by acquiring the city's largest independent insurance agency, Heffron Ingle McDowell & Cooper. Virginia was added to the mix in 1995, when Palmer & Cay opened an office in Richmond. The firm then targeted Tennessee, acquiring McMurray, Daly & Leonard, the largest independent insurance agency in Knoxville, Tennessee. By this point, Palmer & Cay had grown to become one of the 20 largest brokers in the country, involved in 15 cities in six states.

Late 1990s Diversification

In the second half of the 1990s, Palmer & Cay not only expanded its territory, it also diversified its offerings. It forged alliances with major European insurance companies and risk management firms, creating a network of independent representatives on the Continent in order to better serve clients with international scope. More important, during this period Palmer

Key Dates:

1868: Carswell Insurance Group is founded.
1915: Palmer & Cay insurance agency is formed.
1970: John E. Cay, III heads Palmer & Cay.
1985: Palmer & Cay acquires Carswell.
2000: Palmer & Cay Consulting Group Inc. is formed.
2002: Management announces the establishment of the firm's co-headquarters in Atlanta.
2003: The firm enters the field of reinsurance, establishing Palmer & Cay Reinsurance Brokers and Savannah Reinsurance Underwriting Management L.L.C., both in Connecticut.

& Cay took steps to become less dependent on its property-casualty business, which had experienced eroding rates. The firm devoted more resources to its benefits consulting operations, where management believed there was more opportunity for growth. In 1999 Palmer & Cay acquired the employee benefits consulting practice of KPMG L.L.P.'s Mid-Atlantic and Southeastern divisions, with offices in Washington, Baltimore, and Atlanta. Later in the year it acquired Richmond, Virginia-based Slabaugh Morgan & Associates, the 15th largest privately held employee benefits consulting companies in the United States, with offices in six southeastern cities. A year later, Palmer & Cay supplemented its benefits business by acquiring Defrain Mayer, a human resources and actuarial consulting firm, adding offices in St. Louis, Missouri, and Kansas City, Kansas. Palmer & Cay then folded its benefits assets into a new subsidiary, Palmer & Cay Consulting Group Inc.

Palmer & Cay was also active on other fronts at the close of the century. In 1999 it acquired Lexington, Kentucky-based Powell-Walton-Milward Inc., one of the oldest and largest private insurance brokers in the state. Palmer & Cay also expanded in Texas in 1999 by acquiring McDonald & Company, as well as establishing offices in Boston and Minneapolis.

As it entered the new century, Palmer & Cay operated in a rapidly changing landscape. Changes in the law blurred the lines between financial institutions and insurance companies, permitting firms to now offer a smorgasbord of banking services, investment options, and insurance products. Consolidation in the insurance industry also resulted in ever larger concerns, making it increasingly difficult for such independent regional firms as Palmer & Cay to prosper. Moreover, Palmer &

Cay was receiving overtures from larger banks and brokers eager to buy the firm. Management considered the possibility of selling, but in the end concluded that Palmer & Cay should remain independent, although it would have to expand into a national player if it were to remain competitive.

Palmer & Cay developed and began implementing a strategic plan to attract new talent, expand geographically, and diversify into new areas, such as captive management and human resource outsourcing. In 2003 the firm became involved in reinsurance, establishing two entities in Connecticut: Palmer & Cay Reinsurance Brokers and Savannah Reinsurance Underwriting Management L.L.C. Also in 2003, Palmer & Cay opened or expanded brokerage offices in Chicago; Milwaukee; Philadelphia; Cleveland, Columbus, and Cincinnati, Ohio; and Detroit and Grand Rapids, Michigan. But as Palmer & Cay pursued its national ambitions, it found that it could no longer devote the kind of attention necessary to some of its local operations. Thus in 2003 Palmer & Cay sold its Augusta, Georgia, assets to Augusta's Blanchard and Calhoun Insurance Agency Inc. Palmer & Cay also found that Savannah was no longer an ideal location for a firm with larger aspirations and in 2002 management announced that it was making Atlanta its co-headquarters. It was very likely that in the near future, Atlanta would become the firm's permanent home, as Palmer & Cay started yet another chapter in its storied history.

Principal Subsidiaries

Palmer & Cay Consulting Group Inc.; Palmer & Cay Investment Services, Inc.; Palmer & Cay Select; Palmer & Cay Worksite; Palmer & Cay Reinsurance Brokers; Savannah Reinsurance Underwriting Management L.L.C.; Palmer & Cay Outsourcing Solutions.

Principal Competitors

Aon Corporation; Commerce Insurance; Marsh & McLennan Companies, Inc.

Further Reading

Cay, John E. III, ''Palmer Cay, Inc.: Charting a Course for Success,'' Exton, Pa.: Newcomen Society of the United States, 2004.

Jordan, Meredith, ''Insurance Firm Moving Key Execs to Atlanta,'' *Atlanta Business Chronicle,* May 14, 2004, p. A18.

Merx, Katie, ''Staff Additions Fuel Palmer & Cay Growth,'' *Business Insurance,* November 3, 2003, p. 20F.

—Ed Dinger

Payless ShoeSource®

Payless ShoeSource, Inc.

3231 Southeast Sixth Avenue
Topeka, Kansas 66607-2207
U.S.A.
Telephone: (785) 233-5171
Toll Free: (877) 452-7500
Fax: (785) 295-6220
Web site: http//www.payless.com

Public Company
Founded: 1956 as Pay-Less National
Employees: 30,000
Sales: $2.78 billion (2003)
Stock Exchanges: New York
Ticker Symbol: PSS
NAIC: 448210 Shoe Stores; 454110 Electronic Shopping
and Mail-Order Houses

Payless ShoeSource, Inc. is the largest footwear retailer in the United States. The company operates about 4,700 stores in all 50 states as well as Puerto Rico, Guam, Saipan, the U.S. Virgin Islands, Canada, Central America, the Caribbean, Ecuador, and Japan. It also sells footwear via the Internet at www .payless.com. Payless has built its success by offering a large selection of shoes at very low prices, most selling for less than $15 as of 2004. The company has been able to maintain its affordable prices by sticking exclusively to a self-service format, keeping a tight rein on cost structure, and insisting on efficient sourcing and inventory controls. Payless ShoeSource targets as its main customers women from 18 to 44 years of age with household incomes of less than $75,000, and it estimates that in any given year, 40 percent of the women in this target group buy at least one pair of footwear at a Payless store. Payless was acquired by the May Department Stores Company in 1979. The company remained a May subsidiary until 1996, when it was spun off to May shareholders as an independent, publicly traded firm.

Company Origins in the 1950s

Payless ShoeSource was founded as Pay-Less National in Topeka, Kansas, in 1956 by two cousins, Louis and Shaol Pozez.

Three Pay-Less stores were opened in Topeka within a year of the company's founding. The company then expanded into Oklahoma, Texas, and Nebraska, opening 12 new outlets by the end of the decade. From the start, Payless stores were designed to maintain low prices by keeping overhead to a minimum. The first outlets were located in former supermarkets with the original fixtures replaced by simple, unpainted, wooden shelving, constructed in large part by store managers. The self-service format of the stores allowed Payless to limit staff, which usually consisted only of a manager and one or two clerks. This no-frills approach to operations kept the average price for a pair of shoes at the original Payless stores below $3.00.

Payless was not alone in offering budget footwear in a self-service format to American consumers. The self-service shoe industry emerged soon after World War II when cheap imported shoes began to be available on a widespread basis. Growth was fueled by changes in fashion that emphasized a looser fitting, more casual shoe as well as more variety in footwear. The 1950s baby boom also contributed to the rise in large discount shoe stores that catered primarily to middle-income families with children. Like most of these low-end shoe stores, Payless's major market was in women's and children's shoes, which constituted about 60 percent and 30 percent of sales, respectively. By the early 1960s, the $6 million sales rung up in Payless's 38 stores represented only a small fraction of the estimated $270 million volume of the self-service retail shoe industry.

Growth and Acquisitions in the 1960s

In the early 1960s, Pay-Less National, which had been operating retail stores under various names, including Pay-Less Self Service, National Self Service, Gambles Discount Shoes, and Shopper's City, changed its corporate name to "Volume Distributors" in order to reflect the company's diverse operations more closely. In 1962 Volume Distributors went public to raise capital for further growth. The influx of cash from the initial public offering allowed the company to open an average of 12 new stores annually in the early 1960s. In order to cope with the increased inventory, in 1966 Volume Distributors adopted a new computerized inventory system that used stock-keeping units (SKUs) to keep track of the large number of shoe styles and sizes stocked in the company's 50 stores. The new

Company Perspectives:

Strategy: Our primary strategic goal is to be the most successful footwear retailer in the world. We plan to accomplish this goal by expanding our core footwear and accessories businesses, while increasing profitability and maintaining a strong balance sheet. To achieve this goal, we have several key business strategies.

Positioning Payless ShoeSource as the Merchandise Authority: Our strategy is to position Payless ShoeSource as the merchandise authority for value-priced footwear and accessories. We intend to effect this strategy through: new product offerings, featuring merchandise that is right, distinctive and targeted for our customers including an increased selection of leather footwear; new messaging to communicate this positioning to our customers at every point of contact by using our stores as the lead communication vehicle and leveraging with highly identified spokespeople and exposure through influential fashion media; and improved execution, such as: (1) educating our store associates to use key service behaviors identified to impact conversion in their interactions with customers, (2) continuing to implement, through remodelings and new store openings, a new store design intended to be more attractive to consumers and featuring enhanced displays, color, lighting and graphics and improved levels of customer service, and (3) implementing new technologies to enhance our ability to satisfy customers.

system was temporarily sidetracked when a tornado completely destroyed the company headquarters and warehouse in Topeka on the very evening that the first computer-generated inventory report was to be produced. Volume Distributors quickly picked up the pieces from this natural disaster and built new corporate offices at another location in Topeka.

In 1967 "Volume Distributors" was renamed "Volume Shoe Corporation" in order to identify it more closely with the footwear industry. In the same year the company launched an accelerated expansion program that saw the number of stores top 100 and annual sales rise to more than $10 million by the end of the decade. In addition to new store openings in the late 1960s and early 1970s, Volume Shoe implemented a program of acquisitions to further accelerate growth. From 1968 through 1973 Volume Shoe purchased eight smaller retail shoe companies, adding a total of 145 stores to the growing chain. The prosperity of the company during the inflation-plagued early 1970s actually led to a conflict with the Nixon administration in 1971 when Volume Shoe raised its dividend in spite of a government imposed wage-price freeze. Company President Louis Pozez was summoned to Washington to justify the dividend hike in a meeting with the President's "Cost of Living Council," but ultimately no further action was taken against the firm.

Accelerated Expansion in the 1970s

The rate of new store openings continued to accelerate through the mid-1970s. By 1975 Volume Shoe was operating 486 retail units in 31 states with total net sales of almost $75 million, making it the largest chain of family shoe stores in the United

States. The Payless ShoeSource name was adopted in 1978 for the bulk of Volume Shoe retail outlets and the company logo was changed to the now familiar yellow, orange, and brown. The success of Volume Shoe and its Payless ShoeSource outlets was due in part to the company's skill at choosing locations for its stores. Although early stores were primarily freestanding, in the late 1970s Payless outlets also opened in major malls across the country. By 1979, 40 percent of all Payless stores were mall-based. The distribution of Payless units in a variety of real estate locales, including suburban strip developments, central business districts, shopping centers, and shopping malls, promoted the visibility and consumer recognition of the bold yellow logo as well as increasing the range of customers who would feel comfortable shopping at Payless stores.

From the start, Payless's relationship with its suppliers was key to the company's success. In the early years, the company bought their shoes "off the shelf" from American as well as foreign manufacturers, protecting themselves from shortages and sudden price increases by using a large number of suppliers. In the early 1960s no single manufacturer supplied more than 6 percent of Payless's merchandise. By the mid-1960s Payless was having shoes made to their own specifications to ensure that the shoe styles available in their stores matched the expectations of increasingly demanding consumers. These company-specific shoe styles would eventually evolve into private-label brands that would become the staple of Payless ShoeSource outlets from the mid-1970s. The development of in-house brands allowed Payless to maintain tight control over style and quality, the two issues that had driven customers away from many discount chains in the 1970s.

The May Department Stores Era: 1979–96

In 1979 Volume Shoe, with its 739 Payless ShoeSource stores generating annual sales of $191 million, was acquired by the May Department Stores Company in a $160 million stock swap. May was one of the leading retailers in the United States, with annual sales near $3 billion. The retail giant owned 11 department and discount store chains, but Volume Shoe was May's first entry into the discount shoe business. Volume Shoe was considered an excellent acquisition by analysts. The self-service shoe chain was earning operating profits of $28 million or almost 15 percent of sales, one of the best performances in the retail sector. May's capital allowed the Payless chain to expand at an accelerated pace and by 1981 there were 1,089 Payless outlets in 34 states. More than half of these stores were located in the Sunbelt states, where an influx of population was creating record retail growth. In the early 1980s, the Payless chain included 246 outlets in Texas and California alone. In 1983 Payless's presence in California was further strengthened by the acquisition of 66 Koby Shoe Stores, a California-based chain formerly owned by Kobacker Co.

To accommodate the growing number of Payless stores, Volume Shoe constructed a new 300,000-square-foot distribution center in Topeka. The new center, which would be expanded twice over the course of the following decade, became the heart of the Payless network of stores as its computerized inventory and picking system ensured the delivery of the 20,000 pairs of shoes sold annually by the average Payless store in the early 1980s. With changes in the worldwide economy, Volume Shoe began to rely more heavily on Asian manufacturers to

---

Key Dates:

1956: Pay-Less National is founded in Topeka, Kansas, by two cousins, Louis and Shaol Pozez, to open self-service stores selling budget footwear.

1962: The company goes public as Volume Distributors.

1967: The company is renamed Volume Shoe Corporation; an accelerated expansion program is launched.

1978: The Payless ShoeSource name is adopted for the bulk of the company's retail outlets.

1979: Volume Shoe is acquired by the May Department Stores Company.

1991: The company name is changed to Payless Shoe-Source, Inc.

1996: May spins Payless off to shareholders, making it once again an independent, publicly traded firm.

1997: The mid-priced shoe chain Parade of Shoes is acquired from J. Baker, Inc.; the first Canadian Payless stores open.

1999: The firm launches e-commerce at payless.com.

2000: Payless enters into a joint venture to expand into the Central American region.

2004: As part of a major restructuring, Payless announces that it will close down the Parade chain and close hundreds of Payless ShoeSource outlets.

---

supply these shoes and in 1983 the company opened an international office in Taipei, Taiwan, to coordinate overseas production. By the beginning of the next decade, factories in China were producing 80 percent of Payless's merchandise and the Taipei office became the center of the company's sourcing subsidiary, Payless ShoeSource International.

Louis and Shaol Pozez stayed on to facilitate the transition to the new ownership but retired in the early 1980s to be succeeded by former Executive Vice-President Harry Berger. In 1985 Berger was in turn replaced as president by Richard Jolosky, who ran the company through 1988. After an eight-year hiatus Jolosky returned to Payless as president in 1996. Jolosky's distinctive management style, which on one memorable occasion included dressing up as General Patton to rally the sales troops, was instrumental in the development of the aggressive competitiveness that marked Payless's approach to business through the 1980s and 1990s. Jolosky had spent a number of years as a senior vice-president of Wal-Mart Stores, Inc., the giant discount chain that dominated the industry in the 1980s and 1990s, and said that he learned a lot from founder Sam Walton. "When I visited stores with Sam, he never looked to see the things that we were doing better than the competition," Jolosky recalled in a 1996 interview with *Forbes*. "He always looked for the things that the competition was doing better than us." As president of Payless, Jolosky turned this lesson against Wal-Mart as he made certain that Payless always remained competitive in both price and product with the huge discounter.

May continued the vigorous expansion of the Payless Shoe-Source chain through the late 1980s and early 1990s, opening about 200 new stores each year. With almost all of these stores now known under the Payless name, in 1991 the corporate name

also was changed from Volume Shoe to Payless ShoeSource. During the early 1990s, Payless also introduced Payless Kids stores, which were added adjacent to existing Payless Shoe-Source outlets. In 1985 there were 1,662 Payless stores. By 1991 this number had almost doubled to 3,295. Sales during the same period rose from near $700 million to $1.5 billion.

Although Payless's earnings also increased through the late 1980s, return on sales failed to keep pace with the company's earlier performance or with May's core department store holdings. Earnings as a percentage of sales had been about 15 percent when May purchased Volume Shoe, but flat sales in the discount shoe sector saw this figure fall to about 11 percent in the late 1980s and then tumble again to less than 8 percent in 1995. Growing competition from giant discount chains such as Wal-Mart and Kmart as well as an overall decline in the off-price apparel market contributed to this downturn. In addition, the consolidation and conversion of 679 shoe stores acquired from Kobacker Co. and Shoe Works Inc. in 1994 added substantially to operating costs. Payless, whose contribution to May's overall sales shrank from 20 to 14 percent from 1993 to 1996, was no longer considered a key part of May's long-term strategy for growth, and in 1996 May spun off Payless Shoe-Source to shareholders.

Newly Independent and Growing in the Late 1990s

As Payless ShoeSource embarked on its new life as an independent publicly traded company, the company operated 4,270 stores, including 775 Payless Kids outlets. Plans were quickly implemented to close or relocate about 500 of the less profitable locations and to continue opening new stores. Among the new store openings in 1996 were the first Payless outlets in Alaska, giving the company a presence in all 50 states. Leading the firm post-May was Steven J. Douglass as chairman and CEO and Jolosky as president. Douglass was a longtime May veteran who joined Payless in 1993 and was named CEO in 1995.

The late 1990s saw Payless aggressively seek growth on numerous fronts. In 1997 the company went up-market by acquiring Parade of Shoes from J. Baker, Inc. Parade of Shoes was a struggling chain selling mid-priced footwear at 186 shoe stores in 14 states. Revenues in 1995 totaled $113 million. Payless set up Parade as a separate division, maintaining its existing sourcing, distribution, systems, real estate, and financial organizations. Having blanketed the United States with Payless outlets, the company next sought growth in foreign markets. In October 1997 the first Canadian Payless stores opened in the Toronto area. Buoyed by their initial success, the company stepped up plans for further openings and by the end of 1999 had 180 stores in Canada.

Early in 1999 Ken C. Hicks was named president of Payless ShoeSource, having most recently served as executive vice-president of Home Shopping Network, Inc., the Florida-based electronic retailer. Jolosky was appointed vice-chairman. He retained a seat on the board of directors and focused his attention on product development and Parade of Shoes. Meantime, the company ventured into e-commerce in 1999 by offering shoes for sale at its payless.com web site. In another growth initiative Payless entered into a joint venture with ShopKo Stores Inc., a discount retailer based in Green Bay, Wisconsin.

Payless began operating shoe departments inside ShopKo stores under the Payless ShoeSource name. After the first such stores-within-a-store opened successfully in the later months of 1999, the entire 160-unit ShopKo chain was outfitted by the end of 2000. For the fiscal year ending in January 2000, Payless posted strong results: $136.5 million in net income on revenues of $2.73 billion. By this time the company was operating nearly 4,500 Payless ShoeSource stores and more than 220 Parade of Shoes stores.

Struggling in the Early 2000s

As it was opening 56 more stores in Canada in 2000, bringing the total to 236, Payless began looking south for additional growth. In September 2000 the company entered into a joint venture with local partners to operate Payless ShoeSource stores in the Central American region, specifically Costa Rica, Guatemala, El Salvador, the Dominican Republic, Honduras, Nicaragua, Panama, and Trinidad and Tobago. By January 2004 there were 150 Payless stores in the region. Next, a similar joint venture was created in November 2001 to pursue the South American market. This venture was operating 57 Payless stores in Ecuador, Chile, and Peru by January 2004. In 2003 Payless joined with the Japanese trading company Nichimen Corporation in another venture, which opened a test store in Japan in November 2004.

As the early years of the new century began to unfold, Payless was under increasing competitive pressure, in a brutal retail environment, from several challengers: discount chains, most notably Wal-Mart and Target Corporation; department stores, particularly the surging Kohl's Corporation; and specialty chains, such as Foot Locker and Shoe Carnival. The fairly steady rise in both profits and revenues of the late 1990s came to a halt. Another problem area was Parade of Shoes, which was posting disappointing profits. This and other concerns prompted a restructuring in the fourth quarter of the fiscal year ending in January 2002. Payless closed 104 underperforming stores (67 Parade units and 37 Payless ShoeSource outlets), cut 230 positions from the payroll, and took a $43 million after-tax restructuring charge. The operations of Parade also were consolidated with those of the flagship chain. For the year, Payless's earnings plummeted 62.3 percent to $45.4 million, while sales fell 1.2 percent to $2.91 billion. A longtime Payless veteran, Duane Cantrell, was named president in February 2002.

From 2001 to 2003, not only did net sales fall each year, but same-store sales (sales at stores open at least one year) fell each year as well. Payless furthermore suffered a net loss of $100,000 in 2003, and at its annual meeting in May 2004 it had to fight off a challenge from a dissident group of shareholders aiming to gain three seats on the company board. Having already committed to closing or relocating 230 Payless stores during 2004, the company announced a major overhaul in August of that year. The plan, expected to cost about $75 million, included closing down the 181-unit Parade chain, shutting down an additional 260 Payless ShoeStore outlets, exiting the Peruvian and Chilean markets, reducing certain wholesale businesses, and cutting expenses. The moves were intended to enable Payless to heighten its focus on a stronger core operation, though some analysts believed that they were insufficient to revive the struggling firm. By the end of 2004

Payless was operating a little more than 4,700 stores, compared with its peak total of about 5,100. Late in 2004 Cantrell resigned as president, and Payless announced that it was reviewing its agency account relationship for its North American advertising. It also reported that through December, same-store sales for the year were down 0.8 percent.

Principal Subsidiaries

Payless ShoeSource Canada Inc.; Dyelights, Inc.; Payless Shoe-Source International Limited (Hong Kong); Payless ShoeSource Andean Holdings (Cayman Islands); Payless ShoeSource Asia PTE. LTD. (Singapore); Payless ShoeSource Japan Co. Ltd.; Payless ShoeSource Spain, S.L.

Principal Competitors

Wal-Mart Stores, Inc.; Target Corporation; Kmart Holding Corporation; Sears, Roebuck and Co.; Kohl's Corporation; J.C. Penney Company, Inc.

Further Reading

Appelhanz, Christie, "Payless Strides into New Territories," *Topeka (Kans.) Capital-Journal*, May 29, 1999.

Grove, Mary Beth, "The Odd Couple," *Forbes*, November 18, 1996, pp. 178–80.

Hooper, Michael, "Payless Retains Current Board: N.Y. Investor's Bid for Spot Blocked by Company," *Topeka (Kans.) Capital-Journal*, May 28, 2004, p. A1.

——, "Payless ShoeSource Steps into South America," *Topeka (Kans.) Capital-Journal*, May 25, 2002, p. A1.

——, "Payless Slashes Payroll," *Topeka (Kans.) Capital-Journal*, September 3, 2004, p. A1.

Houser, Douglas, "Volume Shoe Maintains Program to Expand Shoe Store Network," *Investment Dealers' Digest*, February 15, 1972, p. 30.

La Monica, Paul, "May Department Stores: The Shoe Doesn't Fit," *Financial World*, April 8, 1996, pp. 16, 18.

LoRusso, Mayann, "Even Steven," *Footwear News*, December 6, 1999, p. 14.

Malone, Scott, "Payless to Add Parade of Shoes to Retail Stable," *Footwear News*, January 20, 1997, pp. 1+.

Mann, Jennifer, "Payless Averts Shareholder Showdown," *Footwear News*, May 31, 2004, p. 2.

——, "Under Pressure: New Competitors Put the Squeeze on Payless Sales," *Footwear News*, July 14, 2003, p. 1.

"May Department Stores Agrees to Buy Volume Shoe Corp.," *Wall Street Journal*, July 24, 1979, p. 2.

"May's Return to Its Roots," *Business Week*, October 19, 1981, pp. 89–92.

McNally, Pamela, "Penetrating the Great Wall of Payless," *Footwear News*, August 16, 1993, pp. 1+.

Patterson, Gregory, "May Stores Buys Shoe Outlets from Two Stores," *Wall Street Journal*, July 28, 1994, p. 8B.

"Payless Making a Move on Latin America," *Footwear News*, September 11, 2000, p. 2.

Quintanilla, Carl, "May to Spin Off Payless to Holders, Close or Move Stores," *Wall Street Journal*, January 18, 1996, 4B.

Sanger, Elizabeth, "Productivity by the Square Foot," *Barron's*, January 13, 1986, pp. 41–42.

Solomon, Goody, "Best Foot Forward: Self-Service Shoe Stores Are Growing by Leaps and Bounds," *Barron's*, February 22, 1965, pp. 11–12, 15.

"Volume Distributors Walk Profit March on Self-Service Sales," *Investment Dealers' Digest,* December 30, 1963, pp. 19–20.

"Volume Shoe Building Sole Base for Extensive Expansion Effort," *Investment Dealers' Digest,* December 25, 1967, pp. 37–38.

"White House Talks with Six Firms on Payout Rises Are Inconclusive," *Wall Street Journal,* September 8, 1971, p. 3.

Zmuda, Natalie, "Analysts: Mass Competition Continues to Hinder Payless," *Footwear News,* September 13, 2004, p. 8.

——, "Payless Trims Down to Beef Up," *Footwear News,* August 16, 2004, p. 2.

——, "Will Payless Closings Help Revive Chain?," *Footwear News,* October 25, 2004, p. 8.

—Hilary Gopnik
—update: David E. Salamie

New York **Philharmonic**
Founded 1842

Philharmonic-Symphony Society of New York, Inc.
(New York Philharmonic)

Avery Fisher Hall
10 Lincoln Center Plaza
New York, New York 10023
U.S.A.
Telephone: (212) 875-5900
Fax: (212) 875-5715
Web site: http://www.newyorkphilharmonic.org

Nonprofit Company
Incorporated: 1842 as New York Philharmonic Society
Employees: 200
Sales: $34.7 million (2003)
NAIC: 711130 Musical Groups and Artists

Philharmonic-Symphony Society of New York, Inc., better known as the New York Philharmonic, is the oldest symphony orchestra in the United States and one of the world's most prestigious. The group began as a small cooperative of local musicians and rose to become the leading orchestra of the nation's cultural capital, New York City. The group is housed in New York's vast performing arts complex, Lincoln Center. The New York Philharmonic gives approximately 180 concerts a year, and tours both the United States and abroad. The group is financed through subscriptions and ticket sales, government grants, an endowment fund, and through corporate and individual charitable donations. The New York Philharmonic has long attracted all the biggest names in classical music as soloists and conductors. Its long roster of famed conductors includes Arturo Toscanini, Leonard Bernstein, Zubin Mehta, and Kurt Masur. Since 2002, the orchestra has been led by Music Director Lorin Maazel.

Early Years

The orchestra now known as the New York Philharmonic began as a cooperative of professional musicians, the New York Philharmonic Society, which banded together to provide three concerts a year to subscribers. The group was organized by violinist and conductor Ureli Corelli Hill and other musicians. Proceeds of the orchestra's season were divided equally among the members. The New York Philharmonic gave its first performance in a rented hall called the Apollo Rooms in December 1842, playing what was only the second New York hearing of Beethoven's Fifth Symphony. New York was a growing metropolis, already one of the ten largest cities in the world, and it boasted a strong cohort of musicians, many of them immigrants from Germany. In 1842, larger orchestras of more than 60 players were becoming quite popular. The Philharmonic Society began with 70 members, about 40 percent of them of German origin. In its first year, the group brought in $1,855, and in its second year raised that to almost $2,500. As ticket sales increased, the cooperative paid out a bigger dividend to its members, and also put money aside for members in need—the rudiments of a health benefits and pension plan.

The young orchestra was an immediate success. It brought in as a soloist one of the world's leading violinists, Henri Vieuxtemps, in 1843, and invited such illustrious guest conductors as Louis Spohr and Felix Mendelssohn (neither Spohr nor Mendelssohn was able to travel to New York, but they did become honorary members of the cooperative.) The group played what was cutting-edge contemporary music of the era: Beethoven, Hummel, Rossini, Berlioz and Verdi. Encouraged by its warm reception in New York, the orchestra made plans to build a permanent concert hall for itself. To aid in fundraising (and collection of debts), the group decided to incorporate. With some governmental foot dragging, this finally occurred in February, 1853. By its 1856–57 season, the orchestra was bringing in as much as $14,000 annually. Ticket sales grew when it decided to admit women as subscribers in 1847, and then to allow single ticket sales for friends of season subscribers. The group weathered financial panics, fires, and the Civil War, as well as competition from other orchestras and glamorous soloists in New York.

The New York Philharmonic had an array of conductors in its early years, and played at many different venues. In 1879 it hired conductor Theodore Thomas, who brought some stability to the group by remaining its head until 1891. Thomas had been

Company Perspectives:

Founded in 1842 by a group of local musicians led by American-born Ureli Corelli Hill, the New York Philharmonic is by far the oldest symphony orchestra in the United States and one of the oldest in the world. In continuous operation throughout two-thirds of our nation's history, the Philharmonic has played a leading role in American musical life and development. In 2002–03, the Philharmonic celebrated its 160th anniversary. Currently, the Orchestra plays some 180 concerts a year, most of them in Avery Fisher Hall, Lincoln Center, during its September-to-June subscription season.

the conductor of the Brooklyn Philharmonic, and that group had siphoned off many of the New York Philharmonic's best players. The two groups often performed on the same night, and contemporary critics generally preferred the Brooklyn ensemble. The New York Philharmonic enticed Thomas with the princely salary of $2,500. His tenure was a time of growing financial stability for the Philharmonic Society. It moved to better quarters in the just-built Metropolitan Opera House in 1886. In 1891, Thomas abruptly decamped to Chicago. He was replaced with the Hungarian-American conductor Anton Seidl. Seidl was well-respected by critics and audiences. He notably premiered Anton Dvorak's Ninth Symphony, the American-influenced ''From the New World,'' in 1893.

Changes in Structure in the Early 20th Century

The New York Philharmonic Society maintained its cooperative governing structure until 1909. Yet as early as the 1880s, the group's direction was influenced by wealthy New York patrons. The Society's president handled the business affairs of the group, and this position had been filled by professional musicians until 1867, when a chemist, R. Ogden Doremus, took the job. Doremus and other succeeding presidents were devoted music-lovers, though not professionals. In the 1880s, the job of president was filled by a series of extremely prominent New Yorkers, known for their great wealth. International banker Joseph Drexel held the post from 1881 to 1888, when the job passed to corporate lawyer E. Francis Hyde. In 1902, the Philharmonic's presidency passed to one of the most prominent men in the nation, Andrew Carnegie. The orchestra had found a new home in the concert hall Carnegie endowed, Carnegie Hall, in 1893 (after the Metropolitan Opera House was destroyed by fire.) Under Carnegie's leadership, the Philharmonic Society began to invest in European celebrity conductors. The orchestra had made do with two unpopular conductors after the sudden death of Anton Seidl in 1898, and ticket receipts fell. Carnegie came up with a plan to give the orchestra a large permanent endowment fund, and to bring in exciting guest conductors from Europe. Instead of one principal conductor, the Philharmonic's season was split among as many as seven European superstars. Then from 1906 to 1909, the orchestra had one principal conductor, the Russian Vassily Safonoff.

Though the Philharmonic brought in exciting and world famous conductors, it was not the only high-caliber orchestra in

the region. Walter Damrosch, who had led the New York Philharmonic for one miserable season, had his own acclaimed orchestra in the city, the Symphony Society of New York. The Metropolitan Opera was also enjoying enormous success in the early years of the 20th century. Boston and Pittsburgh too had large symphony orchestras with dynamic leaders. The New York Philharmonic often suffered from the comparison when these orchestras toured New York.

By the 1890s, the orchestra was relying increasingly on substitutes rather than actual members to play its concerts. By 1909, out of the 100-piece orchestra, only 37 players were Philharmonic Society members. The orchestra had ballooning expenses as it paid thousands of dollars in advertising. Its big-name conductors and soloists were paid for out of separate funds raised by its philanthropist board members, while the members' dividends remained modest, and many played dance music at other venues to make ends meet. The orchestra's cooperative governing structure was seeming less and less able to meet the group's needs.

In 1909, the Philharmonic's wealthy backers took over the orchestra in order to guarantee its continued existence. Elections for board members were suspended, and business affairs were instead turned over to a Committee of Guarantors. These Guarantors were able to put up tens of thousands of dollars of their own money towards the orchestra's expenses, and in exchange, the committee gained the authority to hire the conductor and business manager, and to contract with the musicians. The orchestra players were guaranteed a salary of $35 a week. The Philharmonic Society voted to suspend its old governance system, and the group became, like most of its competitors, a professional orchestra subsidized by wealthy backers. The new governors immediately made waves by hiring none other than composer Gustav Mahler as the Philharmonic's next conductor. Mahler brought in his own concertmaster and made many other changes in personnel. Mahler took the orchestra on tour for the first time, and offered an expanded menu of concerts, including a series in Brooklyn and a series of ''educational'' Sunday concerts.

Mahler was apparently too radical in his musical tastes for New York, and audiences shrank. He died in 1911 and was replaced by Josef Stransky. The orchestra had changed greatly under Mahler's leadership, with very few of the pre-1909 players left in the orchestra. On its sounder financial footing, the orchestra was now able to guarantee its players a decent salary, and to play more concerts and tour. In 1911, the newspaper magnate Joseph Pulitzer died, and willed the New York Philharmonic $500,000 plus other sums, to be used as a permanent endowment. This was another crucial step in guaranteeing the orchestra's future and the expansion of its capabilities. The Philharmonic made its first recordings in 1917, and reached broader audiences through radio beginning in 1923. The orchestra also began a summer stadium concert series, which ran from 1922 until 1951, and began offering special children's concerts in 1924. In 1928 the Philharmonic finessed a merger with one of its major New York competitors, the National Symphony Orchestra. The group, though still colloquially known as the New York Philharmonic, took the official name the Philharmonic-Symphony Society of New York.

Key Dates:

1842: New York Philharmonic is founded as cooperative society.
1886: Orchestra moves to Metropolitan Opera House.
1909: Philharmonic changes corporate structure from co-operative to nonprofit subsidized orchestra.
1911: Joseph Pulitzer wills money to Philharmonic for use as an endowment.
1928: Philharmonic merges with Symphony Society and becomes Philharmonic-Symphony Society of New York, Inc.
1930: Philharmonic takes first tour of Europe.
1962: Orchestra moves from Carnegie Hall to Lincoln Center.
1991: Kurt Masur becomes Music Director.
2002: Lorin Maazel succeeds Masur.

Growth Mid-Century

After the merger with the National Symphony Orchestra, the New York Philharmonic came into its own as *the* New York orchestra. Following several seasons under principal conductor Willem Mengelberg and various guest conductors, the Philharmonic landed the most acclaimed conductor of the era, Arturo Toscanini. After sharing the top billing with Mengelberg, Toscanini became the principal conductor in 1930, when he took the group on its first European tour. Toscanini was the most charismatic of conductors, handsome, with a terrible temper, known for the purity and discipline of his interpretations. He brought enormous crowds to Carnegie Hall. Nevertheless, during the years of the Great Depression, the Philharmonic found itself in financial difficulties. Toscanini was paid a high salary, reputedly $100,000 for ten weeks of performances, and ticket sales tended to die down for the part of the season when the great man was not on the podium. The orchestra players agreed to a 10 percent pay cut in the early 1930s, giving them on average about $90 a week for a 30-week season. Yet by 1934, the Philharmonic's financial position had grown so precarious that the group started an emergency fundraising campaign. The orchestra hoped to raise $500,000 in order to meet immediate needs. Other arts groups in the city also suffered from the severe economic cutbacks of the time. As an economizing measure, it was suggested that the New York Philharmonic and the Metropolitan Opera merge. But Toscanini did not approve, and the merger plans were abandoned.

Toscanini left the Philharmonic in 1936. He was replaced by a much more modest conductor, the Englishman John Barbirolli. He was principal conductor from 1936 to 1941. During that time, the orchestra retrenched. It brought its number of players down to 102 from 107, played a 24-week season instead of 30, and cut costs by almost 25 percent, mostly by saving on guest conductor and guest artist fees. The orchestra returned to financial stability by the late 1930s, and the Philharmonic went on several lengthy tours.

During World War II, the Philharmonic played at military camps, bases, and hospitals. Members of the orchestra were able to donate two ambulances to the Red Cross. The Philhar-

monic was headed by a series of guest conductors after Barbirolli left in 1941, and then it hired Artur Rodzinski in 1943 as principal conductor and Musical Director. Rodzinski remained in place until 1949, presiding over a time of relative financial ease for the Philharmonic. The orchestra instituted a formal pension plan in 1944, which was a model for orchestras across the nation. The orchestra also began broadcasting summer Sunday radio concerts nationwide during Rodzinski's tenure, supplementing existing fall and winter broadcasts. The summer broadcast concerts featured some of the leading soloists and guest conductors of the time, and led to a grand tour of 17 states in the summer of 1947.

Rodzinski resigned in 1947, and the job of principal conductor went to the eminent German Bruno Walter. Walter also took the title of Musical Adviser (sic), overseeing a very broad repertoire and an assortment of guest conductors. Walter was already in his 70s when he took the post, and he had apparently not planned to stay for long with the Philharmonic. Two conductors, Leopold Stokowski and Dimitri Mitropoulos, shared the principal conductor role for the 1949 to 1950 season. Mitropoulos was principal conductor alone from 1950 to 1957. One of the most significant changes in the orchestra's history came in the mid-1950s, when it finalized plans to leave its home in Carnegie Hall and move to a proposed new midtown arts center, Lincoln Center.

The Move to Lincoln Center

The Philharmonic's management had been involved in planning for a new arts center since at least 1953. A section of midtown Manhattan known as Lincoln Square was to be razed, and various groups came together to propose building a performing arts complex there. The Philharmonic's home, Carnegie Hall, was scheduled to be knocked down, and the orchestra thus was under pressure to find new quarters by 1959. A nonprofit group, Lincoln Center for the Performing Arts, Inc., incorporated in 1956, and ground was broken for the new center in 1959. The Philharmonic moved into its new home, Lincoln Center's Philharmonic Hall, in 1962.

The new Philharmonic Hall at first proved a big disappointment. Carnegie Hall was at the last minute saved from the wrecking ball, and audiences and performers alike wistfully recalled the warmer acoustics of the old place. The new hall had been meticulously engineered, but it was nevertheless not acoustically balanced, and a few months after it opened, it had to undergo a substantial overhaul. One of the Philharmonic's frequent guest conductors, George Szell, gave this scathing account of the result of the refurbishment (as quoted in Howard Shanet, *Philharmonic: A History of New York's Orchestra*): "Imagine a woman, lame, a hunchback, cross-eyed and with two warts. They've removed the warts." More changes were made in 1964 and 1965. Finally a three-month, $1.25 million renovation in 1969 made the hall, now Avery Fisher Hall, a satisfying place to play and hear music. The hall was redesigned yet again in 1976.

The Bernstein Years: 1958–69

During the years the Philharmonic was moving into its new quarters, it gained a new conductor, the American Leonard Bernstein. Bernstein had been an assistant conductor with the

Philharmonic in 1943 when he was 25 years old, and the young man had made a thrilling debut, filling in at the last minute for Bruno Walter. Bernstein was a flamboyant, warm-hearted conductor, one of the few American conductors the orchestra had ever had, and his character was very much attuned to the times. He became well-known to television audiences, and he was immensely popular as the conductor of the Philharmonic's children's concerts and free concerts in the park. Bernstein, a composer himself, championed American music in a way few of the Philharmonic's conductors had. During his tenure, the orchestra vastly increased the number of concerts it gave. Its subscription series was generally completely sold out during the 1960s, and the Philharmonic's free outdoor concerts attracted huge audiences. One outdoor concert in 1966, with Bernstein conducting Beethoven and Stravinsky, attracted an audience estimated at more than 75,000 people.

The New York Philharmonic became firmly identified with Bernstein, who embodied a certain verve and glow that made him enduringly popular. The orchestra made as many as 200 recordings under Bernstein. These sold well, and royalties from recordings became a significant source of income for the Philharmonic Society. The orchestra expanded its repertoire in the Bernstein years, playing everything from Baroque music to electronic compositions to musical theater. Bernstein also stretched the roster of guest conductors the orchestra called on, bringing in many canonical European conductors such as Nadia Boulanger and Herbert van Karajan and varied composer-conductors such as Aaron Copland, Duke Ellington, and Darius Milhaud.

The 1970s and 1980s

The orchestra reached a musical high point under Bernstein. Nevertheless, it was not free of financial worries. It had greatly expanded its programming, and by the end of the 1960s its musicians had a 52-week contract. Expenses always outran income, though the gap was made up by contributions from patrons and from the Philharmonic's endowment. In 1969, the Philharmonic banded together with the four other leading American orchestras—the Boston Symphony, the Chicago Symphony, the Cleveland Orchestra, and the Philadelphia Orchestra—and hired a management consultant firm to analyze the financial outlook of the groups. Of the five, the New York Philharmonic was in the best financial shape. The others were all running deficits, while the Philharmonic had a small surplus. But the economic picture such organizations presented was not bright. The five-orchestra group, led by the Philharmonic's board president, decided to petition the federal government for aid through the National Endowment for the Arts (NEA). Despite the federal government's own fiscal worries, in 1970 President Nixon signed a bill authorizing some $40 million for the NEA. Only a small percentage of this actually reached the Philharmonic, but it represented a milestone in U.S. government support of symphony orchestras. The New York Philharmonic on its own then asked the New York state legislature for a grant. To its immense surprise, the legislature complied with a broad appropriation to go to many of the state's nonprofit arts groups. The fundraising and business aspect of running the Philharmonic had become so complex by the early 1970s that the board decided for the first time to make the job of president a full-time salaried position. Back when the post had been filled by such

figures as Andrew Carnegie, it was not considered a full-time job but an extra obligation, and wealthy men like Carnegie had no need of a salary from the Philharmonic Society. The hiring of a salaried executive was a sign that running the Philharmonic had become much more daunting.

Leonard Bernstein conducted his farewell concert in 1969. He was followed by several guest conductors, until Pierre Boulez took over in 1971. Boulez presided until 1978. He was known as a daring modernist, and he presented quite a contrast with Bernstein. Subscription sales dropped somewhat during Boulez's tenure. He was followed in 1978 by Zubin Mehta. From the mid-1970s to the late 1980s, the orchestra grew and prospered in many ways. Salaries for the players rose markedly. In the mid-1970s, the annual minimum salary for a Philharmonic player was just under $20,000. The minimum rose to almost $60,000 by 1990. The number of season ticket subscribers also grew, from a little more than 27,000 for the 1977–78 season to more than 37,000 subscribers in 1990. The orchestra's endowment fund rose from under $10 million in the mid-1970s to $69 million by 1990. Audiences seemed to appreciate Mehta's warmth. He enjoyed a very long stay as principal conductor, leaving in 1991, when he was replaced by Kurt Masur.

New Directions in the 1990s and 2000s

When Mehta resigned, so did the Philharmonic's managing director, who had been with the orchestra since 1975. The new managing director, Deborah Borda, came to a difficult task of keeping balance between the orchestra's artistic needs and financial possibilities. Government support for the Philharmonic dropped off in the 1990s, as many arts groups across the country turned increasingly to private donations. The Philharmonic maintained balanced budgets through the mid-1990s, though not without work. Many orchestras, both large like the Philharmonic and smaller regional groups, suffered poor labor relations in the 1990s, with strikes, lockouts, bitterly contested pay cuts, and much wrangling over the cost of health benefits. The New York Philharmonic came close to a strike over contract negotiations in 1995, while in 1996 and 1997 the orchestras in Atlanta, Philadelphia, and San Francisco all walked off the job. In 1997, the Philharmonic players signed a six-year contract, though three-year contracts were the industry norm. The contract guaranteed small annual increases in base pay and pensions for most players. The long contract gave the orchestra more years in which it did not have to worry about contentious financial issues.

The orchestra seemed to do well in many ways under Kurt Masur. Joseph Horowitz, writing in the *New York Times* (September 15, 2002), stated, ''For the first time in memory, the orchestra can be depended upon to play with virtuosity and commitment, and not merely when the boss is in charge.'' But the critic also noted that there had been times when Masur had ''stopped conducting, and even left the podium, because the Philharmonic's listeners were quite audibly not listening.'' Jay Nordlinger, writing for the *National Review* (July 23, 2001), summed up Masur's stay at the Philharmonic similarly as one of mixed effect, saying ''Masur has made this orchestra one of the mightiest in the world, restoring a glory that had been lost. Yet he has been grossly underappreciated here, by his own management, his own players, and the city's critics.'' Masur was first scheduled to leave in 1998, apparently because of friction between the conductor, the Philharmonic's board, and the players. He then extended his contract through 2002 while the orchestra looked for a replacement.

Masur was followed by the American conductor Lorin Maazel. Maazel had led the Cleveland Orchestra for ten years and was one of the grand names in the international orchestral scene, yet he had not appeared as a guest conductor for the Philharmonic since the 1970s. Maazel seemed to quickly make his mark on the orchestra, and he boasted to the press that subscription ticket sales had risen by 4 percent in his first month as Music Director. The next order of business was apparently to get the orchestra a new hall, as the Philharmonic's Avery Fisher Hall was still plagued by less than satisfactory acoustics. In June 2003, the Philharmonic announced that it was leaving Lincoln Center and moving back to Carnegie Hall. The orchestra and the nonprofit that ran Carnegie Hall would then merge. The decision was prompted in part by a consultant's report on the cost of rebuilding or renovating Avery Fisher Hall, which made moving out seem like the most economical option.

Yet a mere four months later, Carnegie Hall's management and the orchestra announced that the merger plans were off. The Philharmonic was scheduled to remain at Lincoln Center until at least 2011, and Avery Fisher Hall would undergo extensive refitting. The next year, the Philharmonic announced that it had extended Lorin Maazel's contract through 2009. Maazel had originally planned on staying only four years, or through 2006. But the Philharmonic Society's managing director claimed that Maazel was unexpectedly happy at the podium, and he and all other parties involved wanted him to stay on. Also in 2004, the orchestra's musicians ratified another three-year labor contract, assuring some stability to the group.

Further Reading

Conrad, Willa J., ''Harmony Reigns with N.Y. Philharmonic Pact,'' *Star-Ledger* (Newark, N.J.), December 20, 1997, p. 37.

Gates, David, ''The Philharmonic's New 'Admiral' Takes Command,'' *Newsweek*, July 9, 2001, p. 56.

Horowitz, Joseph, ''Anybody Listening? A Hapless History,'' *New York Times*, September 15, 2002, sec. 2, p. 28.

Isherwood, Charles, ''N.Y. Phil, Carnegie Hall Scuttle Wedding Plans,'' *Daily Variety*, October 8, 2003, p. 4.

Kozinn, Allan, ''Philharmonic Appoints Its New Chairman,'' *New York Times*, September 18, 1996, p. C15.

——, ''Who Pulled the Big Five's Plug?'' *New York Times*, February 7, 1993, p. H1.

Malitz, Nancy, ''Arriving on the Fast Track,'' *New York Times*, September 15, 1991, p. H25.

''New York Philharmonic's New Conductor Says Sales Up,'' *Europe Intelligence Wire*, October 21, 2002.

Nordlinger, Jay, ''Mere Excellence,'' *National Review*, July 23, 2001.

Pogrebin, Robin, and Ralph Blumenthal, ''Philharmonic Deal, Completed Quickly, Left Some in Dark,'' *New York Times*, June 3, 2003, pp. A1, B7.

Rockwell, John, ''Administrator Quits Philharmonic,'' *New York Times*, October 6, 1990, p. 11.

Shanet, Howard, *Philharmonic: A History of New York's Orchestra*, New York: Doubleday & Co., 1975.

Smith, Patrick J., ''Filling the Philharmonic's Podium,'' *New Criterion*, April 2001, p. 52.

''3-Year Deal for N.Y. Philharmonic,'' *Star-Ledger* (Newark, N.J.), October 13, 2004, p. 41.

Tindall, Blair, ''The Plight of the White-Tie Worker,'' *New York Times*, July 4, 2004.

—A. Woodward

Pixelworks, Inc.

8100 SW Nyberg Road
Tualatin, Oregon 97062
U.S.A.
Telephone: (503) 612-6700
Fax: (503) 612-0848
Web site: http://www.pixelworks.com

Public Company
Incorporated: 1997
Employees: 241
Sales: $176.2 million (2004)
Stock Exchanges: NASDAQ
Ticker Symbol: PXLW
NAIC: 334413 Semiconductor and Related Device
  Manufacturing

Pixelworks, Inc. designs, develops, and markets semiconductors and software for advanced televisions, multimedia projectors, and flat-panel monitors. Its system-on-a-chip integrated circuits (ICs) or interface IC products integrate a microprocessor, memory, and image processing circuits that function as a computer on a single chip. Its customers include Dell, Epson, Hewlett Packard, InFocus, LG Electronics, NEC-Mitsubishi, Philips, Samsung, Sanyo, Sony, Tokyo Electron Device, and ViewSonic. Close to 90 percent of the company's sales come from its Asian customers.

1997–99: Pioneering a New Technology and Management Style

In 1986, Allen Alley, acting as a venture capitalist, invested in a start-up company called InFocus Systems, which produced projector systems that display output from personal computers and other electronic devices. InFocus founders were convinced that a new program called PowerPoint was the trend of the future. Once the market caught on and InFocus became an international force, Alley who had a background in mechanical engineering and business, became an employee of InFocus Systems and worked there for four years.

Then, in 1996, Alley along with a group of InFocus employees that included Michael West, Robert Greenberg, Bradley Zenger, and Ken Hunkins, decided that they wanted to "make money, have fun, and play fair" and founded Pixelworks. At the time other, larger companies were moving into selling component technology. Pixelworks instead focused on designing and building semiconductors that let flat panel displays translate output signals from such video sources as digital television receivers, digital video disc players, and computers.

At first, Pixelworks focused on the computer market. Its self-contained modules featuring an embedded operating system, source code, and the software tools needed to customize display devices replaced a handful of electronics in flat panel displays and helped flat-display makers reduce the cost of their products. Displays with a Pixelworks controller could show web pages, spreadsheets, and a television broadcast in different windows on the same screen.

Recognized for its innovative product, Pixelworks also stood out in its industry for its distinctive management approach. In its earliest days, Alley ran the company without a strict budget, a style that grew out of his stints at Ford, Boeing, and InFocus Systems. "Most of the metrics and reports you get are like trying to drive the car by looking in the rearview mirror," he said in *Oregon Business* in 2001. "What I rely on is feedback from customers and employees. I can tell you the health of our business by talking with customers much better than I can by reading any report."

Management's goals in 1997 were to grow revenues in the millions; secure customers in Europe, Japan, Asia, and the United States; and introduce Pixelworks chips into three basic markets, televisions, monitors, and projectors. It achieved those goals and reached $12 million in revenues in its first year. "The problem with any [technology] market is you can't figure out how big any of these things is going to grow and when," Alley asserted in the same *Oregon Business* article. His solution: "[Y]ou don't bet on it happening next quarter or next year. You build a platform that can survive an up, down or sideways market."

Pixelworks also kept costs down by keeping a small staff and asking its employees each to do a variety of tasks. Every new employee that joined Pixelworks was literally issued a set of juggling balls when he reported to work as a simple, physical expression of the company's expectations of its workers. Most learned to juggle. They also all flew coach and competed to see who could spend the least on lunch.

Pixelworks' founders also believed that their system-on-a-chip ICs would someday be used in televisions, and they thus positioned Pixelworks to influence television design. "We looked at the business model for computers and said if the model works for computers, the model should work for televisions," said Allen Alley, the new company's chief executive officer in a retrospective 2003 *Wall Street Journal* article.

When, in 1998, the recession in Asia led some Asian high-tech corporations to create partnerships and joint ventures with Northwest firms, Pixelworks had the opportunity to enter the television market. Toshiba Corporation, eager to lure work for its new semiconductor plant in Oita, Japan, agreed to absorb some of the cost of developing Pixelworks' first semiconductor for use in flat-panel monitors and high-definition televisions in exchange for assuming its manufacturing business. Toshiba extended a line of credit to Pixelworks on manufacturing and rushed the production of the first batch of test chips.

In 1999, Pixelworks' staff of 45 workers moved into the company's new 23,000-square-foot office building, and Pixelworks held its third round of venture capital financing, bringing its total capital raised to close to $20 million. This third round of money went to develop the next generation of the company's ImageProcessor products designed to take advantage of the surge in liquid crystal display (LCD) monitors. That year, ViewSonic, the top-selling monitor manufacturer in the United States, chose the ImageProcessor to power the first flat panel displays to incorporate digital, analog, and video inputs into one display.

Although the company lost $5 million on revenues of almost $13 million in 1999, Red Herring magazine named it one of the country's ten young companies to watch in mid-1999. Moreover, Pixelworks continued to grow during troubled financial times. When the company held its initial public offering (IPO) in the spring of 2000, the NASDAQ was past its crest and declining steadily. "A lot of people thought we were crazy to go out," recalled Alley in a 2001 *Oregon Business* article, "but one of my philosophies has been, if I can raise the money, raise the money." The money from the IPO went toward working

capital and general corporate purposes. Shares, issued at $10 per share in May 2000, reached more than $50 per share by October. Named Technology Company of the Year by the Oregon Entrepreneurs forum in 2000, Pixelworks became profitable in the quarter ending June 2000 and remained so. Total revenues climbed to $52.6 million for the year 2000, and Pixelworks began to supply products to Compaq and IBM, among others.

2000–01: Increasing Its Technological Capabilities Through Acquisitions

Beginning in 2000, some of the major electronics manufacturers began to integrate Pixelworks' ImageProcessor architecture into their products. Samsung Electronics employed the ImageProcessor in a line of its flat panel displays in 2000 to provide its monitors with the flexibility to offer video and computer graphics on the screen simultaneously. In 2001, NEC-Mitsubishi Electronics Displays high resolution, premium-quality LCD monitors incorporated the ImageProcessor.

Also in 2001, Pixelworks expanded its scope through acquisitions. With the purchase of Panstera Inc., which manufactured fully integrated handheld devices, it entered the low-cost XDA market. This acquisition also brought with it the technology to offer screenmakers a single-chip solution that combined analog capabilities with an extended graphics array. Pixelworks' second acquisition, nDSP Corporation, strengthened its advanced video processing product and technology portfolio with the addition of low-cost, high-performance video processing ICs and the technology to enhance the image quality of mainstream consumer televisions and other digital display products. The addition of nDSP Corporation, which had two offices and 24 employees in Beijing and Shenzhen, also established Pixelworks' presence in China.

By 2001, the global economic downturn had caused the projector market growth rate to slow to 25 to 30 percent annually, but growth in flat panel displays more than made up for the decline for Pixelworks. Alley acknowledged his company's luck in *Oregon Business:* "I absolutely believe it is sometimes better to be lucky than good. We've done quite well. It's fundamentally because the markets we sell our products to are still robust." Pixelworks had grown from its five original founders to 150 employees and had revenues of $90 million.

2002–05: Looking to the Future of High Definition Television and Internet Appliances

The following year, Pixelworks put together a complete design for the electronics inside LCD and plasma televisions. When Xoceco decided to use this design as the base for its first flat-screen television, Pixelworks' engineers taught the company how it worked and how it could be modified via software. It also acquired rival Jaldi Semiconductor Corporation as part of the move toward consolidation among the manufacturers of chips used in television and computer displays.

Pixelworks finished work on a new video-processing chip, code-named Photopia, in the fall of 2003. Photopia integrated many functions onto one chip, saving space and cost. Alley took the product first to his customers in China, the fastest-growing market for the company's fastest-growing product line. That

Key Dates:

1996: Allen Alley and partners from InFocus found Pixelworks.
1997: Pixelworks incorporates.
1998: Toshiba Corporation helps Pixelworks develop its first semiconductor for use in flat-panel monitors and high-definition televisions in exchange for assuming its manufacturing business.
1999: Pixelworks hold its third round of venture capital financing; moves into its new office building.
2000: Pixelworks holds its first public offering.
2001: The company acquires Panstera, Inc. and nDSP Corporation.
2002: Pixelworks acquires Jaldi Semiconductor Corporation.

summer, Royal Philips Electronics joined with Pixelworks to announce their LCD television reference design targeting the lowest-priced, highest-volume segment of the LCD television market. Techsan, a leading manufacturer of set-top boxes and LCD monitors, introduced Europe's first LCD television with a fully integrated DVB-T digital tuner using Pixelworks' Image-Processor and software kit.

By 2004, consumer trends were leaning toward flat panel and high definition televisions and Pixelworks decided that its immediate future lay in high definition television. Thus, early in 2004, it partnered with byd:sign and Xoceco to introduce a complete line of flat-panel plasma and LCD televisions for sale in the United States. The plan moved Pixelworks into the position of becoming a dominant supplier of microchips for flat panel LCD televisions. In fact, 2004 revenues for the company were $176.2 million, up 25 percent from $140.9 million in 2003. However, the limited capabilities of the manufacturers LCD panels used in computers and televisions, mostly in Asia, kept prices for 30-inch LCD televisions above $1,000 and out of reach of many consumers. Not to have all of its chips in one basket, Pixelworks also began to look to the next logical extension of its technology by adding browsing capability to its products and moving into Internet appliance space.

Principal Subsidiaries

Pixelworks Japan, LLC; Pixelworks Taiwan, LLC; Panstera, Inc.; nDSP Delaware, Inc.; nDSP Corporation; Pixelworks Ltd.; Pixelworks Nova Scotia; Jaldi Semiconductor.

Principal Competitors

Genesis Microchip Inc.; Macronix International Co., Ltd.; Micronas Semiconductor Holding AG; National Semiconductor Corporation; Philips Semiconductors; Silicon Image, Inc.; Silicon Optix Inc.; STMicroelectronics N.V.; Texas Instruments Incorporated.

Further Reading

Grund, John M., ''Juggling Opportunities,'' *Oregon Business*, November 1, 2001, p. 16.
Jones, Steven D., ''Asian Flu Can Be a Shot in the Arm for Some Firms,'' *Wall Street Journal*, January 27, 1999, p. NW1.
''Pixelworks Chairman and CEO—Interview with Bill Griffeth,'' *CNBC/Dow Jones Business Video*, July 31, 2000.
Ramstad, Evan, and Phred Dvorak, ''Big Picture: Off-the-Shelf Parts Create New Order in TVs, Electronics,'' *Wall Street Journal*, December 16, 2003, p. A1.

—Carrie Rothburd

Spode

The Porcelain and Fine China Companies Ltd.

Spode, Church Street
Stoke-on-Trent
ST4 1BX
United Kingdom
Telephone: +44 1782 744011
Fax: 44 1782 747317
Web site: http://www.spode.co.uk

Private Company
Incorporated: 1976 as Royal Worcester Spode
Employees: 1,290
Sales: £48 million ($90 million) (2004 est.)
NAIC: 327112 Vitreous China, Fine Earthenware and
    Other Pottery Product Manufacturing

The Porcelain and Fine China Companies Ltd. is better known for its world-famous china brands, Spode and Royal Worcester. Based at the Spode works in Stoke-on-Trent, where the company has been producing its fine porcelain and china since the late 18th century, The Porcelain and Fine China Companies Ltd. is the holding company set up for the company's U.K. operations, known as Royal Worcester Spode, and its U.S. business, based in New Jersey and known as Royal China and Porcelain Companies. The company also owns Caithness Glass, acquired in 2001. Among the company's products are its flagship Spode ranges, including the Timeless, Blue Collection, Nostalgic, Elegant, and Festive series. U.S. customers are especially familiar with Spode's famed Christmas Tree design, introduced in 1939, which remains a company bestseller. Over the decades, more than ten million sets of that design have been sold. Many of Spode's other designs stem from the company's early period under founder Josiah Spode I and son Josiah Spode II, and many of these designs are still produced using the original templates designed by the Spodes. In addition to operating the Spode works, The Porcelain and Fine China Companies Ltd. oversees the Royal Worcester works in Worcester, England, which remains one of England's largest producers of fine bone china and porcelain, retaining traditional craft techniques. The company also operates a num-

ber of factory shops, including the Spode Factory and Spode Clearance stores, shops for Royal Worcester and Caithness Glass, and a Spode Traditional Cook store. A privately held company, The Porcelain and Fine China Companies Ltd. generates sales of approximately £48 million ($90 million) each year.

Founding China History in the 18th Century

Born in 1733, Josiah Spode was 16 when he apprenticed with Thomas Whieldon, one of England's most prominent potters, where he worked alongside another famed name in English china, Josiah Wedgwood. Yet Spode himself went on to establish one of the world's most renowned names in china and porcelain.

Spode left Whieldon at the age of 21 and went to work with other potters before setting up his first factory in 1761, in the town of Shelton, but soon after moved to Stoke, where he became manager of a factory owned by Turner and Banks, which was likely founded in 1751. Spode took over that site after Turner's death, but did not begin producing earthenware under his own name until 1776.

Spode began experimenting with new formulas and decorative techniques. By 1784, Spode had developed a technique of applying blue underglaze printing to the ceramic surface, an innovation that was to transform the British ceramics industry into one of the world's most important centers for fine china and porcelain.

Spode also had recognized the importance of being close to his core customer base—the British nobility and members of the elite class. In 1778, he sent his son, Josiah II, to open a store in London. Spode's designs met with success in the city, and Spode moved to larger premises by 1884, then again in 1888.

After his father's death in 1797, the younger Spode returned to Stoke-on-Trent to take over the Spode factory. The company's London business was turned over to a friend, William Copeland, a tea merchant, who became the company's chief salesman. Josiah II's later designs borrowed heavily from the Chinese imagery on Copeland's imported tea packaging.

Josiah II proved as much an innovator as his father. Spode began experimenting with the formula for producing china,

Company Perspectives:

Spode's craftsmen have been designing and manufacturing some of the finest ceramics ever produced for over 200 years.

working with the addition of feldspar. By 1799, Spode had perfected his formula, and is credited with the creation of bone china. Soon after, many of his contemporaries adopted Spode's techniques, and British bone china became a world standard by the early 19th century. Spode continued experimenting with production techniques, developing a new china type, called stone china, in 1805. In 1813 Spode launched a new line of stoneware, featuring blue transfer and polychrome paintings of Oriental motifs, which became known as Spode's Stone China.

Josiah II was joined by son Josiah III—who was forced to retire from the family business after losing an arm to a factory accident. Josiah III took over the business briefly after his father's death in 1827. But Josiah III died just two years later. In 1833, the Spode family sold the business to longtime partner family, the Copelands, led by William Taylor Copeland. Joining Copeland was the company's chief sales agent, Thomas Garrett, and the company was renamed as Copeland and Garrett that year.

William Taylor Copeland, who later became mayor of London, took over the business after Garrett's death, and the company was renamed W.T Copeland in 1847. Joined by his sons in 1867, Copeland changed the company's name again, to W.T Copeland & Sons, which remained in use for the next 100 years.

Throughout this period, Copeland maintained the commitment to quality and fine design of its founders, and remained one of England's preeminent producers of fine china and porcelain. The company became a favorite producer to the British royal family, and other British notables. One of these was Charles Dickens, who after visiting the Spode factory in 1852, included a description of it in his *Household Words*. A major success for the company, which had seen increasing interest in its products from the United States, came from the launch of its famed Christmas Tree series in 1939, designed by Harold Holdway, whose designs included, among many others, the so-called "Queen's Bird," which had been a favorite of Queen Elizabeth. Despite Holdway's never having seen an American Christmas tree, his design captured the American imagination and became a perennial bestseller for the company. By the early 2000s, the Spode works estimated that it had sold more than ten million sets featuring the Christmas Tree design.

Merging in the 1970s

The once thriving British china and porcelain industry, which boasted some 70 major producers by the 1940s, began to decline toward the end of the 1950s. A key factor in the decline was the rise of competition from elsewhere in the world, and particularly from the Far East. This competition forced many of the United Kingdom's smaller potters out of business by the early 1960s. Others, including Spode, sought mergers as a means of becoming more competitive. In 1964, Spode entered merger talks with Josiah Wedgwood and Sons, which would

have combined the two most legendary names in British china in a single company. Those talks broke down, however.

Instead, the Copeland family sold the Spode works and name to the United States' Carborundum Company in 1966. Under Carborundum, the Spode works, which continued operating as W.T Copeland & Sons, under the leadership of Ronald Copeland, joined two other china producers, Hammersley China and the Royal Windsor Pottery.

In 1970, in honor of Spode's 200th anniversary, the company changed its name back to Spode. Ronald Copeland retired the following year, marking the end of the Copeland family's nearly 200-year association with the company.

In the mid-1970s, Carborundum decided to exit the pottery business and announced that the Spode works were for sale. Wedgwood once again stepped up as a suitor for the company, but once again was unable to agree on the purchase price. Royal Worcester, another venerable British porcelain maker, emerged with its own bid. After rejecting Royal Worcester's initial bid, Carborundum agreed to spin off Spode into a new company, Royal Worcester Spode, held at 55 percent by Royal Worcester and 45 percent by Carborundum.

Royal Worcester had been in business even longer than Spode. In 1751, Dr. John Wall led a group of 14 local businessmen in establishing a pottery workshop in Worcester. The company opened a showroom in London in 1854, and two years later, Robert Hancock, working at the Worcester workshop, invented a technique for printing on porcelain. In 1783, the workshop was acquired by Thomas Flight, who turned its operations over to his sons, John and Joseph. In that year, a rival workshop was founded in Worcester by Robert Chamberlain. The Chamberlain and Flight companies merged together in 1830, becoming the Worcester Royal Porcelain Company.

The second half of the 19th century saw the Worcester factory expand tenfold. At this time, the company focused its production on figurines and vases, with a range of some 2,500 decorative pieces. In 1862, the company adopted the name of Royal Worcester. A major success for the company came with the launch of its Painted Fruit series in 1880.

Royal Worcester grew by acquisition as well. In 1889, the company acquired the Grainger Porcelain Company, which was later closed and moved to the main Worcester site. In 1905, the company purchased Hadley & Sons Art Pottery, also based in Worcester.

In 1914, Royal Worcester supported the British war effort through the production of hard porcelain for use in hospitals, schools, and the like. Similarly, during World War II, the company began producing spark plugs and electrical resistors. Following the war, after returning its production to decorative porcelain, Royal Worcester went public, listing on the London exchange in 1953.

Porcelain and China Leaders in the New Century

Royal Worcester acquired complete control of Royal Worcester Spode in 1978, after Carborundum's takeover by Kennecott. By then Royal Worcester had begun developing a

Key Dates:

1751: A Worcester ceramics workshop, which becomes Royal Worcester, is founded.
1770: Josiah Spode founds a porcelain and china factory in Stoke-on-Trent.
1833: Spode is renamed as Copeland & Garrett.
1847: Copeland & Garrett is renamed as W.T. Copeland.
1867: W.T. Copeland becomes W.T. Copeland & Sons.
1889: Royal Worcester acquires Grainger Porcelain Company.
1905: Royal Worcester acquires Hadley & Sons Art Pottery, also based in Worcester.
1953: Royal Worcester goes public.
1966: Carborundum acquires W.T. Copeland & Sons.
1970: W.T. Copeland is renamed as Spode.
1976: Royal Worcester acquires control of Spode, forms Royal Worcester Spode.
1984: Royal Worcester Spode is acquired by LRC International.
1988: Royal Worcester Spode is acquired by Derby International; the U.S. operation splits off as a separate business, renamed as Royal Porcelain and China, and the U.K. business becomes The Porcelain and Fine China Companies Ltd.
2001: Caithness Glass Ltd., maker of decorative glass objects, is acquired; Vista Alegre acquires a 25 percent stake in The Porcelain and Fine China Companies.
2004: Spode launches a line of candles in a move to expand its range of decorative items.

second line of business, that of ceramics-based electronics components. That operation, however, brought Royal Worcester to the attention of Crystalate, which sought to merge Royal Worcester's electronics business into its own, then spin off the Royal Worcester china and porcelain division.

Crystalate acquired Royal Worcester in a hostile takeover in 1983 and began taking bids for the Spode and Royal Worcester porcelain operations. In 1984, Crystalate agreed to sell the division to LRC International, a U.K.-based producer of rubber gloves, paint rollers and paintbrushes, and contraceptives. Soon after its acquisition, Royal Worcester Spode launched its largest-ever collection of dinnerware, adding some 60 new patterns, in large part to step up the company's sales in the United States, which represented just 30 percent of its total revenues.

Yet a major reason behind LRC's acquisition of Royal Worcester Spode was its interest in acquiring Wedgwood as well, then merging the two groups together to form the United Kingdom's leading porcelain group. LRC's bid for Wedgwood failed, however, after being rejected by the British mergers and monopolies commission. In 1988, after Royal Worcester Spode slipped into losses, LRC sold off the division to Derby International, which also owned the Raleigh bicycle group.

Under Derby, the U.S. branch of the china and porcelain group was split off as a separate and independently operating

company, renamed as Royal China and Porcelain Companies, in part to better differentiate the Worcester and Spode brands in the U.S. market. Yet the U.S. business continued to work closely with its U.K. counterpart, renamed as The Porcelain and Fine China Companies Ltd.

Both the Spode and Royal Worcester brands remained among the world's most well-known porcelain and china brands into the dawn of the 21st century. The Porcelain and Fine China Companies began extending its operations in the 2000s to include a wider range of complementary decorative items. For this reason, the company acquired Caithness Glass Ltd., based in Perth, in Scotland, from Royal Doulton, adding its decorative glassworks. The company also launched a line of Spode-branded candles in 2004—the low price of the candles was designed to introduce and lead consumers to Spode's higher-end core products.

A new suitor for Spode's ownership appeared in the early 2000s as well. In 2001, the Portuguese ceramics group Vista Alegre reached a partnership agreement with The Porcelain and Fine China Companies, which included the acquisition of a 25 percent stake in the company. That agreement included an option for Vista Alegre to acquire full control of Royal Worcester Spode by as early as 2005. Regardless of its owner, The Porcelain and Fine China Companies retained the legacy of two of the world's most important china and porcelain brands.

Principal Subsidiaries

Caithness Glass Ltd; Royal Worcester Spode Ltd.; Royal China and Porcelain Companies Inc. (U.S.A.).

Principal Competitors

American Greetings Corporation; Waterford Wedgwood PLC; Villeroy und Boch AG; Longaberger Co.; Kyocera Fineceramics GmbH; Rosenthal AG; Lladro S.A.; Pamesa Ceramica S.L.; Josiah Wedgwood and Sons Ltd.

Further Reading

Clarke, Arthur, "Obituaries: Harold Holdway: Creative Spirit Behind the Fauna and Flora on Some of the World's Favorite China," *Guardian*, September 27, 2002, p. 22.

Mandel, Sarah, "Christmas Classic: Spode's Tree Design Is a True Evergreen at 65," *Gifts & Decorative Accessories*, August 2003, p. 149.

Moran, Michelle, "Spode and Wallace Expand Christmas Tree Pattern," *Gourmet Retailer*, August 2004, p. 33.

"Royal Worcester/Spode Acquires Caithness Glass," *Home Accents Today*, August 2001, p. 66.

"Spode Draws on History," *HFN The Weekly Newspaper for the Home Furnishing Network*, April 27, 1998, p. 57.

Warren, Jane, "A Country Gent As Smooth As His China," *Express*, April 19, 2002, p. 45.

Webb, Carla, and Allison Zisko, "Companies See the Light with Candle Assortments," *HFN The Weekly Newspaper for the Home Furnishing Network*, October 11, 2004, p. 124.

Wise, Peter, "Ceramicist Makes Bid for Global Brand Recognition," *Financial Times*, May 4, 2001, p. 45.

—M.L. Cohen

Portugal Telecom SGPS S.A.

Avenida Fontes Pereira de Melo 4
Lisboa
P-1069-300
Portugal
Telephone: +351 21 500 17 01
Fax: +351 21 355 66 23
Web site: http://www.telecom.pt

Public Company
Incorporated: 1994
Employees: 24,872
Sales: $7.53 billion (2003)
Stock Exchanges: Bolsa de Valores de Lisboa
Ticker Symbol: PT
NAIC: 517110 Wired Telecommunications Carriers;
515210 Cable and Other Subscription Programming;
517212 Cellular and Other Wireless Telecommunica-
tions; 517910 Other Telecommunications; 551112
Offices of Other Holding Companies

Portugal Telecom SGPS S.A. (PT) is not only Portugal's largest telecommunications company, it is also Portugal's largest company. Lisbon-based PT, formed in the privatization of the country's telephone services sector, provides a full range of fixed-line and wireless telecommunications services, including high-speed and ADSL-based voice and data transmission and mobile telephone services, to the Portuguese market. The company is also one of the country's leading multimedia groups, overseeing Portugal's largest cable television network, through which it also provides broadband internet services. PT claims to be one of the most efficient telecommunications providers in Europe, and enjoys one of the lowest net debt-to-earnings ratios in the sector. PT remains the dominant telecommunications group at home, controlling 92 percent of the country's fixed-line services, 80 percent of data transmission traffic, 52 percent of the mobile telephone market, and 84 percent of the cable television market. PT, however, has been transforming itself into a global telecommunications group in the early 2000s, targeting the Latin American market, and specifically Brazil, for

its future expansion. PT has invested strongly in the Brazilian market since the late 1990s, in large part in cooperation with Spanish partner Telefonica Moviles. Together the companies control Brasilcel, which operates Vivo, the leading mobile telephone provider in Brazil, with 17 million active customers and, with a geographic penetration of more than 90 percent, access to a potential market of more than 125 million. PT also holds an 18 percent share of UOL, Brazil's leading Internet access provider, and is active in data and voice transmission, the Dedic call center service, and the Mobitel message transmission service. Together with Telefonica Moviles, PT has begun to expand into the larger Latin American market, targeting the mobile markets in Peru, Chile, Argentina, Venezuela, and Colombia. Unlike most of its European counterparts, which also were created from the former state-owned telecoms, PT is now nearly 100 percent privatized as the Portuguese government has retained just 500 "golden shares" in the company. PT is listed on the Lisbon and New York Stock Exchanges. In 2003, the company, led by Miguel Horta e Costa, generated more than $7.5 billion in revenues.

Founding Portugal's Telecom Industry in the 19th Century

The first telephone system appeared in Portugal in 1877—just one year after Bell claimed the invention of the telephone itself. King D. Luis I, impressed by the new technology, ordered that a private telephone network be set up for him linking Lisbon to Carcavelos.

The first full-fledged telephone networks appeared in the country only five years later, however. In 1881, the British-owned Edison Gower Bell Company of Europe was granted the exclusive right to establish telephone systems in the principal cities of Lisbon and Oporto. The Bell company installed separate networks for each city that year. The networks were quite small at the outset, boasting just 22 and 19 subscribers, respectively.

Before the end of the decade, the concession for the two cities' phone services was transferred to a new company, the Anglo Portuguese Telephone Company (APTC). APTC's initial

Mission and Outlook

   We intend to be the largest Portuguese business group and to be amongst the largest international infocommunications groups.

   To reach this aim we will keep up the strong growth and will create shareholder value through: Leadership in all national business; International growth and leadership; Belief in businesses of high growth; Reinforcement of alliances and partnerships; Maintenance of the excellence and innovation standard.

contract ran out in 1901. The contact's renewal, as well as subsequent renewals, were made conditional on APTC's agreement to invest in technology improvements and upgrades, such as the installation of double circuit lines, better switching equipment, and underground cabling within the city centers.

Building demand for telephone service led to the extension of the country's telephone network beyond its capital cities at the dawn of the 20th century. This task was turned over to the country's postal and telegraph department, Correios e Telégrafos, which was subsequently renamed as Correios e Telecomunicaçoes de Portugal (CTT) in 1911. CTT's original mandate made it responsible for building not only the country's continental telephone network (apart from Lisbon and Porto), but also for extending its telecommunications reach to include the Madeira and Azores Islands and the country's colonial holdings in Africa and elsewhere.

By 1905, CTT had successfully connected Lisbon and Oporto for the first time, and by 1906 had begun providing service to Braga and Coimbra as well. CTT continued building up the country's telephone network through the end of the decade.

The overthrow of the monarchy in 1910 and the political and economic upheaval that followed brought a reduction in CTT's expansion, particularly its plans for developing the country's intercontinental telephone connection. The new Portuguese government decided to turn over this part of the country's telecommunications sector to a private operator instead.

Portugal's vast colonial empire, which stretched around the world, made developing and operating its intercontinental system an extremely attractive prospect for the continent's private wireless telephone groups, including Telefunken in Germany and Marconi, from the United Kingdom. Marconi finally won out, signing a contract with the government in 1912. The government in its turn agreed to build the infrastructure needed for the installation of Marconi's equipment.

The intervention of World War I made it impossible for the Portuguese government to hold up its end of the agreement and no progress was made on the wireless network. In 1922, the two parties formed a new agreement, creating the Lisbon-based Companhia Portuguesa Rádio Marconi (CPRM) with both Portuguese and British owners. CPRM then took over the exclusive concession for developing the country's wireless intercontinental networks, finally becoming operational only in 1925 under a

40-year contract. CPRM struggled heavily through the next decade, however, in part because of the costs of keeping up with rapid technological developments, in part because of the strong competition with the submarine-based international cable systems, but also because of illegal commercial wireless activity conducted through the Portuguese Navy.

APTC in the meantime had signed a new 40-year contract in 1928, which enabled it to make its own push to extend its Lisbon and Oporto phone networks. Yet APTC, too, struggled through the next decade: from nearly 16,500 phone lines in 1928, the company barely reached 37,000 ten years later. The installation of the first automatic exchanges, in Lisbon in 1930 and in Oporto in 1952, helped boost the company's range, with 100,000 telephone lines by 1950 and a waiting list of some 23,000. Nevertheless, connections between the two cities remained manually operated until 1961.

The arrival to power of the Salazar government spelled a new era for both CPRM and CTT. The government recognized that the telecommunications sector played an important role in its political aims, in particular the maintenance of control over the country's colonial empire. The new government brought about greater cooperation between CPRM and CTT, and also ended the illegal wireless transmissions during the 1930s and 1940s. The need to ensure strong communications between Portugal and its colonies, which were more and more subject to growing nationalist unrest, helped make CPRM's success a priority of the Portuguese government.

During the 1950s, as its contract renewal date approached, CPRM worked to make itself indispensable, forging agreements with submarine cable operators Italcable and Cable and Wireless, in which CPRM took over the role as coordinator of long-distance communications among the three providers. The government ultimately renewed CPRM's contract in 1966, if only because it lacked the technological capacity and personnel to operate the intercontinental wireless network.

Control and Reform in the 1970s

The increasing unrest in Angola, Mozambique, Guinea-Bissau, and other Portuguese colonial possessions transformed the telecommunications sector into a vital and politically sensitive sector. The Salazar government became particularly anxious about the country's situation, in which much of its telecommunications sector remained part-owned by foreign interests. In 1968, therefore, it nationalized the 51 percent of CPRM controlled by Portuguese interests, effectively taking control of the company. CPRM's British shareholders finally sold out their stake in the company to the government in 1972.

APTC, meantime, had continued investing in its networks in Oporto and Lisbon, bringing the total number of lines in those cities to more than 312,000 by the mid-1960s. Yet, recognizing that its contract would most likely not be renewed by the Salazar government, APTC more or less ended further investments in the early 1960s, and instead began raising its rates. In 1967, as APTC lapsed, the government took control of its operations and placed them under a newly formed, state-owned company, Telefones de Lisboa e Port (TLP). CTT in its turn also was restructured, and converted into a state-owned for-profit corporation.

Key Dates:

1877: The first telephone service is installed between Lisbon and Carcavelos.

1887: APTC (Anglo Portuguese Telephone Company) takes over the telephone concession for Lisbon and Oporto.

1905: CTT takes over the creation of domestic telephone service outside of Lisbon and Oporto and connects two cities for the first time.

1925: Companhia Portuguesa Rádio Marconi (CPRM) is created to develop Portugal's wireless intercontinental telecommunications system.

1930: APTC installs the first automatic exchange in Lisbon.

1952: APTC installs an automatic exchange in Oporto.

1967: The Portuguese government takes over APTC's operations, which are placed under Telefones de Lisboa e Port (TLP).

1968: The government nationalizes 51 percent of CPRM, then buys out its British shareholders.

1989: The passage of the Basic Telecommunications Act paves the way for privatization of the telecommunications sector.

1992: CN is created as a holding company for government-owned communications interests.

1994: Portugal Telecom (PT) is created as a single national telecommunications company; the government begins privatization of PT.

1998: PT and partner Telefonicas Moviles acquire Telesp Celular in Brazil, entering that market's mobile telephone sector.

2000: Privatization of PT is completed.

2004: PT and Telefonicas Moviles acquire the South American regional operations of BellSouth.

The change in government, which saw Marcello Caetano replace Salazar in the late 1960s, had a major impact on the telecommunications sector. Whereas Salazar had sought to control the telecommunications sector as a means to assert and develop his political control, Caetano recognized the telecommunications market as a means of reviving Portugal's flagging economy. Under the Caetano government, therefore, the telecommunications market became the focus of massive government investment throughout the 1970s.

The Caetano government also sought to streamline the country's three-headed telecommunications industry, pushing for a merger between TLP and CTT. Yet the *coup d'état* of 1974 and the resulting political upheaval led the government to abandon the plan. Successive minority governments, as Portugal struggled toward democratic stability into the mid-1980s, continued to hamper the expansion of the country's telecommunications network. By the late 1980s, Portugal's telecommunications sector lagged far behind its Western European counterparts. Indeed, with penetration rates as low as just 15 lines per 100 people, it placed behind many Soviet-dominated Eastern European countries as well.

Reform of the country's telecommunications industry began in earnest after Portugal was accepted into the European Community in 1986. In that year, the government commissioned a study of the industry, resulting in a series of recommendations that led to the adoption of a new Basic Telecommunications Law in 1989. The new legislation represented a landmark in the Portuguese telecommunications industry and pointed the way to the creation of a single national company, Portugal Telecom.

That reform gained momentum in 1992, when legislation was passed to separate CTT into its postal and telecommunications operations, with the latter renamed as Telecom Portugal. In that year, also, the Portuguese government set up a new holding company for its various communications interests. That company, called Comunicaçoes Nacionais (CN), then became the umbrella for CTT, Telecom Portugal, CPRM, TLP, and the country's television broadcasting arm, Teledifusora de Portugal (TDP).

Global Operations in the 2000s

CN proved short-lived, however. By 1994, the company had completed a series of mergers among its subsidiaries, resulting in the fusion of Telecom Portugal, TLP, CPRM, and TDP into a single, national telecommunications powerhouse, Portugal Telecom.

Through the remainder of the 1990s, the Portuguese government carried out a privatization program for PT. This occurred in several steps, starting with the public offering of 27.26 percent in 1995. By 1996, the government's stake had dropped to just 51 percent and by 1997, PT became privately controlled at 75 percent. The Portuguese government nonetheless continued in its privatization, and by the end of 2000 had sold all but 500 so-called "golden shares" in the company. In this way, PT had become the most privatized of the European telecoms.

PT in the meantime began investing heavily in new technologies, such as mobile telephone services starting in the early 1990s and internet access services under the Sapo name in 1995. In 2002, the company rolled out Sapo ADSL, bringing broadband to Portugal. By 2003, the company had firmly embraced the digital age, with the avowed goal of transforming Portugal into a digital society. In that year, the company rolled out its PT Wi-Fi service as well.

In the meantime, PT also had begun to expand internationally. For this, the company targeted the world's Portuguese markets, especially the huge Brazilian telecom market. In 1998, PT joined with partner Telefonica Moviles to enter Brazil, acquiring state-owned Telesp Celular in what was then considered the world's largest privatization offer. The purchase marked the start of a $5.5 billion investment in the Brazilian telecommunications market by PT, leading to the launch of the nationally operating VIVO service, with more than 17 million customers and a potential market of more than 125 million subscribers.

By 2004, PT and Telefonica Moviles signaled their intention to build a major presence in the South American market, with the announcement of an agreement to acquire BellSouth's operations in the region for $5.8 billion. This purchase brought the company into Argentina, Chile, Peru, Colombia, and Venezuela. Led by Miguel Horte e Costa, PT now laid claim to the title of being one of Europe's most efficient telecoms, with a debt-to-equity ratio of just 1.75. Indeed, as Horte e Costa proudly told the *Financial Times,* PT had grown into "the jewel in the crown" of Europe's telecommunications industry.

Principal Subsidiaries

Brasilcel N.V. (Brazil); PT Prime - Solucoes Empresariais de Telecomunicacoes e Sistemas S.A.; Telepac II - Comunicacoes Interactivas S.A. TELEPAC; TMN - Telecomunicacoes Moveis Nacionais S.A.; TV Cabo Portugal S.A.

Principal Competitors

Turk Telekomunikasyon End A.S.; Deutsche Telekom AG; France Telecom S.A.; TRACTEBEL S.A.; Telefonica S.A.; British Telecommunications PLC; Bouygues S.A.; MCI Inc.; Sprint Corporation.

Further Reading

"Portugal Telecom Will Not Bid for Antenna Hungaria," *Hungarian News Agency (MTI),* December 22, 2004.

Sousa, Helena, *Communications Policy in Portugal,* London: City University, 1996.

Wheatley, Jonathan, "European Mobile Groups Accelerate LatAm Push," *Financial Times,* August 26, 2004, p. 26.

Wise, Peter, "Portugal to Become 'Digital Nation,'" *Financial Times,* October 31, 2003, p. 19.

——, "PT Chief Seeks to Put Investors in the Money," *Financial Times,* June 24, 2003, p.31.

——, Rationalisation Is the Right Call," *Financial Times,* October 7, 2003, p. 5.

—M.L. Cohen

Raymond James Financial Inc.

880 Carillon Parkway
St. Petersburg, Florida 33716
U.S.A.
Telephone: (727) 567-1000
Fax: (727) 573-8365
Web site: http://www.rjf.com

Public Company
Incorporated: 1969
Employees: 5,000
Total Assets: $7.62 billion (2004)
Stock Exchanges: New York
Ticker Symbol: RJF
NAIC: 523110 Investment Banking; 551112 Offices of
   Other Holding Companies

Raymond James Financial Inc., a diversified financial services company, earned national recognition from a mixture of investment savvy and high-profile placement of its name. Subsidiary Raymond James & Associates provides securities brokerage, investment banking, and financial advisory services. Raymond James Financial Services, the independent contractor unit, offers both individual and institutional clients financial planning and brokerage services. Asset management, trust, and retail banking also fall under the umbrella of the holding company.

Financial Business Family Beginnings: The 1960s to the Mid-1980s

Robert A. James Investments incorporated in 1962, producing revenue of less than $100,000 for the fiscal year. The St. Petersburg, Florida-based business started out selling mutual funds. Membership on the Philadelphia-Baltimore-Washington Stock Exchange allowed the company to fulfill orders for stocks and bonds.

During 1964, the company expanded into the Bradenton-Sarasota region through a merger with Raymond and Associates, another family named company. The combined company was renamed Raymond James & Associates (RJ&A). Thomas

A. James joined his father's firm after his 1966 graduation from Harvard business school. Following his arrival, the company began handling private placements of debt and equity offerings for small local companies.

During the late 1960s the company expanded its services, beginning investment banking and general insurance agency activities. Raymond James Financial (RJF) incorporated as a holding company in 1969. That same year, Thomas James became CEO and Robert James became chairman. Thomas recruited other Harvard M.B.A. graduates to the firm, Francis S. ''Bo'' Godbold, among them, who would be named company president in 1987.

Revenue topped $5 million in fiscal 1972. During 1973, RJ&A gained membership on the New York Stock Exchange. Thomas James put his business background into high gear when the 1973–74 recession and stock market crash created havoc for small stocks and, consequently, RJF. Emphasis had to change from sales to administration and finance. Five of 14 offices were closed and neither Thomas James nor his father collected a salary until the market revived, according to a 1991 *Forbes* article.

Revenue began climbing again in 1975, a trend that continued for the remainder of the decade. In 1979, the company was cited for its leadership in the area of financial planning services. RJF had been ahead of the curve when it came to providing this service to small investors.

In 1980, RJF's net income exceeded $1 million for the first time. The company completed a $14 million initial public offering in 1983.

In the Public Eye: The Late 1980s Through 1999

In the late 1980s, RJ&A opened international offices, first in Paris, France, in 1987, then in Geneva, Switzerland, in 1988. Overseas expansion aside, the difficult days of the early 1970s riveted the need for cost control in Thomas James's mind and continued to be a priority.

The stance aided the company during volatile times. In 1991, the vast majority of RJF's nearly 700 offices paid their

Company Perspectives:

Our Pledge: We, the Associates of Raymond James Financial, commit our energies, intellect and knowledge to attaining the financial objectives of our clients by providing the highest possible level of service and delivering superior investment alternatives. We believe that putting the financial well-being of our clients first ultimately serves the best interests of our shareholders, our communities and ourselves. Remaining responsive to the needs of our clients in a financial environment characterized by constant change is our continuing challenge.

own fixed costs and overhead out of sales commissions, according to *Forbes.* The measure helped keep the company's net margins up even during a market decline during the last half of 1990. RJF's net margins were 7.6 percent versus an industry average of 2.7 percent.

By 1994, RJF had established a national presence. The company's stock pick record gained recognition from the *Wall Street Journal.* Fiscal 1993 marked the posting of a fifth straight year of record results. Expansion plans were in the works, including entry into the banking industry.

The general trend toward broadening services drove a spike in buyouts in the financial industry. RJF, with about 50 percent of shares controlled by Thomas James, his family, firm officers, and employees, looked like an unlikely prospect for an unfriendly bid. But the company did look appetizing. ''We've done three times as much business in the past six years as we did in the entire first 29,'' Godbold told *Florida Trend* in 1997.

RJF had 1,100 offices versus 680 for Merrill Lynch and 250 for Charles Schwab, *Florida Trends* reported, yet was still billed as a regional broker by many despite its size and nationwide business. According to the publication, RJ&A's $475 million offering of Miami's CHS Electronics stock was the largest underwriting done outside New York on the year. In addition, nearly 20 percent of the offering went to large foreign institutional investors via its European offices.

RJF was intent on matching its promotion package to its size and in 1998 purchased naming rights for Tampa's football stadium, housing its NFL Buccaneers team. The 2001 Super Bowl would provide the company name with national television exposure. On a local level, the company's name was now synonymous with a significant landmark.

The company's independent contractor subsidiaries Investment Management & Research (IM&R) and Robert Thomas Securities merged in 1999 to form Raymond James Financial Services. IM&R, established in 1967, served independent financial planners. Robert Thomas Securities, established in 1981 as a discount office, worked with independent stock and bond brokers.

Robert Thomas Securities, named after father and son, found early success in the discounting business in Milwaukee. But when brokers from other discounters came on board and found themselves paying their own costs the practice fell by the wayside.

Just as businesses change over time so does an industry. The merger trend continued among financial concerns into the new century. According to a 2001 *American Banker* article, 30 broker-dealers had dropped off the radar since 1997, the majority due to consolidation. An RJF competitor, St. Louis-based A.G. Edwards & Sons Inc., was among the companies warding off suitors.

Earlier consolidation had surged with the stock market as banking companies sought firms in order to get into the game. Brokerages, in turn, were looking for the financial gains made from selling out. When the bear market hit, a new wave of consolidation ensued, this time driven by brokerages hurt by declining commissions and investment banking fees. Lack of capital, increased competition, and need for larger distribution systems also made larger look better to some independents, but not to RJF.

Both RJF and A.G. Edwards continued to stick with their traditional retail brokerage business despite the capital market downturn and subsequent drop in consumer business, according to *American Banker.* Baltimore-based Legg Mason Inc., on the other hand, had been recreating itself as an asset management concern and was buffered somewhat from falling brokerage revenue.

Chet Heick, an executive vice-president and chief recruiter for the firm's independent contractor subsidiary, was appointed RJF's first ever COO in March 2002. Among his goals was an increase in coordination among the company's retail units.

In 2003, RJF was reshaping its board of directors, placing more weight on outside directors than management, in line with Congress-mandated reforms prompted by misdeeds in the financial industry.

In fiscal 2003, RJF posted a 9 percent increase in profits, reversing a two-year downturn. The company earned $86.3 million on revenue of $1.49 billion versus $79.3 million in 2002 on revenue of $1.51 billion. The third and fourth quarters of the fiscal year were bolstered by increases in commissions and fees thanks to an upswing in the stock market. The company's best year was 2000, when net revenue reached $125.2 million on revenue of $1.7 billion.

During 2003, more than 66 percent of revenue was generated by individual clients, 22 percent from institutional sales and investment banking, 8 percent from asset management, 2 percent from Raymond James Bank, and 2 percent elsewhere. The company managed or co-managed 58 U.S. stock offerings on the year, a 50 percent increase from 2002.

In early 2004, *American Banker* reported that RJF was among six financial securities companies that had agreed to settle with the Securities and Exchange Commission regarding allegations of failure to give customers promised mutual fund discounts during 2001 and 2002. The companies were to pay fines and reimburse customers.

RJF posted records for sales and profits in fiscal 2004. Net revenue was $1.8 billion, up 23 percent over the previous year. Net income climbed 48 percent to $127.6 million. Securities commissions, along with a nearly 50 percent jump in invest-

Key Dates:

1962: Robert A. James Investments is incorporated.
1964: Raymond James and Associates (RJ&A) is formed with the merger of Raymond and Associates into Robert A. James Investments.
1969: Raymond James Financial (RJF) incorporates as a holding company.
1973: RJ&A gains membership on the New York Stock Exchange.
1980: RJF's net income tops $1 million for the first time.
1983: RJF completes a $14 million initial public offering.
1987: RJ&A opens its first international office in Paris, France.
1994: The Raymond James Bank subsidiary forms.
1998: RJF purchases naming rights for Tampa stadium.
1999: Investment Management & Research and Robert Thomas Securities merge.
2001: RJF is named to the *Fortune* 500.
2004: RJF posts record revenue and profits.

ment banking revenue, elevated the company's numbers. Their performance outweighed the effects of a lagging stock market performance and questions regarding interest rates, both of which had put a damper on trading, according to the *St. Petersburg Times.* "James said investors are likely to regain their confidence 'once the uncertainty about the election is resolved and investors realize that the economy is still growing relatively well,'" Helen Huntley reported for the *Times.*

The weather in Florida late in the year prompted expansion of offices in the Midwest. RJF, headquartered in St. Petersburg, found itself in an evacuation zone during the hurricane season. "The Detroit center is equipped only to take over 'mission critical' processing in an emergency, and workers have to be brought in from St. Petersburg to handle it. When Hurricane Ivan was churning in the Gulf, Raymond James sent 100 people to Detroit for two days," wrote Huntley for the *Times.* The company decided to create a more comprehensive backup of its computer operations in its Detroit office to offset the effects of any disaster, natural or otherwise.

Principal Subsidiaries

Raymond James & Associates, Inc.

Principal Competitors

A.G. Edwards & Sons Inc.; Jones Financial Companies; Morgan Keegan.

Further Reading

Ackermann, Matt, "Deal Seen in 'Breakpoint' Probes," *American Banker,* February 2, 2004, p. 6.

Gray, Tim, "Florida's Raymond James Financial Expands Banking," *Knight Ridder/Tribune Business News,* January 2, 1996.

Huntley, Helen, "Raymond James Has a Banner Year," *St. Petersburg Times,* October 21, 2004, p. 1D.

——, "Raymond James to Expand in Detroit," *St. Petersburg Times,* November 5, 2004, p. 1D.

Hutchins, Dexter, "What Now, Tom?," *Florida Trend,* November 1997, pp. 40+.

Johnston, Jo-Ann, "St. Petersburg, Fla.-Based Financial Company Changes Its Board of Directors," *Knight Ridder/Tribune Business News,* January 9, 2003.

Mandaro, Laura, "For Indy Brokers, Being Solo Is Key Retail Driver: Second of Two Parts," *American Banker,* September 6, 2001, p. 1.

——, "The Joys (and Pressures) of Staying Independent: First of Two Parts," *American Banker,* September 5, 2001. p. 1.

Meeks, Fleming, "Why Small Is Still Beautiful," *Forbes,* November 11, 1991, pp. 226+.

Phillips, Dana, "South Florida's a Bull Market: St. Pete Brokerage Expanding Offices, May Open in Miami," *South Florida Business Journal,* March 25, 1994, pp. 1A+.

"Raymond James Bucking Merger Trends," *Knight Ridder/Tribune Business News,* June 2, 2001.

"Raymond James Should Bestow 'Buy' Recommendation on Itself," *South Florida Business Journal,* September 2, 1991, p. 25.

Stockfisch, Jerome R., "St. Petersburg, Fla., Financial Services Company on Rebound," *Tampa Tribune* (Tampa, Fla.) (via *Knight-Ridder/Tribune Business News*), October 23, 2003.

Uzelac, Ellen, "Raising Standards: Raymond James Financial's New President, Chet Heick, Says Advisors Today Must Aspire to Be True Professionals," *Research,* July 2002, pp. 30+.

—Kathleen Peippo

falabella.

S.A.C.I. Falabella

Rosas 1665
Casilla (P.O. Box) 1737
Santiago
Chile
Telephone: (56) (2) 380-2000
Toll Free: (56) 600 395-2000 or 395-6500
Fax: (56) (2) 380-2077
Web site: http://www.falabella.com

Public Company
Incorporated: 1937
Employees: 25,813
Sales: CLP 1.06 trillion ($1.79 billion) (2003)
Stock Exchanges: Bolsa de Comercio de Santiago
Ticker Symbol: FALABELLA
NAIC: 314129 Other Household Textile Product Mills;
    444110 Home Centers; 445110 Supermarkets and
    Other Grocery (Except Convenience) Stores; 452111
    Department Stores (Except Discount Department
    Stores); 522210 Credit Card Issuing; 522291
    Consumer Lending; 531312 Nonresidential Property
    Managers; 561510 Travel Agencies

S.A.C.I. Falabella is one of the largest companies in Chile and the second largest operator of retail chains in Latin America. Under the Falabella name, it operates the largest department store chain in Chile and also such stores in Argentina and Peru, plus hypermarkets (supersized supermarkets) in the latter country. It also operates the HomeStore and Sodimac chains of home furnishings and construction supplies in Chile. Through subsidiaries, Falabella also manufactures textile fabrics and clothing and offers travel agency services. Also through subsidiaries, the company offers banking and financial services, sells insurance, engages in real estate development and related services, and administers shopping centers in Chile.

A Century of Retailing: 1889–1989

The origins of Falabella date back to 1889, the year in which Salvatore Falabella, an Italian immigrant from Genoa, opened, in Santiago, the first large tailor shop in Chile. It eventually became a clothing store for the family. Falabella was incorporated in 1937, when Alberto Solari joined the firm. He added new products and points of sale. Falabella became a department store, with a vast array of home products, in 1958.

Under the left-wing government of President Salvador Allende, in the early 1970s, Falabella was requisitioned by the state, but its loyal employees are said to have kept the designated administrators from entering the premises. Business was so bad, according to Juan Cúneo Salari, who later became vice-president of the firm, that at times the employees passed the hours playing chess in the office "because there was nothing to sell," as he explained to the business magazine *Gestión* in a 2003 interview. Cúneo credited Jorge Mellafe with rescuing Falabella by planting the idea of extending credit to customers, in spite of inflation running at about 20 percent a month, by negotiating 60-day credits from the company's suppliers. But Falabella was always very much a family business, and it was Cúneo, a nephew and protégé of Solari, who became its general manager. He was responsible for the promulgation of Falabella's CMR credit card in 1980. Cúneo also decided that the firm should move its 70-year-old store from central Santiago to the recently vacated site of the Sears department store in the posh Parque Arauco area. When Solari demurred, Cúneo threatened to resign, impelling Solari to call in his three daughters for advice. They, and Solari's brother Reinaldo, supported the move, which was completed in 1983.

The 1980s saw other major changes after the death of the president—the founder's son Arnaldo—and the retirement of Alberto Solari, Arnaldo's son-in-law. Most members of the Falabella family and related Peragallo family sold their shares. Some 75 percent of the company was acquired by a group composed of Reinaldo Solari Magnasco, Cúneo, Mellafe, Sergio Cardone Solari, and the Lombardi family. Cúneo was the driving force behind the ensuing expansion of the Falabella chain and its diversification into finance, insurance, real estate, and tourism. His management style included promotion within the company and the formation of autonomous management teams. At the beginning of the 1990s the company created an expansion plan composed of four steps: internationalization, potential in the financial area, real estate growth by means of malls, and other retail areas.

Expansion in the 1990s

Falabella, in 1990, took a stake in the Mall Plaza group, which opened Mall Plaza Vespucio, the first of several Santiago shopping centers catering to the middle class. This was the first Chilean mall that incorporated features such as a food court, a play area for children, and the nation's first multiplex cinema. Mall Plaza group later opened six more centers in Chile: Oeste, Tobalaba, and Norte in Santiago; El Trébol in Concepción; and one each in La Serena and Los Angeles, with Falabella holding a half-share in each. By 1996 Falabella had annual sales of some $500 million and 13 stores in Chile. At the end of 1996 there were 22, plus more than one million names in the chain's database, more than any other Chilean retailer. The company also had established the financial services affiliates Serva Ltda. and Venser Ltda.; the real estate firm Aseger, S.A. for Falabella's real estate projects; and the textile firms Italmod S.A. and Mavesa S.A.

The first Falabella store outside of Chile opened in Mendoza, Argentina, in 1993. This was followed by stores in the Argentine cities of Córdoba, Rosario, and San Juan. In 1995 Falabella entered Peru by acquiring 70 percent of Sociedad Andina de Grandes Almeneces (Saga), the nation's only department store chain. This company owned two Saga (formerly Sears, Roebuck & Co.) department stores in Lima. A third, in the center of Lima, was added in 1998 at a cost of $15 million. Inverfal S.A. was established as the subsidiary charged with investments in Argentina and Peru. Falabella also acquired, in 1996, García Hermanos y Cía. La Favorita S.A., an Argentine-based company engaged in buying and selling goods for large stores and offering financial and other services.

Falabella became a publicly traded company in 1996, when it first sold shares on the Bolsa de Comercio de Santiago. The

following year it entered a new field of business when it established a partnership with Home Depot Inc., taking a one-third share in its commercial ventures in Chile. Also in 1997, it established a travel agency, Viajes Falabella S.A., and an insurance agency, Seguros Falabella. In 1998 the first two Chilean Home Depot stores opened, and Banco Falabella was established by purchasing the license held by ING Bank Chile. The new bank oriented itself principally to consumer credit in the form of mortgages and auto loans in small offices located within the stores. Falabella began, in 1999, making sales via the Internet in Chile and opened a $30 million department store in Buenos Aires. During the same year it purchased a 20 percent stake in Farmacias Ahumada S.A., the largest drugstore chain in Chile. The associations with Home Depot and Farmacias Ahumada gave CMR cardholders access to credit at these chains. In its turn, Falabella began selling the latter's cosmetics and personal care products in its own stores. The company acquired Textil Viña Ltda. in 1998 with the purpose of making and selling its own clothing. The following year it sold half of the enterprise to the U.S. firm Spring Industries, with which it formed a joint venture to produce textiles for the home for sale in the United States, Chile, Argentina, and Peru.

Entering the 21st Century

In a poor year for business, 2001, Falabella excelled, and it was voted company of the year by the Chilean business magazine *Capital*. It maintained its position as the largest department store chain in the nation, with 43 percent of the market. The five Argentine stores registered gains in sales in spite of the severe recession that gripped that country and a general unfamiliarity with department stores. In Peru, where Falabella now had ten stores, the company was seeking to expand to the nation's northern part. Falabella acquired the two-thirds of Inverfal S.A.—its real estate development arm—that it had not previously held. The number of CMR cardholders reached 3.7 million, and the card gained access to McDonald's and the Copec chain of gas stations. (Its popularity rested on lower monthly payment credit cards than the ones issued by banks.) Before the end of the year Falabella bought out Home Depot's two-thirds interest in the Chilean home furnishings and construction equipment chain for $54.4 million, also assuming its debts. The annual revenues of this five-unit chain, which was renamed HomeStore, had reached $120 million, but it was losing money. To pay for the acquisition and further expansion of its department stores, Falabella successfully floated $100 million worth of bonds.

Falabella's bet on HomeStore paid off immediately, as the chain reversed three years of losses under the Home Depot name. The parent company saw this chain as the vehicle it lacked to continue growing in retail sales and made plans to invest about $70 million each year for the construction of new outlets. But, with only a few existing stores, HomeStore's share of the $4 billion-a-year Chilean retail market in this field was much smaller than that of the leader, Sodimac S.A., with 51 stores in Chile (and six in Colombia). After extended negotiations, Falabella, in 2003, purchased Sodimac by issuing to its owners new shares of its stock valued at $550 million for 80 percent of the company and paying cash for the remainder. The result was that three sisters, Liliana, María Luisa, and María

Teresa Solari Falabella, retained 39 percent of Falabella, compared with 54 percent before. Reinaldo Solari, their uncle, emerged with 12.8 percent, Cúneo with 12.6 percent, and Cardone with 2.4 percent. The Del Río family, owners of Sodimac (and of Genoese origin, like the Falabellas and Solaris) received 22.4 percent, and other shareholders, 10.8 percent.

The negotiations, over a nine-month period, that led to this merger were long and tedious. In the final weeks, the families involved practically disappeared from the social map. An accord not only had to satisfy the families but also meet legal norms and take into account the interests of minority shareholders, some of them administrators for pension funds. Much time was spent before arriving at a valuation of CLP 730 (about $1.23) per Falabella share of stock. During the closing sessions the parties remained in conference until three and even five in the morning. After the pact was confirmed, the parties spoke enthusiastically about extending Falabella's reach, possibly as far as Brazil and Mexico, and, after Mexico, even to the United States.

Pablo Turner González, the hyperenergetic general manager of Falabella, caused a stir when he left the company in 2004, after 21 years, to join its closest rival in the department store field, Almacenes Paris Comercial S.A. There was speculation that under the new ownership structure, this longtime Falabella executive had to accept certain restrictions that displeased him. He was succeeded by Juan Benavides Feliú, the general manager of the credit card subsidiary, which was accounting for more than half of the parent company's profits. (Substantially more than half of Falabella's department store customers were paying for their purchases with the CMR credit card.)

Falabella had net sales of CLP 1.06 trillion ($1.79 billion) and net income of CLP 98.41 billion ($165.72 million) in 2003. Department store merchandise included a number of private labels, such as Recco (for appliances), University Club, Basement, Sybilla, Vamp, and Doo Australia. A shoe line was added in 2003. In Chile, the company had 29 Falabella stores and 57 Sodimac and HomeStores. There were five Falabella department stores in Argentina and ten company-owned stores in Peru, including two Tottus hypermarkets opened in Lima during 2002–03. There were seven Sodimacs in Colombia. Falabella had a half-share in six commercial centers (including one in Santiago and one in Los Angeles that opened in 2003) and held 50 percent of the Mall Plaza group, the largest operator of such centers in Chile. Banco Falabella, whose services included mortgage and auto loans, had 40 branches inside and outside the department stores and 5 percent of the consumer banking market in Chile. Viajes Falabella, the Chilean leader in individual travel, had 29 offices. The Falabella web site included an Internet service provider, Falabella Free. S.A.C.I. Falabella had a stock market valuation of $4.65 billion in mid-2004, almost three times its valuation when it entered the stock market in 1996.

Principal Subsidiaries

Aseger S.A. (50%); Banco Falabella; CMR Falabella S.A.; Falabella Uruguay S.A.; Home Trading S.A.; Inverfal S.A.; Italmod S.A. (50%); Mavesa S.A.; S.A.C.I. Falabella Argentina Islas Cayman (Cayman Islands); Serva Ltda.; Venser Ltda.

Principal Divisions

Banco Falabella; CMR; Department Stores; Falabella Argentina; Falabella Peru; Home Improvement.

Principal Competitors

Almacenes Paris Comercial S.A.; Cencosud S.A.; Comercial Eccsa S.A.; Distribuidos & Servicios D&S S.A.; Parque Arauco S.A.

Further Reading

Barahona, Marcela, ''Meritocracia pura,'' *Capital*, October 22– November 4, 2004, pp. 46–48.

——, ''La revancha de Falabella,'' *Capital*, April 26–May 9, 2002, pp. 52–55.

Burgos A., Sandra, ''Cuál crisis?,'' *Capital*, December 28, 2001– January 11, 2002, pp. 52–53.

——, ''Hasta cuándo crece Falabella?,'' *Capital*, November 16–29, 2001, pp. 34–37.

Fazio, Hugo, *Mapa actual de la extrema riqueza en Chile*, Santiago: LOM Ediciones, 1997, pp. 300–02.

——, *La transnacionalización de la economía chilena*, Santiago: LOM Ediciones, 2000, pp. 98–99.

Medel, Lorena, ''Antes de partir,'' *Capital*, October 8–21, 2004, pp. 38–41.

Moraga, Javiera, ''La plaza de la clase media,'' *Capital*, August 14–28, 2003, pp. 37–40.

''Muchos No Entienden que uno Salude y se Sepa los Nombres de 300 o 400 Trabajadores,'' *Gestión*, November 2003, pp. 4–6, 8.

''New Tricks for Old Stores,'' *Business Week*, June 26, 2000, p. 32.

Pérez, Soledad, and Roberto Sapag, ''El parto del año,'' *Capital*, August 1–14, 2003, pp. 27–32.

''This Latin Tiger Is Friendly,'' *Chain Store Age*, April 1996 supplement, pp. 13–14.

—Robert Halasz

The Sanctuary Group PLC

Sanctuary House
45-53 Sinclair Road
London W14 0NS
United Kingdom
Telephone: +44 (0)20 7602 6351
Fax: +44 (0)20 7603 5941
Web site: http://www.sanctuarygroup.com

Public Company
Incorporated: 1976 as Smallwood-Taylor Enterprises
Employees: 600
Sales: £151.7 million (2003)
Stock Exchanges: London
Ticker Symbol: SGP
NAIC: 512210 Record Production; 711410 Agents and
    Managers for Artists, Athletes, Entertainers, and Other
    Public Figures; 512240 Sound Recording Studios;
    512110 Motion Picture and Video Production

The Sanctuary Group PLC is the largest independent music company in the world, with rights to more than 150,000 recordings, and is also a leading artists management agency, with nearly 100 acts under contract, including Beyonce, Destiny's Child, The Who, Nelly, Iron Maiden, and Guns 'N' Roses. The company owns a number of record labels as well, including Sanctuary, Castle, Metal-Is, and Trojan. The Sanctuary Group offers a ''360 degree'' service approach, which includes management, recording studios, record labels, merchandising, financial advice, travel arrangements, and more. Founders Andy Taylor (executive chairman) and Rod Smallwood (head of artist services) continue to run the company and own stakes in it. Sanctuary has offices in London, Berlin, New York, Los Angeles, and Houston.

Beginnings

The roots of The Sanctuary Group can be traced to 1969, when Andy Taylor and Rod Smallwood met at Cambridge University's Trinity College. Natural science student Taylor had as a teenager organized dances in his hometown of Newcastle, and engineering and structural architecture student Smallwood was an avid music lover. The two, born just days apart in February 1950, hit it off immediately, and soon began helping to organize the college's May Balls, booking acts that ranged from Dadaist rockers The Bonzo Dog Band to the Royal Philharmonic Orchestra. With another student, they went on to form TWS (Taylor Wallace Smallwood), which organized events and provided catering services, though their partner left after a year.

After college Taylor and Smallwood continued to work together in the music business. Seeking to develop his skills in the financial end, Taylor began training with Robson Rhodes in London, an accountancy firm. He was eventually made a partner, and then took a job as financial director of Perstorp, a Swedish multinational firm with a division in the United Kingdom.

Smallwood, meanwhile, was working for musical agency MAM, which handled such acts as The Kinks, Judas Priest, and Golden Earring. After a year and a half, he left to become a junior partner at a management company that represented Steve Harley and Cockney Rebel. With Taylor, he continued to take on outside projects, including catering the Reading Festival. Their business, which was run out of the two-bedroom apartment they shared in London, was incorporated in 1976 as Smallwood-Taylor Enterprises, and they began selling shares in it a year later. By this time they were handling a range of projects including booking of concerts, catering, and running a mobile discotheque.

Discovery of Iron Maiden in 1979

In early 1979 Smallwood decided to quit his agency job and go off on his own. Although not certain he wanted to continue in the music business, he heard through a rugby player friend about a musician named Steve Harris, who was in an up-and-coming heavy metal rock band called Iron Maiden. After screening a recording they had made, he negotiated a contract for them with record industry giant EMI (home to The Beatles), and signed on as their manager. Their first album, released in February 1980, debuted at number four on the British charts and went on to sell 350,000 copies worldwide.

Taylor and Smallwood soon dropped their other activities to focus exclusively on building the band, obtaining financing

314

from a bank with which Taylor had worked in Sweden. Iron Maiden's music struck a chord with British youth, and by 1982 annual sales of its records and merchandise were worth £50 million. Smallwood and Taylor later renamed their business Sanctuary, after an Iron Maiden song. They also assembled a group of companies and accountants for each member of the band, and set up a tax-avoidance scheme that, in large part, kept the group out of the United Kingdom between 1982 and 1988.

In 1983 the firm again began taking on other acts. In addition to management, Sanctuary offered related services including financial advice, merchandising, and travel planning. This diversity was a key element in Smallwood and Taylor's success, as was their professionalism, which set the firm apart in the often flaky, fly-by-night music promotion world of that time.

In the 1980s Sanctuary branched out to the United States, but the firm had problems with the British executives it sent there, who did not acclimate well to the more cutthroat American music promotion business. After being sidetracked by a legal dispute with the band Poison, the firm hired more American-born staff for its U.S. unit, and matters there improved. Smallwood himself was now living in Los Angeles, in a home that had been built by 1930s Hollywood star James Cagney, though he spent much of the year on the road. By this time Sanctuary was managing a number of different acts, including Metallica, Blur, and Wet Wet Wet. New Sanctuary units formed during this period included Platinum Travel International, Focus Business Management, and concert booking agency Helter Skelter.

Focus on Intellectual Property Rights in the 1990s

In the 1990s Sanctuary began to work on establishing a portfolio of intellectual property rights, which would grow to include recordings, television programs, and books. Baronsmead Venture Capital and ABN Amro provided the initial financing for this expansion. The company also started a television division that formed a partnership with CLT/Utd. of Luxembourg, which owned stakes in many European broadcasters. With funding from CLT/Utd., programs would be made by a production company, Cloud 9, that was created as a joint venture with Ray Thompson, one-time head of BBC drama series development. Productions were typically aimed at children, and included a series based on the novel *The Swiss Family Robinson,* another based on the books of Enid Blyton, and a "teenage soap opera" called *The Tribe.*

In 1996 Sanctuary Records was formed to release recordings by acts the company managed, some of which, past their hit-making days, felt they were being ignored by the major labels.

Sanctuary later bought smaller labels Air Raid and Mayan to serve its younger acts.

In December 1996 a 40 percent stake in Sanctuary's records, publishing, and studio group (known as Sanctuary Music Productions) was offered on London's Alternative Investment Market. The success of this sale led to a full listing of the entire Sanctuary Group a year later on the London Stock Exchange, which was followed by a complete reorganization of the company from four divisions to three: music, television, and facilities.

After the sale, Taylor and Smallwood each owned 20 percent of the firm. Taylor was named CEO, and Smallwood continued as head of music management. Forty percent of revenues was derived from music, with an equal amount earned from television. For its most recent year, Sanctuary had sales of £18 million.

In August 1998 the firm acquired a holding company, Ted D Bear, for a reported £2.1 million. It consisted of three businesses, including Chop Em Out, a mastering, recording, and tape duplicating firm; and Probe Media, a database marketing company. They were combined with existing Sanctuary operations to form a new production division. During 1998 the company also signed a number of acts, including the Pet Shop Boys, Lodger, and Marillion, and in early 1999 it acquired classical record label ASV.

In the summer of 2000 Sanctuary signed an agreement with Bug Music, Ltd. to administer the firm's music publishing interests worldwide. The year 2000 also saw the repositioning of the Probe Media business into a "New Media" division within the company, which would handle creation of band web sites and other multimedia offerings. Former Pearson New Entertainment CEO Nick Alexander was hired to run it.

Doubling Revenues with Acquisition of Castle and CMC in 2000

In 2000 Sanctuary acquired record labels Castle Music and U.S.-based CMC International, which were merged into Sanctuary Records. CMC had released albums by Sanctuary artists Iron Maiden and W.A.S.P. in the past, along with other "classic rock" acts including Lynyrd Skynyrd and Styx, and was distributed by industry major BMG. Castle had a large back-catalog that included classic older albums by a number of major heavy metal acts, including Iron Maiden, Black Sabbath, Motorhead, Uriah Heep, and Hawkwind. Heavy metal was experiencing a major upswing, with older acts that had been reduced to appearing in clubs now touring auditoriums and larger venues to strong attendance. The CMC/Castle acquisitions would nearly double Sanctuary's revenues. For the fiscal year ended September 2000, the firm reported sales of £44.1 million ($64.9 million). Profits were £4.1 million ($6 million).

In early 2001 the company reached an agreement to acquire German record label Modern Music Records GmbH, which owned imprints Noise, T&T, Dynamica, Machinery, and AGR. After the purchase its name was changed to Sanctuary Records GmbH.

In June 2001 Sanctuary bought the catalog of Trojan records, which was one of the top labels for reggae music and owned thousands of classic recordings by such artists as Bob Marley and Desmond Dekker. The deal included Trojan imprints Rialto, Mooncrest, Receiver, Indigo, and Jet, which collectively offered music ranging from blues and jazz to punk rock. The deal was valued at £10.4 million ($14.5 million).

The year also saw development of a joint venture with Rough Trade Records to develop new acts, and the acquisition of merchandising company Bravado International Group and music management firms MM&M and Big FD. For 2001 sales rose more than 86 percent, to £82.3 million ($119 million), while profits increased to £17.7 million ($22.7 million). Records made up more than half this figure (£52 million/$75.3 million), with television/movies second (£13.8 million/$20 million), artist services third (£12.1 million/$17.5 million), and group services contributing £4.3 million ($6.3 million). At this time the firm was seeking to raise an additional £20.5 million ($28.7 million) through an issue of 27 million new shares of stock.

In 2002 the firm bought publishing company Air-Edel for £1.2 million, and the following year Sanctuary partnered with U.K. financial firm Gerrard to create Gerrard/Sanctuary Wealth Management Service, which offered investment management, banking, financial planning, and insurance services. Along with musicians, the unit hoped to attract sports stars, actors, and other performers. In May the firm reached an agreement for industry giant BMG to distribute its audio and video recordings worldwide, and later in the year Sanctuary sold the Cloud 9 television production unit back to partner Ray Thompson. The Sanctuary Visual Entertainment division would continue to produce music-related documentaries and advertising and to issue DVDs and videos. Sanctuary Group was now reorganized into three units: Recorded Product (both audio and video), Artist Services (management and other services), and Group Services (recording studios and corporate support).

Purchase of MWE in 2003

In September 2003 Sanctuary bought Music World Entertainment (MWE), owned by Mathew Knowles, for a reported £6.1 million. The management company's clients included Knowles's daughter Beyonce and her mega-platinum group Destiny's Child, along with other artists in the R&B, hip-hop, and gospel genres. The company subsequently launched a new division called Sanctuary Urban, headed by Knowles, to expand its offerings in these areas. The new unit, which had offices in New York and Houston, also would include a publishing operation and a record label.

In the fall of 2003 Sanctuary raised £20 million from Merrill Lynch and Highbridge International to make acquisitions and pay down debt. Shortly thereafter, the firm acquired Creole Records, another reggae label, and early 2004 saw a deal signed for Sanctuary Music Publishing to administer a Nashville company called Ten Ten Music's catalog in the United Kingdom. In April, merchandising and visual rights company World Online Merchandising was acquired and folded into the Bravado operation.

In the spring of 2004 Taylor, Smallwood, and several of the firm's directors sold blocks of shares in the company to allow large institutional investors to buy into it. The move was made to widen Sanctuary's shareholder base in preparation for seeking more funds to make large acquisitions. The firm was now hoping to buy publishing catalogs and record companies in the United States, where it earned 40 percent of its revenues, with country music a primary target.

In the summer, Sanctuary's profitable Urban division bought Erving Wonder, a Philadelphia-based artist management firm, and took over Mary J. Blige's company, MJB Management. The Urban unit's record label also was preparing to release new albums by The O'Jays and Earth, Wind & Fire. In the fall, the firm bought Tony Davis Management, Inc., which managed hip-hop artist Nelly, among others, and signed a distribution deal with Drive-Thru Records, which specialized in independent rock/punk bands including Dashboard Confessional and New Found Glory.

In late 2004 the company appointed Sanctuary US CEO Merck Mercuriadis, age 41, to the position of CEO of The Sanctuary Group. Andy Taylor remained executive chairman, in charge of commercial and financial strategy, while Rod Smallwood remained head of Artist Services.

In nearly 30 years, The Sanctuary Group PLC had grown into one of the largest and most diverse music businesses in the world. With its roster of hit-making artists, its huge intellectual property rights collection, its record labels, and its integrated services approach, the firm had carved out a unique niche for itself within the industry.

Principal Subsidiaries

Sanctuary Artist Services Ltd.; Sanctuary Artist Management Ltd.; Focus Business Management Ltd.; Helter Skelter Agency Ltd.; Platinum Travel International Ltd.; Sanctuary Publishing Ltd.; Sanctuary Studios Ltd.; Sanctuary Music Publishing Ltd.; Sanctuary Visual Entertainment Ltd.; Sanctuary Records Group Ltd.; Sanctuary Copyrights Ltd.; Sanctuary Records GmbH (Germany); Trinifold Management Ltd.; Bravado International Group Ltd.; Sanctuary Group Inc. (U.S.A.); Sanctuary Artist Management Inc. (U.S.A.); Sanctuary Records Group Inc.

(U.S.A.); Bravado International Group Inc. (U.S.A.); MW Entertainment Productions and Management Inc. (U.S.A.).

Principal Competitors

Universal Music Group; Sony BMG Music Entertainment; Warner Music Group; Eagle Rock Entertainment Ltd.; Snapper Music; Creative Artists Agency, Inc.; William Morris Agency, Inc.; International Creative Management, Inc.

Further Reading

Adams, Richard, "Rock By Numbers: Interview: Andy Taylor, Chief Executive, Sanctuary Group," *Guardian,* May 31, 2003, p. 34.

Ashton, Robert, "Sanctuary Unveils New Urban Division," *Music Week,* October 11, 2003, p. 7.

Ashworth, Jon, "Charting the Market for Heavy Metal: A Working Week for Rod Smallwood," *The Times,* December 16, 1995, p. 1.

Bonutto, Dante, "The Billboard Interview: Rod Smallwood—President of Sanctuary Music Division," *Billboard,* September 23, 2000, p. S4.

——, "A Q&A with Andy Taylor: CEO of the Sanctuary Group PLC," *Billboard,* September 23, 2000, p. S6.

Cope, Nigel, "Record Breaking Run at the 'Rest Home for Pop Music Has-Beens,' " *Independent,* December 2, 2002, p. 19.

Fletcher, Ester, "Giving Sanctuary to Creative Talent," *Accountancy,* December, 1998, p. 38.

Goldsmith, Charles, "U.K. Music Firm Sets a New Beat By Moving Beyond Record Sales," *Wall Street Journal,* May 28, 2003, p. B6.

"An Interview with Merck Mercuriadis: CEO of the Sanctuary Music Group U.S. & Sanctuary Music Management," *Billboard,* September 23, 2000, p. S8.

Masson, Gordon, "Sanctuary's Expansion Yields Financial Results," *Billboard,* January 27, 2001, p. 8.

——, "U.K.'s Sanctuary Posts Record-Breaking Results," *Billboard,* January 26, 2002, p. 45.

Mitchell, Gail, "R&B Acts Find Sanctuary," *Billboard,* August 7, 2004, p. 5.

Reesman, Bryan, "Sanctuary Goes Global: By Merging and Expanding, the Company Has Boosted Its Profile Around the World," *Billboard,* September 23, 2000, p. S10.

Rigby, Elizabeth, "Everything's Coming Up Guns N' Roses," *Financial Times,* June 30, 2001, p. 4.

"Sanctuary Move Heralds U.S. Growth," *Music Week,* March 20, 2004, p. 7.

"Sanctuary to Focus on Country and Publishing," *Music Week,* June 19, 2004, p. 6.

Solomons, Mark, "U.K.'s Sanctuary Music Seeks Investors," *Billboard,* January 31, 1998, p. 63.

Wylie, Ian, "Gimme Sanctuary," *Fast Company,* January, 2005, p. 31.

—Frank Uhle

Shriners Hospitals for Children

1900 Rocky Point Drive
Tampa, Florida 33607-1460
U.S.A.
Telephone: (813) 281-0300
Fax: (813) 281-8174
Web site: http://www.shrinershq.org/hospitals

Nonprofit Corporation
Incorporated: 1937 as Shriners Hospitals for Crippled
    Children
NAIC: 622000 Hospitals

Shriners Hospitals for Children is a nonprofit subsidiary of The Shrine fraternal organization, which in turn is composed of Master Masons in the Freemasonry fraternity. Shriners Hospitals operates a network of 18 orthopedic hospitals, three hospitals dedicated to the treatment of severe burns, and one hospital that handles spinal cord injuries as well as orthopedic and burn care. Twenty of the 22 Shriners hospitals are located in the United States, with single units in Mexico and Canada. Shriners Hospitals also funds some 100 research projects in the orthopedic and burn care fields. Care is available at Shriners hospitals at no cost to any child under 18 years of age if, in the opinion of surgeons, they can be helped. In addition, the hospitals spend millions of dollars each year in transporting patients. In recent years, Shriners Hospitals has had to contend with an American healthcare system that is now dominated by health maintenance organizations (HMOs), many of which are reluctant to refer patients out of its network. Despite offering free services, Shriners Hospitals has had to market itself to find enough referrals to keep facilities fully utilized. A downturn in the stock market also has eaten away the organization's endowment fund, forcing Shriners Hospitals to cut costs and even consider closing some of its facilities. Moreover, the parent organization, The Shrine, has experienced a deep erosion in membership over the last quarter-century, placing a greater burden of responsibility on fewer volunteers.

19th Century-Founding of The Shrine

Shriners Hospitals is at the heart of the mission of The Shrine, whose 500,000 members are best known to the public for the red fez hats they wear and clown brigades that appear in parades across the country. The roots of the organization are traced to 1870s New York City, where a group of Masons often met for lunch and discussed the idea of setting up a secondary fraternity where fellowship and fun would take precedence over ritual. Two of those men were Walter M. Fleming, a doctor, and world-renowned actor William J. Florence. It was Florence's sense of theatrics that led to much of the pageantry surrounding The Shrine. While performing in France, Florence attended a party hosted by an Arabian diplomat featuring a comedy routine that concluded with all the guests being indoctrinated into a secret society. He took notes on the ceremony and passed them on to Fleming, who then used aspects of the comedy routine to develop a new fraternity for Master Masons, calling it the Ancient Arabic Order of the Nobles of the Mystic Shrine. The initials—A.A.O.N.M.S.—could be rearranged to spell ''A MASON.'' Fleming and his friends then developed the ceremonial aspect of the organization, including a ritual costume that featured the red fez with black tassel. On September 26, 1872, the First Shrine Temple in the United States was organized by Fleming, Florence, and 11 other men.

The Shrine spread from Manhattan to Rochester in 1875 and then throughout the United States and Canada. By the end of the century there more than 50,000 Shriners belonging to approximately 80 Temples. Although The Shrine was created with fellowship in mind, its members early on became involved in charitable work on a local level. Shriners contributed money to help the victims of the 1888 yellow fever epidemic in Jacksonville, Florida, and the 1889 Johnstown flood. The national office contributed $25,000 to help San Francisco rebuild after the 1906 earthquake, and during World War I it donated $10,000 for European war relief. Following the war Shriners, who now numbered close to 400,000, began clamoring for an official Shriners' philanthropy rather than simply reacting to catastrophes. Heading the organization at the time was Freeland Kendrick, who was inspired to create Shriners Hospitals after paying a visit to the Scottish Rite Hospital for Crippled Children in Atlanta and becoming aware of how many children in the country were crippled and in need of help. The Salk vaccine was still decades away and polio was a scourge, afflicting thousands of children each year. In 1919 Kendrick proposed establishing ''The Mystic Shriners Peace Memorial for Friendless, Or-

318

phaned and Crippled Children,'' but the idea was not grand enough for the Shriners. Over the next year, Kendrick visited most of the Temples, drumming up support for an official philanthropy, and modifying his idea. At the 1920 Imperial Session, he proposed establishing the ''Shriners Hospital for Crippled Children,'' to be funded by a $2 assessment from each Shriner each year. After the resolution passed unanimously, a committee was formed to work out the details. Its members came back the next year proposing that instead of a single hospital, the Shriners should establish a network of hospitals throughout the country. Membership agreed and construction of the first Shriners hospital was underway by the time of the next Imperial Session.

Building Several Hospitals in the 1920s

The first Shriners hospital opened in Shreveport, Louisiana, in 1922. Initially, children had to be under 14 years old to receive treatment, but the age limitation would soon be increased to 18. Thirteen other hospitals followed during the 1920s. In 1923 hospitals were opened in Honolulu, Minneapolis, and San Francisco. A year later hospitals opened in St. Louis, Spokane, and Portland. In 1925 the Shriners added facilities in Salt Lake City; Springfield, Massachusetts; and Mexico City. A pair of hospitals opened in 1926, in Philadelphia, Pennsylvania, and Lexington, Kentucky. Finally, in 1927 the Shriners opened a children's hospital in Greenville, South Carolina. It was also during the 1920s that The Shrine established one of its most enduring fundraising events, the East-West Shrine College All-Star Football Game, played each year in San Francisco. Not only did it raise money, it raised the profile of the Shriners hospitals, especially after the advent of television.

The Shriners building program came to an end as the nation lapsed into the Great Depression of the 1930s. Shrine membership fell off during this period, placing a financial burden on the fraternity. The organization began to draw money from its endowment fund to support its hospitals, putting the long-term stability of the Shriners in jeopardy. As a result, in 1937 two nonprofit corporations were created to provide financial separation between the fraternal organization and the hospital network. Despite the difficulties imposed by the Depression, however, Shriners Hospitals was able to scrape by and did not have to close any of its facilities.

As the U.S. economy recovered during the early 1940s, primarily due to defense spending, Shriner membership once again began to grow. Shriners Hospitals also was able to resume

its expansion. In 1945 the organization opened a hospital in Mexico City. Then, in 1952, the Shriners opened three more hospitals, in Houston, Los Angeles, and Winnipeg. Funding during the 1950s also increased rapidly. Shriners Hospitals during this period faced the pleasant problem of a decreasing waiting list for services due to medical advances, in particular the introduction of the Salk vaccine for polio, the impact of which was dramatic. In 1955 there were 28,985 cases of polio. Two years later that number fell to 14,647, in 1957 it dropped below 6,000, and soon the one-time scourge of childhood was eradicated. The Shriners now had to decide how to best use its largesse, and it began to apply more resources to clinical research, in which network hospitals had been involved since the beginning. In the late 1950s Shriners Hospitals began creating a computer database of patient records, made available to its own staff and others by way of microfilm, a project that was a boon to clinical research. Then in the early 1960s Shriners Hospitals began to dedicate funds to specific research projects to enter the structured research field, which became another major part of the organization's mission.

Also in the 1960s Shriners Hospitals formed a special committee to look for new areas of concentration. It reported back in 1962 that the burn care field for children, both in terms of treatment and research, was severely limited in North America. In fact, the only burn treatment center in the United States was located on a military base. The matter was brought before the Imperial Session and Shriners Hospitals was directed to immediately pursue this new area. Burn units were initially established within non-Shriner hospitals. The first, a seven-bed ward for the care of severe burns in children, was opened in November 1963 in the John Sealy Hospital in Galveston, Texas. A few months later, in February 1964, a similar unit was established in the Cincinnati General Hospital, followed two months later by a five-bed ward in the Massachusetts General Hospital in Boston. At the same time, Shriners Hospitals began constructing 30-bed pediatric burn hospitals in the vicinity of these units. The first, located in Galveston, opened in March 1966, followed by Cincinnati in February 1968 and Boston in November 1968. Aside from treatment, Shriners Hospitals committed funds for burn research and teaching. Due in large measure to its efforts, a child's chance of surviving severe burns has more than doubled since the 1960s. Also of note, during the 1960s Shriners Hospitals opened a pediatric hospital in Erie, Pennsylvania, in 1967.

Shriners' membership reached 960,000 in 1979, but the organization had no way of knowing that this would be the high-water mark. The rolls would begin to decline steadily, placing an increasing burden on a graying membership. But Shriners Hospitals, the beneficiary of a large endowment fund, was actually ready to embark on an era of major expansion. In addition to burns, the organization now began to focus on spinal cord injuries in children. In 1980 the Shriners Hospital in Philadelphia opened the first ward in the United States dedicated to spinal cord injuries in children and teenagers. Other units were opened in the San Francisco and Chicago Shriners hospitals in 1984. Another new area of focus in the 1980s was spina bifida, a birth defect where the backbone and spinal canal do not close before birth. A number of the Shriners Hospitals developed programs to provide care for afflicted children. Moreover, during the 1980s Shriners Hospitals expanded its prosthetic services and research efforts, and the burn hospitals developed a re-entry program to help patients make the difficult adjustment in returning home from the hospital. The Cincinnati hospital started the first air ambulance service dedicated to the transportation of burn patients.

Launching an Expansion Program in the 1980s

Early in the 1980s the Shriners decided to launch an expansion and reconstruction program. In 1985 Shriners Hospitals opened a pediatric hospital in Tampa, Florida, the first new Shriners hospital to be built in nearly 20 years. The Winnipeg facility had closed in 1977, so the addition of Tampa returned the network to 22 hospitals in size. Over the course of the 1980s and 1990s, the other 21 hospitals would be either renovated or replaced. The Cincinnati and Galveston burn hospitals were replaced in 1992. The San Francisco hospital was closed and replaced with a new hospital in Sacramento in 1997. It became the flagship facility, the only one in the Shriners system to offer all of the organization's major disciplines, providing orthopedic, burn, and spinal cord care, as well as conducting research.

During the 1990s, Shriners Hospitals changed its corporate name, dropping the word "crippled," a move that not only reflected the hospitals' involvement in burn care and other pediatric areas, but also removed any stigma that might be attached to the term. Appearances, as the Shriners well knew, mattered. One of the problems the organization now faced was convincing more people to take advantage of what the Shriners Hospitals had to offer. For one, the Shriners with their red fezzes and motorcycle clown brigades had unintentionally cultivated a public image of a fun-loving and unserious group. Moreover, people wanted the highest quality healthcare for their children, and most of them assumed that anything free had to lack quality, which was far from the truth about what Shriners Hospitals had to offer. Starting in the 1980s Shriners Hospitals took pains to change this public perception in order to drive up demand for its services. In 1986 it became one of the first healthcare organizations in the country to provide an electronic press kit to television news departments. It also used marketing ploys such as shopping cart signage, the Goodyear blimp, and newspaper stand rack cards to promote its message.

When Shriners Hospitals celebrated its 75th anniversary in 1997, it was operating in an environment decidedly different from when the organization was founded. The most significant

change resulted from the rising dominance of HMOs, which affected patient referrals. Many doctors who had once sent patients to Shriners Hospitals were now required by their managed care contracts to keep patients within the HMO network. At the same time, the organization did not want to be put into a situation in which it was subsidizing an HMO. Traditional government relationships also were changing, as some states now assigned Medicaid patients to HMOs and other managed care systems rather than to Shriners Hospitals. As a result, occupancy rates at Shriners hospitals declined, especially in Houston, Lexington, and Minneapolis.

Marketing a free service, however, would lessen in importance as Shriners Hospitals moved into a new century. Shriners membership continued to fall, dipping below 500,000, or roughly half the 1979 number. The Shriners took cold comfort in knowing that other service clubs—such as the Kiwanis, Lions, and Rotary clubs—found themselves in similar straits. The networking opportunities that once made such organizations appealing were less attractive to many people, who were overextended and opted to spend free time with their families. Moreover, the concept of giving back to the community had lost some of its importance in contemporary society. As a result, the Shriners had half the number of people doing twice as much work, and because the money that came out of members' dues earmarked for Shriners Hospitals was reduced, the system was increasingly dependent on the money earned by its $8 billion endowment fund. But with a sharp drop in the stock market in the early 2000s the fund lost about one-quarter of its value.

Facing a financial crunch as well as a changing healthcare landscape, Shriners Hospitals formulated a restructuring plan, announced in late 2002. Under consideration was the idea of establishing satellite clinics, whereby Shriners staff could bring healthcare to the children, a less expensive approach than paying the transportation costs of parents and children to Shriners hospitals. The hospitals also looked to make more use of videoconferencing. But the most controversial recommendation was the closing of the Minneapolis hospital, which had experienced declining occupancy rates, which now averaged around 25 percent. There were also rumors that several other system hospitals might be closed as well. The Shriners voted against closing the Minneapolis hospital in July 2003, electing to study the matter further. Clearly, Shriners Hospitals was entering a period of change and uncertainty. What was not questioned, however, was the organization's commitment to its mission: providing the highest quality healthcare to children at no cost.

Further Reading

Andrews, Michael C., "Today the Goodyear Blimp, Tomorrow the Moon," *Public Relations Quarterly,* Spring 1993, p. 39.
Keen, Russ, "Shriner Discusses Possible Closure of Minnesota Hospital, Rising Costs," *American News* (Aberdeen, S.D.), November 14, 2002.
"Shriners Prepare to Close Some of Their Children's Hospitals Because of Financial Problems," *New York Times,* July 6, 2003, p. A10.
Ward, Tyler E., "A Noble Cause—With Concerns About Its Future," *Tampa Bay Business Journal,* January 24, 1997.

—Ed Dinger

Sidney Frank Importing Co., Inc.

20 Cedar Street
New Rochelle, New York 10801-5247
U.S.A.
Telephone: (914) 637-5700
Fax: (914) 633-5637
Web site: http://www.sidneyfrankco.com

Private Company
Incorporated: 1972
Employees: 75
Sales: $23.7 million (2004 est.)
NAIC: 312130 Wineries

Sidney Frank Importing Co., Inc. is a New Rochelle, New York-based distributor of specialty liquors. The company is best known for growing the sales of Jagermeister, an herbal liqueur, and Grey Goose vodka. The company's highly successful marketing approach relies little on advertising, focusing instead on direct marketing efforts at key urban bars by hosting promotional parties, courting bartenders, offering giveaways to patrons, concocting wild stunts, and hiring attractive young women and men to give out samples. The company is owned by its chairman, Sidney Frank, who remains highly involved in running the business despite being in his mid-80s. Well known in the spirits industry, he has used some of his marketing genius to craft his own persona—part 1940s Hollywood agent, part Winston Churchill. He likes to conduct business in his bedroom, complete with large screen television, art collection, and kitchen, dressed in either his pajamas or a colorful jacket, and is forever smoking an expensive cigar, which has resulted in his signature sandpaper voice. Although the company headquarters are located in a New Rochelle office park, Frank winters in San Diego, where he still oversees his business. Aside from distributing Jagermeister (Frank sold Grey Goose in 2004), the company represents brands such as Gekkeikan Sake, Gekkeikan Plum Wine, Tequila Corazon de Agave, Barenjager Honey Liqueur, Jacques Cardin XO Brandy, Jacques Cardin Napoleon VSOP Brandy, Henri Savard Sparkling Wines, Reynac Pineau des Charentes Cognac, Hudson's Bay Scotch, St. Vivant Armagnac, and Genofranco Wines.

Founder's First Taste of the High Life in the 1930s

Sidney Frank was born in 1919 in Montville, Connecticut, one of four children, and grew up on a small farm that raised chickens and maintained an orchard. Because money was tight, his mother sewed their sheets out of flour bags and bought day-old bread. The young Frank grew up longing for the rich life, his dreams fueled by the New York skyline he watched from the train window when visiting relatives in Brooklyn. Like a true Horatio Alger hero, he would rely on pluck and luck to make his fortune in the world. During high school at the Norwich Free Academy he found work at a local hotel, where he worked as a busboy in the morning and a waiter at night. He also worked construction during the summer months, and saved his money for college, determined to be the first one in his family to attend college. Other than in French class, he was a straight-A student. Despite his modest circumstances, Frank set his sights on the Ivy League and in 1937 applied to Brown University. He was admitted, supposedly due in large part to the firm handshake he offered the admissions officer (and that he played football). The luck involved in his rise to riches was the chance assignment of his freshman roommate, Eddie Sarnoff, son of RCA president David Sarnoff. During holidays Frank visited the Sarnoffs' New York mansion, where the "chicken farmer's son" began to use his good looks and winning personality to make connections. He also learned first hand about the life to which he aspired. After staying with the Sarnoffs, Frank told *Forbes* in a 2004 profile, "I knew I had to marry a rich girl." It was through Eddie Sarnoff that he would meet his future wife, Louise "Skippy" Rosenstiel, who was indeed one of the richest girls in the country, the daughter of Lewis Rosenstiel, owner of Schenley Co., at the time the largest liquor distiller in the world.

Marrying Skippy was no easy feat. She turned him down six times before accepting his proposal. In the meantime, Frank had to contend with a lack of money. At the end of his freshman year at Brown he was forced to drop out. He found work at Pratt & Whitney Motors, and represented the company in India and China during World War II as a troubleshooter, investigating crashes and testing airplane engines. After the war he continued to woo Skippy but had quicker success with her father, who hired him to work for Schenley. In his first assignment, Frank was sent

Company Perspectives:

Sidney Frank Importing Co., Inc. was founded in 1972 with the ambition to turn import specialty liquor items into national brands.

to London to check out a money-losing scotch distillery Schenley had recently purchased. He quickly discovered that the operation was operating only two days a week, a practice that was in keeping with outdated laws but no longer necessary. Frank simply ramped up production, an obvious decision in his opinion but one that established his reputation at Schenley. He turned to sales and worked his way up to sales manager, married the boss's daughter, and from there became president of the company in 1960. It was not always smooth sailing working for his father-in-law, however. He reportedly did not get along with Rosenstiel's many successive wives. Whatever the reasons, Frank was fired, rehired, and fired again. As a result, he became an art dealer for a few years. When Skippy died in 1972, Frank decided to go into the business with his brother Eugene. He sold his personal art collection and launched the liquor importing and distribution company Sidney Frank Importing.

Struggling in the 1970s

The first ten years or so was a struggle for Sidney Frank Importing. Most of that time, Frank devoted his efforts to building a limited number of brands, in keeping with the liquor business of the 1940s, an era dominated by family-run firms willing to patiently grow a brand. Frank's first product was Gekkeikan Sake, which he sold to sushi restaurants. Next, Frank discovered Jagermeister, which would become a veritable cash cow but at the time was a very unlikely prospect to serve as the foundation for a distributorship. The German after-dinner drink, made from a secret recipe of 56 herbs and spices and possessing a 35 percent alcohol content, was introduced in 1935. It was popular in Europe more for its medicinal value than for its taste. As described by *Forbes,* reddish-brown Jagermeister at room temperature tasted "like a mixture of root beer, black licorice and Vicks Formula 44." Frank stumbled upon the drink at a New York City bar in 1974. Learning that only 600 cases were being sold in the United States, he sensed an opportunity, believing he could do a much better job promoting the beverage. He flew to West Germany to visit Jagermeister's distillery and convinced the brand's owner to give him the rights to sell the product in the southeastern United States.

Frank soon learned that marketing warm Jagermeister in a warm climate was not an ideal combination. Selling Gekkeikan Sake and Jagermeister was a tough go for the first six years, as Sidney Frank Importing consistently lost money. Frank was eventually forced to sell 500 acres of beachfront property in Antigua to raise $500,000 to stay in business. He was not the only one having trouble selling Jagermeister, but he was the most persistent, and gradually he picked up more territories as other suppliers dropped out. By 1985 he had the rights to the entire United States. Although Frank had succeeded in growing the brand, annual sales by this point were still just 55,000 cases. But once again in his life, Frank's pluck would be followed by a dose of good luck. He came across a story published in the May

12, 1985 edition of the *Baton Rouge Advocate* that told about a cult drink, nicknamed "Liquid Valium," which was being served in a New Orleans Bourbon Street bar. It was actually shots of cold Jagermeister, poured from a bottle kept in the freezer. Moreover, there were rumors that the drink was doped with opium, Quaaludes, and aphrodisiacs.

Frank seized the opportunity the article presented and ran with it. Although he denied the drug rumors if asked, he printed thousands of copies of the newspaper article and passed them out at college bars around the country. He also convinced other Bourbon Street bars to begin serving freezing cold shots of Jagermeister. College students who came to New Orleans for the Sugar Bowl, Mardi Gras, and other events brought bottles back to school and helped spread the growing fad. Frank tried an ad campaign that failed to work, then fell back on bar promotions to grow Jagermeister sales. In 1988 he hired an attractive young woman and clothed her in a sexy outfit to become the first Jagerette. Her job was to talk young men into having shots of Jagermeister sprayed into their mouths using a specially made bottle. The idea took hold and hundreds of Jagerettes were hired across the country, paid $25 an hour for three hours of work each night. In addition to spraying shots, the Jagerettes handed out promotional items including T-shirts, pennants, and Frisbees. Eventually the Jagerettes would be supplemented by male counterparts called Jagerdudes. Frank also invented a tap machine to dispense Jagermeister: It was capable of chilling three bottles to three degrees and with the push of a button meted out a measured shot.

After a dozen years of promoting Jagermeister as an ice cold drink, Sidney Frank Importing had increased annual sales to 430,000 cases, and the brand would continue to grow at a torrid pace. But success did not come without some complications. In 1997 the company and its marketing subsidiary, All State Promotions Inc., were hit with a sexual harassment lawsuit, filed by the United States Equal Employment Opportunity Commission and initiated two years earlier by a pair of former Jagerettes and that now represented more than 100 women. The suit alleged that Sidney Frank and other executives of the companies, as well as bar employees and patrons, kissed, groped, and made improper advances toward the women. In particular, Frank was accused of requiring the women to attend company functions where he offered them clothing, trips, and jobs to accept his sexual advances. Moreover, the company was alleged to have required the women to sign a restrictive arbitration agreement that waived their rights to compensatory and punitive damages and a trial by jury. Frank denied the charges. The matter would not be settled for another two years when in June 1999 the company settled the matter by agreeing to pay $2.6 million to 104 women, the largest settlement of its kind in New York State. It did not admit any wrongdoing, and in a released statement contended the company settled because of the mounting costs of litigation and a desire to put the matter to rest. The company also agreed to provide sensitivity training to supervisors and to create a 24-hour toll-free phone line to accept employee complaints.

Turning to Vodka in the Late 1990s

Having succeeded with Jagermeister, in 1997 Frank turned his attention to vodka, which he believed offered another excellent opportunity, especially in the "superpremium" liquor

Key Dates:

1972: Sidney Frank founds the company.
1974: Frank first tastes Jagermeister.
1985: A newspaper article spurs Jagermeister sales.
1997: Grey Goose vodka is launched.
2004: Grey Goose is sold for $2 billion.

category that Absolut had defined and that was showing strong growth during the booming economy of the late 1990s. Frank explained his reasoning to *Forbes* in 2004: "A bottle of Absolut sells for $20 a bottle. Vodka is just water and alcohol, so if I sold a bottle for $30, the $10 difference is almost all profit." Thus he set out to produce the world's best vodka, or at least one of the world's priciest. He dispatched executives to France to have the vodka distilled and coined the brand name Grey Goose. He also used a frosted bottle that featured a Cezanne painting and asked for a price in the $30 range. Grey Goose was launched in late 1997 with some print advertising in such magazines as *Cigar Aficionado* and the *Wine Spectator,* but mostly Frank relied on the playbook he developed for Jagermeister, as well as tapping into the good will he had engendered with distributors and retailers for making them considerable sums of money with Jagermeister over the years. He also hired Grey Goose girls to hand out samples at nightclubs and trendy lounges and continued his practice of courting bartenders. The approach worked and Grey Goose enjoyed unprecedented growth in a short period of time, increasing from 20,000 cases a year initially to 100,000 cases in 1999 and 1.2 million cases by 2003, making it the third best-selling imported vodka in the United States, trailing only Absolut, with 4.5 million cases, and Stolichnaya, with 1.6 million cases.

In promoting Grey Goose, Sidney Frank Importing became involved in a tiff with competitor Belvedere vodka. They initially fought over similarities between their bottles, a matter that was settled confidentially but resulted in changes to the Grey Goose packaging. A more important disagreement grew out of the Grey Goose print advertising campaign that relied heavily on a 1998 Beverage Testing Institute blind test that rated Grey Goose as the number one tasting vodka in the world. Given that for many people vodka was odorless and tasteless, Frank needed some way to promote Grey Goose as the best brand available. He found it in the Beverage Testing Institute survey. It was one thing to boast about the strong showing of Grey Goose, but it was another to also print the lower scores of its rivals. Five years later, when Grey Goose continued to rely on the 1998 results, Belvedere cried foul, because more recent taste tests elicited higher scores for its brand. Because 1998 was the last year Grey Goose had been tested, Sidney Frank Importing argued that it was not proper to mix results from different years. The National Advertising Review Board asked Sidney Frank

Importing to discontinue the ads, which it called "inaccurate and misleading," but the company refused. In September 2003 the matter was referred to the Federal Trade Commission and the Alcohol and Tobacco Tax and Trade Bureau.

The Grey Goose flap with Belvedere would soon be of little consequence to Frank. In June 2004 he sold the brand to Bacardi Ltd. for $2 billion. For Frank it was a windfall profit, the result in large measure attributable to the need of Bacardi to distinguish itself from rival Diageo PLC, which in 2000 had outbid Bacardi for Seagram Co.'s liquor business. The addition of Grey Goose would give the company greater leverage with distributors. Moreover, Bacardi was considering an initial public offering of stock and very much needed to fill out its product offering. Grey Goose, which controlled about half of the premium vodka market, was especially attractive because premium rums including Bacardi were increasing sales at only a 5 percent clip while superpremium vodkas grew by 25 percent and superpremium tequilas jumped by 30 percent.

Although Frank was in his mid-80s he was not ready to cut back. He gave away considerable sums of money, including $100 million to Brown University, but also plowed a large portion of his earnings back into his business. The popularity of superpremium tequilas did not escape his notice, but he would find it hard going distinguishing his Corazon de Agave brand. He also entered other tough categories, introducing a line of Sicilian wines as well as a pomegranate-flavored energy drink called Crunk. Also in the works were a 50-proof cognac and Blue Goose gin. Frank had succession plans in place, with his 55-year-old daughter, Cathy Halstead, set to replace him, but in 2004 he made it clear he had no intention of retiring for another ten years, when his replacement would herself reach traditional retirement age.

Principal Subsidiaries

All State Promotions Inc.

Principal Competitors

Diageo North America; National Distributing Company, Inc.

Further Reading

Brady, Diane, "The Wily Fox Behind Grey Goose," *Business Week,* September 20, 2004, p. 71.
Lawton, Christopher, "Long Shot," *Wall Street Journal,* May 21, 2003, p. A1.
Miller, Matthew, "Grey Goose Billionaire's Second Act," *Forbes,* September 4, 2004.
Palmeri, Christopher, "Meet the Jagerettes," *Forbes,* September 15, 1993, p. 108.
Whitford, David, "Top-Shelf Marketing," *Fortune Small Business,* March 2004, p. 32.

—Ed Dinger

SINA Corporation

1468 Nan Jing Road, W, United Plz
Shanghai
200040
China
Telephone: 86-21-6289-5678
Fax: 86-21-6279-3803
Web site: http://www.sina.com

Public Company
Incorporated: 1993 as Beijing Stone Rich Sight
   Information Technology Company Ltd.
Employees: 785
Sales: $200.0 million (2004)
Stock Exchanges: NASDAQ
Ticker Symbol: SINA
NAIC: 541512 Computer Systems Design Services

SINA Corporation (Sina) is one of China's leading Internet-based media groups, providing Chinese-language web portals and services, e-mail access, as a well as a variety of value-added services for the mobile telephone market. Sina, based in Shanghai, targets Internet users in mainland China, already the world's second largest Internet population in the mid-2000s, as well as in Hong Kong and Taiwan, and the Chinese community in North America. The company operates four localized web sites (sina.com.cn; sina.com.tw; sina.com.hk; and sina.com) targeting each market, with an array of news, information, and online ''department'' stores. The company's online services include SinaSearch; SinaChat; Club Yuan, an online dating club; e-Card, an online greeting card service; SinaBaby, a virtual parenting game; and MySina, a home page personalization service. Sina lays claim to more than 115 million registered users worldwide, making it the leading Chinese Internet brand name. Sina's background as the creator of the first Chinese interface for Windows software, and one of the first Chinese-language Internet browsers, also positions it as an important provider of Chinese-language software for Internet and online use, including web search and e-commerce tools. A major part of Sina's revenues comes from its range of value-added services for China's fast-growing mobile telephone market. The company offers value-added services based on multimedia messaging (MMS) protocols and short-messaging services (SMS) protocols, as well as wireless access protocol (WAP), including games, news, and messaging. Sina has been listed on the NAS-DAQ since 2000. In 2004, the company posted $200 million in revenues.

Chinese Net Pioneers in the 1990s

Wang Zhidong, who created the present Sina Corporation through the merger of U.S.-based Sinanet and his own company, Beijing Stone Rich Sight Information Technology Company Ltd., in 1999, is widely considered one of the great visionaries of China's fast-growing Internet market. Wang, the son of a poor rural school teacher in Guangdong province, had displayed an early interest in electronics, and an aptitude for math and chemistry as a young boy. Yet, as Wang himself told *Asia Week:* ''Before I went to university in Beijing, I never touched a computer.''

At university, Wang studied radio electronics, and became such a good student that his professor refused to allow him to switch to computer technology, where Wang's real interest lay. Instead, Wang taught himself at home, and by the end of the 1980s had already begun writing software for the growing number of computer companies in the Haidian area of Beijing. In 1989, after graduating at the age of 21, Wang decided to go into business for himself. Wang reportedly shut himself in his little apartment and began working on Chinese-language software for personal computers. In this way, Wang saved up enough money to launch his own company, Chinese Star, in order to produce software that enabled Western applications to run on Chinese-language personal computers (PCs).

The emergence of Windows as the dominant force in the PC market encouraged Wang to change his direction. After leaving Chinese Star, Wang decided to formulate a new software, this time to create an interface that could translate Windows for Chinese PCs. In this venture, Wang was joined by Yan Yanchou.

Yan himself had already earned a reputation as one of China's most respected computer experts. The son of a former government official (jailed under the Mao regime), Yan had excelled in school, and was admitted to the prestigious National Research Institute in Beijing in 1978. There, Yan taught himself how to design hardware systems and the software to run them. Yan was credited with designing China's first two computer systems, the first for a dedicated payroll system, the second for a computer-controlled flour mill system. By 1983, Yan had been assigned one of only two computers in China at the time. Yan then created CC-DOS, for Chinese Character DOS, adapting the early Microsoft code for Chinese characters.

Wang and Yan set up a new company, Suntendy Electronic Technology and Research, and set to work developing a new program, a software-based shell program that provided Chinese-language conversion for the new graphics-based Windows operating system. The pair developed RichWin, and went looking for financing. After an investment from the Stone Group, a Hong Kong-based electronics distributor, Wang and Yan renamed their company Beijing Stone Rich Sight Information Technology Company (SRS).

Launched in 1993, three years before Microsoft's own Chinese-language version, RichWin became an essential component in the growth of the Chinese PC market. By the mid-1990s, nearly 80 percent of the country's three million computers ran the RichWin shell.

A trip to the United States by Wang in 1995 changed the course of SRS. There, Wang discovered the Internet for the first time, and quickly grasped its potential. As Wang Yan, a Sorbonne-educated lawyer who joined the company soon after to help it develop its Internet business, explained to *AsiaWeek:* "He got online for the first time, and stayed online for two whole days. It changed him a lot. Right away he started planning his internet strategy. He began to imagine a different future for the company."

Returning home, Wang decided to steer SRS onto the Internet, launching a program he called "Project Surf." Wang met with a great deal of resistance within the company, especially from its software engineers who were more accustomed to writing code than writing web pages. Wang's plan quickly received the nickname "Project Stinky Fish." Another hurdle for the project was the fact that, at the time, only a few thousand hardline members of the Communist Party elite had any kind of access online. Yet as Wang told *AsiaWeek:* "I just felt it was the right move, and that we should do it."

By 1996, RichWin had added its first browser, capable of translating web sites into Chinese characters, along with a built-in dictionary for looking up English words. The browser also came to include its own search engine, developed by Wang's younger brother, Wang Zhidang.

In support of its browser, SRS put up its first online bulletin board. The initial intent of the bulletin board was for users to report bugs and share tips for using the software. Yet the board quickly developed a social aspect, as users met to discuss a wide variety of subjects. Recognizing the potential—and the pent-up need in China for a forum for relatively free expression, SRS stepped up its transition to Internet portal (or "chortal" as the new breed of Chinese portals became called). The company brought in Wang Yan to lead the development of the site, modeling its content after U.S. counterparts such as AOL, Yahoo!, and others. By 1997, the company's service included chat rooms, forums, news and other information, as well as a growing range of multimedia content.

Although other chortals sprang up, SRS gained a clear and early lead as China's most popular web portal. By the summer of 1997, when China participated in the World Cup, the site began registering more than three million hits per day. That year was widely considered as the start of China's Internet boom which was to see the country become the world's second largest Internet market, trailing only the United States, by the mid-2000s.

Emerging As Sina in the 2000s

Despite SRS's rising success in China, Wang became interested in expanding the site's reach to the large Chinese population outside of mainland China, including in Taiwan, Hong Kong, North America, and elsewhere. Wang's attention fell on Sinanet, a small company that had been founded at Stanford University by three Taiwan-born students in the mid-1990s.

Launched in 1995, Sinanet quickly attracted the large Chinese-speaking population in the United States, who also began using the site as a way to communicate with family members in Taiwan and Hong Kong. Sinanet attracted investors as well, such as Stan Saih, who had founded Acer Computer, and who gave the company its own servers and computers, as well as operating funds. With Saih's backing Sinanet moved into its own offices.

The steady growth of the company led the founding partners to seek professional management, bringing in former Trend Micro head Daniel Chang as the company's CEO. The company now began signing on a growing number of content providers and advertisers, and adding new servers to keep up with the fast-growing membership. By the late 1990s, Sinanet had launched a companion site in Taiwan and was prepared to add a site dedicated to the Hong Kong market as well. Yet the company soon realized that its future success required an entry into the mainland Chinese market.

In late 1998, SRS and Sinanet agreed to merge their operations, creating Sina.com. The mainland China chortal was renamed Sina.com.cn, and all of the company's sites were redesigned to offer a similar browsing experience. Nonetheless, due to cultural and political differences, the company's four sites, including the newly launched Hong Kong sites, each maintained their own editorial staff and content.

By 1999, Sina had begun to prepare its initial public offering (IPO). Because the Chinese market was closed to foreign investors, the company decided to list on the NASDAQ, following in the footsteps of another content provider, China.com. As prepa-

Key Dates:

1991: Wang Zhidong and Tan Yanchou establish Suntendy Electronic Technology and Research to develop a Chinese language shell, called RichWin, for the Windows operating system.

1993: RichWin is launched; the company changes its name to Beijing Stone Rich Sight Information Technology Company (SRS).

1995: The company begins developing the first browser capability for RichWin; Sinanet is founded at Stanford University.

1996: The first Internet-capable RichWin version is launched.

1998: SRS and Sinanet merge and form Sina.com.

1999: SINA Corporation (Sina) goes public with a listing on the NASDAQ.

2000: Sina launches value-added services for the mobile telephone market.

2001: A slump in stock price leads to Wang's dismissal as company CEO.

2002: Techur Technology, a B2B portal operator and software developer, is acquired; the company turns a profit for the first time.

2003: MeMeStar, a value-added SMS provider, is acquired.

2004: Crillion Corp., provider of job-search services for SMS, is acquired.

2005: Zhongsou, a web search developer, is acquired.

ration for the offering, Sina brought in a new executive team and board of directors, including investment banker Daniel Mao as COO, and Jim Sha, a cofounder of Netscape, as CEO.

Sha's management, however, quickly came into conflict with Wang's vision of the company. Sha, pointing to the still tiny Internet market, wanted to steer Sina's focus toward its North American and Western markets. Yet Wang remained committed to the vast potential of the Chinese market. As the conflicts increased within the company, Wang began to take control, resulting in what *BusinessWeek* labeled a "purge" of the company's management shortly before the launch of the company's IPO. As quoted by *Wired,* Wang said: "I learned what Sina.com needed to go forward, and felt the need to set the company on a clear, concise course."

Sina's IPO was a success as investors eagerly embraced an entry into what many observers now recognized as the fastest-growing and soon-to-become largest Internet market in the world. Sina's stock soared, valuing the company at its peak at some $1.5 billion, despite the fact that the company's revenues numbered in just the tens of millions and it had yet to turn a profit.

Sina moved to capitalize on its momentum. In 2000, the company formed an alliance with China Telecom (CT) in an effort to boost Internet usage in China. The deal brought Sina into CT's "Home Online" advertising campaign, bundling Sina's browser software, e-mail, news ticker delivery service, and pager service as part of a giveaway of ten million CDs. The

campaign worked growing from just 4.5 million Internet users in 1999, to more than 50 million by 2002, with the actual figure (because people often shared connections) estimated to be double that amount.

Sina also began developing new revenue stream sources. The rising popularity of mobile telephone use in China, especially in value-added services such as SMS, provided the company with a new market. In May 2001, the company unveiled a portfolio of some 60 new subscription-based services taking advantage of SMS to provide Sina's content to the fast-growing mobile market.

Yet the crash of Internet stocks hit China that year, and, as Sina's value plummeted, its investors staged a new boardroom purge. This time out, Wang became the victim, and was forced to resign in June 2001. Taking his place as CEO was Daniel Mao.

The slump in Sina's shares proved short-lived, as the company's value began to climb again, backed by the soaring potential of the Chinese Internet and mobile telephone market. Sina boosted its range of services through acquisition, acquiring Shanghai-based Techur Technology in 2002, an operator of a leading B2B web portal and developer of logistics and Internet software. In 2003, the company purchased MeMeStar Ltd., which provided value-added services to more than two million mobile telephone subscribers. By then, Sina finally had become profitable.

In March 2004, the company acquired Crillion Corp., which operated a popular SMS-based job search service. The company also reached an agreement with Korea's Plenus to introduce that company's games technology into the Sina portals.

Sina continued looking for fresh expansion opportunities at the beginning of 2005. In January, Sina prepared to acquire Zhongsou.com, and its web search engine technologies, in a move designed to help Sina counter the efforts of competitors such as Yahoo! and Google as they entered the Chinese market. As the leading portal to the vast Chinese Internet and mobile markets, Sina emerged as an important player in connecting China to the rest of the world.

Principal Subsidiaries

Rich Sight Investment Limited (Hong Kong); SINA.com (Hong Kong) Limited; SINA.com Online (U.S.A.); SINA.com (BVI) Ltd. (British Virgin Islands).

Principal Competitors

Suho.com; NetEase.com; Beijing Blue IT Industries.

Further Reading

"Ahead of the Curve," *Asiaweek,* July 14, 2000.
"China Looks Beyond Profitability," *China Daily,* January 8, 2003.
"China's Sina Teams with South Korea's Plenus for Game Portal," *Wireless News,* February 20, 2004.
Dickie, Mure, "Sina.com to Acquire Crillion," *Financial Times,* March 2, 2004, p. 30.
"Is This Any Way to Dress Up for an IPO," *Business Week,* October 11, 1999, p. 58.

Kuo, Kaiser, "Back from the Brink," *Time International,* December 16, 2002, p. 43.

Schafer, Susan, "China's Torrid Trio," *Newsweek,* October 20, 2003, p. 40.

"Sina Expands Revenue Stream Through Launch of Comprehensive Subscription-Based Short-Messaging Services," *Wireless Cellular,* July 2001, p. 15.

Sheff, David, "Click Dynasty," *Wired,* December 1999.

Shinkle, Kirk, "Content Provider Reaps Benefits of Expanding Chinese Market," *Investor's Business Daily,* July 15, 2003, p. A09.

Smith, Craig S., "Big Chinese Web Portal About to Issue Stock in U.S.," *New York Times,* April 13, 200, p. C4.

—M.L. Cohen

Sirius Satellite Radio, Inc.

1221 Avenue of the Americas, 36th Floor
New York, New York 10020
U.S.A.
Telephone: (212) 584-5100
Fax: (212) 584-5200
Web site: http://www.sirius.com

Public Company
Incorporated: 1990 as Satellite CD Radio, Inc.
Employees: 375
Sales: $66.9 million (2004)
Stock Exchanges: NASDAQ
Ticker Symbol: SIRI
NAIC: 515112 Radio Stations; 517410 Satellite Telecommunications

Sirius Satellite Radio, Inc. broadcasts more than 120 channels of digital audio via satellite to subscribers throughout the United States. The company's programming includes 65 channels of commercial-free music and 55 channels of news, sports, and talk. Its offerings range from a full-time National Football League (NFL) channel to an all-Elvis music station, and include "shock jock" Howard Stern, who signed a five-year contract to broadcast exclusively for the firm beginning in 2006. Sirius's broadcasts are beamed from three satellites to more than one million subscribers who pay a monthly fee of $12.95. The company also offers a subscription service for businesses that wish to play its music in stores and offices. Automakers including Ford, Chrysler, and BMW offer Sirius-ready radios as options, and retailers including Wal-Mart and Radio Shack sell similar units for home and boat use.

Beginnings

The roots of Sirius Satellite Radio date to 1990, when ex-NASA engineer Robert Briskman formed a company called Satellite CD Radio, Inc. in Washington, D.C. Briskman, the former chief of operations at Geostar, a satellite messaging company, had created technology that could be used to broadcast digital radio signals by satellite. He joined with several other ex-Geostar staffers to start the firm, and they found investors including David Margolese, a Canadian venture capitalist who had founded a pager company and then helped launch Canada's largest cellular telephone company. After investing $1 million in Satellite CD Radio, Margolese began working with the firm, and eventually was named its CEO.

The company's plan was to develop a digital radio service that would be broadcast with satellites to listeners with special receivers, earning its revenues from charging subscription fees. This type of broadcast had not yet been allocated radio bandwidth by the Federal Communications Commission (FCC), and the company faced many hurdles before it could begin to turn a profit.

In 1992 the company became known as CD Radio, Inc., and made Satellite CD Radio, Inc. its sole subsidiary. There were now several different companies seeking to create satellite radio networks, and in 1993 CD Radio bought one of them, Sky Highway Radio Corp., for $2 million.

By 1994 the company had spent $10 million on development costs, but had accumulated a deficit of $9.5 million. That year, the firm made an initial public offering of stock on the NASDAQ, raising close to $7.5 million. Its prospectus claimed that it would offer 30 channels of CD-quality, commercial-free music via "S-Band" radio receivers, which were not yet being made. Its monthly subscription price was projected to be less than $10. The cost of the company's ambitious plan to launch satellites and create programming was estimated at upward of $500 million.

Purchasing Bandwidth in 1997

After the stock sale, CD Radio signed a contract with a unit of Loral Corp. to build two satellites, which it would launch when it obtained a FCC license. In April 1997, after fighting a fierce anti-satellite radio lobbying campaign by the National Association of Broadcasters, the firm bought the first of two licenses granted by the FCC to broadcast digital radio signals, paying $83.3 million at auction. The company had received a discount price under the FCC's "pioneer's preference" program, because it had been the developers of the technology. One

---

Company Perspectives:

Satellite radio is the future of music and audio entertainment. And SIRIUS is satellite radio. We offer over 120 channels of satellite radio: 65 devoted to commercial-free music, in almost every genre imaginable, plus 55 channels of sports, news and talk. From our futuristic studios in NYC's Rockefeller Center, to our fleet of satellites over the continental US, to a full line of SIRIUS satellite radio products—the future of music and audio entertainment has arrived.

---

of its three competitors at this time, American Mobile Satellite Corp., won the second license for $89.9 million. CD Radio soon announced plans to begin broadcasting in 1999, nearly ten years after the firm had been founded.

The late 1990s saw CD Radio actively seeking more funding. In late 1998 Apollo Management L.P. bought $135 million worth of new stock shares and took an option to buy $65 million more within a year. The company's costs had been escalating, with its estimate for building its now three-satellite network standing at $965 million.

In early 1999 the firm filed suit against its sole rival, now known as XM Satellite Radio, alleging that the latter company had infringed on three of its eight patents. In May 1999 CD Radio's financing topped $1 billion when it sold $200 million worth of senior notes to investors. The company was now planning to offer 100 channels of programming, with a start date of late 2000 projected.

In November the firm was renamed Sirius Satellite Radio, after the brightest star in the night sky, and it moved into a new $38 million, 100,000-square-foot space in Manhattan that contained multiple broadcast studios, a music library, and a satellite tracking center. The ribbon-cutting party featured a performance by rocker Sting, who also had been signed by the firm as a consultant for its music channels.

Although the company's projected broadcasting debut was now on hold while technical problems were resolved, it was actively working on developing its content, signing up musicians and well-known disc jockeys to program its music stations, enlisting self-help experts for others, and reaching deals with content providers including National Public Radio and a distributor of classic radio shows from the 1930s and 1940s. The firm also was planning to spend $100 million on a promotional campaign to lure subscribers.

In February 2000 Sirius and XM ended their legal standoff and agreed to jointly develop unified standards for satellite radio. The company expected the bulk of its listeners to tune in while driving, rather than at home, and had lined up a number of automakers to offer its receivers in their vehicles, including Ford, Chrysler, BMW, Mercedes, Mazda, Jaguar, and Volvo, as well as the makers of Freightliner and Sterling trucks. In June 2000 Sirius arranged for $150 million in new credit from Lehman Brothers, which would become available after its system was successfully demonstrated.

In July 2000 the company launched its first satellite from the former Soviet facility in Kazakhstan where Sputnik had taken off in 1957, and the third successfully entered orbit in December. At this point Sirius was well ahead of XM, which had launched neither of the two satellites it planned to use. Both firms also would utilize ground-based "repeaters" to boost the signal in urban areas where tall buildings caused interference, though Sirius's three-satellite system required far fewer of these.

CEO Margolese was now projecting that the company would begin to break even with as few as two million subscribers, which represented just 1 percent of the total number of Americans who listened to radio. He was banking on listeners' unhappiness with the increasing amount of advertising on music stations (typically 15 minutes per hour), the limited playlists and the fact that many types of music were not heard at all, and the company's ability to deliver diverse nonmusic programming, such as sports events from around the country and different news viewpoints. Sirius was continuing to add content, reaching agreements with such performers as comedian Sandra Bernhard, who would have a show on the firm's comedy channel, as well as outside concerns including The Discovery Channel, A&E, CNBC, and the BBC. Total investment in the company now topped $1.5 billion, but it still had generated no revenues.

In early 2001, while it projected that broadcasting would start in the summer, Sirius sold additional stock worth $230 million. Audio equipment manufacturer Kenwood USA Corp. was preparing to ship "Sirius-ready" radios for sale via the automotive aftermarket, though in April Margolese announced that only 20,000 were likely to be sold by Christmas. The firm had contracted out development of the microchip sets that would be installed in the radios, and the unit of Lucent Technologies charged with making them was having problems completing the work. Once again, the company was forced to push back its broadcast launch, even as XM prepared for its own. In May, Sirius announced that it would charge subscribers $12.95 per month, $3 more than originally forecast.

In the fall of 2001, a class-action lawsuit was filed by shareholders who asserted that company executives had inflated the value of Sirius stock by making false claims that its service would be launched in 2001. Shortly after the lawsuit was filed, CEO Margolese quit the firm, though he denied that it was due to the suit. In November, Sirius named Joseph Clayton, 52, to the top job. Clayton had formerly served as executive vice-president of Global Crossing Ltd., a telecommunications firm. After taking control, he inaugurated several money-saving measures, including reducing the company's headquarters from three floors to two.

Starting to Broadcast in 2002

On February 14, 2002, Sirius launched service to four states, and coverage was extended to the rest of the country by July 1. XM, which had officially launched in September 2001, had already gotten a big headstart in finding subscribers, and Sirius was now scrambling to catch up.

The company was facing more competition than just XM, however. Radio giant Clear Channel, with its listener numbers

Key Dates:

1990: Satellite CD Radio is founded in Washington, D.C.
1992: The company becomes known as CD Radio, Inc.
1993: Sky Highway Radio Corp. is purchased.
1994: The company makes its initial public offering of stock on the NASDAQ.
1997: A broadcast license is purchased in a Federal Communications Commission (FCC) auction.
1999: The company name is changed to Sirius Satellite Radio, Inc.; the company moves to new headquarters in New York City.
2000: Three satellites are launched successively into orbit.
2002: Nationwide radio service begins.
2003: A $220 million pact is signed with the NFL.
2004: Howard Stern signs an exclusive contract with Sirius, beginning in 2006; Mel Karamzin is named CEO; the one millionth subscriber signs up for Sirius service.

stagnating, was pledging to reduce the number of ads it broadcast each hour, while free broadcast digital radio was now a reality, courtesy of a company called Ibiquity Digital. AM and FM radio stations could broadcast a digital signal with the addition of a $75,000 digital transmitter module, and all of the nation's broadcast stations were expected to offer digital signals by 2017. Unlike Sirius or XM's offerings, reception would not require a subscription, just the purchase of a digital-ready radio.

In October 2002, reportedly edging close to bankruptcy, Sirius announced a recapitalization plan that would convert $700 million in debt and $525 million in preferred stock into common stock, with Oppenheimer Global Funds, Blackstone Group LP, and affiliates of Apollo Management LP providing an additional $200 million in cash to keep it afloat. The plan was approved by shareholders the following March, and they also agreed to the issuance of $200 million worth of new stock. Following the reorganization, the total number of shares Sirius had outstanding would balloon from 80 million to nearly 1 billion.

By June 2003, Sirius had attracted 75,000 subscribers, far less than XM's 500,000. Many of the latter firm's listeners had been delivered with the help of investor General Motors (GM), which was putting XM receivers in its cars. Sirius was banking on the installation of digital-ready radios to many of its partners' vehicles in the fall, and it also signed a deal with rental car giant Hertz to offer the radios at 33 airports.

Sales in the fall were strong, as newly introduced "plug and play" receivers sold well, and by January 2004, Sirius had 261,000 subscribers, compared with XM's 1.36 million. The firm was projecting a subscriber base of 1.3 million in 2004, 2.5 million in 2005, and 4.9 million in 2006, when it expected to post its first profit.

In December 2003 Sirius signed a seven-year, $220 million deal with the NFL to broadcast its games. A similar deal had already been struck with the National Hockey League. Revenues for 2003 reached only $12.9 million, with a loss of $226.2

million reported. The following year, revenues rose to $66.9 million, while losses expanded to $712.2 million.

In early 2004 an agreement was reached with Standard Radio of Canada to offer Sirius's service in that country, subject to government approval. The firm also began providing traffic and weather reports for the top 20 U.S. markets in late February.

Spring saw a deal signed with DISH Networks to provide Sirius radio programs free of charge to subscribers of certain DISH packages. In June an exclusive all-Elvis Presley radio station was launched, which broadcast from the singer's former home of Graceland in Memphis. In the fall, broadcasts of live football games from the NFL, as well as from 23 major college teams, were begun. The company had also reached agreements with retail giants Wal-Mart and Radio Shack to feature Sirius radio receivers in their stores.

Signing Howard Stern in the Fall of 2004

The company got a major promotional boost in October when it signed controversial radio "shock jock" Howard Stern to a deal worth $100 million per year for five years, which would make him heard exclusively on Sirius beginning in January 2006. The firm had reportedly bid three times what XM was willing to offer, and significantly more than what he was earning from current employer Infinity Broadcasting. Stern, whose morning talk program was syndicated around the country, and who had been fined a total of $2.5 million over the years by the FCC for obscene content, had recently been removed from six Clear Channel-owned stations. A survey by market research firm Odyssey found that 30 percent of Stern listeners said they were "very likely" to subscribe to satellite radio if Stern was only available there, and Sirius anticipated a spike in subscribers.

Following the signing of Stern, Sirius issued $200 million worth of convertible bonds and 25 million new shares of stock, raising a total of $321 million in new capital. Ford also committed to offer Sirius-capable radios as a factory-installed option in 20 of its vehicle lines by the 2006 and 2007 model years, having previously offered the radios as dealer-installed options only. Rival XM was getting half of its subscribers from installations in GM cars, which typically included a free trial subscription, while only a quarter of Sirius's business came from its carmaker partners.

In November the firm hired former Viacom CEO Mel Karamzin for the job of CEO, and gave Joseph Clayton the title of board chairman. In the 1980s Karamzin had built Infinity Broadcasting into a major force in radio, and it was hoped that he could draw on this experience to boost Sirius's fortunes. In late December the company celebrated the signing of its one-millionth subscriber, and in early January it announced a partnership with Microsoft to broadcast video programming to cars, some of which were being equipped with televisions in the back seat.

In 15 years' time, Sirius Satellite Radio, Inc. had spent more than $2 billion developing a digital satellite radio network that boasted 120 channels of music and information programming, though it had yet to earn a profit. The signings of such high-profile franchises as the NFL and Howard Stern were expected to boost its subscriber base, but it remained to be seen whether Sirius could overtake rival XM Satellite Radio, which had been the first to market and had already developed a sizable subscriber base.

Principal Subsidiaries

Satellite CD Radio, Inc.

Principal Competitors

XM Satellite Radio Holdings; Clear Channel Communications, Inc.; Infinity Broadcasting Corporation; DMX Music, Inc.; Ibiquity Digital Corporation.

Further Reading

Adelson, Andrea, "Coming Soon to a Radio Near You," *New York Times,* December 28, 1998, p. C6.

Bary, Andrew, "Interference," *Barron's,* April 21, 2003, p. 13.

——, "Shock Stock," *Barron's,* October 11, 2004, p. 34.

——, "A Sound Idea," *Barron's,* February 17, 2003, p. 17.

Brull, Steven V., "The Cable TV of Radio? Satellite Audio Could Be the Next Big Thing—Or a Big Flop," *Business Week,* January 31, 2000, p. 96.

Cochran, Thomas N., "Offerings in the Offing: CD Radio," *Barron's,* May 30, 1994, p. 48.

Coffey, Brendan, "Big Audio Dynamite," *Forbes,* March 18, 2002, p. 166.

Eisinger, Jesse, "Long & Short: Sirius Satellite May Be Headed for Dog Days; Overspending on Stern, NFL, Plus Too-Optimistic As-

sumptions Look Like Recipe for a Flameout," *Wall Street Journal,* December 8, 2004, p. C1.

"Fledgling Satellite Radio Providers Incur Setbacks with Launch and Chipset Delays," *Satellite News,* January 15, 2001, p. 1.

Helyar, John, "Radio's Stern Challenge," *Fortune,* November 1, 2004, p. 123.

Lewis, Peter, "Sirius Competition," *Fortune,* June 23, 2003, p. 130.

McLean, Bethany, "Satellite Killed the Radio Star," *Fortune,* January 22, 2001, p. 94.

"Nationwide Radio Stations on Way," *Pittsburgh Post-Gazette,* May 5, 1996, p. A7.

Savitz, Eric J., "In Satellite Radio, a Sirius Discrepancy," *Barron's,* January 12, 2004, p. T1.

Sheng, Ellen, "Sirius Bolsters Lineup to Battle XM," *Wall Street Journal,* June 2, 2004, p. 1.

Simmons, Jacqueline, "CD Radio Seeks Auto Audience for Broadcasts," *Wall Street Journal,* February 11, 1994, p. B7.

"Sirius Radio and XM Radio Form Alliance," *Satellite Today,* February 17, 2000, p. 1.

"Sirius Raises $210 Million, Prepares for Aftermarket Receiver Sales with Kenwood," *Satellite Today,* February 26, 2001, p. 1.

Steinberg, Brian, "Satellite-Radio Firms Prepare for 2000 Launch," *Wall Street Journal,* January 25, 1999, p. 1.

Strauss, Robert, "Satellite, But Down to Earth," *New York Times,* October 24, 2004.

Twachtman, Gregory, "Sirius Delays Its Rollout," *Satellite Today,* April 26, 2001, p. 1.

Williams, David, "Margolese Quits As Sirius CEO; Firm Postpones Service Launch," *Satellite Today,* October 17, 2001, p. 1.

——, "Sirius, Top Officers Charged in Shareholder Suit," *Satellite Today,* October 15, 2001, p. 1.

—Frank Uhle

Skidmore, Owings & Merrill LLP

---

224 S. Michigan Avenue
Suite 1000
Chicago, Illinois 60604-2505
U.S.A.
Telephone: (312) 554-9090
Fax: (312) 360-4545
Web site: http://www.som.com

Private Company
Incorporated: 1936
Operating Revenues: $73 million (2003 est.)
NAIC: 541310 Architectural Services; 541330
  Engineering Services; 541990 All Other Professional,
  Scientific and Technical Services

Skidmore, Owings & Merrill LLP (SOM), established in Chicago in the 1930s, attained standing as one of the most prestigious and successful architectural and engineering firms in the United States. SOM reached this stature by creating structures such as Chicago's Sears Tower and John Hancock Center, the Lever House in New York City, the U.S. Air Force Academy located in Colorado, and the Bank of America World Headquarters in San Francisco. Well known for its clean, geometric designs, during the 1970s and 1980s the firm was the preeminent champion of a style of architecture that dominated the landscape of great cities worldwide. Unfortunately, when the style of architecture promulgated by Skidmore, Owings & Merrill was eclipsed by other styles during the late 1980s and early 1990s, the company was hit hard by a decrease in new contracts. Redesigned itself, SOM rebounded and earned an unprecedented second Firm Award from the American Institute of Architects (AIA) in 1996. The new millennium saw the firm working toward regaining its place as the designer of the world's tallest building.

Laying the Foundation: 1920s–40s

While studying architecture and design in Paris during the late 1920s, Louis Skidmore met some of the architects who were planning the Century of Progress Exposition scheduled for 1933 in Chicago. Through his connections, Skidmore was appointed the chief architect for the exposition and hired Nathaniel Owings, his brother-in-law, to help him design the layout and buildings for the entire site.

After the exposition was over, the two men went their separate ways, but they joined together again in 1936 to establish a design firm in Chicago. Named Skidmore and Owings, the company began to draft designs for corporate clients they had met during the Century of Progress Exposition. By the end of the year, the firm had grown large enough for the partners to hire three employees to help with drafting new designs. In 1937 the firm opened an office in New York City, primarily to assist the American Radiator Company in designing a new office building. Using their corporate contacts and emphasizing the experience they had gained from the Century of Progress Exposition in Chicago, the two men won the contract to design the 1939–40 New York World's Fair. In 1939 engineer John Merrill joined the firm as partner, and the name was changed to Skidmore, Owings & Merrill.

By the early 1940s, the firm had developed its own architectural style, emphasizing clean lines and functional designs. It secured its most important contract during this time—the design of part of the facilities used in the Manhattan Project in Oak Ridge, Tennessee—which catapulted the firm into national prominence. Skidmore and Owings also articulated the guiding principles upon which the firm's architectural designs would be based; these included group projects, innovative designs, social change, and "showmanship." By promoting these principles the firm grew rapidly, and after the war ended Skidmore, Owings & Merrill was selected to build such prestigious buildings as Lever House in New York City, the H.J Heinz plant in Pittsburgh, and Mount Zion Hospital in San Francisco.

Golden Glow: 1950s–60s

The decade of the 1950s was the beginning of the firm's golden era. By 1950 the firm had grown to include seven partners, one of whom was Gordon Bunshaft. Joining the firm in 1937, by 1950 Bunshaft had assumed leadership of the New York office with its staff of approximately 40 architects and

Company Perspectives:

Founded in 1936, Skidmore, Owings & Merrill LLP (SOM) is one of the world's leading architecture, urban design, engineering, and interior architectural firms. SOM's sophistication in building technology applications and commitment to design quality have resulted in a portfolio that features some of the most important architectural accomplishments of this century.

designers. Under his direction, the firm began to win numerous large institutional and corporate contracts. The Lever House contract in New York propelled Skidmore, Owings & Merrill into corporate architecture and interior design, and the firm soon garnered a reputation as the leading exponent of an architectural style promulgated by Mies van der Rohe and Le Corbusier.

With accolades heaped upon its distinctively modern designs, the firm became the first to receive an invitation to exhibit at the Museum of Modern Art in New York City. By 1952 the company numbered 14 partners and more than 1,000 employees, with offices in Chicago, New York, San Francisco, and Portland, Oregon.

During the late 1940s, the firm's wealthier corporate clients began to provide funds for items such as plants, sculptures, paintings, and various other decorative objects to provide an attractive atmosphere in their workplaces; they also began to request that Skidmore, Owings & Merrill purchase or design furniture that was particularly comfortable, so that employee morale would remain high and performance during long hours remain effective. Adequate lighting and suitable coloring also became concerns. With more and more clients requesting such services, Skidmore, Owings & Merrill became one of the first architectural firms to include interior design in its contracts, attending to space, lighting, color, furniture, and the overall effect of the enclosed environment.

The combination of architectural design and interior design was reflected in the company's projects during the 1950s. In association with a Turkish firm, Sedat Eldem, Skidmore, Owings & Merrill was contracted to design and decorate the Istanbul Hilton Hotel. Situated on a site overlooking the Bosporus Strait that separates the continents of Asia and Europe, the Istanbul Hilton was a combination of modern architectural and traditional design. The building was constructed of reinforced concrete, with a rigid rectilinear form and a rising facade of recessed balconies. In contrast, the interior of the hotel was embellished with rich and lushly textured materials and colors incorporating traditional Turkish motifs. Completed in 1955, the Istanbul Hilton was hailed as one of the great architectural and interior design achievements of Skidmore, Owings & Merrill.

Another landmark building designed by Skidmore, Owings & Merrill was the Chase Manhattan Bank. The firm was commissioned to design both a 60-story downtown headquarters and a smaller office located at 410 Park Avenue. The larger building would include the bank's executive offices, and the smaller mid-town office was to be used primarily for customer transactions.

Skidmore, Owings & Merrill encouraged Chase to adopt a contemporary design for its offices and to incorporate art into the interior as an element integral to the design of the building. The curator of the Museum of Modern Art was brought in to provide advice in purchasing an art collection; the collection was not only well received by art critics, but also established a precedent for other corporate art collections. When the building was completed in 1959, the exterior was sparse and minimalist while the interior was rich in color and texture. It housed one of the best art collections in the country.

During the 1960s, the company continued its innovative designs both for corporate and institutional commissions. In 1962 Skidmore, Owings & Merrill designed the buildings for the U.S. Air Force Academy in Colorado Springs, Colorado. In 1965 the firm designed the Brunswick Building in Chicago, the entire community at the University of Illinois at Chicago, and the library and museum at the Lincoln Center for the Performing Arts in New York. Perhaps the firm's most distinctive architectural and interior design of this period was the Businessmen's Assurance Company of America. Located in Kansas City, Missouri, and completed in 1963, the design was a strikingly successful mix of contrasting styles and periods, with cool, clear lines on the exterior of the building and a tapestry of Native American artifacts such as Apache baskets, Navaho jewelry, and old arrowheads decorating the interior. One of the notable awards received by Skidmore, Owings & Merrill during this decade was from the American Institute of Architects. Presented by the membership to the firm, it was the first award for architectural excellence presented by the Institute.

At the Summit: 1970s–80s

In the 1970s Skidmore, Owings and Merrill reached the peak of its influence. In 1970 and 1971 the firm designed the John Hancock Center in Chicago, Regenstein Library at the University of Chicago, One Shell Plaza in Houston, the Bank of America Building in San Francisco, the Library at Northwestern University in Evanston, Illinois, and the Lyndon Baines Johnson Memorial Library at the University of Texas in Austin. In 1974 the firm designed the Hirshhorn Museum and Sculpture Garden in Washington, D.C., and the Sears Roebuck Tower in Chicago, then the tallest building in the world. One of the most interesting commissions received during this period was the rehabilitation of one floor of a corporate complex in New York City, for the insurance company Alexander & Alexander. Skidmore, Owings & Merrill combined Queen Anne chairs with glass-topped dining tables to create a remarkable balance between old and new designs.

In 1977 the firm won an important commission to design the National Commercial Bank in Jidda, Saudi Arabia. The clients requested that the firm design one of its greatest buildings, and the result was not disappointing. The triangular 27-story building, situated on a site directly overlooking the Red Sea, was a stunning merger of traditional Islamic elements with modern design and the capacity for modern electronic banking. The facade was interrupted by interlocking incisions and different elevations, giving the impression both of mystery and severity. The interior design was considered one of the best ever conceived by the firm. Furniture was designed in France, Italy, and the United States; carpets were purchased from Hong Kong;

Key Dates:

1936: Louis Skidmore and Nathaniel Owings establish a design firm in Chicago.

1937: The New York City office is opened.

1939: John Merrill joins the firm, prompting a name change.

1952: Skidmore, Owings & Merrill has 14 partners and more than 1,000 employees.

1959: The completion of the Istanbul Hilton represents a feat of architectural and interior design for SOM.

1961: SOM receives the first Firm Award presented by the American Institute of Architects (AIA).

1974: SOM designs the Sears Roebuck Tower in Chicago, then the tallest building in the world.

1982: The completion of the National Commercial Bank in Jidda, Saudi Arabia, marks the end of an era.

1986: First overseas office is opened in London.

1991: David Childs assumes the role of company chairman.

1996: SOM receives its second Firm Award from AIA.

2004: SOM is set to reclaim its status as designer of the world's tallest building.

woodwork was commissioned from Germany; and 15 different types of marble were used in decorating the interior, along with 100 different kinds of fabrics and more than 25 types of wood. Individual executive offices were designed to have their own unique furniture, carpet, and wall coverings. Completed in 1982, this project was the last of the firm's historic designs and signaled the end of an era. The founders had all retired, and Gordon Bunshaft also retired with the completion of the National Commercial Bank.

By the mid-1980s, architectural design and engineering were fully integrated with interior design, and the firm offered a wide range of services, including architectural design, civil engineering, electrical engineering, equipment planning, fire protection engineering, landscape architecture, mechanical engineering, plumbing engineering, site planning, space planning, and structural engineering. With such an inclusive list of services for clients, Skidmore, Owings & Merrill continued to grow, relying heavily on increasing commissions from outside the United States. In 1986 the firm opened its first overseas office, in London, and counted more than 1,400 employees in nine locations.

During the late 1980s, the firm designed the AT&T Corporate Center in Chicago and Rowes Wharf in Boston, two of the most impressive buildings of that era. Gross receipts peaked in 1989 at $157 million.

With the advent of Postmodernism, however, Skidmore, Owings & Merrill's dedication to Modernism began to seem outdated, and the company found itself struggling for lucrative commissions. New management was brought in to solve the problem, but a crisis in the commercial real estate market further exacerbated the firm's declining fortunes.

Back to the Design Table: 1990s

Sales dropped precipitously from a total of $134 million in 1990 to $63 million by 1992, necessitating massive layoffs: between 1990 and 1992 employment dropped from 1,623 to 687.

In 1991 David Childs, a longtime employee at Skidmore, Owings & Merrill, had appointed himself the first chairman of the board. Among the problems he faced were the pressures of debt repayment and legal battles with former partners. Adding insult to injury, the firm found itself in the unfamiliar position of having to go out and stump for business.

Childs moved to steer the firm toward designing and building institutional projects, such as transportation facilities, airports, and religious buildings, including the Chicago Transit Authority building, the Commonwealth Edison building, also located in Chicago, and the Islamic Center in New York. Projects on foreign ground furthered the firm's turnaround.

"By 1995, SOM appeared to be on the rebound, raking in revenues of $117 million and employing nearly 800 people. With offices in Chicago, New York, Washington, San Francisco, Los Angeles, and London, SOM has rebuilt itself on a portfolio of high-rise projects in Asia—approximately 43 percent of its work lies overseas, 26 percent across the Pacific—as well as numerous large scale public and institutional commissions in the U.S.," wrote Bradford McKee for *Architecture*. SOM's successful redesign of itself earned a second Firm Award from the AIA in 1996.

While projects such as the 88-story Jin Mao tower in Shanghai and the Hong Kong Convention Center had helped SOM rebuild its status, a downturn in the Asian economy cut into its growing overseas business as the decade wound down. In an effort to boost its global operations, in 1999, SOM tapped an international manager from General Electric Co. (GE) to be its first president. Bringing in a leader from the business world was atypical to the industry, according to *Crain's New York Business*.

Once Again Reaching for the Heights: 2000–04

As the new millennium rolled in, the firm's New York City endeavors were gaining attention. Three projects alone, the Columbus Centre to house Time Warner and other notable organizations, the new Pennsylvania Station transportation facility, and a new building for the New York Stock Exchange, totaled nearly $2 billion in construction. Moreover, the sheer number of projects the firm had gained in the city was deemed remarkable. "Creating architecture in New York City is notoriously difficult, so SOM's involvement in such a great scope of work is no small feat," wrote Elizabeth Harrison Kubany for *Architectural Record* in March 2000.

In April 2001, Kenneth Brown, the GE executive hired as president just 19 months earlier, departed. Even though the firm had regained its footing on the architectural end, SOM's management system had been a work in progress since the downturn of the early 1990s.

In 2003, SOM was in the running to recapture its position as the designer of the world's tallest building. Both the Freedom

Tower on the Ground Zero site in Manhattan and a tower in Dubai in the United Arab Emirates would exceed the height of Cesar Pelli's Petronas Towers in Kuala Lumpur, which had surpassed the Sears Tower in 1998.

Childs had come under criticism for expressing his interest in rebuilding at the World Trade Center site not long after the towers fell on September 11, 2001. The Freedom Tower project itself would later prove to be a hotbed of controversy, complete with lawsuits, which continued into 2004.

As of December 2004, the Taipei 101 Tower, at 1,674 feet, ranked as the tallest occupied building. Toronto's CN Tower, at 1,815 feet, was the tallest freestanding structure. The Burj Dubai Tower, slated for completion in 2008, would reach nearly one-half mile to the sky at 2,624 feet.

Principal Competitors

Heery International, Inc.; HOK Group, Inc.; RTKL Associates Inc.

Further Reading

Angel, Karen, "Kenneth Brown, Who Recently Headed GE's Southeast Asia Effort, Plans to Ramp Up," *Crain's New York Business,* July 26, 1999, p. 15.

Dunlap, David, "Plans Reveal World's Tallest Tower, But Only 70 Stories Will Be Inhabited," *New York Times,* December 10, 2003, p. B1.

Gates, Charlie, "Tallest Tower Crown Back in SOM's Sights," *Building Design,* July 25, 2003, p. 7.

Iovine, Julie V., "The Invisible Architect," *New York Times,* August 31, 2003.

Kladko, Brian, "Building in Dubai to Tower Over N.Y.," *The Record,* December 13, 2004, p. A1.

Kubany, Elizabeth Harrison, "SOM Takes Manhattan," *Architectural Record,* March 2000, p. 68.

Lubell, Sam, "Liebeskind and Silverstein Reach 'Genius Fee' Settlement," *Architectural Record,* November 2004, p. 34.

McKee, Bradford, "SOM Retrenches," *Architecture,* May 1996, pp. 231 +.

Slavin, Maeve, *Davis Allen: 40 Years of Interior Design at Skidmore, Owings & Merrill,* New York: Rizzoli, 1990.

Ward, Jacob, "The Outsider," *Architecture,* April 2001, p. 60.

—Thomas Derdak
—update: Kathleen Peippo

Swales & Associates, Inc.

5050 Powder Mill Road
Beltsville, Maryland 20705-1913
U.S.A.
Telephone: (301) 595-5500
Fax: (301) 902-4114
Web site: http://www.swales.com

Private Company
Incorporated: 1978
Employees: 925
Sales: $180 million (2004 est.)
NAIC: 336414 Guided Missile and Space Vehicle
    Manufacturing; 336415 Guided Missile and Space
    Vehicle Propulsion Unit and Propulsion Unit Parts
    Manufacturing; 336419 Other Guided Missile and Space
    Vehicle Parts and Auxiliary Equipment Manufacturing

Swales & Associates, Inc., doing business as Swales Aerospace, is an aerospace engineering firm based in Maryland. It is employee-owned through an ESOP. Swales does some manufacturing of aerospace-related products, specializing in structural and thermal management systems—ways to control movement and heat in satellites. Facilities are located in Virginia, Florida, Texas, California, and Maryland, home of the Goddard Space Flight Center. NASA accounts for about 75 percent of business. The U.S. Department of Defense is another key customer. The company has participated in programs such as the Hubble Space Telescope and the International Space Station and has begun producing its own small satellites.

Beltsville Origins

Swales was established in Beltsville, Maryland, on April 17, 1978. Company founder Tom Swales was the first president and CEO. Future CEO Tom Wilson was director of business development. Both Swales and Wilson had structural analysis engineering backgrounds. Ron Luzier, originally senior vice-president and chief engineer, and later chief technology officer, joined Swales and Wilson in founding the company.

The company began with ten employees overall and originally worked from an office at NASA's Goddard Space Flight Center, where it provided analysis for the Hubble Space Telescope. After occupying space at the Maryland Federal Savings and Loan Building and the Nationwide Insurance Building in Greenbelt, Maryland, in 1985 Swales moved into a half-floor suite in the Paulen Industrial Center. It eventually expanded into 18 buildings at the site.

Acquisition Drive Beginning in 1995

Swales set out on an acquisition drive in 1995. Around the same time, it ventured from pure engineering to manufacturing satellite hardware and tools for astronauts, such as a popular power wrench. Revenues exceeded $75 million in 1997. Swales then had 700 employees and was growing quickly. Among other projects, the company was manufacturing components for the International Space Station's thermal control system.

Welch Engineering Ltd. of Pasadena, California, was acquired in December 1998. Welch strengthened Swales's control systems offerings, Tom Wilson told the *Washington Business Journal.* The Pasadena location was convenient to the Jet Propulsion Laboratory. Welch also had an office in Rockville, Maryland, and about 40 employees.

NASA accounted for 70 percent of business. In the late 1990s Swales designed an instrument package for NASA's Far Ultraviolet Spectroscopic Explorer (FUSE). FUSE sought to probe wavelengths that had not yet been observed in a quest to help understand the origins of the universe. According to *Space Business News,* Swales was transferring technology from the FUSE project to the Naval EarthMap Observer (NEMO) remote sensing-satellite.

A team led by Swales was awarded the rights to commercialize NASA's Small Explorer-Lite (SMEX-Lite) spacecraft technology in 1999. AlliedSignal Technical Services Corp. and Hammers Co. were partners in the venture. Swales was prime contractor on the Earth Observer One (EO1), a small satellite launched in November 2001. Swales was also one of three companies NASA chose in 2000 to develop lightweight spacecraft, new conductivity materials, and other technologies.

Big Contracts in 2000

Sales were $90 million in 2000. The company had never had an annual loss, Wilson told the *Washington Post,* because it kept to its engineering niche. Employment hovered at around 800 people. In November of that year, Swales wrested a five-year, $240 million NASA contract from its much larger local rival Federal Data Corp. (later acquired by Northrop Grumman). This contract related to NASA's Langley Research Center. It was soon followed up with a $350 million deal supporting the Goddard Space Flight Center for five years. In both cases, Swales led a team of subcontractors.

NASA accounted for most of the company's revenues. After the September 11, 2001 terrorist attacks against the United States, updating aging defense satellites became a national priority. Defense-related work was soon accounting for about 10 percent of revenues.

In October 2001 Swales acquired most of the assets of Dynatherm, a Hunt Valley, Maryland developer of thermal management systems, from Pressure Systems Inc. of California, which had bought the company three years earlier. Around the same time as the Dynatherm purchase, Swales opened an office in El Segundo, California, to be more accessible to the commercial aerospace industry near Los Angeles. The company also had a new engineering center on Merritt Island, Florida, near Cape Canaveral and the John F. Kennedy Space Center.

Swales opened an office near Houston's Johnson Space Center in early 2002. The company's Beltsville, Maryland site was expanded later in the year with the addition of a 34,000-square-foot office and production facility, bringing its total space there to more than 220,000 square feet. Revenues were $157 million for 2002.

NASA was farming out more of its engineering work in order to reduce its staffing levels, noted the *Daily Press* of Newport News, Virginia. Swales was one of the three largest contractors for NASA's Langley, Virginia facility. Still, with about 900 employees (125 of them at Langley, according to the *Daily Press*), it was not too large to compete as a small business, which conveyed certain advantages in the bidding process. In 2002, Swales took over the lead contractor position in a $225 million, five-year contract to provide NASA Langley with Sys-

tems Analysis and Mission Support (SAMS), displacing previous agreements held by giant Lockheed Martin and Federal Data Corp.

Among the company's high-tech projects was computer simulation work for a powerful hypersonic aircraft engine. Swales was also a partner on a Boeing-led team contracted by NASA to develop nuclear electric power systems deep space exploration. These used electric thrusters powered by nuclear reactors.

The company continued to support the Hubble Space Telescope by participating in repair missions. Swales designed more efficient solar arrays for the Hubble and developed a cooling system for the Hubble's Near Infrared Camera and Multi-Object Spectrometer (NICMOS).

A New Drill in 2002

Swales seemed likely to benefit from President George W. Bush's proposal to put an American on Mars. One relevant technology being tested was a low-energy dry drilling instrument designed to probe for water under the Martian surface. In a 2002 field test, the device drilled ten meters into Arizona sandstone without requiring repairs or a bit change. After slipping $4 million to $140 million in 2002, revenues rose to $157 million in 2003.

An important new product was the SCONCE secondary carrier. It allowed small payloads to share a launch with larger ones. SCONCE successfully launched an experimental microsatellite from an Air Force rocket in May 2003. Its cost savings suggested commercial potential.

Aavid Thermalloy, LLC joined Swales in an alliance to commercialize advanced electronic cooling systems that Swales had developed in thermal management work for government satellite programs. Aavid, the world leader in thermal management for electronics, brought high-volume manufacturing capacity and global marketing connections to the partnership. Wilson told the *Washington Post* that as computer chips became faster and hotter, they could benefit from the heat pipes the company had developed to regulate the temperatures of satellite components.

Swales was named the primary mission assurance director for the U.S. Department of Defense's Missile Defense Agency in September 2004. Swales was supported by a team including Millennium Engineering and Integration Company and subcontractors SRS Technologies and Vanguard Research Inc. The Missile Defense Agency's main role was to develop the Ballistic Missile Defense System.

Sales were expected to exceed $180 million in 2004, when Swales employed 900 people. Expanding the company's customer base was a priority.

Swales was reorganized into four business units effective January 2005. Civil Services included engineering support for NASA customers such as Goddard Space Flight Center, Langley Research Center, the Jet Propulsion Laboratory, and the Johnson Space Center. Commercial Programs and Engineering Services was in charge of supplying commercial space programs with flight hardware and thermal management systems.

Key Dates:

1978: Swales is formed.
1998: Welch Engineering of Pasadena is acquired.
2001: Dynatherm is acquired; the El Segundo, California office is opened.
2002: The Houston office is opened.
2005: Swales is reorganized into four business units.

Civil Programs provided technology and systems for NASA's Exploration and Science programs. The National Security Programs and Engineering Services SBU was dedicated to marketing the company's services to national security space programs.

Swales also was participating in a space weather program called THEMIS, scheduled for launch in October 2006. THEMIS (Time History of Events and Macroscale Interactions During Substorms) was designed to track disturbances in the Earth's magnetosphere using five satellites.

Principal Operating Units

Civil Programs; Civil Services; Commercial Programs and Engineering Services; National Security Programs and Engineering Services.

Principal Competitors

The Boeing Co.; EADS; Lockheed Martin Corporation; Loral Space & Communications; Northrop Grumman Corporation.

Further Reading

"Civil Expanding Commercial Profits: Working with NASA Can Pave the Way," *Space Business News,* May 26, 1999.
Dujardin, Peter, "Beltsville, Md.-Based Aerospace Firm Helps Out at Hampton, Va., NASA Facility," *Daily Press* (Newport News, Va.), August 23, 2002.

——, "NASA Research Center Taps Firms for High-Tech Program," *Knight Ridder Tribune Business News,* September 7, 2000.
Gebhardt, Sara, "Beltsville Firm Rockets; Swales Aerospace Wins Big-Money NASA Contracts," *Washington Post,* January 4, 2001, p. T5.
Hopkins, Jamie Smith, "Proposal to Send Humans to Mars May Mean Boost for Maryland Aerospace Industry," *Baltimore Sun,* January 10, 2004.
Jain, Aruna, "Swales Marks 25th Anniversary, Vies for More Defense Contracts," *Business Gazette,* May 16, 2003.
Klinger, Linda, "Space Station Brings Area Down-to-Earth Contracts," *Washington Business Journal,* August 10, 1998.
Munson, Christian T., "Swales Acquires, Bolsters Small Satellite Business," *Washington Business Journal,* December 28, 1998.
"NASA Awards Boeing-Led Team Contract for Nuclear Propulsion Tech," *Aerospace Daily,* October 4, 2002, p. 2.
"NASA Picks Swales Aerospace Team to Commercialize SMEX-Lite," *Aerospace Daily,* July 1, 1999, p. 4.
"Satellite Maker Swales Buys Dynatherm Assets," *Washington Business Journal,* October 2, 2001.
Sunnucks, Mike, "Swales Aerospace Nabs $240M NASA Contract," *Washington Business Journal,* November 20, 2000.
"Swales Aerospace Opens Calif. Office," *Baltimore Business Journal,* October 15, 2001.
"Swales Aerospace Opens Florida Office," *Baltimore Business Journal,* June 12, 2001.
"Swales Aerospace Strengthens Leadership in Thermal Management Systems, Doubles Capacity in Support of Global Satellite Industry," *Advanced Materials & Composites News,* October 21, 2002.
"Swales Aerospace's Launch Carrier Completes Successful Trip in January," *Daily Record* (Baltimore), May 29, 2003.
"Swales' Approach Illuminates," *Business Marketing,* November 1, 1998, p. 50.
"Technology Powerhitters: Maryland-Grown Swales Aerospace Is a Leading Provider of Satellites and Associated Flight Hardware," *Maryland Business Review,* August 7, 2002, pp. 5–7.
Williams, David, "Swales Aerospace Opens Second West Coast Office," *Satellite Today,* October 16, 2001.

—Frederick C. Ingram

Synopsys, Inc.

700 East Middlefield Road
Mountain Valley, California 94043
U.S.A.
Telephone: (650) 584-5000
Toll Free: (800) 541-7737
Fax: (650) 584-4249
Web site: http://www.synopsys.com

Public Company
Incorporated: 1986 as Optimal Solutions, Inc.
Employees: 4,362
Sales: $1.09 billion (2004)
Stock Exchanges: NASDAQ
Ticker Symbol: SNPS
NAIC: 541512 Computer Systems Design Services

Synopsys, Inc. is the leading developer of software used in designing semiconductors, a field known as electronic design automation, or EDA. The company's products help engineers to develop and test the design of integrated circuits before production, allowing designers to achieve the optimal standards of cost, power consumption, and size in the electronic ''chips'' used in innumerable products. Synopsys sells its products to semiconductor, computer, communications, consumer electronics, and aerospace manufacturers. The company operates more than 60 sales and research and development offices in North America, Europe, Japan, Israel, and the Pacific Rim.

Origins

Beginning in the 1970s, electronic design automation (EDA) software became a key factor in the dramatic advances of the electronics industry. Increasingly complex integrated circuits (ICs) and electronic systems, coupled with a scarcity of qualified IC engineers, created a need for software that could reduce the time to market and product design and development costs, while facilitating the design of reliable, high-speed, high-density ICs.

EDA design methods changed rapidly, with three new generations of enabling technologies. The 1970s brought the first generation of EDA: computer-aided design (CAD). Computer-aided engineering (CAE) was the technology of the 1980s, representing an even greater improvement over the archaic, manual design methods. CAE made great progress in automating the design of complex integrated circuits, but engineers were still spending needless hours connecting the thousands of nodes (or gates) used on silicon chips. CAE could not keep up with the fast-paced changes of the electronics industry, and increasing circuit complexity led to an opening for a third generation design method in the 1980s. It was at the crossroads of the third generation of EDA technology that Synopsys emerged.

Aart de Geus, who led a work team at General Electric Microelectronics Center, developed a set of ideas for a new software technology called Synthesis. With Synthesis, engineers would be able to ''write'' the functionality of a circuit in computer language, rather than describing it in terms of individual gates. The software would automatically create the logic synthesis, saving design time and freeing engineers to focus on creative design solutions rather than manual implementation. Synthesis would create circuit designs from hardware languages (such as VHDL and, later, Verilog), supporting the new generation of EDA technology, hardware language design automation (HLDA).

In 1986, de Geus and several other engineers received support from General Electric and formed Optimal Solutions, Inc., dedicating themselves to the development of Synthesis software. After building the initial prototype, the company relocated to Mountain View, California, renaming itself Synopsys (SYNthesis OPtimization SYStems). In 1987, EDA entrepreneur Harvey Jones became president and CEO of the company, leaving Daisy Systems, where he had been president, CEO, and cofounder.

From 1986 until 1990, the company focused on becoming ''The Synthesis Company,'' as well as on changing the methodology of modern electronic design. Synopsys quickly jumped to the forefront of top-down design companies, launching an era that would be defined by top-down design. In fact, Synopsys had virtually no competitors in the synthesis market.

Synopsys was successful in marketing its new synthesis technology by demonstrating improved circuit design quality through advances in timing optimization. Sales in the 1980s, and in fact throughout Synopsys' history, demonstrated dramatic increases each year. In 1987, Synopsys' revenues were $130,000. The next year, revenues rose by more than 700 percent, to $976,000. An even more dramatic increase occurred in 1989, when revenues skyrocketed by another 700 percent, to $7.3 million. The company entered the 1990s with a 204 percent increase, ending fiscal 1990 with $22.1 million in revenues.

Business Scope Widening in the 1990s

Recognition of the vital importance of hardware description languages (HDLs) led the company to broaden its focus in the 1990s. In 1990, Synopsys purchased a VHDL simulator from Zycad Corp. and introduced test synthesis products, anticipating the acceptance of VHDL as the computer language of choice. Although other companies had used HDLs, including VHDL, before Synopsys entered the market, usage was primarily to meet Department of Defense documentation regulations. Synopsys offered the first synthesis technology that was well supported and marketed, spawning widespread reliance on HDL as a productivity tool. In 1991, Synopsys ended its fiscal year with a 55 percent increase in sales, and revenues of $40.5 million.

By 1992, Synopsys counted among its customers nine of the top ten computer makers, the top 25 semiconductor companies, and many other prominent businesses. Using synthesis, companies cut their custom-chip design time by 30 percent. Synopsys' $50 million operation owned more than 75 percent of the logic synthesis tools market, which was EDA's hottest growth area. In 1992 and 1993, Synopsys would introduce both design-for-test products and Design-Ware methodology for smart design reuse.

Although clearly the industry leader, Synopsys faced its first real competitive challenge in 1992. Vantage Analysis Systems, Inc., the leading VHDL simulator vendor, based in Fremont, California, organized an alliance with eight synthesis vendors. Vantage joined broad-based EDA suppliers including Mentor Graphics, Cadence Design Systems, Racal-Redac, and Viewlogic, who purchased synthesis technology in a joint effort to unseat Synopsys as the synthesis market leader. Although Synopsys no longer had a monopoly on the synthesis market, the company remained in control of more than 50 percent.

Since capital budgets were loosening and only approximately 5 percent of electronics designers used HDLs at all in

1992, some companies looked to displace Synopsys. Cadence Design Systems and Mentor Graphics emerged as Synopsys' primary competitors. Both companies possessed greater financial, technical, and marketing resources, as well as larger installed customer bases than Synopsys. Synopsys' profits had fallen sharply, in large part due to a fivefold increase in the cost of software license revenues (from $722,000 in fiscal 1990 to $3.6 million in fiscal 1991).

In 1992, Peter Schleider, an analyst with Wessels, Arnold & Henderson, predicted in an interview with *Electronic Business* that Synopsys' market share would fall to the 40 percent range. Amidst talk that the company might be bought by a larger competitor, Synopsys announced that it would go public in the spring of 1992. Synopsys President Harvey Jones told *Electronic Business*, "We have no interest in being a tool vendor in someone else's strategy. We feel we can drive a paradigm shift all on our own."

Three corporate shareholders sold stock in Synopsys' 1992 initial public offering: Harris Corp., Sumitomo Corp., and Zycad. Synopsys also was backed by three venture capital firms, none of whom participated in the stock offering: Oak Hill Investment Partners, investment funds affiliated with Technology Venture Investors, and Merrill, Pickard, Anderson & Eyre IV. Synopsys announced the sale of two million shares of stock, at an initial selling price between $13 and $15 per share. The expected $19.6 million proceeds would be used for working capital and general corporate activity, including strategic acquisitions.

Also during the spring of 1992, Synopsys announced that it would link its suite of high-level design tools with Mentor Graphics Corp.'s Falcon framework. This announcement was a surprise to Cadence Design Systems, whose executives had expected their own framework to be chosen for the linkage. According to *Electronic News*, Synopsys' senior product marketing manager, Kevin J. Kranaen, attributed the selection of Mentor's framework over Cadence's to flaws in Cadence's interface, "based on intermediate files with shallow integration."

In June 1992, Synopsys introduced yet another breakthrough in synthesis technology: version 3.0 of its synthesis tools. The new tools further accelerated sequential timing of electric circuits, using a path-based timing verifier. Designers could take advantage of the new tools in applying synthesis to increasingly common multi-clock, multi-cycle, and multi-phase communications designs. In addition, timing-driven design of electronic circuits could be maintained throughout the design process. Although other companies owned products capable of sequential design, Synopsys' version 3.0 was the first product that could optimize sequentially in a timing-driven fashion, by manipulating data through a timing verifier.

In September 1992, Synopsys introduced DesignWare, a new product area that would facilitate the "smart re-use" of electronic designs through methodologies, tools, and libraries. Synopsys entered into a cooperative agreement with Texas Instruments and Comdisc Systems, using DesignWare to link TI's custom digital signal processing (DSP) architectures to Comdisc's Signal Processing Worksystem. To increase the quality of its customer support, in 1993 Synopsys introduced SOLV-IT!, a 24-hour customer service that combined the company's com-

Key Dates:

1986: A team of engineers led by Aart de Geus forms Optimal Solutions, Inc., the predecessor to Synopsys.

1990: Synopsys introduces test synthesis products.

1992: Synopsys completes its initial public offering of stock.

1994: Synopsys acquires Logic Modeling.

1997: Approximately $1 billion is spent to acquire Epic Design Technology and Viewlogic Systems.

2002: Synopsys acquires Avant! Corporation.

plete design knowledge database with information retrieval technology.

Synopsys signed on as a supporter of a new initiative sponsored by Cadence in early 1993. The new effort, VHDL Initiative Toward ASIC Libraries (Vital), initially made Synopsys wary, when it seemed that Vital was focused on tying Verilog libraries into the VHDL language. Verilog, a competing hardware description language, was developed by a company that was later acquired by Cadence. Synopsys initially withdrew its support, not wanting to participate in the development of an initiative that could become competitive with its own products. It became apparent, however, that support of Vital could promote Synopsys as a leading vendor and that, without Synopsys, Vital would not succeed. In January 1993, Synopsys announced that it would support Vital with technical expertise and experience in ASIC libraries for synthesis, simulation, and test tools. This support was provided with the stipulation that the group must encourage the development of a VHDL ASIC library standard.

A new high-level design tool marked the expansion of Synopsys' line of electronic designs in January 1993. The FPGA Compiler was introduced, featuring architecture-specific logic optimization and mapping and state machine optimization to increase performance of FPGA designs. FPGA represented a major growth area for Synopsys, as the complexity and performance requirements of the FPGA marketplace demanded more efficient design methodologies, and only 10 to 20 percent of the people who could be using high-level FPGA design tools were actually using them.

Five years after its spinoff from General Electric Co., Synopsys held a 70 percent share of its chief market, specialized software to speed chip design. Synopsys' HLDA software was used by almost every major chip designer, from Intel Corp. to NEC Corp., as well as by such computer makers as Apple, Sun Microsystems, and Sony. In 1992, Synopsys' sales had skyrocketed, jumping by 56 percent to $63 million. Profits doubled, reaching $7.1 million, and Synopsys' stock closed at $36.50 in January 1993, 50 times its projected 1993 earnings.

One reason for Synopsys' success in 1992 was a 73 percent increase over the previous year in international revenue. This growth was achieved through two major investments. First, Synopsys restructured its European offices. Continental Europe was emerging as a center of electronic design, and Synopsys established its European headquarters in Munich, Germany.

The company continued to cover the continent with additional offices in France and England. This restructuring allowed Synopsys to secure important contracts in growth industries, including three of its top ten clients. Second, Synopsys acquired an 82 percent interest in its former Japanese distributor, Nihon Synopsys, in July 1992. Synopsys maintained Nihon Synopsys offices in Tokyo and Osaka, along with Asia/Pacific offices in Korea and Taiwan. Moreover, two of Synopsys' top ten clients were located in Japan.

In March 1993, Synopsys filed a lawsuit against Cadence, charging misappropriation of trade secrets in connection with the new Leapfrog VHDL simulator developed by Cadence. In a related complaint, Synopsys had filed suit against Seed Solutions, Inc., and its cofounders Paul M. Hubbard and Greg M. Ordy. Hubbard and Ordy served as employees of Zycad Corp. and Endot, a company acquired by Zycad, before founding Seed Solutions in 1988. From 1988 to 1990, they worked as consultants to Zycad in developing VHDL simulation software. In 1990, Zycad sold the rights to simulation software to Synopsys. Synopsys claimed that Hubbard and Ordy had intentionally concealed information and misled Synopsys (and its Zycad subsidiary) about the best path for future software development. The day after Hubbard and Ordy's contract with Synopsys/Zycad was terminated, in October 1990, Seed Solutions had distributed a detailed business plan for Seed Solutions' ''new'' product: VHDL simulation software that would compete directly with the software Synopsys had purchased from Zycad. In 1992, Cadence acquired the rights to Seed's software, leading to the 1993 lawsuit.

In June 1993, Synopsys joined Sunrise Test Systems in the purchase of a failed company, ExperTest. ExperTest had been founded in 1988, and although its fiscal operations failed, its technological advancements were valuable. In the joint purchase of the automatic test pattern generation (ATPG) technology, both companies integrated the technology into their own design-for-test-product lines.

In November 1993, Synopsys expanded its VHDI System Simulator (VSS) line, introducing the VSS Professional and the VSS Expert. These products would help system designers reduce the number of simulators used in design creation. Synopsys targeted the VHDI simulation market as its fastest growing segment. Synopsys identified three factors behind the accelerating sales growth of its simulation products: the market momentum designating VHDL as an industry standard for high-level design, Synopsys' ability to provide increased simulation speed and productivity for all phases of the design process, and the fact that Synopsys' VHDL simulator was the first to achieve application-specific integrated circuit (ASIC) signoff.

Due to both the expansion of its technological focus and the success of its international business in the Japanese market, Synopsys crossed the $100 million mark in sales in fiscal 1993, closing the year at $108 million (a 71 percent increase over the previous year). In addition, Synopsys almost doubled its cash position between 1992 and 1993.

Synopsys began the new year in 1994 with the acquisition of Logic Modeling, a company that marketed a library of software models for more than 12,000 commercially available

ICs, as well as a line of hardware modeling systems. The acquisition was achieved in March through a stock swap with a value of $116 million. Logic Modeling was established as a "differentiated business unit" in Beaverton, Oregon. The relationship was structured as a ten-year partnership with the goal of bridging a developing gap between EDA tools and ASIC process technology.

Later in 1994, Synopsys continued to expand its design re-use operations, acquiring CADIS GmbH of Aachen, Germany, an innovative company specializing in digital signal processing (DSP) design. CADIS was acquired for approximately $4 million, in a strategic move to take Synopsys into the digital signal processing market with second generation technology.

In March 1994, Synopsys signed a marketing deal with Quickturn Design Systems, allowing the companies to jointly design and market products and to provide each other with software to speed product integration. In 1994, Synopsys also began the process of selling its synthesis, VIIDI, simulation, test, and design re-use software and services to Texas Instruments. Another connection was strengthened when Synopsys made it possible for users of Altera's programmable logic devices (PLDs) to use Synopsys' DesignWare and VIIDI System Simulator (VSS). The companies had been working closely together since 1991, with more than 100 mutual clients, but only in 1994 could Altera users perform timing-driven synthesis by specifying clock frequencies and path delays using Synopsys' automation tools.

In what was referred to as the "Blockbuster Video approach to design tools" (by Bill Hood, a program manager at Locklead Sanders), Synopsys lent its expertise to a new plan to rent software over the Internet in April 1994. The rental idea was developed to appeal to military contractors who often needed additional capacity during some phases of a project, but for whom purchase of software would be inefficient in the long term.

Other new developments in 1994 included the announcement of Behavioral Compiler, a synthesis tool that simplified IC design by cutting specification time by five to ten times, allowing designers to use a higher level of programming and facilitating modification and reuse. For the first time, Synopsys announced that bus interface would become available in DesignWare, a kit that can be configured and synthesized into an ASIC design, through an agreement with Intel Corporation to offer Peripheral Component Interconnect (PCI) Local Bus solutions for the systems market.

In the mid-1990s, Synopsys was intent upon establishing itself as a leader in its three technological areas: synthesis, simulation, and test. The company's HLDA tools were marketed to a worldwide network of key accounts and were widely used on UNIX workstations, including Sun Microsystems, Hewlett-Packard, IBM, Digital Equipment Corporation, Solbourne, MIPS, and Sony. Synopsys provided customer service, training, and support as a component of its HLDA offerings. Synopsys had license agreements with more than 250 customers, including the world's leading semiconductor, computer, communications, and military and aerospace companies. In addition, Synopsys had invested in developing and maintaining cooperative market development relationships with leading semiconductor vendors worldwide. As electronics technology continued to experience fast-paced advances in the 1990s, Synopsys expected to continue doing what it did best—creating and marketing solutions that allow engineers to maximize their creative time while taking advantage of the latest technology.

Diversification in the Late 1990s

As Synopsys exited the mid-1990s, it embarked on a definitive period in its development, one that presented de Geus with his most difficult challenge in a decade. By all accounts, de Geus had created a market winner, taking Synopsys' pioneering role in the development of synthesis software and shaping the company into a dominant player. After roughly a decade of progress, the company controlled 80 percent of the synthesis software market, but, as de Geus was one of the first to perceive, the synthesis software market was a slow-growth business by the mid-1990s. De Geus realized he needed to develop a new portfolio of technologies and products "to expand beyond being a one-trick pony," as an analyst remarked in a June 1998 interview with *Electronic Business.*

De Geus pursued his objective by acquiring companies with the technology Synopsys needed to reinvent itself. The company's acquisition of Logic Modeling in 1994 was driven by de Geus's desire to gain new technology to enter new markets. A spate of acquisitions, each meant to give Synopsys new capabilities, followed, greatly expanding the company's revenue volume and its business profile. In 1995, the company purchased Silicon Architects because of its pioneering involvement in the development of next-generation gate-array technology, cell-based array. In 1997, de Geus spent $1 billion on acquiring two companies, Epic Design Technology, whose products were used in deep-submicron analysis, and Viewlogic Systems, which developed high-level simulation products.

As de Geus expanded Synopsys' operations dramatically through acquisitions, he was not the only chief executive officer to strengthen his position by purchasing the technologies developed by other companies. Cadence Design Systems, Inc. and Mentor Graphics Corporation also followed a growth-through-acquisition strategy. By 2002, Synopsys, Cadence, and Mentor, who controlled 45 percent of the EDA market in the early 1990s, controlled 75 percent of the market, creating a race that pitted the three market leaders against one another, with the rest of the industry's competitors trailing far behind. Of the three companies, Cadence ranked as the largest, but de Geus's achievements during the early years of the decade turned Synopsys into the dominant player.

Synopsys chased Cadence for years, at last passing the company in late 2003. One of the decisive moments in the final leg of the pursuit was Synopsys' acquisition of Avant! in 2002, which fleshed out de Geus's capabilities in the EDA's most lucrative market segment: developing software for creating the smallest and most complex chips. In the years that followed, de Geus made sure Synopsys held on to its market leadership, completing strategic acquisitions that bolstered hopes for a profitable future. After canceling a $432 million agreement to acquire Monolithic System Technology Inc. in June 2004, de Geus announced plans to acquire Integrated Systems Engineering AG, a Switzerland-based developer of software used to simulate and test chip manufacturing processes. In December

2004, Synopsys acquired Nassada Corp., a designer of chip design simulation and analysis software, paying $192 million for the company. The acquisition of Nassada was the eighth acquisition completed during the year, suggesting that in the years to follow de Geus would continue to target acquisition candidates to help keep Synopsys ahead of its two closest rivals.

Principal Subsidiaries

Avant! Software & Development Centre/(India) Private Limited; Nihon Synopsys KK (Japan); Numerical Technologies Canada Inc.; Synopsys Denmark ApS; Numerical Nova Scotia Company (Canada); Numerical Subwavelength Technologies B.V. (Netherlands); Synopsys S.A.R.L. (France); Synopsys Finland Oy; Synopsys GmbH (Germany); Synopsys (India) Private Ltd.; Synopsys (India) EDA Software Private Limited; Synopsys International Limited (Ireland); Synopsys Ireland Limited; Synopsys Ireland Resources; Synopsys Israel Limited; Synopsys Italia, S.R.L. (Italy); Synopsys Korea, Inc.; Synopsys (Northern Europe) Ltd. (U.K.); Synopsys Scandinavia AB (Sweden); Synopsys Singapore Pte. Ltd. (Singapore); Synopsys Taiwan Limited; Analogy UK Ltd. (U.K.); Angel HiTech Limited (Bermuda); Avant! Asia Investment Holdings, Ltd. (British Virgin Islands); Avant! China Holdings, Ltd. (Bermuda); Avant! Corporation GmbH (Germany); Avant! Corporation Limited (U.K.); Avant! Europe Manufacturing Ltd. (Ireland); Avant! France S.A.R.L.; Avant! Global Investment Holdings, Ltd. (Bermuda); Avant! Global Technologies Ltd. (Ireland); Avant! HiTech Corporation (Taiwan); Avant! International Distribution Ltd. (Ireland); Avant! Japan Corporation; Avant! Korea Co., Ltd.; Avant! LLC; Avant! Microelectronics (Shanghai) Company Limited (China); Avant! Software & Development Centre (India) Private Limited; Avant! Software (Israel) Ltd.; Avant! Taiwan Holdings, Ltd. (Bermuda); Avant! UK Ltd. (U.K.); Avant! Worldwide Holdings, Ltd. (Bermuda); Avanticorp Hong Kong Limited; CIDA Technology, Inc.; Co-Design Automation Ltd. (U.K.); Compass Design Automation Europe, EURL (France); Compass Design Automation International, B.V. (Netherlands); Crystal VC (Cayman Islands); inSilicon Corporation; inSilicon GmbH (Germany); inSilicon International, Inc.; inSilicon Limited (U.K.); Maingate Electronics, Inc. (Japan); Maude Avenue Land Corporation; Nexus IC Asia Corporation (Cayman Islands); Nexus IC Corporation (Cayman Islands); Nihon Synopsys KK (Japan); Numerical Technologies, Inc.; Numerical Technology, Inc. (Taiwan); Synopsys (India) EDA Software Private Limited.

Principal Competitors

Cadence Design Systems, Inc.; Magma Design Automation, Inc.; Mentor Graphics Corporation.

Further Reading

Dorsch, Jeff, "Synopsys in $116M Deal to Buy Logic Modeling," *Electronic News,* January 10, 1994, pp. 1, 21.

——, "Synopsys Sues Cadence Design Over VHDL Flap," *Electronic News,* March 15, 1993, p. 4.

"Entire Synopsys Line Supports Altera PLDs," *Electronic News,* April 11, 1994, p. 46.

Garner, Rochelle, "Artistic Vision," *Electronic Business,* June 1998, p. 50.

Hof, Robert D., "Chip-Design Shortcuts Are Synopsys' Long Suit," *Business Week,* January 25, 1993, p. 93.

Kharif, Olga, "A Promising Story Line for Synopsys," *Business Week Online,* August 18, 2003, p. 32.

"LSI Logic, Synopsys Spurred by User Integrations," *Electronic News,* May 2, 1994, p. 56.

Meyer, Cheryl, "Synopsys: Don't Blame Us," *Daily Deal,* April 27, 2004, p. 43.

Morrison, Gale, "De Geus: We're on the Launching Pad," *Electronic News,* December 4, 2000, p. 2.

——, "EDA's Cold War: Real-Life Intrigue Rocks Sector's Oldest, Most Vital Technology," *Electronic News,* November 4, 2002, p. 1.

——, "Synopsys Steers Through Garage," *Electronic News,* August 21, 2000, p. 38.

"Quickturn, Synopsys Sign Marketing Deal," *Electronic News,* March 7, 1994, p. 22.

Roberts, Bill, "Fortunate Reversal," *Electronic Business,* December 1998, p. 23.

"Sequential Timing Version Added to Synopsys Tool Line," *Electronic News,* June 22, 1992, p. 20.

Sperling, Ed, "Feeding Frenzy Ends for EDA," *Electronic News,* June 24, 2002, p. 1.

"Synopsys Buys Nassada for $192M," *Daily Deal,* December 2, 2004, p. 32.

"Synopsys Endorses ASIC Initiative," *Electronic News,* January 11, 1993, p. 10.

"Synopsys Introduces FPGA Design Tool," *Electronic News,* January 18, 1993, p. 10.

"Synopsys Joins RASSP; Will Rent Software," *Electronic News,* April 25, 1994, p. 44.

"Synopsys Set to Buy Logic Modeling," *Electronic News,* January 10, 1994, p. 21.

"Synopsys Software Recycles Design Elements," *Electronic News,* September 21, 1992, p. 18.

"Synopsys, Sunrise Buy ExperTest Tech," *Electronic News,* June 7, 1993, p. 12.

"Synopsys Surprises Cadence, Picks Mentor for High-End Link," *Electronic News,* April 27, 1992, p. 15.

"Synopsys Tries to Stay #1 with IPO," *Electronic News,* February 24, 1992, p. 21.

"Synopsys Unveils VHDL Software Aimed at Cutting Simulator Count," *Electronic News,* November 22, 1993, p. 14.

—Heidi Feldman
—update: Jeffrey L. Covell

Telenor ASA

Snaroyveien 30
Fornebu
N-1331
Norway
Telephone: +47- 810-77-000
Fax: +47-678-91-554
Web site: http://www.telenor.com

Public Company
Incorporated: 1995
Employees: 19,450
Sales: $7.93 billion (2003)
Stock Exchanges: Oslo NASDAQ
Ticker Symbol: TELN
NAIC: 517110 Wired Telecommunications Carriers;
    515210 Cable and Other Subscription Programming;
    517212 Cellular and Other Wireless Telecommuni-
    cations; 517910 Other Telecommunications

Telenor ASA is Norway's leading telecommunications group. As the former state-owned telephone monopoly, Telenor remains the dominate provider of fixed-line telecommunications services in the country. Fixed-line network operations continue to account for 35 percent of the group's revenues. Telenor also controls 56 percent of Norway's mobile telephone market, through subsidiary Telenor Mobil. Yet the small size of its domestic market has led Telenor to look elsewhere for growth, and in the early 2000s, Telenor has emerged as one of the most geographically diversified of Europe's major telecom groups. For its international expansion, Telenor has targeted especially the mobile telephone market. In Scandinavia, the company operates djuice, through subsidiary Telenor Mobile in Sweden, and owns Sonofon, the number two mobile service in Denmark. Beyond Scandinavia, the company owns 100 percent of Hungary's Pannon GSM, that country's second largest cellular service provider, and 100 percent of Promonte, the leading mobile service in Montenegro. Telenor also has entered Ukraine through a 56.5 percent stake in Kyivstar GSM; Russia, with a 29 percent stake in VimpelCom; and Austria, where it owns 17.5 percent of that country's ONE mobile service. Further abroad,

Telenor has entered Malaysia, through a 61 percent stake in that country's DiGi cellular phone group; Bangladesh, with 51 percent of GrameenPhone; and Thailand, with a 40.3 percent stake in DTAC. Telenor also owns a license to roll out cellular phone service in Pakistan. Telenor's other operations include television broadcasting via cable and satellite. The company owns 100 percent of satellite broadcaster Canal Digital. Telenor is led by CEO Jon Fredrik Baksaas and is listed on the Oslo and NASDAQ Stock Exchanges. The Norwegian government holds more than 53 percent of the company but has passed legislation allowing its stake in Telenor to drop below 49 percent. In 2003, Telenor posted revenues of $7.9 billion.

Norwegian Telecom Origins in the 19th Century

Norway, like its Scandinavian counterparts, emerged as one of the world's most technologically savvy markets at the start of the 21st century, boasting some of the highest penetration rates for technologies such as mobile telephones, high-speed Internet, and the like. Yet this represented somewhat of a tradition for the country, which had built its first telegraph line in 1855, and its first telephone network, connecting Arendal and Tvedestrand, in 1878. By 1880, the country already had its first telephone company, The International Bell Company, which began operating a telephone network in Oslo. Within six months, the service had attracted 300 subscribers. International service began in the country in 1893, linking Christiania and Stockholm.

For the most part, development of the country's early telephone grid was performed by private companies. In 1901, however, the state-owned Norwegian Telegraph Administration (NTA) made its first move to establish control over the sector, taking over the telephone exchange serving Christiania. The NTA gradually took over the privately controlled players in the market. Yet the last private exchange was absorbed into the NTA only in 1967, and the last privately owned telephone company, Andebu Telephone Association, became part of the NTA only in 1974.

By then, NTA had pointed the way toward Telenor's future mobile telephone interests. In 1967, Norway introduced one of the world's first mobile telephone systems, an analog-based, manually operated system. Two years later, after the NTA inaugurated Denmark's first data transmissions, the NTA changed its name, to Televerket, otherwise known as Norwegian Telecommunications. With the purchase of Andebu, Televerket gained control of the monopoly on telephone and telecommunications services, a position it retained until the 1990s. Nonetheless, the process of deregulating the Norwegian market began as early as the late 1980s, when Televerket lost its monopoly on the sale of telephone handsets in 1988.

Expansion in the 1990s

By then, however, Televerket had launched what was to become its most dynamic operation at the onset of the 21st century. In 1981, the state-owned company became one of the first in the world to roll out automated mobile telephone services, launching its Norwegian Mobile Telephone subsidiary, or NMT. By the beginning of the next decade, Televerket had begun preparation to launch a new generation of mobile telephone service, based on the GSM protocol soon to be adopted throughout Europe.

Televerket launched its GSM service in 1993. By then, the company also had expanded into television broadcasting, with the acquisition of the Thor satellite a year earlier. The move enabled Televerket to emerge as the dominant provider of satellite-based broadcasting in the Scandinavian region. The company also began restructuring ahead of the Norwegian telecommunication market's deregulation and its future privatization. The restructuring effort required some four years to complete, and included Televerket's transformation from a state-owned enterprise to a public corporation in 1994.

In the meantime, Televerket had begun to leverage its early experience in mobile telephony and with the GSM protocol in particular. In 1993, the company joined the consortium setting up the Pannon GSM mobile telephone network in Hungary. Televerket's initial share of Pannon GSM stood at just 14 percent. Over the next decade, however, the company boosted its stake in the Hungarian provider, which claimed the number two share in that market, to 100 percent control. The company also acquired a 13 percent stake in Northwest GSM, which launched cellular phone services in St. Petersburg in 1995.

Televerket changed its name to Telenor in 1995 as it prepared to extend its international operations. In 1995, the company won a license for establishing a GSM-based mobile network in Montenegro. For the Montenegro license, Telenor joined the European Telecom Luxembourg (ETL) consortium, which also included W-Com Investments, Westsouth Telecom, and TopStar Shipping and Trading. ETL then formed a joint venture with Montenegro's PTT to launch ProMonte, the country's first and largest mobile phone service, which became operational in 1996.

The following year, Telenor bought a 51 percent stake in GrameenPhone, in Bangladesh. That group had been granted a license to build a GSM-based network in Bangladesh in 1996, and by 1997 had launched commercial mobile telephone services in the country. Into the 2000s, GrameenPhone remained the only mobile phone provider offering nationwide coverage in Bangladesh.

Telenor continued seeking out deals as the full deregulation of its domestic market approached. The company joined consortiums acquiring licenses and building GSM-based networks in Germany, Ireland, Greece, and Austria in 1997 alone. In that year, Telenor also boosted its satellite television division, through an alliance with NetHold BV/Canal Plus that ultimately led to Telenor acquiring a stake, then full control of Canal Digital in 2004.

Mid-Sized Telecom Group in the 2000s

The full deregulation of the Norwegian market was completed in 1998. Telenor soon began an effort to reposition itself among Europe's major telecom groups. In 1998, the company began negotiating with Swedish counterpart Telia for a merger of the two companies. The combination of the two groups held a great deal of promise and was greeted enthusiastically, except by the Norwegian and Swedish governments and, indeed, by Telenor and Telia themselves.

The initial round of talks quickly broke down. In 1999, the two sides tried again, and this time came so far as to announce an actual merger agreement. Yet the merger never materialized, as a variety of factors, not least of which was national pride, seemed to have doomed the merger from the outset. Hopes remained strong that the two companies might eventually work out their differences. The merger between Telia and Finland's Sonera in 2002, however, put an end to those hopes as well.

Despite the collapse of the Telia merger, Telenor pushed ahead with its public offering, listing on the Oslo stock exchange and the NASDAQ. As part of the offering, the largest ever in Norway, the Norwegian government reduced its holding to 77 percent and later passed legislation allowing it to reduce its stake to below 49 percent in order to facilitate Telenor's ability to make cross-border deals. The government continued to reduce its stake into the 2000s, reaching less than 53 percent by the end of 2004.

Telenor became an active deal-maker in the 2000s. After a hostile takeover attempt for Ireland's Esat group failed, the company turned instead to Denmark, where it acquired majority control of the country's second largest mobile service provider, Sonofon, for DKK 14.7 billion ($1.9 billion). The company also entered Thailand, acquiring a 30 percent stake in TAC/UCOM. These purchases came on top of Telenor's entry into Malaysia, where it had purchased a 33 percent stake in the country's DiGi mobile network in 1999.

Telenor began restructuring its holdings in 2001, selling off its minority stakes in Germany and Ireland, as well as its position in Northwest GSM. Telenor also sold off a number of noncore holdings, such as its Telenor Media directories busi-

Key Dates:

1855: The Norwegian Telegraph Administration (NTA) completes its first telegraph line.

1878: The first telephone network is completed in Norway.

1901: NTA takes over the Christiania telephone exchange and gradually becomes the dominant telephone services operator.

1966: NTA introduces the first manual mobile telephone system.

1969: NTA launches its first data transmissions and changes its name to Norwegian Telecommunications Administration (Televerket).

1974: The last privately operated telephone company in Norway is acquired.

1981: The first automated mobile telephone system is launched.

1992: The company expands into satellite broadcasting and transmission with the purchase of Thor satellite.

1993: The company launches a GSM mobile network in Norway; the company joins a consortium developing Pannon GSM in Hungary (later acquires full control).

1994: Televerket is converted to a public corporation.

1995: The company changes its name to Telenor.

1998: The Norwegian telecommunications market is deregulated; Telenor enters merger talks with Telia of Sweden.

1999: The merger attempt with Telia is abandoned.

2000: Telenor is privatized with the largest ever public offering in Norway; the company acquires a stake in Sonofon, in Denmark.

2002: The company opens a new centralized headquarters in Oslo; Utfors, in Sweden, is acquired.

2003: Telenor acquires full control of Sonofon.

2004: Tiscali's Norwegian operation is acquired; the company wins a license to build a GSM network in Pakistan.

ness, to Texas Pacific Group. Instead, the company concentrated on building up majority positions, if not full ownership. In 2001, for example, Telenor acquired full control of Pannon GSM in Hungary, and boosted its share of DiGi in Malaysia past 60 percent. The company also acquired full control of Canal Digital, and bought up Comsat Mobil Communications from Lockheed that year to become the world's leading provider of satellite-based mobile telecommunications services. In addition, in 2001 Telenor launched the next-generation UTMS mobile platform in Denmark, which provided high-speed voice and data transmissions.

A turning point in Telenor's conversion from government body to publicly held company came in 2002, when Telenor opened its new headquarters. Where the former Telenor's offices had been scattered among some 35 sites throughout Oslo, the new headquarters brought more than 6,000 of the company's employees together into a single site. The move to new headquarters coincided with the naming of Jon Fredrik Baksaas as the company's CEO.

After acquiring a majority stake in Ukraine's Kyivstar in 2002, Telenor returned to its home region, acquiring struggling Swedish telecom group Utfors for SEK 264 million ($30 million). The following year, Telenor took full control of Sonofon, buying out the stake held by BellSouth. The company also returned to Russia, now acquiring a stake in VimpelCom, the country's number two mobile telephone company. By 2004, Telenor's stake in VimpelCom had increased to 29 percent.

Telenor's expansion continued into 2004, with the formation of the Starmap alliance with nine mobile service providers in Europe. The company also won a license to introduce GSM-based services in Pakistan that year. At home, the company acquired the Norwegian Internet operations of Italy's Tiscali, then bought up the Swedish Internet group Spray's corporate Internet customers at the end of the year. Telenor closed out 2004 with the purchase of an additional stake in Grameen-Phone, boosting its position to 62 percent of the Bangladesh operator. Telenor had successfully transformed itself from a single-country monopoly into a fast-growing global mobile telecommunications group.

Principal Subsidiaries

Canal Digital; GrameenPhone (Bangladesh; 51%); Kyivstar GSM (Ukraine; 56.51%); ONE (Austria; 17.5%); Pannon GSM (Hungary); Promonte (Montenegro); Sononfon (Denmark); Telenor Mobil; Telenor Mobile (Sweden); Telenor Pakistan; VimpelCom (Russia; 29%).

Principal Competitors

Deutsche Telekom AG; Vivendi Universal S.A.; Vodafone Group PLC; France Telecom S.A.; TRACTEBEL S.A.; Nokia Corporation; Telefonica S.A.; Royal KPN N.V.; TDC A/S.

Further Reading

Brown-Humes, Christopher, ''Telenor Sale Set to Raise Dollars 1bn,'' *Financial Times,* July 1, 2003, p. 29.

Brown-Humes, Christopher, and Claire MacCarthy, ''Telenor Agrees to Take Control of Sonofon,'' *Financial Times,* December 11, 2003, p. 35.

Criscione, Valeria, ''Big Cross-Border Deal Still Eludes Telecom Operator,'' *Financial Times,* October 26, 2001, p. 2.

——, ''Boss Acts to Scrap Division of Labour,'' *Financial Times,* April 29, 2002, p. 29.

''Telenor,'' *Financial Times,* February 14, 2004, p. 16.

''Telenor Acquires Tiscali's Norwegian Branch,'' *Wireless News,* August 29, 2004.

''Telenor ASA Acquires Additional Shares,'' *Nordic Business Report,* December 29, 2004.

''Telenor of Norway Reaffirms Commitment to Thai Cellular Operator,'' *Knight Ridder/Tribune Business News,* November 26, 2004.

—M.L. Cohen

Texas Roadhouse, Inc.

6040 Dutchmans Lane, Suite 400
Louisville, Kentucky 40205
U.S.A.
Telephone: (502) 426-9984
Toll Free: (800) 839-7623
Fax: (502) 426-3274
Web site: http://www.texasroadhouse.com

Public Company
Incorporated: 1993 as Texas Roadhouse, LLC
Employees: 9,700
Sales: $286.5 million (2003)
Stock Exchanges: NASDAQ
Ticker Symbol: TXRH
NAIC: 722110 Full-Service Restaurants; 533110 Owners
  and Lessors of Other Non-Financial Assets

Texas Roadhouse, Inc. operates a chain of casual-dining restaurants catering to blue-collar families, offering a menu of steak, chicken, side dishes, and made-from-scratch rolls. Texas Roadhouse operates 182 restaurants in 34 states. The company's restaurants feature a southwestern décor, hand-painted murals, neon signs, and jukeboxes, offering patrons a free, unlimited supply of peanuts and inexpensive entrées. The per guest check average is $13.53, roughly two-thirds less than the per guest check average of the company's largest competitor, Outback Steakhouse, Inc. Texas Roadhouse targets secondary markets for expansion, preferring communities with populations above 60,000 and a high concentration of working-class families. The company is controlled by its founder and chairman, W. Kent Taylor, who owns approximately 60 percent of Texas Roadhouse stock.

Origins

Kent Taylor's first passion was the state of Colorado, not Texas, specifically the mountains in Colorado. The Texas Roadhouse founder, a self-described skiing addict, moved to Colorado after earning an undergraduate degree at the University of North Carolina. To help pay for his skiing equipment and lift tickets, Taylor managed nightclubs and restaurants in Colorado. His idyllic life of splitting time between work and the slopes came to an end when troubles in his personal life forced a retreat to his hometown. Taylor and his wife divorced in 1990, an event that forced him decidedly off pitch and back to Louisville, Kentucky.

Back in his hometown, Taylor began rebuilding his life. He worked as a manager for KFC Corporation, the operator of the massive fast-food chicken chain. He managed a Hooters of America restaurant. Taylor's thoughts were on Colorado, however, propelling him to hatch plans to open his own restaurant, a Colorado-themed bar and grill. His desire turned to reality when John Y. Brown, the former Governor of Kentucky, agreed to help financially support the opening of Taylor's own restaurant. Brown gave Taylor $80,000, a sum used to open Buckhead Hickory Grill. The Louisville restaurant did well, quickly turning a profit, which convinced Brown to invest more. Brown wanted to open a second Buckhead in Clarkesville, Indiana, but as Taylor began making preparations for his second grand opening the partnership collapsed. Brown, according to Taylor, was unwilling to divide the profits from the second restaurant evenly.

Taylor's hopes of opening a second restaurant appeared dashed. The Clarkesville project gained new life, however, after Taylor solicited the financial backing of three cardiologists. With the money obtained from his new backers, Taylor opened his restaurant in Clarkesville, but he was forced to choose another name and to abandon his Colorado theme. The Clarkesville restaurant opened in February 1993, debuting as Texas Roadhouse. One year later, Taylor sold his interest in Buckhead. The Kentucky native, educated in North Carolina and emotionally attached to Colorado, would stake his business future on a casual-dining brand inspired by Texas and first begun in Indiana.

The opening of the Clarkesville restaurant represented the beginning of a chain of Texas Roadhouse restaurants, although it would be several years before the company could be discerned as operating a chain of restaurants. Expansion did occur in the years immediately following the Clarkesville opening. However, there appeared to be no strategic cohesion. Taylor, earlier in his life, had competed in a track meet in Gainesville,

Company Perspectives:

We wanted to provide a place that the whole family could enjoy. Texas Roadhouse is about a hearty, good meal with service that is friendly, energetic, and enthusiastic. Life should be fun—so the workplace needs to reflect that as well—and that is why we put our employees first.

Florida, leaving the city with positive memories. The second Texas Roadhouse opened in Gainesville. "We were all over the map the first few years," the Gainesville restaurant's first manager noted in a March 2003 interview with *Chain Leader*. The Gainesville restaurant proved to be successful, but poor site selection afflicted Taylor during his first years in business. Within a year of their opening, restaurants in Cincinnati, Ohio, and in Clearwater and Sarasota, Florida, were forced to close their doors.

Despite some bad decisions made early on, Taylor's business strategy proved to be sound. He emphasized service and quality food—objectives of nearly every restaurateur, but objectives that were far easier to proclaim than to fulfill. Taylor achieved his objectives, creating a new entrant in the casual-dining steakhouse category of the industry that would present concern for the three, publicly held and well-funded leaders of the industry segment. As Taylor built his chain, he was competing against the industry stalwart, Outback Steakhouse, Inc., and the two other biggest contenders, Lone Star Steakhouse & Saloon, Inc. and RARE Hospitality International, Inc.'s LongHorn Steakhouse chain. As Taylor's chain expanded and matured, it created its own identity in the fiercely competitive steakhouse category, one described by an investment banker and investor in Texas Roadhouse. "I call the place a redneck Outback," George Rich said in a March 2003 interview with *Chain Leader.*

Texas Roadhouse expanded at a moderate pace during its formative years. The pace of expansion was dictated in large part by the lack of financial resources at Taylor's disposal. Although Taylor was intent on building a chain of restaurants, he demonstrated an unwillingness to obtain money from outside sources, his partnerships with Brown and the three cardiologists aside. Once Texas Roadhouse was up and running, Taylor avoided dealing with venture capitalists and other external sources of raising cash saying in a 2003 interview in *Chain Leader,* "I'm not interested; I don't need their money." Taylor only completed one private placement during his first decade in business, but that private placement, a $5 million deal completed in 1997, was raised primarily from employees, with the average investment being $75,000, which left Taylor in firm control.

Rapid Expansion in the Late 1990s

The cash raised in 1997 ignited Texas Roadhouse's first substantial burst of expansion. Again, Taylor made some bad decisions in terms of site selection. Restaurants were opened in Utah, Idaho, and Colorado for the wrong reasons. "Back when we jumped out there because of my ski addiction," Taylor conceded in his March 2003 interview with *Chain Leader,*

"that was definitely not the right thing to do. I don't think I'd do that anymore." Taylor also experienced the hazards of overly aggressive expansion, attempting in 1999 to open 30 new restaurants. The hallmarks of his success—service and food quality—suffered as a result of the overzealous expansion. "Back in the late 1990s everything was go-go-go," Taylor explained in his interview with *Chain Leader*. "The economy was doing great and everyone was getting excited. That's when we realized we were rushing people to get them ready to take on stores. That was a real education."

Mistakes were made during Texas Roadhouse's development into a chain, but on balance, the good decisions outweighed the bad. Instead of relinquishing control to outside investors, Taylor helped pay for the expansion of the chain by franchising the concept, typically signing franchise agreements with former employees. By relying on a franchise network and by securing loans from banks, who were more than willing to help finance the chain's expansion in the "go-go-go" late 1990s, Taylor constructed a modestly sized chain. By the end of the decade, there were 67 restaurants operating under the Texas Roadhouse banner. Together, the restaurants generated $71 million in revenue in 1999 and registered $4.4 million in net income.

Texas Roadhouse experienced another growth spurt as it entered a new decade. Taylor and his management team focused on establishing restaurants in secondary markets, focusing on communities with a high concentration of blue-collar families. The company chose communities with populations above 60,000, but below the figures reflective of a large metropolitan market. In December 2000, for instance, the company opened one of its 250-seat units in Columbia, South Carolina, its fourth restaurant in the state, adding to units already operating in Greenville, Spartanburg, and Anderson. The following year, at a time when the company was opening an average of 25 restaurants each year, Texas Roadhouse moved into Oklahoma, opening a 5,000-square-foot unit along Interstate 240 in Oklahoma City. In 2003, the company entered New Hampshire, opening a restaurant in Nashua.

As the company expanded, it developed a managerial structure that gave considerable control to personnel on the local and regional level. Taylor created a performance-based compensation program for managers working out in the field. Restaurant managers, in the company's terms, were referred to as "managing partners," and regional managers were referred to as "market partners." To those two groups fell much of the responsibility for selecting sites and creating restaurants that drew some of their décor from the communities in which they operated. One of the largest murals in the company's Columbia, South Carolina restaurant, for example, depicted a scene from a University of South Carolina football game.

By the company's tenth anniversary, the Texas Roadhouse chain stood as a likely candidate to break into the ranks of the industry's elite, the upper echelon occupied by Outback Steakhouse, Longhorn Steakhouse, and Lone Star Steakhouse & Saloon. There were 162 restaurants in more than 30 states in operation at the end of 2003, nearly 100 more units in existence than four years earlier. Annual revenue growth during this period reflected the physical growth, swelling from $71 million to $286 million. Profits leaped upward as well, jumping from

Key Dates:

1993: The first Texas Roadhouse restaurant opens in Clarkesville, Indiana.
1997: Texas Roadhouse raises $5 million in a private placement.
1999: By the end of the year, there are 67 Texas Roadhouse restaurants in operation.
2004: Texas Roadhouse completes its initial public offering of stock.

$4.4 million in 1999 to $24.2 million during the company's tenth anniversary year. When George Rich, the investor who referred to Texas Roadhouse as a "redneck Outback," offered his analogy to *Chain Leader* in March 2003, his comments were not disparaging. "That means we have a similar offering in terms of service and menu," he continued. "But our price points are lower and our check average is only about $12.50. If you are two-thirds the price [of Outback Steakhouse], you have to do 40 percent more business. And we do."

As he celebrated his tenth year in business, Taylor presided over a proven business model. Profitable and growing, Texas Roadhouse drew covetous attention from the financial community, which wanted to invest in Taylor's model of success, particularly because the chain had yet to fully assert itself nationwide. Outback Steakhouse, with more than 800 restaurants, had little room for future expansion. Texas Roadhouse, in contrast, was perceived as having substantial room for future expansion. Taylor continued to shun outside involvement in the company, however, stating to *Chain Leader* in March 2003, "If you have a long-term outlook in a low-interest-rate environment and a strong balance sheet, you can continue to secure funds from banks." An initial public offering (IPO) of Texas Roadhouse stock was, in Taylor's estimation, "inevitable," he conceded to *Chain Leader,* but the timing was not right in his mind in 2003. By the following year, Taylor's mindset had changed, giving Wall Street the opportunity to take a stake in the future expansion of the chain.

Initial Public Offering of Stock in 2004

Texas Roadhouse completed its IPO in October 2004. The company, which previously had operated under the corporate title Texas Roadhouse LLC, changed its official name to Texas Roadhouse, Inc. Slightly more than nine million shares were sold to the public at $17.50 per share, raising $159.3 million and netting Taylor $100.2 million. After the offering, Taylor remained in financial control of the company, holding 61.6 percent of Texas Roadhouse stock. He planned to use the proceeds from the IPO to repay the company's debt, which totaled $65.8 million at the time of the offering.

Taylor, with the hopes of shareholders and his decade of success fueling great expectations, faced a future of opportunity following the IPO of Texas Roadhouse. Industry observers were waiting and watching for the chain to sweep the nation with its restaurants and complete its development into a national giant. The company, according to its web site, planned to open "many more locations" in the years immediately following its debut as a publicly traded company, years that would determine whether the Texas Roadhouse name would be included among the elite of the casual-dining segment.

Principal Competitors

Lone Star Steakhouse & Saloon, Inc.; Outback Steakhouse, Inc.; RARE Hospitality International, Inc.

Further Reading

Adams, Tony, "Another Steakhouse Enters Market in Columbus, Georgia," *Knight Ridder/Tribune Business News,* March 24, 2001.

Blossom, Debbie, "Texas Roadhouse to Open First Eatery in Tulsa, Okla.," *Knight Ridder/Tribune Business News,* August 28, 2002.

Farkas, David, "Beef Stakes: Western-Themes Texas Roadhouse Is Rounding Up Impressive Numbers," *Chain Leader,* March 2003, p. 64.

Kennedy, Eileen, "State's First Texas Roadhouse Eatery Opens in Nashua, N.H.," *Knight Ridder/Tribune Business News,* August 29, 2003.

Lockyer, Sarah E., "Texas Roadhouse Rakes in $159.3 Million from Public Offering," *Nation's Restaurant News,* October 18, 2004, p. 11.

Mortland, Shannon, "Texas Roadhouse Puts Down Stakes Here," *Crain's Cleveland Business,* May 7, 2001, p. 12.

Thomas, Maurice, "Columbia, S.C.-Area Neighborhood Adds Two More Restaurants," *Knight Ridder/Tribune Business News,* December 12, 2000.

—Jeffrey L. Covell

Tha Row Records

8200 Wilshire Boulevard
Los Angeles, California 90211
U.S.A.
Telephone: (323) 852-5000
Fax: (323) 852-5029
Web site: http://www.tharow.com

Private Company
Incorporated: 1992 as Death Row Records
Employees: 10
Sales: $33 million (2004 est.)
NAIC: 512210 Record Production

Tha Row Records specializes in rap music. Originally known as Death Row Records, the firm continues to use that name on its recordings. Death Row once had major hits with artists including Dr. Dre, Snoop Dogg, and Tupac Shakur, but after the departures of Dre and Dogg and the murder of Shakur, as well as CEO Marion "Suge" Knight's lengthy prison stay, the company lost much of its momentum. Since his release in 2001, Knight has vowed to return the label to prominence through new releases by such artists as Kurupt. Tha Row also releases videos through its Suge Knight Films, Inc. subsidiary.

Beginnings

Tha Row Records was founded in Los Angeles in 1992 by successful rap music producer Dr. Dre (Andre Young), of the popular group N.W.A., and Marion "Suge" Knight. Knight, born in the L.A. suburb of Compton, had gotten his nickname from being called "Sugar Bear" as a child. Reputedly a member of the Bloods street gang, Knight had played football for the University of Nevada and then tried out for the Los Angeles Rams. The 6-foot 3-inch, 315-pound Knight began working as a bodyguard for rhythm and blues singers including Bobby Brown, then became a music promoter before publishing white rapper Vanilla Ice's lone hit "Ice Ice Baby."

After starting out as Future Shock Records, the company took the more ominous name of Death Row, with a logo depicting a man strapped to an electric chair. CEO Knight reportedly liked the new name because many of the label's artists had been in trouble with the law. Funding for the endeavor came in part from Interscope Records, which would handle distribution. Before starting work with the label, Dr. Dre was released from his contract with Ruthless Records, allegedly after Knight threatened N.W.A. founder Eric "Eazy E" Wright with bodily harm. A lawsuit filed by Wright was later settled out of court by Knight, who admitted no wrongdoing.

Death Row's first release, in December 1992, was Dr. Dre's solo album *The Chronic,* which featured vocals from guests including Snoop Doggy Dogg, Nate Dogg, Kurupt, and Daz. It quickly became a major hit, and the following September the label's second album, Snoop Dogg's *Doggystyle,* entered the *Billboard* charts at number one and sold four million copies. Just prior to the album's release, Dogg (birth name Calvin Broadus) had been involved in a shooting incident in which a gang member was killed, and the ensuing media attention helped boost sales. After several years and a reported $2.5 million in lawyer's fees, the rapper was ultimately exonerated.

The label's chosen name, and its artists' troubled lives, mirrored the type of music in which it specialized, known as "gangsta rap." Whereas earlier forms of rap often had celebrated party life or uninhibited sexuality, gangsta rap featured songs with highly graphic lyrics about violent street life. Although popular among the young in the urban, mainly black communities from which the artists came, gangsta rap was increasingly embraced by suburban whites who apparently enjoyed fantasizing about a lifestyle of guns, money, and women.

In 1994 Death Row released two new albums, both movie soundtracks featuring rap songs. The label's hits were now filling the coffers of distributor Interscope, which was partly owned by Time Warner. Due to controversy over the lyrical content of 1995 Death Row release *Dogg Food* by Tha Dogg Pound, Time Warner sold its stake in Interscope under pressure from stockholders.

In 1995 future Death Row artist Tupac Shakur and company CEO Suge Knight were sentenced to jail time (4½ years and 30 days, respectively) for various offenses. After eight months in prison, Shakur was released when Knight put up $1.4 million in bail, and he soon joined Death Row.

1996: Tupac Shakur's Death Row Debut

In 1996 Shakur's first Death Row record, *All Eyez on Me,* was released. The double album quickly became a bestseller and boosted the stature of both Shakur and the label. In its first four years of business, Death Row had sold 18 million albums worth more than $325 million at retail. Its annual revenues were pegged at approximately $100 million. The company, which had thus far been exclusively tied to the Los Angeles area, was now reportedly laying plans for an East Coast division.

In the summer of 1996, cofounder Dr. Dre parted ways with the firm. He had apparently grown tired of both the negativity and the stylistic limitations of the gangsta rap genre. Leaving his master tapes and publishing rights with Death Row, he formed a new company, Aftermath Entertainment, to release his projects. Dre would later have major success with artists like the white rapper Eminem.

On September 7, 1996, at a Las Vegas intersection, a gunman opened fire on a vehicle driven by Suge Knight, hitting both Knight and passenger Tupac Shakur. Although the Death Row CEO was only grazed by a bullet, Shakur was hit four times, and he died a week later. The next month, Knight was jailed for violating parole, having allegedly participated in beating the man who, some said, had later shot him and Shakur. In the midst of this turmoil, the label was preparing for the release of new product, and four albums came out before year's end, including new titles from both Shakur and Snoop Dogg.

In February 1997, Knight was sentenced to nine years in prison for violating his parole. After being imprisoned, he was barred from running the label, and half of its staff was laid off. Knight's brother-in-law, Norris Anderson, was given initial control of the firm, before more experienced management personnel were brought in. Numerous lawsuits were now swirling

around Death Row, including several claiming underpaid royalties or unpaid bills. Another suit had been filed by relatives of a man stomped to death at a Death Row event in 1995, which was later settled out of court.

In March 1997 East Coast rapper Notorious B.I.G. (Christopher Wallace) was murdered in Los Angeles, which brought a feud between East and West Coast rappers (already aggravated by threatening lyrics on their albums) to fever pitch. Some speculated that the killing had been in retaliation for the still unsolved murder of Tupac Shakur, and Knight was later investigated for possible involvement, but he was not charged.

In January 1998 Interscope dropped Death Row from its distribution roster under pressure from new co-owner Seagrams, but the company soon found another distributor in Priority Records. The year after Knight's incarceration saw several artists defect, including Snoop Dogg, Daz Dillinger, and old-school rapper MC Hammer. The handful of new albums released made little headway, with the exception of the fall release *2Pac Greatest Hits,* a double album that would become Death Row's best seller to date.

In 1999 Daz Dillinger returned to Death Row for releases under the DPG Records imprint, but in October he and a bodyguard were shot and killed in a Los Angeles recording studio. Another Death Row rapper, Javon Jones, was wounded. Several more artists left the label during the year, including Rage and Chocolate Bandit. Releases included another featuring posthumous Shakur material, *Still I Rise,* credited to Tupac and the Outlaws.

Activity for 2000 was slow, with an exclusive license for audio downloads signed with Musicmaker.com in March, and two albums released in October, including one of unreleased Snoop Dogg material, *Dead Man Walkin'.* The following year brought another compilation of unissued Tupac material, *Until The End of Time,* and a Dogg Pound album. The label's distribution arrangement with Priority lapsed in 2001, and the firm signed a new agreement with a smaller independent company, DNA, to release remastered, enhanced versions of 16 Death Row albums.

Also in 2001, Death Row's video unit, Suge Knight Films, prepared for the release of *J. Lo Uncut: The Real Story,* which purportedly contained home-video sex footage of actress/singer Jennifer Lopez (the then girlfriend of Knight rival Sean ''Puff Daddy''/''P. Diddy'' Combs). Legal action ensued, and Lopez successfully blocked the release, whereupon a Death Row spokesman admitted that no sex tape actually existed. Suge Knight Films already had released several direct-to-video titles including the documentary *Welcome to Death Row.*

August 2001: The Return of Suge Knight

In August 2001, Suge Knight was released from prison, having served slightly more than half of his nine-year sentence. Although he had been banned from running the label from jail, his presence was still strongly felt, and upon release he vowed to restore Death Row to its former luster. He also announced that the label would henceforth be known as Tha Row, and would broaden its scope to include Rhythm and Blues artists.

Knight later signed with a talent agency, hoping to pursue film roles and write an autobiography.

In January 2002 a joint investigation of Tha Row by the FBI, Los Angeles police, and other agencies ended with the company agreeing to pay a fine of $100,000 and back taxes. Rumors of drug money laundering and murder had been investigated, but Knight and the label were not charged. In November, police raided Knight's home and offices, arresting three of his associates in connection with another murder investigation, but they were later released. Knight's legal troubles were mounting, and included a multitude of lawsuits, claims of unpaid child support from his ex-wife, and a reported $6 million in back taxes sought by the Internal Revenue Service. Clear Channel Outdoors, Inc. was also seeking damages from Death Row because the label had used a Clear Channel billboard atop its headquarters without permission. The sign, which advertised a Crooked I album, generated complaints from some passersby, but Death Row had refused to take it down or give Clear Channel workers access to the roof.

In 2003 Knight was jailed twice for parole violations, the second time for punching a parking lot attendant, for which he was sentenced to ten months in jail. In early 2004 Death Row also was ordered to pay $162,000 to a man who had been beaten by the firm's security guards in a recording studio. The label countered that the altercation had begun after the man brandished a gun.

In the summer of 2004 Tha Row released its first all-new recording since 1996, *Against Tha Grain* by Dogg Pound co-founder Kurupt. A hits compilation, *The Best of Death Row*, was slated for release in early 2005. Artists on the label at this time included Kurupt, Danny Boy, Eastwood, Michel'le, Crooked I, Virginya Slim, and Gail Gotti. Tha Row now claimed to have sold more than 50 million albums worldwide since its inception, accounting for $750 million in retail sales.

Although Tha Row Records had once been the leading label for ''gangsta rap'' music, it had fallen victim to the same kinds of violence and legal problems that were portrayed in its artists' songs. CEO Marion ''Suge'' Knight was still a force within the industry, however, and he vowed to restore the label to prominence with new releases by artists including Kurupt.

Principal Subsidiaries

Suge Knight Films, Inc.

Principal Competitors

Interscope Records; The Island Def Jam Group; Tommy Boy Music; Bad Boy Worldwide Entertainment Group; TVT Records.

Further Reading

Bing, Jonathan, ''New Life for Death Row,'' *Daily Variety,* June 10, 2002, p. 1.

''Escaping Death Row,'' *OC Weekly,* January 29, 1999, p. 22.

Gumbel, Andrew, ''Guns 'N' Poses: Marion 'Suge' Knight Is the Biggest, Baddest Man in Gangsta Rap,'' *Independent (London),* August 9, 2001, p. 1.

——, ''Rap Label Boss Cuts a Deal to End Criminal Inquiry,'' *Independent (London),* January 10, 2002, p. 12.

Harrington, Richard, ''Is Death Row in Death Throes?; Legal Troubles, Talk of Sale Dog the Once-Hot Rap Label,'' *Washington Post,* August 22, 1997, p. D1.

Kennedy, Dana, ''Deadly Business,'' *Entertainment Weekly,* December 6, 1996, p. 34.

Lee, Jr., McKinley ''Malik,'' *Chosen By Fate: My Life Inside Death Row Records,* West Hollywood: Dove Books, 1997.

Morris, Chris, ''DNA to Distribute Death Row Catalog,'' *Billboard,* March 3, 2001.

——, ''Knight Sentenced to 9 Years; Impact on Death Row Uncertain,'' *Billboard,* March 15, 1997, p. 12.

——, ''New Questions Over Funding of Death Row,'' *Billboard,* September 13, 1997.

Pollock, Danny, ''Rap Pioneer Facing Challenges to Rebuilding Legendary Label,'' *Associated Press,* July 12, 2003.

Ro, Ronin, *Have Gun Will Travel—The Spectacular Rise and Violent Fall of Death Row Records,* New York: Doubleday, 1998.

Samuels, Allison, ''Suge Knight Is Back in Business,'' *Newsweek,* April 23, 2001, p. 54.

Strauss, Neil, ''Rap Empire Unraveling As Stars Flee,'' *New York Times,* January 26, 1998, p. D1.

Waxman, Sharon, ''A Rap Cast to Make Your Head Spin; Death Row Boss in a Courtroom Muddle,'' *Washington Post,* October 31, 1996, p. B1.

Wielenga, Dave, ''Nighty Knight: Suge Knight Is in Jail, Death Row Records Is in Disarray,'' *New Times Los Angeles,* December 18, 1997.

——, ''Reeling and Dealing; 'Suge' Knight Is Behind Bars, Tha Doggfather Is on the Shelves, and the Future of Death Row Records Hangs in the Balance,'' *Phoenix New Times,* November 28, 1996.

——, ''Stacked Deck: With Suge Knight Behind Bars, Death Row Galvanizes Behind Tha Doggfather,'' *New Times Los Angeles,* November 7, 1996.

——, ''Who's the Man?; With Suge Knight in Prison, Onetime Receptionist Norris Anderson Is Now the Big Man on Death Row,'' *Phoenix New Times,* March 27, 1997.

—Frank Uhle

II-VI Incorporated

375 Saxonburg Boulevard
Saxonburg, Pennsylvania 16056
U.S.A.
Telephone: (724) 352-4455
Toll Free: (888) 558-1504
Fax: (724) 352-4980
Web site: http://www.ii-vi.com

Public Company
Incorporated: 1971
Employees: 1,094
Sales: $150.84 million (2003)
Stock Exchanges: NASDAQ
Ticker Symbol: IIVI
NAIC: 333314 Optical Instrument and Lens Manufacturing; 334419 Other Electronic Component Manufacturing

II-VI Incorporated develops and manufactures optical and optoelectronic devices used in laser and sensor systems. The company's products are used in industrial, medical, military, security, and aerospace applications. II-VI maintains production facilities in Pennsylvania, New Jersey, Florida, and California. Overseas, where the company generates 41 percent of its annual sales, II-VI operates manufacturing plants in Singapore and China. The company also has sales and marketing subsidiaries in Japan, the United Kingdom, Belgium, and Switzerland.

Origins

II-VI's development nearly spanned its founder's entire professional career, representing the life's work of Carl J. Johnson. Described, in the August 31, 1997 issue of the *Pittsburgh Business Times* by a rival as "a real capable scientist and manager," Johnson earned his bachelor's degree at Purdue University, his master's degree at Massachusetts Institute of Technology, and his doctorate in electrical engineering at the University of Illinois. He received his Ph.D. in 1964 and began what would be a brief period of working for an employer, starting out with a two-year stint as a member of Bell Laboratories' technical staff. Next, Johnson joined Essex International

Inc., an automotive products maker, where he served as the director of research and development for five years. In 1971, Johnson, in his late 20s, founded II-VI, starting a company that would count him as its leader for more than 35 years.

Johnson based his entrepreneurial creation in Saxonburg, Pennsylvania, a city 25 miles north of Pittsburgh. The name of the company, pronounced "two-six," referred to groups II and VI of the Periodic Table of Elements, the two groups of elements that served as the basis for many of the components and materials made by Johnson's company. II-VI's name had deeper meaning than most other corporate titles chosen by companies since the name reflected Johnson's strategy. Industry pundits pointed to Johnson's decision to focus his efforts on the elements found in groups II and VI as the primary reason for his company's financial success. Starting out, Johnson's record of success was impressive, as II-VI remained profitable and increased its revenues every year during its first 15 years of business.

II-VI's achievements during this period not only created a sturdy financial base but also advanced the science and engineering driving the development of laser technology. Thanks in part to II-VI's research with a number of zinc-, cadmium- and gallium-based compounds, engineers were able to improve the materials used in devices that controlled and directed laser energy. One measure of the advances in laser technology propelled by II-VI's work was in the power generated by some lasers, which leaped from 300 watts in 1971 to 5,000 watts in 1987, an important year in II-VI's history.

Initial Public Offering in 1987

By 1987, Johnson was ready to offer the public an opportunity to invest in his company. He had created, according to his own assessment quoted in the August 31, 1987 issue of the *Pittsburgh Business Times,* "a leading researcher in the area of infrared materials and a leading producer for precision infrared optical devices," and he wanted to leverage his company's stature to gain capital from Wall Street. II-VI filed for an initial public offering (IPO) of stock in August 1987, planning to issue one million shares at between $6.50 and $7.50 per share with the hope of raising $8 million for capital investment and to fund research and development efforts.

When Johnson announced his intention to go public, he presided over a nearly $10 million-in-sales business, one that derived nearly 40 percent of its sales from overseas customers. The company's product line included precision components found in high-powered infrared lasers used for industrial, military, and medical applications, constituting the optics (lenses and reflectors) that controlled the type and amount of energy passing through a laser. Although the company received some of its income from the medical and military markets, the majority of its business was involved in supplying components for lasers used in industrial settings. II-VI equipped lasers were used to weld everything from automobile bodies to heart pacemakers and to cut, drill, and heat treat in scores of other industrial applications. II-VI sold its components to the more than 960 companies worldwide that manufactured lasers and related equipment.

Johnson owned 31 percent of II-VI following its IPO and guided the company into the 1990s, a decade of significant growth. Much of the company's growth during that decade was achieved through acquisitions, a strategy employed in earnest after Johnson and his management team resolved problems in one of the company's most important markets. By the early 1990s, II-VI collected nearly half its annual sales from foreign customers, conducting much of its international business in Japan. For years, the company faced little competition there, relying on a distributor, Material Technology Trading Corp. (25 percent owned by II-VI) to develop a leading position in the Japanese market.

The end to the years of relative ease came in the early 1990s, when Japan's Ministry of International Trade and Industry began promoting increased involvement, by Japanese companies, in the industrial laser business, including the production of advanced optical lenses. "Our first reaction was one of curiosity," II-VI's chief financial officer remarked in a November 29, 1993 interview with the *Pittsburgh Business Times*. "We weren't sure what we would do," CFO John Sherbin continued. "But I think we felt we just simply couldn't do the same as usual. We then made the assessment that, really for the long run, we would have to take a direct position." The management team found itself facing a wave of new competitors, such as the massive conglomerate Sumitomo Corp., and felt inadequately supported by its Japanese distributor, Material Technology. In February 1993, the company sold its 25 percent stake in Material Technology and gave the distributor a one-year termination notice, a customary practice when severing a long-term business relationship in Japan. Next, the company began working to establish its own subsidiary to directly sell its products in Japan, an objective realized in July 1993, when II-VI Japan Ltd. began operating as a wholly owned sales-and-support subsidiary.

After shoring up business in Japan, Johnson directed his energies to expanding II-VI's domestic business. His expansion program consisted largely of acquiring other companies. In 1995, II-VI acquired the Tampa, Florida-based Virgo Optics division of Sandoz Chemical Corp. Johnson merged this acquisition with a company he acquired the following year, Tarpon Springs, Florida-based Lightning Optical Corp., to create a new subsidiary named VLOC based in New Port Richey, Florida. The addition of this business helped II-VI generate $52.7 million in revenue in 1997, nearly triple the total collected three years earlier.

The Pursuit of Laser Power: 1990s–2000s

II-VI's most important acquisition was first targeted at the end of the 1990s. The object of Johnson's desire was a San Diego-based company named Laser Power Corp., one of his competitors. Laser Power, a $31 million-in-sales company founded by a former II-VI employee, manufactured infrared optics products used in carbon dioxide lasers purchased by industrial and military customers. Half of the company's sales were derived from contracts with the military, the part of Laser Power's business that interested Johnson in particular. Laser Power made domes for the front end of missiles that functioned as infrared eyes for the weapon, window assemblies for tanks and helicopters, and optical coatings for space-based lasers, additions that would enable Johnson to increase the less than 10 percent II-VI collected in sales from military work.

Johnson coveted Laser Power, demonstrating an ardent desire to purchase the company. He made his first move quietly, acquiring 100 shares of Laser Power's stock in June 1999. In late September 1999, his intentions were made public when II-VI paid $2.75 million for 14.7 percent of Laser Power, part of Johnson's plan to purchase the entire company in a stock-and-cash transaction valued at $25.5 million. Industry analysts supported Johnson's decision to buy Laser Power, noting that the acquisition would rid II-VI of a competitor, give it a manufacturing presence on the West Coast, and, most important, broaden its customer base by quintupling its military-related business. Laser Power's management, however, did not rush to complete the deal. Months passed and the new year came without any further action, as Johnson began to realize that acquiring Laser Power would be one of the most trying experiences in his career.

In mid-2000, Johnson's attempt to acquire Laser Power became a battle. In early June, II-VI's opportunity to acquire Laser Power appeared lost when another company, a Brussels-based non-ferrous metals producer named Union Minière SA, offered $39 million for Laser Power. Union Minière, which owned 10 percent of Laser Power, signed an agreement to merge with the San Diego company, prompting Johnson to counter with another, higher bid. Johnson offered $43 million for the company, setting the stage for a bidding war between II-VI and Union Minière. "Obviously," Laser Power CEO Dick Sharman said in a June 6, 2000 interview with the *Press-Enterprise*, "we are an attractive takeover target."

Key Dates:

1971: II-VI is founded by Carl J. Johnson.
1987: II-VI completes its initial public offering of stock.
1997: II-VI's VLOC subsidiary is formed by merging two acquisitions.
2000: II-VI acquires Laser Power Corp.
2004: II-VI acquires Marlow Industries, Inc.

In the weeks following the merger agreement between Union Minière and Laser Power, the II-VI executives in charge of the effort to acquire Laser Power scrambled to come up with a response. A bidding war ensued, as Sharman sat back and watched the value of his company escalate. By the end of the month, a winner was announced. II-VI offered $53 million for Laser Power, an amount Union Minière executives were unwilling to match. Johnson, a year after he began pursuing Laser Power, achieved his objective, paying more than twice the amount he originally expected to pay. Despite the increase in price, analysts applauded the deal, an acquisition that increased II-VI's annual revenues by 66 percent and elevated its military-related business from 5 to 25 percent of its revenue volume.

Once Laser Power was integrated into its operations, II-VI continued to strengthen its market position through acquisitions during the first half of the decade. In 2001, the company's 30th anniversary, it acquired Litton Systems, Inc.'s Silicon Carbide Group. Recessive economic conditions forced the company to halt its expansion program following the Silicon Carbide purchase, but by 2003, when the invasion of Iraq boosted prospects for military contractors, Johnson and his team again began pursuing acquisition candidates. In September 2003, the company purchased the ultraviolet filters materials business owned by rival Coherent, Inc. The filters were used by military aircraft to detect ground-launched missiles, which emit an ultraviolet plume when burning rocket fuel.

As II-VI prepared for the future, the breadth of its product line distinguished it from competing optics makers. The company, primarily from achievements during the 1990s, became a comprehensive developer and manufacturer of high technology materials, developing a portfolio of products that was diverse yet reflected the company's adherence to using elements from groups II and VI of the Periodic Table. The breadth of the company's product line translated into robust financial growth, as II-VI increased its annual revenue volume from $18.6 million in 1994 to $150 million in 2004. In the years ahead, the company was expected to build on its broad business founda-

tion by continuing to complete acquisitions, a strategy it employed as it entered the mid-2000s. In December 2004, II-VI signed an agreement to acquire Marlow Industries, Inc., a $26 million-in-sales manufacturer of thermoelectric solutions for both cooling and power generation. II-VI marked the occasion with a press release issued December 13, 2004: "The Marlow acquisition represents a tremendous opportunity for II-VI Incorporated. Marlow's leading portfolio of thermoelectric cooling solutions complements our strong position in optical and optoelectronic components. . . . Our combined company will offer one of the broadest product arrays to space, defense, medical, industrial, and telecommunications markets."

Principal Subsidiaries

VLOC Incorporated; Exotic Electro-Optics, Inc.; II-VI Acquisition Corp.; II-VI Delaware, Incorporated; II-VI Holdings B.V. (Belgium); II-VI Deutschland GmbH (Germany); II-VI/L.O.T. GmbH (Germany; 75%); II-VI Singapore Pte., Ltd.; II-VI International Pte., Ltd. (Singapore); II-VI Optics (Suzhou) Co. Ltd. (China); II-VI Japan Incorporated; II-VI U.K. Limited; II-VI L.P.E. N.V. (Belgium); II-VI/L.O.T. Suisse S.a.r.l. (Switzerland; 75%); II-VI Beijing (China).

Principal Competitors

Röhm and Haas Company; Sumitomo Corp.; Ophir Optronics; Northrop Grumman Corporation; Raytheon Corporation.

Further Reading

Bates, Daniel, " 'Gutsy' II-VI Goes It Alone in Pacific Rim Market," *Pittsburgh Business Times,* November 29, 1993, p. 11.

Faustina, Sean Monique, "Pittsburgh-Based Firm Eyes Murrieta, Calif., Optical-Products Maker," *Business Press,* June 12, 2000, p. B3.

Gannon, Joyce, "Saxonburg's II-VI Inc. Launches IPO to Raise $8 Million," *Pittsburgh Business Times,* August 31, 1987, p. 1.

Guzzoo, Maria, "II-VI Looks to Narrow Playing Field, Grow Customer Base," *Pittsburgh Business Times,* October 1, 1999, p. 4.

Lott, Ethan, "II-VI Refuses to Concede, Ups Offer for San Diego-Based Competitor," *Pittsburgh Business Times,* June 9, 2000, p. 4.

McAuliffe, Don, "French Valley, Calif., Optics Maker Gets Sweeter Bid from Pittsburgh Rival," *Press-Enterprise,* June 6, 2000, p. B2.

——, "Pennsylvania Firm Emerges As Victor in Battle for California Laser Producer," *Press-Enterprise,* June 23, 2000, p. B1.

Reeves, Amy, "II-VI Inc.," *Investor's Business Daily,* July 7, 2004, p. A7.

Tucker, Darla Martin, "Pennsylvania-Based Optic Components Maker Lands on Market Radar," *Business Press,* January 28, 2002, p. 13.

—Jeffrey L. Covell

Ultimate Electronics, Inc.

321 West 84th Avenue, Suite A
Thornton, Colorado 80260-4824
U.S.A.
Telephone: (303) 412-2500
Fax: (303) 412-2501
Web site: http://www.ultimateelectronics.com

Public Company
Incorporated: 1968 as Pearse Electronics, Inc.
Employees: 3,497
Sales: $712.9 million (2004)
Stock Exchanges: NASDAQ
Ticker Symbol: ULTEQ
NAIC: 443112 Radio, Television, and Other Electronics
    Stores; 443130 Camera and Photographic Supplies
    Stores; 451220 Prerecorded Tape, Compact Disc, and
    Record Stores; 811211 Consumer Electronics Repair
    and Maintenance

Ultimate Electronics, Inc. is a leading specialty retailer of home entertainment and consumer electronics products in the Rocky Mountain, Midwest, and Southwest regions of the United States. At the end of 2004 the company was operating 65 stores: 54 Ultimate Electronics stores in Arizona, Idaho, Illinois, Iowa, Kansas, Minnesota, Missouri, Nevada, New Mexico, Oklahoma, South Dakota, Texas, and Utah; and 11 SoundTrack outlets in Colorado. The company's stores specialize in mid- to high-end audio, video, television, and mobile electronics products, sold by a knowledgeable staff of commissioned salespeople. Ultimate's future was in doubt, however, following its filing for Chapter 11 bankruptcy protection in January 2005. The filing was precipitated by a brutally competitive environment in consumer electronics retailing, as Ultimate Electronics found its sales and market share declining primarily as a result of the voracious growth of the two industry giants, Best Buy Co., Inc. and Circuit City Stores, Inc.

Pearse Electronics: 1968–93

Ultimate Electronics was founded as Pearse Electronics, Inc. by William Pearse, a business administration graduate of West-

ern Michigan University, and his wife, Barbara. William Pearse was working as a management trainee at the Gates Rubber Co. before he and Barbara started a Team Electronics audio/video franchise store in Arvada, Colorado—a suburb of Denver—in 1968, with $15,000 in personal funds. This franchise was abandoned in 1974, when the retail business was renamed Sound-Track. The second SoundTrack opened in Denver in 1976. During the 1980s six more SoundTrack stores were opened in the Denver area and Colorado's Front Range: in Aurora (1983), Littleton (1984), Boulder and Thornton (1985), a second Littleton store (1986), and Colorado Springs (1989). A Fort Collins store opened in 1990. Audio-related equipment was Sound-Track's core business at this time.

The SoundTrack chain grew not only by the establishment of new stores but also by the expansion of existing ones and the number of products each location carried. Pearse believed his employees, about 70 percent of whom were paid through incentive compensation, could make their own decisions and direct their own efforts without much supervision. Consequently, he kept down overhead by maintaining a management team of only four. All store managers were promoted from within the company. Customer service was given the highest priority: one of the company's top executives told a reporter, "The customer will generally get through [on the telephone] quicker than you would."

Pearse Electronics was willing to spend on advertising, however, publicizing SoundTrack through humorous commercials intended to distinguish the chain from hard-sell price-oriented rivals such as Best Buy and Fred Schmid. In 1990 the company's ads featured a hippopotamus. The following year it introduced a spokesperson/ventriloquist named Taylor Mason and his puppet, Romeo, who wore different costumes, such as a white jumpsuit for an Elvis Presley spoof. Interviewed in the *Denver Post,* an ad agency executive handling the SoundTrack account said, "Everybody is saying they have the lowest prices in town, so after a while there's a believability gap. We're having more fun and getting across a very competitive message as well."

Pearse Electronics had net sales of $53.7 million in fiscal 1992 (the year ended January 31, 1992) and net income of $1 million. In 1993 sales and income increased to $62.6 million and $2.1 million, respectively. The company changed its name to Ultimate

Electronics, Inc. in August 1993 and went public in October 1993, raising nearly $16 million by selling a minority of its common stock at $8.50 a share. The Pearse family, formerly the sole owner, retained about 60 percent of the company stock after the offering, and William Pearse continued to head the company as chairman and chief executive officer. The company said it planned to use the net proceeds of the offering to finance expansion into new markets. At this time SoundTrack was specializing in middle-market to upscale stereo equipment, television sets, and videocassette recorders and had about 375 employees.

Ultimate Electronics: 1993–96

In the fall of 1993 two new stores opened under the Ultimate Electronics name, in Salt Lake City and Orem, Utah—the first company outlets outside Colorado. These were also the company's largest, with about 19,000 square feet in selling space, compared with between 8,000 and 17,000 square feet for the earlier ones. One advantage of locating in Utah was that the market was yet untouched by huge retailers such as Best Buy and Circuit City, although Ultimate's company president pointed out, "There are lots of aggressive independents with low costs that can put products out there at low prices."

As part of a new strategy, the Ultimate Electronics stores expanded the home-office and television selections found in the SoundTrack stores. They added 100 to 200 CD-ROM titles and selections from the top 100-selling personal computer (PC) software titles and gave increased emphasis to PC accessories. The PC lineup was increased from four to five lines, including Packard Bell and Compaq, and from 10 to 15 models. Facsimile machine offerings were boosted from 10 to 15 models, including products from Brother International, Murata, Panasonic, and Sharp. The number of direct-view television sets up to 40 inches was expanded from 100 to 200 models, and a big-screen viewing room had a selection of 35 rear-projection sets starting at 40 inches. Each store had two home-theater rooms packed with audio/visual receivers, speakers, and other products as well as television sets, and two cars placed on the showroom floors to display car-stereo products.

Instant acceptance in Utah enabled Ultimate Electronics to end the fiscal year with net income of $3.4 million on net sales of $88.2 million. In September 1994 the company closed its Denver SoundTrack store and opened a 31,000-square-foot superstore in the city in what had been the Century 21 movie theater. It featured 200 television sets 32 inches or smaller, 40 large-screen projection televisions, a $30,000 home entertainment system with theater seats, and an automobile displaying a dashboard-mounted TV monitor.

During 1994 Ultimate Electronics opened new stores in Murray, Utah; Albuquerque, New Mexico; and Las Vegas, Nevada. In 1995 it opened stores in Layton, Utah; Boise, Idaho; Tulsa, Oklahoma; and a second one in Las Vegas. The new stores typically incorporated five separate audio demonstration rooms, three car-stereo demonstration rooms, two demonstration cars fully equipped with the latest in mobile electronics, two to three home-theater rooms, and a wide selection of television sets, with particular emphasis on big-screen televisions. Wall-unit furniture was among the product categories added.

Opened on Thanksgiving Day, 1995, the 51,700-square-foot, $4 million Tulsa location was Ultimate Electronics' biggest one yet. It had four auto sound rooms, five home-theater rooms, and at least 45 big-screen TVs. An in-house service department accommodated all products sold by Ultimate except computers (covered by a third-party service contract) and included repairs either under warranty or out of warranty.

During 1995 and 1996 Ultimate Electronics moved its two warehouses near Stapleton International Airport, its Wheat Ridge administrative offices, and its Thornton store to the abandoned 28-acre site of a former Thornton drive-in theater. Here the company built a 285,000-square-foot, $15 million complex, including a new headquarters and distribution warehouse, a service center, and a 40,300-square-foot retail superstore. The latter, which opened in April 1996, had five audio demonstration rooms, three home theaters, two cars on the showroom floor displaying the latest in mobile-audio technology, and a children's play area named "Kid City."

For the Colorado Rockies, the expansion major league baseball team that began playing in Denver in 1993, Ultimate Electronics sponsored an advertising display in the ballpark and player appearances. Popular manager Don Baylor became a spokesperson for the chain. In 1995, and again in 1996, the company ran commercial spots of Baylor to promote its Mitsubishi television products.

Ultimate Electronics' sales increased to $165.1 million in 1995 and to $251.8 million in 1996. Net income, which had been a record $4.9 million in 1995, dropped to $2.8 million, but this partly reflected a charge of nearly $1 million due to a change in the accounting method for preopening expenses. A decrease of comparable-store sales of 2 percent in 1996 compared with a 29 percent gain for such stores in 1995 was attributed to a sluggish retail environment, increased competition in the company's markets, and the opening of new stores within markets the company already served.

Ultimate Electronics adopted a shareholder rights plan in 1995 to discourage the possibility of a hostile takeover. The Pearse family owned about 46 percent of the stock in 1995. Long-term debt, chiefly to finance expansion, grew from $3.3 million at the end of 1994 to $33.7 million at the end of 1996.

1997 Acquisition of Audio King and Its Aftermath

By early 1997 Ultimate Electronics was operating 18 stores in six states. The company made its biggest expansion move yet in June 1997, snapping up Audio King Corporation in a deal valued at about $5.7 million. Like Ultimate, Audio King was a retailer specializing in the middle to upper end of the consumer electronics market. Based in Minneapolis, Audio King operated 11 stores: eight in Minnesota, two in Iowa, and one in South Dakota. It also owned Fast Trak Inc., the Midwest's largest independent audio/video electronics repairs service. Audio King reported a loss of $300,000 on sales of $65.6 million for 1996. Leading the newly enlarged company was Pearse, who remained chairman, and J. Edward McIntire, who was named CEO in August 1997. McIntire had been vice-president of operations, having joined Ultimate in 1995 from Standard & Poor's, a division of McGraw-Hill Cos.

During 1998, six of the Audio King stores were remodeled. Two of them were converted to the larger Ultimate Electronics format. (The largest Audio King unit had been 25,000 square feet in size, whereas the typical Ultimate Electronic/SoundTrack store encompassed 30,000 to 40,000 square feet.) Sales for 1998 jumped 10 percent, reaching $337.4 million, while the closely watched same-store sales figure was up 2 percent. Late in the year, the company shifted its merchandise mix. It got rid of most of its personal computer lines, which were generating little in the way of profits, in favor of an increased emphasis on such high-end products as high-definition television sets, DVD players, digital camcorders, and home theater systems. This overhaul paid immediate dividends. Through the second quarter of 2000, Ultimate Electronics enjoyed six consecutive quarters of same-store sales growth between 13 percent and 20 percent. Fiscal 2000 ended up being the company's best year yet, as net income surged nearly 74 percent to $14.6 million, while net sales amounted to $484.4 million, a 26 percent increase from the previous year. In July 2000 Ultimate expanded into Arizona via the opening of two stores in the Phoenix area. Helping to fund this expansion was a late 1999 secondary stock offering that raised more than $35 million. The proceeds also were used to pay down debt.

Early 2000s: Aggressive Expansion, Downfall into Bankruptcy

Ultimate Electronics launched an aggressive expansion program during 2000. By January 2004 the company had more than doubled in size, opening five new stores in 2000, ten in 2001, twelve in 2002, and seven in 2003. In addition to the aforementioned Phoenix, new markets established during this period were Oklahoma City, St. Louis, Dallas/Fort Worth, Kansas City, Wichita, and Austin. Further funding for this ambitious plan came from another secondary stock offering, completed in May 2002, yielding net proceeds of $84.8 million.

The timing for this expansion was inauspicious. The U.S. economy went into a prolonged slump, consumer confidence fell, and sales of consumer electronics dropped. Competition heated up, not only from arch-rivals Best Buy and Circuit City, but also from mass merchants such as Wal-Mart Stores, Inc. and Target Corporation, which began selling more consumer electronics gear. While the large number of new store openings helped propel Ultimate Electronics to double-digit growth in net sales through 2002, same-store sales fell 2 percent in both 2001 and 2002, a considerable cause for concern.

Ultimate responded during 2003 with a number of initiatives. The company dropped computer products from its stores altogether, converted the remaining Audio King outlets to the Ultimate Electronics brand, and launched several efforts to cut expenses. Despite these efforts, Ultimate suffered a net loss of $16 million for the fiscal year ending in January 2004. The company blamed the loss on continued high expenses, difficulties with a new $27 million management information system, which resulted in some items being out of stock during the all-important holiday selling season, and tough competition. Net sales grew only 1 percent for the year, while same-store sales fell 9 percent.

In January 2004 McIntire retired as CEO and was replaced by David J. Workman, who had served as president and chief operating officer since 1992. Workman placed further expansion on hold while trying to turn the company's fortunes around. Through the first nine months of 2004, however, Ultimate suffered a net loss of $31.1 million. Its cash was down to $1.9 million, suppliers began cutting off its credit lines, and it verged on the brink of bankruptcy. In December 2004 Mark J. Wattles, the founder and CEO of video rental giant Hollywood Entertainment Corporation, paid $1.9 million for a 10 percent stake in Ultimate Electronics. In mid-January 2005 he increased his stake to 31 percent, concurrent with the company filing for Chapter 11 bankruptcy protection. The holiday season failed to save Ultimate, as sales fell 8 percent in November and 18 percent in December. Various observers conjectured that the company had expanded too aggressively during an industry downfall and that the stores were too large to support a product lineup focused on the high end. Speculation about possible store closings began almost immediately. In any event, it seemed certain that Wattles, who was named chairman of Ultimate Electronics, faced a difficult turnaround task given the entrenched competition. Workman remained onboard as CEO, but Pearse resigned, along with the rest of the board of directors, some 36 years after founding the company.

Principal Subsidiaries

Fast Trak Inc.

Principal Competitors

Best Buy Co., Inc.; Circuit City Stores, Inc.

Further Reading

Alexander, Steve, "Turnaround Troubles at Ultimate," *Minneapolis Star Tribune,* September 21, 2004, p. 1D.

Baca, Stacey, "Thornton Lands Ultimate Power," *Denver Post,* January 30, 1995, p. B2.

Bunn, Dina, "Economy Sparks Merger," *Rocky Mountain News,* March 5, 1997, p. 1B.

Forgrieve, Janet, "Incoming CEO Ready to Make Ultimate Jump," *Rocky Mountain News,* December 24, 2003, p. 1B.

——, "SoundTrack Faces Ultimate Test: As Sales Drop, Market Changes, Analysts Wonder About Future," *Rocky Mountain News,* September 7, 2004, p. 1B.

——, "Struggling Ultimate on Brink of Chapter 11," *Rocky Mountain News,* December 14, 2004, p. 1B.

Heller, Laura, "In Search of the Ultimate CE Niche," *DSN Retailing Today,* February 25, 2002, pp. 21–23.

——, "Ultimate Electronics Ramps Up Short-Term Expansion Plan," *Discount Store News,* July 23, 2001, pp. 2, 26.

Johnson, Kimberly S., "SoundTrack Parent Will Try to Reorganize with Cash from Hollywood Video CEO," *Denver Post,* January 12, 2005.

Johnson, Kimberly S., and Aldo Svaldi, "Video Chief Buys Stake in Ultimate," *Denver Post,* December 24, 2004, p. C1.

Lieber, Ed, "More Consolidation: Ultimate and Audio King," *HFN—The Weekly Newspaper for the Home Furnishing Network,* March 10, 1997, p. 4.

Mahoney, Michelle, "Hippo Catches Attention for Evans, Sound-Track," *Denver Post,* June 18, 1990, p. C3.

——, "SoundTrack Projects Humor," *Denver Post,* February 10, 1992, p. C2.

Masters, Greg, "Another CE Chain Rides the Digital Wave," *Retail Merchandiser,* November 2002, p. 38.

McDonald, Natalie Hope, "Ultimate Electronics: The Big (and Bigger) of It," *Dealerscope,* August 2002, p. 28.

McGovern, Tim, "SoundTrack Eyes Top Slot in 2 States," *HFD—The Weekly Home Furnishings Newspaper,* September 19, 1994, p. 122.

McWilliams, Gary, "Electronics Seller Ultimate Files for Chapter 11," *Wall Street Journal,* January 12, 2005, p. B6.

Moore, Janet, "The Ulimate Merger," *Minneapolis Star Tribune,* June 4, 1997, p. 1D.

Parker, Penny, "Newest SoundTrack May Be Last in Colorado," *Denver Post,* September 24, 1994, pp. D1–D2.

Pate, Kelly, "Ultimate Tuned in to Digital Change," *Denver Post,* October 8, 2000, p. L1.

Seavy, Mark, "SoundTrack Expands into Utah," *HFD—The Weekly Home Furnishings Newspaper,* August 16, 1993, p. 83.

"Shareholder-Rights Plan Approved to Fight Takeovers," *Wall Street Journal,* February 2, 1995, p. A8.

"SoundTrack Parent to Go Public, Raise $16 Million," *Denver Post,* September 3, 1993, p. C2.

Sweeney, Patrick, "Ultimate Electronics: A Retail Success Story," *Denver Business Journal,* October 12, 2001.

"Ultimate Blames Poor Holiday Promotion Tack for 64% Profit Slide," *Warren's Consumer Electronics Daily,* March 14, 2003.

Vasquez, Beverly, "SoundTrack Benefits from Home Team Link," *Denver Business Journal,* April 12, 1996, p. A20.

—Robert Halasz
—update: David E. Salamie

United Road Services, Inc.

10701 Middlebelt
Romulus, Michigan 48174
U.S.A.
Telephone: (734) 946-3232
Fax: (734) 947-7902
Web site: http://www.unitedroad.com

Public Company
Incorporated: 1997
Employees: 1,726
Sales: $248.7 million (2002)
Stock Exchanges: Pink Sheets
Ticker Symbol: URSI
NAIC: 488410 Motor Vehicle Towing

United Road Services, Inc. (URSI) is a Romulus, Michigan-based company that provides towing services from operations located across the United States and Canada. URSI offers a variety of towing services in addition to road service, including automobile transport, heavy equipment transport, law enforcement towing, insurance salvage towing, private impound towing, and repossession services. Customers include government agencies, automakers, auto dealers, corporate fleets, motor clubs, insurance companies, and lending institutions. Created as a consolidator of the highly fragmented towing industry, URSI has been stifled in its attempts to become a national powerhouse. Instead, it has gone through a series of management changes, and seen its shares delisted and reduced to penny stock status. The company is owned by KPS Special Situations Funds, a New York private equity firm known as a buyer of last resort. Its shares are now sold on a pink sheet basis.

Towing Industry Highly Fragmented in the 1990s

URSI was incorporated in July 1997 as a roll-up vehicle in the towing industry, as had been done in any number of industries in recent years. The idea was inviting, given that towing and transport services generated about $15 billion a year in North America, and it certainly appeared viable because the towing industry was composed of thousands of mom-and-pop operations, perhaps 90 percent of the 50,000 towing companies operating in the United States. Moreover, many of these companies were owned by people ready to retire and who were willing sellers. Some of the eight towing companies that joined forces to create URSI fell into this category. Other trends also favored launching a national towing and transport company. There were more cars on the road than ever, a factor that would naturally increase demand for towing services. Across the country police were cracking down on unlicensed, unregistered, uninsured, and intoxicated drivers and contracting towing companies to remove the vehicles involved. An increasing number of vehicles were now under lease, about one out of three, and after coming off lease they had to be trucked to dealerships or auction houses to be resold. Finally, automakers were turning to transport companies to deliver vehicles to market and were inclined to contract with a reliable national supplier.

Heading the new enterprise as CEO and chairman was Edward T. Sheehan, who came to the towing industry from United Waste Systems, Inc., where he was familiar with the nature of consolidation. During his tenure at United Waste from 1992 to 1997, when Sheehan served as president and chief operating officer, United Waste was rolled up by USA Waste Services, Inc. Sheehan also spent two years as the chief financial officer of Clean Harbors Inc., a Massachusetts environmental services company. Prior to that stint he served in a variety of financial and operational positions with General Electric Company.

URSI's eight founding firms were Northland Auto Transporters Inc./Northland Fleet Leasing Inc. of Detroit; Milne Tow & Transport Service of Reno, Nevada; Quality Towing of Las Vegas; Caron Auto Works Inc./Caron Auto Brokers Inc. of East Hartford, Connecticut; Absolute Towing and Transporting Inc. of Los Angeles; Keystone Towing Inc. of Los Angeles; Falcon Towing and Auto Delivery Inc. of Los Angeles; and ASC Transportation Services of Sacramento. All told, these companies maintained 17 operations in Arizona, California, Connecticut, Florida, Michigan, Nevada, and New Jersey. In 1997 their combined assets totaled $76 million, and together they generated revenues of $46.5 million. In February 1998 URSI filed to make an initial public offering (IPO) of stock. The company hoped to raise $66 million, of which $32.3 million was ear-

360

Company Perspectives:

Our mission is to provide the highest standard of automobile and equipment towing, recovery, and transport services to customers on a local, regional, and national basis and to continuously strive for flexibility in servicing our customers' needs in an expedient and cost efficient manner.

marked to purchase the founding firms. The idea of a towing company roll-up was so well received by investors, however, that URSI raised $86 million when the offering was completed in May 1998. The stock then began trading on the NASDAQ, where it soon rose from its IPO price of $13 to a peak of $19.50.

Torrid Acquisition Pace Following 1998 IPO

Although URSI had no towing operations in the area, it established corporate headquarters in Colonie, New York, close to Albany, where Sheehan made his home. The company took a ''hub-and-spoke'' approach, with Colonie serving as the centralized hub for management, administration, dispatch, and maintenance operations, essentially offering support to the individual towing companies. The owners of the founding firms stayed on to manage their local operations and became directors of United Road. But Sheehan's focus was not on running the business as much as it was on growing the business. He was eager to begin acquiring towing companies as well as transport businesses, with the goal of creating an integrated national transport network. In this way, the regional towing operations could serve as feeders for the transport services. On the day it completed its IPO, URSI spent $32 million to acquire seven more companies, adding 15 operations in six states. Then, in July, it spent $40 million for another 12 companies. In August 1998, URSI announced a slate of 11 acquisitions, including Central Service Inc. of Albany, a deal that added a local flavor to the company. It was a fast pace, one well ahead of schedule, yet Sheehan was far from finished for the year: He had signed letters of intent for more than 60 additional purchases. By the end of the year he added a total of 41 companies to the fold at a cost of $210 million.

In November 1998, Sheehan arranged a $75 million infusion of cash by selling convertible subordinated debentures to Charterhouse Group International Inc., a New York City private investment firm. With these funds Sheehan was able to continue URSI's roll-up activity in 1999. In January of that month, the company bought four transport firms located in Montana, Tennessee, and Utah, and two towing companies located in Indiana and Tennessee. Moreover, Sheehan had another $265 million in additional acquisitions under discussion. But the buying spree would soon come to an end. The company was not performing up to expectations, quarterly earnings were poor, and investors responded by bidding down the price of URSI stock to around $4. In June the URSI board met, shortly after the announcement of disappointing second quarter numbers, and Sheehan was ousted as chairman and CEO. The company maintained that from the outset it anticipated that Sheehan would ultimately be replaced by a CEO who could make the assembled parts work more efficiently together, but no one expected the company to

grow as quickly as it had nor perform so poorly. Instead of achieving a 15 percent profit margin on the towing side of the business, URSI managed just 8.4 percent. Transport services had an 18 percent margin instead of the desired 20 percent.

While board member Donald F. Moorehead stepped in as acting chairman, and President and COO Allan Pass handled the day-to-day running of the business, a New York City executive recruitment firm, Korn Ferry International, was hired to find a new chief executive. As the search lingered, the company put a hold on further acquisitions in order to begin digesting what URSI had already bought. In October URSI finally settled on its new CEO, hiring Gerald Riordan. In addition, Richard Molyneux, an outside director, replaced Moorehead as chairman. Riordan came to URSI from Ryder Systems Inc., where he spent 24 years and held major management positions in a number of business segments, including inventory control, marketing, operations, pricing, and quality. He became president of two business units, consumer truck rental and public student transportation, and was instrumental in the revitalization of Ryder's consumer truck rental business.

Once in charge of URSI, Riordan moved quickly to stop the bleeding. He terminated a $225 million credit facility Sheehan had arranged before leaving, thus ending URSI's acquisitive ways, at least temporarily. He then formed separate committees to examine the state of the towing business and the transport side. After hearing back that the two groups had their own sets of problems to address, in early 2000 he effected a reorganization of the business, creating two operating units: towing/recovery and transport. Effectively out of a job, Pass resigned, and Riordan subsequently hired unit presidents: Harold Borhauer for towing and recovery and Michael Wysocki for transport. Borhauer had 28 years of experience in the field and was the founder of one of URSI's acquisitions, Phoenix-based Towing Professionals Inc. Wysocki brought 27 years of experience in the trucking industry and was the founder of URSI's largest acquisition, vehicle carrier MPG Transport Ltd. of Charlestown, Massachusetts. Both men would operate out of their home cities—Borhauer in Phoenix and Wysocki in Detroit—while Riordan worked out of the Colonie office. Riordan then for the first time brought together in Las Vegas all of the company's 66 managers, many of whom had never even met. Riordan said of that meeting to *Capital District Business Review,* ''The company didn't have that synergy, that 'team' feeling you want to draw on in good times and in bad. There were a lot of upset people in this company. Some of them own millions of shares of stock they got when they sold their companies, and they are as upset, if not more upset, than any outsider shareholders.'' By January 2000 URSI stock had fallen to about $1.50 per share.

During the Las Vegas gathering, URSI drew up a list of objectives, implemented a performance incentive program, and developed an action plan. A major objective was to become more efficient and to cut daily operating costs. To achieve this goal, URSI forged deals with suppliers to reduce the cost of gasoline, tires, and truck parts. To save money on workers' compensation claims, URSI also improved its safety training programs. The company also made some changes to the employee benefits program to cut costs. Riordan then took steps to shore up URSI's finances. He lined up a $25 million investment by Blue Truck Acquisition LLC, an affiliate of KPS Special

Situations Fund, L.P. KPS specialized in small companies that were in need of operational, financial, or strategic restructuring. The private equity firm also pledged to bring in other lenders. Because KPS was entitled to name 6 of the 11 directors on the URSI board, it effectively controlled the company. Riordan faced another serious challenge in the price of the company's stock, which in early May 2000 was trading at 75 cents per share, a far cry from the $20 range of a year before. Now the company was in danger of being delisted by the NASDAQ. To boost the price to more than $5 in order to remain listed, Riordan engineered a reverse 1-for-10 stock split. The gambit failed, however, and the stock was delisted and relegated to over-the-counter status.

A GE Capital affiliate, CFE Inc., bought $2 million in preferred shares and provided URSI with a $93 million credit facility in the summer of 2000. With the company's financial situation in good shape, Riordan hoped that URSI could now turn the corner, but the business continued to slip. After losing $29.7 million on revenues of $255 million in 1999, the company reported a loss of $159 million (including a $129 million impairment charge) on revenues of $247 million in 2000. The company sold off a number of underperforming units and took several steps to control costs, but 2001 offered little improvement. Throughout the year, the price of its stock hovered between 25 cents and 50 cents—or less than a nickel if viewed in terms of the price before the reverse split. The company man-aged to reduce its loss to $13.7 million in 2001, but that was hardly positive news for investors.

In January 2002 URSI made its first acquisition in almost three years, buying Auction Transports Inc., a Missouri transport company. It was a hopeful sign, but little more. Despite selling off unprofitable units, or simply closing them down, and initiating further cost cuts, URSI offered another disappointing balance sheet when the results of 2002 were tallied. The company lost another $84.7 million, on sales of $248.7 million. The company continued to perform poorly in 2003, and in April, Riordan resigned in order "to pursue other opportunities." He was replaced as CEO by Wysocki, who then moved the company's headquarters to the Detroit suburb of Romulus. He was able to convert some debt to stock, which helped to cut URSI's significant debt load, but it remained very much in doubt whether he would ever be able to turn around the business. The thought of being an industry consolidator, for the time being at least, was simply out of the question.

Principal Subsidiaries

URS Midwest, Inc.; URS Northeast, Inc.; URS Southeast, Inc,; URS Southwest, Inc.; URS West, Inc.; URS Leasing, Inc.

Further Reading

Boyer, Jeremy, "United Road Services Moves Headquarters from Colonie, N.Y., to Detroit," *Times Union,* May 14, 2003.

Johnston, Jo-Ann, "Albany, N.Y.-Area Towing Company Has National Aspirations," *Times Union,* May 26, 1999.

Pinckney, Barbara, "New Firm Carries Lots of Weight," *Business Review (Albany),* March 6, 1998.

——, "United Road Finds Itself Still Stuck in Ditch," *Business Review (Albany),* April 5, 2002, p. 7.

——, "United Road Pins Hopes on Radical Restructuring Program," *Capital District Business Review,* January 17, 2000, p. 6.

—Ed Dinger

W.C. Bradley Co.

1017 Front Avenue
Columbus, Georgia 31902
U.S.A.
Telephone: (706) 571-6056
Fax: (706) 571-6084
Web site: http://www.charbroil.com

Private Company
Founded: 1887 as Carter and Bradley
NAIC: 335221 Household Cooking Appliance
  Manufacturing

Family owned and operated by a fourth generation, the W.C Bradley Co. is a Columbus, Georgia-based company best known for its Char-Broil barbecue grill division, which is a major producer of gas, charcoal, and electric grills sold under the Char-Broil and Thermos labels. It also manufactures grills for Costco and Sears under the Kenmore brand. Char-Broil is part of the W.C Bradley Co. Home Leisure Group, which includes several other businesses. A full-service fulfillment company, Bradley Direct oversees the company's Grill Lover's catalog and web site business while also offering third parties its call center services, order processing, and shipping capabilities. Operating out of Menomonee Falls, Wisconsin, the Lamplight subsidiary offers indoor lamps and scented candles and outdoor torches, sold under the Lamplight and Tiki labels. Zebco is a Tulsa, Oklahoma-based company that designs and makes fishing tackle. The W.C Bradley Co. also runs the PGA Tour Stop, a 31,000-square-foot golf apparel, shoe, equipment, and gift store located in the World Golf Village in St. Augustine, Florida. Finally, the company operates the W.C Bradley Co. Real Estate Division, which develops and manages more than 60 commercial and residential properties in the Columbus, Georgia market.

Company's Founding in the 1800s

The W.C Bradley Co. has been involved in a wide range of commercial activities since it was founded in 1887 by William Clark Bradley and his brother-in-law, Samuel A. Carter. Bradley was born in 1863 on his family's plantation in Alabama. He

moved to Columbus, Georgia, in 1885 and went to work at a cotton factoring company called Bussey-Goldsmith. In 1887 he married Sarah M. Hall and soon became partners with her brother. They bought Bussey-Goldsmith, renaming it Carter and Bradley. They quickly moved beyond cotton factoring and began producing fertilizer for cotton farmers as well as launching a wholesale grocery business. Bradley also became involved in the banking business, acting as one of the founders of the Third National Bank and the Columbus Savings Bank, which would eventually merge and one day form the basis of a major financial services company, Synovus Financial. Bradley bought out Carter in 1895 and changed the company's name to W.C Bradley Co.

During the final years of the century, Bradley entered the textile industry. In 1896 he and a partner took over the largest textile operation in the South by acquiring the massive Eagle and Phenix Mills. He then supplemented the business by constructing the largest cotton warehouse in the South, which also would be put to good use by another venture in which Bradley participated during this period. As head of the Merchant and Planters Steamboat shipping line, he began shipping groceries and fertilizer, as well as passengers, down the Chattahoochee River to cotton plantations as far away as Florida. The boats then returned with cotton for his warehouses and mills. In 1917 he bought five of those downriver plantations, establishing a farming division that would grow into one of Georgia's largest family operations.

As successful as Bradley was in his many endeavors, the venture that made him an immensely wealthy man was the investor group he helped to organize with Earnest Woodruff. In 1919 they paid $25 million to acquire a struggling Coca-Cola Company, a purchase that almost did not materialize. Because the group was unable to borrow the money as a syndicate, Bradley had to personally borrow $4 million in New York to save the deal. Coca-Cola was first concocted in the 1880s by Dr. John S. Pemberton, and under the leadership of druggist Asa G. Candler the company became a thriving enterprise and a well-known brand. But Coca-Cola's growth was slowed by sugar rationing during World War I and slipped into a state of flux when Chandler retired in 1916. A bad sugar purchase after the war threatened the company's existence and ruptured relations

Company Perspectives:

The goal of the W.C Bradley Co. is to attain leadership as a multi-brand supplier of high quality consumer goods focused primarily on home leisure lifestyle markets and distributed through a variety of channels.

with its bottlers. Coca-Cola was in need of modernization, both in terms of equipment and leadership, and the company received both in the new ownership group. Bradley became chairman of the board, and Woodruff's son, 33-year-old Robert Woodruff, soon became president. Woodruff guided the company through the Great Depression of the 1930s and then oversaw a period of tremendous growth during and after World War II when Coca-Cola become an American icon and the company emerged as one of the country's first multinational corporations. Bradley served as chairman of Coca-Cola's board until 1946, after which members of his family continued to hold significant interests in Coca-Cola stock.

Bradley had one child, Elizabeth, who in 1917 married D.A Turner. Turner then became involved in Bradley's business ventures and was groomed to succeed his father-in-law. Nevertheless, Bradley remained very much in charge and active for another three decades. The W.C Bradley Co. continued to diversify during the 1920s. It established the Bradley Manufacturing Company after buying the Hamburger Cotton Mills in 1920 and later in the decade bought a majority interest in the Columbus Iron Works. A maker of armaments during the Civil War, the Iron Works in the 1870s produced the first commercial ice-making machines. Bradley expanded the plant's product lines to include wood and coal burning heaters and stoves and horse-drawn farming equipment, products without much future potential. In 1949 the Iron Works introduced a new item, producing its first Char-Broil Barbecue Grill.

Along the way, many of Bradley's ventures became outdated. In addition to dropping cast iron stoves and horse-drawn plows, the company exited the steamboat business and during the 1940s sold off its textile mills. In the final years of his life, Bradley, a very religious man, established the W.C and Sarah H. Bradley Foundation in 1943, an organization that would contribute millions of dollars to a wide range of charitable, cultural, and educational causes. Bradley died in July 1947 and was replaced as chairman of W.C Bradley Co. by Turner.

Grilling Gaining in Popularity After World War II

Although the bulk of the Turner family's wealth continued to come from Coca-Cola, much of its business activities centered around its barbecue grill product. Prior to this time, many houses featured brick or stone fireplaces in the backyard where outdoor cooking was done, and sometimes incinerators were modified to accommodate grilling. Many people created their own barbecue grills and smokers out of wine barrels, oil drums, trash cans, water heater tanks, and metal roofing. The wood they used as fuel, however, was far from convenient. Then, Henry Ford found a way to convert the sawdust and scrap wood that were left over from the making of wood frames for his Model T

automobile to fashion charcoal briquettes. His new business, The Ford Charcoal Company, would become better known for its location, Kingsford, Michigan. Although intended as a heating fuel, Kingsford charcoal was soon discovered to be perfectly suited for outdoor grilling. After World War II many veterans took advantage of the G.I. Bill to purchase vast numbers of suburban homes complete with backyards and patios. Barbecuing became even more widespread, although makeshift grills were still the order of the day. The introduction of the Char-Broil grill was perfectly timed, as manufactured grills now began to replace homemade affairs. In the early 1950s, George Stephen, part owner of Weber Brothers Metal Works, a Chicago sheet metal shop that produced half-spheres welded together to make buoys for Lake Michigan, invented the kettle grill by joining two of those half-spheres with a hinge. The Weber grill would go on to become a major force in the fast-growing grilling industry and Char-Broil's chief competitor.

For many years charcoal grills dominated the marketplace, but in the 1960s gas became a viable fuel, although these early units were connected to natural gas lines and thus anchored in place. Char-Broil added gas grills in the 1960s while Weber continued to concentrate on high-end charcoal grills. In 1973 the W.C Bradley Co. moved its manufacturing operations out of the Iron Works and into a modern plant in Bradley Industrial Park. (The Iron Works would be preserved as part of the Columbus Iron Works Trade and Convention Center.) Around the time of the move, propane tanks were introduced, marking a significant change in the grilling industry. Propane made gas grills portable, so that they could now be stored indoors during the winter. Weber made an attempt to incorporate gas into its line of grills, but quickly gave up, deciding instead to focus on charcoal grills. But by the mid-1980s, however, gas grills were beginning to make significant gains, despite a price that was much higher than charcoal grills. Many consumers were simply won over by the speed and convenience of gas. Sales of charcoal grills peaked in 1988, then steadily lost ground to gas grills. Char-Broil, and other competitors like Sunbeam, had claimed a major stake in the gas grill market before Weber was able to use its brand recognition to seriously enter the race with its Genesis line of high-end gas grills.

Fourth Generation Taking the Helm in the Late 1980s

While Char-Broil grew into an industry leader, the W.C Bradley Co. underwent changes in leadership. D.A Turner's son, William B. Turner, took over as chief executive officer in 1973, and after the elder Turner passed away in 1982 he assumed the chairmanship as well. By this time, a fourth generation was also active in the family business in the form of William B. Turner, Jr., and Stephen Turner Butler. The latter first went to work in the warehouse as a teenager and joined the company on a full-time basis in 1974. In 1987 William B. Turner retired, and his son became president and chief operating officer of W.C Bradley Co., and Butler was elected CEO and chairman.

Under new leadership, W.C Bradley Co. entered the 1990s very much focused on its grilling business, especially gas grills, which finally outsold charcoal grills in 1995. In fact, Char-Broil sales tripled from 1988 to 1995, growing at an average annual clip of nearly 20 percent, prompting W.C Bradley Co. to spend

Key Dates:

1887: William Bradley and Samuel Carter buy a cotton factoring company.
1895: The company is renamed W.C Bradley Co. after Bradley buys out Carter.
1919: Bradley becomes chairman of Coca-Cola Company and serves until 1946.
1947: Bradley dies.
1949: The company make its first Char-Broil grill.
1973: The third generation of the family begins running the company.
1987: Stephen Turner Butler becomes the fourth generation to head the company.
1998: Lamplight Farms Inc. is acquired.
2001: The company adds to its lighting business by acquiring Tiki Corp.; the company acquires Zebco Corp.
2002: The company forms its Home Leisure Group.
2004: The company announces the closure of its plant in Columbus and the transfer of manufacturing to China.

$14 million to expand its Columbus plants by 400,000 square feet. In addition to gas grills, the company also produced a small number of charcoal and electric grills, smokers, and other barbecue products and accessories. But the industry was highly competitive and now beginning to consolidate, forcing W.C Bradley Co. to keep growing or risk losing its place in the market. In December 1996 the W.C Bradley Co. acquired the barbecue grill division of Thermos Co. Only weeks later, in February 1997, the W.C Bradley Co. made a second acquisition, buying New Braunfels Smoker Co., a Texas company that manufactured heavy-duty charcoal grills, smokers, and accessories. It was an important addition, because charcoal was enjoying a resurgence, and Char-Broil had devoted little attention to charcoal grills during the previous decade. Moreover, it was clear that a large portion of the grilling market were purists dedicated to charcoal and would never buy a gas grill, and the W.C Bradley Co. wanted to make sure it earned a share of this sizable market as well. Another major acquisition followed in May 1998 with the purchase of Oklahoma Joe's, a Stillwater, Oklahoma company that manufactured upscale grills and smokers, as well as accessories, seasonings, and sauces. Oklahoma Joe's was a solid complement to New Braunfels, and its operations were transferred to the larger New Braunfels plant later in the year.

As the grilling industry evolved, the patio began to be seen as another room in the house, and because grills were often at the center of that space, grill manufacturers were well positioned to join the race to furnish that space. In 1998 the W.C Bradley Co. acquired Lamplight Farms Inc., a Menomonee Falls, Wisconsin company that made decorative outdoor torches as well as indoor lamps and oil and scented indoor candles. The W.C Bradley Co. then added to its lighting business in late 2001

by acquiring Tiki Corp. and its well-known brand of Tiki torches, plus the Longlighter brand of general-purpose lighters. Tiki was folded into the Lamplight subsidiary, although it would remain an autonomous business. In 2001 the W.C Bradley Co. completed another acquisition, but one that was out of keeping with the company's other recent additions. It bought Zebco Corp., a Tulsa-based fishing tackle subsidiary of The Brunswick Corp. What primarily attracted the W.C Bradley Co. to Zebco was the company's similar distribution system. In 2002 the W.C Bradley Co. formed its Home Leisure Group, which included Char-Broil, Lamplight, Zebco, and Bradley Direct. Bradley Direct began in 1980 and was a full-service third-party call center and order fulfillment operation that grew out of the grilling business. This step was part of the company's effort to become less dependent on the barbecue industry, as was the launch of the PGA Tour Stop store in Florida's World Golf Village.

But the W.C Bradley Co. remained one of the leading grill makers and was willing to spend the marketing dollars to battle Weber and make Char-Broil the most recognizable name in the industry. The company launched its "Keepers of the Flame" series of television commercials, which became all but ubiquitous on sports telecasts, in an effort to reach the target audience of men, ages 25 to 49. Although the Bradley company enjoyed a good measure of success on the marketing front, it was forced to face the unpleasant reality that it could no longer manufacture its Char-Broil grills in the United States and remain competitive. Because the products could be manufactured for 25 percent less in China, the W.C Bradley Co.'s management believed it had no choice but to close its plant in Columbus, where the company had been making grills for more than 50 years, and to transfer manufacturing to China. The decision was announced in November 2004, but management promised not to begin cutting the workforce until the summer of 2005.

Principal Divisions

Char-Broil; The W.C Bradley Co. Home Leisure Group; The W.C Bradley Co. Real Estate Division.

Principal Competitors

Maytag Corporation; Weber-Stephen Products Co.; Whirlpool Corporation.

Further Reading

Adams, Tony, "Columbus, Ga.-Based Company Buys Popular Outdoor Torch Firm," *Columbus Ledger-Enquirer,* December 13, 2001.
MacArthur, Kate, "Boy Meets Grill," *Advertising Age,* April 2, 2001, p. 10.
Wells, Garrison, "Georgia-Based Char-Broil, Grill Maker, to Buy Thermos Co.," *Columbus Ledger-Enquirer,* December 14, 1996.
Williams, Chuck, "Columbus, Ga.-Based Grill Maker to Move Manufacturing Operations to China," *Columbus Ledger-Enquirer,* November 17, 2004.

—Ed Dinger

Westfield Group

1 Park Circle
Westfield Center, Ohio 44251
U.S.A.
Telephone: (330) 887-0101
Toll Free: (800) 243-0210
Fax: (330) 887-0840
Web site: http://www.westfield-cos.com

Private Company
Incorporated: 1848 as Farmers Mutual Fire Insurance
   Company of Medina County
Employees: 2,000
Sales: $1.3 billion (2004 est.)
NAIC: 524126 Direct Property and Casualty Insurance
   Carriers

Based in Westfield Center, Ohio, Westfield Group (unrelated to the identically named Australian real estate conglomerate) is a major regional collection of eight insurance companies, serving customers in 26 states. Westfield offers a wide range of personal and commercial insurance products and services, including automobile, homeowners, burglary, general liability, business owners, inland marine, farm and livestock, fire, and fidelity and surety bonds. The firm's products are represented by more than 1,200 independent insurance agencies. In recent years, Westfield has expanded into the banking business, launching Westfield Bank, offering personal and business banking services as well as a mortgage division. Westfield also has started Westfield Services, providing data management and business processing services to insurance companies as well as outsourcing services to insurance agencies. In addition, Westfield has established Westfield Group Foundation, dedicated to positively impacting young people through sports, in particular golf. The foundation sponsors the national Junior PGA Championship.

Lineage Dating to the 1800s

The Westfield Center region of Ohio was first settled in 1820 and the town was founded in 1826, named after an early settler's hometown of Westfield, Massachusetts. During this period, Ohio quickly grew into a major agricultural state with a large number of farmers in need of fire insurance. Always a threat, whether one lived in town or in the country, fire was particularly dangerous for farmers, who lived too far from neighbors to receive help and could easily be put out of business or rendered homeless should a fire occur. There was no lack of ways for a fire to start, given the prevalence of oil lamps and later the use of straw-burning wooden threshing machines that habitually threw off sparks. The best protection, economically at least, was for farmers to pool their risks, in much the same way that they joined forces to build barns for one another. Private companies, generally based in the East, sprang up to offer fire insurance to Ohio farmers, but there was no guarantee that the well-groomed salesman driving a fine buggy pulled by a handsome set of horses would ever honor a claim. In the late 1840s Westfield Center was visited by such an insurance agent, who convinced most of the area's farmers to insure their property against fire with his company. When one of them suffered a loss in late 1847, however, and tried to make a claim, they soon learned that the salesman represented no one but himself and that they had been duped. During this period, mutual insurance companies also were being formed to offer honest coverage, but rather than paying a set premium, policyholders were assessed an equal amount at the end of the year to cover claims. Farmers and townspeople were lumped together, and because the cities suffered far less fire damage, farmers believed they were paying more for fire insurance than was fair.

There was one mutual insurance company, Western Farmers Mutual Insurance Company of Batavia, New York, that placed farmers and townspeople in separate pools. Westfield Center farmers became familiar with how this company did business when a traveling lecturer from Batavia, Andrew W. Young, paid a visit. After his talk, Young held court at the general store where he explained Western Farmers' approach to insurance. The locals were inspired to come together, despite their political, religious, and personal differences, to discuss whether they wanted to induce Western Farmers to provide coverage in their area or to form their own mutual fire insurance company along the same lines. The latter view won out handily and that same night a petition to the Ohio Legislature was drawn up, requesting a charter. It was approved on February 8, 1848, and the Farmers Mutual Fire Insurance Company of Medina County was born. Its first home was a room over the general store

Company Perspectives:

A Leader Today. A Leader Tomorrow. Westfield today is a leading regional insurance group. Our strength comes through relationships we have built with employees, independent agents, policyholders, and business partners. The product we offer is peace of mind, and our promise of protection is supported by a commitment to service excellence.

owned by Ben Austin. Three years later the company became known as Ohio Farmers Insurance Company, a name that would be kept for the next 114 years. (The same could not be said for Westfield Center, which for uncertain reasons also became known as LeRoy, Ohio, a name that was officially adopted in 1914; then in 1971 the town reverted to its original 1826 name of Westfield Center.)

In April 1848 an organizational meeting was held, at which time the board and officers were named. The first president was George Collier, a surveyor who in 1818 had fallen in love with the area while surveying the township and had moved his family there. The first agent the company hired was a Baptist minister named Thomas E. Inman, but no policies could be issued, according to the terms of incorporation, until the mutual had received $25,000 in insurance applications. The board was even more cautious, waiting until the total topped $50,000 in June 1848 before issuing its first policy to Jonathan Simmons, one of the founders, whose early enthusiasm was key to the company's creation. He soon replaced Collier as president of the insurance company, a post he held until 1851. The inexperienced managers of Ohio Farmers were fortunate that the company did not have to pay out any claims until a year after its formation, allowing the business to get on its feet. In September 1849, at its annual meeting, the company reported that it had 2,101 fire insurance policies in effect, covering more than $1.6 million in property. It had only paid out $752 while accumulating some $70,000 in cash and notes.

During the early decades of its existence, Ohio Farmers improved its name recognition through a pair of disparate events, helping to produce steadily increasing business. In 1854 the company honored a claim from a man named Michael Hagenbaugh, who had purchased a farm covered by Ohio Farmers but had failed to transfer the policy to his name before fire struck, destroying some of his property. The company was under no legal obligation to make reparations, but the board agreed to honor Hagenbaugh's request. Each director wrote down what he believed was a fair amount, and a check was written for the average: $327. It was money well spent, going a long way in convincing farmers that the company was honest and trustworthy. Eleven years later Ohio Farmers gained wider recognition, not from an act of generosity but by being a victim of an audacious robbery. On the night of April 3, 1865, thieves broke into the office, cracked the safe, and absconded with some $60,000 in cash and bonds, of which $8,000 belonged to townspeople who were sharing the safe. Tallied together, the company's assets at this time amounted to little more than $100,000, so the loss was substantial and occurred at a time when the company's prospects were far from assured. To

reassure policyholders the company had all of its agents place placards in their windows that read, "Losses paid in cash on the spot by the Ohio Farmers Insurance Company!," flanked by towers of dollar bills. Ironically, the theft provided more in the way of advertising than the money the company lost, as the mystery of the cracked safe made good newspaper copy and the Ohio Farmers name was spread to all corners of the state, resulting in an increased demand in business and the opening of new agencies across Ohio. The legendary Allan Pinkerton was hired to investigate the matter, and although he was able to track down, to his satisfaction, the three men who committed the crime, the perpetrators were able to use law enforcement connections to avoid prosecution, and in the end Ohio Farmers recovered less than $10,000 of the stolen money and bonds. The company would have to be content with an unexpected windfall in free publicity.

Fifth President Beginning 42-Year Tenure in 1870

In 1870 James C. Johnson became Ohio Farmers' fifth president. A lawyer and former speaker of the Ohio House of Representatives, he would serve as president for 42 years until his death at the age of 93 in 1912. He saw the company through the panic of 1873 and ensuing five years of depression. Despite a significant loss of business during this period, in 1877 he led Ohio Farmers into neighboring Indiana, marking the first time the company ventured outside Ohio to do business. Within a matter of years it was operating in more than a dozen states. It was also during this period that Ohio Farmers first began using a picture of a bearded farmer sitting on a fence as its logo, a variation of which is still used today. By 1891 the company reached the $1 million mark in direct premiums. Two years later another of the periodic economic panics gripped the nation, followed by a four-year depression. Ohio Farmers also had to contend with a series of heavy losses, including a major fire in Milwaukee, and a $300,000 investment in bridge bonds that were falsely rumored to be worthless. Many policyholders lost faith in the company and either canceled their policies or opted not to renew them. Johnson met the matter head on, stuffing a satchel with cash and taking to the road in his horse and buggy to personally pay out claims on the spot in crisp, slick greenbacks. Word of his visits got around, confidence was restored, and policy renewals began to trickle in.

Johnson was replaced as president in 1912 by Frank H. Hawley, whose family members had served the company since the beginning. Under Hawley, Ohio Farmers began doing business on the East Coast, added automobile insurance, and started an inland marine department. In 1929 the company established Ohio Farmers Indemnity Company to write more comprehensive casualty coverage than Ohio Farmers Insurance was permitted to offer. Hawley held the top post for 28 years, until 1940, thus putting Ohio Farmers in the hands of just two men for 70 years and providing the kind of continuity that helped the small-town insurer to grow into a major company. To help guide Ohio Farmers through the difficult Depression years of the 1930s Johnson leaned on vice-president and lawyer Charles Don McVay, who then succeeded Johnson as president in 1940, providing even more stability in the top spot, as he headed Ohio Farmers until 1956. During his tenure, Ohio Farmers celebrated its 100th anniversary, at which point it had $10 million in net premiums and assets of more than $14 million between the Ohio Farmers companies.

Strong Growth in the 1960s

McVay was replaced by Jean C. Hiestand, who served as president for just two years before being succeeded by Charlie E. Curtis. General Counsel since 1939 and vice-president since 1949, Hiestand was instrumental in taking steps to ensure the company's rapid growth in the 1960s. In 1963 the company became involved in life insurance, forming Colonial Heritage Life Insurance Company. In 1965 Hiestand oversaw the formation of Ohio Farmers Insurance Group, consisting of Ohio Farmers Insurance Company, Colonial Heritage, and Superior Risk Insurance Company (the name Ohio Farmers Indemnity Company took in 1959). In that same year, Hiestand stepped down in favor of the company's tenth president, Thomas B. Rowe, who had been with the company for more than 30 years. In 1968 Ohio Farmers expanded further, adding three new companies to the group—Ohio Farmers Investment Company, O.F. Equity Sales Company, and Ohio Farmers Growth Fund—to market mutual funds and other financial products through existing agents. A year later Westfield Investment Fund, Inc. was incorporated, and in 1970 it changed its name to Westfield Income Fund, Inc. Also in 1968 Westfield Insurance Company was created and joined the Ohio Farmers stable of companies. Although it was adding to its products and services, the company also was narrowing its geographic focus. The East Coast business launched in 1912 was sold in 1969, and soon the company began to focus on Ohio and other Midwestern states, and the Pacific Coast. In 1971, the group was renamed the Westfield Companies for the sake of continuity, although Ohio Farmers Insurance Company remained the legal parent company. Also during Rowe's tenure, Westfield added to the professionalism of the organization, starting the company's first formal in-house training program and launching a profit-sharing plan. It was under Rowe's successor as president, Charlie Bishop, that Westfield in the mid-1970s sponsored its first national golfing event, the National Insurance Youth Golf Classic.

It was not until 1992 that Westfield made the first acquisition in its 145 years of existence, paying $89.7 million for Beacon Insurance Company of America, a move that removed a competitor and significantly expanded agency representation in Ohio. It was also the start of an extended period of expansion.

At this stage Westfield generated revenues in excess of $670 million. Guiding the company through these times was the company's 13th president, Cary Blair, who assumed the post in 1986. Westfield completed another acquisition in 1995, adding the Economy Farm business in Indiana, Illinois, Iowa, and Wisconsin. Westfield also introduced niche products for home, auto, and businesses in 1995. Faced with rapid consolidation in the insurance industry, in 1998 Westfield formulated an acquisition strategy in an effort to become a major regional property-and-casualty insurer, focusing on companies in the Southeast and Midwest. To fund this expansion, rather than go public Westfield elected to exit the life insurance business, selling Westfield Life Insurance Co. to Guarantee Life Cos. for $90 million in cash and $10 million in Guarantee Life stock. In that same year, Westfield achieved some diversity by forming Westfield Services, Inc. to provide outsourcing services to insurance companies and agencies, including data management and customer service.

Westfield completed another acquisition in May 2000, paying approximately $45 million for Old Guard Group Inc., a Lancaster, Pennsylvania-based insurer. It was also in 2000 that the company, after a year's worth of research, decided to replace the Ohio Farmers Insurance Group with Westfield Group. In addition, it launched Westfield Group Foundation, a charitable organization devoted to the promotion of scholarship, benevolence, competitive spirit, and ethical conduct among young people. Late in 2000 Westfield received permission from the Office of Thrift Supervision to open a federally chartered bank, like many insurers taking advantage of lowered regulatory barriers to enter the banking field. By the same token, banks were now encroaching on the traditional territory of insurance companies, making for increased competition across both industries. Westfield Bank immediately began doing business on the Internet and in 2002 opened a new home office in Westfield Center. The new bank offered checking, savings, money market accounts, certificates of deposit, individual retirement accounts, as well as a full range of business and real estate loans, and consumer, mortgage, and home equity loans. Much of the lending business was the result of referrals from independent insurance agents working for Westfield Group.

By 2004 Westfield was generating $1.3 billion in annual sales. While the insurance industry continued to undergo consolidation, there was every reason to believe that Westfield, now more than 150 years old, would find a way, as it had in the past, to continue to prosper and grow for the foreseeable future.

Principal Subsidiaries

Ohio Farmers Insurance Company; Westfield Insurance Company; Westfield National Insurance Company; American Select Insurance Company; Old Guard Insurance Company.

Principal Competitors

The Allstate Corporation; Prudential Financial, Inc.; State Farm Mutual Automobile Insurance Company.

Further Reading

Condon, George E., and Willard Largent, *History of Ohio Farmers Insurance Company,* Westfield Center, Ohio: Westfield Companies, 1985.

Gjertsen, Lee Ann, "For Ohio Insurer's Thrift, Name of Game Is Referrals," *American Banker,* February 28, 2001, p. 6.

O'Boyle, Maureen, "Ohio Farmers, Beacon Adjusting to Marriage," *Business First-Columbia,* April 5, 1992, p. 7.

Reynolds, Victoria, "A Brand New Day," *SBN Magazine – Akron,* January 2002.

Serres, Christopher, "Westfield Plans Acquisitions to Insure Its Future," *Crain's Cleveland Business,* September 14, 1998, p. 1.

—Ed Dinger

Wincor Nixdorf Holding GmbH

Heinz-Nixdorf-Ring 1
Paderborn
D-33106
Germany
Telephone: +49 5251 69 98 0
Fax: +49 5251 693 67 67
Web site: http://www.wincor-nixdorf.com

Public Company
Incorporated: 1952 as Labor für Impulstechnik
Employees: 6,000
Sales: EUR 1.58 billion ($1.9 billion) (2004)
Stock Exchanges: Frankfurt
Ticker Symbol: WNXDF
NAIC: 334111 Electronic Computer Manufacturing;
   333313 Office Machinery Manufacturing; 423430
   Computer and Computer Peripheral Equipment and
   Software Merchant Wholesalers; 511210 Software
   Publishers; 541512 Computer Systems Design
   Services; 811211 Consumer Electronics Repair and
   Maintenance

Wincor Nixdorf Holding GmbH is one of the world's leading manufacturers of automated teller (ATM) and electronic point-of-sale (EPOS) machinery, equipment, and software. The company, based in Paderborn, Germany, is that country's market leader, and number three in the world, in both categories. Wincor Nixdorf is also number one in Europe for EPOS equipment for the retail sector, and number two in Europe for ATMs. Production takes place in Germany and at its Asian-region headquarters in Kallang, Singapore. Wincor Nixdorf focuses on two core sectors, including the retail banking market for its ATM and self-service terminal systems, such as information terminals and statement and voucher printers. The company also sells its ProClassic/Enterprise software, adding international support for Internet and telephone banking services. Retailers form Wincor Nixdorf's other major area of operation, for which the company provides POS systems as well as shelf-labeling, "reverse vending systems" (for returns of items such as refillable bottles and containers), and other retail-oriented systems. The company supports these products with inventory management and related information software. In addition to its hardware and software production, Wincor Nixdorf also provides a range of support services for its bank and retailer customers, including call-screening and part supply logistics, as well as IT outsourcing services. Once one of Germany's major computer companies, then part of Siemens, before being spun off in the late 1990s, Wincor Nixdorf returned to the Frankfurt Stock Exchange in 2004. In that year the company posted sales of EUR 1.58 billion ($1.9 billion).

Germany's Pride in the 1950s

For much of the postwar era Nixdorf Computer epitomized the Wirtschaftswunder, Germany's extraordinary recovery from the devastation of war. From its headquarters in the provincial town of Paderborn, Nixdorf built a worldwide reputation for quality and innovation in the field of small- and medium-sized computers, becoming a source of considerable pride in a country still suffering from the war's physical and psychological wounds. In the year following the death of Heinz Nixdorf, the charismatic founder and owner of the corporation, Nixdorf was honored as 1987's "most admired German company." By the end of the 1980s, after a decade of more than 20 percent annual sales growth, there was talk of Nixdorf eventually challenging the world's computer leaders.

Yet by 1989, the erstwhile pride of Germany was headed for bankruptcy, a victim of one of the sudden storms that periodically lash the international computer industry. By early 1990 the company had been sold to German industrial giant Siemens. Heinz Nixdorf's miraculous creation remained Nixdorf in name alone, but Germany as a whole maintained control of one of its symbols of economic strength.

Heinz Nixdorf was born in Paderborn in 1925, the son of a railway clerk. After service in the Luftwaffe at the end of World War II, he enrolled at Frankfurt University to study physics and business but left before taking a degree. With a small amount of borrowed capital, Nixdorf founded his own company, the Labor für Impulstechnik, in a basement workshop in Essen in 1952. He devised and built a calculator using radio tubes and sold it to

---

West Germany's largest electrical utility, the Rheinische Westfalische Elektrizitatswerke. Word spread of Nixdorf's innovative machines, and Impulstechnik began supplying some of Europe's leading electrical manufacturers with products they later sold under their own names. Chief among these customers were Groupe Bull of France and Wanderer Werke in West Germany.

When the former was bought out by General Electric in 1964 the resulting drop in Nixdorf sales taught its founder an important lesson. Henceforth his company would not rely on such unpredictable relationships with industrial giants. It would manufacture and sell its own equipment. Nixdorf developed a line of calculators and billing machines superior to those it supplied to Wanderer and quickly proceeded to out-sell its own best customer. Nixdorf soon simplified matters by buying out Wanderer—considered a remarkable coup for a 15-year-old company. Nixdorf thus acquired extensive production facilities and a widespread sales force, with which it set about revolutionizing the use of computers in small businesses and banking.

In the mid-1960s few people yet envisaged any but IBM's theory of computer utilization, in which ever-larger central processing units handled a growing amount of corporate data from a single location. Heinz Nixdorf recognized that most companies did not need more computational muscle. They needed to put such tools to work efficiently. To do so, they required two elements IBM was not particularly interested in supplying including small, versatile computers and a sales force willing to tailor such machines to the specific needs of each customer. This strategy was not only generally sound but also addressed the realities of the West German economy, whose companies tended to be smaller, family-owned concerns not capable of IBM-style investments but still in need of computing efficiency. For these users Nixdorf brought out its 820 general-purpose minicomputer in 1968, adding both the sales force and software needed to adapt such a machine to the daily needs of each small-business client. As a result of this campaign, Nixdorf sales rose from DEM 28 million in 1966 to DEM 263 million four years later, beginning the pattern of explosive growth that did not end until the debacle of 1989.

During the 1970s Nixdorf continued to defy conventional wisdom by exploiting the niche it had uncovered. The company's first international sale provided the Swedish banking industry with 1,000 terminals for its various branch locations, and by 1972 Nixdorf had opened sales and manufacturing centers in 21 other countries as well. The most important foreign target was the United States, but Nixdorf met with only limited success in the U.S. market. In 1969 it bought the electronic division of Victor Comptometer, a U.S. manufacturer of office equipment, and in 1977 it added the Massachusetts-based Entrex, Inc., but at no time was Nixdorf able to gain more than 1 percent of the U.S. market. It was not that the company seemed in need of additional sales. By 1978 Nixdorf had passed DEM 1 billion in sales and employed some 10,000 people around the world.

Heinz Nixdorf and his family still owned 100 percent of the company stock, which some observers felt gave Nixdorf a decided advantage over its main German competitor, Siemens, a multibillion-mark conglomerate unable to keep up with the rapidly changing computer world. Although such a concentration of ownership offered more flexibility and the ability to move quickly, it also limited the company's capital base, and in 1978 Nixdorf dallied with a number of suitors eager to buy up large chunks of the corporation. However, the entrepreneur refused to relinquish control, instead making a conditional sale of 25 percent of his stock to longtime ally Deutsche Bank in 1979.

Siemens to the Rescue in the 1990s

In addition to its traditional strength in small businesses and banking, Nixdorf expanded in 1974 to provide information services for the retail sector. Nixdorf's retail involvement primarily involved point-of-sale equipment, an area in which the company became one of the European leaders. The fourth leg of Nixdorf's marketing platform was in place by 1982, when its new telecommunications division created Germany's first digital telephone switching system. Heinz Nixdorf predicted that telecommunications would provide 50 percent of corporate revenue by the century's end, as the gradual convergence of telecommunication and computer systems opened a vast new field known as integrated service digital networks.

To pursue such goals Nixdorf needed yet more capital, and in 1984 the company made its initial public offering (IPO) of stock, first in West Germany and then also on the Swiss markets. Response was outstanding, as expected for a company whose 1984 sales had reached DEM 3.27 billion and continued to climb at about 21 percent per year. Heinz Nixdorf had become something of a legend in his native land; the employer of 20,000 skilled German workers was a symbol of that country's unflagging determination to remain a world leader in the crucial computer industry.

When the founder died unexpectedly of a heart attack while dancing at a company party in March 1986 his employees were stunned, but none doubted that under new Chairman Klaus Luft the Nixdorf ascent would continue. At that time the company offered both a full line of IBM-compatible minicomputers, workstations, and terminals, and a new series of TARGON machines using the UNIX "open" operating system which was the only real competitor to that of IBM.

Nixdorf was Europe's largest seller of software and had built perhaps the world's most dedicated, knowledgeable sales force to help its many smaller customers make intelligent use of the machines and programs they purchased. The company always

Key Dates:

1952: Heinz Nixdorf founds Labor für Impulstechnik in Paderborn, Germany, and begins supplying calculators to third parties.

1964: Nixdorf begins selling calculators and billing machines under its own name.

1968: The company develops the minicomputer.

1969: The company acquires the United States' Victor Comptometer.

1982: A telecommunications division is established.

1984: The company makes its first public offering of stock on the Frankfurt Stock Exchange.

1986: Heinz Nixdorf dies at a company party.

1989: Nixdorf's losses top DEM 1 billion and the company is acquired by Siemens.

1992: The company is renamed as Siemens Nixdorf Informationssysteme (SNI).

1996: The company refocuses on the personal computer market, becoming the largest in Germany and the second largest in Europe.

1998: The company sells its personal computer division to Acer; Siemens spins off SNI as a new company, Siemens Nixdorf Retail and Banking Systems GmbH, specializing in ATM and electronic point-of-sale (EPOS) markets.

1999: The company is acquired by venture capital firm Kohlberg Kravis Roberts and Goldman Sachs Capital Partners, renamed as Wincor Nixdorf, and delisted from the Frankfurt Stock Exchange.

2000: The company begins providing IT services, including IT outsourcing.

2004: Wincor Nixdorf is re-listed on the Frankfurt Stock Exchange.

worked from the customer to the machine, not vice versa, in that way earning the kind of loyalty that ensures repeat sales. For all of these reasons, therefore, the financial community was puzzled when it became apparent that 1988 profits were not going to be as spectacular as Nixdorf had expected. As the months went by, a rather embarrassed Klaus Luft admitted that profits would indeed not be spectacular at all, except in a wholly negative sense: Profits for the year were DEM 26 million, down 90 percent from the previous year's record DEM 264 million.

The year 1989 proved to be an unprecedented nightmare for Nixdorf. A first half loss of DEM 297 million snowballed into a second half nearly twice as bad. By the end of the year, the company's losses had topped DEM 1 billion, wiping out nearly all of the company's profit from the decade before. Since Deutsche Bank and the Nixdorf family, who still controlled 100 percent of the voting stock, were determined to keep the company in German hands, the Siemens buyout was the most advantageous solution.

Nixdorf was overcome by an unfortunate combination of factors mostly outside its control. The company suffered a triple blow from the economy at large. The price of computer chips skyrocketed; the Nixdorf mix of sales shifted rapidly from high-margin bank installations to low-margin office and retail work; and, most important, increased world competition and standardization of products severely depressed hardware prices. The international movement toward so-called open systems meant that an increasing percentage of equipment was interchangeable, which drove standard part prices down and forced competitors to "add value" to their own products in order to justify a higher final price. Nixdorf thus found itself paying more for the computer chips with which it assembled machines that sold only at lower prices. The element the company could have better managed was the excessive growth of its highly paid personnel, most of them software designers and engineers.

Despite such difficulties, Siemens was happy to pay $350 million for its smaller cousin. The acquisition gave Siemens a strong position in the midrange computer market, where it was previously weak, and made the parent company the seventh largest computer maker in the world. For the Nixdorf family, the deal brought to an abrupt end one of Germany's most successful postwar economic creations, as another maverick entrepreneur was swallowed up by a larger competitor whom only a few years before it had consistently outperformed in the marketplace.

Independent and Focused in the 2000s

Renamed as Siemens Informationssysteme, and then as Siemens Nixdorf Informationssysteme (SNI), the marriage between Siemens and Nixdorf quickly floundered. Indeed, some observers recognized that Siemens's acquisition had been doomed from the start. This was in large part due to Nixdorf's overemphasis on the micro-computer market. While this market had been one of the major sectors in the computer industry in the 1980s, by the early 1990s it had become in large part obsolete—crushed by the rise of the personal computer (PC) and the development of efficient networking systems. With the collapse of the microcomputer market, Nixdorf had little left to offer other than operations in a few small niche areas.

SNI's losses remained high in 1991, topping DEM 780 million, which did not include more than DEM 200 million in additional "restructuring charges." Yet, despite a thorough restructuring, the group's losses continued into the mid-1990s. In 1992, the company's losses were still greater than DEM 500 million, and dropped slightly, to DEM 420 million, at the end of 1993.

In response, SNI brought in a new CEO, Gerhard Schulmeyer, who formerly had been with Asea Brown Boveri. Schulmeyer represented the first time an outsider had come in to run Nixdorf, and the company now began a massive shift in its operations, refocusing its production on the one hand on the PC market, and on the other on financial transaction support machinery and equipment, such as ATMs and EPOS systems.

By the mid-1990s, SNI had regained some of Nixdorf's former glory. In 1996, the company appeared reborn, posting sales of nearly DEM 14 billion ($9 billion), placing it as Germany's number one computer company, and number two in Europe, trailing only IBM. Yet the company had made few inroads in penetrating the all-important U.S. computer market. As such, into the late 1990s, amid a surge in PC sales, SNI fell behind competitors such as IBM, Compaq, Hewlett-Packard, Dell, and fast-growing Acer. Unable to compete, Siemens announced its decision to sell off its PC operations to Acer in 1998.

The sell-off led to a spinoff that year of what was left of SNI into a new company, Siemens Nixdorf Retail and Banking Systems GmbH. That company was set up as a separate and independent company from Siemens, and refocused to target the retailing and retail banking markets with its ATM and EPOS systems. In 1999, Siemens sold off the former SNI entirely, in a buyout led by the venture capital firm Kohlberg Kravis Roberts and Goldman Sachs Capital Partners.

The company then took on its new name, Wincor Nixdorf, and began building its stature not only as one of Europe's leading manufacturers of ATMs and EPOS systems, but as a global player, with operations in more than 60 countries supported by a subsidiary network in more than 30 countries.

In the early 2000s, Wincor Nixdorf added a range of IT support services to its portfolio, responding to an increasing cross-industry trend toward outsourcing services. As such Wincor Nixdorf not only developed support services for its own range of equipment and software, but also for third parties. By the middle of the decade, the company had begun to offer full-service IT outsourcing services for its retail banking customers.

Wincor Nixdorf reincorporated as a joint stock company, leading to its IPO in May 2004. The listing on the Frankfurt Stock Exchange represented one of the first major IPOs since the crash of Germany's IPO market in the early 2000s. By the end of its 2004 year, Wincor Nixdorf had posted profits of EUR 116 million on sales of nearly EUR 1.6 billion ($1.9 billion). The company now turned its attention to further expansion, with a particular focus on growth in the Asian markets. Wincor Nixdorf carried the legacy of one of Germany's great economic successes into the new century.

Principal Subsidiaries

Pt. Wincor Nixdorf (Indonesia); Siemens Nixdorf B.V. (Netherlands); Wincor Nixdorf A/S (Denmark); Wincor Nixdorf AB (Sweden); Wincor Nixdorf AS (Norway); Wincor Nixdorf Asia Pacific (Singapore); Wincor Nixdorf Bilgisayar Sistemleri A.O. (Turkey); Wincor Nixdorf C.A. (Venezuela); Wincor Nixdorf Ltd. (Korea); Wincor Nixdorf Ltd. (Ireland); Wincor Nixdorf Oy (Finland); Wincor Nixdorf Retail & Banking Systems Ltd. (China); Wincor Nixdorf Retail and Banking Systems Sp. z.o.o. (Poland); Wincor Nixdorf S.R.L. (Italy); Wincor Nixdorf Sdn. Bhd. (Malaysia); Wincor Nixdorf Soluçoes em Tecnologia da Informaçao Ltda. (Brazil).

Principal Competitors

International Business Machines Corporation; NEC Corporation; Motorola Inc.; Teradata Corporation; NCR Corporation.

Further Reading

Chen, Sandy, "Acer Acquires Siemens Unit," *Electronic Buyers' News,* April 27, 1998, p. 10.
Panni, Aziz, "Nixdorf's Salvation Army," *International Management,* June 1994, p. 40.
"Siemens Nixdorf Makes Plans for New U.S. Market Push," *Chain Store Age,* July 1995, p..36.
"Wincor-Mehrheit jetzt im Streubesitz," *Borsen-Zeitung,* June 22, 2004.
"Wincor Nixdorf Plant zukaufe in China und Nordafrika," *Handelsblatt,* December 14, 2004.
"Wincor Nixdorf Reopens German IPOs After Two Year Gap," *Euroweek,* May 21, 2004, p. 28.

—Jonathan Martin
—update: M.L. Cohen

XEROX®

Xerox Corporation

800 Long Ridge Road
Stamford, Connecticut 06904
U.S.A.
Telephone: (203) 968-3000
Toll Free: (800) 828-6396
Fax: (203) 968-3218
Web site: http://www.xerox.com

Public Company
Incorporated: 1906 as The Haloid Company
Employees: 59,300
Sales: $15.7 billion (2003)
Stock Exchanges: New York Chicago Boston Cincinnati
   Pacific Philadelphia London Swiss
Ticker Symbol: XRX
NAIC: 333315 Photographic and Photocopying
   Equipment Manufacturing; 334119 Other Computer
   Peripheral Equipment Manufacturing; 333313 Office
   Machinery Manufacturing; 518210 Data Processing,
   Hosting, and Related Services

Xerox Corporation, though virtually synonymous with photocopying, makes printers, scanners, fax machines, multifunction devices, and digital printing and publishing systems in addition to its flagship black-and-white and color copiers. The firm's related services operations encompass consulting, imaging, content management, and document outsourcing services. Increasingly expanding beyond its black-and-white offerings, Xerox now derives more then 20 percent of its revenues from color printers, copiers, digital presses, and related services and supplies. Approximately 45 percent of revenues are generated by the company's numerous overseas offices, subsidiaries, and joint ventures. Fuji Xerox Co., Ltd., a joint venture with Fuji Photo Film Co., Ltd., 25 percent owned by Xerox and 75 percent by Fuji, develops, manufactures, and distributes document processing products in Japan and the Pacific Rim (including Australia, New Zealand, Indonesia, Malaysia, the Philippines, Singapore, South Korea, Taiwan, Thailand, Vietnam, China, and Hong Kong).

Origins As The Haloid Company in 1906

Xerox can trace its roots to 1906, when a photography-paper business named The Haloid Company was established in Rochester, New York. Its neighbor, Eastman Kodak Company, ignored the company, and Haloid managed to build a business on the fringe of the photography market. In 1912 control of the company was sold for $50,000 to Rochester businessman Gilbert E. Mosher, who became president but left the day-to-day running of the company to its founders.

Mosher kept Haloid profitable and opened sales offices in Chicago, Boston, and New York City. To broaden the company's market share, Haloid's board decided to develop a better paper. It took several years, but when Haloid Record finally came out in 1933 it was so successful that it saved the company from the worst of the Great Depression. By 1934 Haloid's sales were approaching $1 million. In 1935 Joseph R. Wilson, the son of one of the founders, decided that Haloid should buy the Rectigraph Company, a photocopying machine manufacturer that used Haloid's paper. To help pay for the acquisition, Haloid went public in 1936, and selling Rectigraphs became an important part of Haloid's business.

In 1936 Haloid's 120 employees went on strike for benefits and higher wages. When Mosher proved intransigent, Wilson stepped in and offered concessions. Tension and resentment between labor and management persisted until World War II. During the war the Armed Forces needed high-quality photographic paper for reconnaissance, and business boomed. When the war ended Haloid faced stiff competition from new paper manufacturers.

Amidst this, Haloid needed to come up with new products, particularly following a showdown between Mosher, who wanted to sell Haloid, and Wilson, who did not. Wilson won, and in 1947 Haloid entered into an agreement with Battelle Memorial Institute, a nonprofit research organization in Columbus, Ohio, to produce a machine based on a new process called xerography.

Xerography, a word derived from the Greek words for "dry" and "writing," was the invention of Chester Carlson. Carlson was born in Seattle, Washington, in 1906 and became a patent lawyer employed by a New York electronics firm. Frustrated by the difficulty and expense of copying documents, Carlson in 1938 invented a method of transferring images from one piece of paper to another using static electricity. In 1944 Battelle signed a royalty-sharing agreement with Carlson and began to develop commercial applications for xerography.

Debut of the XeroX Copier in 1949

In 1949, two years after Haloid signed its agreement with Battelle, Haloid introduced the XeroX Copier, initially spelled with a capital X at the end. The machine, which required much of the processing to be done manually, was difficult and messy to use and made errors frequently. Many in the financial community thought that Haloid's large investment in xerography was a big mistake, but Battelle engineers discovered that the XeroX made excellent masters for offset printing, an unforeseen quality that sold many machines. Haloid invested earnings from these sales in research on a second-generation xerographic copier.

In 1950 Battelle made Haloid the sole licensing agency for all patents based on xerography, but Battelle owned the basic patents until 1955. Haloid licensed the patents liberally to spread the usage of xerography to such corporations as RCA, IBM, and General Electric. In 1950 Haloid sold its first commercial contract for a xerographic copier to the State of Michigan. Meanwhile, Haloid's other products were again highly profitable, with paper sales increasing and several successful new office photocopying machines selling well.

In 1953 Carlson received the Edward Longstreth Medal of Merit for the invention of xerography from the Franklin Institute. In 1955 Haloid revamped its 18 regional offices into showrooms for its Xerox machines instead of photo-paper warehouses, hired 200 sales and service people, began building the first Xerox factory in Webster, New York, and introduced three new types of photography paper. Haloid also introduced the Copyflo, Haloid's semiautomatic copying machine. In 1956 Haloid President Joe Wilson, Joseph R. Wilson's son, formed an overseas affiliate called Rank Xerox with the Rank Organisation Plc, a British film company seeking to diversify. This arrangement paved the way for Xerox factories in Great Britain and a sales and distribution system that brought Xerox machines to the European market.

1960: The Xerox 914 Copier, an Instant Hit

In 1958 Haloid changed its name to Haloid Xerox Inc., reflecting its belief that the company's future lay with xerography, although photography products were still more profitable. That balance quickly changed with the success of the Xerox 914 copier. Introduced in 1960, it was the first automatic Xerox copier, and the first marketable plain-paper copier. The company could not afford a blanket advertising campaign, so it placed ads in magazines and on television programs where it hoped business owners would see them. The company also offered the machines for monthly lease to make xerography affordable for smaller businesses.

Demand for the 650-pound 914 model exceeded Haloid Xerox's most optimistic projections, despite its large size. *Fortune* later called the copier "the most successful product ever marketed in America." Sales and rental of xerographic products doubled in 1961 and kept growing. In 1961 the company was listed on the New York Stock Exchange, changed its name to Xerox Corporation, and photography operations were placed under the newly created Haloid photo division. In 1962 Xerox formed Fuji Xerox Co., Ltd. in Japan with Fuji Photo Film Co., Ltd. Also during the 1960s Xerox opened subsidiaries in Australia, Mexico, and continental Europe. The company had sunk $12.5 million into developing the 914 copier, more than Haloid's total earnings from 1950 to 1959, and the 914 had led the company to more than $1 billion in sales by 1968. In 1963 Xerox introduced a desktop version of the 914, Although this machine sold well, it was not very profitable, and Xerox depended on its larger machines thereafter.

With its suddenly large profits, Xerox began a string of acquisitions, purchasing University Microfilms in 1962 and Electro-Optical Systems in 1963. The market for copiers continued to expand at such a rate that they remained Xerox's chief source of revenue. The 1960s were a tremendously successful time for Xerox, which became one of the 100 largest corporations in the United States and, in 1969, moved its headquarters to Stamford, Connecticut.

In the late 1960s Xerox began to focus its efforts on the concept of an electronic office that would not use paper. With this end in mind the corporation bought a computer company, Scientific Data Systems, in 1969, for nearly $1 billion in stock, only to have it fail and close down in 1975. Xerox also formed Xerox Computer Services in 1970, bought several small computer firms in the next few years, and opened the Xerox Palo Alto Research Center (PARC) in California.

In 1973 scientists at PARC invented what may have been the world's first personal computer. So innovative was the work of the PARC scientists that many features they invented later appeared on Apple Macintosh computers. In fact, in December 1989 Xerox would sue Apple Computer for $150 million, alleging that Apple had stolen the technology that helped make its computers so successful. Apple cofounder Steven Jobs, who later hired some researchers from PARC, claimed that his company had refined Xerox's work, and thus made it original.

PARC's innovations were largely overlooked by Xerox. The computer division and the copier division competed for resources and failed to communicate. Products were released by the office products division in Dallas, Texas, which PARC had never seen before. Disagreements broke out at Xerox headquarters at the suggestion of change, which further stifled innovation.

Struggling Through the 1970s and 1980s

In April 1970 IBM introduced an office copying machine, giving Xerox its first real competition. IBM's machine was not

Key Dates:

1906: The Haloid Company is founded in Rochester, New York, as a photography-paper business.

1935: Haloid buys Rectigraph Company, a maker of photocopying machines.

1936: Haloid makes its first public offering of stock.

1938: Chester Carlson invents a method of transferring images from one piece of paper to another using static electricity, a process dubbed xerography.

1947: Haloid enters into an agreement with Battelle Memorial Institute to produce a photocopying machine based on xerography.

1949: Company introduces the XeroX Copier.

1956: Haloid expands into Europe through the creation of Rank Xerox, a joint venture with the Rank Organisation Plc, a British film company.

1958: Company changes its name to Haloid Xerox Inc.

1960: Introduction of the Xerox 914, the first automatic, plain-paper copier, proves to be a huge success.

1961: Company is renamed Xerox Corporation, and its stock is listed on the New York Stock Exchange.

1962: Xerox joins with Fuji Photo Film Co., Ltd. in creating the 50–50 joint venture Fuji Xerox Co., Ltd.

1969: Headquarters for Xerox are moved to Stamford, Connecticut.

1970: Xerox Palo Alto Research Center opens in California.

1982: The 10-Series copier line debuts.

1994: Xerox begins touting itself as The Document Company and increases emphasis on digital products.

1995: Company increases its stake in Rank Xerox to 80 percent.

1997: Xerox buys out its European partner in Rank Xerox, which is subsequently renamed Xerox Limited.

1998: XLConnect Solutions Inc. is acquired.

2000: Xerox acquires Tektronix, Inc.'s color printing and imaging unit; as red ink begins to flow, massive restructuring is launched.

2001: Xerox sells half of its stake in Fuji Xerox to Fuji Photo Film for more than $1.3 billion; manufacturing outsourcing relationship with Flextronics International Ltd. begins.

2002: Company agrees to pay $10 million civil penalty to settle the charges of accounting fraud.

as fast or as sophisticated as the Xerox copiers, but it was well built and was backed by IBM's reputation. Xerox responded with a suit charging IBM with patent infringement. The dispute was settled in 1978 when IBM paid Xerox $25 million. Meanwhile, Xerox itself became a defendant in several antitrust violation investigations, including a lawsuit by the Federal Trade Commission. Distracted from its market by legal battles, Xerox lost its lead in the industry when Kodak came out with a more sophisticated copier. IBM and Kodak followed a strategy similar to that of Xerox, leasing their machines and attracting many large accounts on which Xerox depended.

According to most critics, Xerox had become inefficient during this time, as its executives had concentrated too heavily on growth during the 1960s. Xerox had spent hundreds of millions of dollars on product development but introduced few new products. Engineers and designers were divided into small groups that fought over details as they missed deadlines. While the company sought to perfect the copying machine, it failed to challenge the new products on the market, and Xerox's market share dropped.

By 1985 Xerox's worldwide plain-paper copier share had dropped to 40 percent, from 85 percent in 1974. Yet Xerox's revenues grew from $1.6 billion in 1970 to $8 billion in 1980, partially because Xerox began to sell the machines it had been renting, thus depleting its lease base.

Beginning in the mid-1970s, Japanese products emerged as an even more dangerous threat. Xerox machines were big and complex and averaged three breakdowns per month. The Japanese firm Ricoh Company, Ltd., however, introduced a less expensive, smaller machine that broke down less often. The Japanese strategy was to capture the low end of the market and move up. By 1980 another Japanese competitor, Canon Inc., was challenging Xerox's market share in higher-end machines.

In the late 1970s Xerox began reorganizing, making market share its goal and learning some lessons about quality control and low-end copiers from its Japanese subsidiary. The company also cut manufacturing costs drastically. Xerox regained copier market share, but intense price competition kept copier revenues around $8 billion for most of the 1980s.

In 1981 Xerox finally began releasing new products, beginning with the Memorywriter typewriter. This typewriter soon outsold IBM's and captured over 20 percent of the electric typewriter market. By January 1983 Xerox had unveiled a Memorywriter that could store large amounts of data internally. In 1982 the 10-Series copiers, the first truly new line since the 1960s, was introduced. These machines used microprocessors to regulate internal functions and were able to perform a variety of complicated tasks on different types of paper. They were also smaller and far less likely to break down than earlier Xerox copiers. The 10-Series machines used technology developed at PARC, which was becoming more integrated with the company. Xerox began gaining market share for the first time in years, and morale improved.

Xerox also released computer workstations and software and built a $1 billion business in laser printers. The workstations proved an expensive flop, however, and by 1989 the company closed its workstation hardware business. Xerox also moved to protect its 50 percent share of the high-end market in the United States with machines that made 70 or more copies per minute. The major high-end competition was Kodak, but the Japanese, led by Ricoh, were again launching a drive for this market.

During the 1970s Xerox had also diversified into financial services. In 1983 it bought Crum and Forster Inc., a property casualty insurer, and in 1984 it formed Xerox Financial Services, Inc. (XFS), which bought two investment-banking firms in the next few years. By 1988 XFS supplied nearly 50 percent of Xerox's income—$315 million of the $632 million total. XFS performed well, able to raise funds at a low cost because it was backed by the Xerox "A" credit rating.

Xerox spent more than $3 billion on research and development in the 1980s looking for new technologies, such as those for digital and color copying, to promote growth. Xerox was a leader in developing technologies, but often had trouble creating and marketing products based on them, particularly computers.

A Late 1980s Comeback

In 1988 Xerox underwent a $275 million restructuring, cutting 2,000 jobs, shrinking its electronic typewriter output, dropping its medical systems business, and creating a new marketing organization, Integrated Systems Operations, to get new technologies into the marketplace more effectively. Xerox's comeback was so impressive that in 1989 its Business Products and Systems unit won the U.S. Congress's Malcolm Baldridge National Quality Award for regaining its lead in copier quality. Xerox had demonstrated its ability to change in the late 1970s when it responded to the first wave of Japanese competition.

In 1990 when David T. Kearns, CEO since 1932, retired to become U.S. Deputy Secretary of Education, and Paul A. Allaire, a career Xerox man, was named to replace him, industry analysts speculated that Allaire would have to repeat the feats of the 1970s if Xerox were to survive as an independent corporation. A restructuring of company management occurred almost immediately. The office of the president was transformed into a document processing corporate office led by Allaire and including Executive Vice-Presidents A. Barry Rand and Vittorio Cassoni, and Senior Vice-Presidents Mark B. Myers and Allan E. Dugan. Two years later, Xerox announced plans to restructure the company as well. Three customer service operations units were created in Connecticut, New York, and England. In addition, nine document processing business units were established, each of which was headed by a president responsible for the profitability of the unit.

During the seven-month period from September 1990 to March 1991, Xerox introduced five new types of computer printers: the Xerox 4350, Xerox 4197, Xerox 4135, Xerox 4235, and Xerox 4213. These printers were designed to handle a wide variety of office needs from two-color printing to desktop laser printing. In October 1990 the Docu-Tech Production Publisher signaled Xerox's intent to take advantage of what the company foresaw as an industry move from offset printing to electronic printing and copying.

The introduction of the Xerox 5775 Digital Color Copier was met with great fanfare and was expected to rejuvenate sales. Xerox also continued to update and improve its facsimile machines by developing a personal-sized model that could be used as a copier as well as a telephone, and by developing thermal, recyclable fax paper. In May 1992 Xerox introduced Paperworks, software making it possible to send documents to a fax machine directly from a PC.

Despite these new products, financial and legal woes continued to plague Xerox in the early 1990s as American economic conditions worsened. After earnings of $235 million in the fourth quarter of 1990, Xerox reported only $91 million in profits for the same period the following year. Earlier in 1990, just four months after the creation of the X-Soft division, which was to develop and market the company's software products, Xerox announced that it would lay off 10 percent of X-Soft's employees. In February 1992 the company offered severance pay to 6,000 of its American employees in an attempt to reduce the workforce by 2,500 by July.

By the end of 1991, Xerox was announcing the sale of three of its insurance wholesalers. Crum and Forster sold Floyd West & Co. and Floyd West of Louisiana to Burns & Wilcox Ltd. London Brokers Ltd. was sold to Crump E & S. Moreover, several lawsuits resulted in losses for Xerox during this time. In February 1992 Xerox was ordered to pay Gradco Systems, Inc. $2.5 million to settle a patent dispute, and a suit settled in favor of Monsanto a month later was expected to cost Xerox $142 million to clean up a hazardous waste dump site.

Emergence of The Document Company in the Mid-1990s

With its core office products businesses on the upswing, Xerox announced in January 1993 that it intended to exit from insurance and its other financial services businesses. Later that year Crum and Forster was renamed Talegen Holdings Inc. and was restructured into seven stand-alone operating groups in order to facilitate their piecemeal sale. This exit took several years, however, and was delayed when a 1996 deal to sell several units to Kohlberg Kravis Roberts & Company for $2.36 billion collapsed. During 1995 two of the groups were sold for a total of $524 million in cash. In 1997 three more were sold for a total of $890 million in cash and the assumption of $154 million in debt. Then in January 1998 Xerox completed the sale of Westchester Specialty Group, Inc. to Bermuda-based ACE Limited for $338 million, less $70 million in transaction-related costs. Finally, Xerox in August 1998 sold its last remaining insurance unit, Crum & Forster Holdings, Inc., to Fairfax Financial Holdings Limited of Toronto for $680 million.

As it was exiting from financial services, Xerox was also beginning to shed its image as a copier company. In 1994 Xerox began calling itself The Document Company to emphasize the wide range of document processing products it produced. A new logo included a red "X" that was partially digitized, representing the company's shift from analog technologies to digital ones. A number of new digital products were developed over the next several years, including digital copiers that also served as printers, fax machines, and scanners (so-called multifunction devices). From 1995 to 1997 revenue from analog copiers was virtually stagnant, even falling slightly, whereas revenue from digital products enjoyed double-digit growth, increasing to $6.7 billion by 1997.

Xerox also shifted focus from black-and-white to highly sought-after color machines, with revenues from color copying and printing increasing 46 percent to $1.5 billion in 1997. The most notable introduction here was the DocuColor 40, launched in 1996, which captured more than 50 percent of the high-speed color copier market based on its ability to print 40 full-color pages per minute. Revitalized new product development at Xerox resulted in the introduction of 80 new products in 1997 alone, the most in company history and twice the number of the previous year. More Xerox products were being developed for the small office/home office market, with prices low enough that the company increasingly marketed its products via such retailers as CompUSA, Office Depot, OfficeMax, and Staples.

However, the new Xerox was about more than just office products. The company introduced DocuShare document-management software in 1997, providing a system for users to post, manage, and share information on company intranets. Xerox also gained the leading market share position in the burgeoning document outsourcing services sector through the 1997-created Document Services Group. This group offered such services as the creation of digital libraries, the design of electronic-commerce systems for Internet-based transactions, as well as professional document consulting services. In May 1998 Xerox bolstered its Document Services Group through the $413 million acquisition of XLConnect Solutions Inc. (renamed Xerox Connect) and its parent Intelligent Electronics, Inc. XLConnect specialized in the design, building, and support of networks for companywide document solutions.

The mid-1990s also saw Xerox launch a restructuring in 1994, leading to 10,000 job cuts over a three-year period. In February 1995 the company paid The Rank Organisation about $972 million to increase its stake in Rank Xerox to 80 percent. Then in June 1997 Xerox spent an additional $1.5 billion to buy Rank out entirely. With full control of the unit, Xerox renamed it Xerox Limited. That same month G. Richard Thoman, who had been senior vice-president and chief financial officer at IBM, was named president and chief operating officer of Xerox, with Allaire remaining chairman and CEO.

In April 1998 Xerox announced yet another major restructuring, as its shift to the digital world led it to spend more on overhead than its competitors. The company eliminated 9,000 jobs over the next two years, taking a $1.11 billion after-tax charge in the second quarter of 1998 in the process. The cuts came at a time when Xerox was enjoying record sales and earnings as well as a surging stock price, so the company was clearly proactive in maintaining the momentum it had gained through its impressive 1990s resurgence.

Late 1990s Downfall/Early 2000s Turnaround Effort

This resurgence, however, came to a crashing halt during the later months of 1999. For both the third and fourth quarters, Xerox was forced to issue warnings that its profits would be well below the expectations of Wall Street analysts, sending its stock tumbling. Sales and profits were hurt by a number of factors, several of which were out of the company's control: the strength of the dollar against European currencies; heightened competition from Japanese rivals, particularly Canon, which launched new lines of midrange and high-end copiers that ate into Xerox's market share; a slump in the sales of high-end copiers and printing systems late in the year because of Y2K fears; and a severe economic downturn in Brazil, a longtime key market for Xerox that had been responsible for about 10 percent of sales and an even-larger portion of profits. On top of these challenges, Xerox shot itself in the foot by botching two corporate restructurings. A consolidation of customer administration centers launched in 1998 led to chaos, including delayed and lost orders, unreturned phone calls, and billing errors. During 1999 Xerox reorganized its worldwide sales force, shifting about half of the 30,000-person operation from a geographic

focus to an industry focus. Although this change was long overdue, it was not implemented smoothly, leading to disgruntled staffers, furious customers, and lost sales. Also burdening the company was servicing some $16 billion in total debt.

Early in 2000 Xerox acquired the color printing and imaging unit of Tektronix, Inc. for $925 million. The move made Xerox the number two player in the U.S. market for color laser printers, trailing only Hewlett-Packard Company. The deal was an important one, coming at a time when in many offices the proliferating computer printer was taking over some of the functions of the copier. Before it could bear fruit, however, a management shakeup jolted the company. As the firm's financial performance deteriorated, Thoman was forced to resign as CEO in May 2000. Allaire temporarily reassumed that position, and company veteran Anne M. Mulcahy was named president. By this time, Xerox's stock had fallen 60 percent from its level one year earlier.

In October 2000 the company reported a third-quarter loss of $167 million—its first quarterly loss in 16 years—and initiated the first of a string of restructuring programs. Aiming to slash $1 billion in annual operating expenses (6 percent of its total costs), Xerox placed a number of assets on the block. Late in the year it sold its subsidiaries in China and Hong Kong to Fuji Xerox for $550 million. Then in March 2001 Xerox sold half of its stake in Fuji Xerox itself to Fuji Photo Film for more than $1.3 billion in cash, reducing its interest in the joint venture to 25 percent. In another key move, Xerox outsourced about half of its worldwide manufacturing operations to Flextronics International Ltd., at the same time selling to Flextronics plants in Canada, Mexico, Malaysia, the Netherlands, and Brazil. Several other noncore operations were also sold off as part of this overhaul, which in total culled 11,200 positions from the payroll. During 2001 a separate restructuring, which aimed to sharpen the company's focus, saw Xerox eliminate product lines aimed at the small office/home office business segment. Approximately 1,200 more employees were laid off. Xerox eliminated its stock dividend that year in order to conserve cash, and in August, Mulcahy was named CEO. She replaced Allaire as chairman in early 2002.

Late in 2000 the Securities and Exchange Commission (SEC) launched an investigation into Xerox's accounting practices for the period from 1997 to 2000. The SEC eventually found that the company had been improperly accounting for revenues associated with office equipment it leased to customers, booking more of the lease revenue up front than was proper and thereby artificially—if temporarily—inflating revenue and, according the SEC, misleading investors. In April 2002 Xerox agreed to pay a record $10 million civil penalty to settle the charges. A few months later it restated its results for 1997 to 2001, shifting $1.41 billion in pretax income among the years. For instance, for 1998 the company now reported a pretax loss of $13 million rather than the previously reported pretax profit of $579 million, whereas the pretax loss for 2001 of $293 million was trimmed to $71 million. The SEC went after several Xerox executives as well. In June 2003 the agency reached an agreement with six executives (five former and one current, including Allaire, Thoman, and former CFO Barry Romeril), who agreed to pay $22 million in fines and other penalties. The

SEC was highly critical of the managers, contending that they had personally profited from bonuses and stock sales that had been based on false financial results.

In addition to shedding unprofitable businesses and lines of business, and eliminating tens of thousands of workers from the workforce (which was reduced by one-third from the beginning of 2001 to the end of 2003, from 92,500 to 61,100), Xerox vastly improved its balance sheet. During 2002 a $7 billion line of credit was successfully renegotiated, while the following year saw the completion of a $3.6 billion recapitalization plan that included public offerings of common stock, the issuance of convertible preferred stock, and the securing of a new $1 billion credit facility. Total debt was reduced from $18.64 billion in 2000 to $11.17 billion in 2003. Perhaps most importantly, Xerox moved aggressively to regain lost market share by introducing 38 new products during 2002 and 2003 as well as a wide range of new document-related services. The product line placed particular emphasis on digital and color copiers and enhanced multifunction devices capable of printing, copying, scanning, faxing, and e-mailing.

Through Mulcahy's able leadership and dogged pursuit of a turnaround, Xerox was able to post strong results for 2003. Net income of $360 million was the firm's highest profit level since 1999. Xerox's stock rebounded in 2003 and 2004, although it remained well below the levels of 1999 and early 2000. Debt was reduced further during 2004 to less than $10 billion, and the now cash-rich company was poised to begin pursuing acquisitions again. From the real possibility of bankruptcy when she took over, Mulcahy had engineered at least the beginnings of a remarkable comeback, though the competitive environment showed no sign of becoming less brutal.

Principal Subsidiaries

Palo Alto Research Center Incorporated; Xerox Credit Corporation; Xerox Financial Services, Inc.; Xerox Canada Inc.; Xerox GmbH (Germany); Xerox Limited (U.K.). The company also lists some 250 additional subsidiaries in the United States, Canada, Mexico, Argentina, Brazil, Chile, Colombia, Costa Rica, Dominican Republic, Ecuador, Guatemala, Haiti, Honduras, Nicaragua, Panama, Peru, Venezuela, Austria, Belgium, Bulgaria, Czech Republic, Denmark, Finland, France, Germany, Greece, Hungary, Ireland, Italy, Luxembourg, the Netherlands, Norway, Poland, Portugal, Romania, Russia, Slovenia, Spain, Sweden, Switzerland, Turkey, Ukraine, the United Kingdom, Yugoslavia, Egypt, Morocco, China, India, and elsewhere.

Principal Competitors

Canon Inc.; Ricoh Company, Ltd.; Hewlett-Packard Company; Sharp Corporation; Konica Minolta Holdings, Inc.

Further Reading

Alexander, Robert C., and Douglas K. Smith, *Fumbling the Future: How Xerox Invented, Then Ignored, the First Personal Computer,* New York: William Morrow, 1988, 274 p.

Arner, Faith, and Adam Aston, "How Xerox Got Up to Speed," *Business Week,* May 3, 2004, p. 103.

Bandler, James, and John Hechinger, "Six Figures in Xerox Case Are Fined $22 Million," *Wall Street Journal,* June 6, 2003, p. A3.

Bandler, James, and Mark Maremont, "Xerox to Pay $10 Million in SEC Case," *Wall Street Journal,* April 2, 2002, p. A3.

Bianco, Anthony, and Pamela L. Moore, "Downfall X: The Inside Story of the Management Fiasco at Xerox," *Business Week,* March 5, 2001, pp. 82–88, 90, 92.

Brady, Diane, Ira Sager, and Janet Rae-Dupree, "Xerox: Can New CEO Rick Thoman Turn Its Digital Dreams into Reality?," *Business Week,* April 12, 1999, pp. 92–96, 98, 100.

Byrne, John A., "Culture Shock at Xerox," *Business Week,* June 22, 1987, pp. 106+.

Byrnes, Nanette, "Xerox Is Dreaming in Color," *Business Week,* December 13, 2004, p. 70.

Byrnes, Nanette, and Anthony Bianco, "Xerox Has Bigger Worries Than the SEC," *Business Week,* August 12, 2002, pp. 62–63.

Campanella, Frank W., "Versatile Xerox: Company Builds Up Basic Copier Line, Moves to Diversify," *Barron's,* September 29, 1980, pp. 9+.

Dessauer, John H., *My Years with Xerox,* Garden City, N.Y.: Doubleday, 1971.

Deutsch, Claudia H., "Original Thinking for a Digital Xerox," *New York Times,* April 15, 1997, pp. D1, D6.

Driscoll, Lisa, "The New, New Thinking at Xerox," *Business Week,* June 22, 1992, pp. 120+.

Eisenberg, Daniel, "An Image Problem at Xerox," *Time,* October 30, 2000, pp. 63–64.

Hamilton, David P., "United It Stands: Fuji Xerox Is a Rarity in World Business: A Joint Venture That Works," *Wall Street Journal,* September 26, 1996, p. R19.

Jacobson, Gary, and John Hillkirk, *Xerox: American Samurai,* New York: Macmillan Publishing, 1986, 338 p.

Kahn, Jeremy, "The Paper Jam from Hell," *Fortune,* November 13, 2000, pp. 141–42, 146.

Kearns, David T., and David A. Nadler, *Prophets in the Dark: How Xerox Reinvented Itself and Beat Back the Japanese,* New York: Harper Business, 1992, 334 p.

Moore, Pamela L., "She's Here to Fix the Xerox," *Business Week,* August 6, 2001, pp. 47–48.

Morris, Betsy, "The Accidental CEO," *Fortune,* June 23, 2003, pp. 58–60+.

Narisetti, Raju, "Pounded by Printers, Xerox Copiers Go Digital," *Wall Street Journal,* May 12, 1998, pp. B1, B6.

——, "Xerox Aims to Imprint High-Tech Image," *Wall Street Journal,* October 6, 1998, p. B8.

——, "Xerox to Cut 9,000 Jobs Over Two Years," *Wall Street Journal,* April 8, 1998, pp. A3, A6.

——, "Xerox to Sell Crum & Forster for $565 Million," *Wall Street Journal,* March 12, 1998, p. B6.

——, "Xerox to Sell Resolution Group for $612 Million in Cash, Securities," *Wall Street Journal,* September 10, 1997, p. B4.

Nevans, Ronald, "Xerox's Billion-Dollar Mistake," *Financial World,* June 18, 1975, p. 9.

——, "Xerox Comes Through Its Mid-Life Crisis," *Financial World,* July 15, 1979, p. 18.

"The New Lean, Mean Xerox: Fending Off the Japanese," *Business Week,* October 12, 1981, pp. 126+.

Norman, James R., "Xerox Rethinks Itself—and This Could Be the Last Time," *Business Week,* February 13, 1989, pp. 90+.

Palmer, Jay, "Ready to Copy?," *Barron's,* May 29, 2000, pp. 27–28, 30.

Rudnitsky, Howard, "World's Largest Up and Comer," *Forbes,* May 18, 1987, pp. 78+.

Santoli, Michael, "Copy This: Xerox Image Is Brightening Again," *Barron's,* November 1, 2004, pp. 13–14.

Sheridan, John H., "A CEO's Perspective on Innovation," *Industry Week,* December 19, 1994, pp. 11–12, 14.

Siwolop, Sana, "Man of the Year: Xerox Chairman and CEO David T. Kearns," *Financial World,* December 12, 1989, pp. 56+.

Smart, Tim, "Can Xerox Duplicate Its Glory Days?," *Business Week,* October 4, 1993, pp. 56, 58.

——, "So Much for Diversification," *Business Week,* February 1, 1993, p. 31.

Smart, Tim, and Peter Burrows, "Out to Make Xerox Print More Money," *Business Week,* August 11, 1997, pp. 81+.

The Story of Xerography, Stamford, Conn.: Xerox Corporation, n.d.

Taub, Stephen, "Will Xerox Keep on Fading?," *Financial World,* February 15, 1983, pp. 14+.

Uttal, Bro, "Xerox Xooms Toward the Office of the Future," *Fortune,* May 18, 1981, pp. 44+.

Verespej, Michael A., "Xerox at a Crossroads," *Industry Week,* May 28, 1984, pp. 21+.

Vogel, Todd, "At Xerox, They're Shouting 'Once More into the Breach,'" *Business Week,* July 23, 1990, pp. 62+.

Weber, Thomas E., "Xerox to Pay $1.5 Billion to Buy Rank's Stake in Copier Venture," *Wall Street Journal,* June 9, 1997, p. B4.

Wysocki, Bernard, Jr., "Change Machine: Xerox Recasts Itself As Formidable Force in Digital Revolution," *Wall Street Journal,* February 2, 1999, p. A1.

"Xerox Tries to Capture Some IBM Territory," *Business Week,* October 12, 1974, p. 28.

Ziegler, Bart, "Success at IBM Gives Thoman Edge at Xerox," *Wall Street Journal,* June 13, 1997, pp. B1, B8.

Ziegler, Bart, and Leslie Scism, "Xerox Shares Fall 5.6% After Collapse of the Sale of Insurance Units to KKR," *Wall Street Journal,* September 13, 1996, pp. A2, A4.

Zweig, Phillip, "A Pale Copy," *Financial World,* October 20, 1987, pp. 20+.

—Scott M. Lewis
—updates: Mary McNulty; David E. Salamie

XM Satellite Radio Holdings, Inc.

1500 Eckington Place NE
Washington, D.C. 20002-2194
U.S.A.
Telephone: (202) 380-4000
Toll Free: (866) 962-2557
Fax: (202) 380-4500
Web site: http://www.xmradio.com

Public Company
Incorporated: 1992 as American Mobile Radio
    Corporation
Employees: 500
Sales: $244.4 million (2004)
Stock Exchanges: NASDAQ
Ticker Symbol: XMSR
NAIC: 515112 Radio Stations; 517410 Satellite
    Telecommunications

XM Satellite Radio Holdings, Inc. broadcasts more than 120 channels of digital radio via satellite to subscribers throughout the United States. The company's programming includes nearly 70 channels of commercial-free music and more than 50 of news, sports, and talk. Its offerings range from broadcasts of Major League Baseball and NASCAR events to channels featuring content from CNN, Playboy, MTV, ABC News, Disney, Sesame Street, and Discovery. XM's's broadcasts are beamed from two satellites to more than three million subscribers who pay a monthly fee of $9.95. Automakers including General Motors, Honda, and Toyota offer XM-ready radios as options, and the company has gained half of its subscribers through installations in vehicles. Others listen via XM-ready boomboxes or personal stereos, and over the Internet. XM has also created a radio channel for the Starbucks coffee shop chain, and provides data services such as traffic information for Cadillac and Acura owners.

Beginnings

The origins of XM Satellite Radio date to 1988, when a consortium was formed to buy a license for satellite broadcasting of telephone, fax, and data signals. It was made up of eight organizations including Hughes Aircraft Co., McCaw Communications, Inc., and Mobile Telecommunications Technologies Corp. The U.S. Federal Communications Commission (FCC) had ruled that sufficient bandwidth existed for only one license to be issued for such broadcasting, which forced the competing firms to form the joint venture. It was named American Mobile Satellite Corporation (AMSC).

In 1990 AMSC announced that a $100 million satellite would be built for it by Hughes and launched by the mid-1990s. Before that took place, the firm would lease space on other satellites for its data transmission services. The company was also looking into offering other satellite-based services, and in June 1992 formed a unit called American Mobile Radio Corporation to develop a satellite-based digital radio broadcasting service. In December 1993 AMSC went public on the NASDAQ.

AMSC's first satellite was launched in April 1995 from Cape Canaveral. The company was now planning to offer a bulky $2,000 satellite telephone to customers which would work anywhere in the United States. The growth of cellular telephone networks was mushrooming at this time, however, and the usefulness of AMSC's phone service was decreasing almost daily. As a result, the firm signed up far fewer customers than expected, primarily trucking companies, boaters, and airplane owners.

In April 1996 AMSC reported that it was close to bankruptcy, but it was bailed out when Hughes and several other firms granted it a $225 million line of credit. In the spring and summer there were a number of management changes, with new board members, a new chief financial officer, a new chairman, and a new CEO in Gary Parsons, who had been recruited from MCI Communications Corp.

In 1997 AMSC's radio unit spent $89.9 million to buy an FCC license to broadcast digital radio by satellite. It was one of just two licenses the agency granted, the other going to a firm called CD Radio, Inc., which had been working since 1990 on developing the digital radio concept.

In 1998 AMSC hired former journalist, Time Warner Cable executive, and Request TV head Hugh Panero to run its radio unit, with Gary Parsons serving as its chairman. Shortly after

---

Company Perspectives:

One big idea can change everything. And XM Satellite Radio is one big idea. Radio to the Power of X. *America's most popular satellite radio service gives you the power to choose what you want to hear—wherever and whenever you want it.*

---

being hired, Panero renamed the operation XM Satellite Radio. In June 1999 XM received a $250 million investment in the form of convertible debt from General Motors, DirecTV, Inc., Clear Channel Communications, Inc., and three investment firms. The company was now planning to launch two stationary satellites which would beam down signals to listeners across the United States. In large cities, where the signal would be impaired by tall buildings, XM planned a network of 1,700 repeating towers to ensure uninterrupted coverage.

Going Public: Fall 1999

In October 1999 AMSC spun off XM Satellite Radio Holdings, Inc. via an initial public offering of stock on the NASDAQ. The sale raised nearly $110 million of the $1 billion it anticipated spending to build a satellite network. AMSC would retain 17 million shares of its stock and controlling interest in the firm. XM hoped to begin broadcasting in 2001, following the anticipated start of rival Sirius (formerly known as CD Radio), which was planning to launch its satellites during 2000.

XM soon leased an old, unused printing plant building in Washington, D.C., and spent $62 million to renovate it. The company's new headquarters would house 82 digital studios, one of which was large enough to record a full orchestra, as well as providing space for the 400 employees the firm was planning to hire.

To put together the 100-plus channels it would offer, XM hired well-known FM radio consultant Lee Abrams. Famed for developing the research-based approach to radio programming which had helped make FM radio both immensely popular and highly profitable (but also increasingly homogenous and stale, according to critics), Abrams had recently quit the business out of his own frustration over the industry's focus on the bottom line at the expense of creativity and quality. Asked to recommend someone to head XM's programming department, he became excited by the opportunity it offered, and took the job himself.

Abrams soon began working to create a diverse range of programming that would enable it to entice listeners to pay a $9.99 monthly fee, as well as $300 for a digital radio. To CEO Panero, it was important that the channel lineup consist of more than just a library of CDs set to shuffle play mode. He told the *Washington Post,* "We have to make this real and authentic, so that on the blues channel you feel like you're in a blues club drinking whiskey, and on a classical channel you feel like you're in a symphony hall."

For XM's music stations, Abrams hired experienced hands like Bobby "The Mighty Burner" Bennett, a popular rhythm and blues disc jockey of the 1960s, who would program soul music for an XM channel devoted to that genre, as well as doing

a show of his own. Other channels were devoted to the music of each decade between the 1940s and 1990s, as well as various forms of rock, country, jazz, and classical music. The firm was also starting to sign up outside providers such as Discovery Communications, Inc., the Associated Press, and Bloomberg to provide content for its talk channels.

In the fall of 2000 the company began preparing for the launch of its two satellites, which had been christened "Rock" and "Roll." The first was scheduled to take off on Elvis Presley's 66th birthday, January 8, 2001, but its countdown was halted just 11 seconds before liftoff when a minor technical glitch was discovered. On March 18 it successfully reached a stationary orbit 22,236 miles above Texas, and the second satellite was launched in May. XM was now seeking additional funding, and sold $201 million in stock and notes to pay for operational expenses until broadcasting could begin.

Deals continued to be signed for content, and the company reached agreements with ABC Radio Networks and affiliate Disney, MTV Networks, CNN, and USA Today. Some of the informational channels would be heard on both XM and rival Sirius, while others were exclusive to XM. The company was also working with retailers including Best Buy, Circuit City, and Sears to sell its radios.

Broadcasting Beginning in Fall of 2001

The company was now planning to begin broadcasting on September 12, 2001, to Dallas and San Diego. A $100 million advertising campaign was launched in August with movie trailer spots depicting David Bowie, B.B King, and rapper Snoop Dogg falling from the sky along with piles of musical instruments.

On September 11, 2001, as company officials flew to the firm's first two broadcast cities, terrorists crashed planes into buildings in New York City and Washington, D.C. In the aftermath of the attacks, in which numerous people had fallen to their deaths at the World Trade Center, XM's ads were pulled and re-edited, and the company's broadcast launch was put on hold for two weeks. It officially debuted on September 25, and by October XM's signal extended to the entire Southwest. On November 12, it was available from coast to coast.

In late September the firm had discovered that, due to a manufacturing defect, its satellites would have shorter lifespans than the 12 to 15 years originally anticipated. The company soon announced that it would need to raise an additional $250 million to $300 million to continue operating, and it scaled back its ad campaign and cut other costs. XM subsequently restructured $31 million in debt, got a loan for $35 million, and raised $129 million through a new offering of stock. It was the fifth time the company had issued stock.

By the end of 2001, XM had signed up close to 30,000 subscribers. Though it had been perceived as the "Johnny Come Lately" of digital satellite radio, competitor Sirius was still not on the air because of problems with the microchip sets in its radios, and XM was winning major kudos in the media, with *Fortune* magazine calling its radio service the product of the year and *Time* honoring it as the invention of the year. The total amount invested in XM now stood at $1.4 billion.

XM's radios were initially sold as aftermarket items for cars, built by Sanyo, Pioneer, and others, but they were soon offered as options on 2002 Cadillac Seville and Deville models. Though Cadillac maker GM was a major shareholder in the firm, XM paid part of the cost of each radio it installed, as well as for the associated advertising. In February 2002 XM reached an agreement with satellite television broadcaster and 10 percent stakeholder DirecTV to offer the radio service to its viewers.

By June 2002 XM had signed up 135,000 subscribers. The firm was still recording heavy losses, however, and in November laid off 80 of its workforce of 480. It also adjusted its programming lineup, dropping teen talk channel BabbleOn and USA Today News, and adding an audio feed of CNN's television broadcast and XM Live, which featured concert recordings, some done in the company's studios. The firm was also preparing to offer a premium-priced service for an additional $2.99 per month that was programmed by Playboy and featured sexually explicit talk.

New Funding Arrangement: December 2002

In late December 2002 XM cut a deal with its major stakeholders including GM, American Honda Motor Co., and Hughes Electronics Corporation for $475 million in new funding from debt deferral and the sale of stock. The stake owned by GM and affiliates Hughes and DirecTV would rise to 19.6 percent, while Honda would own 8.3 percent.

Aftermarket XM radios now cost $200, and Wal-Mart had made a commitment to begin selling them in 2003, while car rental firm Avis was offering XM in its cars for $3 per day. The radios were available in three-quarters of GM vehicles as factory-installed options, for a price of $150 to $300. For fiscal 2002 the firm reported sales of $20.2 million and a loss of $495 million.

In April 2003 XM signed up its 500,000th subscriber, while announcing new deals to put its radios in Toyota and Audi cars. In August the company reported that a $400 million insurance claim for the defects in its satellites had been denied, though it continued to seek restitution. Following this setback, the firm raised an additional $150 million from the sale of 11 million new shares of stock. The money would be used to build a new

$130 million spare satellite, as the existing spare would have to be launched in 2004 at a cost of some $190 million.

The end of 2003 saw XM's subscriber base grow to 1.36 million, five times that of rival Sirius. In early 2004 the company announced that it would begin broadcasting local traffic and weather information in 21 U.S. cities. The move was protested by the National Association of Broadcasters (NAB), who contended it violated the company's license to provide only a national radio service. The FCC did not interfere, however, as the channels were broadcast to the entire country.

The NAB was one of the most powerful lobbying groups in Washington, and had managed to place numerous restrictions on satellite broadcasters, including forcing them to pay performer royalties in addition to songwriter royalties. As a result, XM was spending an estimated $10 million per year on the former, in addition to the hefty amount it paid songwriter agencies BMI and ASCAP. Though AM and FM radio operators had for many years paid songwriters, they were not required to pay performers.

The first quarter of 2004 saw XM's revenues exceed fixed costs for the first time, though the company continued to lose money overall. The cost of adding a subscriber had dropped to $106 from $156 a year earlier, much less than what Sirius was spending. In May, new TV ads were launched to coincide with the annual surge in electronics sales tied to Father's Day and high school and college graduation.

In the summer, XM signed popular National Public Radio host Bob Edwards, who had been let go after nearly 25 years as anchor of the network's Morning Edition program. Many listeners had been angered by the move including CEO Panero, who made Edwards an offer to work for XM. Although rival Sirius had an exclusive contract to broadcast the programs of National Public Radio, XM was licensing content from other educational radio firms including Public Radio International, WBUR in Boston, and American Public Media. In the fall, a new "shock jock" morning talk team, Opie and Anthony, were added to the company's offerings, at the same time that rival Sirius signed controversial talk-show host Howard Stern to a five-year, $500 million deal which would start in January 2006.

In October 2004 XM signed a $650 million, 11-year agreement with Major League Baseball. The company would broadcast all of the games played during the season, devoting as many as 15 of its channels to them when all 30 teams played on a given day, with an additional baseball channel featuring archival and Spanish-language games. The broadcasts would use the established radio voices of each home team, who would continue to be heard on regular radio.

October also saw the introduction of the $350 Delphi XM MyFi. A small, personal-sized unit akin to a Walkman, it could pick up XM's signal and also record up to five hours of programs. Television ads featuring rock star Elton John hawked the new item. Competitor Sirius was reportedly still months away from offering such a product.

XM's receivers had always included a small information screen that showed the artist and song being played, and the firm was now experimenting with new ways to use this function, such as displaying the stock market ticker. XM's service also enabled listeners to select favorite artists or songs, and when one of its channels broadcast them the radio would automatically switch to that station. XM was readying another service called NavTraffic, a continuously updated mapping system that showed traffic problems and suggested alternate routes, initially available for owners of certain Cadillac and Acura models.

The firm was also preparing a dedicated music channel for Starbucks coffee shops, and had begun to offer its programming via the Internet. By the end of 2004, XM boasted more than three million subscribers, triple the count of Sirius. Revenues for the year would hit $244 million. Losses, however, would exceed $642 million. The company's stock price, often volatile, now was in the mid-$30 range, after having reached a low of $1.66 in 2002. During the 2004 model year, GM had installed more than one million XM radios in cars, while Honda had put them in 200,000.

In just over a decade, XM Satellite Radio Holdings, Inc. had spent more than $2 billion putting together a satellite radio service that offered more than 120 channels of music and informational programming. The firm had gotten the jump on rival Sirius Satellite Radio by going on the air first and had built up a sizable subscriber base, but the industry was not yet profitable, and it would take time to see whether XM's business plan was truly viable.

Principal Subsidiaries

XM Satellite Radio Inc.; XM Equipment Leasing LLC.

Principal Competitors

Sirius Satellite Radio, Inc.; Clear Channel Communications, Inc.; Infinity Broadcasting; DMX Music, Inc.

Further Reading

Adelson, Andrea, "Coming Soon to a Radio Near You," *New York Times,* December 28, 1998, p. C6.

Ahrens, Frank, "Can XM Put Radio Back Together Again?," *Washington Post,* January 19, 2003, p. W12.

Brull, Steven V., "The Cable TV of Radio? Satellite Audio Could Be the Next Big Thing—Or a Big Flop," *Business Week,* January 31, 2000, p. 96.

Feder, Barnaby, "A New Temptation for the Ears, Via Satellite," *New York Times,* June 2, 2002, p. C9.

——, "Satellite Radio Gains Ground with Right Mix of Partners," *New York Times,* April 21, 2003, p. C1.

"Fledgling Satellite Radio Providers Incur Setbacks with Launch and Chipset Delays," *Satellite News,* January 15, 2001, p. 1.

Frey, Jennifer, "Former NPR Host Bob Edwards to Be XM's New Morning Host," *Washington Post,* July 29, 2004, p. A1.

Irwin, Neil, "XM Radio Turns It On," *Washington Post,* September 10, 2001, p. E1.

Knight, Jerry, "CD Radio, XM Satellite Tune Up for Pay-to-Listen Programs," *Washington Post,* June 28, 1999, p. F7.

——, "Picking Up a Stronger Signal on XM," *Washington Post,* September 9, 2002, p. E1.

——, "Rivals in the Satellite-Radio Business Share Brunt of Wall Street's Wariness," *Washington Post,* April 9, 2001, p. E1.

Markels, Alex, "100 Channels, But Where Are the Subscribers?," *New York Times,* November 3, 2002, p. C4.

McLean, Bethany, "Satellite Killed the Radio Star," *Fortune,* January 22, 2001, p. 94.

Merle, Renae, "XM Faces a Rough Start," *Washington Post,* October 10, 2001, p. E5.

Mills, Mike, "The Launch That Languished: American Mobile Satellite Struggles to Catch Up," *Washington Post,* October 21, 1996, p. F19.

"Nationwide Radio Stations on Way," *Pittsburgh Post-Gazette,* May 5, 1996, p. A7.

Shin, Annys, "At XM, Boldly Going; Under Hugh Panero, Satellite Radio Is a Hit," *Washington Post,* November 29, 2004, p. E1.

"Sirius Radio and XM Radio Form Alliance," *Satellite Today,* February 17, 2000, p. 1.

Steinberg, Brian, "Satellite-Radio Firms Prepare for 2000 Launch," *Wall Street Journal,* January 25, 1999, p. 1.

Wooley, Scott, "Broadcast Bullies," *Forbes,* September 6, 2004, p. 134.

—Frank Uhle

INDEX TO COMPANIES

Index to Companies

Listings in this index are arranged in alphabetical order under the company name. Company names beginning with a letter or proper name such as Eli Lilly & Co. will be found under the first letter of the company name. Definite articles (The, Le, La) are ignored for alphabetical purposes as are forms of incorporation that precede the company name (AB, NV). Company names printed in bold type have full, historical essays on the page numbers appearing in bold. Updates to entries that appeared in earlier volumes are signified by the notation (upd.). Company names in light type are references within an essay to that company, not full historical essays. This index is cumulative with volume numbers printed in bold type.

INDEX TO INDUSTRIES

Index to Industries

565

AUTOMOTIVE

BIOTECHNOLOGY

CHEMICALS

CONSTRUCTION

MINING & METALS

TEXTILES & APPAREL

UTILITIES

WASTE SERVICES

GEOGRAPHIC INDEX

Geographic Index

Algeria

Sonatrach, IV; 65 (upd.)

Argentina

Aerolíneas Argentinas S.A., 33; 69 (upd.)
Arcor S.A.I.C., 66
Atanor S.A., 62
Coto Centro Integral de Comercializacion
   S.A., 66
Cresud S.A.C.I.F. y A., 63
Grupo Clarín S.A., 67
Grupo Financiero Galicia S.A., 63
IRSA Inversiones y Representaciones S.A.,
   63
Ledesma Sociedad Anónima Agrícola
   Industrial, 62
Molinos Río de la Plata S.A., 61
Nobleza Piccardo SAICF, 64
Penaflor S.A., 66
Quilmes Industrial (QUINSA) S.A., 67
Renault Argentina S.A., 67
Sideco Americana S.A., 67
Siderar S.A.I.C., 66
Telecom Argentina S.A., 63
Telefónica de Argentina S.A., 61
YPF Sociedad Anonima, IV

Australia

Amcor Limited, IV; 19 (upd.)
Ansell Ltd., 60 (upd.)
Aquarius Platinum Ltd., 63
Aristocrat Leisure Limited, 54
Arnott's Ltd., 66
Australia and New Zealand Banking Group
   Limited, II; 52 (upd.)
AWB Ltd., 56
BHP Billiton, 67 (upd.)
Billabong International Ltd., 44
Bond Corporation Holdings Limited, 10
Boral Limited, III; 43 (upd.)
Brambles Industries Limited, 42
Broken Hill Proprietary Company Ltd., IV;
   22 (upd.)
Burns, Philp & Company Ltd., 63
Carlton and United Breweries Ltd., I
Coles Myer Ltd., V; 20 (upd.)
CRA Limited, IV
CSR Limited, III; 28 (upd.)
David Jones Ltd., 60
Elders IXL Ltd., I
Foster's Group Limited, 7; 21 (upd.); 50
   (upd.)
Goodman Fielder Ltd., 52
Harvey Norman Holdings Ltd., 56
Holden Ltd., 62
James Hardie Industries N.V., 56
John Fairfax Holdings Limited, 7
Lend Lease Corporation Limited, IV; 17
   (upd.); 52 (upd.)
Lion Nathan Limited, 54
Lonely Planet Publications Pty Ltd., 55
Macquarie Bank Ltd., 69
McPherson's Ltd., 66

Metcash Trading Ltd., 58
News Corporation Limited, IV; 7 (upd.);
   46 (upd.)
Pacific Dunlop Limited, 10
Pioneer International Limited, III
Publishing and Broadcasting Limited, 54
Qantas Airways Ltd., 6; 24 (upd.); 68
   (upd.)
Ridley Corporation Ltd., 62
Rinker Group Ltd., 65
Smorgon Steel Group Ltd., 62
Southcorp Limited, 54
TABCORP Holdings Limited, 44
Telecom Australia, 6
Telstra Corporation Limited, 50
Village Roadshow Ltd., 58
Westpac Banking Corporation, II; 48 (upd.)
WMC, Limited, 43

Austria

AKG Acoustics GmbH, 62
Andritz AG, 51
Austrian Airlines AG (Österreichische
   Luftverkehrs AG), 33
Bank Austria AG, 23
BBAG Österreichische Brau-Beteiligungs-
   AG, 38
Erste Bank der Osterreichischen
   Sparkassen AG, 69
Gericom AG, 47
Glock Ges.m.b.H., 42
Julius Meinl International AG, 53
Lauda Air Luftfahrt AG, 48
ÖMV Aktiengesellschaft, IV
Österreichische Bundesbahnen GmbH, 6
Österreichische Post- und
   Telegraphenverwaltung, V
Red Bull GmbH, 60
RHI AG, 53
VA TECH ELIN EBG GmbH, 49
voestalpine AG, IV; 57 (upd.)
Zumtobel AG, 50

Bahamas

Bahamas Air Holdings Ltd., 66
Kerzner International Limited, 69 (upd.)
Sun International Hotels Limited, 26
Teekay Shipping Corporation, 25

Bahrain

Gulf Air Company, 56
Investcorp SA, 57

Bangladesh

Grameen Bank, 31

Belgium

Agfa Gevaert Group N.V., 59
Almanij NV, 44
Bank Brussels Lambert, II
Barco NV, 44
Belgacom, 6

C&A, 40 (upd.)
Cockerill Sambre Group, IV; 26 (upd.)
Delhaize ''Le Lion'' S.A., 44
DHL Worldwide Network S.A./N.V., 69
   (upd.)
Electrabel N.V., 67
Etablissements Franz Colruyt N.V., 68
Generale Bank, II
GIB Group, V; 26 (upd.)
Groupe Herstal S.A., 58
Interbrew S.A., 17; 50 (upd.)
Kredietbank N.V., II
PetroFina S.A., IV; 26 (upd.)
Punch International N.V., 66
Roularta Media Group NV, 48
Sabena S.A./N.V., 33
Solvay S.A., I; 21 (upd.); 61 (upd.)
Tractebel S.A., 20
NV Umicore SA, 47
Xeikon NV, 26

Bermuda

Bacardi Limited, 18
Central European Media Enterprises Ltd.,
   61
Frontline Ltd., 45
Jardine Matheson Holdings Limited, I; 20
   (upd.)
Sea Containers Ltd., 29
Tyco International Ltd., III; 28 (upd.); 63
   (upd.)
White Mountains Insurance Group, Ltd., 48

Brazil

Aracruz Celulose S.A., 57
Banco Bradesco S.A., 13
Banco Itaú S.A., 19
Brasil Telecom Participaçoes S.A., 57
Companhia de Bebidas das Américas, 57
Companhia Energética de Minas Gerais
   S.A. CEMIG, 65
Companhia Vale do Rio Doce, IV; 43
   (upd.)
Empresa Brasileira de Aeronáutica S.A.
   (Embraer), 36
Gerdau S.A., 59
Ipiranga S.A., 67
Lojas Arapua S.A., 22; 61 (upd.)
Perdigao SA, 52
Petróleo Brasileiro S.A., IV
Sadia S.A., 59
Souza Cruz S.A., 65
TAM Linhas Aéreas S.A., 68
TransBrasil S/A Linhas Aéreas, 31
VARIG S.A. (Viaçâo Aérea Rio-
   Grandense), 6; 29 (upd.)

Canada

Abitibi-Consolidated, Inc., V; 25 (upd.)
Abitibi-Price Inc., IV
Air Canada, 6; 23 (upd.); 59 (upd.)
Alberta Energy Company Ltd., 16; 43
   (upd.)

NOTES ON CONTRIBUTORS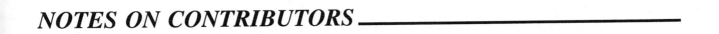

Notes on Contributors

COHEN, M. L. Novelist and researcher living in Paris.

COVELL, Jeffrey L. Seattle-based writer.

CULLIGAN, Susan B. Minnesota-based writer.

DINGER, Ed. Writer and editor based in Bronx, New York.

HALASZ, Robert. Former editor in chief of *World Progress* and *Funk & Wagnalls New Encyclopedia Yearbook*; author, *The U.S. Marines* (Millbrook Press, 1993).

HEER-FORSBERG, Mary. Minneapolis-based researcher and writer.

INGRAM, Frederick C. Utah-based business writer who has contributed to *GSA Business, Appalachian Trailway News,* the *Encyclopedia of Business,* the *Encyclopedia of Global Industries,* the *Encyclopedia of Consumer Brands,* and other regional and trade publications.

PEIPPO, Kathleen. Minneapolis-based writer.

RHODES, Nelson. Editor, writer, and consultant in the Chicago area.

ROTHBURD, Carrie. Writer and editor specializing in corporate profiles, academic texts, and academic journal articles.

SALAMIE, David E. Part-owner of InfoWorks Development Group, a reference publication development and editorial services company.

UHLE, Frank. Ann Arbor-based writer; movie projectionist, disc jockey, and staff member of *Psychotronic Video* magazine.

WOODWARD, A. Wisconsin-based writer.